Contents

Foreword 5

Acknowledgements 7

Notes to the Reader 8

Chapter One
Light Tanks 9

Chapter Two
Early-War Medium Tanks 62

Chapter Three
Late-War Medium Tanks 111

Chapter Four
Heavy Tanks 157

Dedication

The author would like to dedicate this book to the memory of
Major General Adna R. Chaffee Jr. who is considered the father of the
US Army Armoured Forces.

IMAGES OF WAR

ALLIED TANKS OF THE SECOND WORLD WAR

RARE PHOTOGRAPHS FROM WARTIME ARCHIVES

Michael Green

Pen & Sword
MILITARY

First published in Great Britain in 2017 by
PEN & SWORD MILITARY
An imprint of
Pen & Sword Books Ltd
47 Church Street
Barnsley
South Yorkshire
S70 2AS

ISBN 978-1-47386-676-8

A CIP catalogue record for this book is available from the British Library.

Typeset by Concept, Huddersfield, West Yorkshire HD4 5JL.
Printed and bound in India by Replika Press Pvt. Ltd.

Pen & Sword Books Ltd incorporates the imprints of Pen & Sword Archaeology, Atlas, Aviation, Battleground, Discovery, Family History, History, Maritime, Military, Naval, Politics, Railways, Select, Social History, Transport, True Crime, and Claymore Press, Frontline Books, Leo Cooper, Praetorian Press, Remember When, Seaforth Publishing and Wharncliffe.

For a complete list of Pen & Sword titles please contact
PEN & SWORD BOOKS LIMITED
47 Church Street, Barnsley, South Yorkshire S70 2AS, England
E-mail: enquiries@pen-and-sword.co.uk
Website: www.pen-and-sword.co.uk

Foreword

During the interwar years, great debates began about the use of tanks in land warfare. This debate – led by the acrimonious tauntings between J.F.C. Fuller and Basil Liddell Hart in England – was only the beginning of the salvos soon to be fired during the Second World War. At issue was the role of the tank: was it an infantry support weapon, a weapon to achieve breakthroughs in the enemy lines or a vehicle for reconnaissance and pursuit? This debate would influence tank design and doctrine throughout the Second World War. So this is the perfect place for this latest work by Michael Green to fit into the historiography of that conflict.

Many volumes, for instance, track the enormity of the job of building an army in the United States. The manufacturing marvels turned out by industry – a feat of men, muscle and matériel – could in some aspects be the decisive factor in the war. What the author has done is take the tactics, doctrine and industrial capacity and boiled them down into the products made by the allied countries facing the German *bewegungskrieg* or war of operational manoeuvre.

Modern-day programme managers talk about the trade-offs they have to make on vehicle development around the 'iron triangle' of power/performance/protection. The author takes the reader down this same road in the Second World War and shows why tanks were accepted or rejected for service by the military. Lack of armoured protection, too heavy, too light, not enough power, too slow or lack of firepower and numerous engine designs and fuels were just some of the many issues faced by tank developers. The importance of this work cannot be overstated. The author clearly shows the vital link between what is possible and what is probable in building light, medium and heavy tanks. Take the US army M3 Medium Tank as an example of a good idea gone bad.

Prior to 1940, all American tanks were hand-crafted, one at a time, at Rock Island Arsenal in Illinois. There was no facility to build tanks, nor was there a workforce or the industrial know-how and capacity to mass-produce tanks. The building of the Chrysler Tank Arsenal (Detroit Arsenal Tank Plant) was the first facility built in the United States solely devoted to tank design and mass-production. With the help of the US army, the first tank off the assembly line was the M3 Medium Tank.

The M3 was obsolete before it even left the drawing board and its design left something to be desired. Viewed as an infantry support weapon, the Infantry Branch demanded a 37mm gun on the tank. The 75mm gun was for blowing holes through defensive positions for the infantry to storm through. The result was an ineffective design, a limited use and capability of the main gun (housed in a pulpit-like enclosure on the right side with limited ability to shoot left/right or up/down), and a limited-use 37mm main gun in the turret. Before the production run was complete on the M3, the M4 Sherman production began on adjacent assembly lines.

Randy R. Talbot
Command Historian (retired)
US Army TACOM Life Cycle Management Command

Acknowledgments

As with any published work, authors must depend on a great many people for assistance. These included, over many years, my fellow author and long-time mentor the late Richard Hunnicutt. Other friends who kindly supplied information and pictures for this work are credited in the captions.

Both the paid and volunteer staff of the now-closed Patton Museum of Armor and Cavalry provided the author with a great deal of assistance over many years. For the sake of brevity all images from the former Patton Museum of Cavalry and Armor will be credited to the 'Patton Museum'.

I am also indebted to David Fletcher, fellow author and the long-time former librarian at the Tank Museum located in Bovington, England. He has greatly assisted the author in locating photographs for many of his books. All images from the Tank Museum in Bovington will be credited to just the 'Tank Museum' for brevity.

A US army entity that assisted the author in acquiring historical photographs of American tanks for this work was the Command Historian's Office of the TACOM Life Cycle Management Command (LCMC). All pictures from this organization are credited to 'TACOM' for the sake of brevity.

Notes to the Reader

1. Due to the size and format of this series of books the author will concentrate on the gun tank versions of the vehicles described in the text. What is not covered will be those vehicles converted to support-based versions such as bridge-layers, self-propelled artillery, command and control vehicles, recovery vehicles, anti-aircraft vehicles, etc.

2. Prior to the Second World War and during the conflict armies generally classified their tanks as light, medium or heavy, based on the weight of the tank. Some armies also classified them by their missions. Each country's system was unique, sometimes arbitrary and in some cases was changed during the course of the war. What one army might classify as a light tank would be considered a medium tank by another army or vice versa.

Chapter One

Light Tanks

In the decades following the First World War those countries with the industrial capability to design and build tanks tended to concentrate on light tanks. This came about for different reasons: they were what the existing industrial base was capable of designing and building, and they were more affordable than medium and heavy tanks when funding constraints were in place. Armies were also limited by their nation's transportation infrastructure which dictated a tank's maximum weight as well as exterior dimensions.

French Light Tanks

It was the French army that pioneered the development and fielding of the earliest light tank during the First World War. That vehicle was the two-man Renault FT that weighed approximately 15,000lb. It was armed with either a machine gun or a 37mm main gun. As it was not intended to engage enemy tanks, it was considered an infantry support tank. After the First World War the vehicle became unofficially known as the Renault FT17 or the Renault FT-17, a tradition that continues to this day.

Approximately 3,000 Renault FTs were built between 1917 and 1918 for the French army, with 534 slightly modernized machine-gun-armed units surviving in service long enough to see combat during the German military invasion of their country in May 1940, which led to a German victory the following month. All the variants of the Renault FT series were powered by gasoline engines.

French Infantry Light Tanks

Funding for the development of a new infantry support tank to replace the Renault FT light tank for the French army was in very short supply during the 1920s. The French army therefore went looking for a new light tank that would be very affordable to purchase in large numbers. What they got instead was the Char (tank) D1 that was neither affordable nor lightweight.

The Char D1 had a three-man crew and weighed approximately 31,000lb. Due to production problems it was originally fitted with the 37mm main gun armed turret of the Renault FT light tank. It was eventually equipped with a new turret design armed with a 47mm main gun. It was also armed with two machine guns: a coaxial and another mounted in the front hull.

A total of 160 units of the Char D1 were delivered to the French army between 1931 and 1935. Considered obsolete by 1937, most were shipped to French overseas colonies in North Africa. Some were returned to France shortly before the German invasion and were thrown into combat.

Even before the first Char D1 entered French army service, there was a call for an improved version. That vehicle was referred to as the Char D2 and 100 units would be built between 1937 and 1940. Like its predecessor, the three-man tank was armed with a 47mm main gun and two machine guns. Reflecting an increase in the level of armour protection, the Char D2 weighed approximately 44,000lb. It would see combat during the German invasion.

French Cavalry Light Tanks

During the 1920s the French army relied on armoured half-tracks for their cavalry branch reconnaissance needs. By the early 1930s, it was clear to the French army that armoured half-tracks were a technological dead-end, with poor off-road mobility. This resulted in a push to replace them with gasoline-engine-powered light tanks that performed much better off-road due to their full-tracked suspension systems.

The first of the new cavalry light reconnaissance tanks was the machine-gun-armed Renault AMR 33, with the initial examples delivered in 1934. By the time production ceased the following year, a total of 120 units of the Renault AMR 33 had been completed. It weighed 11,023lb and proved unpopular because it was small and cramped as well as under-gunned.

The Renault AMR 33 replacement was supposed to have been the two-man Renault AMR 34 armed with a 25mm main gun. Only twelve units were built starting in 1935 before it was decided that the tank was under-gunned and under-armoured when compared to the latest German army developments in the field of tanks and anti-tank guns. The replacement for the Renault AMR 34 was an up-armoured and up-gunned version labelled as the AMR Renault 35 ACG-1.

The AMR Renault 35 ACG-1 had a three-man crew and weighed 14,330lb. Armament consisted of a 47mm main gun and a coaxial machine gun. Because the AMR Renault 35 ACG-1 was an interim vehicle for the cavalry branch of the French

---

French Army Light Tank Designations

The French army divided its tanks by weight, with those under 15 tons being considered light tanks. Those same light tanks were also divided by their jobs. Those intended for employment by the cavalry branch of the French army were labelled as the AMR or the AMC. The AMR light tanks were intended to acquire information by stealth. The better-armed and armoured AMC light tanks were intended to fight for information if required.

army until a new medium tank was fielded, only forty-eight units were ordered and delivered between 1938 and 1940. They would see action during the German invasion during the summer of 1940.

Hotchkiss Light Tanks

Due to political pressure the infantry branch of the French army was forced to take into service the two-man Hotchkiss H35 between 1936 and 1937. It weighed approximately 24,000lb and was armed with the same 37mm main gun as fitted to the Renault FT light tank. It was also armed with a coaxial machine gun. The cavalry branch of the French army was also forced to take into service 300 units of the Hotchkiss H35, much against their wishes.

Poor performance characteristics of the Hotchkiss H35 led to an upgraded version labelled as the Hotchkiss H39 for the infantry branch of the French army, with a total of 680 units delivered between 1939 and 1940. A longer-barrelled 37mm main gun was fitted to the Hotchkiss H39 production line, beginning in 1940.

Renault Light Tanks

The French army infantry branch adopted the Renault R35. It was a two-man tank weighing approximately 22,000lb. Its production began in 1936. Only 945 units of the Renault R35 were in service with the French army prior to the German invasion, out of a planned order of over 2,000 units.

The Renault R35 was originally armed with the same 37mm main gun as mounted on the Renault FT. However, beginning in 1939, all new-built Renault R35s were armed with a longer-barrelled 37mm main gun. In addition, the tank was armed with a coaxial machine gun. Despite the improvement in armament, it would prove to be a major disappointment for the French army due to its poor off-road mobility.

To overcome the mobility shortfalls of the Renault R35, a new suspension system was introduced into the R35 production line in 1939 but only 155 were completed before the German invasion. These vehicles were labelled as the Renault R40.

FCM 36 Light Tank

Another light infantry support tank adopted by the French army in the 1930s was the FCM 36. It had a two-man crew and was armed with the same 37mm main gun as fitted to the FT. In addition, it was fitted with a coaxial machine gun. The FCM 36 weighed approximately 24,000lb.

Despite the FCM-designed and built light tank being more advanced in comparison to its competitor's light tank counterparts, only 100 units were built for the French army between 1938 and 1939. This happened for a number of different reasons. There were production bottlenecks and the French army thought the company was asking for too much money for their product. In addition, the French army wanted the firm to concentrate on building a heavy tank to which it assigned a higher priority.

British Light Tanks

The British army saw its interwar light tanks as reconnaissance vehicles. In 1928, the British army awarded a contract for four prototype vehicles labelled as the Light Tank Mk I. They had a two-man crew and were armed with a single machine gun. From this original order sprang an evolutionary line of light tanks ranging from the Mk II up through to the Mk VI.

The Mk VI was the only light tank in the series to see combat with the British army during the Second World War. Total production of the Mk VI amounted to approximately 1,150 units. A small number were supplied to both the Canadian and Australian armies by the British army.

The three-man tank was armed with two machine guns and quickly demonstrated that it was both under-gunned and under-armoured. Even worse, it proved both unreliable and extremely fragile. By 1943, it was withdrawn from British army service.

End of the Line

As a possible replacement for the Mk VI, the British army authorized the production in 1938 of the Mk VII Light Tank, eventually named the 'Tetrarch'. The tank was also assigned the designation A18. The first example of the Tetrarch drove off the factory floor at the end of 1940. By the time production ceased in 1942, a total of 177 units had been constructed.

The Tetrarch was a three-man tank armed with a 2-pounder (40mm) main gun and a coaxial machine gun. Reflecting the small numbers built, the Tetrarch saw only limited combat. The best-known employment of the Tetrarch came as a glider-delivered airborne tank on 6 June 1944 during Operation OVERLORD, the invasion of France, with British army airborne forces. A few Tetrarchs also saw combat with the Red Army.

A larger and heavier version of the Tetrarch was the four-man Mk VIII named the 'Harry Hopkins'. It was also labelled as the A25 Light Tank. The Harry Hopkins was armed like the Tetrarch with a 2-pounder (40mm) main gun. Only ninety-nine units were built between 1942 and 1944, with none ever seeing combat.

The real Harry Hopkins was an important advisor to American President Franklin D. Roosevelt during the Second World War. He was a key player in setting up the Lend-Lease programme that greatly assisted Great Britain during the war years, therefore the British army named this tank in his honour.

Soviet Light Tanks

The first post-First World War mass-produced light tank built in the Soviet Union was designated the MS-1. It was a redesigned version of the Renault FT light tank. Production began in 1928 and continued until 1931 with 959 units constructed. The two-man tank was originally armed with the same French 37mm main gun as mounted in the Renault FT light tank. However, this was later replaced by a Soviet-built 37mm main gun. The tank was also armed with two small-calibre machine guns.

The approximately 15,000lb MS-1 would first see combat with the Red Army during the Sino-Soviet conflict of 1929. By the time the German military invasion of the Soviet Union began in June 1941, none remained operational. However, some would be pressed into service as static pillboxes and rearmed with a Soviet-built 45mm main gun.

Borrowed Light Tank Design

The Red Army began a programme to acquire examples of existing foreign light tank designs in the late 1920s and early 1930s, in part with the assistance of a secret German-Soviet production agreement. This was done because the Soviet Union then lacked the engineering talent needed to design satisfactory tanks. Those foreign light tank designs deemed worthy would be acquired by various means and in most cases modified over time by Soviet tank designers to better meet the requirements of the Red Army.

In the amphibious light tank category the Red Army purchased an example of the single machine-gun-armed Vickers-Armstrong Carden Lloyd (VCL) Amphibian Tank in 1929. It was upon this design that the Red Army would base their two-man T-37A amphibious light tank, also armed with a single machine gun.

A total of 1,552 units of the approximately 7,000lb T-37A were built for the Red Army between 1933 and 1936. A modernized version that had a wider hull was assigned the designation T-38. A total of 1,228 units were built between 1937 and 1939. It retained the two-man crew and the single machine-gun armament of its predecessor.

The T-37A and T-38 would see combat against the Japanese army in the Far East in 1939 and later that same year during the Russo-Finnish War (November 1939–March 1940). They would continue to see use in ever-decreasing numbers until the end of the Second World War.

Replacement Amphibious Tank

The Red Army replacement for the T-37A and T-38 amphibious tank was the larger and heavier two-man amphibious T-40 light tank armed with a single large-calibre machine gun. It first appeared in Red Army service in 1940, with approximately 310 units rolling off the assembly line before the German invasion, with twenty-five examples not being fitted with a propeller. The T-40 weighed approximately 12,000lb.

With the huge losses of all tank types during the initial German military invasion of the Soviet Union, there arose a desperate need by the Red Army to fill that void in its inventory. Because light tanks are simpler and quicker to build than medium or heavy tanks, Soviet industry concentrated on their construction as a stopgap measure.

To speed up light tank production it was decided to completely drop the amphibious capability from the T-40. Such vehicles were labelled as the T-30 with approximately 300 being built before production concluded in late 1941. An even more simplified version of the non-amphibious T-40 that was armed with a 20mm automatic cannon was labelled the T-60. A total of 5,662 units were constructed of the approximately 11,000lb T-60, not all of which were gun tanks.

Light Tanks

In the original non-amphibious light tank category the Red Army bought two different versions of a Vickers-Armstrong three-man light tank in 1931, which was referred to as the Type E. One model had two one-man turrets each armed with a single machine gun. The other had a 47mm main gun fitted in a single two-man turret.

Upon the British-designed Type E light tank, which the British army did not adopt, the Red Army would base its T-26 infantry support light tanks series. In total, the Red Army would take into service 8,079 units of the T-26 series between 1933 and 1941. Of that number, not all were gun tanks as this included those equipped with flame-throwers or modified into prime movers or engineering vehicles.

The original model of the T-26 taken into Red Army service is now referred to as the T-26 Model 1931. It weighed approximately 20,000lb and had two single-man machine-gun-armed turrets. Some later had one of their two turret-mounted machine guns replaced by a 37mm main gun. The exact number converted is unknown.

The T-26 Model 1931 was followed into service by the T-26 Model 1933, which was armed with a 45mm main gun and a coaxial machine gun. It would prove to be the most numerous model of the T-26 light tank series with 4,135 units built.

On the heels of the T-26 Model 1933 there appeared progressively-improved versions of the tank almost yearly. The follow-on variants continued to be armed with a 45mm main gun and coaxial machine gun. Officially, production of the T-26 series ended in January 1941 but forty-seven more were built after the German invasion in the summer of 1941.

Red Army Tank Designations

Unlike other armies, the Red Army had no consistent policy of assigning designations to the various sub-variants of their tanks. Post-war authors on the subject have taken it upon themselves to develop a practice of assigning model numbers to Red Army tanks based on the year they were first introduced into service. This is done in order to distinguish between sub-variants. This method has been adopted by the author to assist the reader in identifying the often many different versions of tank produced for the Red Army.

Borrowing an American Design

The Red Army was not above using subterfuge if there was a foreign tank design that proved of interest to them. This was the case with a prototype tank designed by American inventor J. Walter Christie who named it the M1930 Convertible Tank. Two examples were shipped to the Soviet Union in December 1930 without their turrets and labelled as farm tractors.

The M1930 Convertible Tanks featured an innovative suspension system that came to be known as the 'Christie suspension system'. It allowed them to reach unheard-of speeds for tanks. They could also be operated with or without their tracks, hence the use of the word convertible in their designation. It was upon this vehicle's design that the Red Army would base its BT series of light tanks, of which approximately 8,000 units were built between 1931 and 1941.

The prefix 'BT' is an abbreviation for the Russian words '*Bystrokhodny Tank*' that translated means 'fast tank' or 'high-speed tank'. Unlike the slower-moving T-26 series intended strictly as infantry support vehicles, the BT series had been intended for an exploitation role.

The first tank in the BT series was designated as the BT-2. It was intended that all would be armed with a 37mm main gun, but a shortage at one factory led to some being armed with only two machine guns as a temporary measure.

The follow-on BT-5 was armed with a 45mm main gun and up to four machine guns. The last model in the series was the BT-7, still armed with a 45mm main gun and two machine guns. It weighed approximately 31,000lb.

Combat experience gained with the BT series prior to the German invasion demonstrated that they were under-armoured. A great many would be lost in the early months of the German invasion. However, enough would survive in the Far East for them to take part in the Red Army invasion of Japanese-occupied Manchuria in August 1945.

Post-German Invasion Light Tanks

Following the German invasion a number of new light tanks appeared in Red Army service. Most were in development prior to that time but did not enter into production until after the German invasion. These would include the four-man T-50 light tank armed with a 45mm main gun and two coaxial machine guns. It first rolled off the assembly lines in July 1941 and weighed approximately 31,000lb.

The T-50 was intended as the replacement for the T-26 series in the infantry support role. It was a fairly complex vehicle, which meant that it took longer to build and therefore was also more costly. This resulted in only seventy-five units being completed before it was cancelled in January 1942 in favour of simpler and cheaper to build light tanks such as the T-60. The last T-50 came off the production line in February 1942.

The planned Red Army replacement for the T-60 was the up-armoured T-70 Model 1942 light tank. It was armed with a 45mm main gun and a coaxial machine gun. It weighed approximately 22,000lb and had a crew of two. As the original production model of the vehicle had some design shortcomings, it was quickly redesigned and referred to as the T-70M. Production of the T-70 series began in April 1942 and ended in October 1943, with 8,321 units constructed. More than 60 per cent were the T-70M.

There would be a third version of the T-70 labelled the T-80. However, only seventy-seven units of the four-man vehicle were built before production was cancelled at the same time as the T-70M. It was at this time that the Red Army decided that light tanks were no longer viable on the battlefield. Their reconnaissance role would be better served by armoured cars and their infantry support role by a fully-tracked self-propelled gun.

American Light Tanks

It took the Spanish Civil War (July 1936–April 1939) to convince the US army's senior leadership that its existing light tank designs were not as modern as they could be. In response, there would appear the four-man M2A4 light tank armed with a 37mm main gun and up to five machine guns. Production of the tank began in May 1940 and continued until April 1942, with 375 units completed. It weighed approximately 27,000lb.

In US army service the M2A4 was employed only in the training role; however, with the US Marine Corps (USMC) it saw combat during the fighting on the island of Guadalcanal between August 1942 and February 1943. The USMC had originally requested thirty-six light tanks in July 1940 of a newer model from the US army but made do with the M2A4 as that was the only vehicle available.

M3 Light Tank

The US army was well aware that the M2A4 was only a stopgap vehicle and that testing had uncovered a number of design shortcomings. In its place the US army fielded a redesigned and better-protected model labelled the M3.

The gasoline-engine-powered M3 retained the four-man crew arrangement of the M2A4 and its 37mm main gun and up to five machine guns. Production of the approximately 28,000lb M3 began in March 1941 and concluded in October 1942, with 4,526 units completed.

The M3 would initially see combat with the British army in North Africa beginning in November 1941. In British army service the tank was named the 'Stuart'. A big improvement over existing British-designed and built light tanks, especially in overall reliability, it still proved to be a major disappointment in action as it was quickly deemed to be under-gunned and under-armoured.

US Army Designation Code Meanings

In the US army the letter 'M' at the beginning of a tank designation means that it had been 'standardized' (approved for production). The following number/numbers identifies its sequence of production. However, there can be gaps in the number sequence because of cancelled vehicles or due to possible designation confusion with other US army tanks. Hence there was no M4 light tank, only the M4 medium tank.

The letter 'A' added to a vehicle's designation code meant that it underwent a minor design modification, with the number following the letter 'A' denoting its sequence of production. A major design modification would typically be reflected in the vehicle's designation code by the application of a higher number. An example is the redesigned M2A4 light tank being designated as the M3 light tank.

Under Lend-Lease the Australian army began receiving the M3 in the autumn of 1941. These were used successfully to help rid the island of New Guinea of Japanese forces between September 1942 and January 1943. The positive results achieved by the M3s in New Guinea came about because the Japanese lacked any modern anti-tank weapons in that area of operation.

The M3 initially saw combat with the US army in the Philippines between December 1941 and April 1942. The first combat use of the tank by the USMC took place during the conquest of the island of Guadalcanal, which lasted from August 1942 until February 1943. However, the M3 did not make a positive impression on the USMC as it proved too light to push through the jungle undergrowth and its 37mm main gun lacked the penetrative capabilities to destroy well-protected Japanese defensive positions.

M3A1 Light Tank

The US army never stopped incorporating design improvements into the M3 production line. Eventually enough modifications had been made to the tank to warrant a designation change to M3A1. It retained the 37mm main gun of the M2A4 and M3 as its turret lacked the space for anything larger. The M3A1 would come in both a gasoline- and diesel-engine-powered version.

Production of the gasoline-engine-powered M3A1 began in May 1942 and ended in February 1943, with 4,410 units constructed. There were also 211 units of the diesel-engine-powered M3A1 constructed between August and October 1942. The US army employed the latter version for training purposes only.

Despite the improvements made to the M3A1, the USMC found the tank just as useless during the Battle of Tarawa in November 1943 as it had on Guadalcanal with the M3. There were no jungles to worry about on Tarawa but the 37mm gun on the M3A1 still proved unequal to the task of destroying Japanese defensive positions.

A total of 2,433 units of the gasoline-engine-powered version of the M3A1 were passed on to other armies as part of Lend-Lease. The British army received 1,594 units and classified them as the 'Stuart III'. The Red Army was supplied with 340 units of the same version under Lend-Lease. The remaining 499 units went to other countries' armies under Lend-Lease. Only twenty units of the diesel-engine-powered version of the M3A1 were allocated to Lend-Lease.

M5 Light Tank

The next light tank in service with the US army would be the M5. It featured a sloping front hull arrangement, referred to as a 'glacis'. As with its predecessors, the M5 had a four-man crew and was armed with a 37mm main gun and up to three machine guns. It retained the turret from the M3A1. Production of the approximately 33,000lb M5 began in April 1942 and ended in December 1942, with 2,074 units built.

M3A3 Light Tank

The last model in the M3 series was the approximately 32,000lb M3A3. It came about because the US army requested that an M3A1 be modified to have the same sloping glacis as the M5. The M3A3 was also designed with sloping hull upper side plates and came with a new turret design that had a bustle added for a radio as per a British army request.

Production of the gasoline-engine-powered M3A3 began in January 1942 and did not end until September 1943 with a total of 3,427 units completed. The majority built went overseas under Lend-Lease. The British army received 2,054 units of the M3A3 and referred to them as the 'Stuart V'. The Free French army was supplied with 277 units of the M3A3, with another 100 units being sent off to serve with the Chinese Nationalist Army.

M5A1 Light Tank

An improved model of the M5 light tank entered into production in November 1942 and was designated as the M5A1 light tank. The major external feature of the M5A1 that distinguished it from the earlier M5 was the addition of the turret from the M3A3. Construction of the M5A1 continued until June 1944, with 6,810 units built. It was the most common light tank to see service with the US army in Western Europe from June 1944 until the German surrender in May 1945.

The M5A1 entered into USMC service in late 1943. All would be discarded by the USMC in late 1944 in favour of more capable better-armed and better-armoured medium tanks.

The British army would receive 1,431 units of the M5A1 under Lend-Lease. They labelled it as the 'Stuart VI'. In turn, the British army would pass many of them on to the various Commonwealth armies, from Australia, Canada, New Zealand and South Africa. The Free French would also acquire 226 units of the M5A1 under Lend-Lease, while the Red Army would only receive five units. Both the M5 and M5A1 were driven by gasoline-powered engines.

M24 Light Tank

In August 1942 the US army began planning for the design and development of a next-generation light tank to replace the M3 series. The M5 and M5A1 were not yet in service at that time. The replacement for the M3 and eventually the M5 and M5A1 was the four-man gasoline-engine-powered M24. It rode on a torsion bar suspension system in contrast to the vertical volute spring suspension (VVSS) system of the M2A4 through M5A1.

The M24 first rolled off the assembly line in April 1944. By the time production concluded in September 1945, a total of 4,371 units had been constructed. The M24 was larger than the M5 and M5A1 and weighed approximately 40,000lb. It was armed with a 75mm main gun originally developed for an Army Air Forces (AAF) medium bomber optimized for the ground-attack role. The tank was also armed with up to three machine guns.

The first units of the M24 arrived in Western Europe in December 1944 as the replacement for the M5 and M5A1. The M3 series was already out of service with the US army by that time. Under Lend-Lease the British army received 289 units of the M24, which they assigned the name 'Chaffee'. However, none would see combat with the British army during the Second World War. The Red Army was provided with two examples of the M24.

Airborne Light Tank

The US army was very impressed by the German military employment of para-troopers and glider-delivered infantry during the early part of the Second World War. It was also aware of the pre-war experiments by the Red Army of attaching light tanks to the bottom of multi-engine aircraft that were envisioned as being flown to enemy airfields captured by its paratroopers. This concept would lead to the US army adoption of the approximately 16,000lb M22 Light Tank.

The M22 had a crew of three men and was armed with a 37mm main gun and a coaxial machine gun. Production of the gasoline-engine-powered M22 began in April 1943 and concluded in February 1944, with a total of 830 units completed. As plans for the airborne invasion of France in the summer of 1944 did not call for the seizure of any enemy airfields, the M22 proved to be a vehicle without a mission in the US army.

The American government eventually transferred 260 units of the M22 to the British army under Lend-Lease and they named it the 'Locust'. Its only combat action with the British army occurred on 24 March 1945. Nine were loaded into gliders and took part in Operation VARSITY, a joint Anglo-American airborne operation over the River Rhine into Germany.

Light Tank Odds and Ends

Such was the fear of a Japanese invasion of the west coast of the United States following the attack on Pearl Harbor in December 1941 that the US army impressed into service approximately 600 Marmon-Herrington Company-designed and built light tanks. These had been intended for shipment to friendly foreign armies. The majority were armed only with machine guns, although some were armed with 37mm main guns. All were disposed of by 1942 when the threat of a Japanese invasion of the United States receded.

Prior to acquiring the M2A4 from the US army, the USMC had tested and eventually purchased thirty-five machine-gun-armed light tanks in three different versions that had been designed and built by the Marmon-Herrington Company. Testing of these vehicles showed them to be under-armoured and mechanically unreliable. None would be committed to combat by the USMC and all were disposed of before the end of the Second World War.

Pictured is a First World War-era battle-damaged French-designed and built FT light tank on display in France. It can be identified by the wooden boards employed in the construction of the vehicle's large front idler wheels. The slightly modified American-built version designated as the 6-ton Tank M1917 had all-steel front idler wheels. *(Pierre-Olivier Buan)*

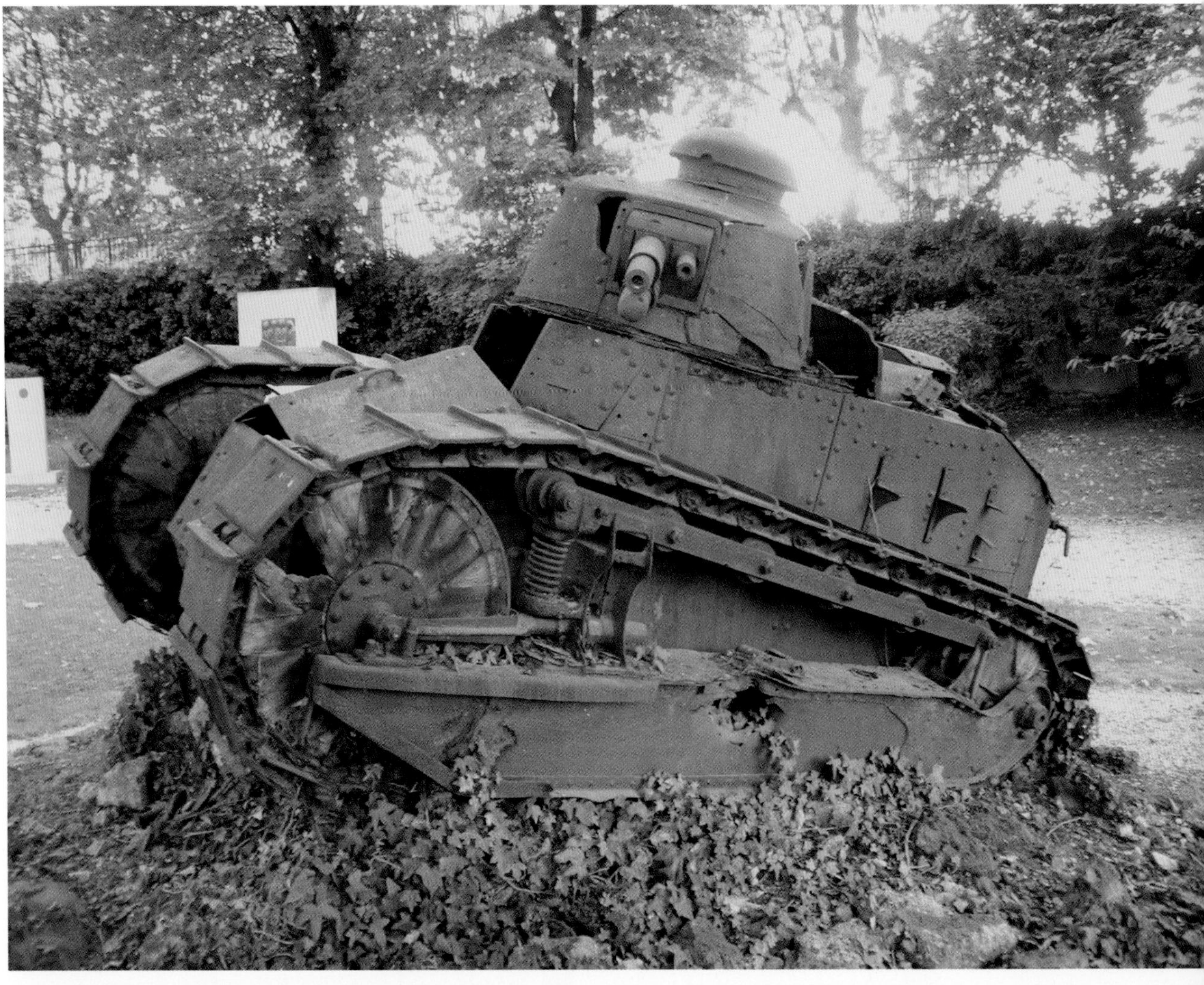

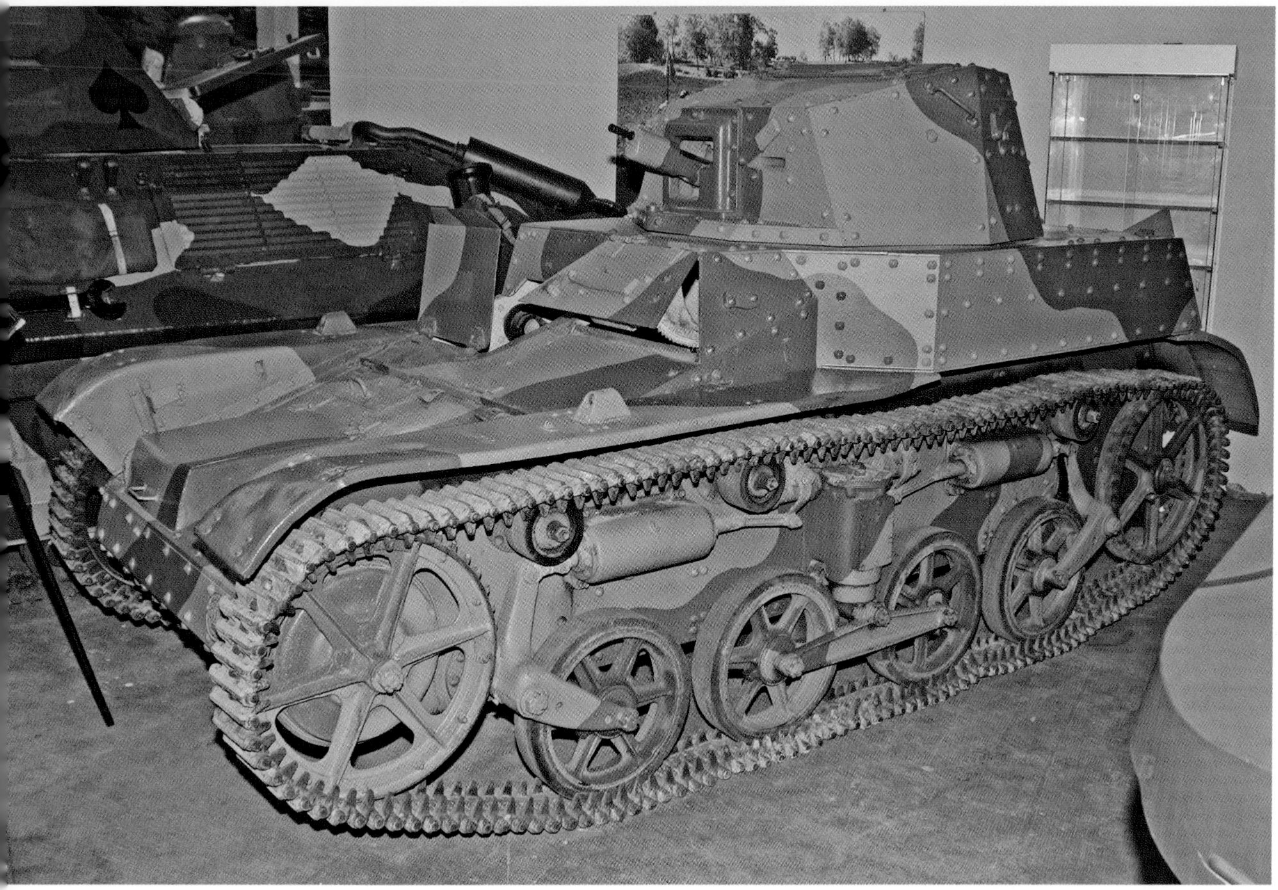

Located at the French Tank Museum is an AMR33. The vehicle's engine was located in the front hull. Prior to ordering the tank into production the French army had five pilot examples, each built with a different suspension system. A Renault design was judged superior to that of its competitors, resulting in the firm being awarded a contract to build the tank. *(Christophe Vallier)*

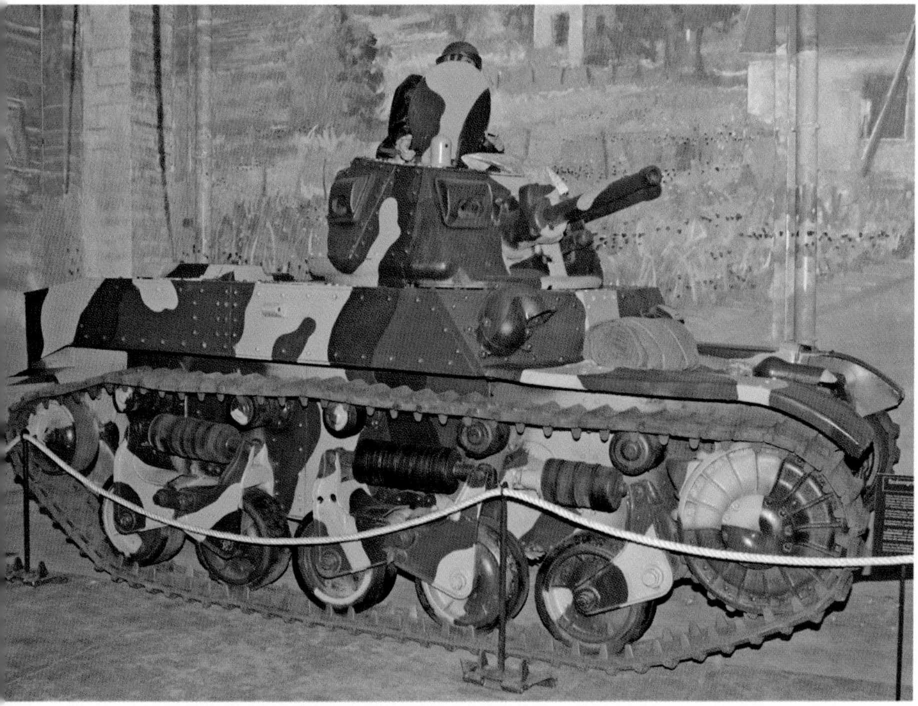

With the threat of war with Germany looming in the late 1930s, the French army sought out better-armed and armoured light tanks. One example of this effort is this Renault-designed and built light tank designated as the AMC35 ACG 1 shown here on display at the French Tank Museum. It was armed with a 47mm main gun and a coaxial machine gun. *(Christophe Vallier)*

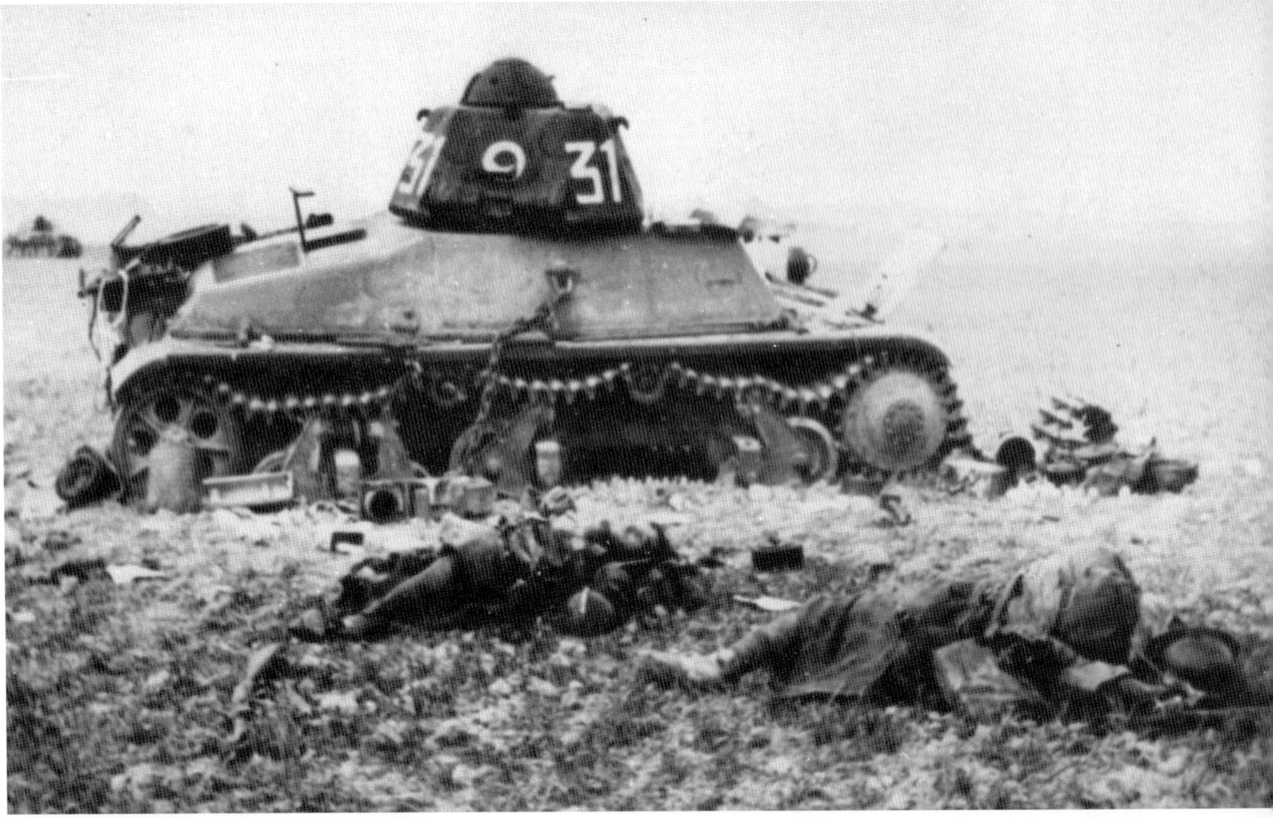
9
31

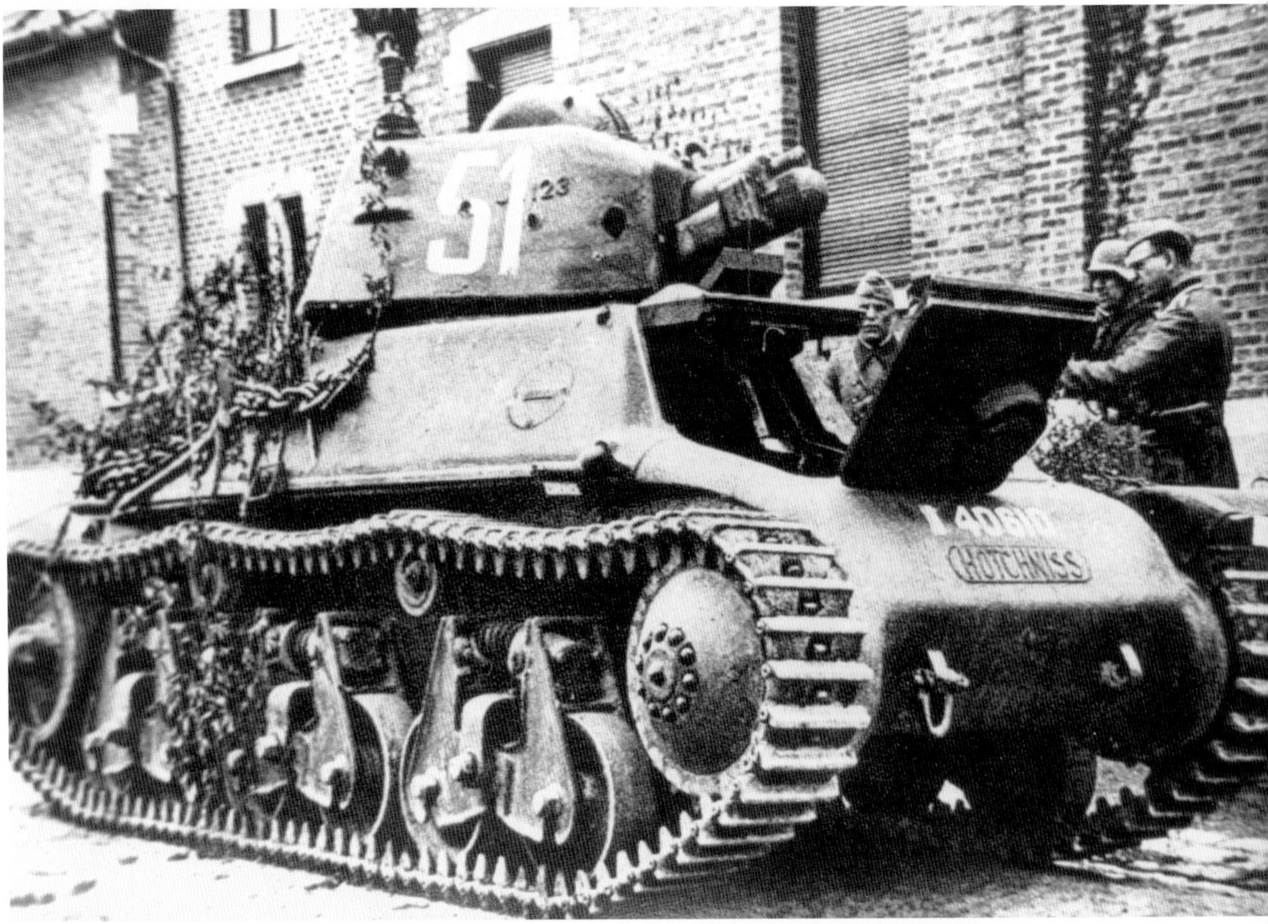
51
HOTCHKISS

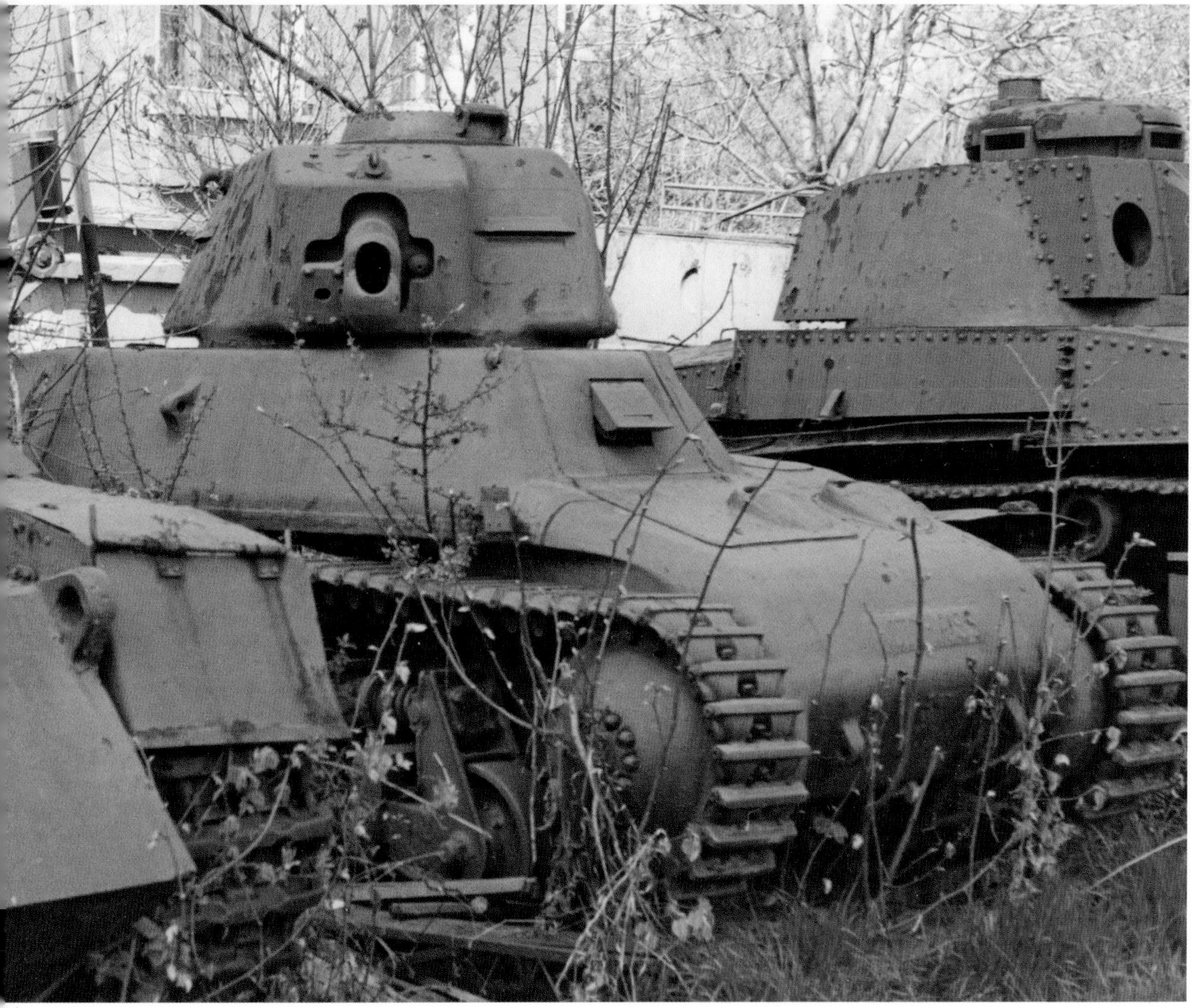

(*Opposite above*) A destroyed French army H35 light tank is pictured in a French field in the summer of 1940. The H35 was a pre-war Hotchkiss-designed and built light tank that can be distinguished from a subsequent improved model by its steeply-sloping rear hull engine deck. Visible on the roof of the tank's turret is the vehicle commander's cupola, which did not open. *(Patton Museum)*

(*Above*) Belonging to the Bulgarian Army Museum is this former French army H39 light tank later employed by the German army as can be discerned by its low-profile vehicle commander's cupola. This particular tank is missing its 37mm main gun. The H39 can be distinguished from the H35 by the near-horizontal rear hull engine deck, which housed a larger and more powerful engine. *(Thomas Anderson)*

(*Opposite below*) German soldiers are shown examining an abandoned French army H39 light tank. The turret and main armament of the H35 and the H39 were identical. The differences between the two versions of the same tank were the mobility upgrades to the latter, which besides a larger and more powerful engine included wider tracks and new steel-rimmed road wheels. *(Patton Museum)*

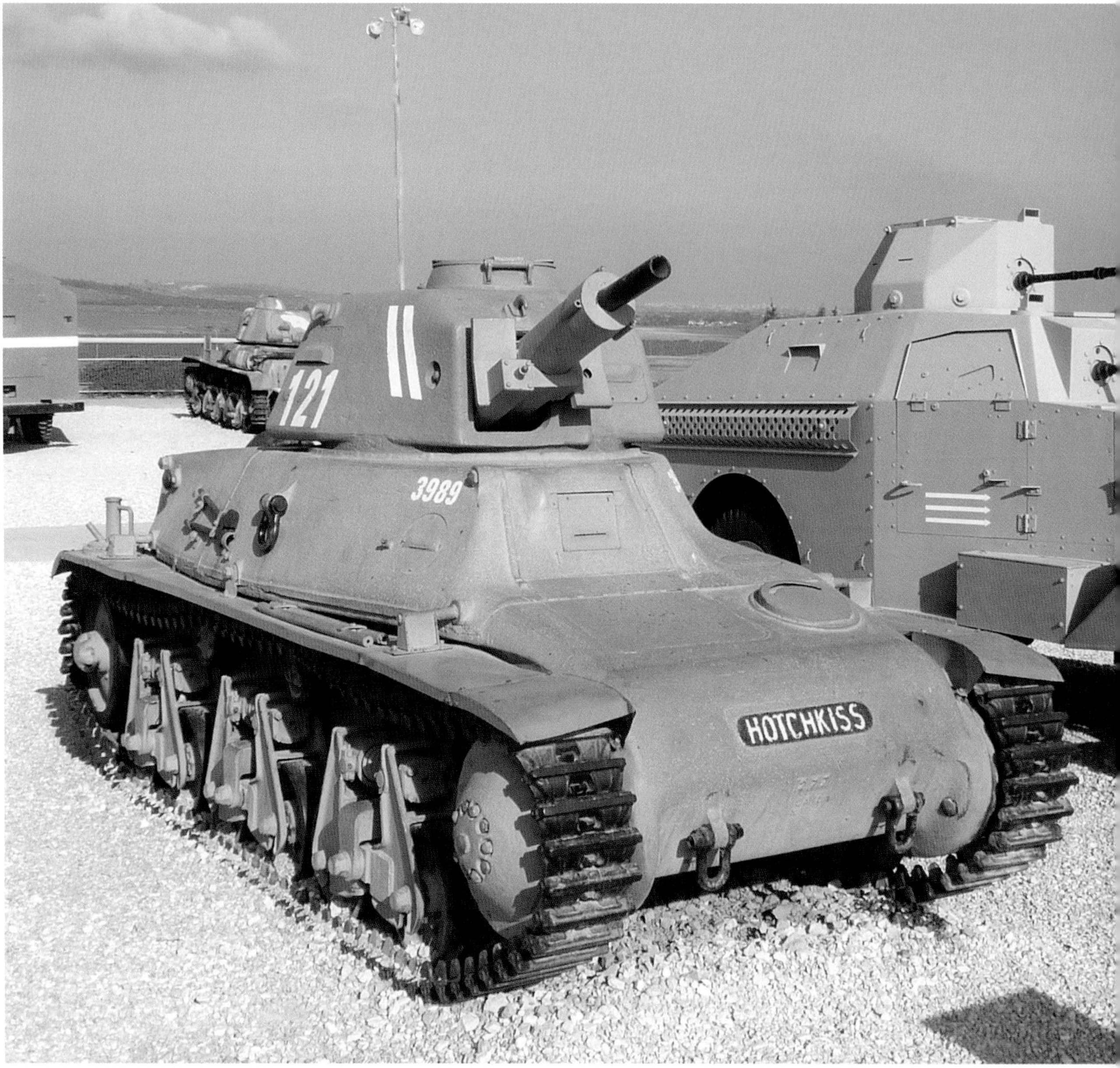

121
3989
HOTCHKISS

(*Above*) Pictured at the Israeli Army Tank Museum is a late-production example of a French army H39 light tank armed with a long-barrelled 37mm main gun designated as the SA38. Unlike the original short-barrelled 37mm main gun on the H39 labelled as the SA18, which had been designed as an infantry support weapon, the SA38 was intended as a tank-killing weapon when designed. *(Vladimir Yakubov)*

(*Opposite above*) On display in France as a monument tank is this late-production H39 armed with the SA38 37mm main gun. Like its predecessor the H35, the H39 had authorized storage space within the vehicle for 100 main gun rounds. Frontal armour protection on both tanks was an impressive 40mm thick, which was far superior to its German light tank counterparts in 1940. *(Pierre-Olivier Buan)*

(*Opposite below*) Located at the Israeli Army Tank Museum is a former French army R35 light tank designed and built by Renault. Its resemblance to the Hotchkiss-designed and built H35 and H39 is due to the fact that both firm's light tanks were designed to meet the same French army light tank requirements. The key external differences between the two company's tanks are in their respective suspension systems. *(Vladimir Yakubov)*

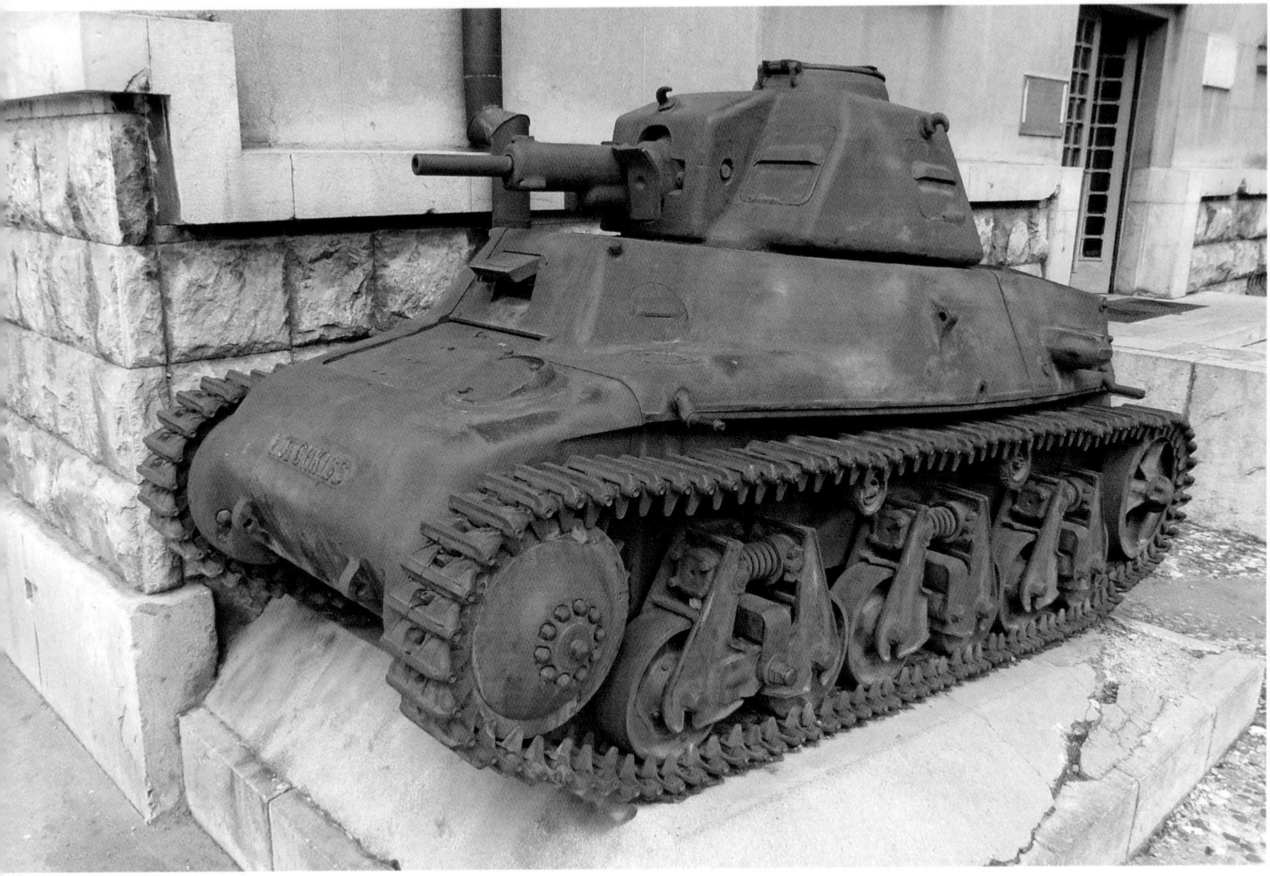
HOTCHKISS

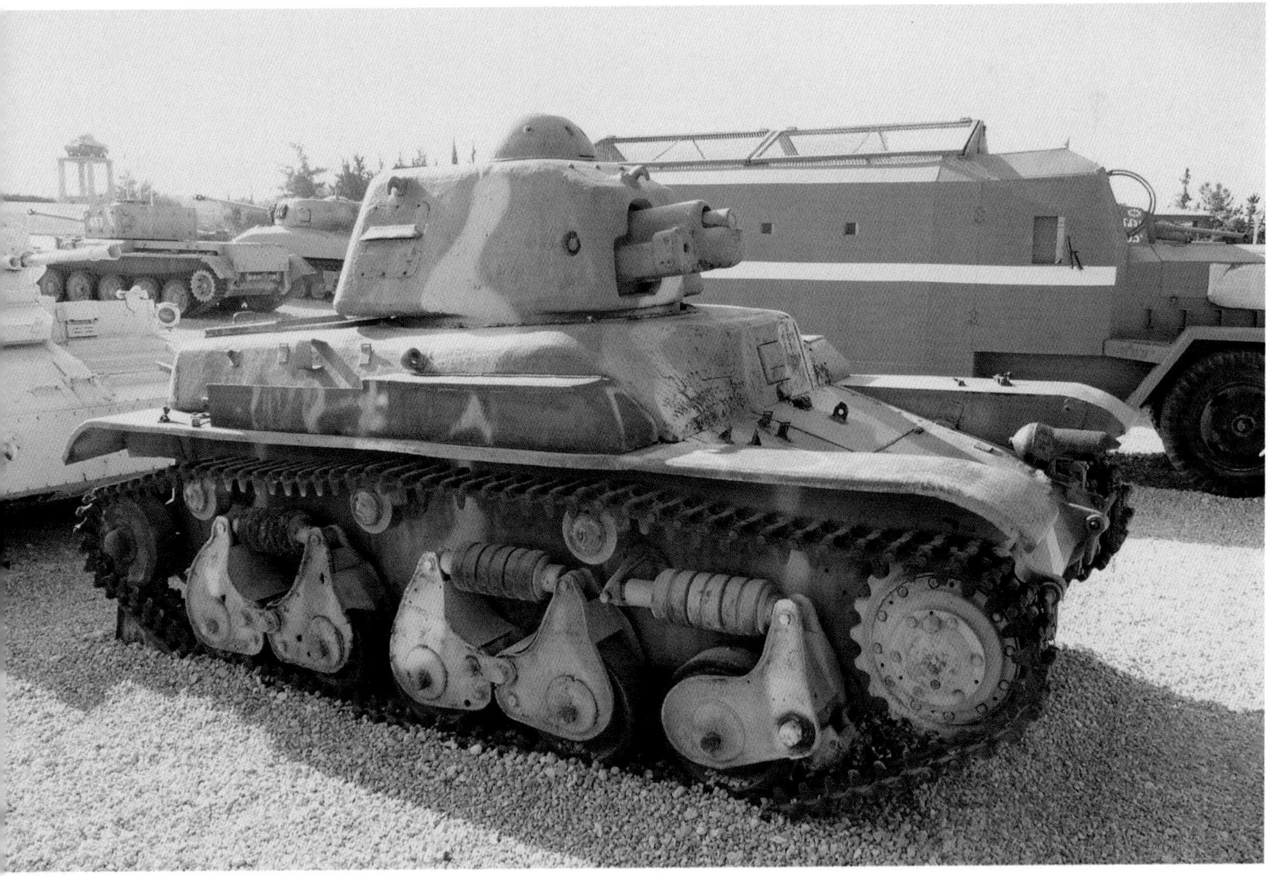

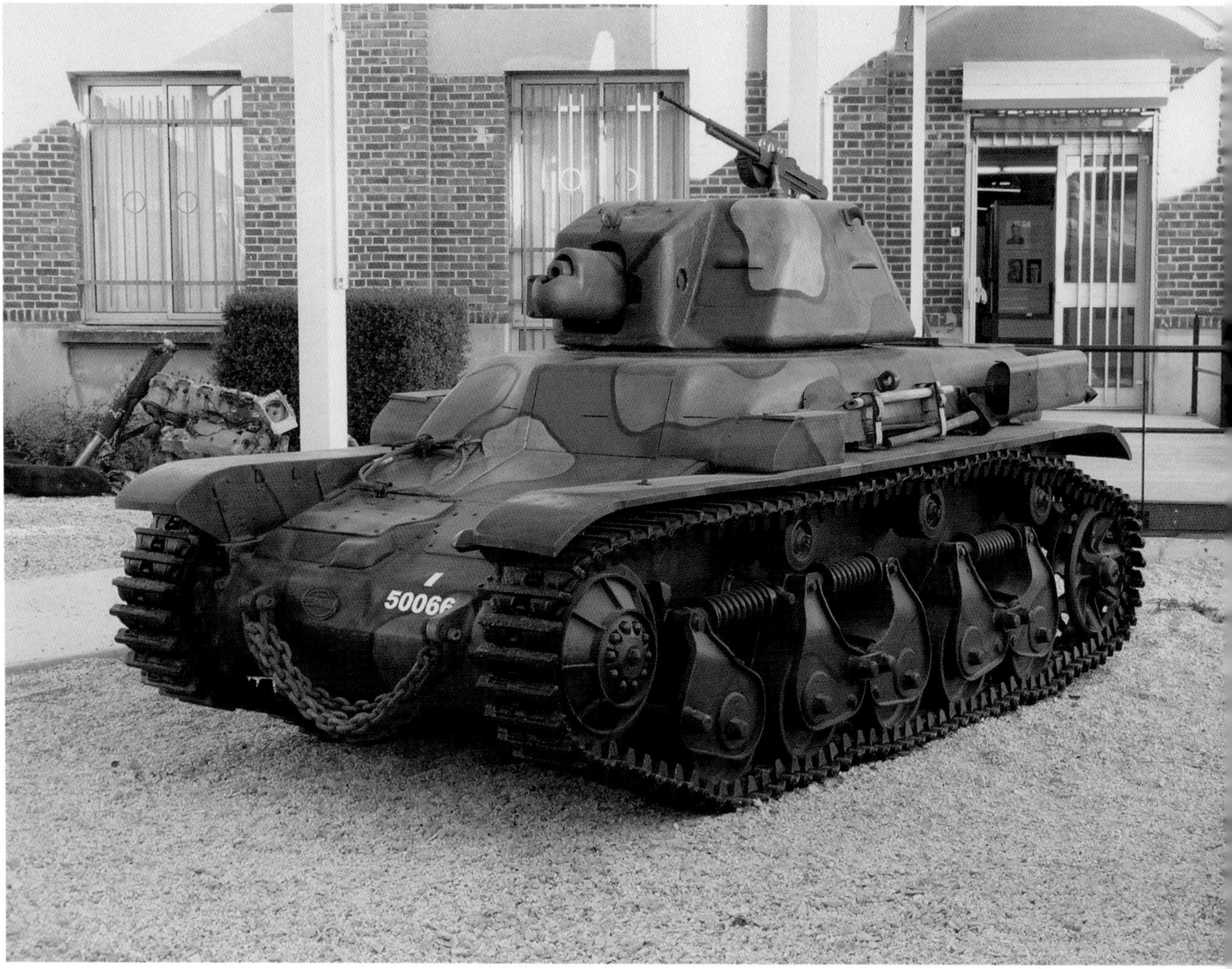

(*Above*) On display in front of the French military museum is this restored R35 light tank, the most numerous in the French army's inventory in 1940. It is missing its original dome-shaped vehicle commander's cupola. The French army was not pleased with the tank suspension system. However, they went ahead and ordered the vehicle into production because of the fear of a coming war with Germany. *(Jean-Claude Poubel)*

(*Opposite above*) Late-production Renault R35s were up-armed with the longer-barrelled SA38 37mm gun as seen here on this restored example belonging to the French Tank Museum. The domed vehicle commander's cupola did open but was not large enough for the vehicle commander to use for entering or leaving the vehicle. The vehicle commanders entered and left their tanks by way of a rearward-folding hatch seen in the photograph. *(Christophe Vallier)*

(*Opposite below*) In sharp contrast to the rounded cast hulls and turrets of the Hotchkiss and Renault light tanks was the welded hull and turret design of the FCM36 seen here on display in the French Tank Museum. There had been some thought given to up-arming the tank with the longer-barrelled SA38 37mm gun but the gun mount proved difficult to reconfigure and work was soon halted on the conversion. *(Christophe Vallier)*

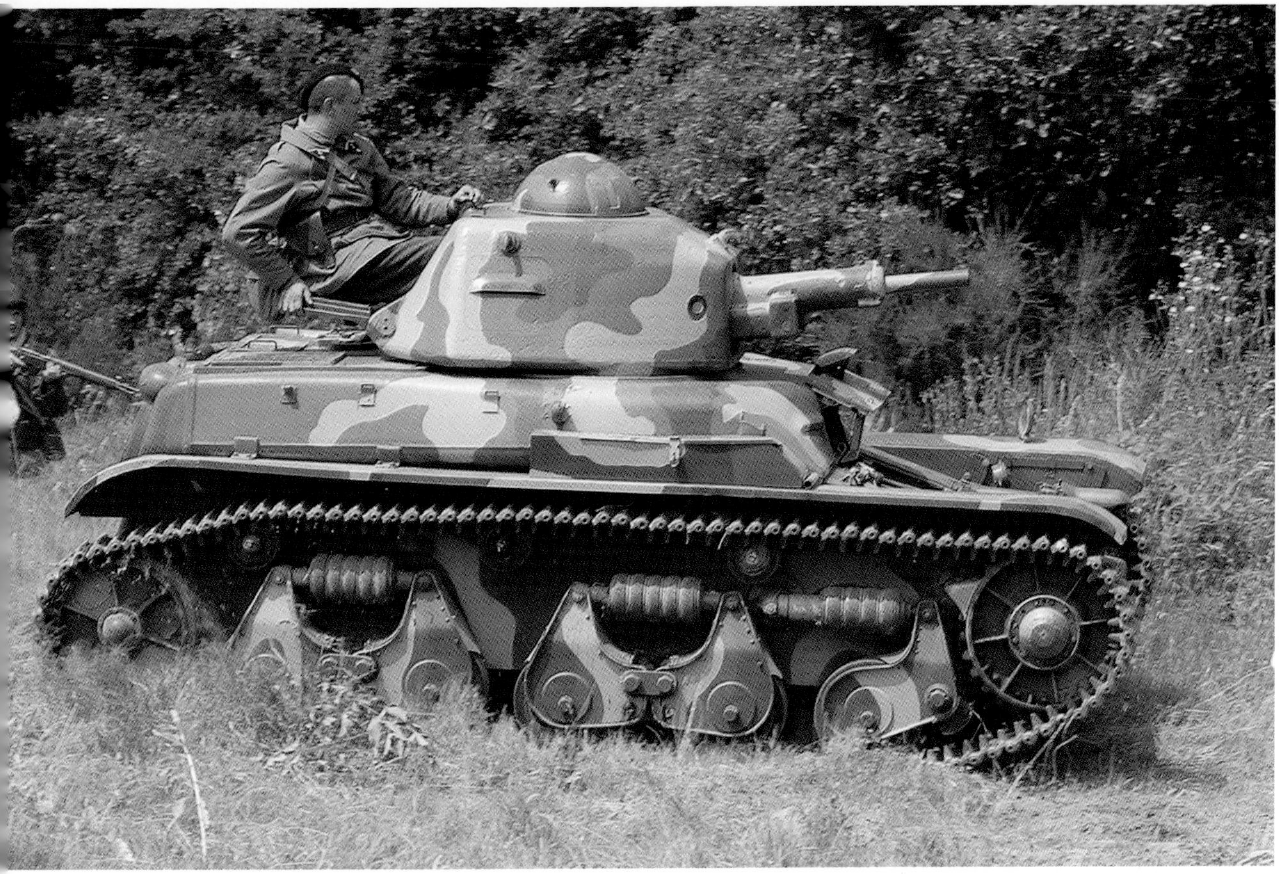

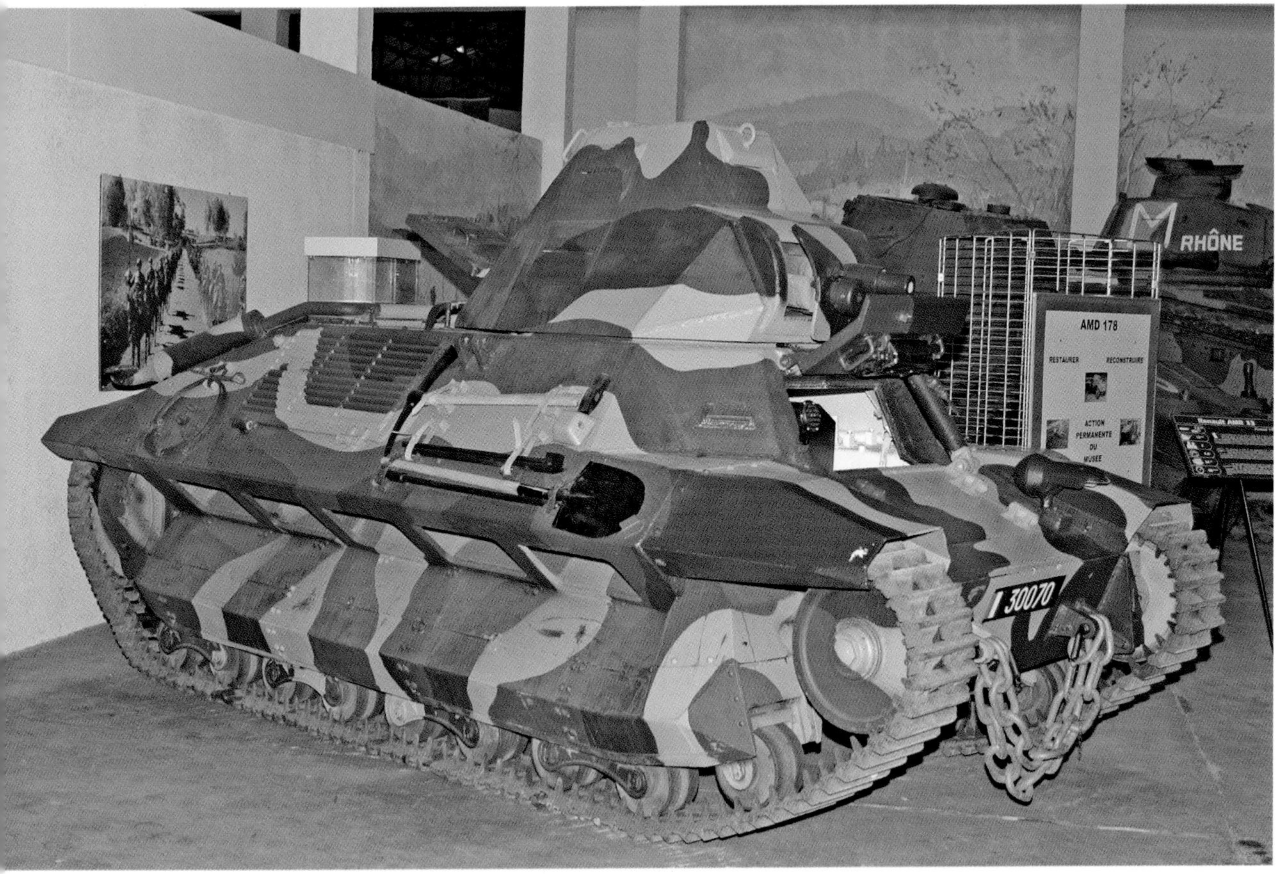
RHÔNE
AMD 178
RESTAURER
RECONSTRUIRE
ACTION PERMANENTE DU MUSÉE
30070

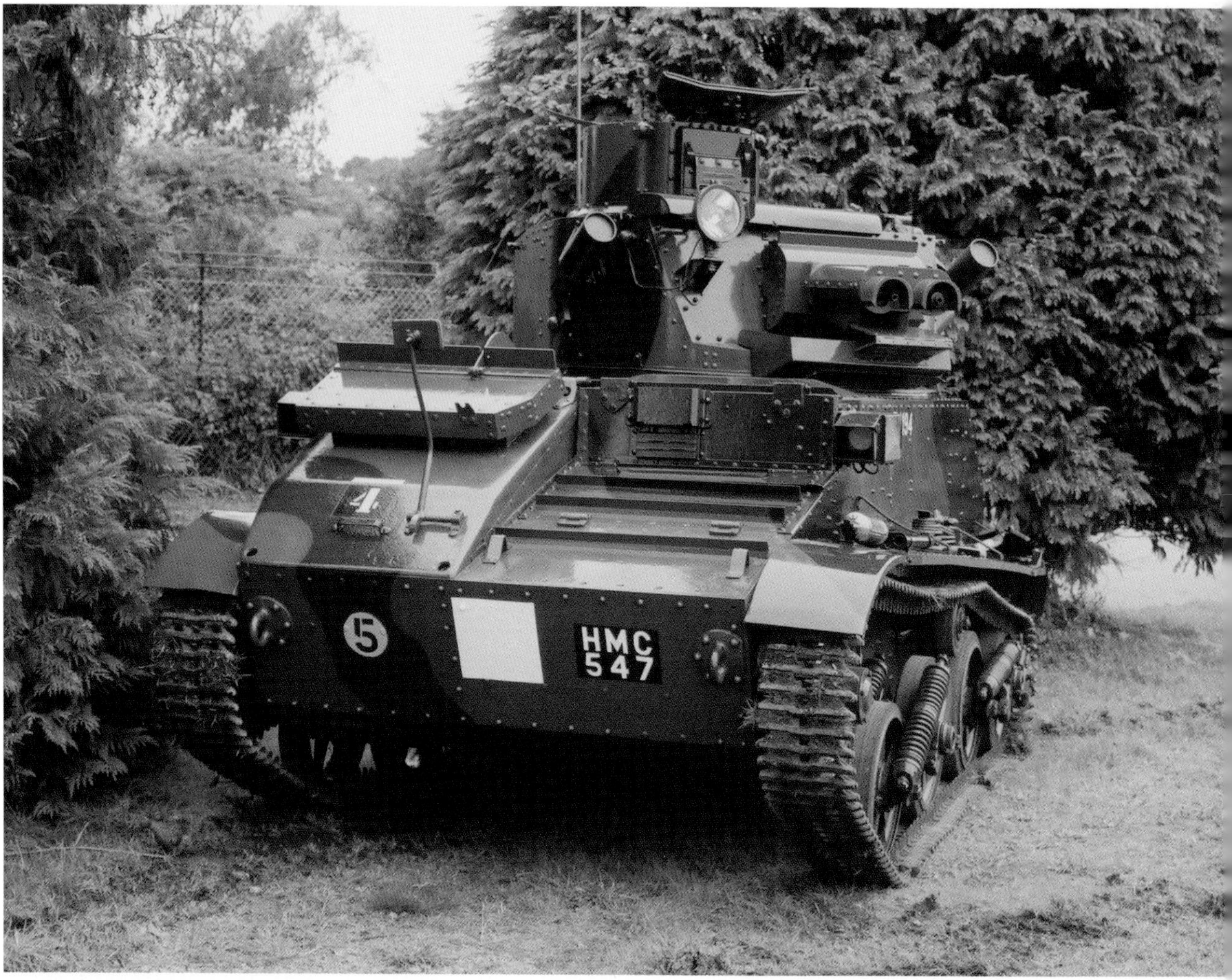
4
5
HMC
547

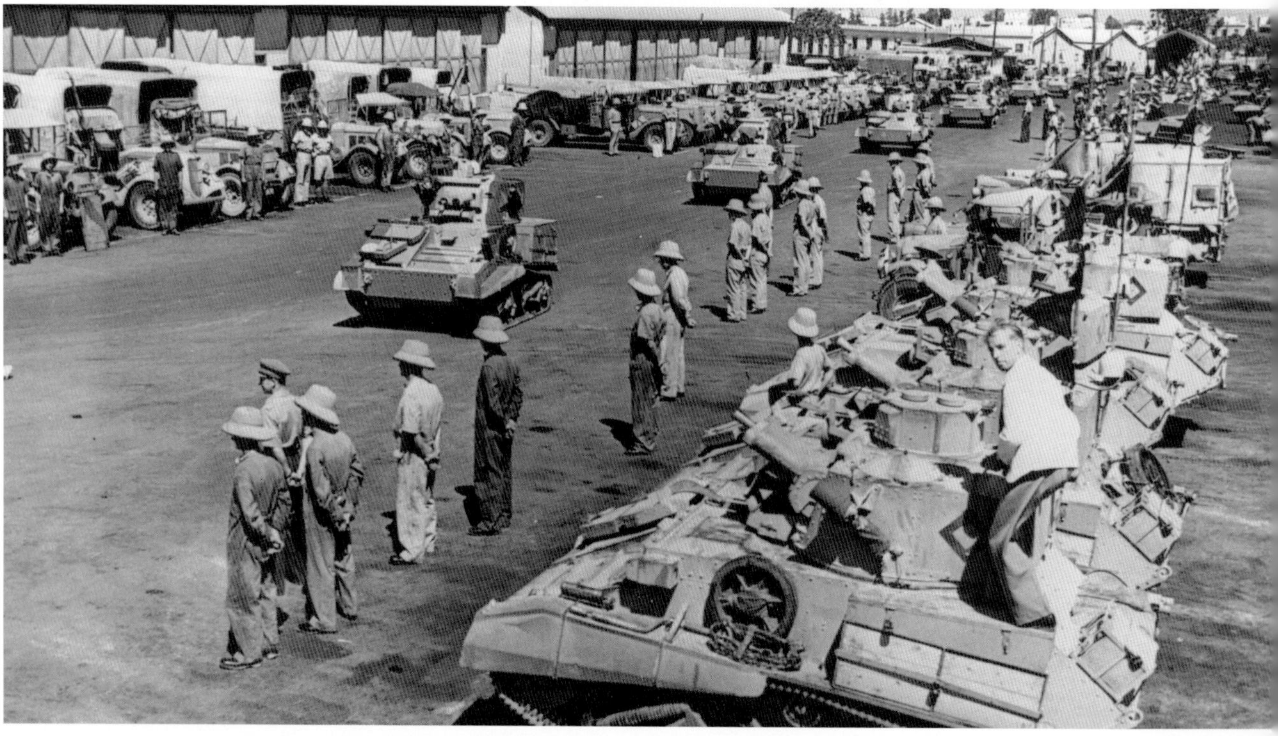

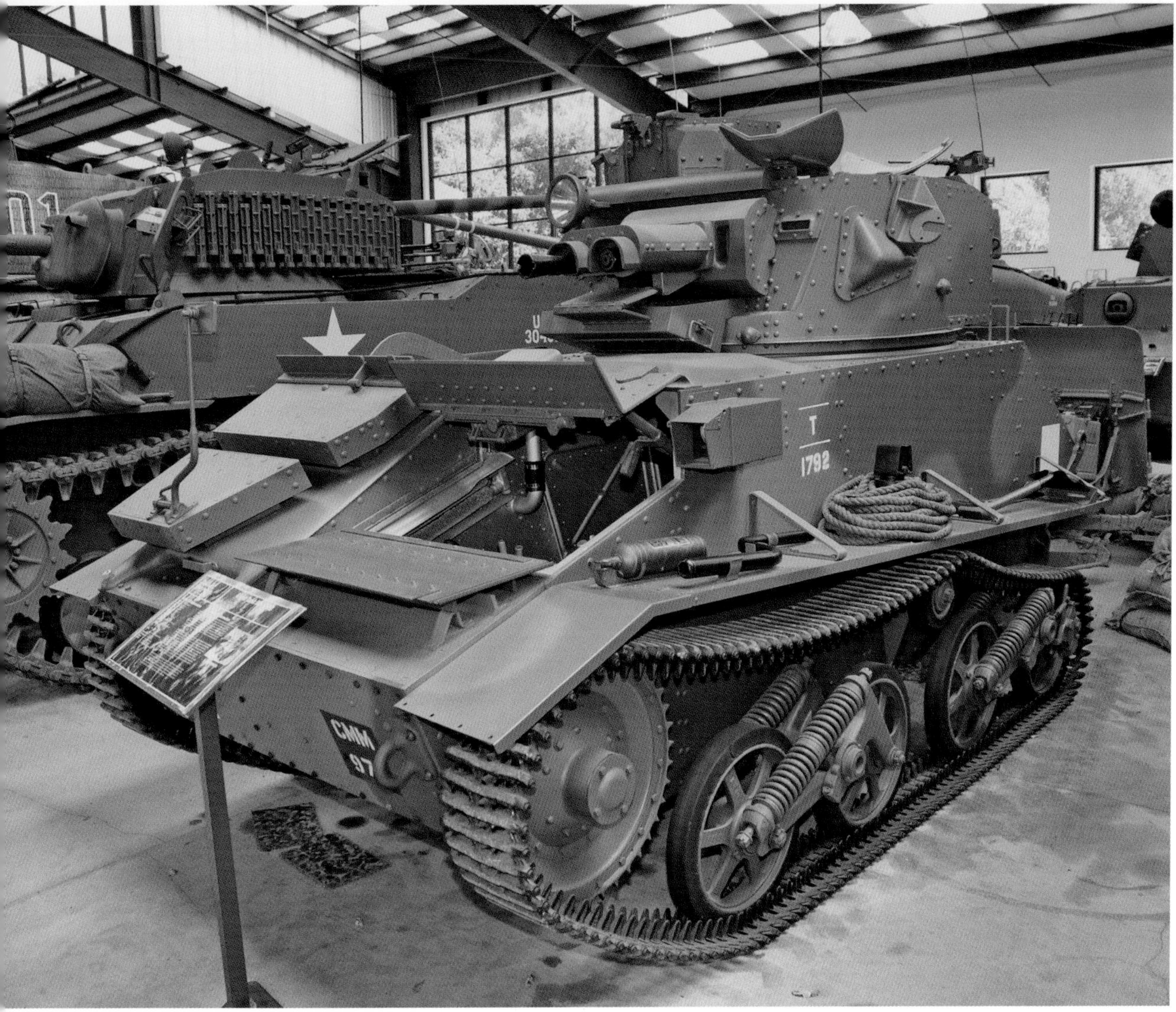
T
1792

(*Opposite above*) The last of the pre-war-designed British army light tanks and the only one to see combat during the Second World War was the Mk VI series. An example of the three-man tank belonging to the Tank Museum's collection is pictured here. The maximum armour protection on the machine-gun-armed tank was 14mm and the minimum was 4mm. *(Tank Museum)*

(*Opposite below*) In this pre-war photograph we see a parade in Egypt of a unit of British army Mk VIA tanks. Armament on the Mk VI series consisted of two turret-mounted machine guns enclosed within a single armoured housing. The vehicle had a top speed on level roads of 35mph and had a maximum range of 130 miles. *(Tank Museum)*

(*Above*) Seen here in one of the display buildings at the former Military Vehicle Technology Foundation is a Mk VI series light tank. The larger of the tank's two water-cooled machine guns was a Vickers 12.7mm. The final version of the Mk VI series was armed with a licence-built Czech-designed machine gun labelled as the 15mm BESA Heavy Machine Gun. *(Chris Hughes)*

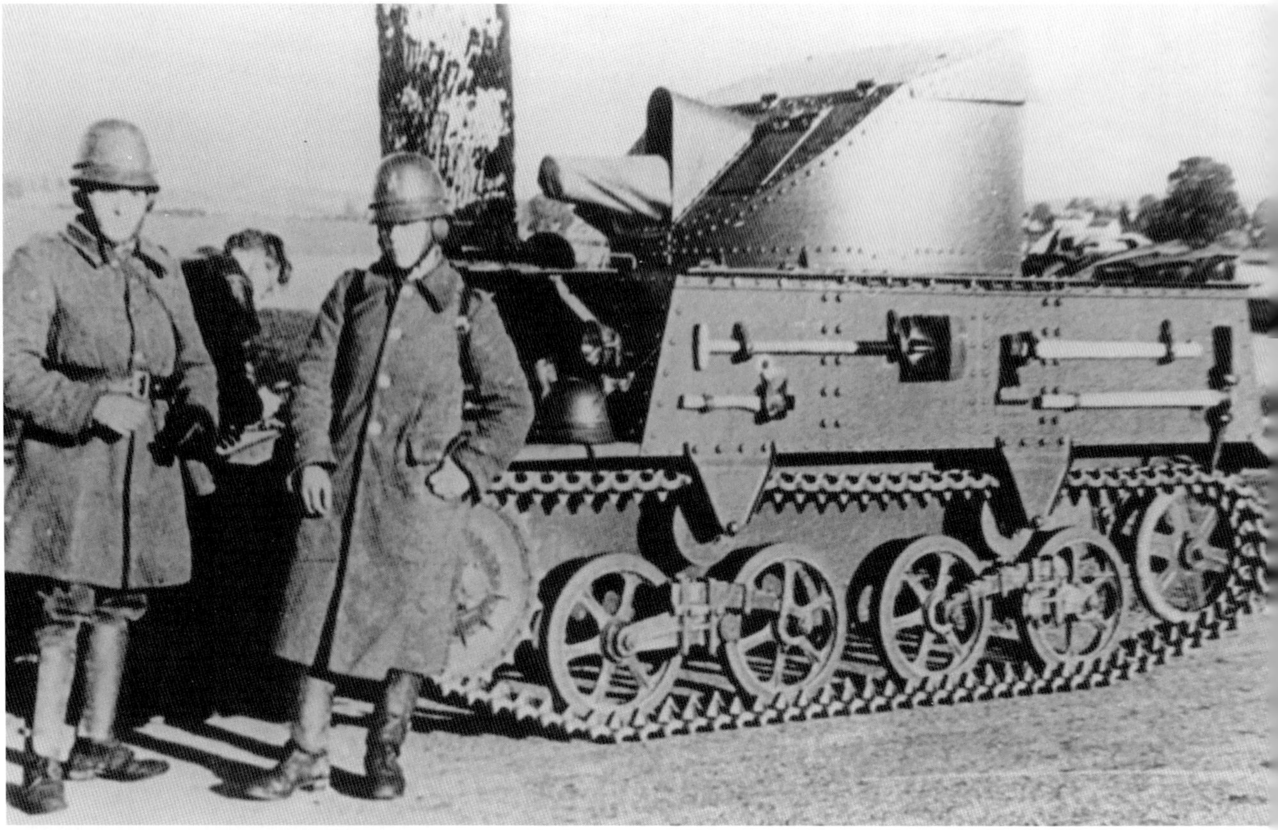

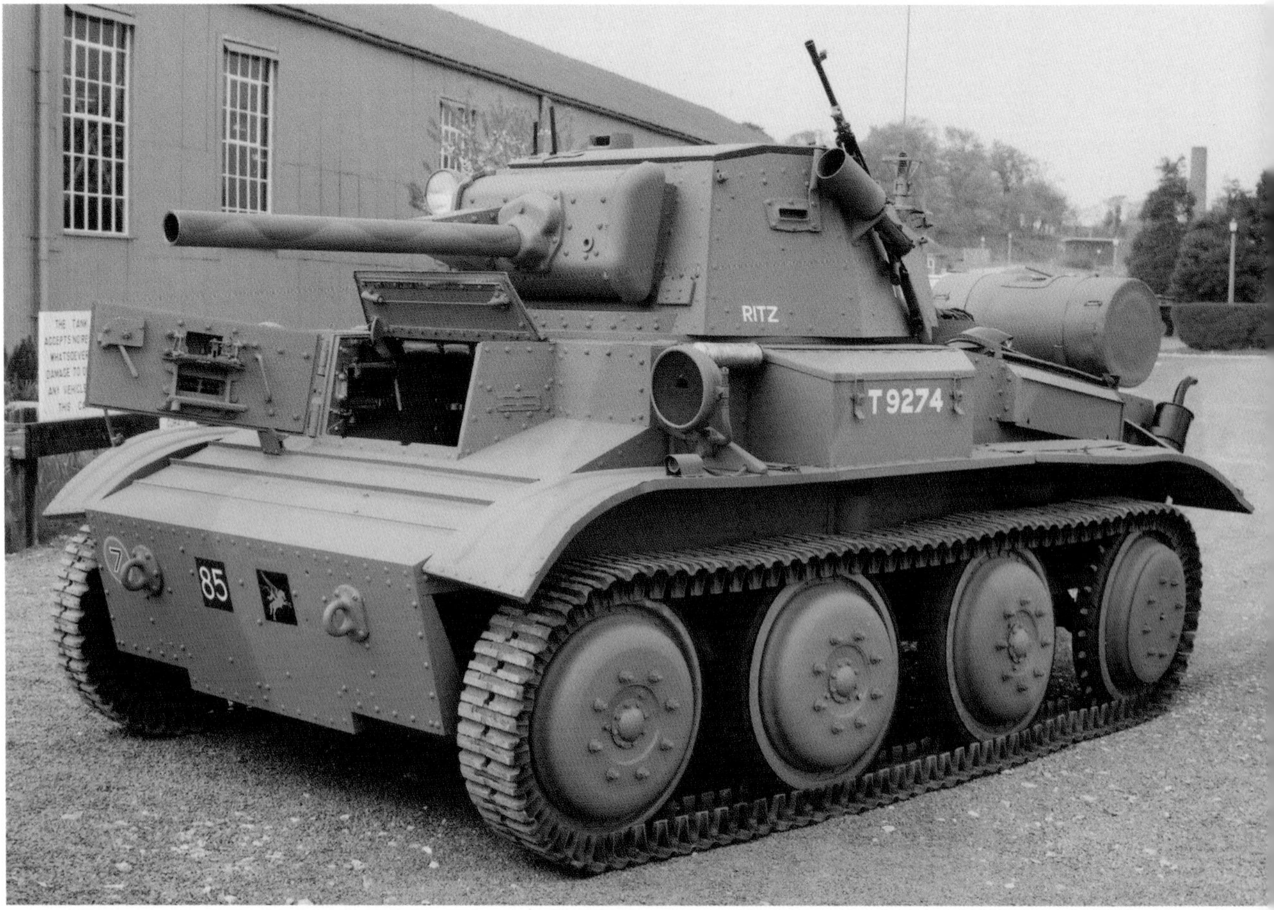
RITZ
T 9274
85

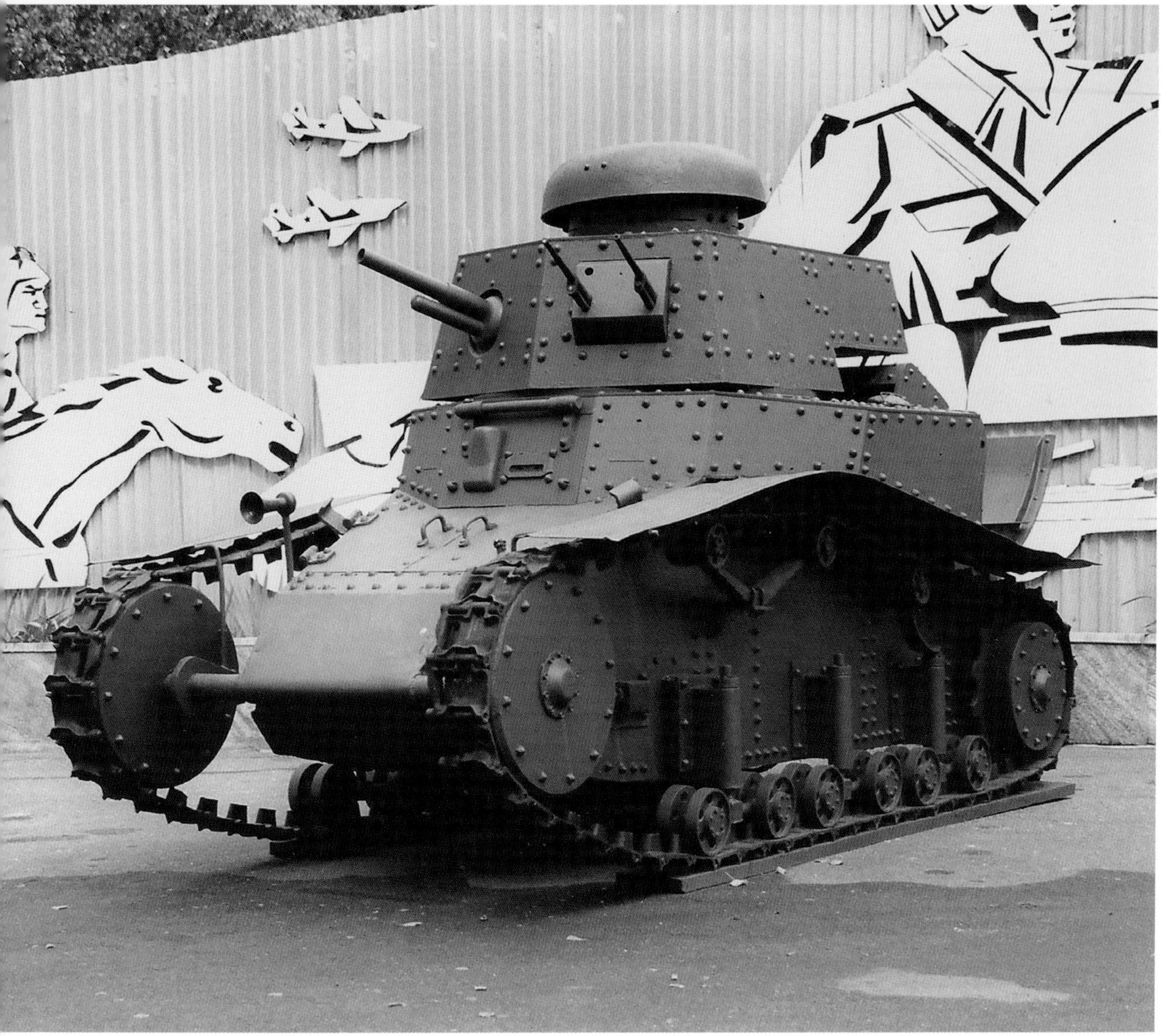

(*Opposite above*) The Belgian army had in its inventory prior to the German invasion of May 1940 a range of commercially-acquired British-designed and built light tanks from the firm of Vickers-Armstrong. The example pictured is armed with a Belgian-designed 47mm main gun and labelled as the T13B3 tank destroyer. (*Tank Museum*)

(*Opposite below*) The Tetrarch light tank pictured was not designed and built to meet any specific British army requirements; rather it was a private venture vehicle from the firm of Vickers-Armstrong. Due to its small size and light weight it was acquired by the British army for its airborne forces as it could fit within the confines of an existing glider. (*Tank Museum*)

(*Above*) Part of the Russian Tank Museum collection is this Red Army T-18 light tank, also referred to as the MS-1. It was based on the general design layout of the French FT light tank with a new Russian-designed suspension system. It was armed with a turret-mounted 37mm main gun and two machine guns. The suspension system shown is a modern reconstruction. (*Bob Fleming*)

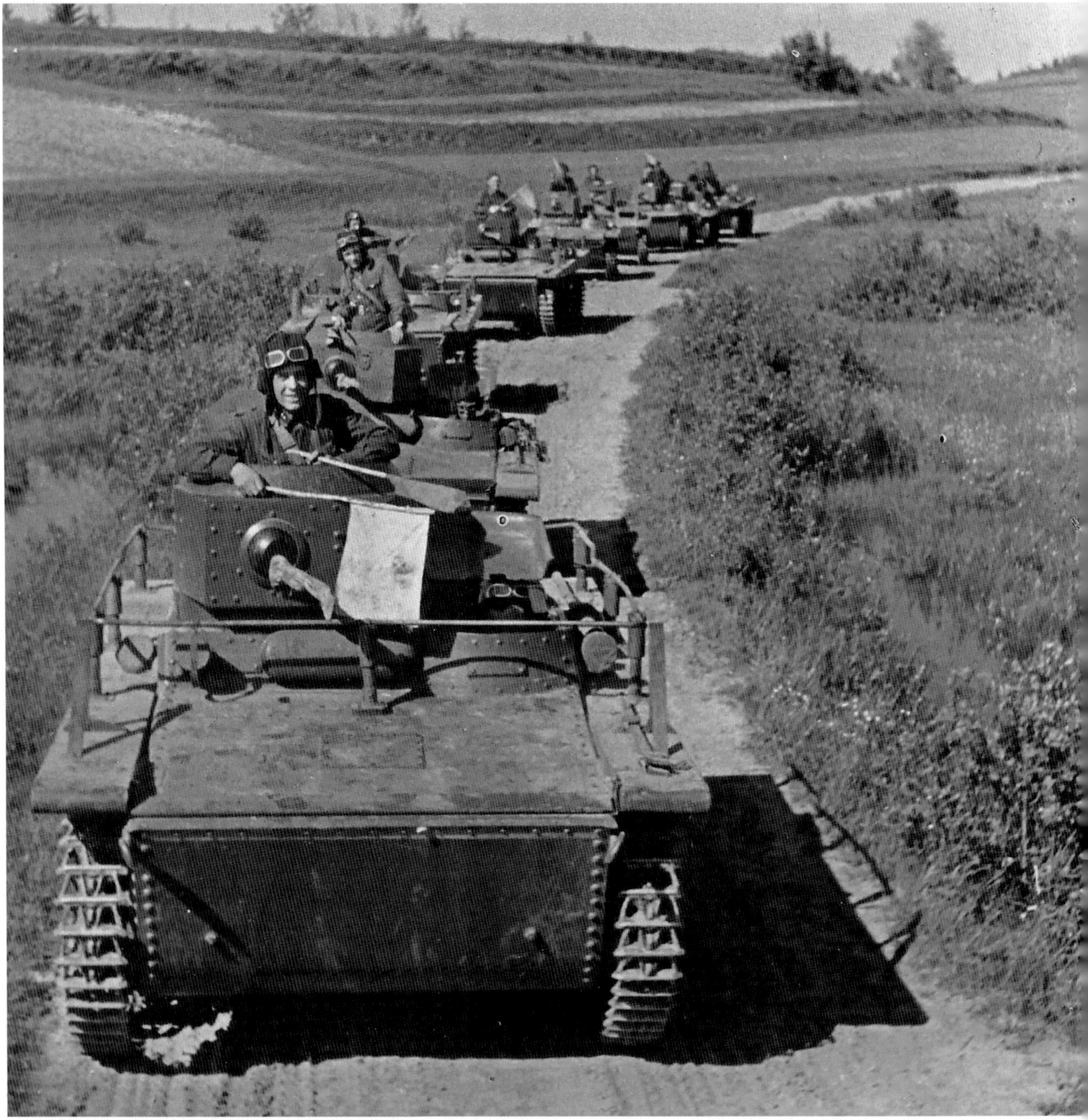

(*Above*) Pictured is a column of T-37A amphibious light tanks led by a radio-equipped command version with its frame antenna. The radio-command vehicle was designated as the T-37RT. The only armament on the T-37 series was a single small-calibre machine gun. The tank's maximum speed was 23.6mph. (*Bob Fleming*)

(*Opposite above*) In the footsteps of the Red Army T-37A amphibious light tank appeared the T-38 amphibious light tank, a column of which is pictured. Besides a redesigned hull, the T-38 had the position of the driver and turret reversed when compared to its predecessor. The T-38 also lacked the thicker cork-filled fenders seen on the T-37. (*Bob Fleming*)

(*Opposite below*) On display at the Russian Army Museum in Moscow is this up-gunned example of the T-38 amphibious light tank armed with a turret-mounted 20mm automatic cannon. The T-38 did not prove to be much of an improvement over the earlier T-37A in field service and its production was stopped in 1937. (*Vladimir Yakubov*)

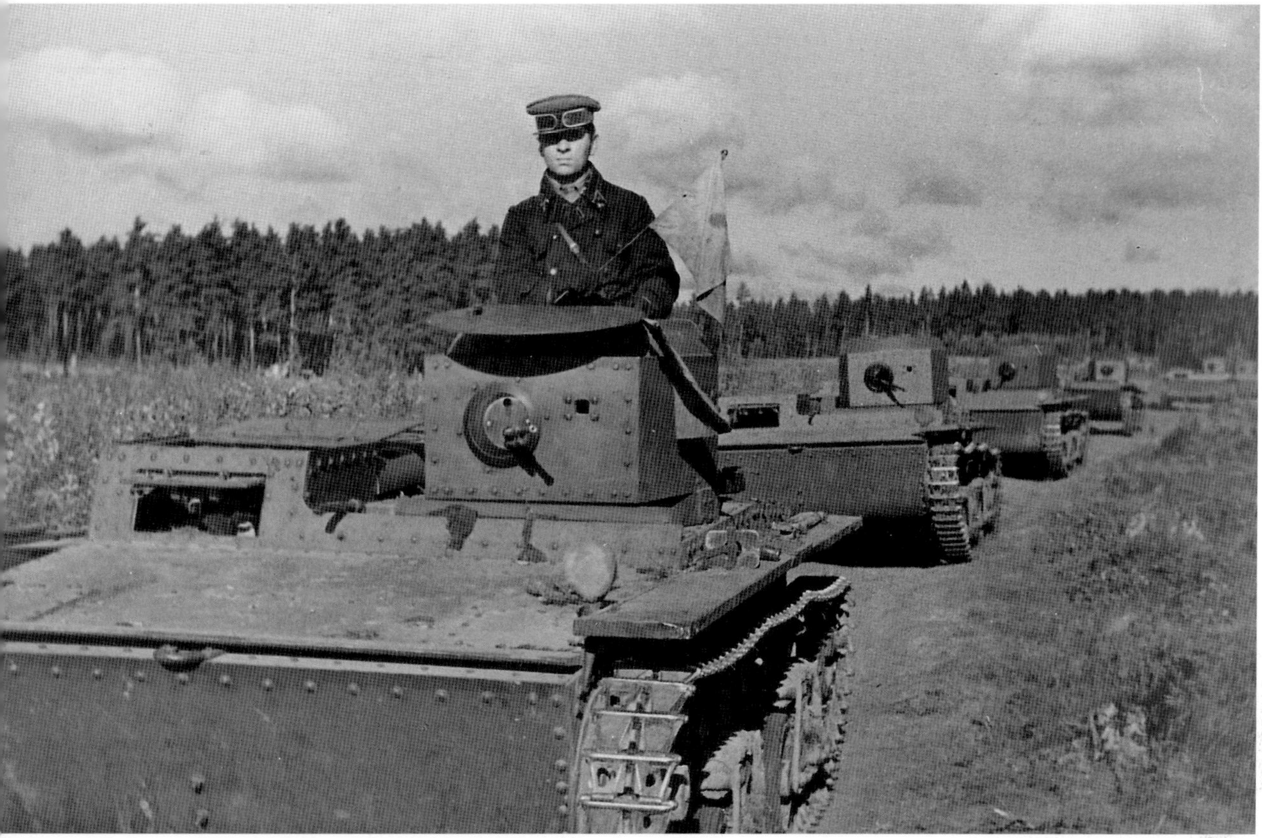

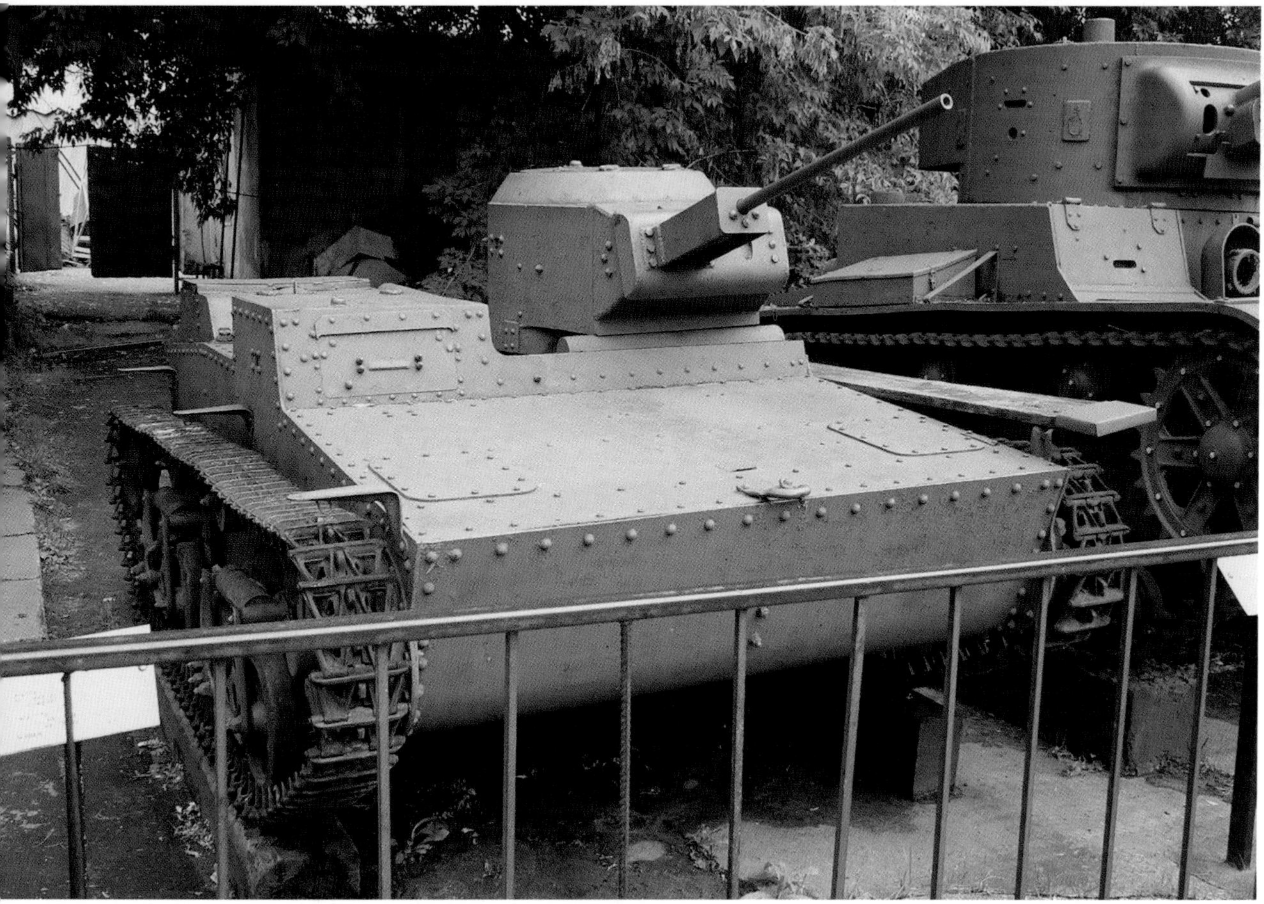

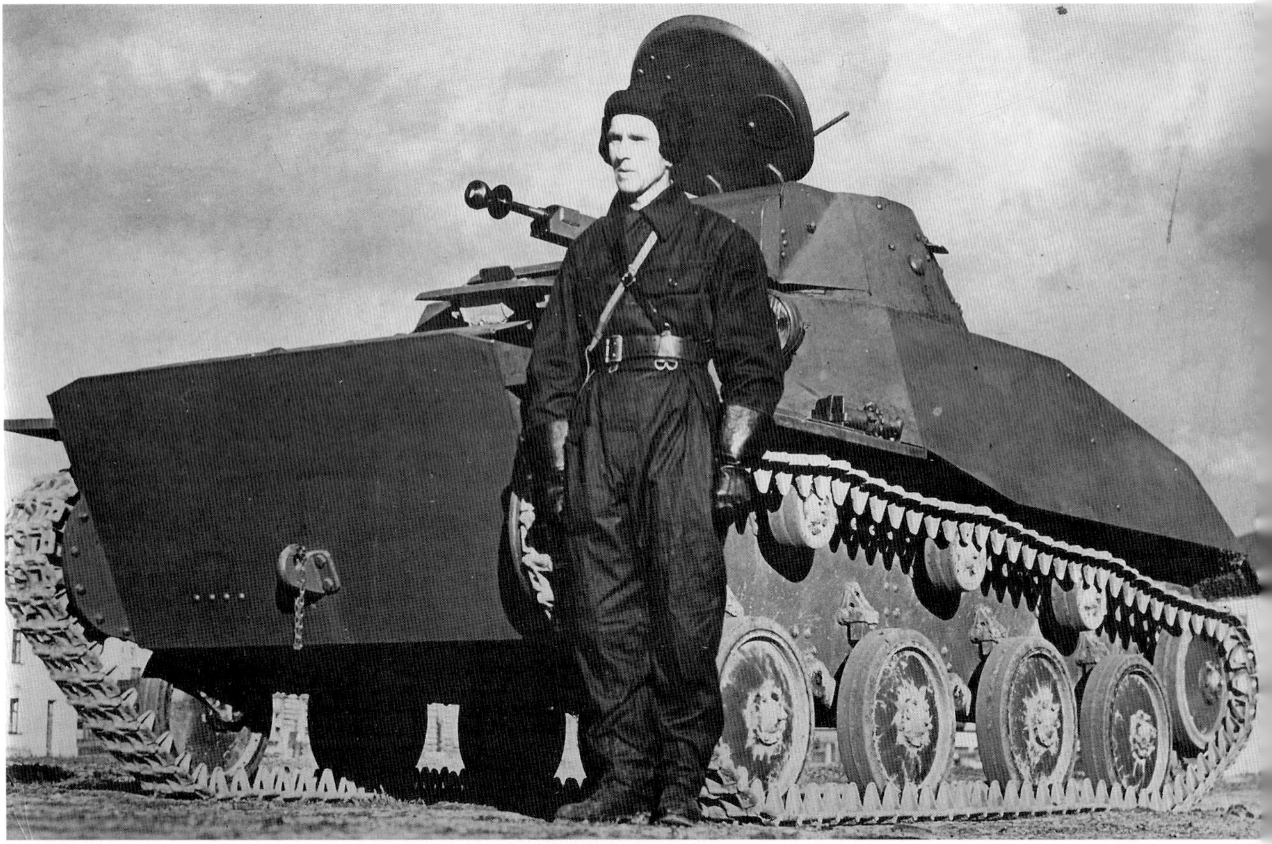

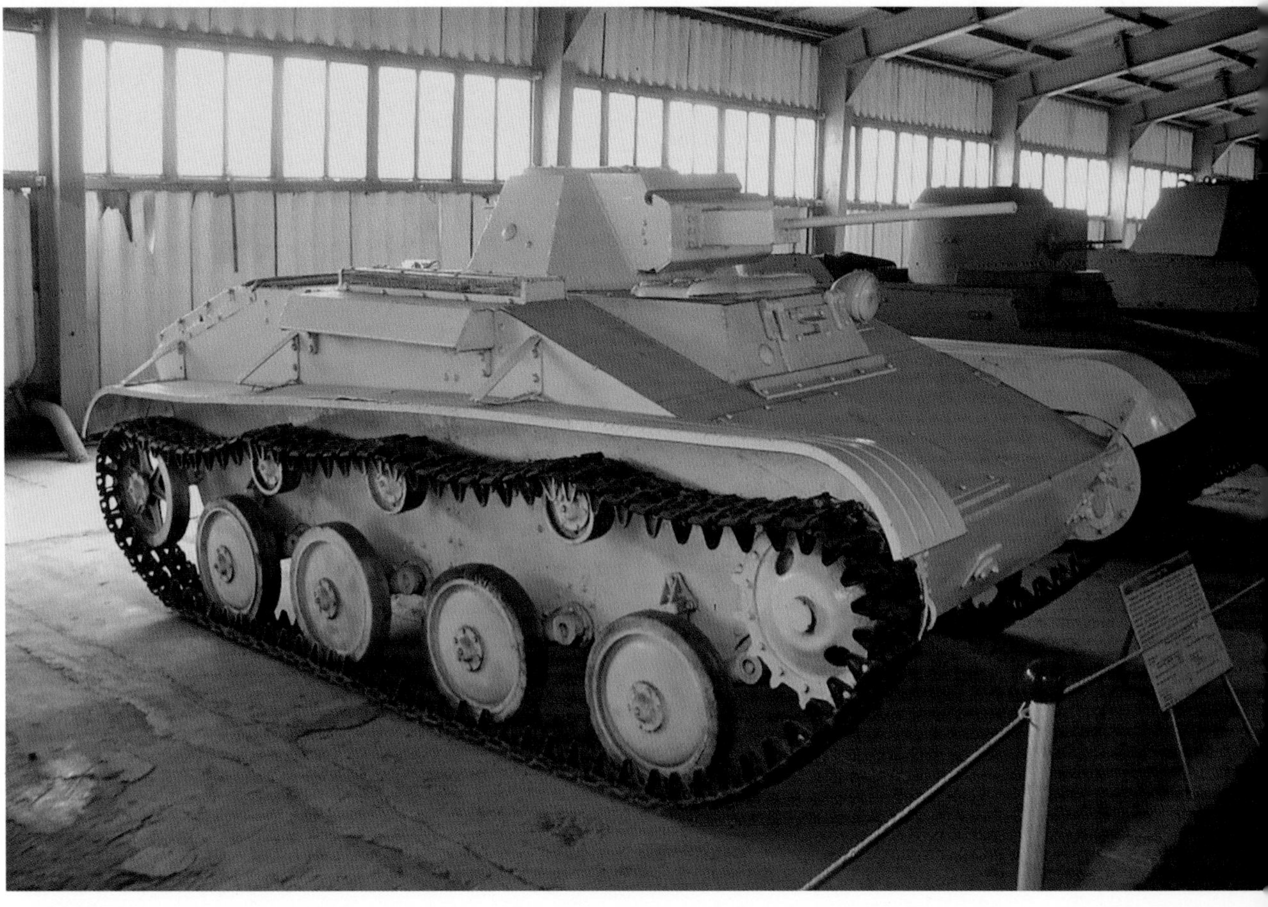

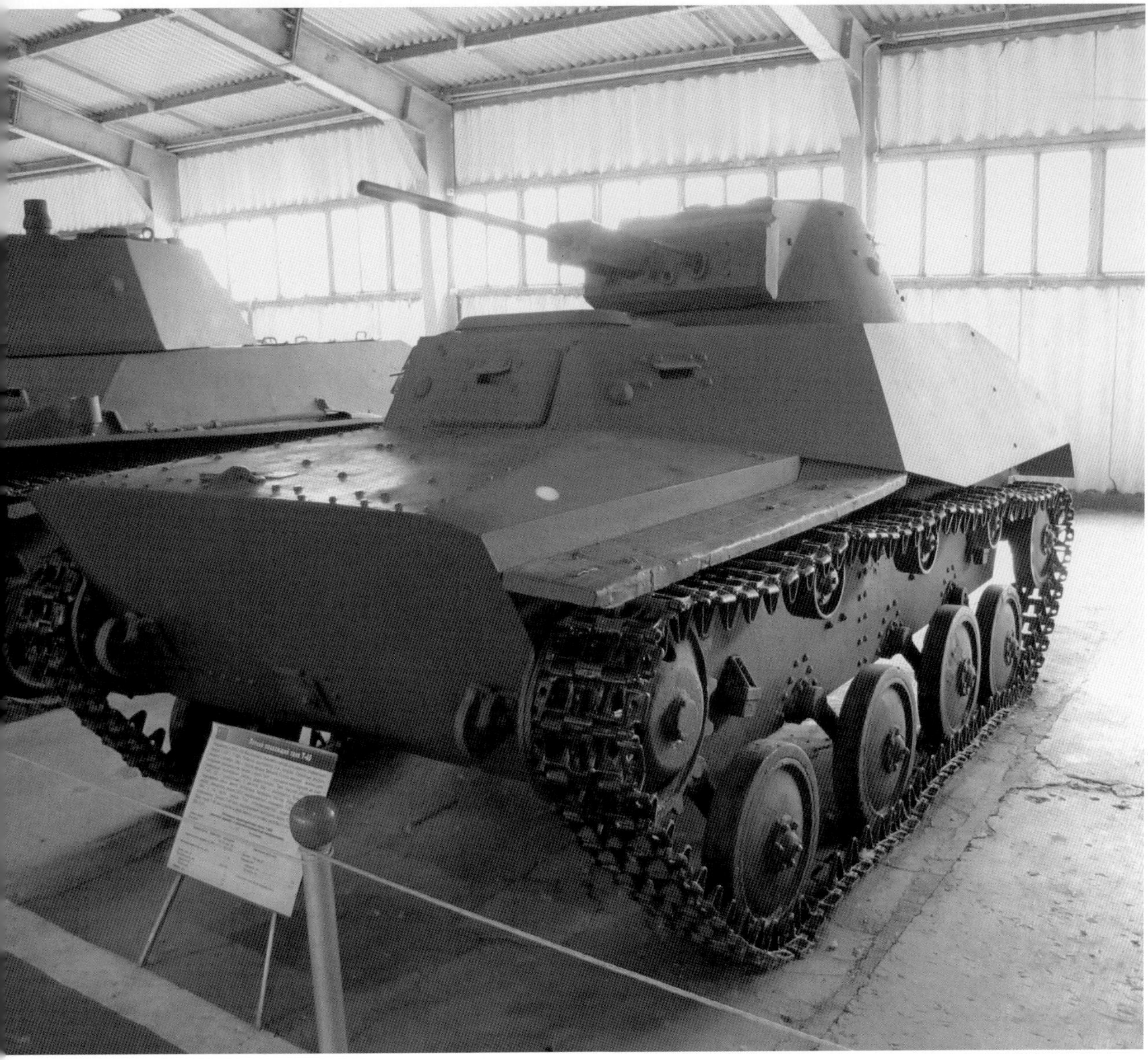

(*Opposite above*) A Red Army tanker poses in front of his T-40 amphibious light tank which was armed with a heavy-calibre 12.7mm machine gun and a smaller coaxial 7.62mm machine gun. It was the planned replacement for the T-37A and T-38. Design work on this vehicle had begun in 1938. It proved to be the first Red Army tank to have a torsion bar suspension system. *(Bob Fleming)*

(*Above*) Production of the T-40 amphibious light tank ended with the German invasion. In its place a non-amphibious version of the tank was built, labelled as the T-30. Late-production units of the tank, an example of which is seen here at the Russian Army Tank Museum, were armed with a 20mm automatic cannon and a coaxial machine gun. *(Vladimir Yakubov)*

(*Opposite below*) On display at the Russian Army Tank Museum is a T-60 light tank armed with a 20mm automatic cannon derived from an aircraft cannon and a small-calibre coaxial machine gun. The T-60 was based on the powertrain and suspension system of the T-40 with a more compact and streamlined up-armoured hull and turret. *(Bob Fleming)*

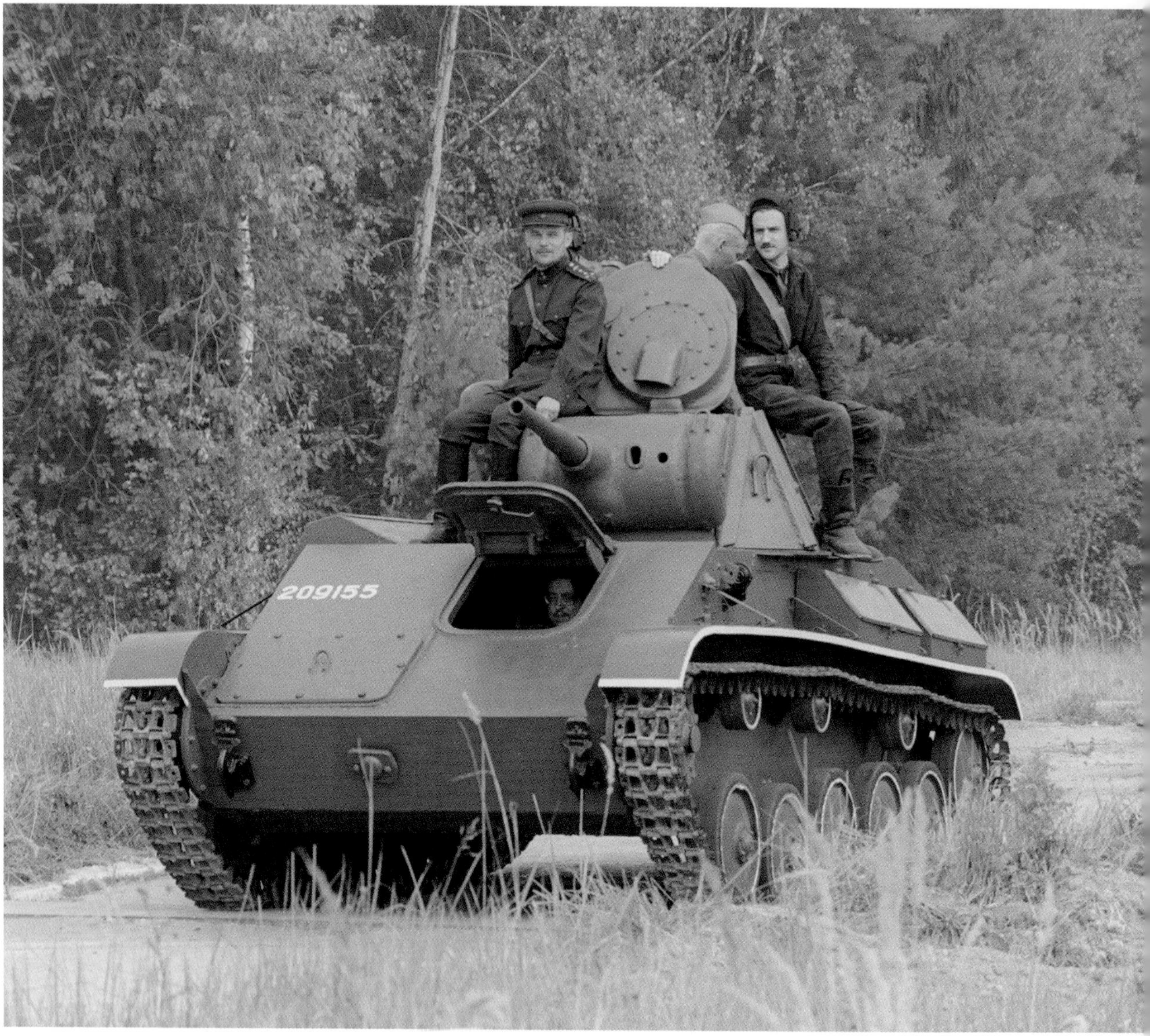
209155

(*Above*) The Red Army decided to use the T-60 as a base upon which to develop a new up-armoured and up-gunned non-amphibious light tank labelled as the T-70. An upgraded version known as the T-70M belonging to the Russian Army Tank Museum is seen here with staff members dressed in period uniforms. (*R. Bazalevsky*)

(*Opposite above*) Shown here in a wartime photograph is a Red Army T-70M. The vehicle's armament consisted of a 45mm main gun and a coaxial 7.62mm machine gun. It was powered by two gasoline engines, one behind the other. The vehicle was 14ft long, 7ft 7in wide and had a height of 6ft 8in. The maximum armour thickness on the T-70M was 45mm. (*Bob Fleming*)

(*Opposite below*) More than a dozen examples of the twin-turreted machine-gun-armed British commercially-available Vickers Mk E light tank were acquired for evaluation in 1930 by the Red Army. Impressed by its design, the Red Army ordered a modified version of the three-man tank into service. The version seen here was designated as the T-26 Model 1931. (*Bob Fleming*)

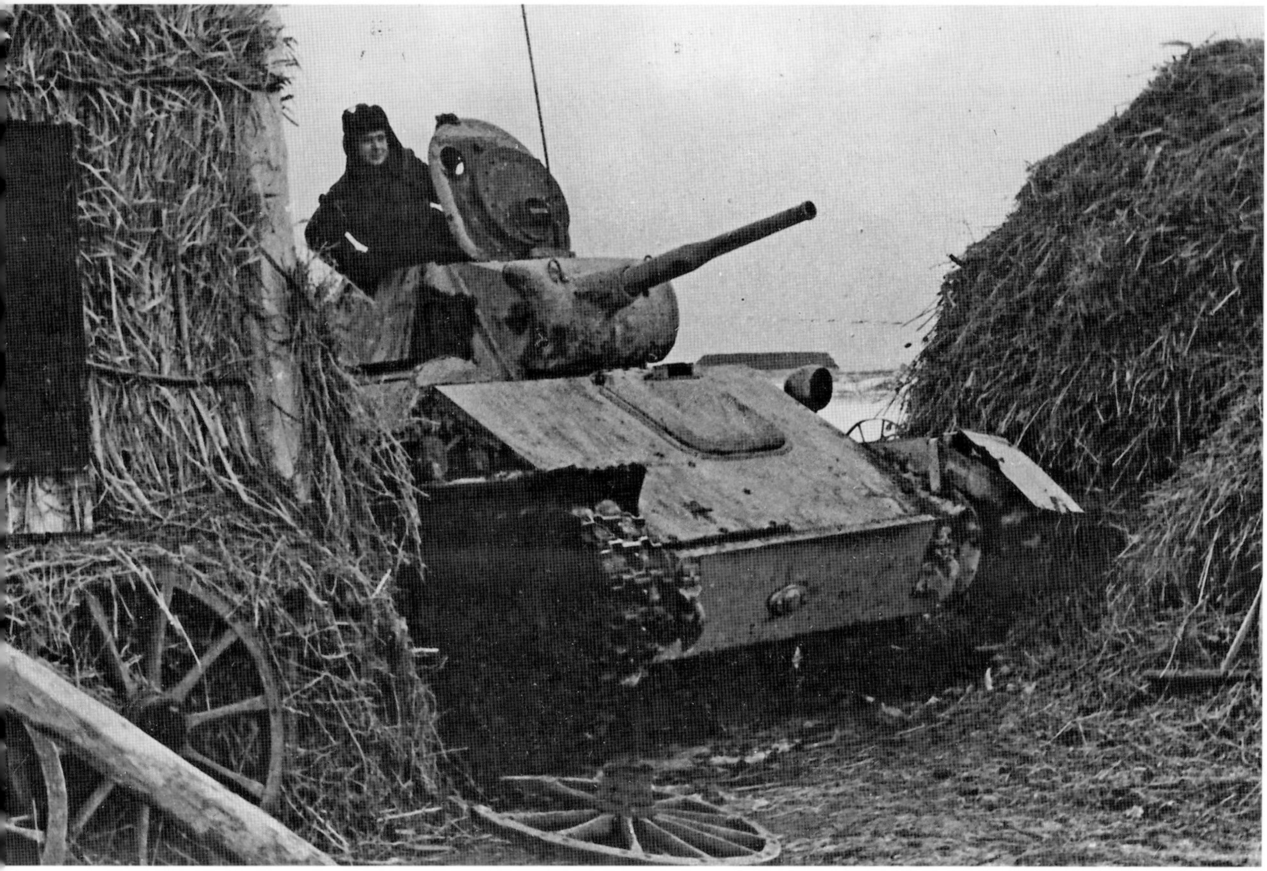

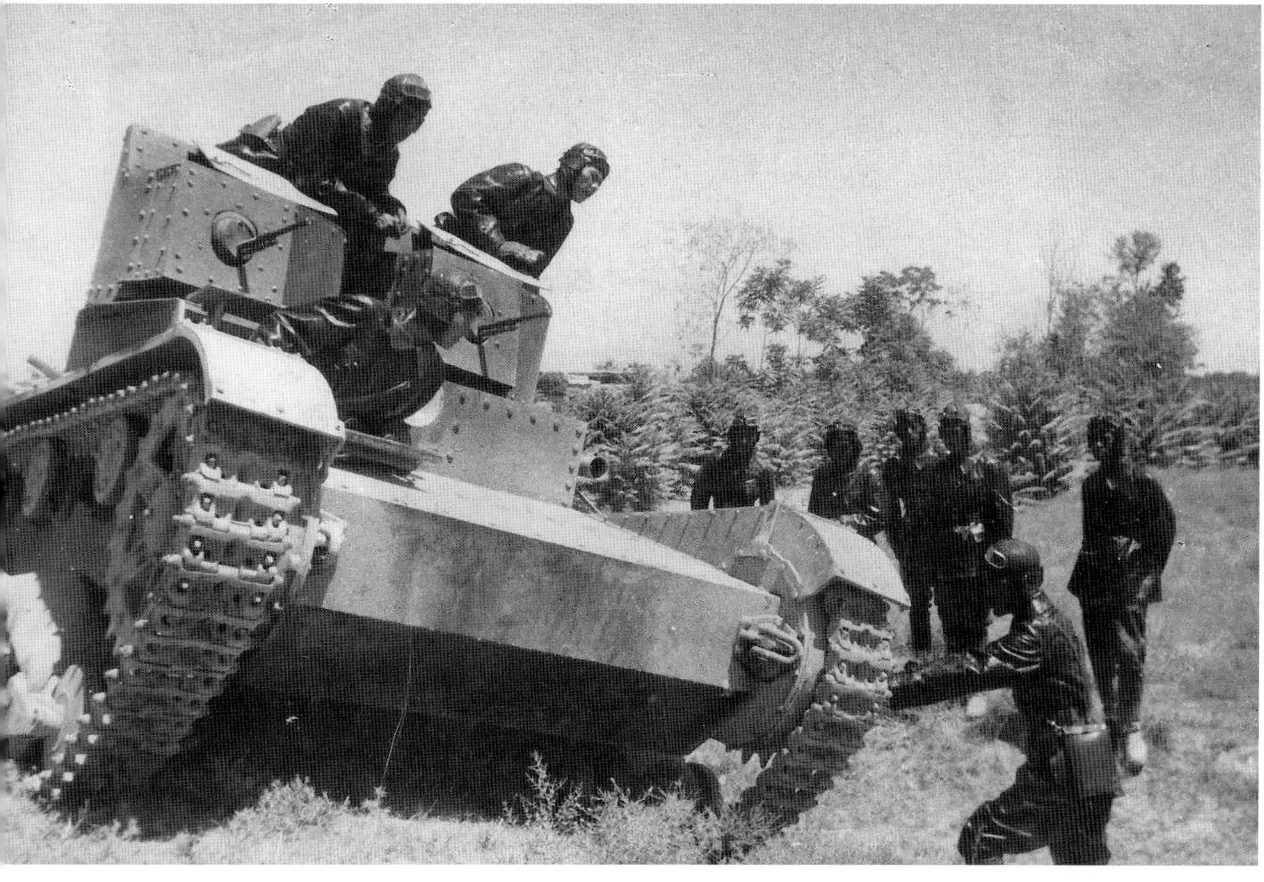

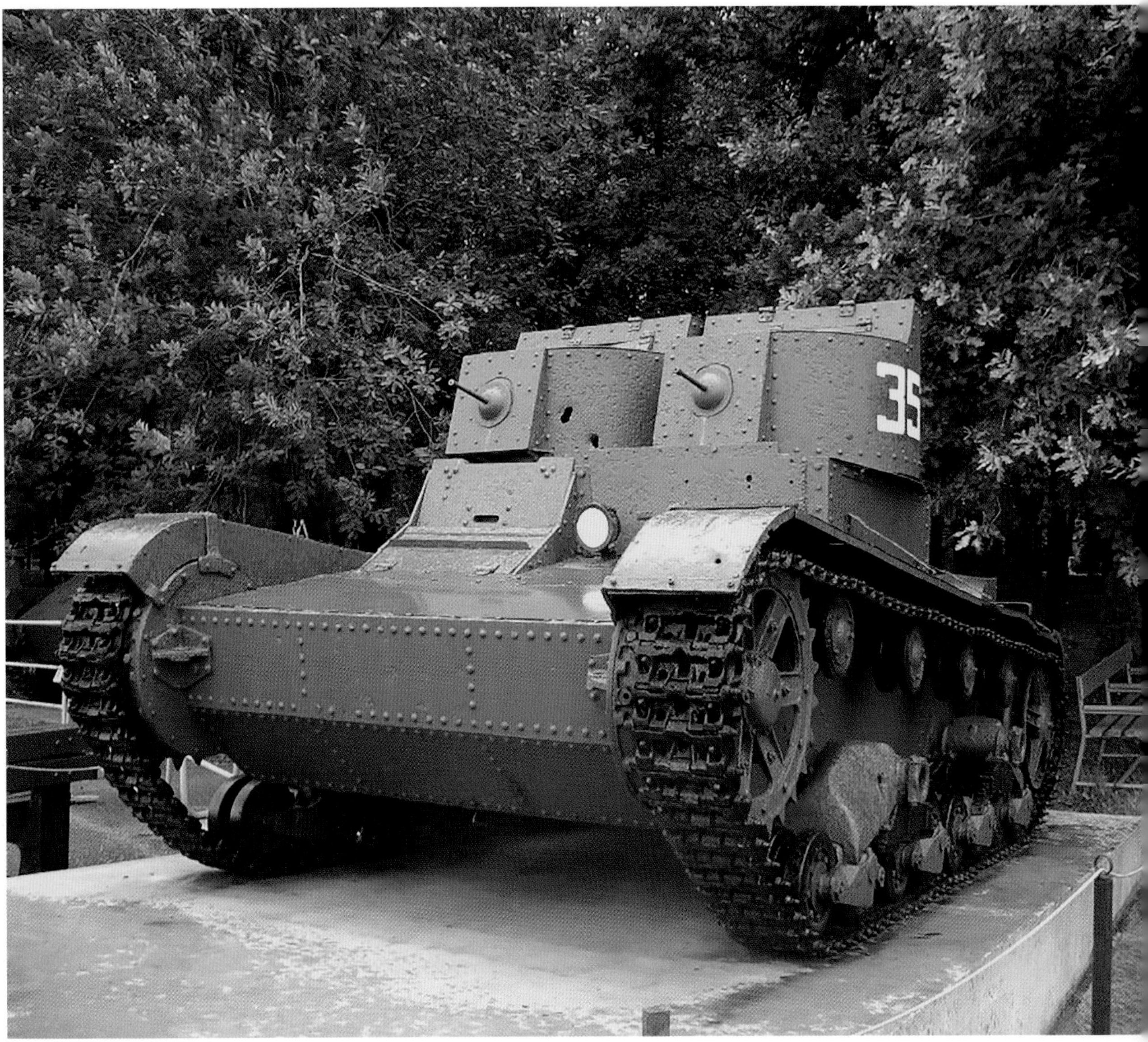

(*Above*) The only surviving example of the T-26 Model 1931 (pictured) resides at the Russian Army Museum in Moscow. Each of the vehicle's two single-man turrets was armed with a single 7.62mm machine gun. The vehicle was 16ft 1in long, 11ft 2in wide and had a height of 7ft 9in. (*Vladimir Yakubov*)

(*Opposite above*) Eventually a new two-man turret armed with a 45mm main gun and a coaxial machine gun was designed and fitted to the T-26 Model 1931 as seen here. The redesigned and up-gunned vehicle was designated as the T-26 Model 1933 and an example in wartime Finnish army markings is seen here on display in a museum. (*Tank Museum*)

(*Opposite below*) It was initially planned by the Red Army that its entire inventory of T-26 Model 1933 light tanks would be equipped with radios. However, production shortages made that impossible, so only command tanks designated as the T-26RT Model 1933 had the horseshoe-shaped metal frame antennas fitted. (*Bob Fleming*)

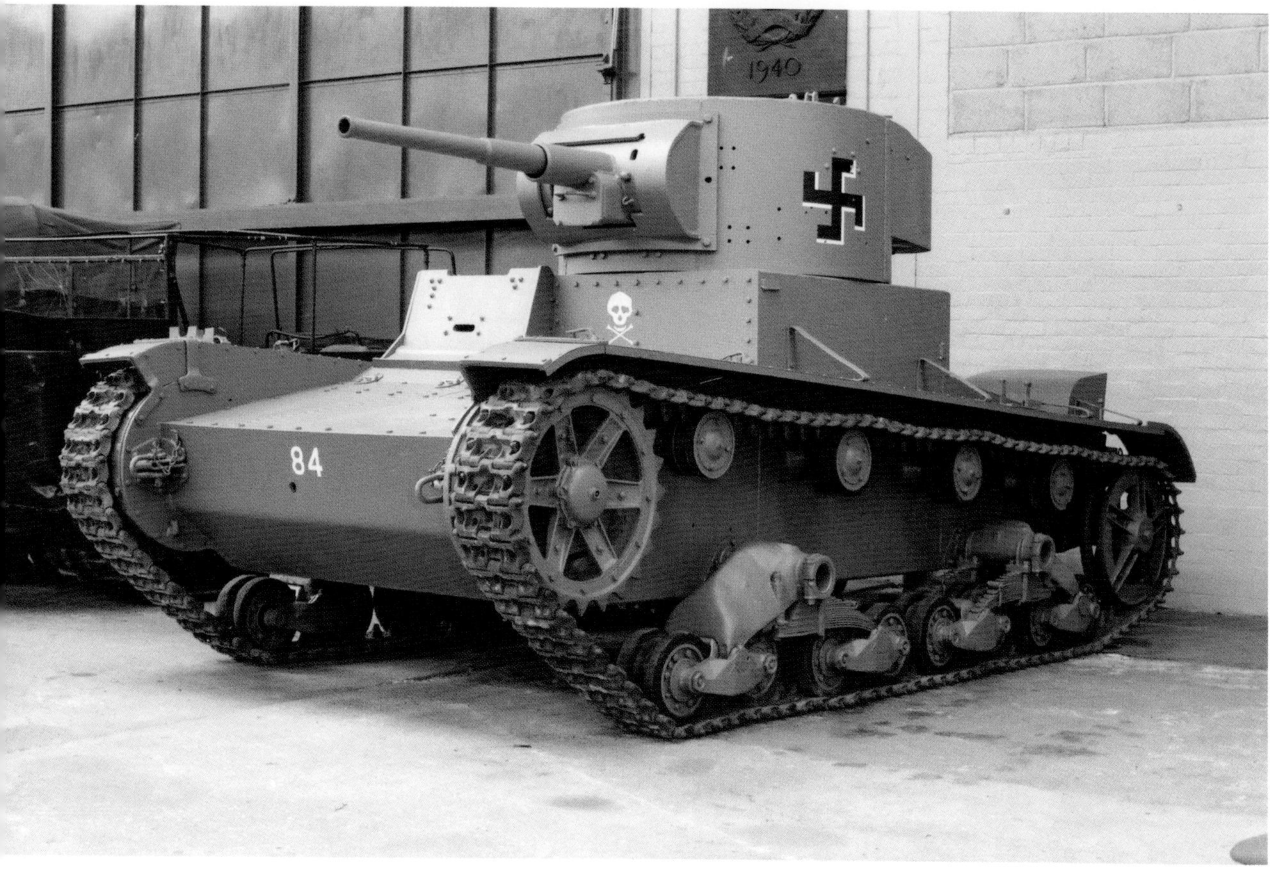
1940
84

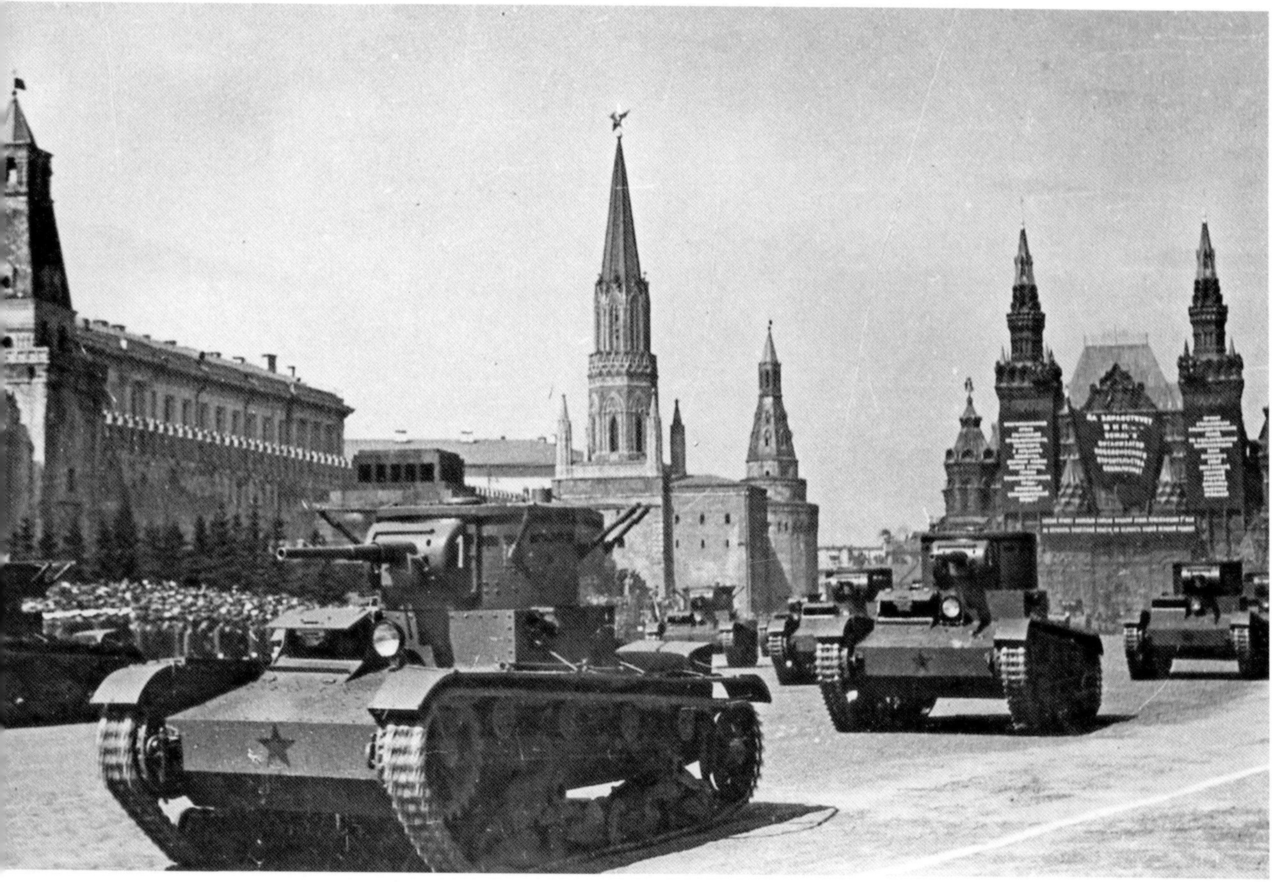
1

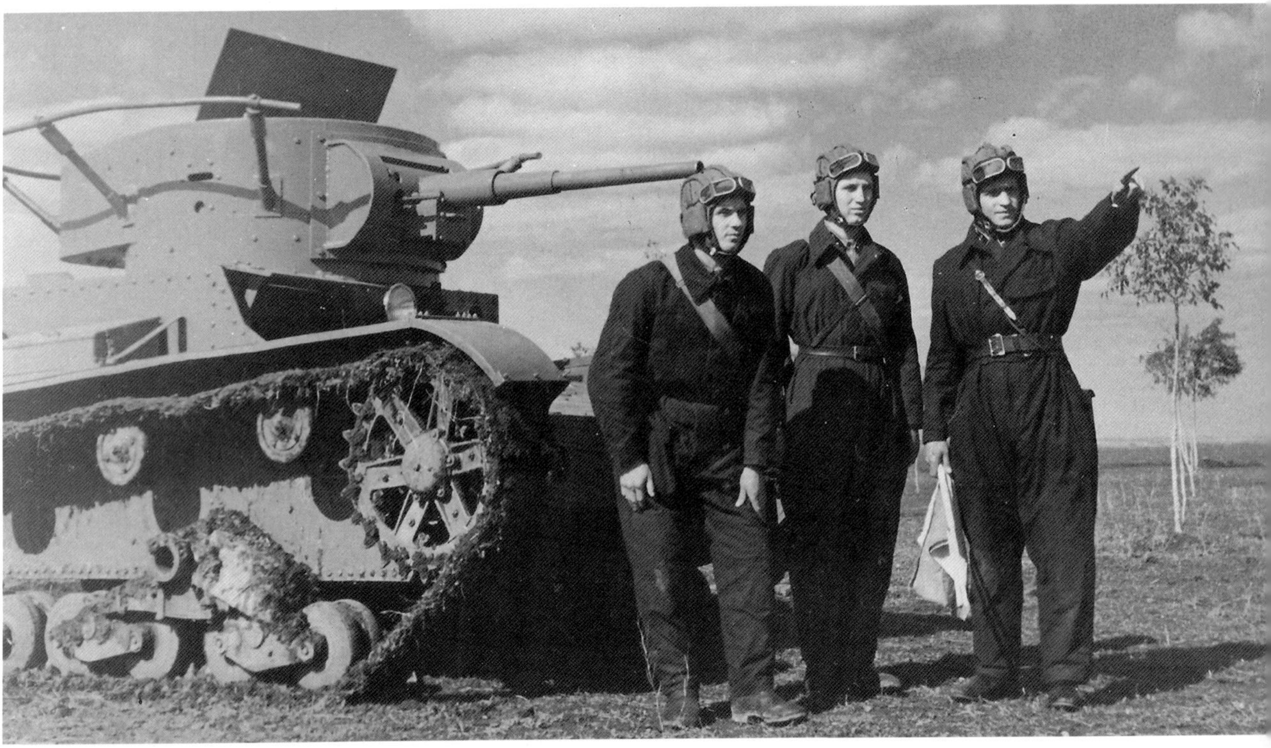

The vehicle commander in this picture of a Red Army T-26RT Model 1933 command tank is holding flags that he would employ when directing his non-radio-equipped counterparts in a training exercise or battle. Production of the two-man turret armed with the 45mm main gun for the T-26 series began in 1932. *(Bob Fleming)*

Crossing a snow-bank is a T-26 Model 1933. It would prove to be the most numerous tank in the Red Army inventory when the Germans invaded the Soviet Union. Eventually, the T-26 series was fitted with an interphone system to allow the crew to communicate with each other. The maximum armour on the tank was originally 15mm thick but later increased to 20mm. *(Bob Fleming)*

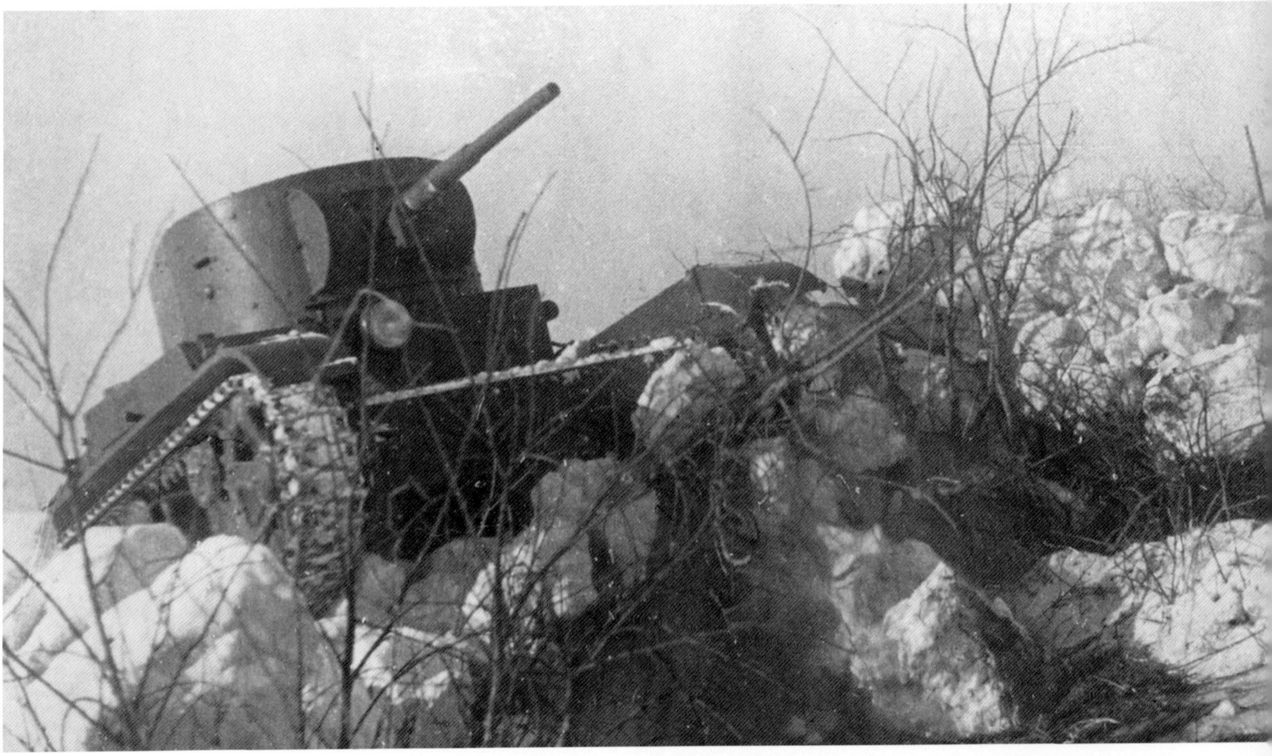

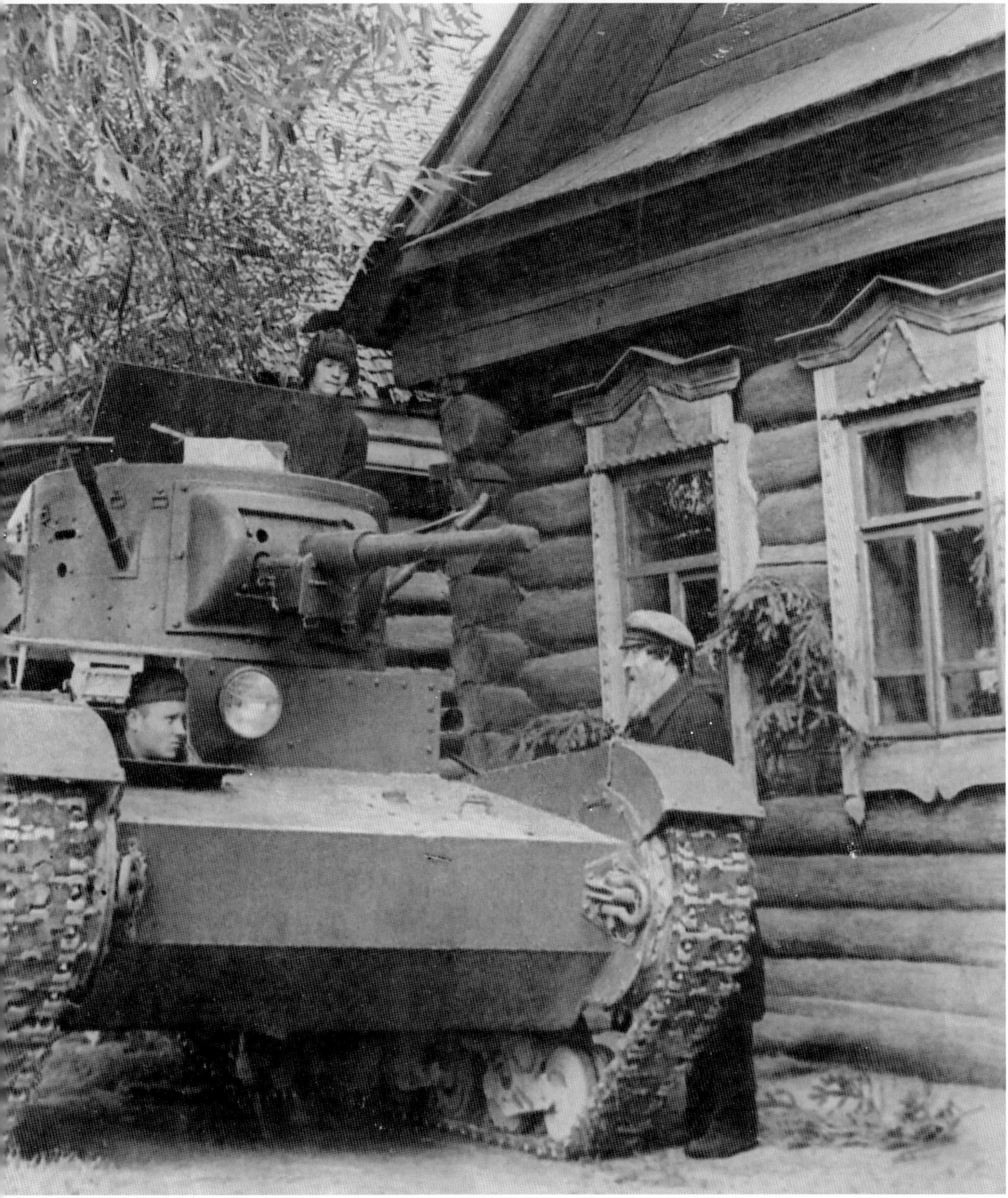

Parked next to a farmhouse is a Red Army T-26RT Model 1933 command tank. The T-26 Model 1933 series originally had authorized storage space for 122 main gun rounds for its 45mm main gun which was later increased to store 147 main gun rounds. The metal frame antenna was eventually dispensed with as it tended to identify command tanks that were quickly targeted for destruction. *(Bob Fleming)*

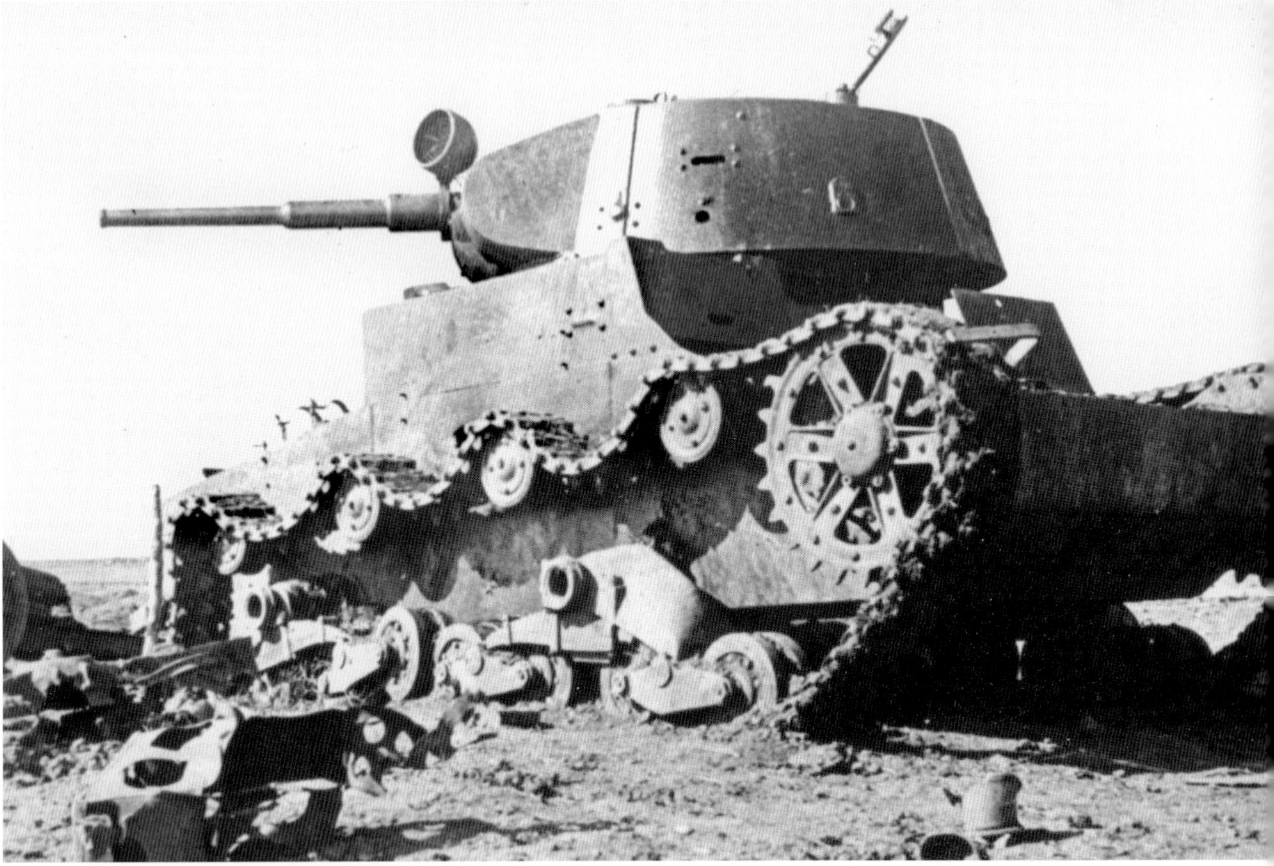

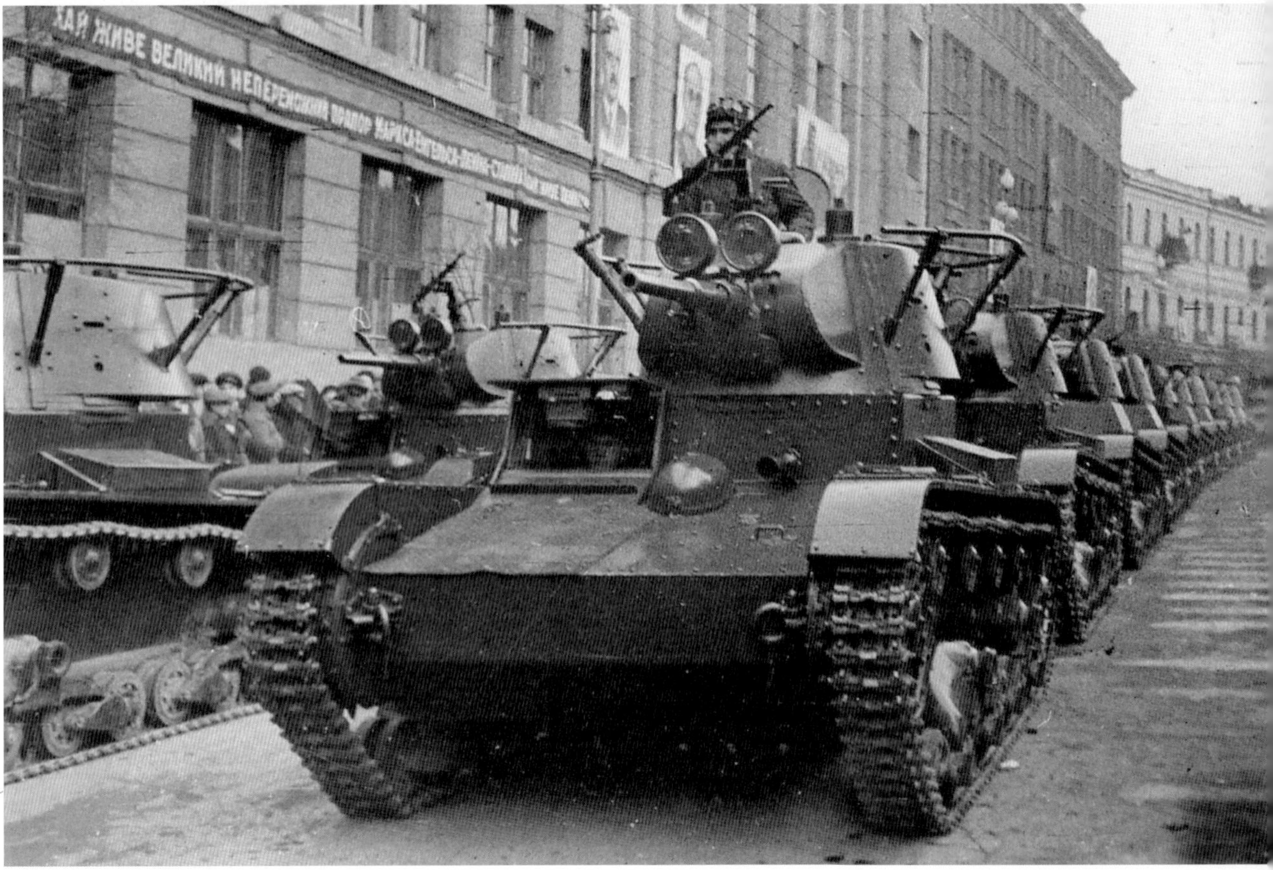
ЖИВЕ ВЕЛИКИЙ

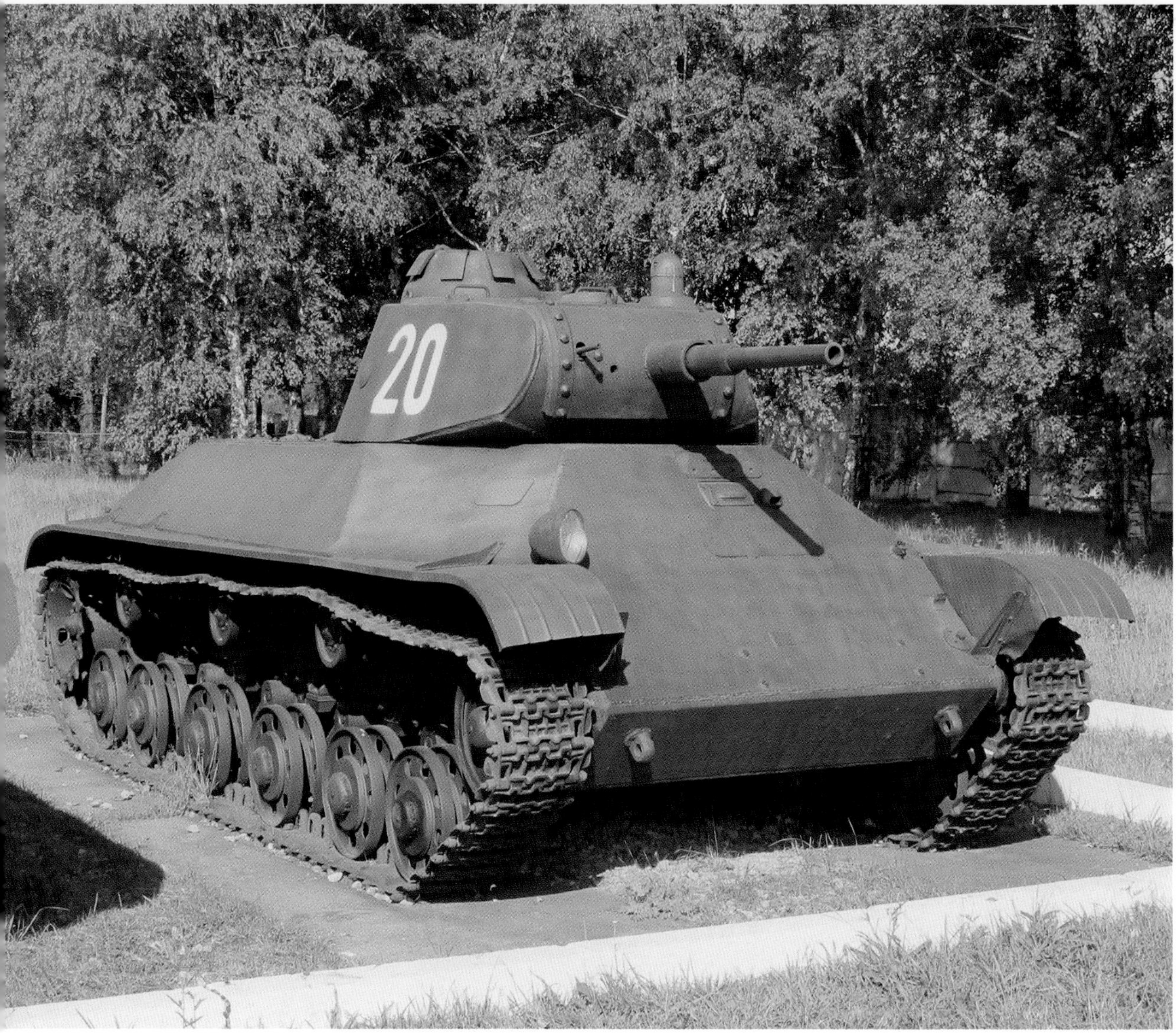
20

(*Opposite above*) Soviet heavy industry mastered the art of electric arc-welding in 1935 and applied that newly-acquired skill to the T-26 series of tanks. An example of that construction method is seen here on the turret of this knocked-out vehicle that was designated as the T-26 Model 1938. Note the sloping sides of this new turret design. *(Patton Museum)*

(*Opposite below*) Lined up for a parade is a formation of T-26 Model 1938 tanks with most being the command version with the metal frame antenna around the turret. The hulls of the vehicles pictured were still being riveted together. Note the headlights attached to the 45mm main gun and the small-calibre anti-aircraft machine gun on the turret roof. *(Bob Fleming)*

(*Above*) The Red Army's pre-war planned replacement for the T-26 series of light tanks was the T-50 light tank seen here on display at the Russian Army Tank Museum. It retained the 45mm main gun of its predecessor but featured a newly-designed turret and hull that took advantage of the additional ballistic protection offered by sloped armour. *(Vladimir Yakubov)*

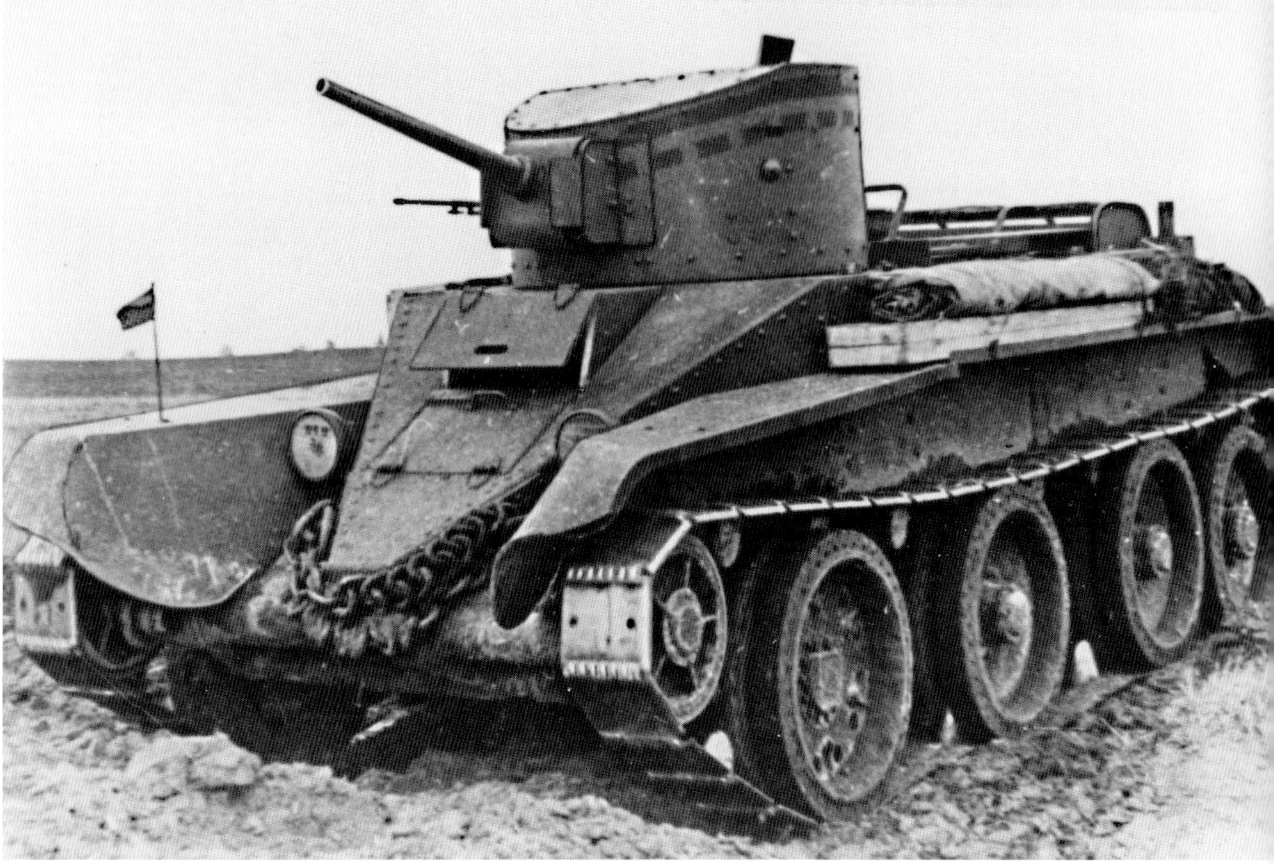

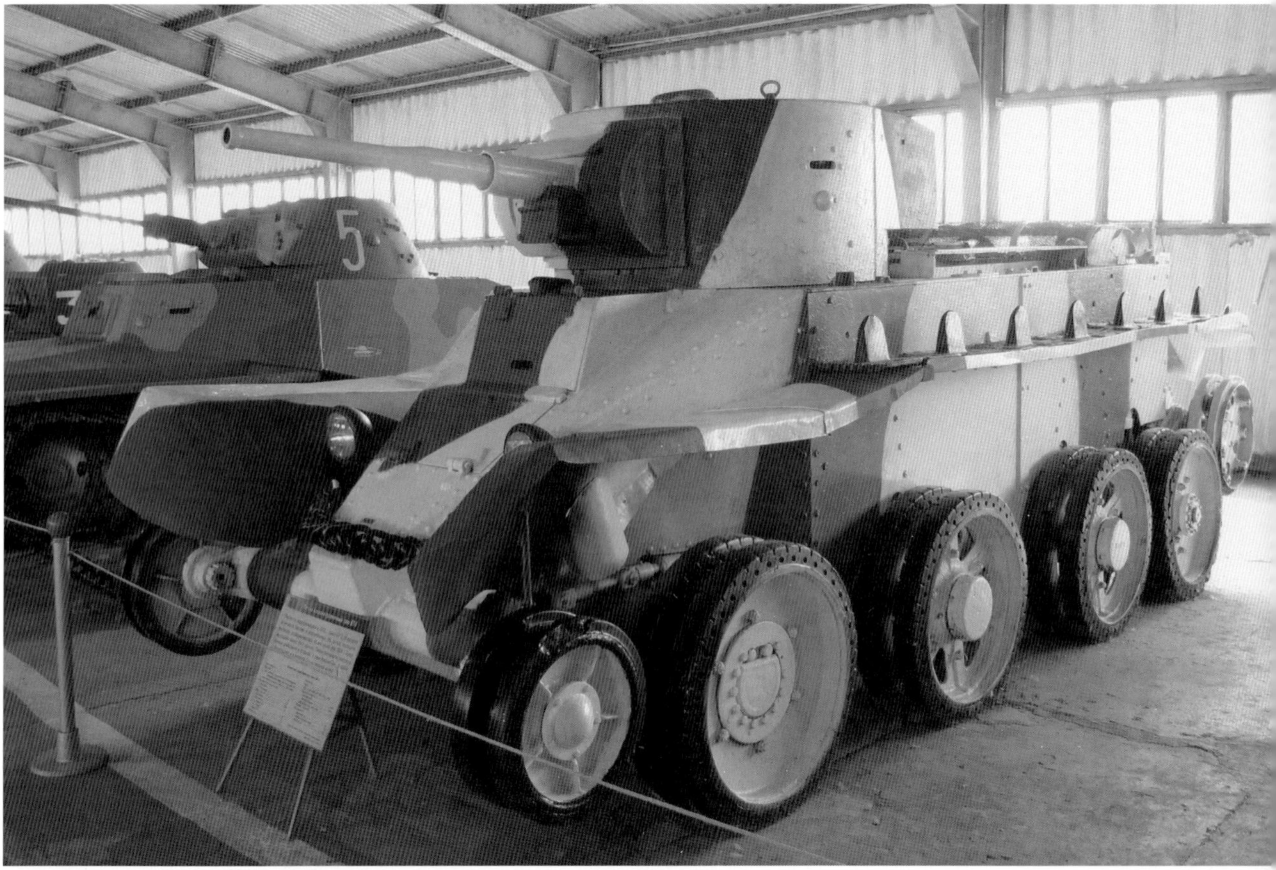
5

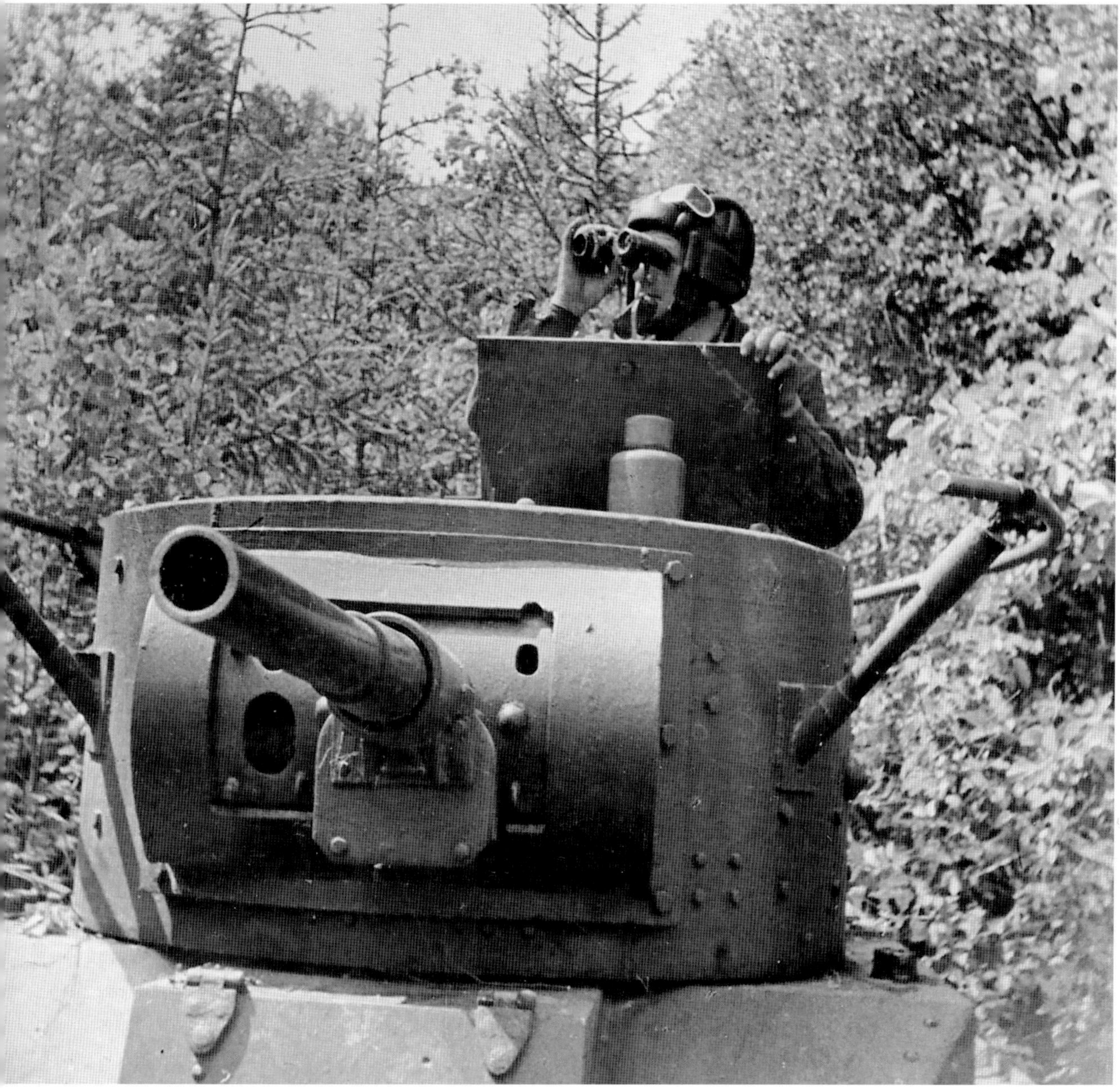

(*Opposite above*) Pictured is a Red Army BT-2 light tank armed with a 37mm main gun and coaxial machine gun. The earliest production units of the tank were armed only with three turret-mounted machine guns. The distinguishing external features of the BT-2 included the sloping front turret roof and the glacis coming to a flat point. *(Bob Fleming)*

(*Above*) As the 37mm main gun on the BT-2 was quickly considered inadequate, the vehicle was soon fitted with a new turret with a flat roof as seen here that was armed with a 45mm main gun and a coaxial machine gun. In this configuration the vehicle was designated as the BT-5 or, in this case, a BT-5RT as it has the metal frame antenna that marks it as a radio-equipped command tank. *(Bob Fleming)*

(*Opposite below*) On display at the Russian Army Tank Museum is this BT-5 in the wheels-only running configuration. A portion of the vehicle's track is stored on top of the visible fender. A distinguishing feature of the BT-2 and BT-5 was the driver's hatch that projected out from the vehicle's glacis plate. *(Vladimir Yakubov)*

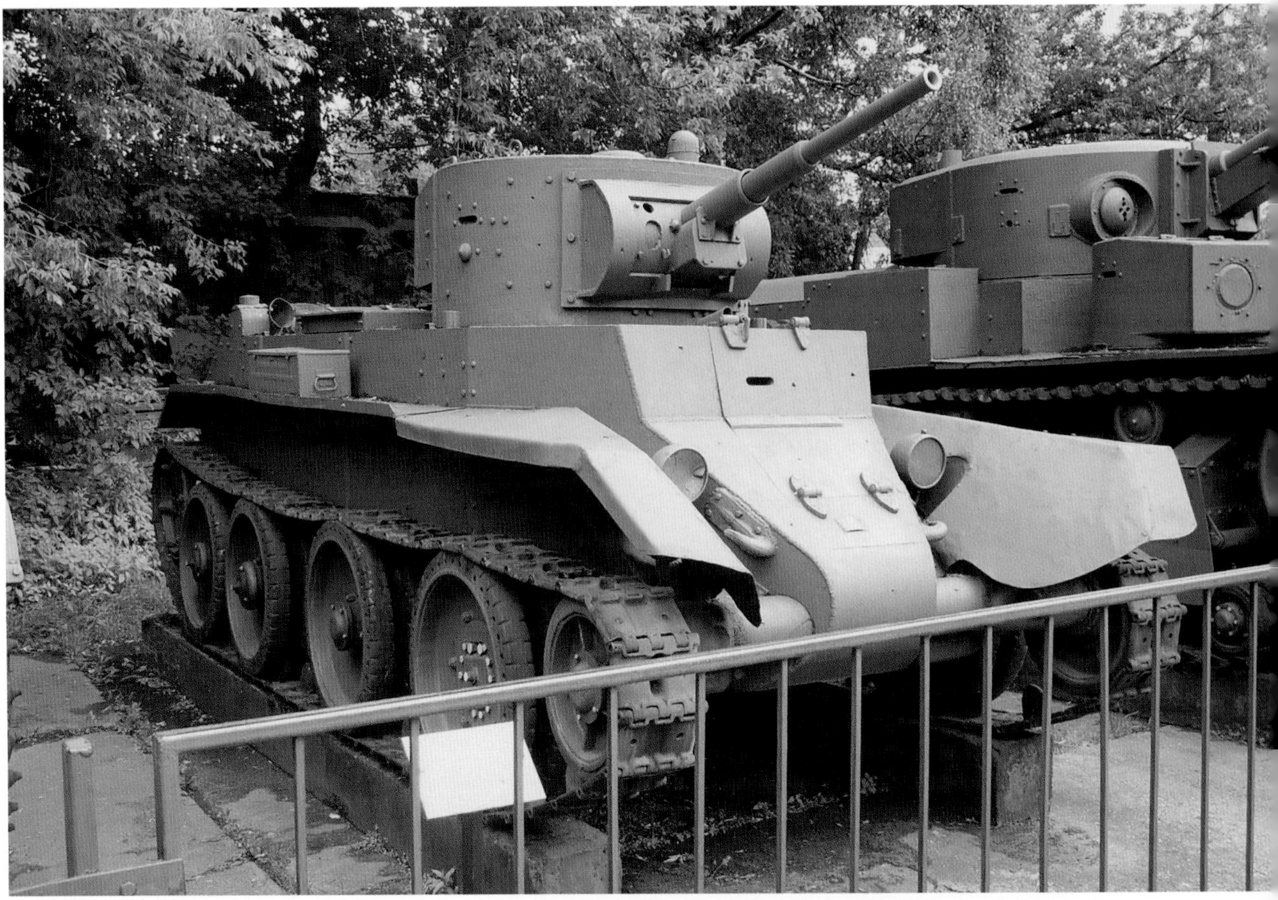

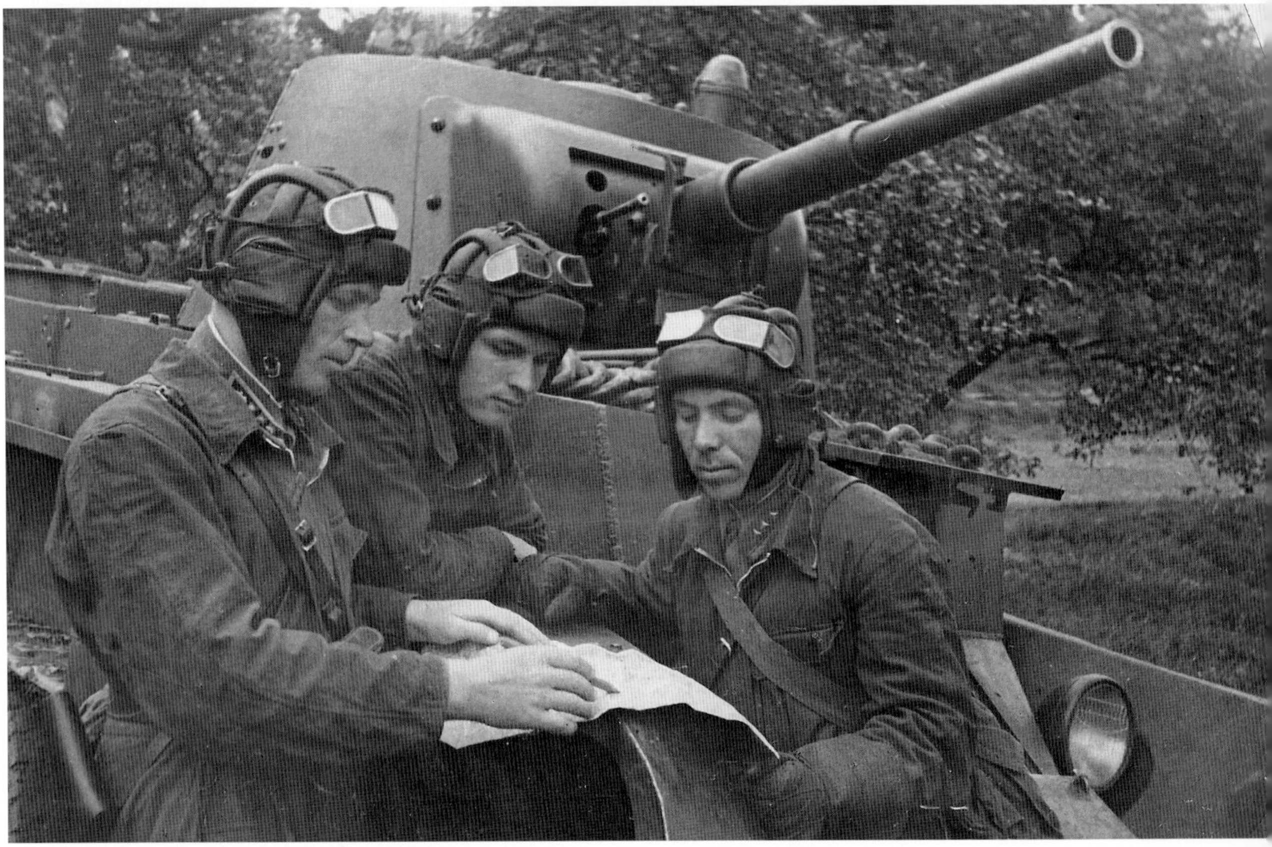

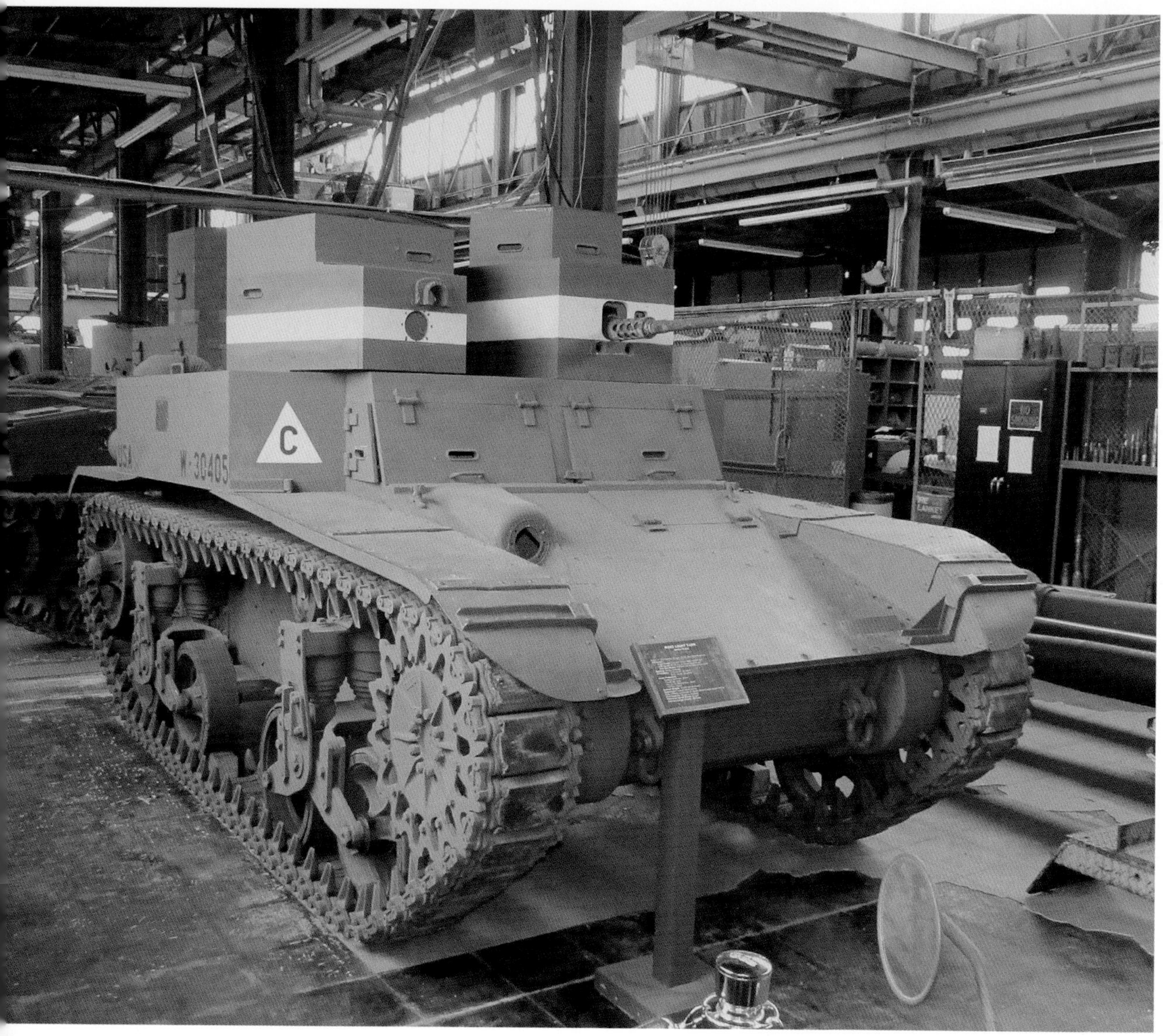

(*Opposite above*) The BT-5 follow-on was the BT-7 Model 1935 seen here on display at a military museum in Moscow. Identifying features of the BT-7 included the incorporation of the driver's hatch seen on earlier versions of the series into the front glacis and a rounded lower front hull. The BT-7 and the BT-5 had a rear turret bustle not seen on the BT-2. *(Vladimir Yakubov)*

(*Opposite below*) In a continuing effort to improve the BT-7, the Red Army adopted a new turret for the light tank seen here that had sloping sides. The main armament remained a 45mm gun. With the new turret the tank was labelled as the BT-7 Model 1937. It was 18ft 6in long, 7ft 6in wide and 7ft 11in tall. *(Bob Fleming)*

(*Above*) A US army M2A3 light tank (of which seventy-three units were built in 1938) is pictured in a storage facility located at Fort Benning, Georgia. Armed only with machine guns, the twin-turreted vehicle was quickly seen as being obsolete. This resulted in the production of a version fitted with a single turret armed with a 37mm main gun and a coaxial machine gun that was designated as the M2A4 light tank. *(Rob Cogan)*

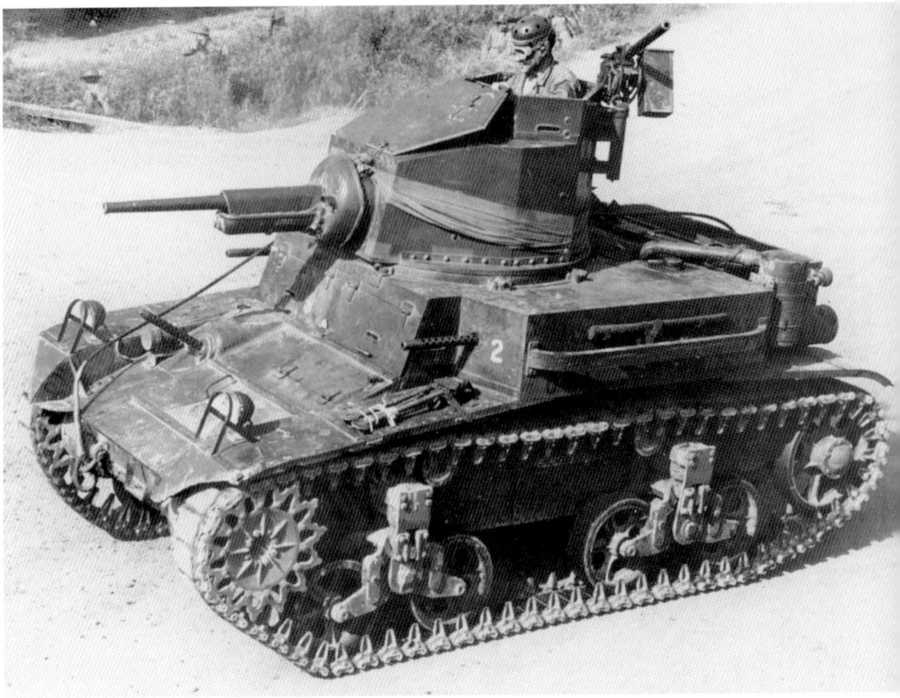
2

The 37mm main gun seen here in the turret of the M2A4 light tank was a 5-inch shorter version of the standard towed version employed by the infantry branch of the US army. Besides the turret-mounted coaxial machine gun, the tank was fitted with three other machine guns: one in a flexible ball mount in the glacis and one fixed forward-firing machine gun on either side of the superstructure. *(Patton Museum)*

An improved version of the M2A4 was the M3 light tank shown here. It featured thicker frontal armour than its predecessor. This particular vehicle is on display at a US army military base located at Fort Hood, Texas. Like the M2A4, the M3 had a very prominent fixed vehicle commander's cupola fitted with an overhead hatch and vision slits. *(Paul and Loren Hannah)*

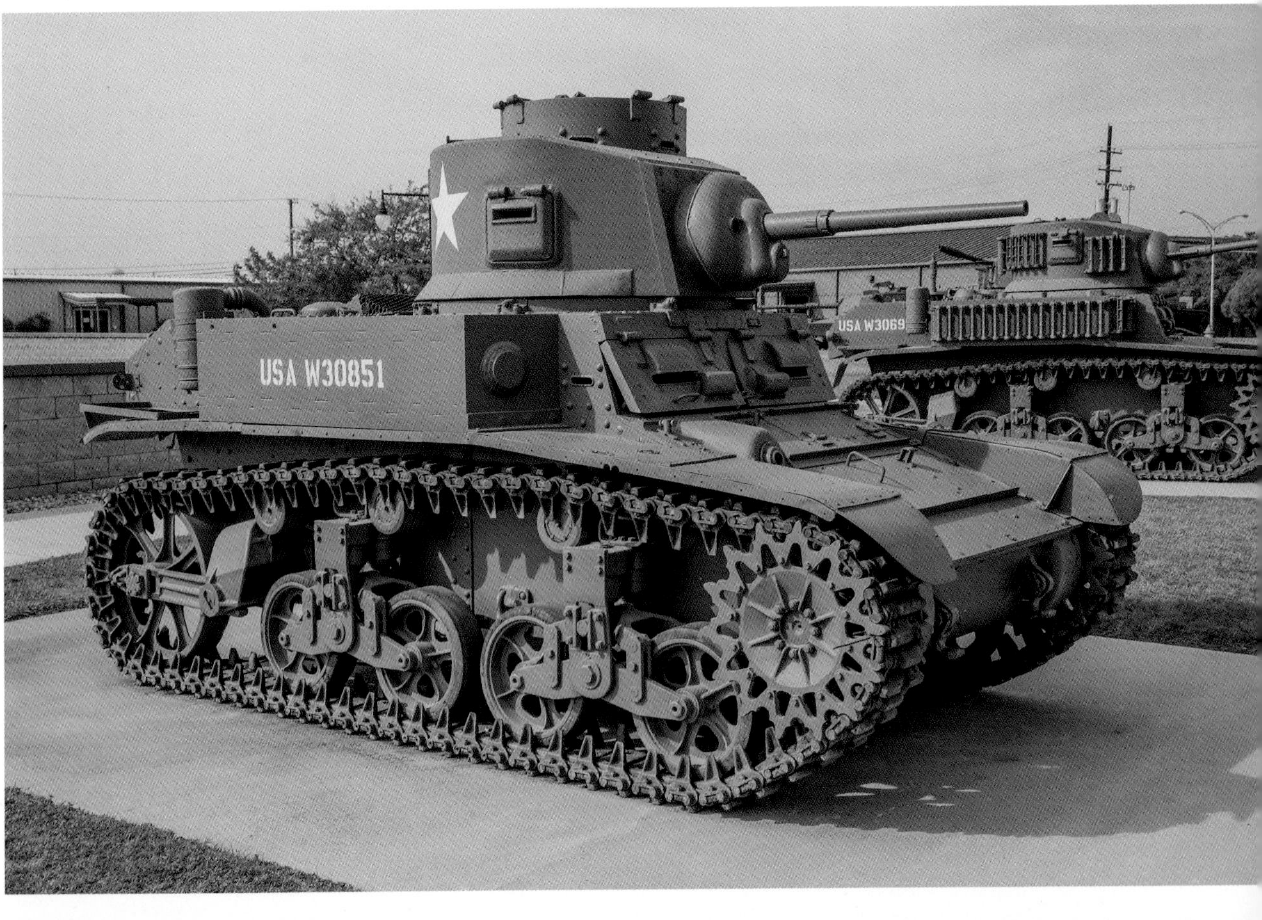
USA W30851
USA W3069

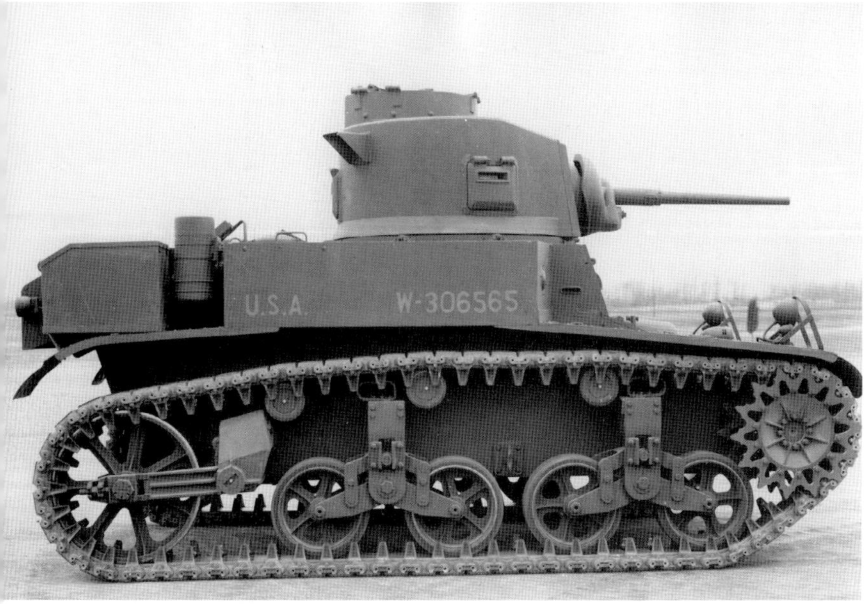
U.S.A.
W-306565

To improve the M3 light tank's off-road mobility it was fitted with a trailing idler visible in this photograph, which was not a design feature seen on the M2A4. Another external identifying feature of the M3 was the shortened recoil mechanism that did not extend out from the bottom of the gun shield as it did so prominently on the M2A4 with its armour-protected sleeve. *(Author's collection)*

Following the M3 off America's assembly lines was the M3A1 light tank. A restored late-production example belonging to a private collector is pictured here. It lacked the vehicle commander's cupola and the fixed forward-firing machine guns mounted on either side of the superstructure that were present on the M2A4 and the M3 light tanks. *(Author's collection)*

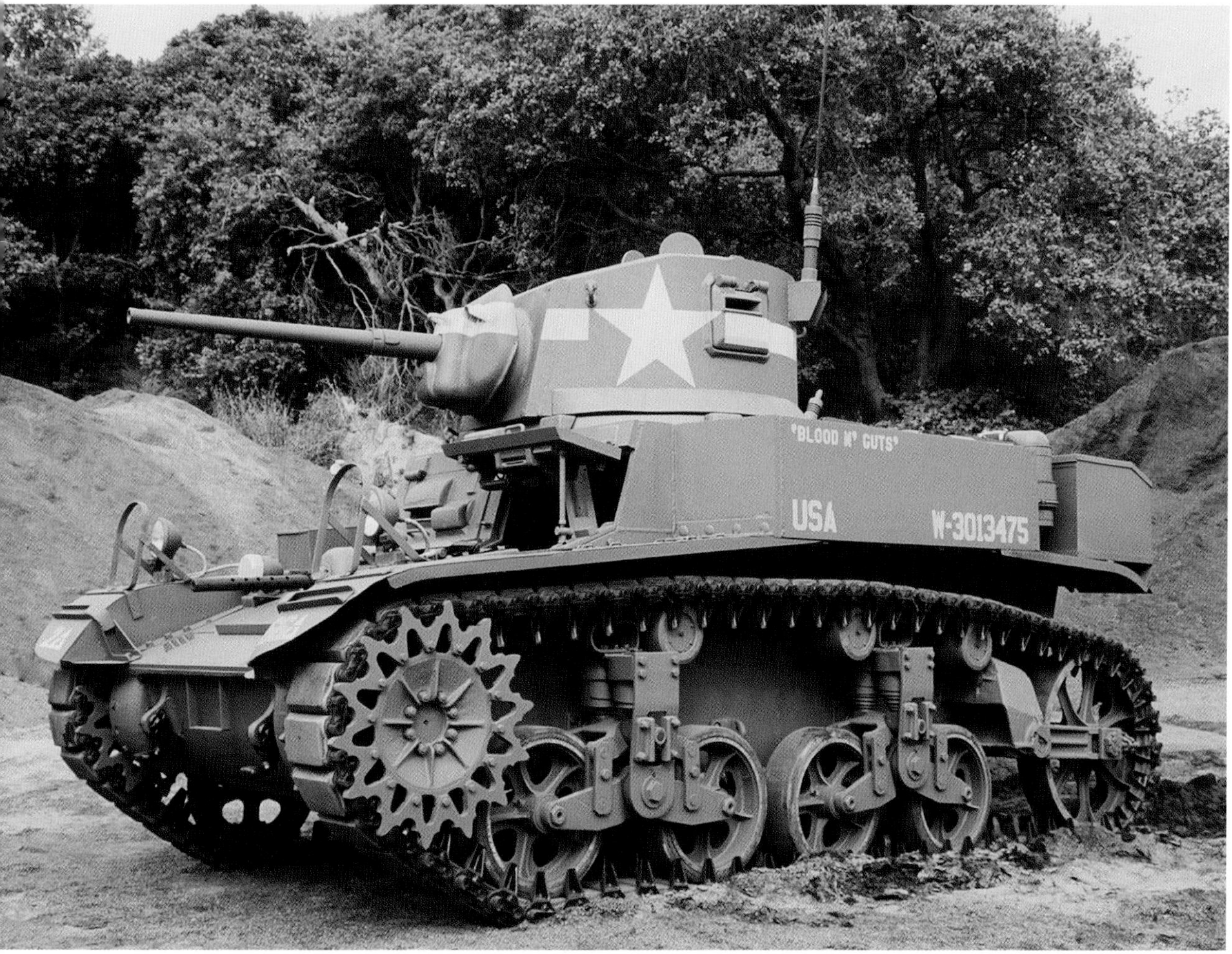
"BLOOD N' GUTS"
USA
W-3013475

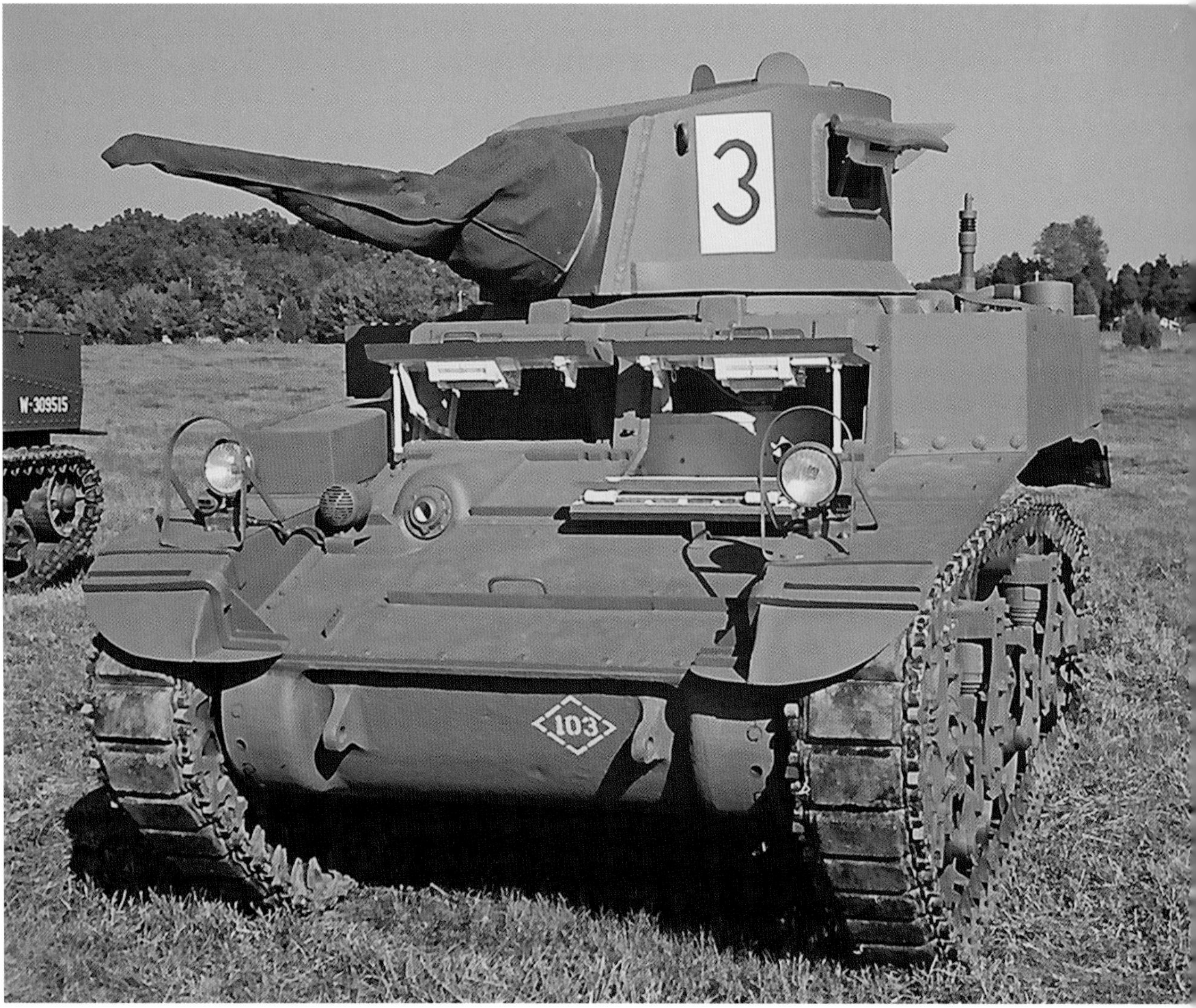
3
W-309515
103

(*Above*) Belonging to the Virginia Museum of Military History is this M3A1 light tank. The wartime crews of the vehicle were provided with an interphone system to better communicate with each over the noise of the tank when in motion. On the M2A4 and the M3 the tank commanders used their feet to tap out on the driver's upper torso a series of pre-arranged instructions that included right turn, left turn, speed up or slow down, etc. *(Author's collection)*

(*Opposite above*) On display at the First Infantry Division Museum located in Wheaton, Illinois is an M5 light tank. The oversized markings on the vehicle are intended to mimic the markings of an M5 that would have landed in French North Africa during Operation TORCH in November 1942. The glacis on the tank pictured was sloped at 48 degrees and had a thickness of 29mm. *(Paul Hannah)*

(*Opposite below*) The M5 light tank retained the turret of the M3A1 light tank as seen in this wartime photograph. A key external identifying feature of the M5 that differed from the light tanks of the M3 series was the raised rear engine deck. On level roads the M5 had a maximum speed of 36mph, with a cruising range of 100 miles. The tank was 14ft 6in long, had a width of 7ft 4in and was 7ft 6in tall. *(Patton Museum)*

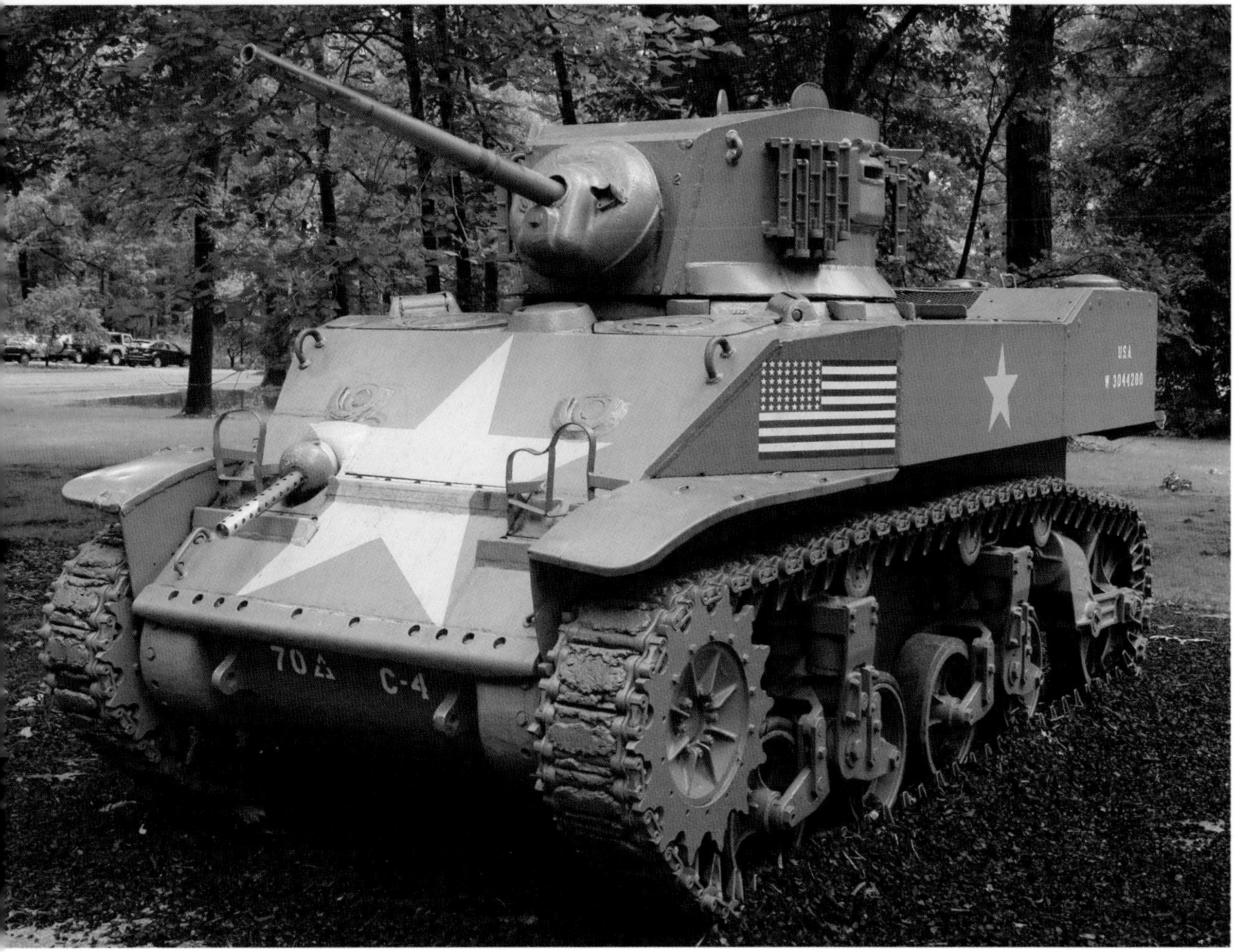
USA
W 3044280
70
C-4

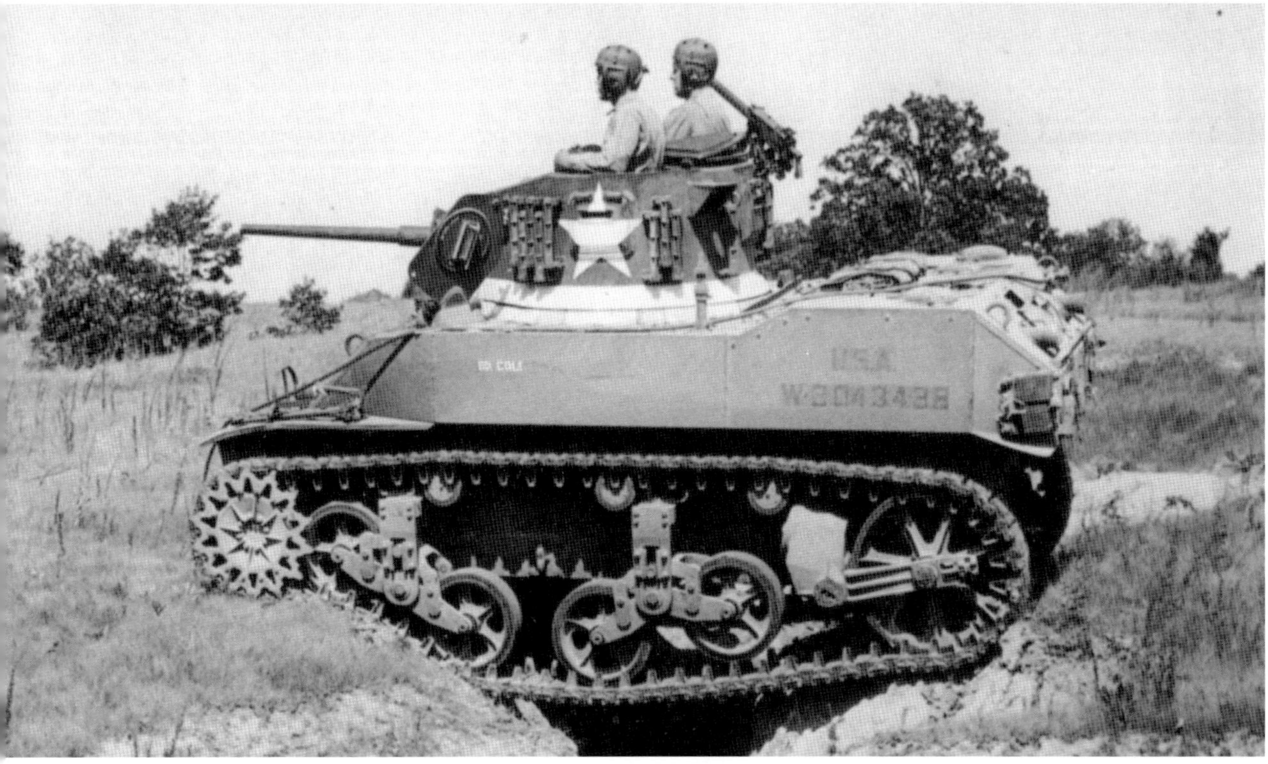
USA
W-3043488

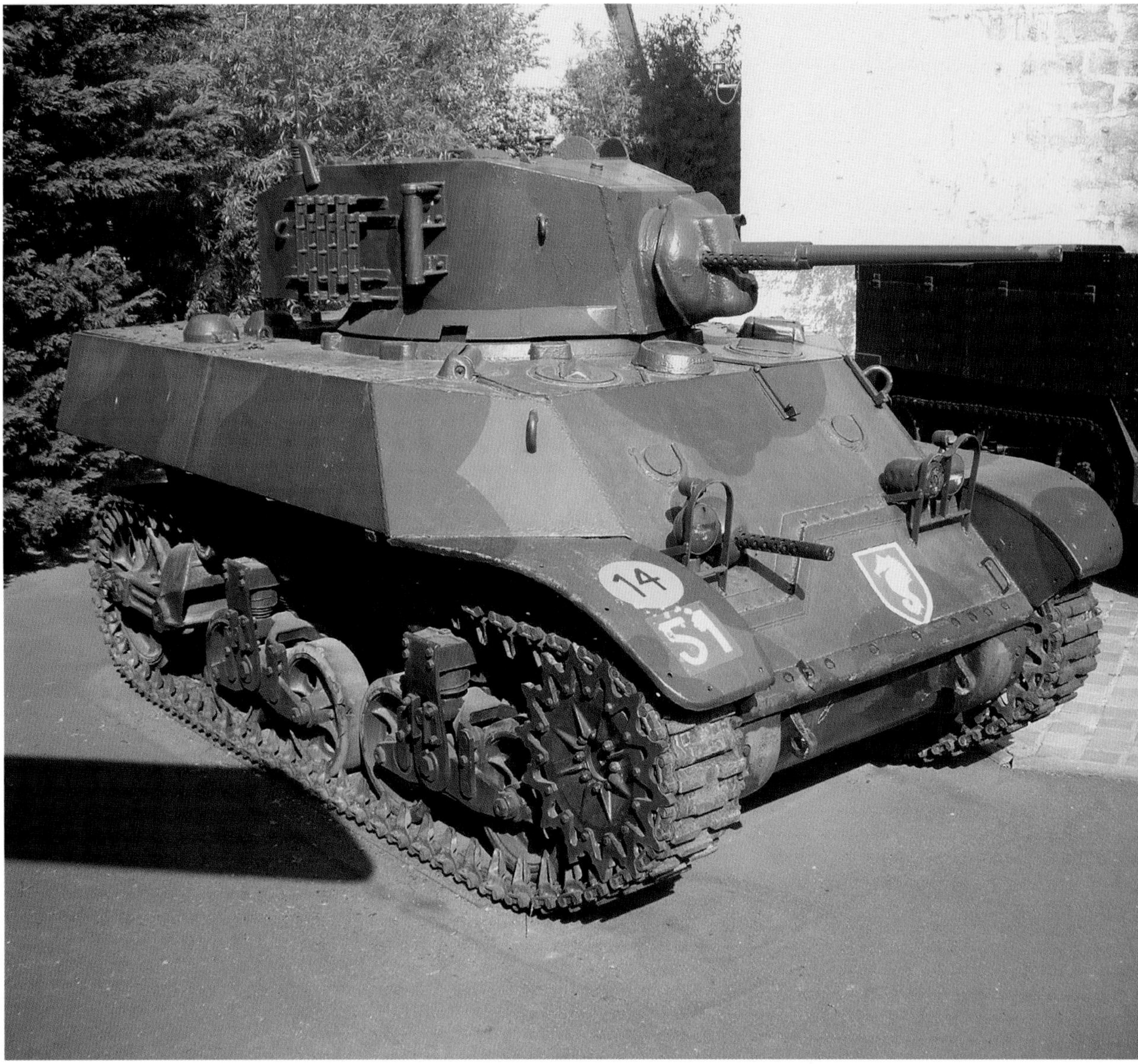
14
51

(*Above*) The added space provided by the sloping glacis of the M3A3 light tank pictured on display in Europe meant that the driver and assistant driver/bow gunner would have their own overhead hatches not seen on earlier versions of the M3 series of light tanks. The M5 had the same overhead hatches for the driver and assistant driver/bow gunner. (*Pierre-Olivier Buan*)

(*Opposite above*) The replacement for the M5 light tank was the M5A1 light tank seen here. An identifying feature of the M5A1 was the extended rear turret bustle that contained a radio. The larger turret on the M5A1 had originally been developed for the M3A3 light tank. The M5A1 could surmount a 60 per cent gradient and cross a trench 5ft 3in in width. (*Author's collection*)

(*Opposite below*) A restored early-production M5A1 light tank is shown decked out with a variety of wartime features. Like the M5, it was powered by two liquid-cooled gasoline-powered Cadillac car engines coupled to an automatic transmission. The M3 series of light tanks employed by the American military were powered by a single air-cooled gasoline-powered aircraft-type radial engine coupled to a manual transmission. (*Pierre-Olivier Buan*)

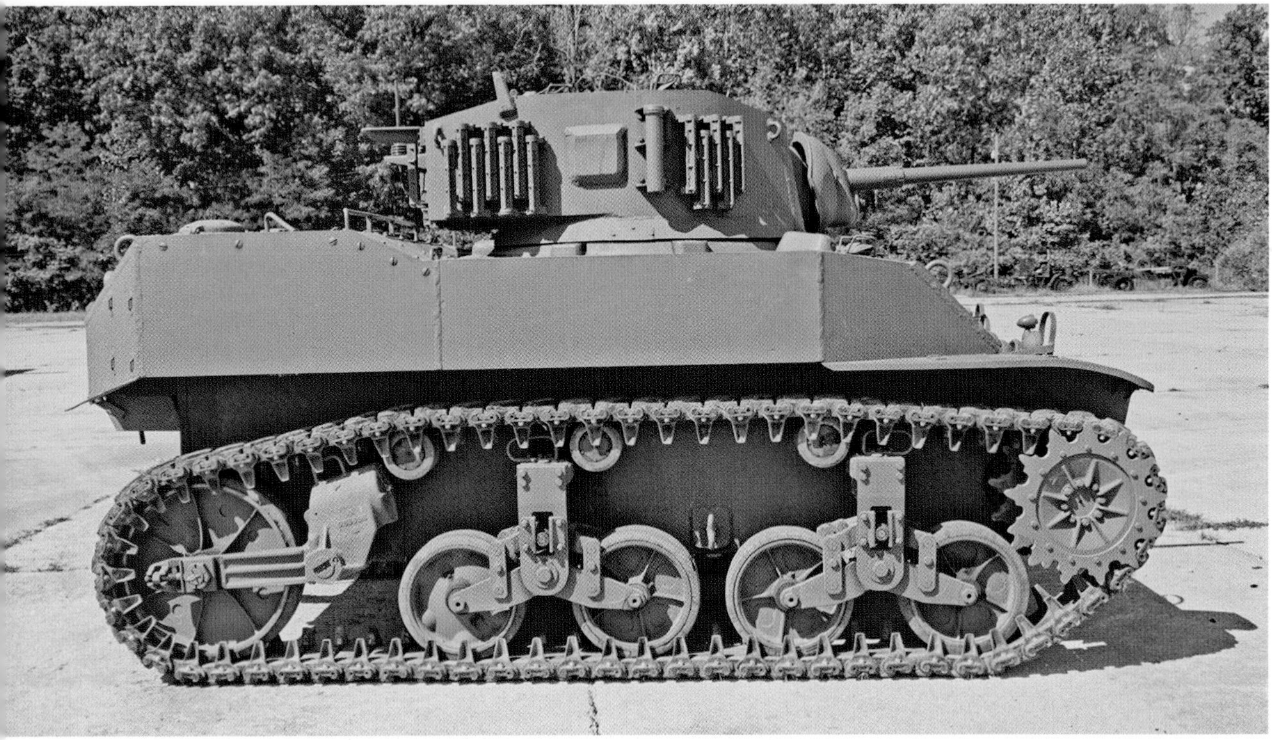

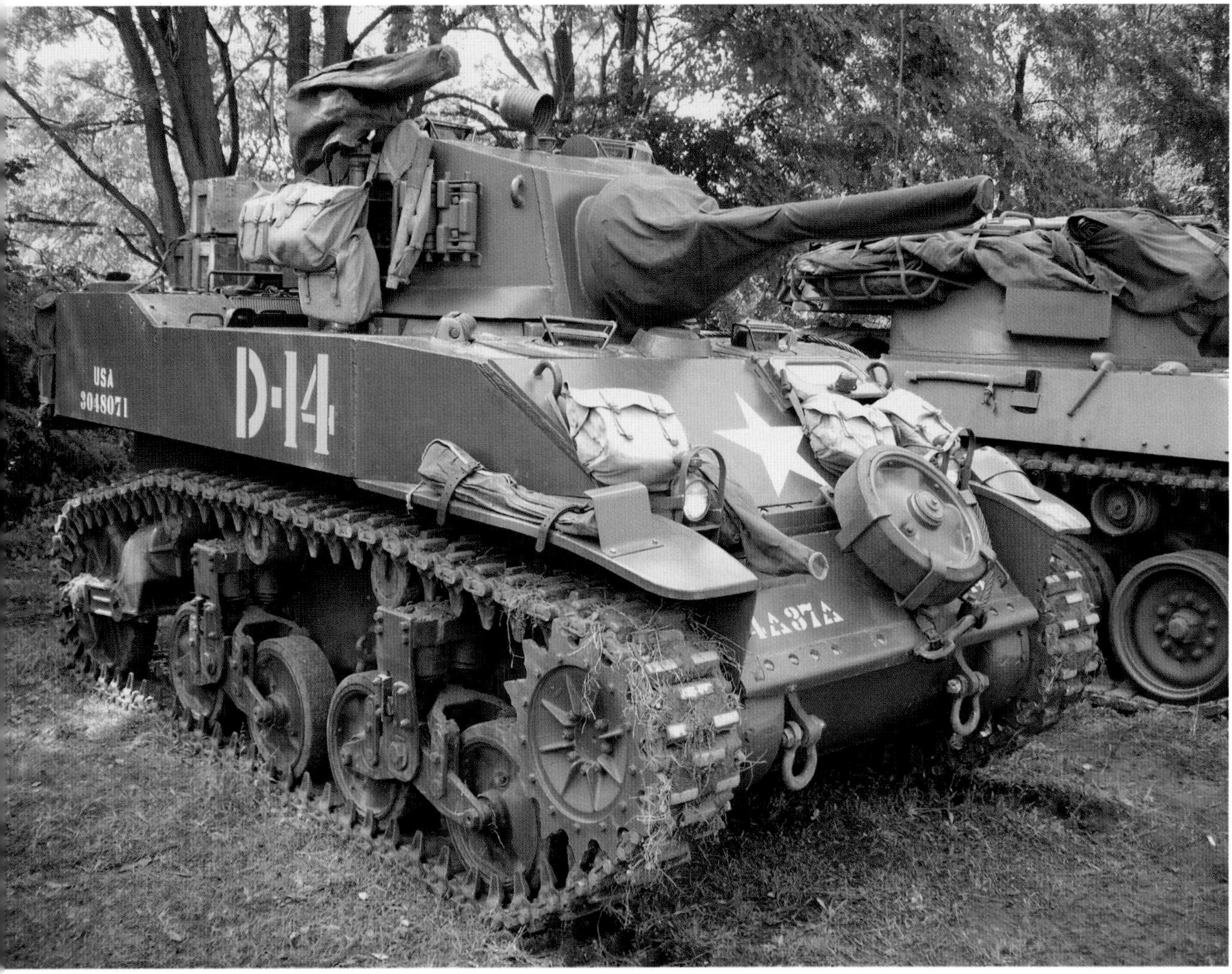
USA
3048071
D-14

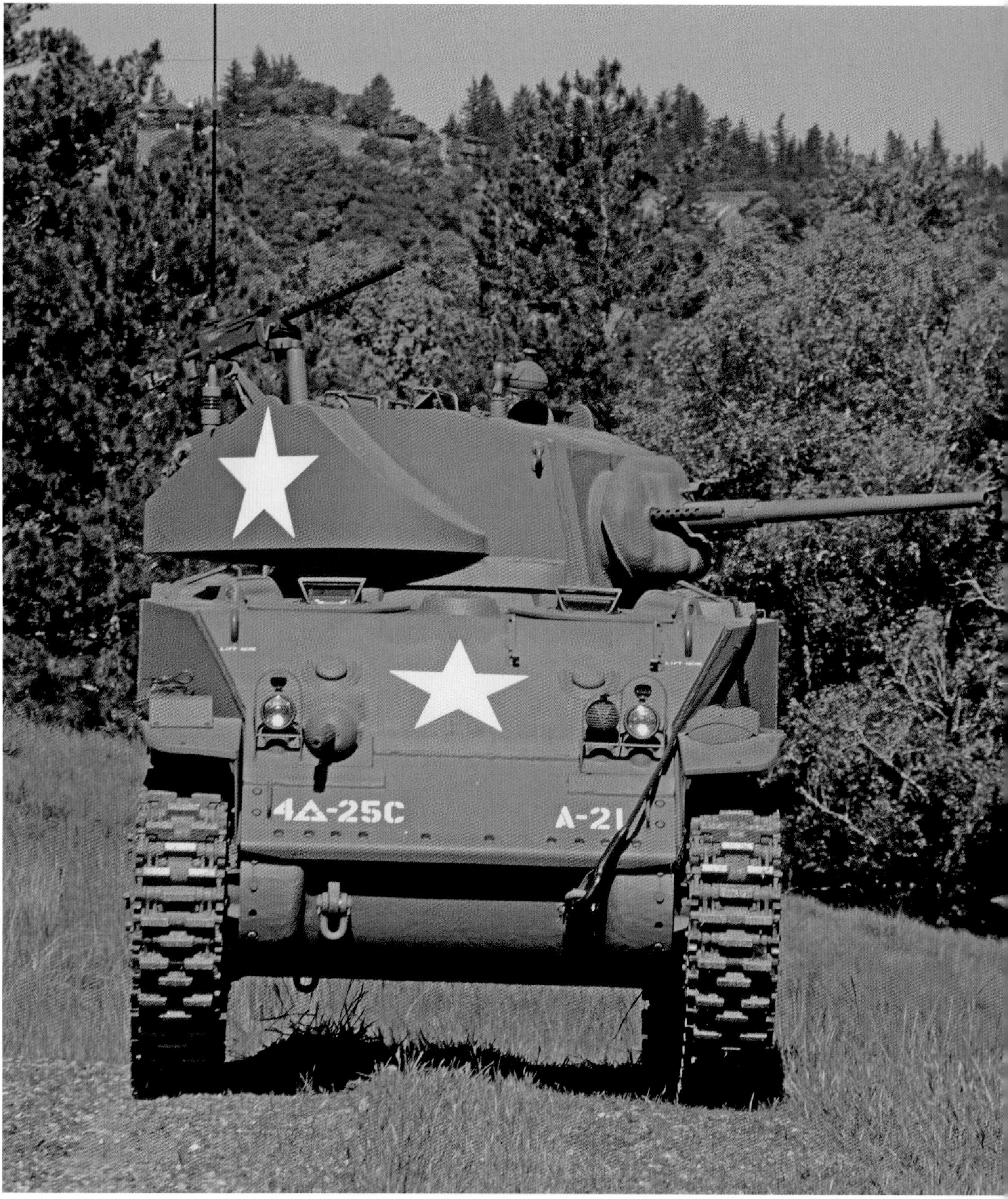
4Δ-25C
A-21

Later-production units of the M5A1 light tank as seen here appeared with a curved armoured storage box located on the right side of the turret to store a small-calibre machine gun. On the M5 the small-calibre machine gun was mounted at the rear of the turret bustle, which meant that a crewman had to climb out of the vehicle to employ it in combat. *(Author's collection)*

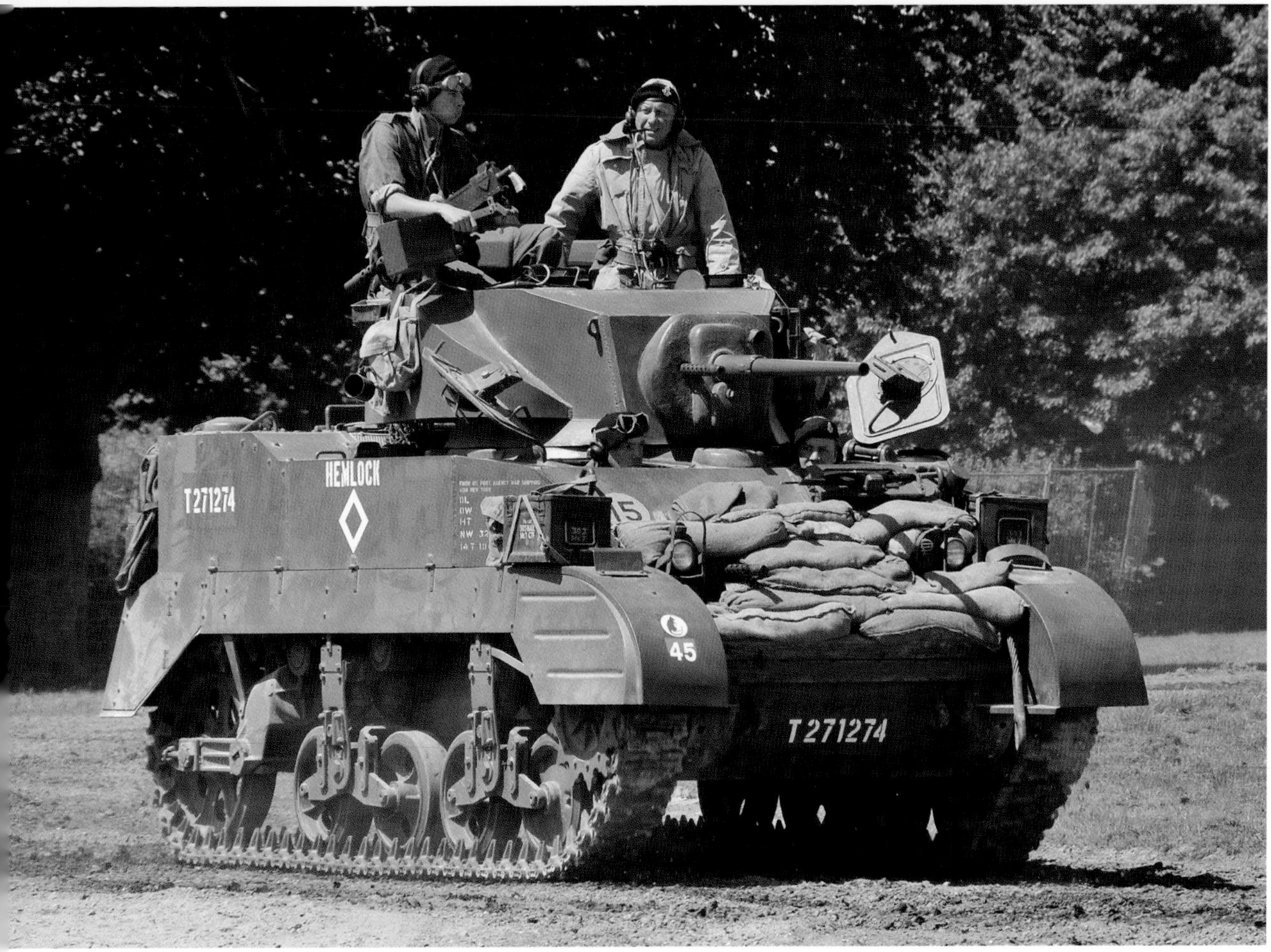

T271274
HEMLOCK
45
T271274

Taking part in a historical vehicle demonstration held by the British Tank Museum and referred to as 'Tankfest' is an M5A1 in British army markings. It was not unheard-of for the crews of these vehicles during the Second World War to add an assortment of sandbags and logs to the glacis of their tanks to hopefully provide some sort of stand-off protection from enemy shaped-charged warheads. *(Christophe Vallier)*

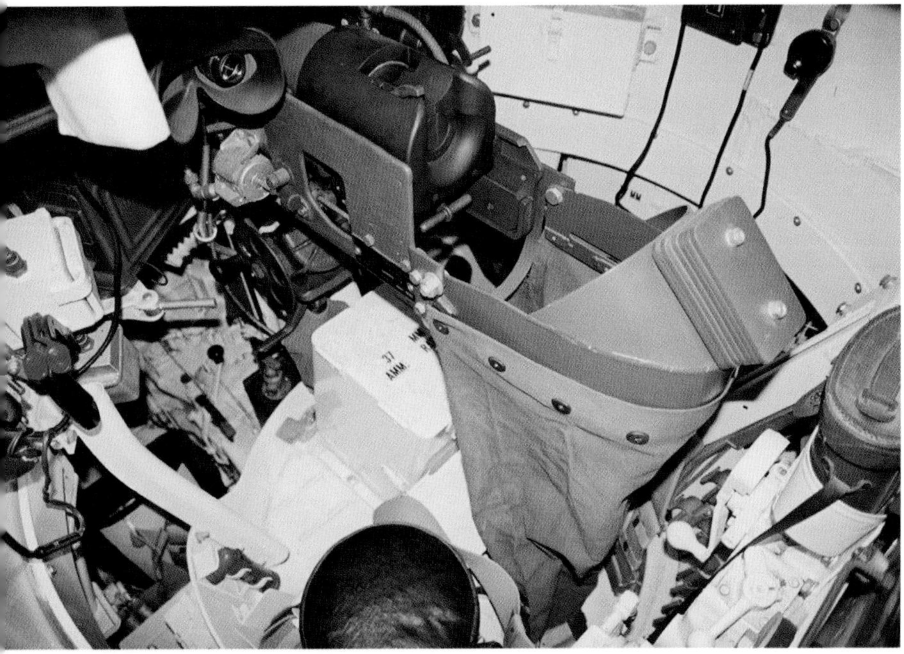

Visible in this picture taken inside the turret of an M5A1 light tank is the fabric bag for catching the spent cartridge cases from the 37mm main gun. The gunner sat on the left side of the turret and the vehicle commander on the right. The gunner's turret-traversing control handle is visible in this picture as well as the two red firing switches; one for the main gun and the other for the coaxial machine gun. *(Author's collection)*

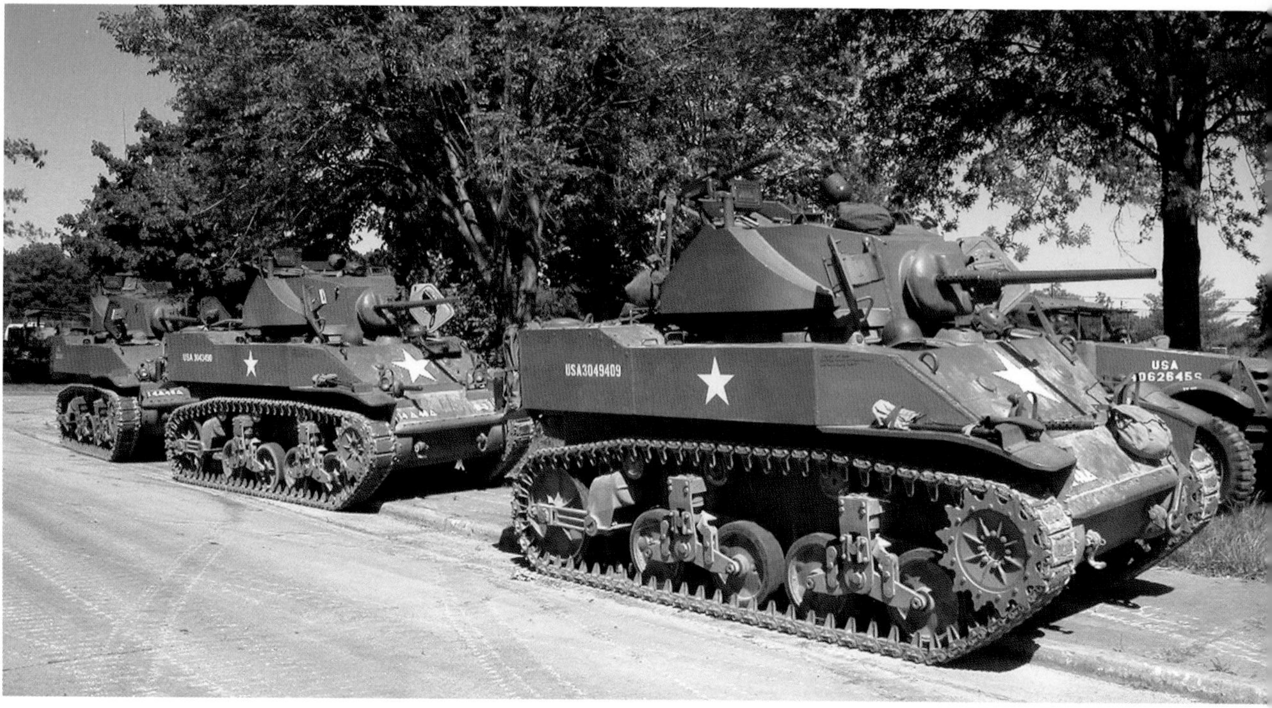
USA3049409

A trio of M5A1 light tanks appears prior to a historical vehicle demonstration that had been an annual event for many years at the now-closed Patton Museum of Armor and Cavalry. Well aware of the limited combat usefulness of the M5 series, the US army in the ETO tended to restrict them to secondary duties that would limit their exposure to enemy anti-tank weapons. *(Chun-lun Hsu)*

The M24 pictured here employed the same powertrain as the M5 series of light tanks. Like the M5 series, the maximum speed of the M24 on a level road was 35mph with an operational range of approximately 100 miles. The vehicle was 18ft 3in in length, had a width of 9ft 10in and a height of 9ft 1in. *(TACOM)*

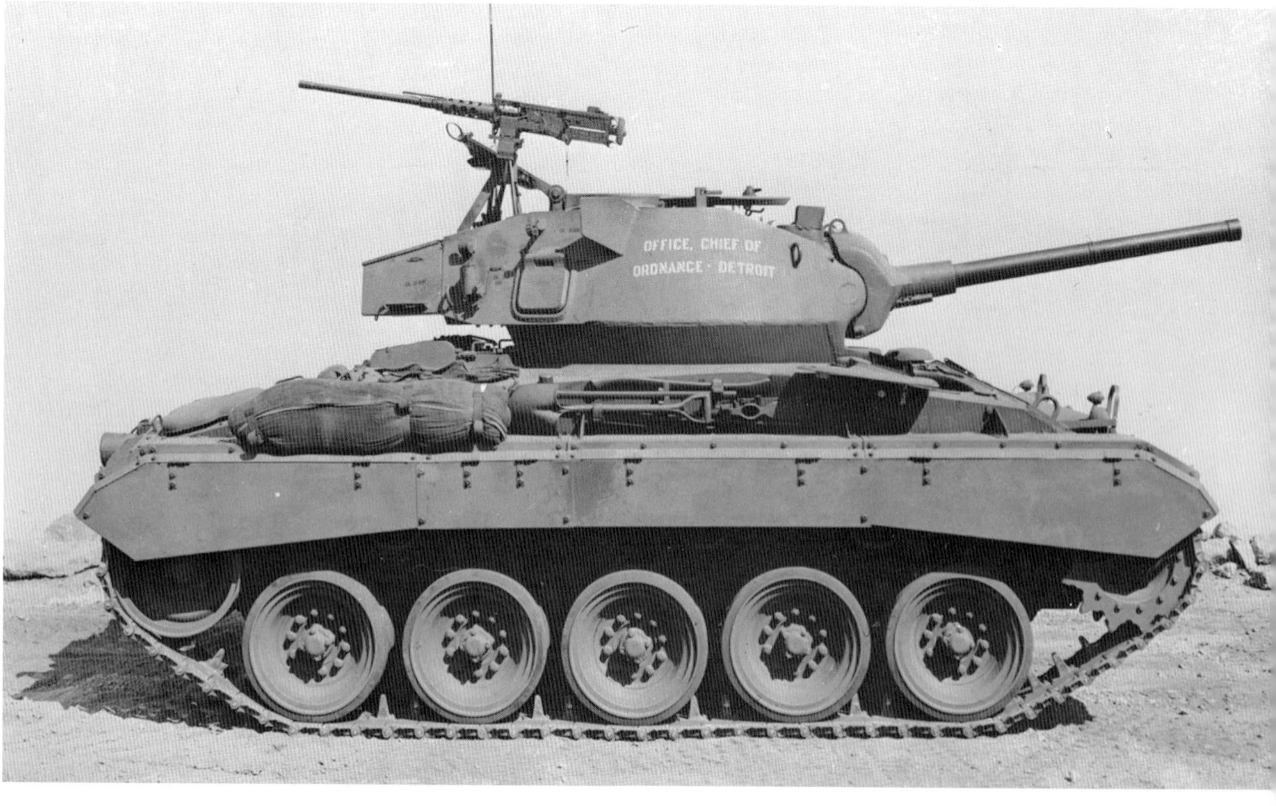
OFFICE, CHIEF OF
ORDNANCE · DETROIT

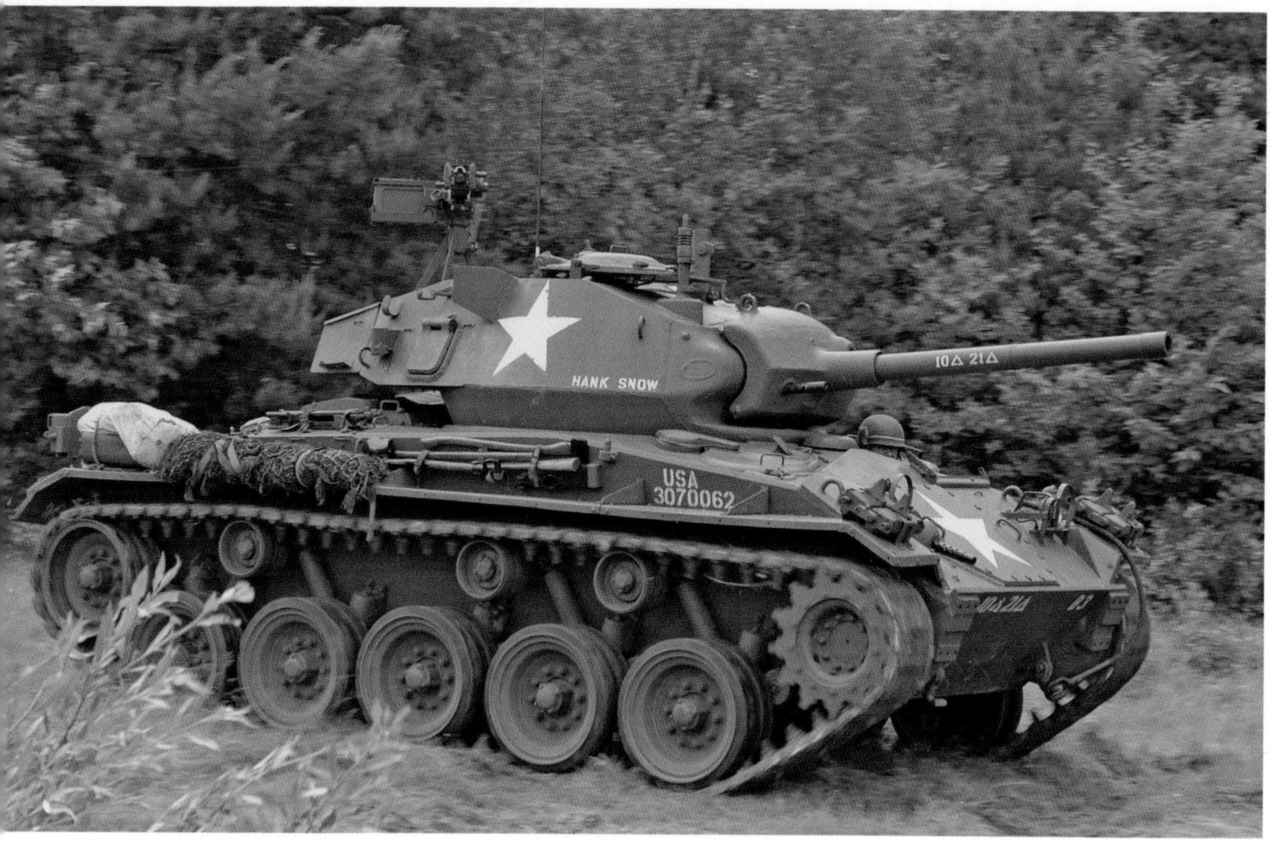
HANK SNOW
USA
3070062

Being run during a historical military vehicle demonstration in Europe is this restored M24. The torsion bar suspension system was adopted by the US army because of its simplicity, combined with its ability to absorb more energy in relation to its weight than previous light tank suspension systems, which consisted of the vertical volute spring suspension (VVSS) system. *(Christophe Vallier)*

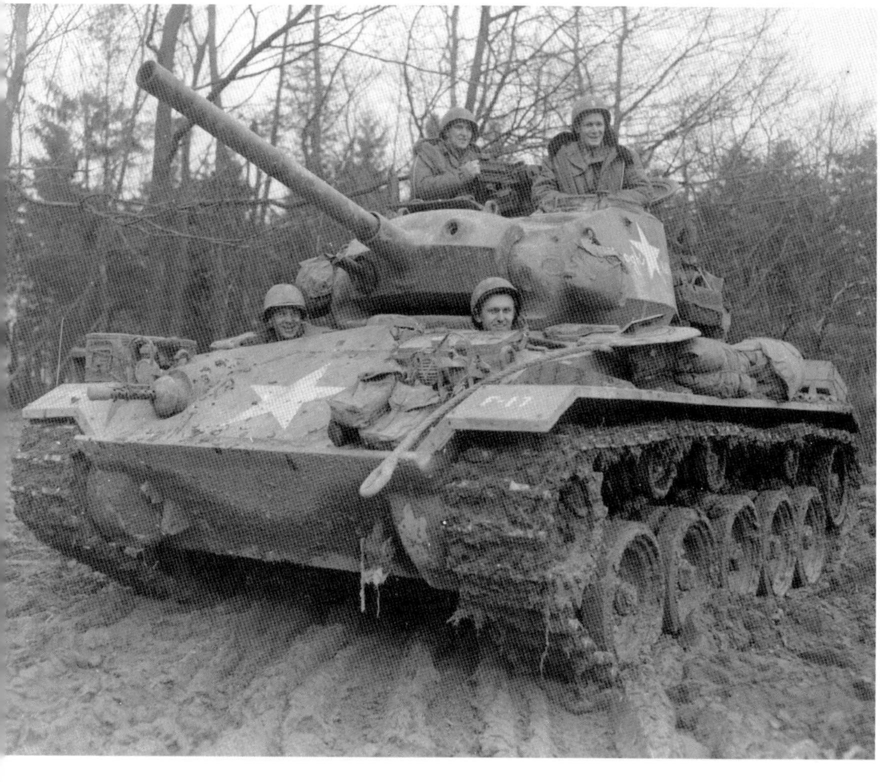

The M24 light tank seen here in a wartime picture was a big improvement on the previous US army light tanks. However, compared to German late-war tanks and self-propelled guns it remained badly under-gunned and under-armoured. The main role of the M24 in North-West Europe was the same as that of the M5 series light tanks; escorting the mechanized infantry and reconnaissance and flank security. *(Patton Museum)*

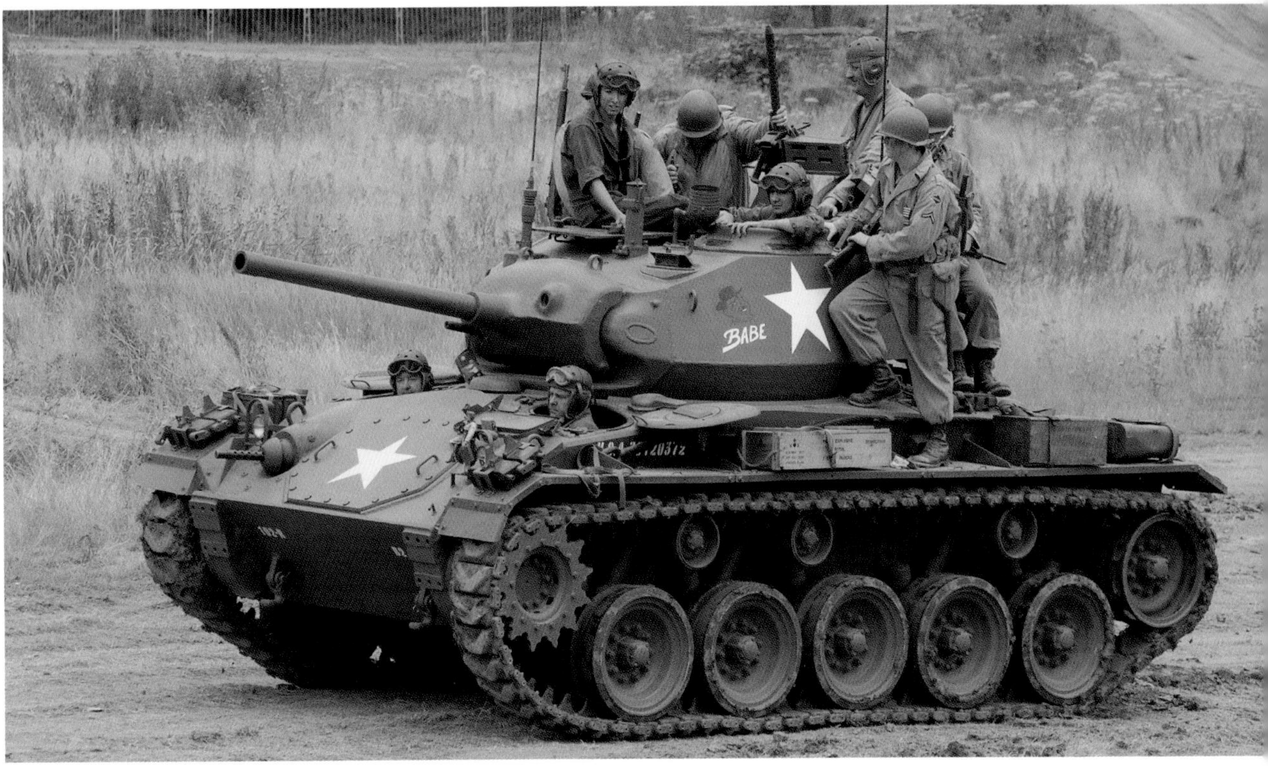
BABE

Re-enactors in period uniforms add a touch of wartime reality to this M24 light tank. Armour thickness on the tank topped out at a maximum of 1.5in (38mm) at the gun shield, typically the best-protected portion of most tanks. The rest of the armour on the tank ranged from as little as 13mm on the turret roof to 25mm on the frontal aspects of the hull and turret. *(Christophe Vallier)*

The restored M22 light tank seen here formerly resided at the now-closed Military Vehicle Technology Foundation founded by the late Jacques Littlefield. Located on the top of the vehicle's fenders and welded to the hull can be seen two of four carrying brackets that were envisioned as holding the hull of the M22 under the fuselage of a four-engine C-54 transport aircraft. *(Author's collection)*

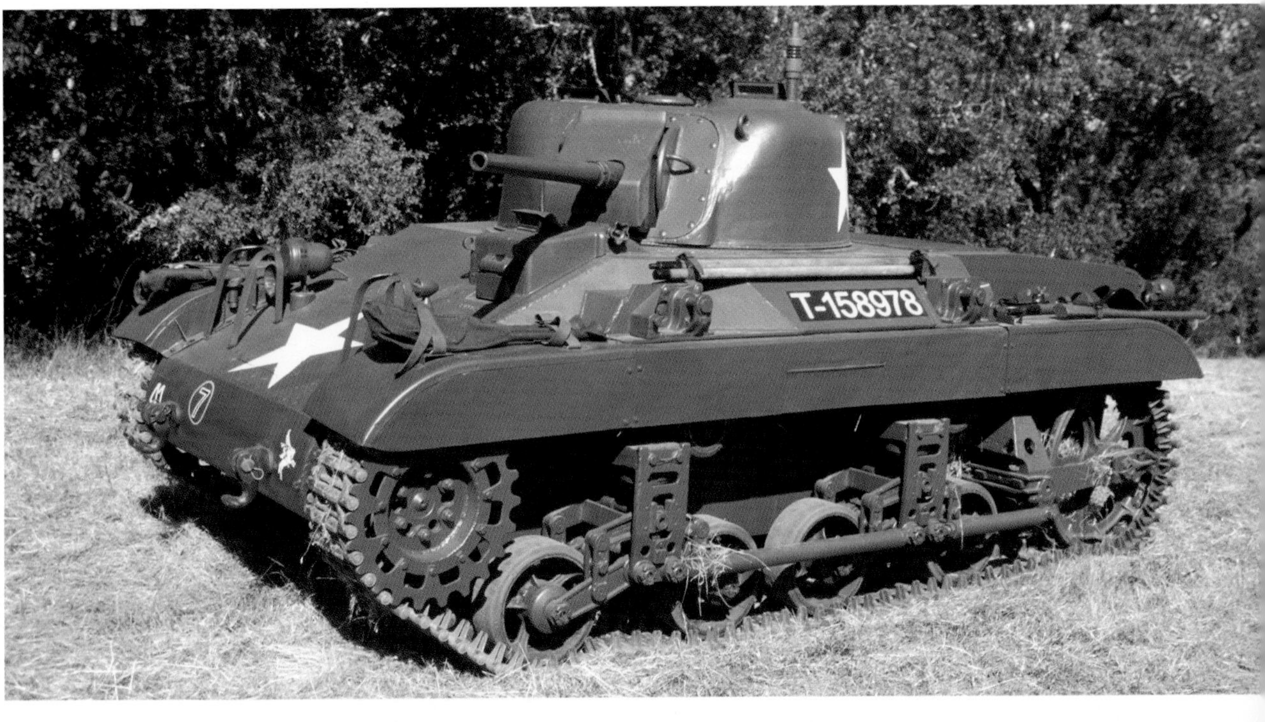
T-158978

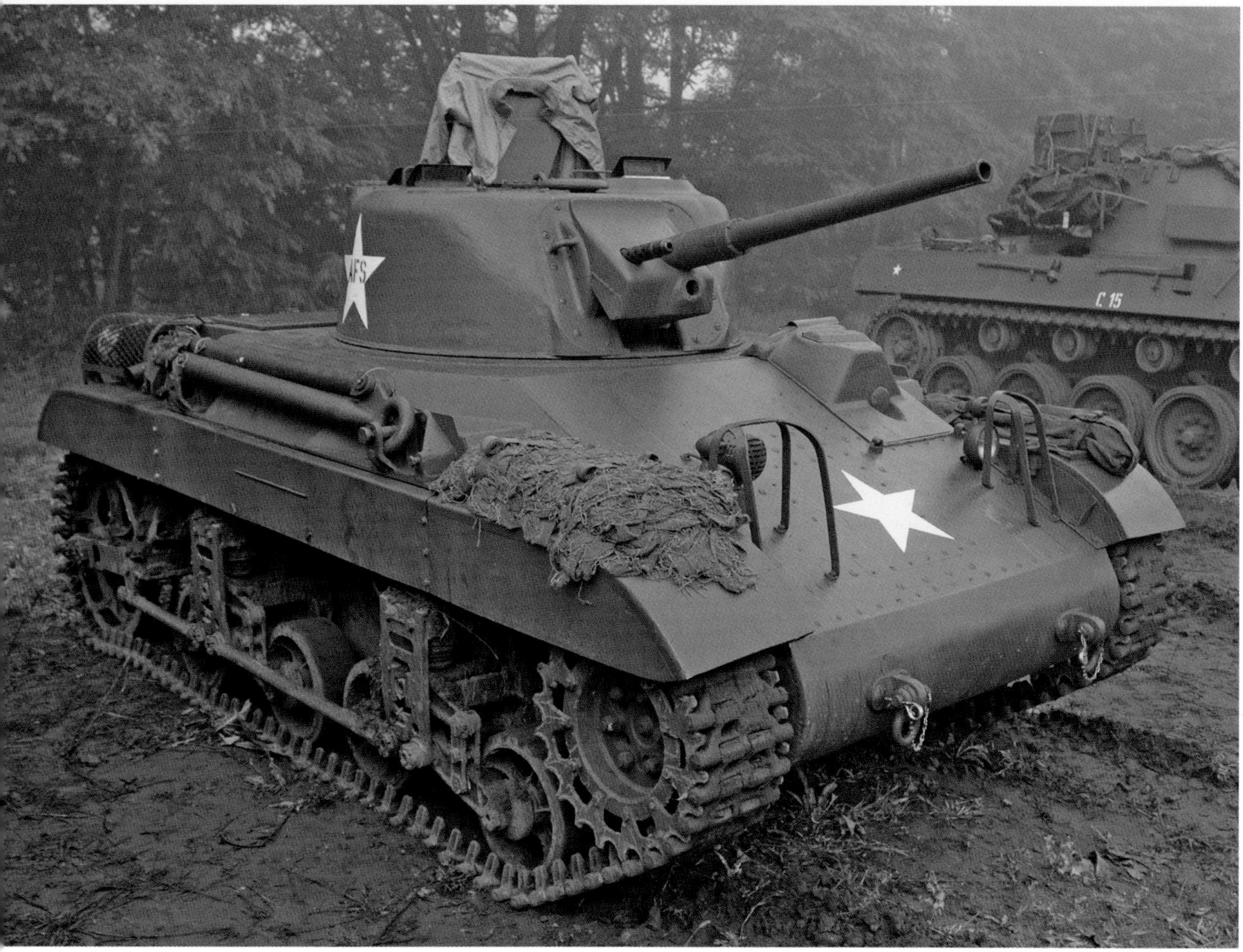

On display during a historical vehicle rally in Europe is this restored M22 light tank. Power for the vehicle came from a 162hp air-cooled gasoline engine that gave it a top speed of 35mph. The sloped glacis of the tank was 13mm thick. To boost the penetrative power of the tank's 37mm main gun the British army would install on some of its inventory of M22 tanks a squeeze-bore device named the 'Littlejohn'. *(Christophe Vallier)*

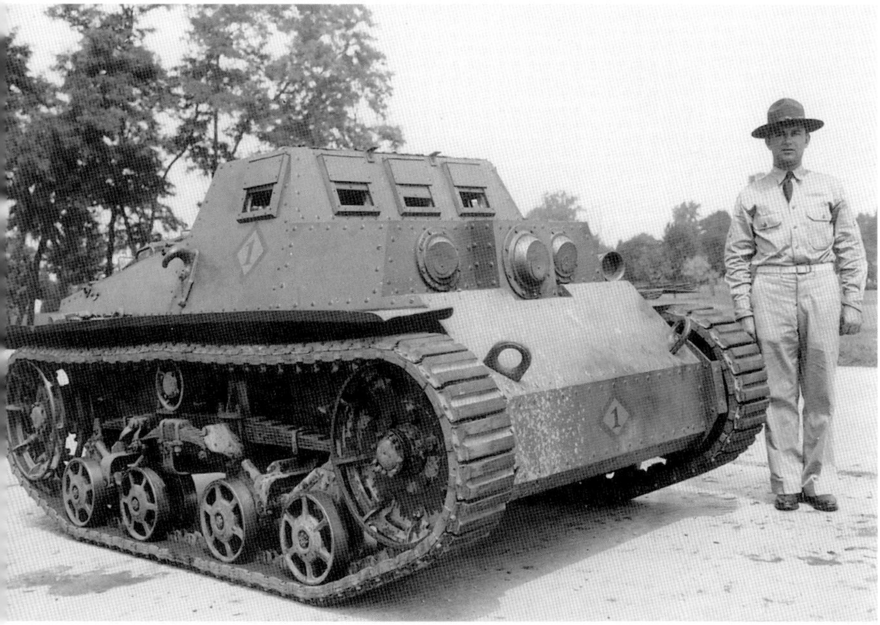

Before America's official entry into the Second World War, the USMC went its own way on tank development. An example of their efforts is this turretless light tank designated the CTL-3. It was designed and built by the Marmon-Herrington Company, the same company that designed and built the M22 light tank for the US army. *(Marine Corps Historical Center)*

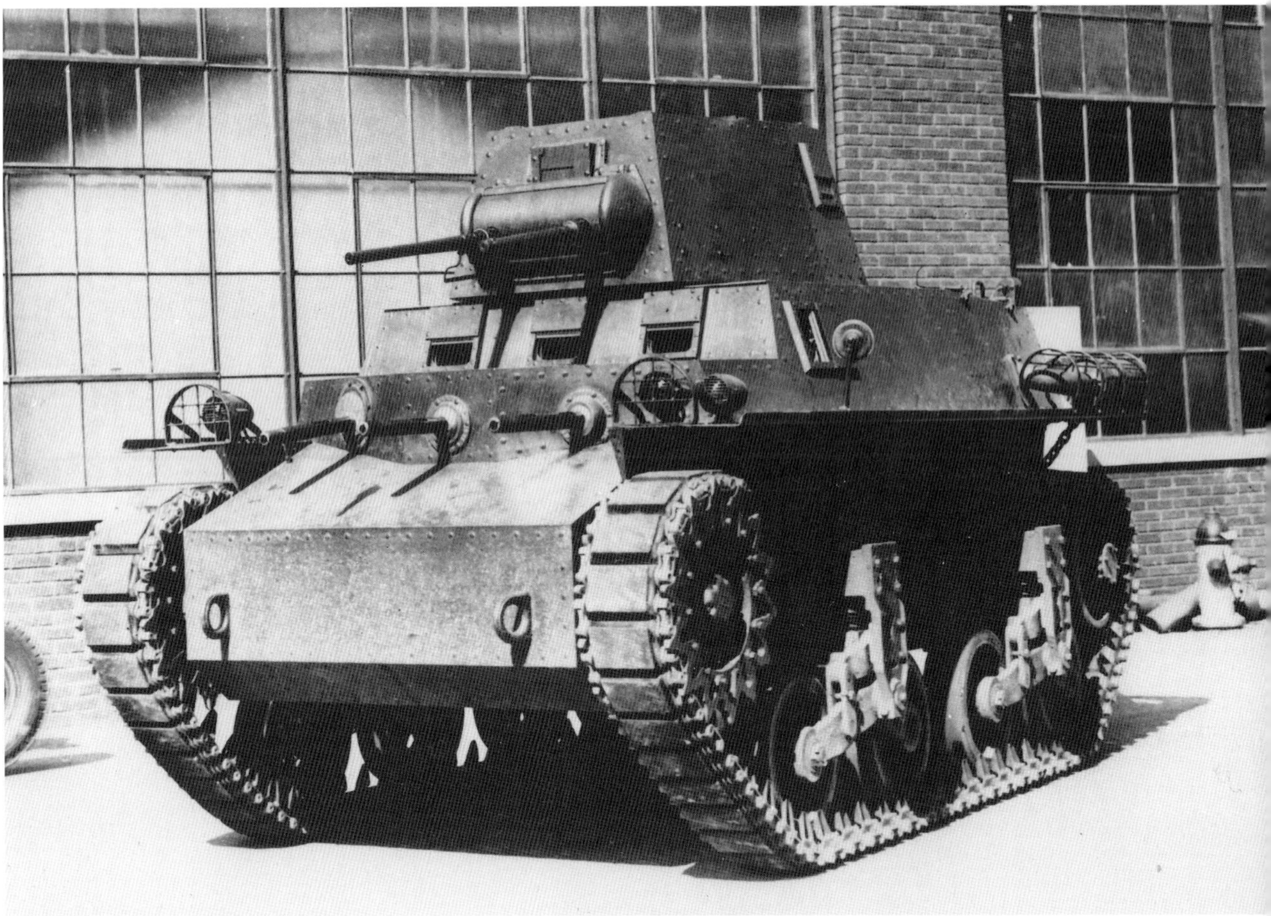

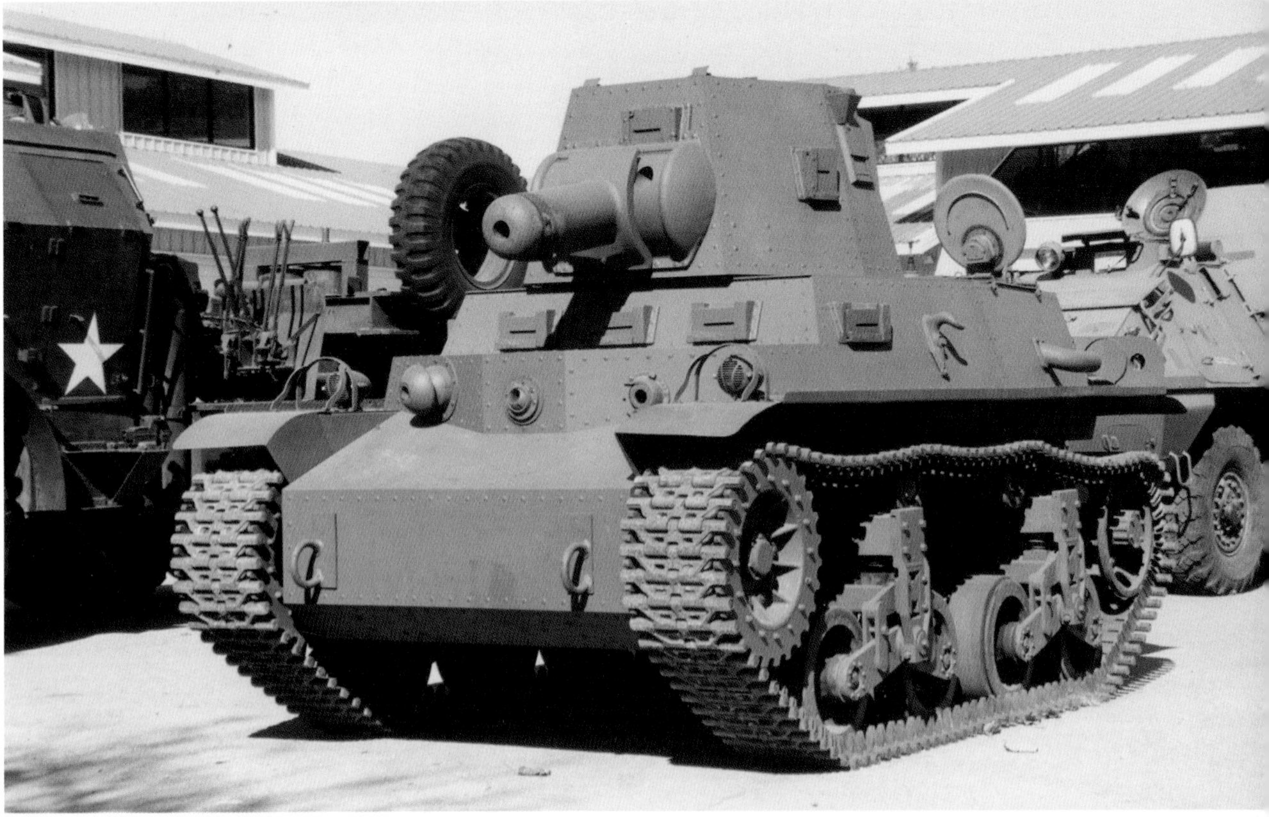

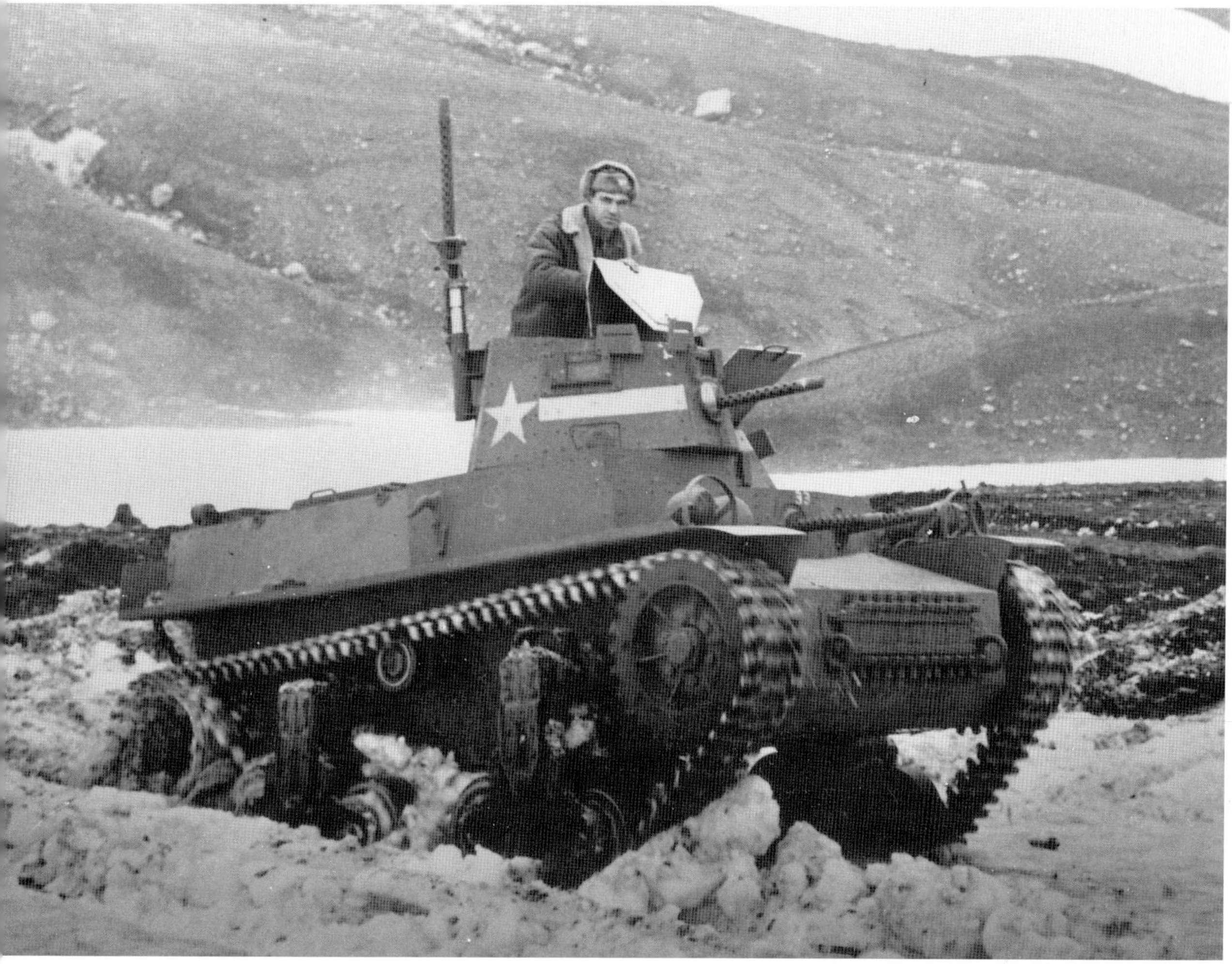

(*Opposite above*) One of the last Marmon-Herrington Company tanks considered by the USMC before the attack on Pearl Harbor, Hawaii is this turreted model designated as the CTM-3TBD. Like all the Marmon-Herrington Company tanks acquired by the USMC it proved mechanically unreliable and, compared to its US army light tank counterpart of the M3 series, was under-armed, being equipped only with machine guns. (*Marine Corps Historical Center*)

(*Above*) Pictured is one of the two-man impressed light tanks designed and built by the Marmon-Herrington Company for foreign buyers but placed into US army service after the Japanese attack on Pearl Harbor. In US army service the machine-gun-armed vehicle was designated as the Light Tank T16. Armour on the front of the tank was 25mm thick and 13mm on the remaining portions of the vehicle. (*Patton Museum*)

(*Opposite below*) A Marmon-Herrington Company-designed and built light tank taken into US army service as an emergency measure after Pearl Harbor was the CTMS-1TB1. An example is seen here at the now-closed Military Vehicle Technology Foundation. Unlike the majority of Marmon-Herrington light tanks armed only with machine guns, this particular model was armed with a 37mm main gun, the barrel of which is missing from the vehicle pictured here. (*Author's collection*)

Chapter Two

Early-War Medium Tanks

The British army was the world's first to field a fully-tracked armoured vehicle classified as a medium tank. Armed only with machine guns, it was assigned the designation Tank, Medium A. Its initial foray into combat occurred in March 1918 during the last year of the First World War. Approximately 200 units of the three-man 'Whippets' were eventually built.

The British army continued to field newer-generation medium tanks in the 1920s, including 160 units of the Mk I Medium Tank and a redesigned version designated as the Mk II Medium Tank. Three units of the Mk III Medium Tank were also built before the British army concluded that the design was no longer worth pursuing.

The Mk I through to the Mk III Medium Tanks were armed with a 3-pounder (47mm) gun and several machine guns. They did not see combat with the British army in the Second World War but were employed as training vehicles early in the war. Some of their turrets were supposedly mounted on pillboxes in North Africa.

New Labels

Up to the early 1930s the British army continued to describe tanks of a certain weight range as medium tanks. Beginning in 1936, they began to classify them by their assigned missions as either 'cruiser' or 'infantry' tanks, regardless of their weight. The cruiser tanks were intended for the exploitation role and as can be surmised the infantry tanks would perform the infantry support role.

The design emphasis for all the pre-war-designed British army cruiser tanks was on high speed. Due to the existing level of powertrain development and suspension systems it was impossible at the time to build a cruiser tank possessing both high speed and thick armour. The British army believed that high speed would make up for the cruiser tank's light armour as they would supposedly be harder to hit on the battlefield. As the infantry tanks had no need for high speed, they could be designed with a higher level of armour protection.

Early Cruiser Tanks

The first of the 1930s-era cruiser tanks to enter into British army service was the Cruiser Tank Mk I (A9). Crewed by six men, it was armed with a 2-pounder (40mm)

British Army Tank Designations

Unlike the Red Army that never bothered much with other than the most basic designation for its tanks, the British army had a bewildering array of tank designations. Even worse, they were inconsistently applied. Most tanks were assigned a General Staff specification number based on their sequence of authorization; however, not all would be placed into production.

The General Staff specification number was always prefixed by the letter 'A' that stood for tank in the British army nomenclature system. Hence the Mk I Medium Tank was also identified as the A2 and the Mk II Medium Tank as the A3. The Mk III was listed as the A6. By the end of the Second World War the General Staff specification numbers had reached A43.

The British army also assigned many of its tanks a second mark number. This was done to denote sub-variants of the same tank due to a change in its design, such as a new main gun or another type of engine being fitted. The British army also adopted the practice of assigning names to many of its tanks beginning in 1940, which has continued up to the present day.

main gun and three machine guns. Two of its machine guns were fitted into individual sub-turrets positioned at the front of the vehicle's hull, reflecting the fact that it had originally been intended as an infantry tank.

The Cruiser Tank Mk I weighed approximately 27,000lb and, like all the cruiser tanks that followed, was powered by a single gasoline engine. A total of 125 units of the tank were built. It would go on to see combat in both France and the Middle East between 1940 and 1941.

The five-man Cruiser Tank Mk II (A10) was a larger and better-armoured version of its predecessor. The first two versions were armed with a 2-pounder main gun and the last version a 37mm howitzer, plus two machine guns. The tank weighed approximately 32,000lb. A total of 170 units were built and they would see combat in both France and North Africa between 1940 and 1941.

Reflecting its increased armour protection level compared to the Cruiser Tank Mk I (A9), the Cruiser Tank Mk II (A10) was also labelled at some point as a 'heavy cruiser tank'. This designation is not employed at the Tank Museum in its description of the vehicle. Rather, it and all the other cruiser tanks that form part of its large collection are labelled as 'Cruiser/Medium Tanks'.

Mk III and Mk IV

Two senior British army officers were invited by the Red Army to witness training manoeuvres in the Soviet Union in 1936. They were impressed both by the large number of tanks the Red Army possessed and the American-designed Christie suspension on their BT series of light tanks. This would result in the Cruiser Tank Mk III (A13) being designed with a version of the Christie suspension system.

The Cruiser Tank Mk III had a crew of four and was armed with a 2-pounder gun and a single coaxial machine gun. A total of sixty-five units were built. It weighed approximately 31,000lb and would see combat in France and North Africa between 1940 and 1941.

Power for the Cruiser Tank Mk III was provided by an American-designed Liberty gasoline engine licence-built by the British firm of Nuffield. The engine's design dated back to 1917 and started life as an aircraft engine. As the British-built Liberty engine only developed 340hp, its continued use on British army cruiser tanks became a serious design problem as the weight of new cruiser tanks rose with each successive model and they became ever more underpowered.

Unhappiness with the Cruiser Tank Mk III led to a redesigned version labelled the Cruiser Tank Mk IV (A13 Mk II). Some 270 units were built of the 33,000lb tank. Like those before it, the main armament was a 2-pounder gun and a coaxial machine gun. The Cruiser Tank Mk IV would see combat in both France and the Middle East between 1940 and 1941.

Covenanter

The continuous up-armouring of the cruiser tank series eventually led to the production of the last of the pre-war-designed cruiser tanks. That was the four-man Cruiser Tank Mk V (A13 Mk III), which was assigned the name 'Covenanter'. It rode on a Christie suspension system. Power for the approximately 40,000lb Covenanter came from a Nuffield Liberty engine.

Armament on the Covenanter consisted of a 2-pounder main gun and a coaxial machine gun. A total of 1,771 units were built between 1940 and 1942. A design failure, it was never committed to combat and retained only for the training role in Great Britain.

Infantry Tanks

There were three pre-war-designed infantry tanks that entered British army service. These included the Infantry Tank Mk I (A11) and the Infantry Tank Mk II (A12), respectively named the 'Matilda' I and II. The third was the Infantry Tank Mk III named the 'Valentine'. It was never assigned a General Staff specification number.

Matilda Infantry Tanks

The two-man Matilda I weighed approximately 25,000lb. It was armed with two machine guns and was powered by an American-designed gasoline engine. A total of 139 units were built between 1937 and 1940. It would see action in France in the summer of 1940 where its armour proved sufficient to protect it from the majority of

German tank and anti-tank guns. However, it was badly under-gunned and therefore of little battlefield utility and was soon pulled from front-line service.

The Matilda II was a completely new tank design intended to make up for the Matilda I's design flaws. Upon the removal of the Mk I Matilda from front-line British army service, the Matilda II became known just as the Matilda. It had a three-man crew and was armed with a 2-pounder main gun and a coaxial machine gun. One version of the tank was armed with a 3-inch howitzer.

The Matilda weighed approximately 59,000lb and was powered by two diesel engines. A total of 2,987 units were built between 1938 and 1943. It would see combat both in France and in the Middle East.

Against under-gunned and under-armoured Italian tanks in North Africa, the Matilda did well. However, upon the arrival of better-armed and better-armoured German medium tanks it was quickly rendered obsolete as a gun tank and pulled from front-line service by the summer of 1942. It would be employed by the Australian army as a gun tank in jungle warfare against the Japanese until the end of the Second World War.

Valentine

Introduced into service with the British army in 1940 was the three-man Infantry Tank Mk III named the 'Valentine'. It weighed approximately 39,000lb and was armed with a 2-pounder main gun and a coaxial machine gun. The first version was powered by a gasoline engine with subsequent versions powered by diesel engines. Although classified as an infantry tank by the British army, the Valentine was also employed as a cruiser tank between 1940 and 1941.

The 2-pounder gun was an effective tank-killing weapon on British army cruiser and infantry tanks up until 1941. By 1942, the increased armour thickness of German medium tanks such as the Panzer III and IV had rendered it useless. To address this issue the British army decided to have a later version of the Valentine up-armed with a 6-pounder (57mm) main gun. Production of this version of the tank designated as the Mk VIII Valentine began in early 1942.

The final production version of the Valentine series was armed with a British-designed 75mm main gun and a coaxial machine gun. It was designated as the Mk XI Valentine. By the time production of the Valentine tank series ended in 1944, a total of 8,275 units had been built. Of that number 1,420 units had been built in Canada with all but thirty of those tanks being provided to the Red Army.

French Cavalry Medium Tanks

There was only a single medium tank in the French army cavalry branch inventory before the German invasion. It was the Somua S35 that weighed approximately 44,000lb and was armed with a 47mm main gun and a coaxial machine gun. It was powered by a gasoline engine. Of the 600 units of the Somua S35 ordered prior to the German invasion, 417 units had been delivered but not all had been placed into service with field units.

Although better-armed and armoured than its German medium tank counterparts, the Somua S35 had some design shortcomings. These included a one-man turret and a less than reliable suspension system that proved difficult to maintain in the field. Despite these disadvantages, the Somua S35 did well at the tactical level but could not overcome the strategic errors made at the highest levels of the French army.

Red Army Medium Tanks

As with its light tanks, the Red Army turned to British industry in the early 1930s for inspiration in looking for a suitable medium tank design. This resulted in the acquisition of more than a dozen examples of the British army Mk II Medium Tank. The Red Army testing of the vehicles left them unimpressed and they never sought to copy the design.

The first Red Army medium tank was labelled as the T-12. It looked much like an enlarged MS-1 and was based on the Christie M1921/1922 experimental tank. Its development began in 1928, with the first prototype being finished in November 1929. Trials of the vehicle began in February 1930. As it continued to be modified, the T-12 was eventually relabelled as the T-24. Officially the Red Army referred to these vehicles as 'manoeuvrable tanks' rather than medium tanks.

The first six production units of the T-24 were completed by October 1931, ten more by November 1931, and by the end of the year another eight. It had a crew of five, whereas the T-12 had a crew of four. Both tanks were armed with a 45mm main gun and up to three machine guns. The T-24 was not a success in Red Army service and it was quickly relegated to training duties. Prior to the German invasion there had been plans to employ the T-24 as dug-in pillboxes, but no pictures exist of that having taken place.

T-28 Medium Tank

The first of the Red Army medium tanks to be built in large numbers was the six-man T-28 Model 1934 medium tank. It had three turrets; one armed with a 76.2mm main gun. It was also armed with four machine guns. The tank's design was inspired by the unsuccessful series of British medium tanks known as the A6 series (the A6E1, A6E2 and A6E3). The suspension system of the T-28 was based on a German prototype tank that never went into production.

In total, 503 units of the T-28 series of medium tanks were constructed between 1934 and 1940. The last ten production units of the series were designated as the T-28 Medium Tank 1940 and came with a new conical main gun turret design borrowed from an existing Red Army heavy tank.

Into Combat

The T-28 would first see action during the Red Army invasion of Poland in September 1939. Combat experience gained during the subsequent Russo-Finnish War that began in November 1939 showed the gasoline-engine-powered T-28 series to be under-armoured. To rectify the problem, add-on armour kits were tacked on to the vehicles. The downside of this was an increase in weight, which compromised the vehicle's off-road mobility.

Those Red Army T-28 series tanks that survived the Russo-Finnish War would face the German army in the summer of 1941. The majority would quickly be lost to non-combat causes such as mechanical failure or lack of fuel due to a logistical breakdown within the Red Army. A few units of the T-28 series would last long enough in service to take part in the defence of Moscow and Leningrad in late 1941.

T-34 Medium Tank

The eventual Red Army replacement for the T-28 series was the T-34 medium tank. The first examples of the approximately 69,000lb tank came off the assembly lines in June 1940. The initial version of the tank is now commonly referred to as the T-34 Model 1940 and, despite a number of teething problems, was the most modern medium tank then in existence. It had a four-man crew: the driver, assistant driver, loader and the vehicle commander who doubled as the tank's gunner.

The T-34 Model 1940 was armed with a 76.2mm main gun and two machine guns. The tank originally had authorized storage for seventy-seven main gun rounds, which was raised to 100 main gun rounds in later models. Many of these were stored on the interior hull sides of the tank. However, the bulk of the main gun ammunition was stored in metal bins on the floor of the fighting compartment. This was normally covered with matting until access to the main gun rounds was required by the loader.

Early Combat

By the time the German invasion began in June 1941, Soviet industry had built 1,066 units of the T-34 Model 1940 of which 892 were in the Red Army inventory. Upon encountering the T-34 Model 1940 during the initial stages of their invasion of the Soviet Union, it became painfully obvious to the German army that it was superior to their own medium tanks.

The superiority of the T-34 over existing German medium tanks and the inability of the towed anti-tank guns of the infantry branch of the German army to deal with the tank was a serious shock to all concerned. It would result in the eventual development and production of the Panther medium tank and the Tiger E heavy tank. For the German army infantry branch, it prompted the development and the fielding of a new generation of towed anti-tank guns.

The design advantages of the T-34 over the German medium tanks during the summer of 1941 was offset by the fact that Red Army field units equipped with the tank had not been sufficiently trained with the vehicle. There were also serious shortages of main gun ammunition, fuel and spare parts. These factors and the superior training and command and control system structure of the German army tank units allowed them to eventually prevail over the Red Army T-34-equipped units they encountered in battle.

T-34 Medium Tank Improvements

Even before the German invasion, the Red Army had decided that the original 76.2mm main gun on the T-34 Model 1940, labelled as the L-11, lacked the desired armour penetration performance. This resulted in the development of a longer-barrelled and higher-velocity 76.2mm tank gun that began appearing on the T-34 production line in March 1941. The gun was labelled the F-34 and the tanks armed with it are now labelled as the T-34 Model 1941.

Progressive improvements made to the T-34 Model 1941 resulted in the T-34 Model 1942. These improvements would include a new driver's hatch, wider tracks and thicker side hull armour. Some factories building the T-34 series tank would incorporate features of both the Model 1941 and Model 1942. This has led to some authors using the designation T-34 1941/1942 in describing those tanks.

The next version of the T-34 series is labelled as the T-34 Model 1943. It can be readily identified by a hexagonal-shaped turret that first appeared in early 1942. A vehicle commander's cupola appeared on the hexagonal-shaped turret in 1943. Despite the larger and roomier turret, the T-34 Model 1943 retained the two-man turret crew of earlier versions.

By the time production of the T-34 series ended in 1944, approximately 35,000 units had been built. First-generation T-34 series tanks armed with a 76.2mm gun would remain in Red Army service until the end of the Second World War in ever-decreasing numbers. It was not retained post-war by the Red Army as a gun tank.

In place of the first-generation T-34 series armed with a 76.2mm main gun there would eventually appear in Red Army service a new second-generation T-34 series tank armed with an 85mm main gun fitted to a new turret.

American Medium Tanks

In late 1936, the US army began looking at the development of a proposed six-man medium tank. Rather than design a brand-new tank, it was decided to merely upscale the design of an existing four-man light tank. After building and testing a progressively-improved series of medium tank prototypes, the decision was made to standardize the vehicle as the Medium Tank M2 in June 1938.

The five-man M2 weighed approximately 41,000lb and was powered by a gasoline engine. It was armed with a 37mm main gun and an assortment of machine guns. Production of eighteen units of the tank began in the summer of 1939.

Tests of the M2 soon revealed a number of design flaws that led to the development of an improved version labelled the M2A1. The successful German military conquest of France in the summer of 1940 resulted in an order being placed in early August 1940 by the US army for 1,000 units of the M2A1.

Shortly after the contract for 1,000 M2A1 tanks had been awarded, the US army began receiving overseas reports indicating that the M2A1 was both under-armed and under-gunned when compared to existing German army medium tanks. This led to the cancellation of the M2A1 contract thirteen days after it was awarded. Only ninety-four were built and these were assigned to training units in the United States.

M3 Medium Tank

The M2A1 replacement on the production line would be the up-gunned and up-armoured M3 Medium Tank also powered by a gasoline engine. The US army ordered 1,000 units at the end of August 1940. The seven-man vehicle was armed with a turret-mounted 37mm gun and a front hull-mounted 75mm gun, plus an assortment of machine guns. Eventually it was decided that the M3 could function with only a six-man crew. The vehicle weighed approximately 61,000lb.

Production of the M3 series began in the summer of 1941. By the time production ended in December 1942, a total of 6,258 units had been built. Of that number 4,924 were of the M3. The other 1,334 units were various models designated as the M3A1, M3A2, M3A3, M3A4 and M3A5.

The M3A3 and M3A5 were powered by diesel engines. Twenty-eight of the 300 cast-hull M3A1s were also constructed with diesel engines. As the US army preferred gasoline-engine-powered tanks for logistical reasons the bulk of these tanks were allocated to Lend-Lease.

The M3A4 was driven by five gasoline-powered engines all combined into one unit. The engine arrangement was thought to be too difficult to maintain, so the design was not approved for US army use. Of the 109 built, all served as training tanks in the United States.

Into Combat

The US army's combat debut of the M3 was in North-West Africa in November 1942. After the Axis surrender in Tunisia in May 1943, they were replaced with the next generation of medium tanks. The only combat employment of the M3 with the US army in the Pacific Theatre of Operation appears to have taken place on Butaritari Island in November 1943 when the 193rd Tank Battalion employed a few M3A5s.

Foreign Users

The British army lost the bulk of its tank inventory with the fall of France in June 1940. The British government therefore turned to American industry as their own industrial capacity was incapable of building the number of tanks needed. Of the 2,887 units of the M3 series acquired by the British army under Lend-Lease, 1,686 were built with a British-designed turret that was both larger and lower than that fitted to the US army version of the M3. The British army named their variant of the M3 series the 'Grant'.

As the British army also received the US army versions of the M3 series they assigned them the name 'Lee'. Both the Grant and the Lee would see their first action with the British army in the deserts of North Africa in May 1942. They initially proved superior to the German army medium tanks they met in battle. However, this battle-field advantage lasted for only a few months as the German army in North Africa was soon re-equipped with up-gunned and up-armoured medium tanks.

Besides seeing combat in North Africa with the British army between 1942 and 1943, the Grant and Lee tanks were also employed by the British and Indian armies during the fighting in Burma between 1944 and 1945. Some saw action with the Australian army during the Papua New Guinea campaign that lasted from 1942 until August 1945.

The Red Army was shipped 1,386 units of the M3 series through Lend-Lease. Due to shipping losses only 976 were actually delivered. Twelve M3s were later recovered from a sunken transport ship and refurbished and then sent into combat by the Red Army. According to Red Army documents, several of the tanks listed as M3s were actually M2A1 tanks.

M4 Medium Tank Series

The US army's M3 series was intended only as a stopgap until such time as American industry could produce a suitable five-man medium tank with a turret-mounted 75mm gun and up to three machine guns. A pilot, designated the T6, was presented in early September 1941. Shortly thereafter it was standardized as the M4 and with a number of revisions was approved for production. Its intended mission was exploitation. Dealing with enemy tanks was to be left to specialized tank destroyers.

The M4 series was developed using two types of construction methods for the upper hull. The version having a welded armour hull was designated M4, while the one made with a cast armour hull was designated M4A1. Both had the same cast armour turret and tipped the scales at approximately 70,000 lb. The first unit of the M4A1 was accepted by the US army in February 1942 and the M4 in July 1942.

Another welded hull M4 series tank powered by a gasoline engine was the M4A3. Series production began in June 1942. Because its liquid-cooled V8 engine was more reliable and powerful than the air-cooled aircraft-type engines in the M4 and M4A1, the M4A3 was chosen as the preferred medium tank model by the US army in 1943.

Other Versions of the M4 Series

Additional models of the first-generation M4 series produced but not adopted for front-line service by the US army included the M4A2 and M4A4. They were, however, suitable as training tanks within the United States. The M4A2 was a welded hull design, powered by a GM Twin Diesel Power Plant. This model was supplied as Lend-Lease to the British, Soviets and French.

Due to a lack of sufficient numbers of M4, M4A1 and M4A3 tanks in late 1943 due to Lend-Lease commitments, the USMC was supplied with 493 units of the M4A2 from the US army inventory. These were later replaced by M4A3 tanks from the same source. The USMC was also supplied with a small number of M4A1 and M4A4 tanks by the US army but these were never considered standard equipment.

The M4A4 was driven by a power plant that consisted of five six-cylinder gasoline engines arranged in a star configuration; this had first been used in the M3A4 medium tank and the engine arrangement was referred to as the 'Chrysler A57 Multibank'. Despite the design complexity of the M4A4 power plant, the tank was well-liked by the British and Commonwealth armies who received 7,167 units under Lend-Lease. The Free French army was provided with 274 units of the M4A4.

The M4A6 was a design dead-end. Less than 100 units of the diesel-engine-powered tank were built before the project was terminated in February 1944. The entire inventory of M4A6 tanks remained in the United States throughout the war years, where they were used as test and training tanks.

By the time production of the M4 series came to an end in February 1944, a total of 30,346 units had been produced. Of the six different models the most numerous version was the M4A2 with 8,053 units completed. Following that were 7,499 units of the M4A4, 6,748 M4s, 6,281 M4A1s, 1,690 M4A3s and 75 M4A6s.

Foreign Employment

The combat debut of the M4 series with the British army in North Africa took place on 24 October 1942. They had received over 300 units (215 M4A1s and 90 M4A2s) under Lend-Lease during the previous two months. Of the 30,346 M4 series tanks produced, the British and Commonwealth armies received 15,253 units, making it the most numerous type of tank in their service.

The most numerous models of the M4 series taken into British and Commonwealth army service were the M4A4 and the M4A2, with 7,167 units of the M4A4 received and 5,041 units of the M4A2 delivered. In descending order the British and Commonwealth armies also received 2,096 units of the M4 and 942 units of the M4A1. The British army was also provided with seven units of the M4A3, which they never employed in combat.

The British army assigned the entire M4 series the name 'General Sherman', later shortened to just 'Sherman'. To further break down the M4 series the British army assigned each model of the vehicle a slightly different label. The M4 would become the Sherman I, the M4A1 the Sherman II, the M4A2 the Sherman III, the M4A4 the Sherman V and the M4A3 became the Sherman IV. Those M4s that arrived in Great Britain with the composite hull were labelled as the 'Sherman I Hybrid'.

The recipient of the second-largest number of the M4 series under Lend-Lease was the Red Army, which acquired 3,664 units of the M4A2 and two units of the M4A4. The remaining 656 units of the first generation of the M4 series were allocated to the Free French army, which included 382 units of the M4A2 and 274 units of the M4A4.

Mid-Generation Upgrades

In the spring of 1943, the US army embarked on a programme to upgrade the thousands of early-production M4 and M4A1 series tanks then employed as training vehicles in the United States. This would involve a number of improvements, which included the up-armouring of certain areas of the tanks identified as ballistic weak spots by overseas combat reports. In addition, the main gun ammunition storage arrangement was redesigned to improve crew safety.

By the summer of 1943, new production M4 series tanks began rolling off the assembly line with the mid-generation upgrades incorporated. Tank depots were also mandated to upgrade any M4 series tanks being processed for overseas shipment.

In addition, upgrade kits were supplied to Great Britain so that the entire US army pool of nearly 1,400 M4 and M4A1 tanks could be brought up to the latest standard before the planned invasion of France in the summer of 1944. These modification kits were also made available to the armies of the British Commonwealth and Free French army units based in the United Kingdom.

Into Combat

The M4 series tanks had their initial combat debut with the US army in December 1942, following the Anglo-American invasion of French North Africa in the month before. Despite numerous setbacks by the US army units equipped with the M4 and M4A1 due to inexperience and leadership shortcomings, the tank was generally well thought of by those who employed it in combat in North Africa. This was because at that point in time it was a fairly even match for the German medium tanks.

Unfortunately, the US army did not keep up with German tank technology developments, despite being kept informed by both the Red Army and British army of what it might encounter on future battlefields. With the invasion of France, the M4 series tanks in service with the US army – the M4, M4A1 and the M4A3 – were quickly shown to be both out-gunned and under-armoured compared to the late-war German medium tanks.

Medium Tank Odds and Ends

Following the fall of France in the summer of 1940 and the loss of the bulk of the British army tank inventory, the Canadian and Australian Commonwealth armies tried to use their own local industry to design and build medium tanks for themselves. None of these efforts proved worthwhile as by the time their respective tanks could have been of use, American production capacity made them unnecessary.

To speed up the design and development of its own medium tanks, Canadian industry decided to use the chassis of the American M3 medium tank with their own upper body and turret design. The effort resulted in the limited production of the five-man Ram series of cruiser tanks that weighed in at approximately 65,000lb. Fifty units armed with a 2-pounder main gun and two machine guns were designated as the 'Ram I' and 1,094 units armed with a 6-pounder main gun and two machine guns as the 'Ram II'. None would see service as gun tanks.

Canadian industry later decided to build a copy of the American-designed M4A1 medium tank, which they named the 'Grizzly I'. Only 188 units were built of the 67,000lb vehicle before production ceased in favour of the American-built model. As with the Ram I and II, the Grizzly I would never see action as a gun tank during the Second World War.

Australian industry also attempted to design and build its own cruiser medium tank. As with Canadian industry, they tried to speed up the process by using certain features of the American-designed M3 medium tank. The eventual result of their hard work was the building of sixty-six units of a vehicle referred to as the Cruiser Tank AC I or 'Sentinel', armed with a 2-pounder main gun and two machine guns. None ever left the country and they were employed only as training vehicles by the Australian army.

Pictured is the first tank classified as a medium tank, the British army Medium A. It was also known as the 'Whippet' or the 'Triton' and entered into combat during the last year of the First World War. The Medium A shown was commanded by Lieutenant Cecil Sewell during the Great War. He was awarded the Victoria Cross for his bravery under fire in rescuing the crew of another tank, losing his own life in the process. *(Tank Museum)*

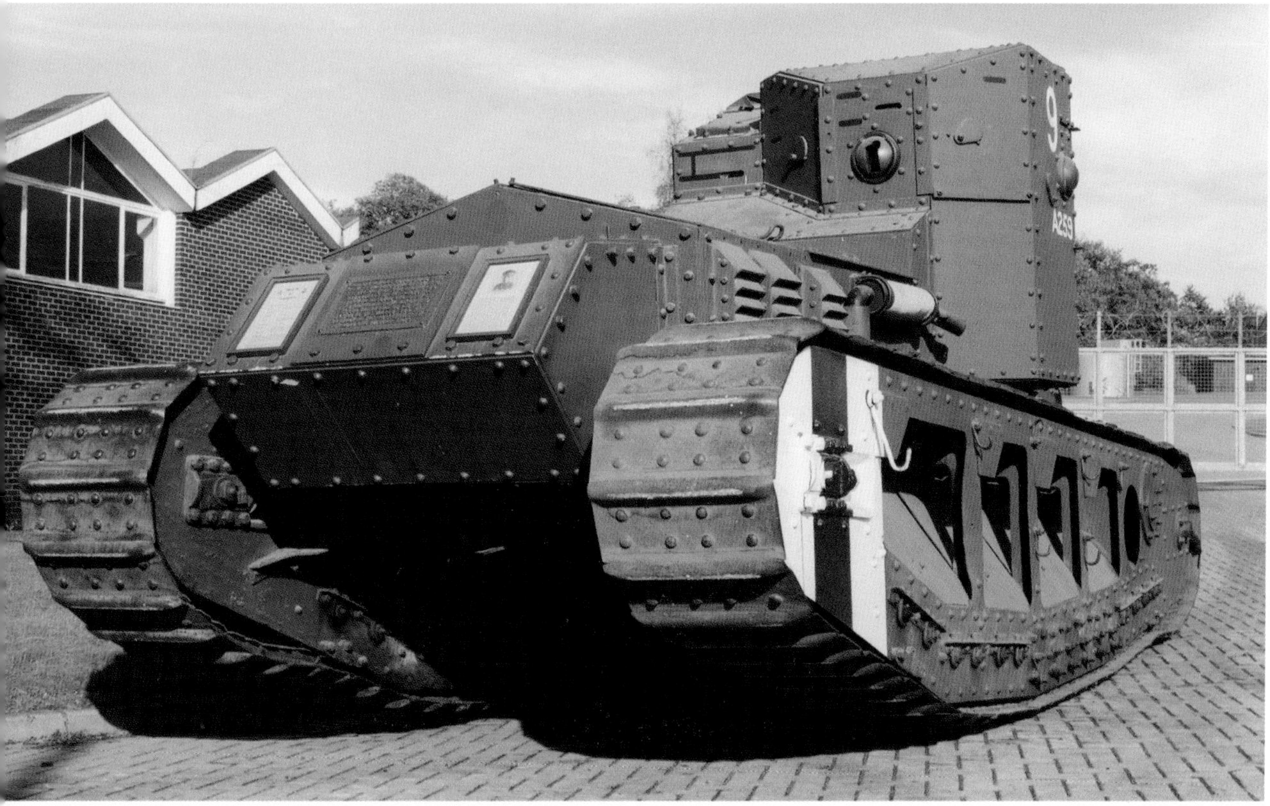
9
A259

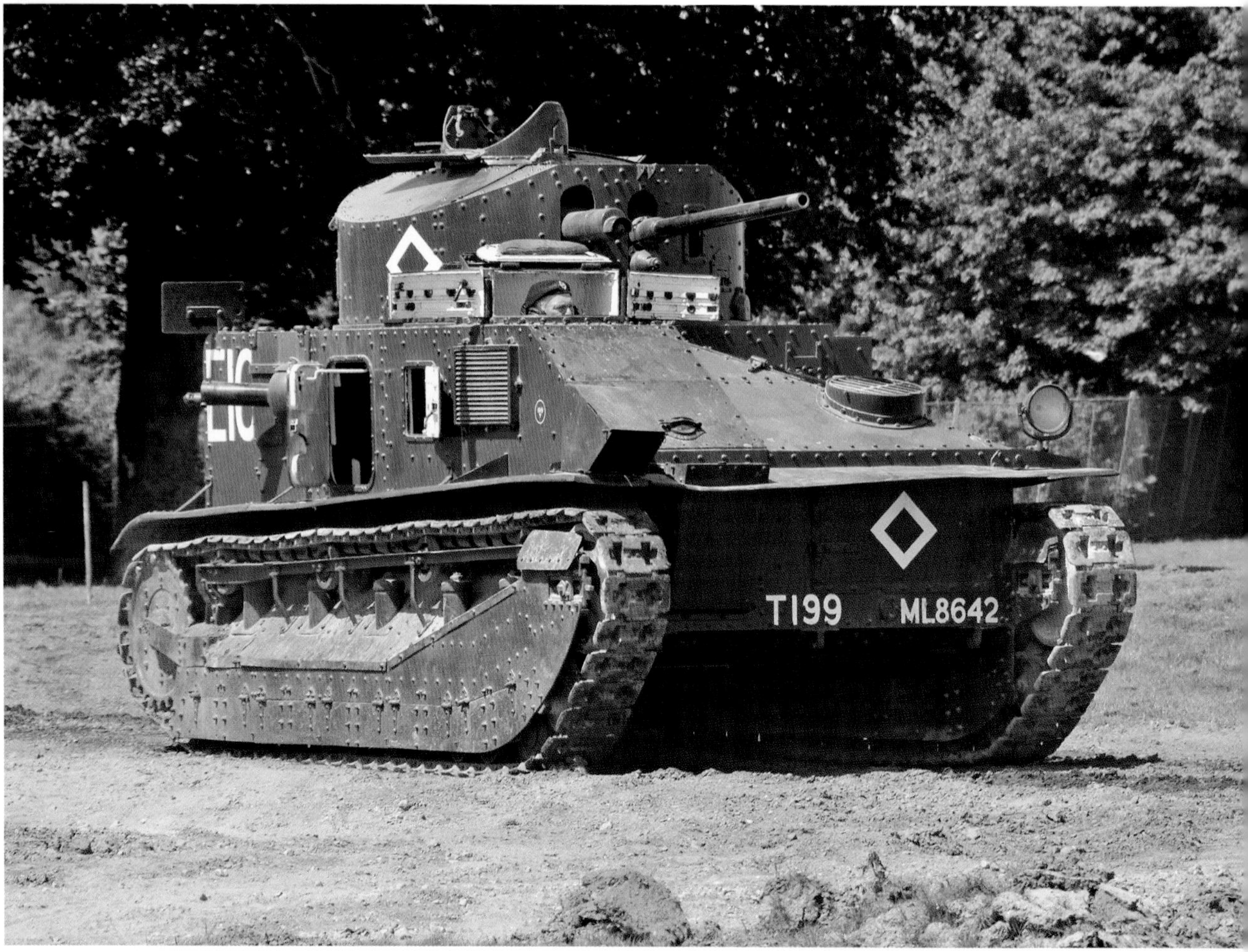
T199
ML8642

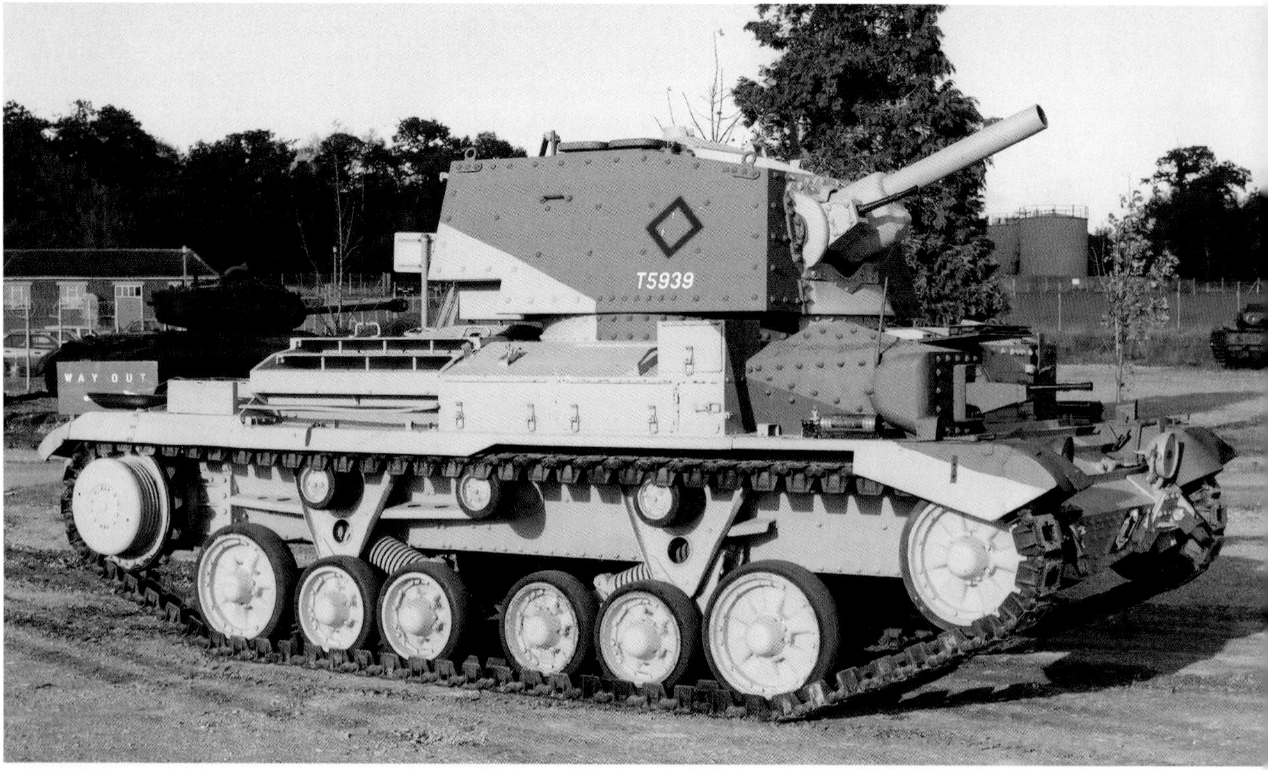
T5939
WAY OUT

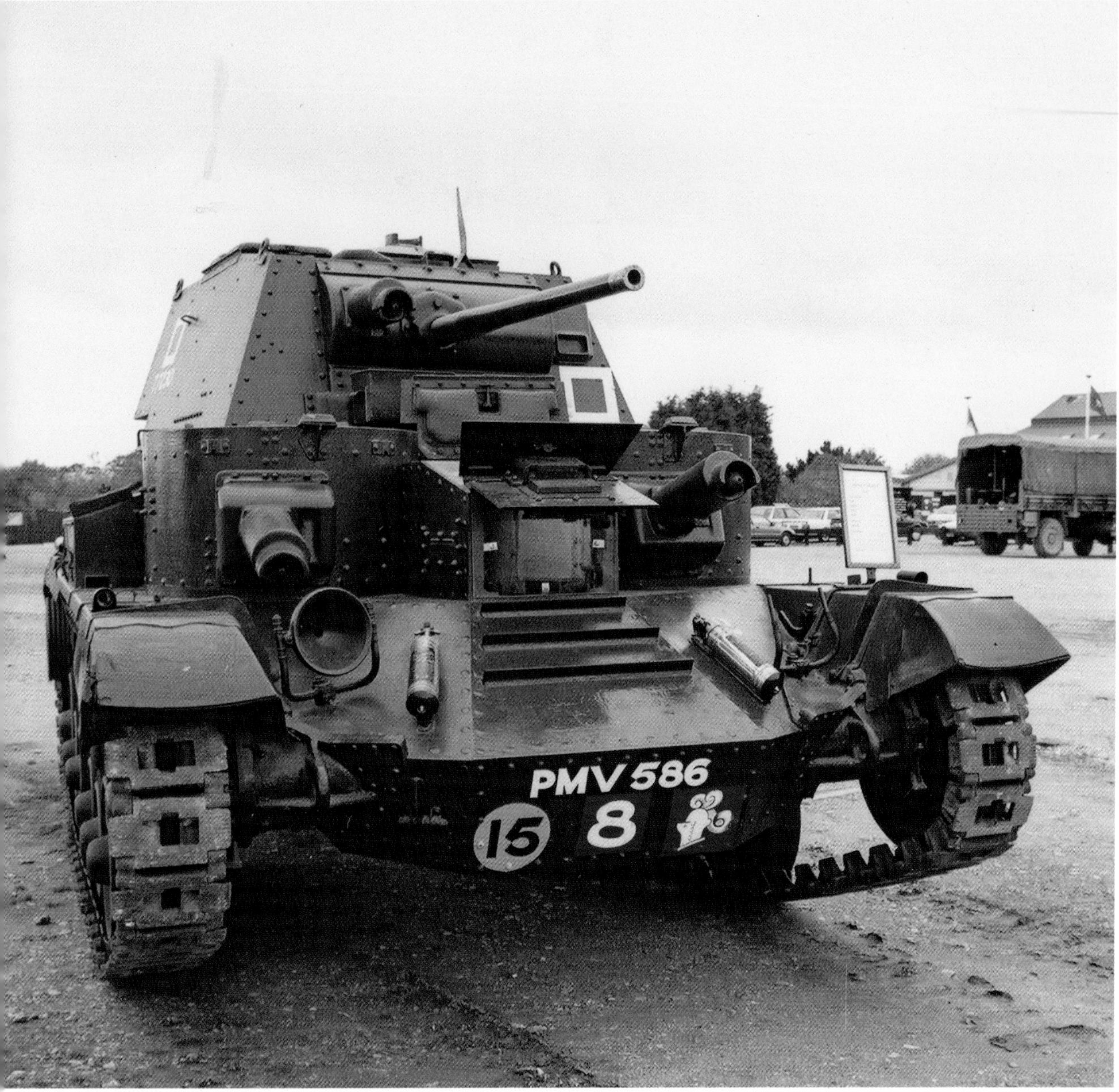
PMV 586
15
8

(*Opposite above*) The first post-war medium tank that lasted in service long enough to see use as a training vehicle by the British army in the Second World War was this preserved Mk II. The tank entered into service in 1925 and had a crew of five. It was 17ft 6in long, had a width of 9ft 2in and the vehicle height was 8ft 10in. *(Tank Museum)*

(*Above*) In the first of a long line of British army pre-war and wartime medium tanks renamed cruiser tanks, we see pictured a preserved Cruiser Tank Mk I (A9). It entered into service in 1938 and had a crew of six. Its length was 19ft, width 8ft 4in and it was also 8ft 4in tall. Maximum speed on level roads was 25mph. *(Tank Museum)*

(*Opposite below*) Following the Cruiser Tank Mk I (A9) into service with the British army was the Cruiser Tank Mk II (A10) shown here in a camouflage paint scheme intended for use in temperate climates. The tank entered into service in 1940 and was 18ft 1in in length, had a width of 8ft 4in and a height of 8ft 6in. *(Tank Museum)*

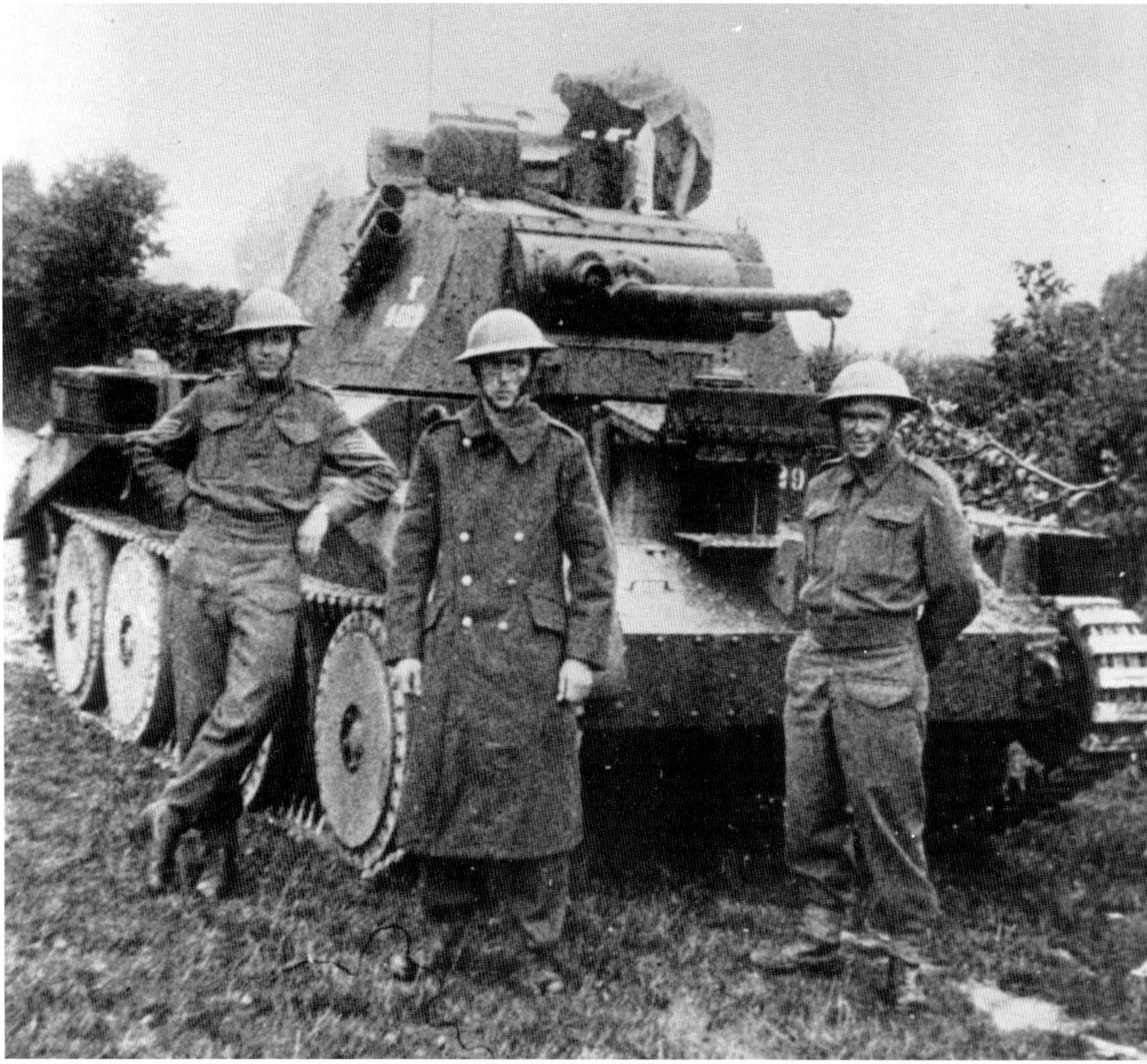

(*Above*) Taken in France in the summer of 1940 is this photograph of a Cruiser Tank Mk III (A13) of the British Expeditionary Force (BEF). Running on the American-designed Christie suspension system, the vehicle had a maximum speed on level roads of 30mph. It was 19ft 9in long and had a width of 8ft 4in. The vehicle height was 8ft 6in. *(Tank Museum)*

(*Opposite above*) The preserved Cruiser Tank Mk IV (A13 Mk II) pictured here entered into service in 1940. Despite being fitted with more armour than its predecessor – the Cruiser Tank Mk III (A13) – a new more powerful engine provided it with the same level of mobility. It was 19ft 9in in length, had a width of 8ft 6in and a height of 8ft 6in. *(Tank Museum)*

(*Opposite below*) Knocked out in France during the summer of 1940 is this British army Cruiser Tank Mk IV (A13 Mk II). Maximum armour protection on the vehicle was 30mm, which was a marked improvement over the earlier Cruiser Tank Mk III (A13) that had a maximum armour thickness of 14mm. An identifying feature of the Cruiser Tank Mk IV (A13 Mk II) was its faceted turret sides. *(Tank Museum)*

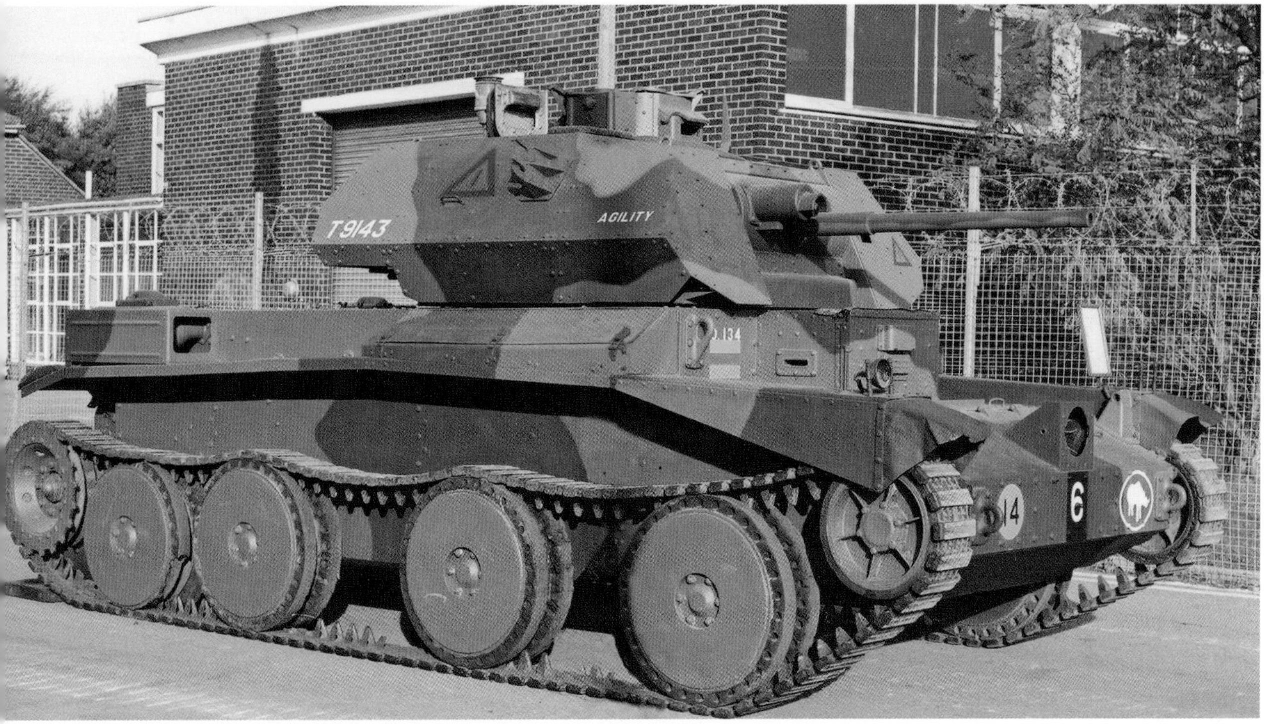
T9143
AGILITY
14
6

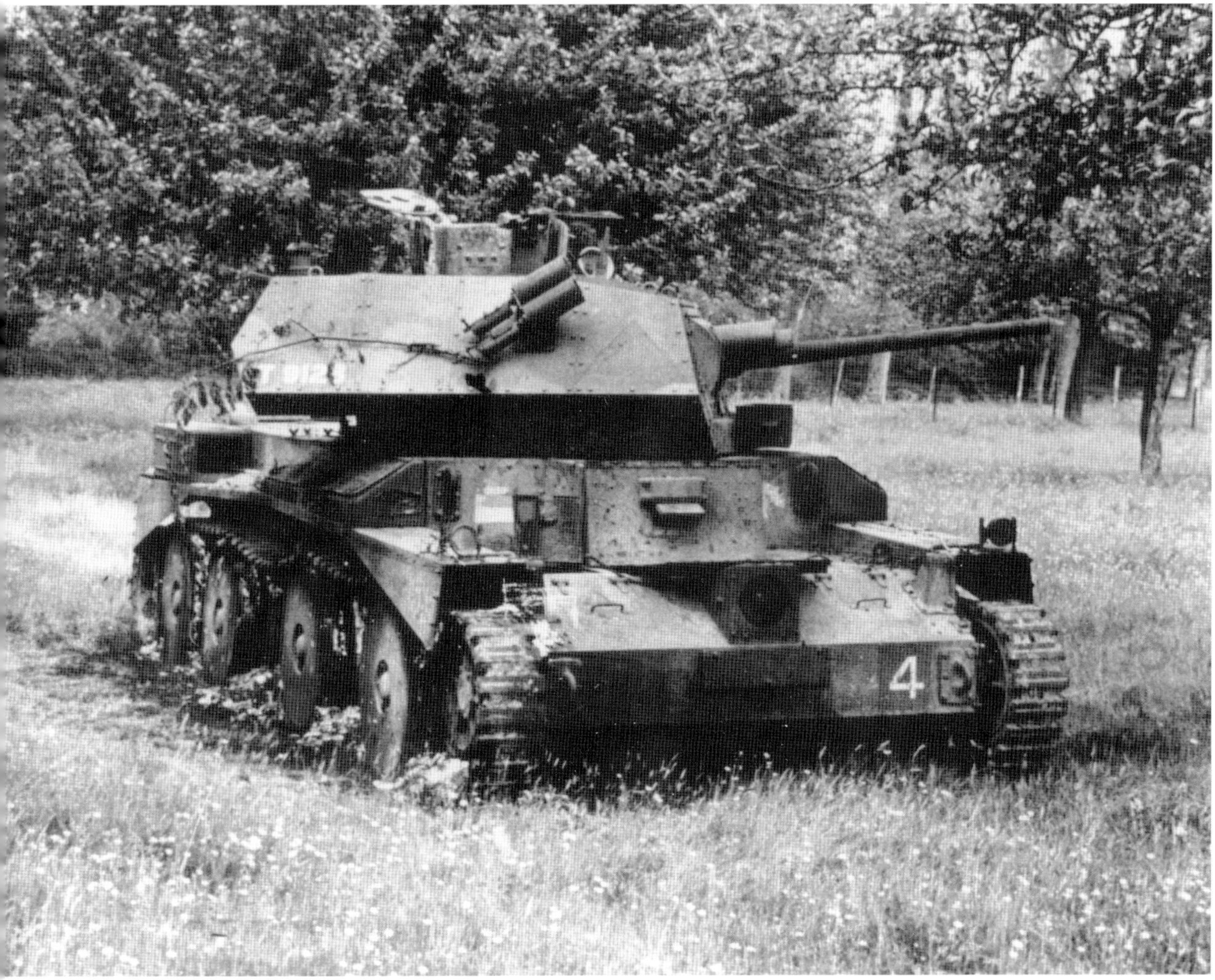
4

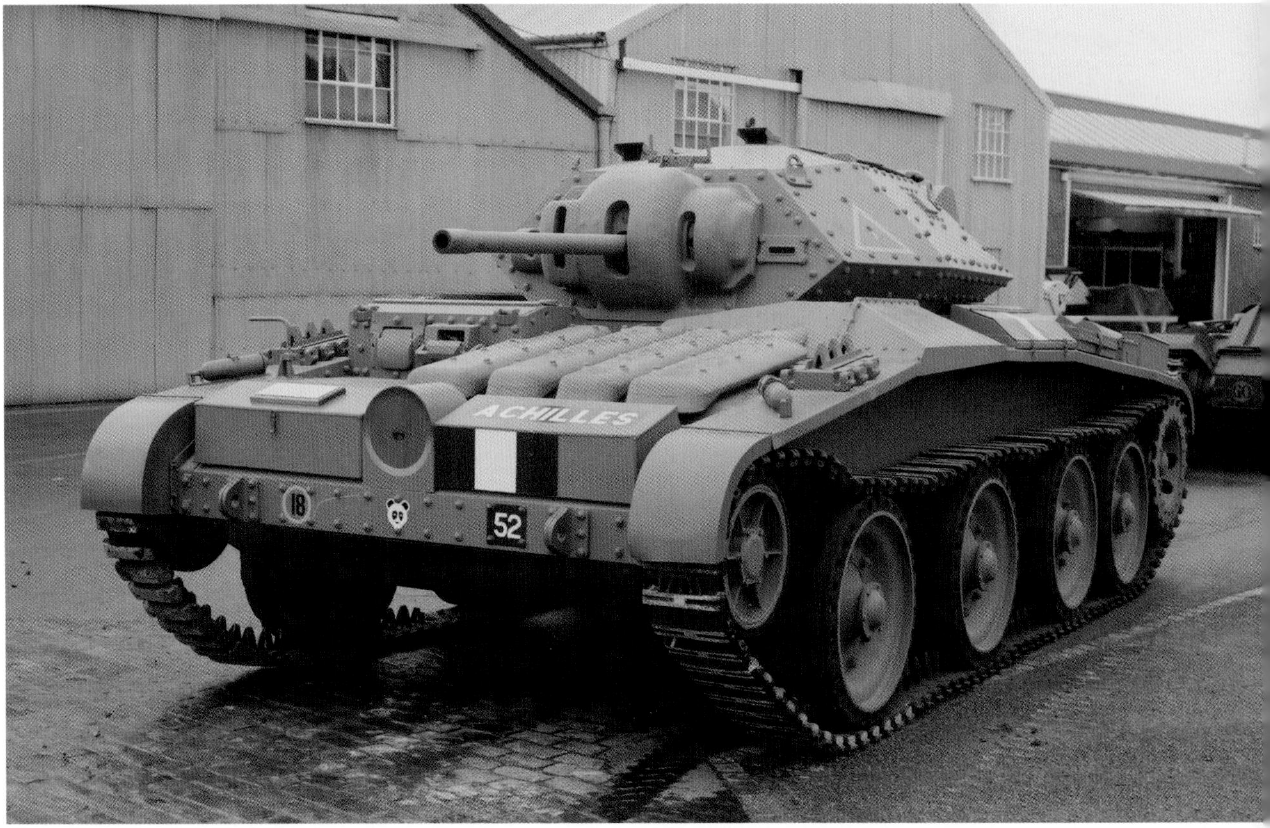
ACHILLES
18
52

The preserved Cruiser Tank Mk V (A13 Mk III) pictured was also assigned the name 'Covenanter'. Based on the design of the Cruiser Tank Mk IV (A13 Mk II), it never saw combat as a gun tank but was used in a number of support roles. It had a crew of four and was 19ft in length with a width of 8ft 7in and a height of 7ft 4in. *(Tank Museum)*

Pictured are two preserved examples of the Infantry Tank Mk I (A11). It entered service with the British army in 1938. Armed only with a single machine gun, the tank had a maximum armour thickness of 60mm. It was 15ft 11in in length, had a width of 7ft 6in and its height was 6ft 1in. *(Tank Museum)*

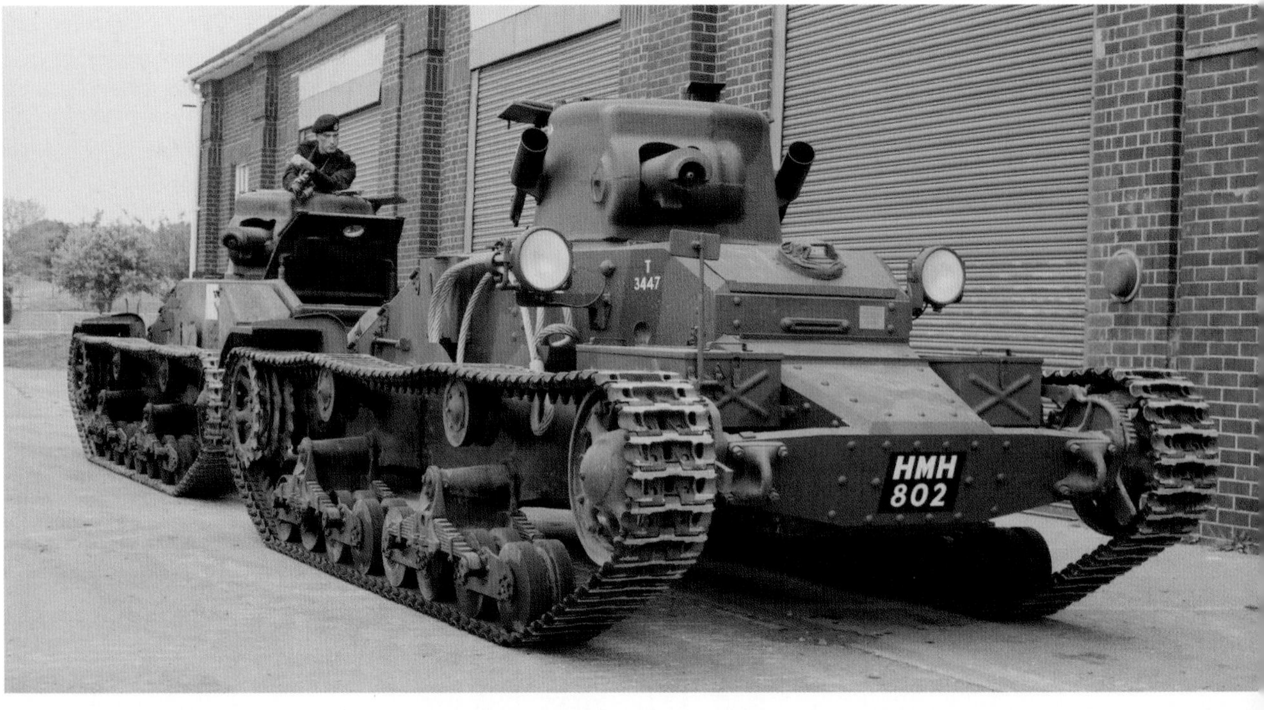
T
3447
HMH
802

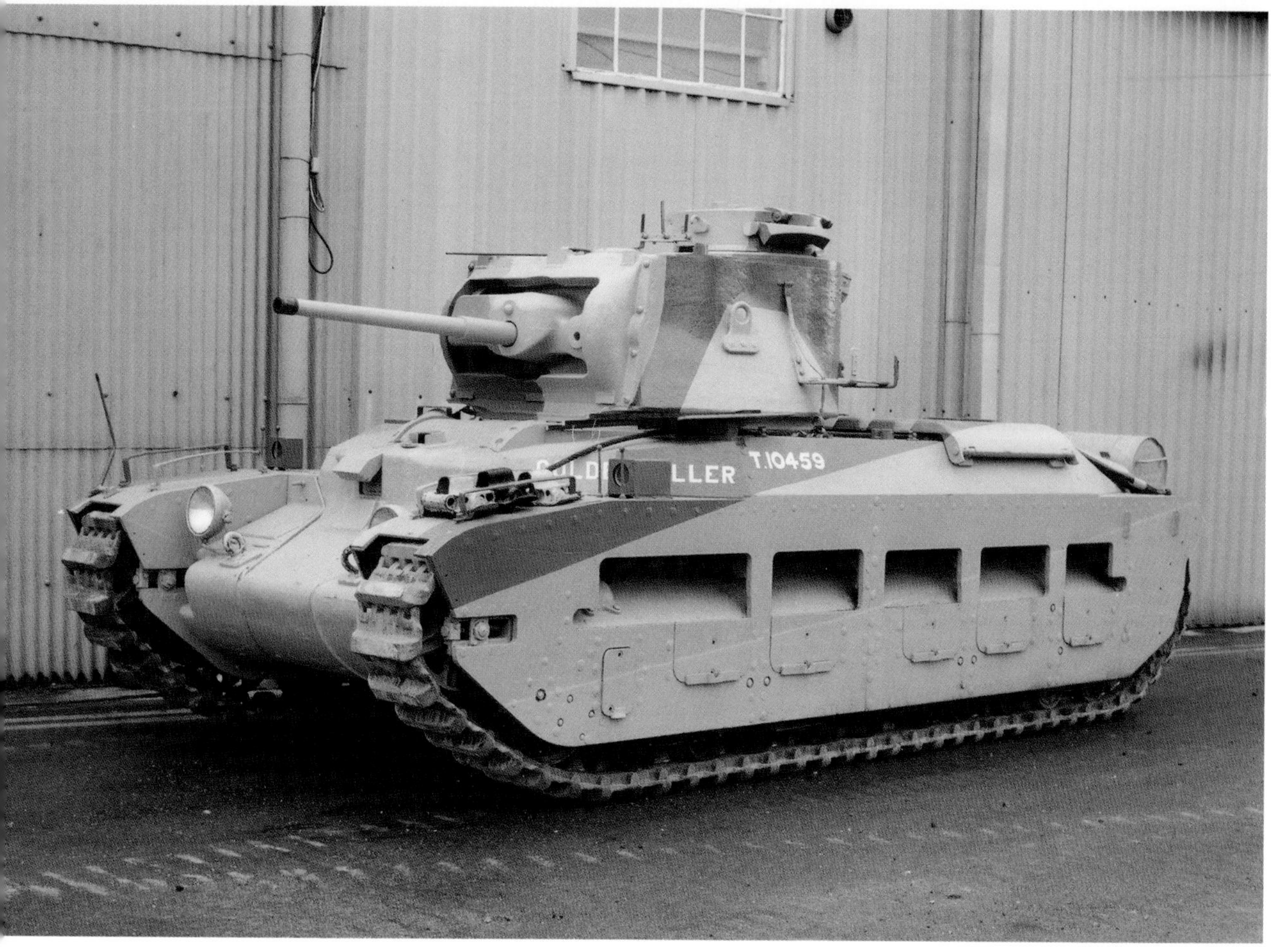
T.10459

The preserved Infantry Tank Mk II (A12) pictured here and best-known as the 'Matilda' is painted in a camouflage scheme that appeared in British army use while fighting the Italian and German armies in North Africa between 1940 and 1942. The tank had a top speed of 8mph. Maximum armour thickness on the vehicle was 78mm. *(Tank Museum)*

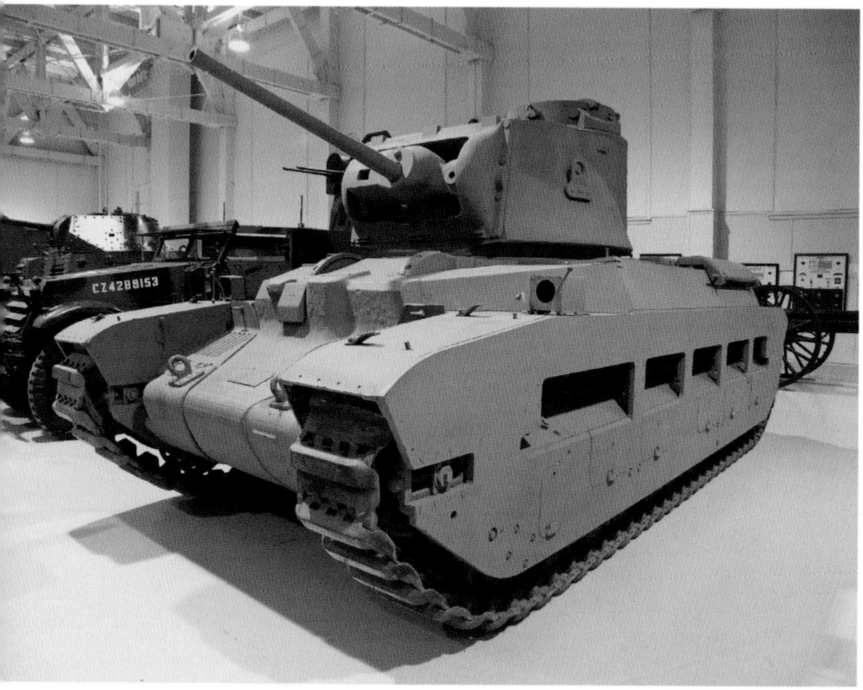

On display at a Canadian army museum is an Infantry Tank Mk II (A12). It entered into service with the British army in 1939 and had a length of 18ft 5in. The tank's width was 8ft 6in and it had a height of 8ft 3in. Once its usefulness as a gun tank was at an end, it was converted into a large number of support variants. *(Paul and Loren Hannah)*

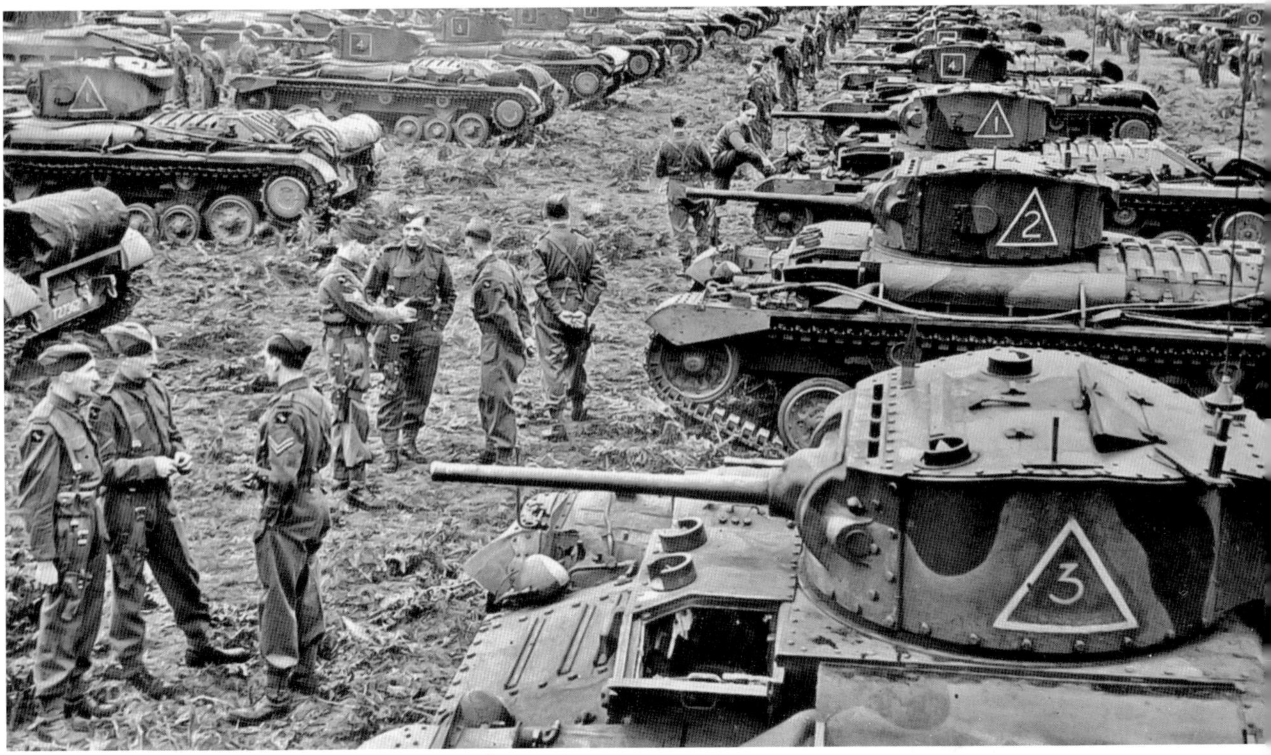

This photograph shows a large number of Infantry Tank Mk III Valentine tanks in British army service. The tank was 19ft 4in in length, had a width of 8ft 8in and the vehicle height was 7ft 6in. Maximum armour protection was originally 65mm thick. Top speed of the tank was 14.9mph with an operational range of 90 miles. *(Tank Museum)*

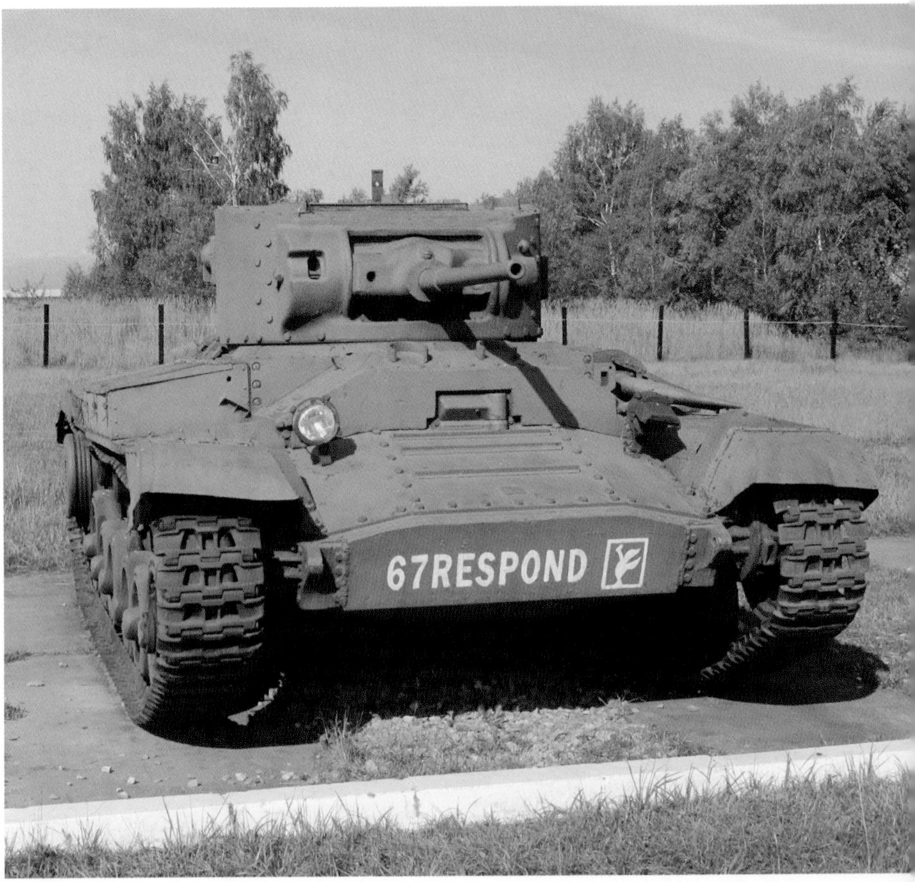
67RESPOND

On display at the Russian Army Tank Museum is one of over 1,000 units of the diesel-engine-powered Canadian-built versions of the Valentine series delivered to the Red Army under Lend-Lease during the Second World War. A spotting feature of these Valentine tanks is a cast glacis, whereas those on British-built examples were bolted together. *(Vladimir Yakubov)*

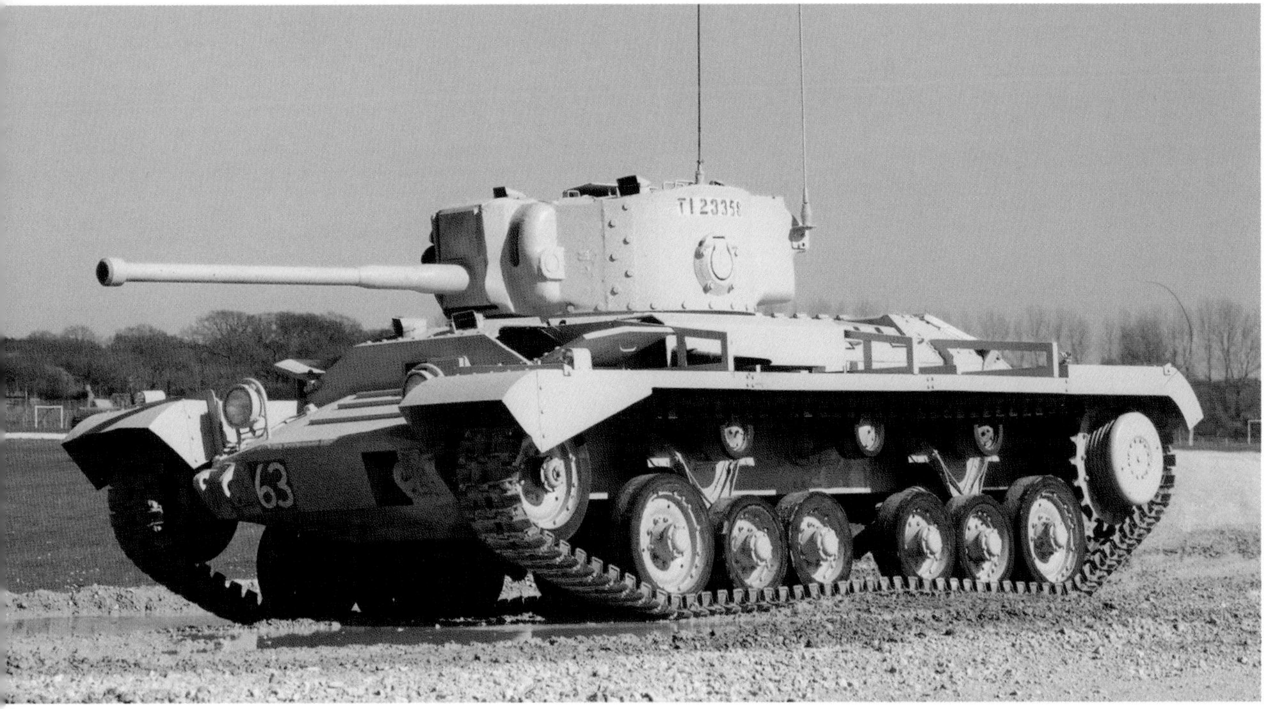
63

In its efforts to keep up with German medium tank development, the British army had the Valentine up-armed with a 6-pounder (57mm) main gun in lieu of its original 2-pounder (40mm) main gun. This up-gunned version of the Valentine tank seen here with a 6-pounder main gun was labelled as the Mk X. *(Tank Museum)*

One of the best-designed tanks in the French army when the Germans invaded was the AMC S35, also known as the Somua S-35 seen here. The restored example pictured is shown on display at the now-closed US Army Ordnance Museum that had been located at Aberdeen Proving Grounds for many decades. The tank is now in long-term storage with the US army. *(Christophe Vallier)*

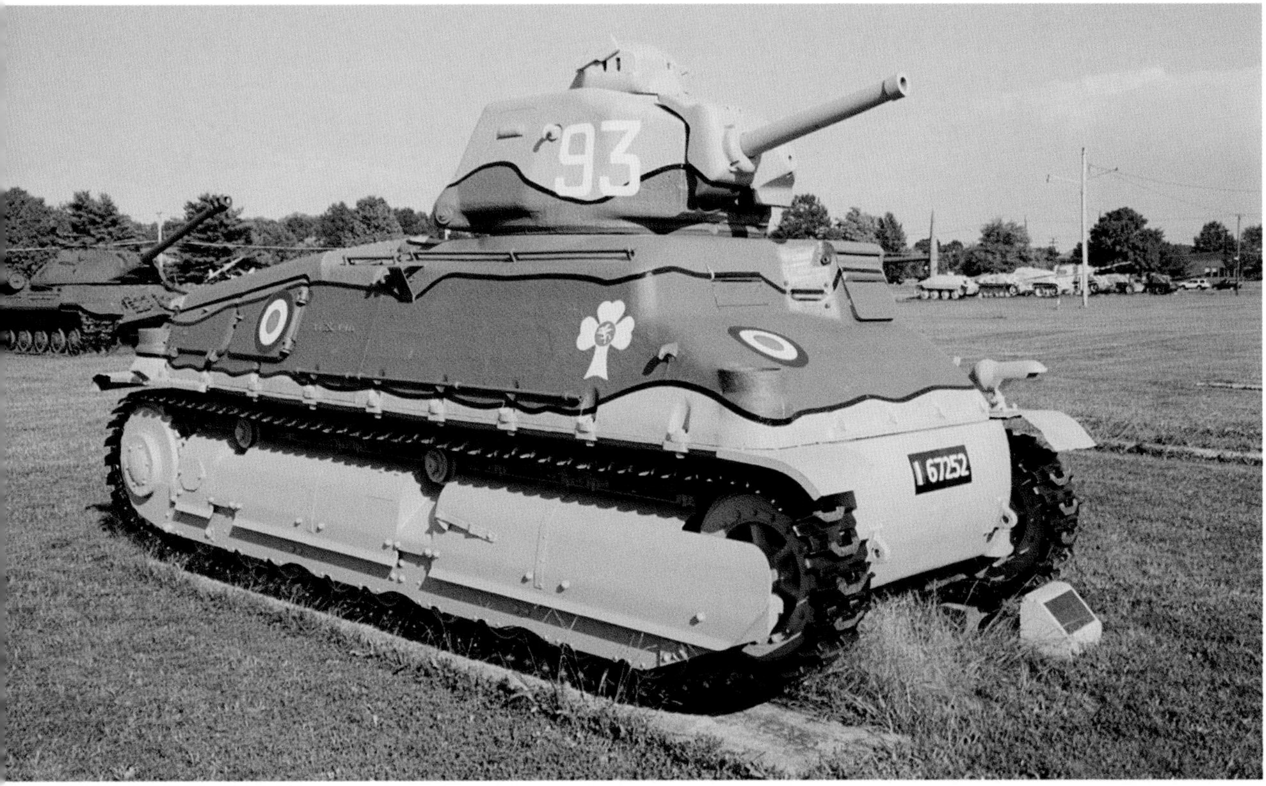
93
1 67252

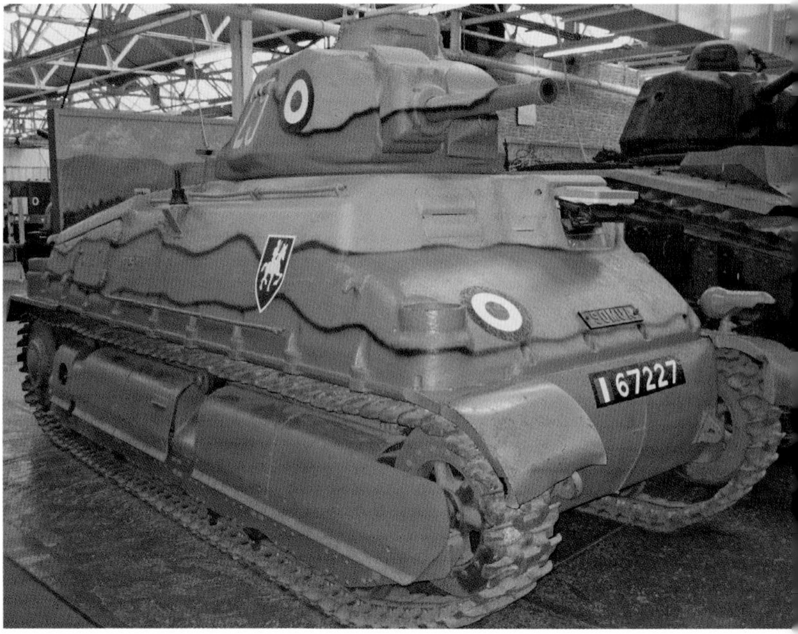
I 67227

Pictured is a preserved example of a French army AMC S35 also known as the Somua S-35. The vehicle had a length of 17ft 8in, a width of 6ft 11in and a height of 8ft 7in. Maximum armour thickness was 40mm. Top speed of the tank was 25.3mph and it had an operational range of 160 miles. *(Tank Museum)*

On display at the Armoured Vehicle Museum in Parola, Finland is this Red Army T-28 medium tank captured by the Finnish army during the Russo-Finnish War, which ran from November 1939 until March 1940. Combat experience gained by the Red Army during their extremely poor showing in the conflict resulted in the up-armoured version of the tank. *(Andreas Kirchhoff)*

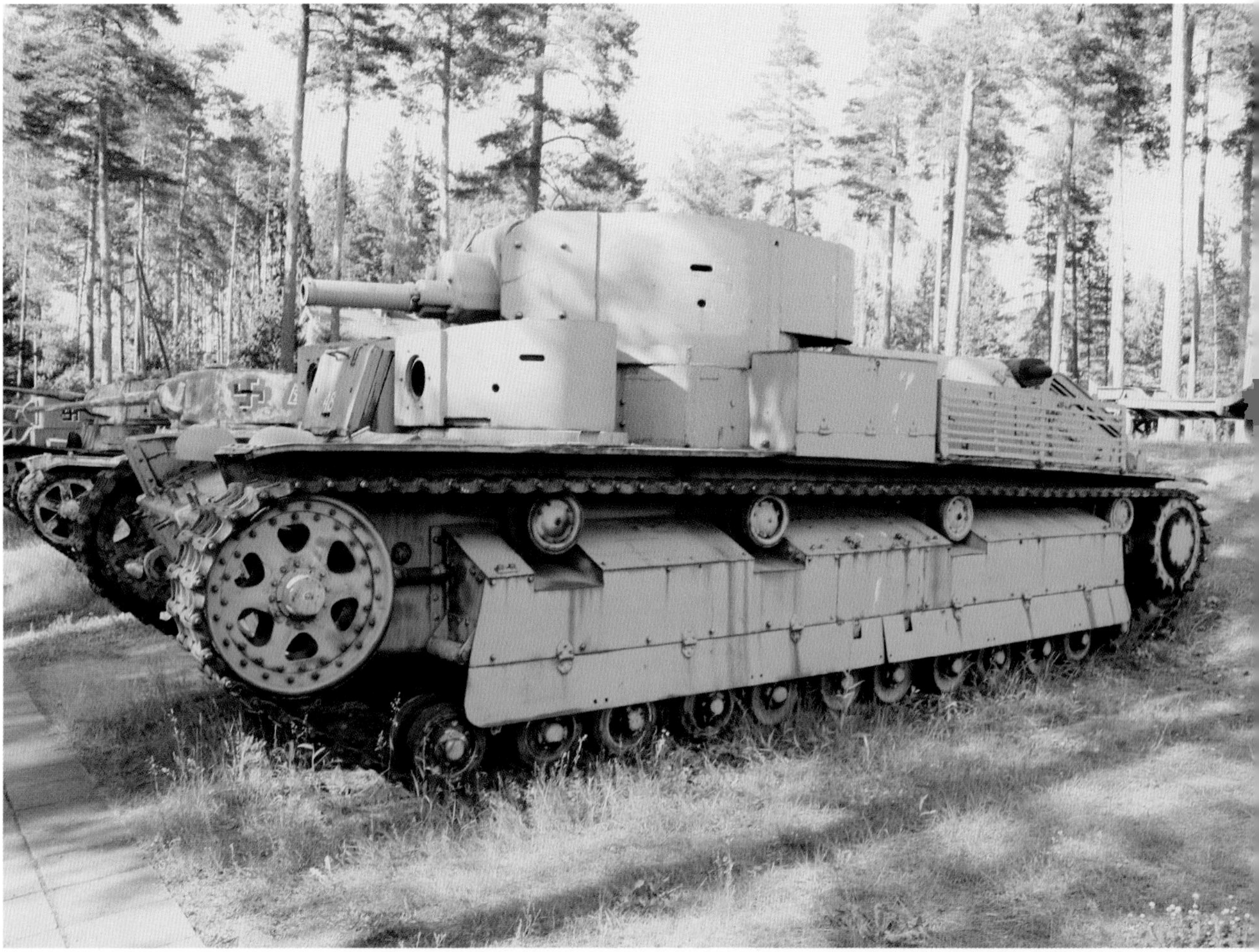

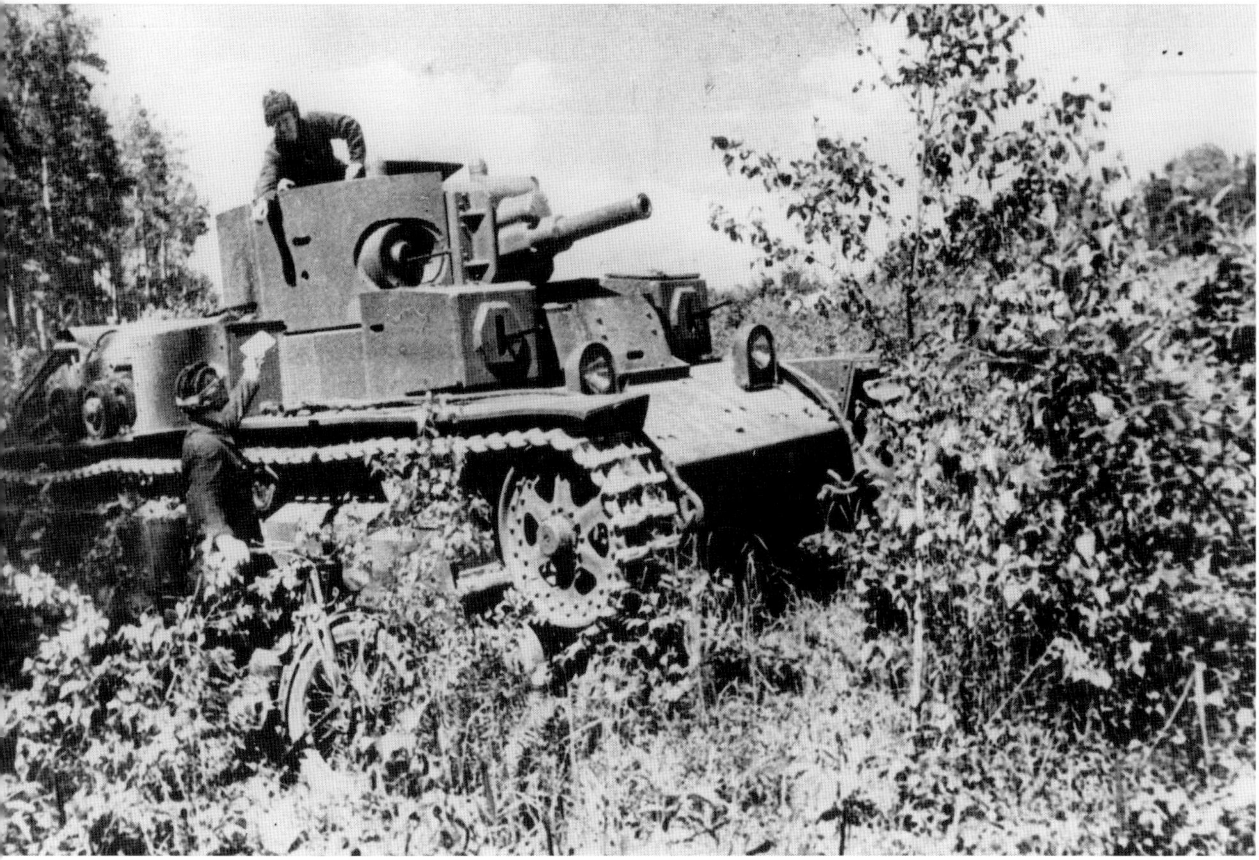

A motorcycle messenger is pictured in this pre-war photograph delivering written orders to the vehicle commander of a Red Army T-28 medium tank. Instead of a coaxial machine gun mounted alongside the vehicle's main gun, there was a separate ball mount for a small-calibre machine gun fitted to the right side of the turret as is visible in this image. *(Patton Museum)*

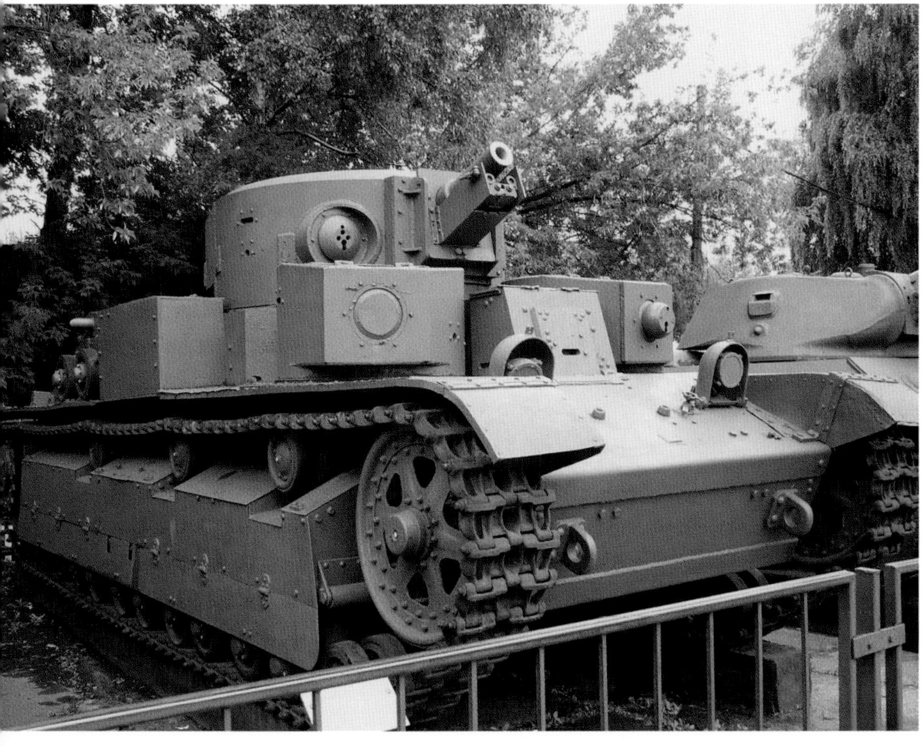

Located at a military museum in Moscow is this example of a Red Army T-28 medium tank. The vehicle had a length of 24ft 5in, a width of 9ft 5in and a height of 9ft 3in. Top speed of the tank was 23mph. It had an operational range of approximately 140 miles. *(Vladimir Yakubov)*

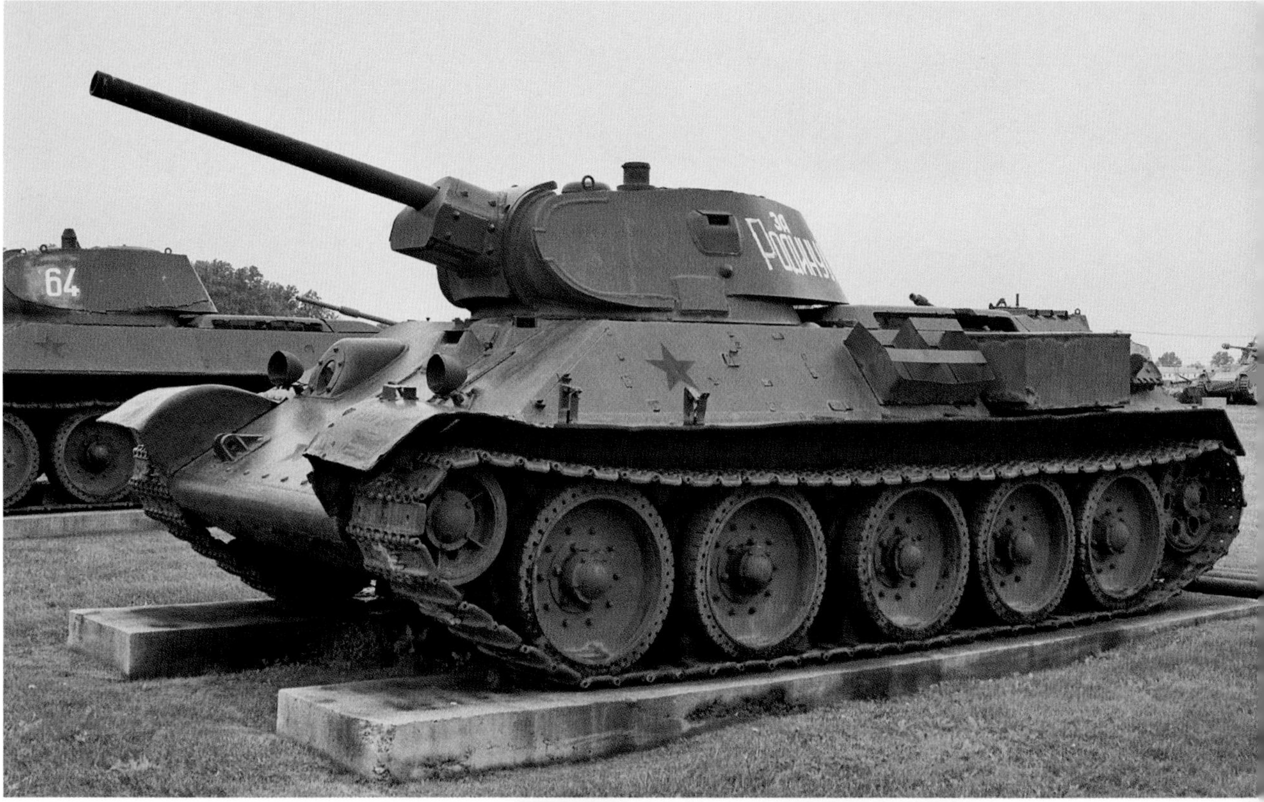
64

The follow-on to the first production version of the T-34 series referred to as the T-34 Model 1940 is the T-34 Model 1941 pictured here when it resided at the now-closed US Army Ordnance Museum. It was armed with a longer-barrelled 76.2mm main gun designated as the F-34. Note the serrated and pierced rubber-rimmed concave road wheels that remained in production till the end of the Second World War. *(Author's collection)*

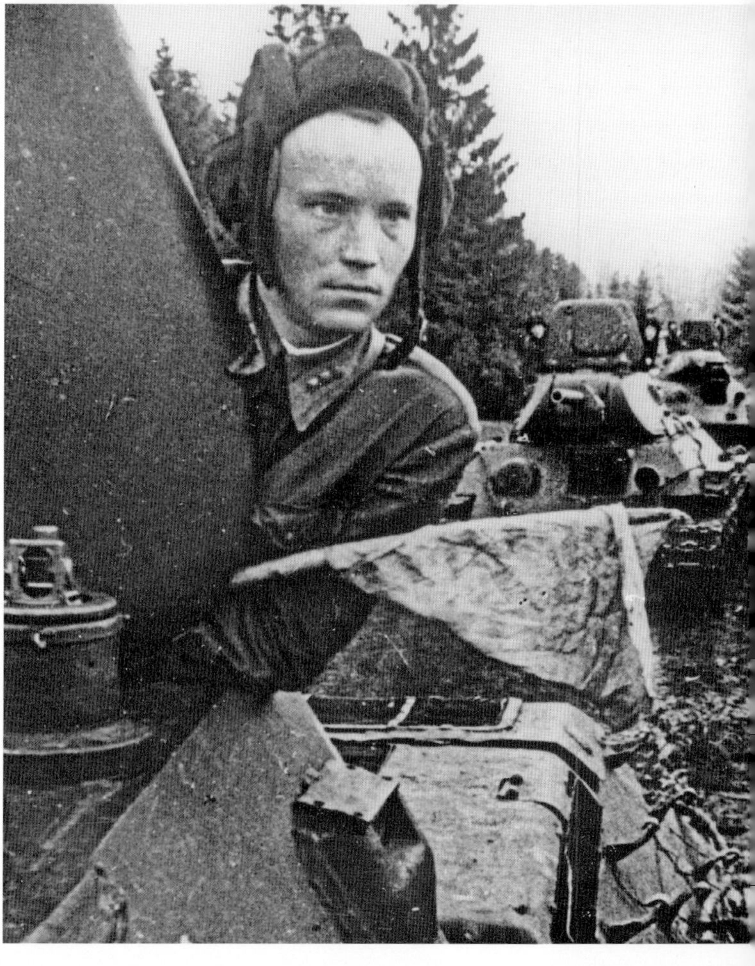

A key external identifying feature of the T-34 Model 1940 and the follow-on Model 1941 and Model 1942 is the large one-piece turret hatch that was hinged forward as is evident in this photograph. The reason for this awkward arrangement is lost to history as it obstructed the forward vision of the vehicle commander when raised. *(Patton Museum)*

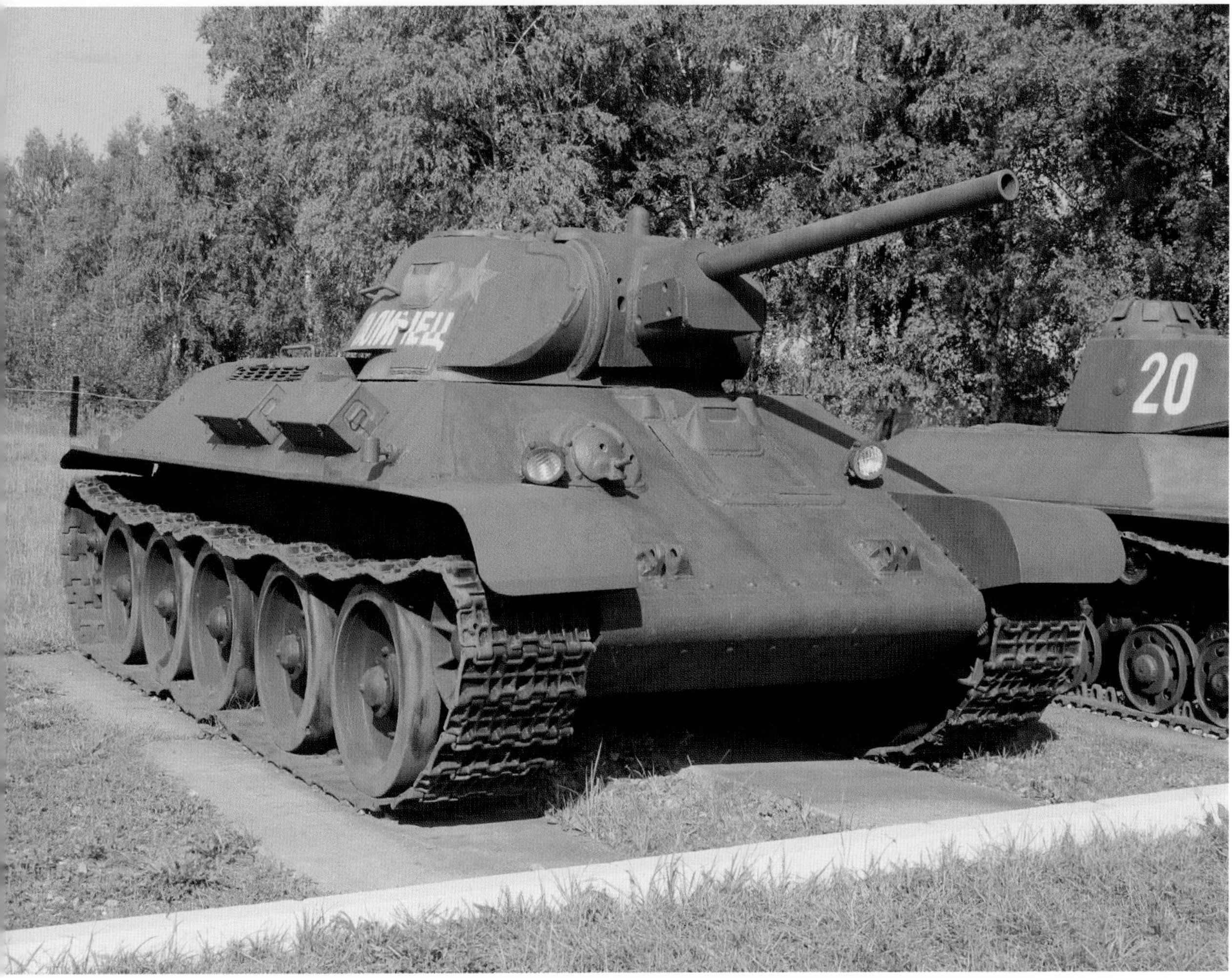
20

On display at the Russian Army Tank Museum is this early-production T-34 Model 1941 with twin headlights, a bolted glacis and an early-style driver's hatch with a single forward-facing periscope. The majority of early-production T-34 series had a welded armour turret as pictured. The low-slung appearance of the tank is attributed to its transmission being located in the engine compartment. *(Vladimir Yakubov)*

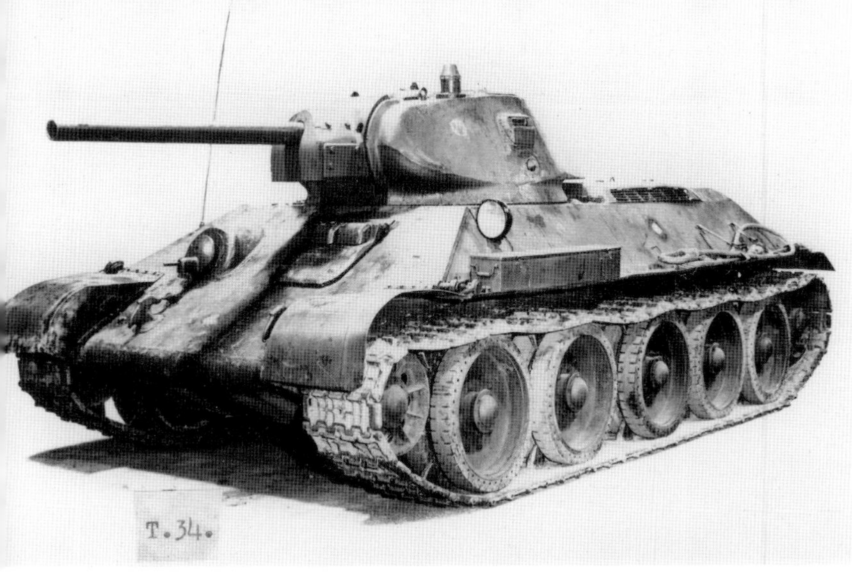
T.34.

Pictured is an example of the less numerous cast armour turreted version of the T-34 Model 1942. This particular vehicle is a late-production unit of that model. It can be identified by several external features. These include the hammerhead towing shackles on the glacis, a single headlight rather than the two seen on early-production units of the tank and two forward-facing periscopes on the driver's hatch. *(Patton Museum)*

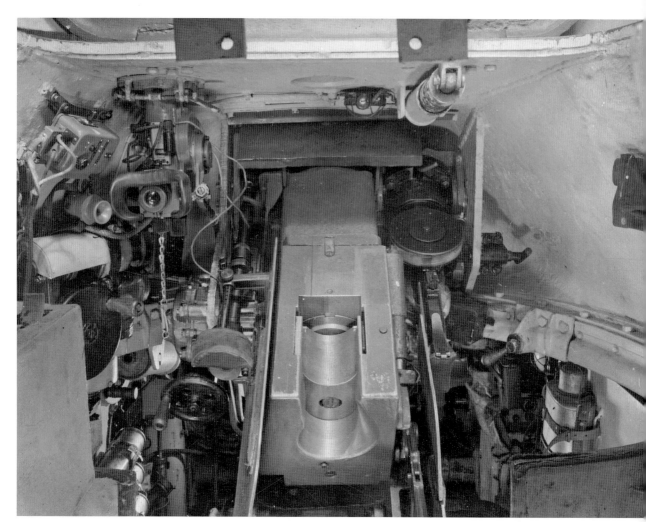

(*Above*) From the rear of the turret of a T-34 Model 1942 looking forward can be seen the breech of the 76.2mm F-34 main gun. The vehicle commander, who doubled as the gunner, sat on the left-hand side of the main gun breech and the loader on the opposite side. The overhead drum magazine for the small-calibre coaxial machine gun is visible on the loader's side of the turret. (*Patton Museum*)

(*Opposite above*) Visible from the driver's seat looking rearward into the hull of a T-34 Model 1942 tank is the vehicle commander/gunner's seat on the right and the loader's seat on the left. Unlike its German medium tank counterparts, the T-34 series did not have a turret basket. Main gun rounds were stored on either side of the hull and under mats on the bottom of the hull floor. (*Patton Museum*)

(*Opposite below*) Unhappiness with the awkward large single-piece turret hatch and the cramped working space due to the narrow turret design of the T-34 Model 1940, 1941 and 1942 led to a new turret design. This resulted in the appearance of the T-34 Model 1943, which featured a larger and roomier hexagonal-shaped turret as pictured here. In lieu of the previous single large turret hatch cover there were now two smaller overhead hatches as seen in this photograph. (*Author's collection*)

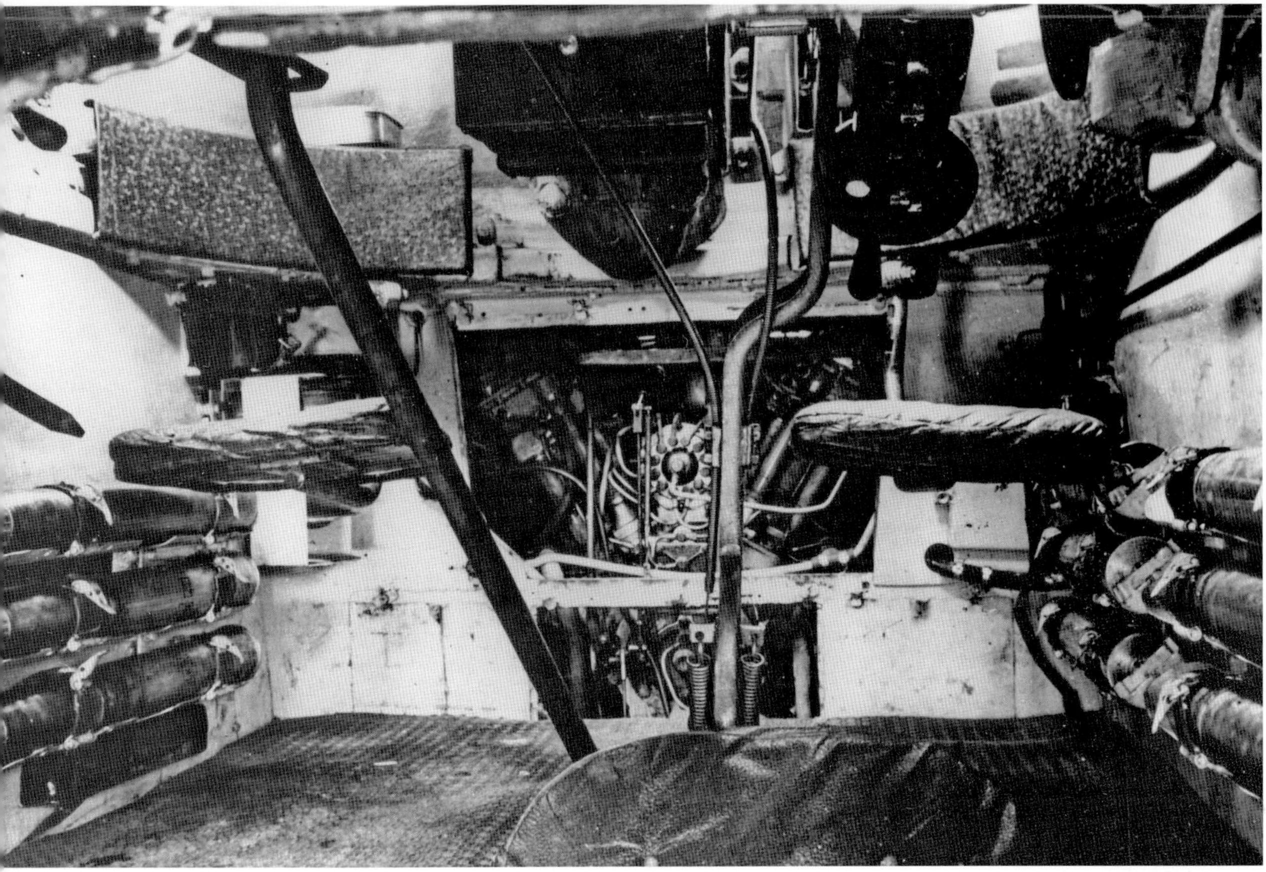

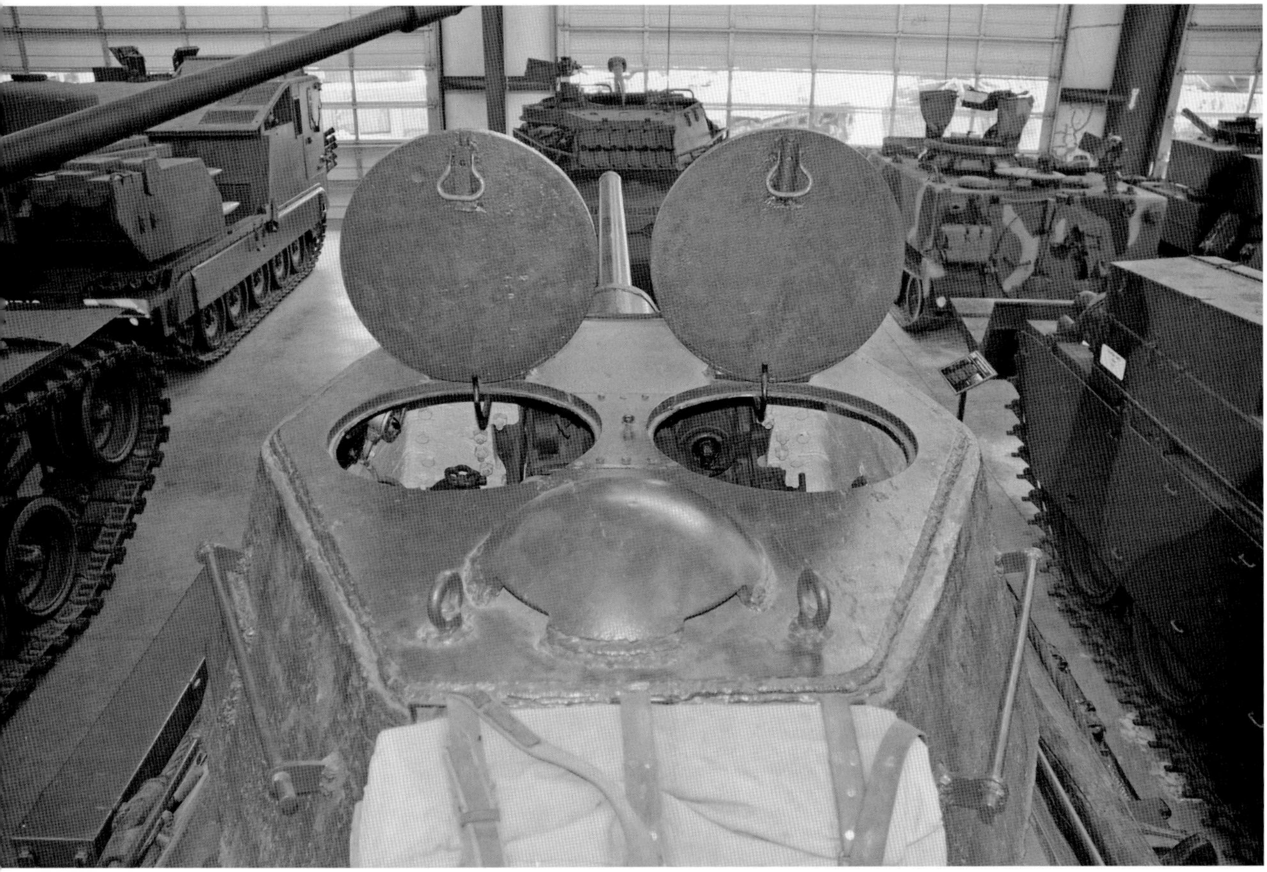

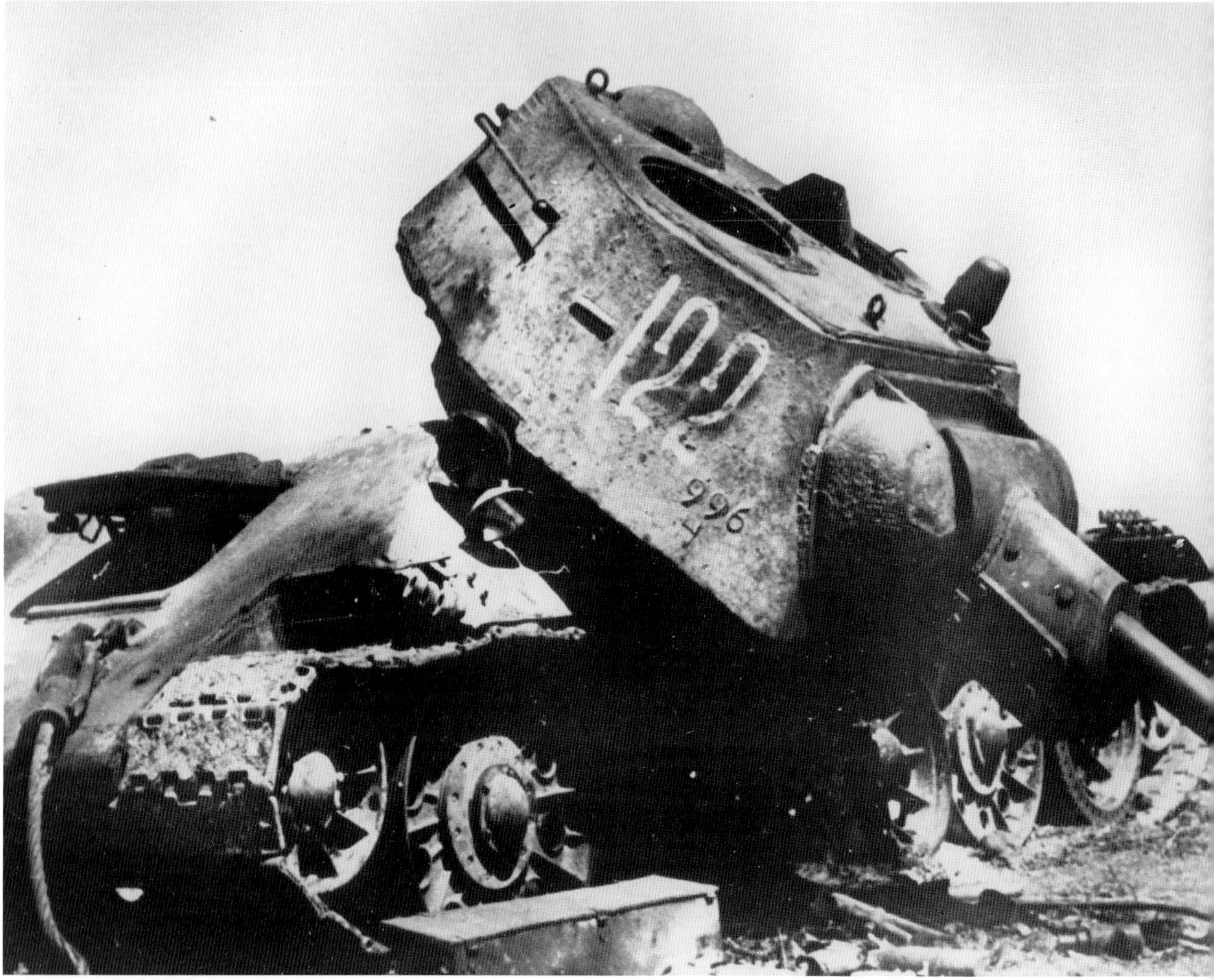

(*Above*) Pictured is a knocked-out T-34 Model 1943 with its cast armour hexagonal-shaped turret and the openings for its two roof hatches. The circular object located at the rear of the turret roof contains the uppermost portion of the electrically-operated ventilating blower. The bottle-shaped object protruding from the front of the turret room is the armoured covering for a periscope sight for the vehicle commander/gunner. *(Patton Museum)*

(*Opposite above*) This restored T-34 Model 1943 was formerly on display at the now-closed Military Vehicle Technology Foundation. An external feature that is common to all T-34 series tanks armed with the 76.2mm F-34 main gun is the bolted armoured housing visible on this tank that extends out from the gun shield partially over the rear portion of the weapon's barrel. Its function was to protect the weapon's hydro-pneumatic recuperator. *(Author's collection)*

(*Opposite below*) From under the breech ring of a T-34 Model 1943 tank's main gun looking forward, the driver's seat is visible on the left and the radioman/machine-gunner's seat on the right. Visible on the right-hand side hull wall is the vehicle's radio. A bit higher and to the left of the radio is the breech end of an incomplete machine-gun reproduction. *(Chris Hughes)*

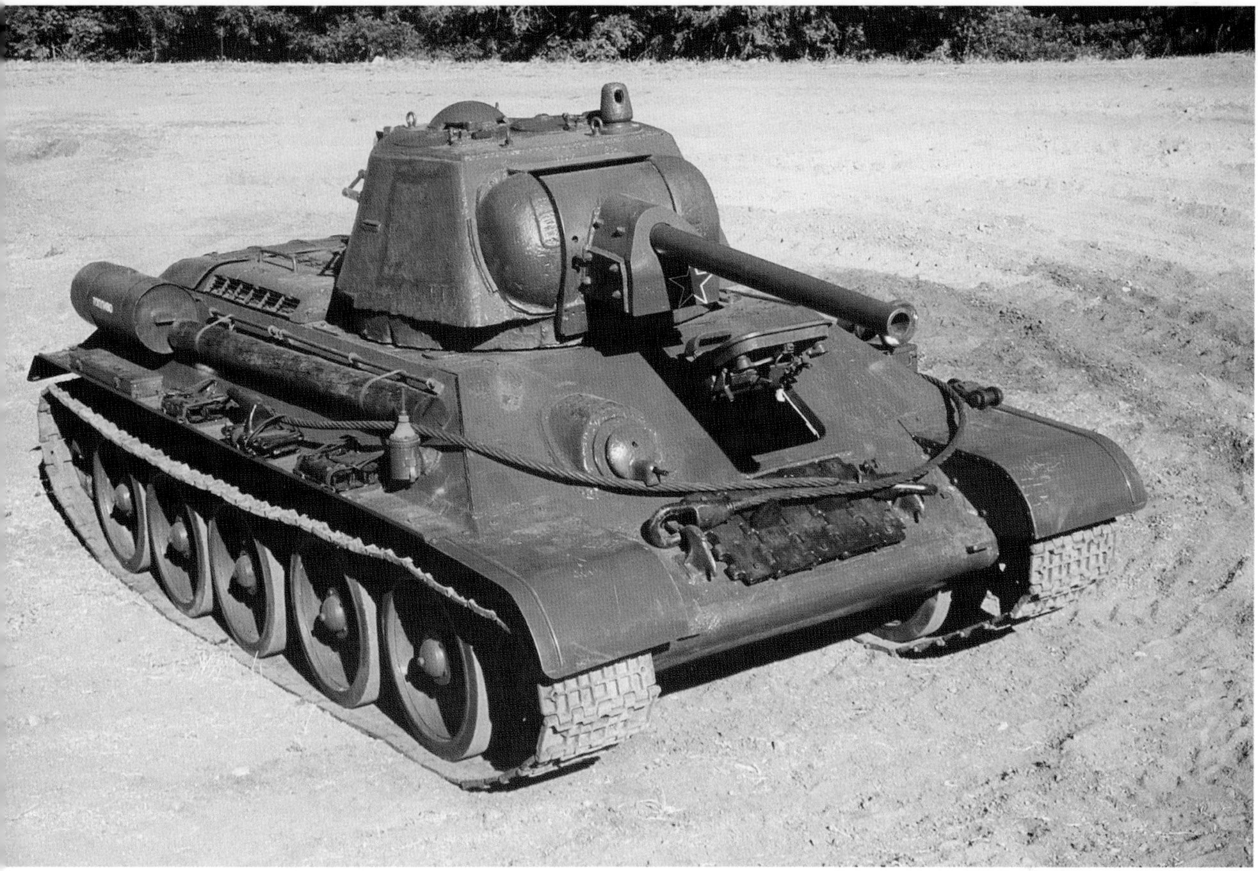

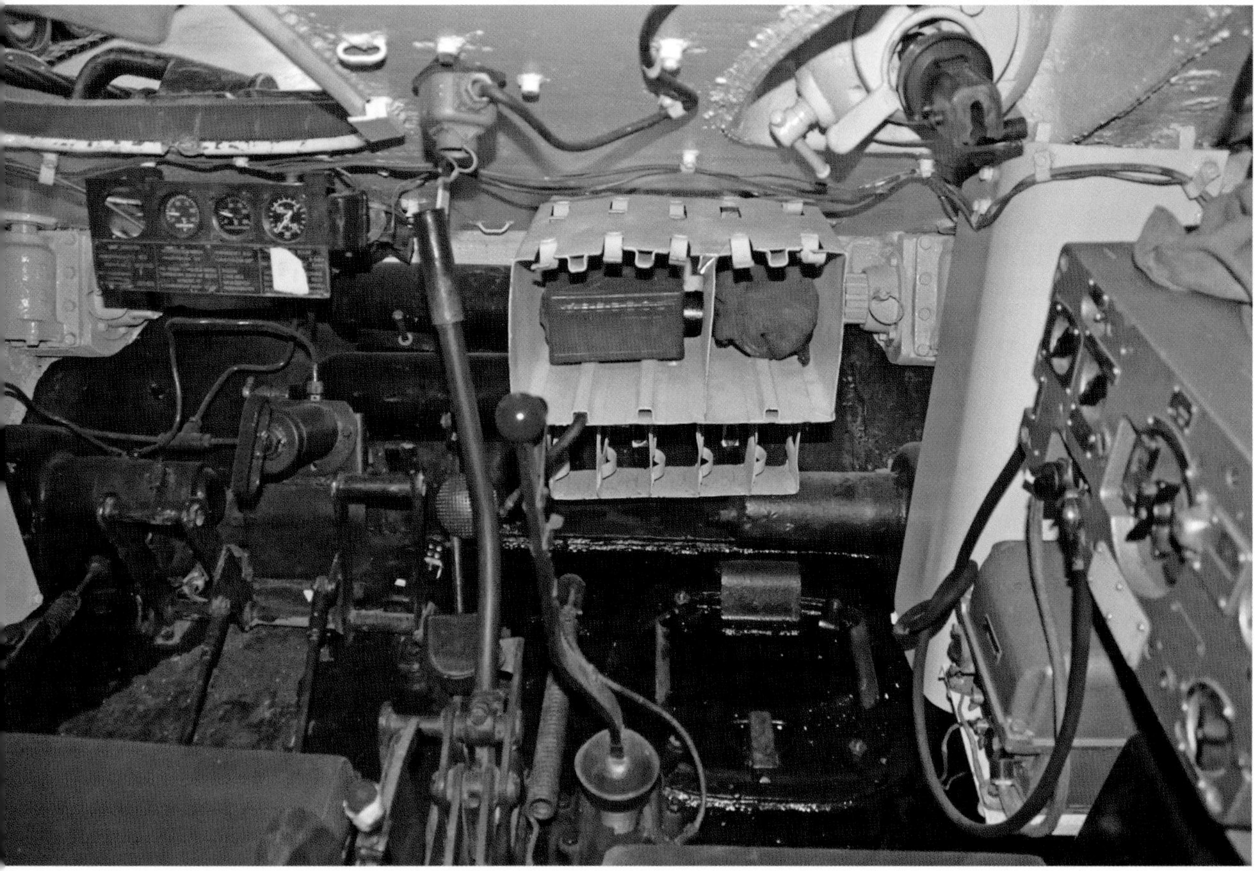

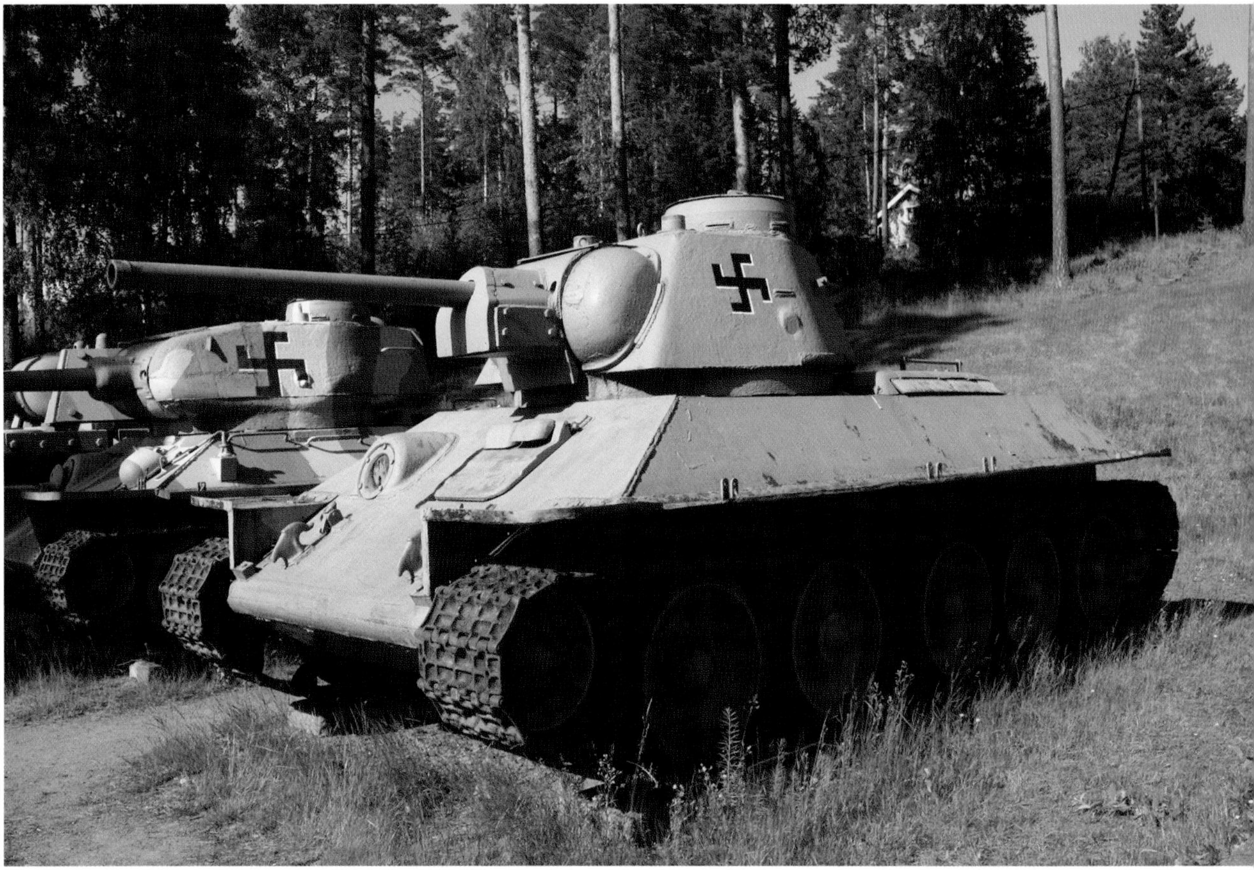

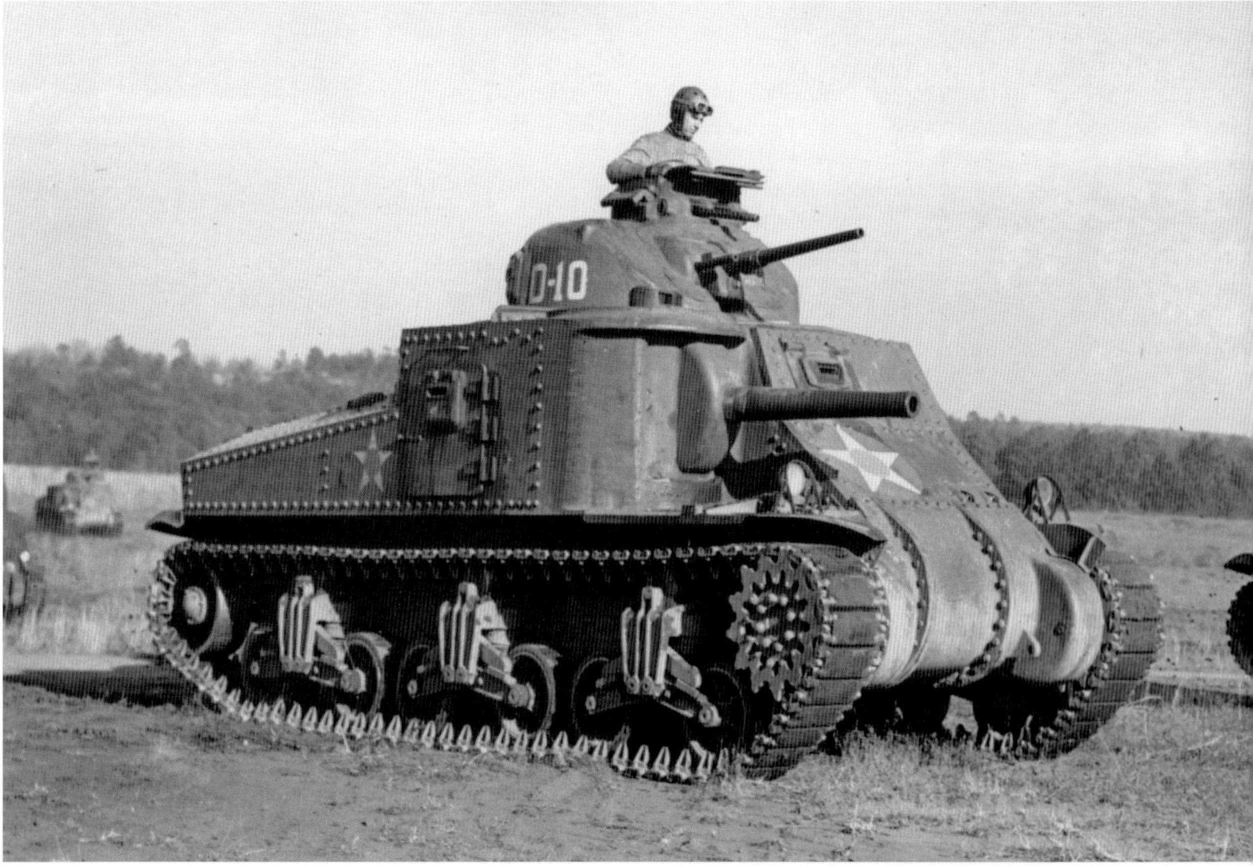
D-10

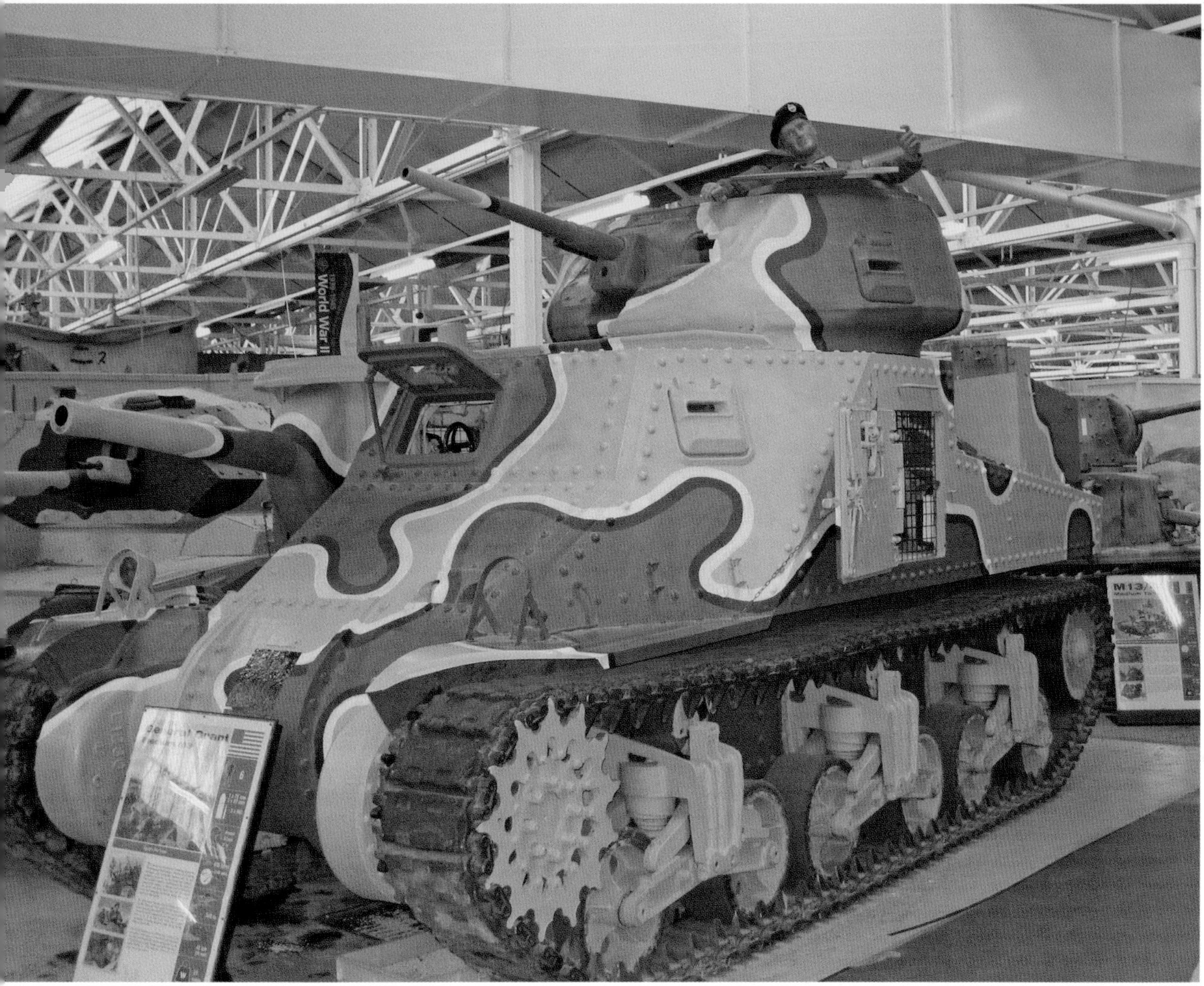
World War II

(*Opposite above*) No doubt influenced by the vehicle commander cupolas seen on German medium tanks, the Red Army eventually adopted a similar component for their very late-production T-34 Model 1943 tanks. This practice is seen here in this captured wartime example on display at a Finnish army museum. The T-34 Model 1940 through to Model 1943 were 22ft in length, had a width of 9ft 6in and their height was 8ft. (*Andreas Kirchhoff*)

(*Opposite below*) An early-production M3 medium tank is pictured on manoeuvres within the United States. The riveted construction of the tank's superstructure is evident in this picture. The M3 was topped off by a small cast armoured machine-gun-armed cupola for the vehicle commander, giving it a height of 10ft 3in. By contrast, the German army Panzer IV medium tank was only 8ft 6in high. (*Patton Museum*)

(*Above*) The British army disliked the height of the US army M3 medium tank and the vehicle's radio being located in the superstructure. British army policy in 1940 called for a tank's radio to be located in the turret with the vehicle commander. The US army therefore gave permission for the British version of the M3 medium referred to as the 'Grant' to be fitted with a larger and lower turret, as seen in this picture of a restored example. (*Author's collection*)

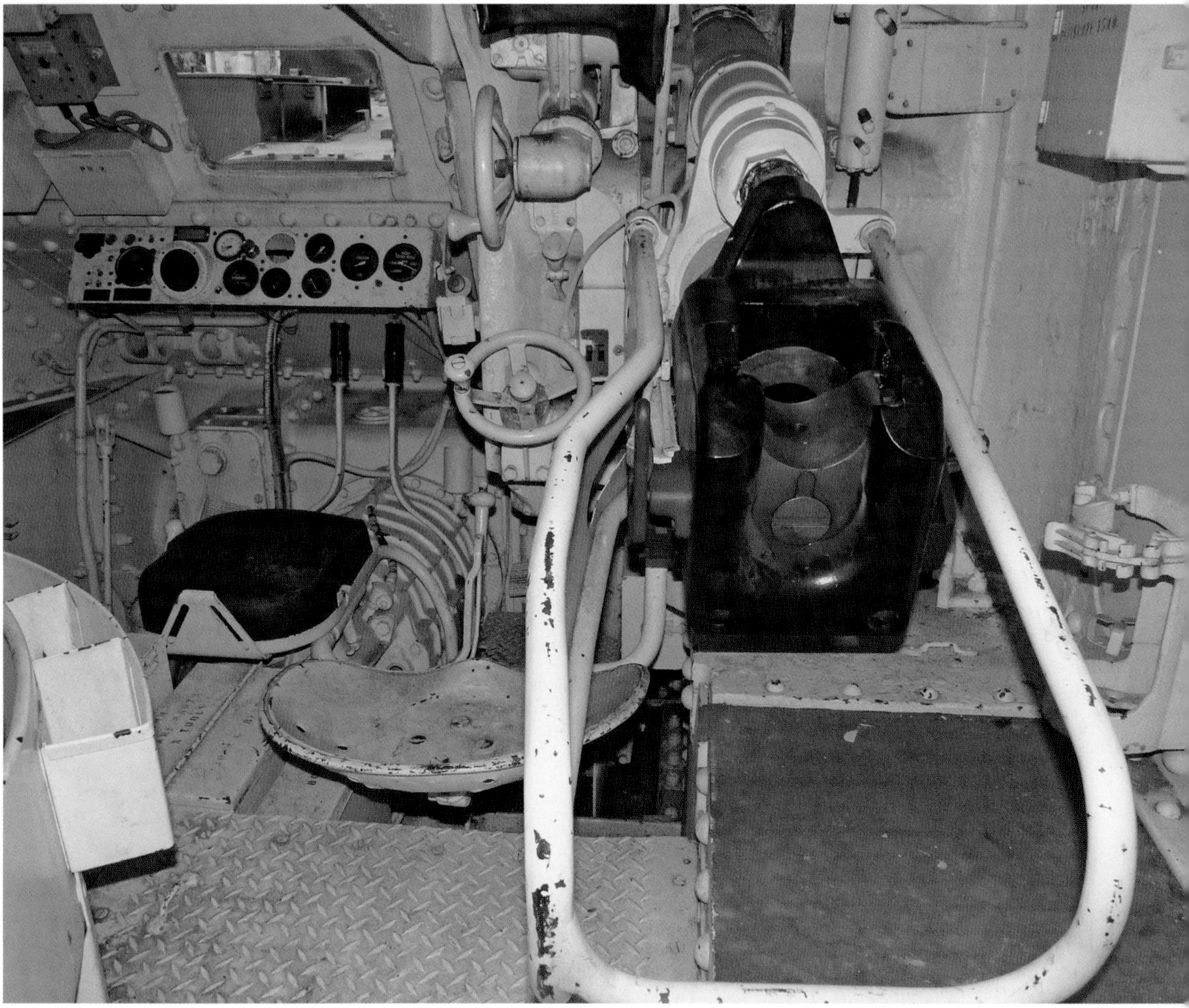

(*Above*) In this photograph we see the superstructure interior of a restored British army M3 Grant. On the right-hand side is the breech end of the tank's forward-firing 75mm gun surrounded by a recoil guard. Visible to the left of the gun are the gunner's seat and controls. On the far left is the driver's seat located on the top of the tank's transmission. *(Paul Hannah)*

(*Opposite above*) In an effort to speed up production of the M3 medium tank, American industry began to build them with a cast armoured superstructure. Those units so built were designated as the M3A1 medium tank by the US army. Seen here is an outwardly-restored M3A1 medium tank when it was on display at the US army's Ordnance Museum, Aberdeen, Maryland. *(Author's collection)*

(*Opposite below*) Pictured in storage at Fort Benning, Georgia is an M3A2 medium tank with a welded superstructure and the standard cast armour turret. The M3A2 came about because there turned out to be an insufficient number of foundries in the United States capable of making the large superstructure required for the M3A1. It retained the same air-cooled aircraft-type radial engine that powered the M3 and M3A1 medium tanks. *(Rob Cogan)*

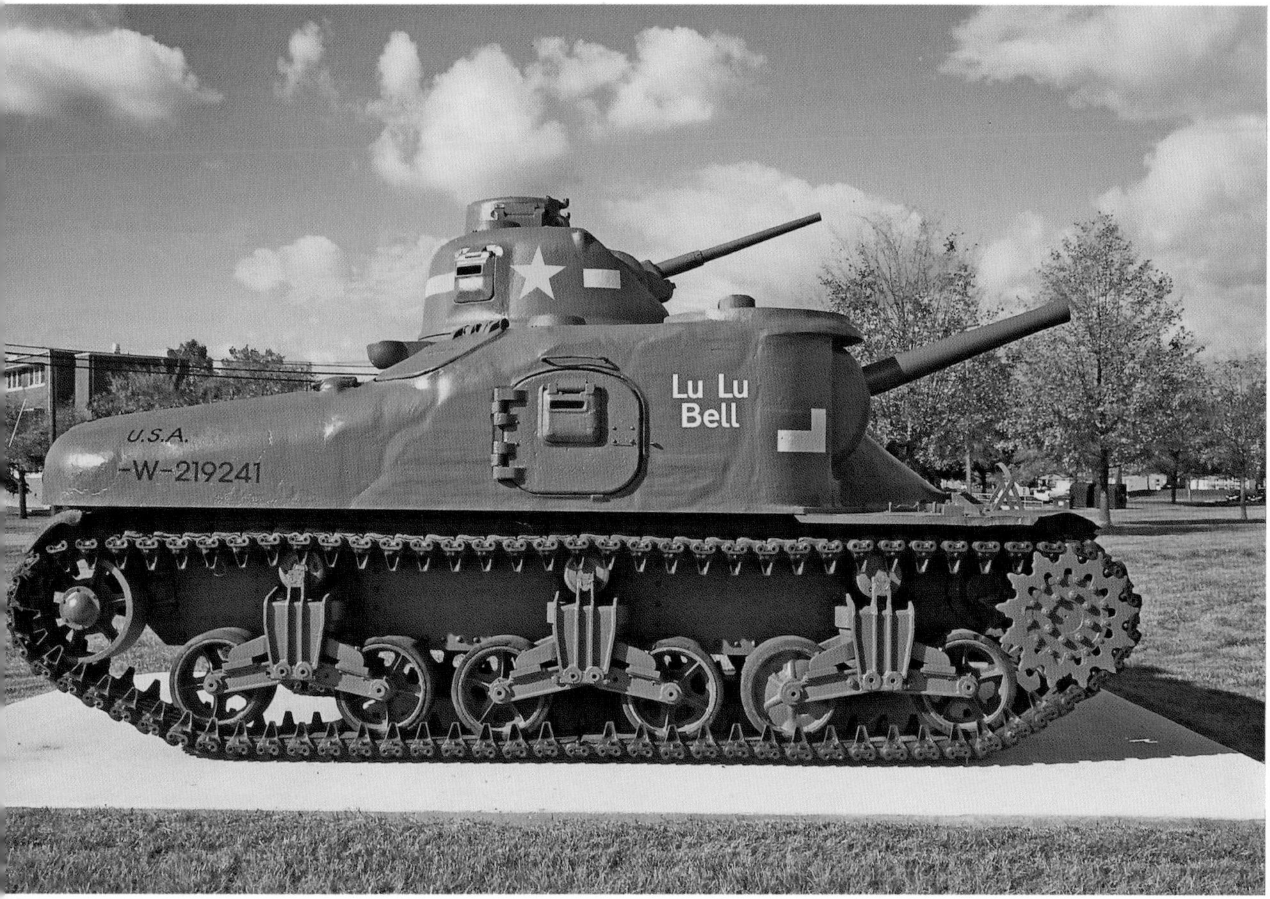
Lu Lu
Bell
U.S.A.
-W-219241

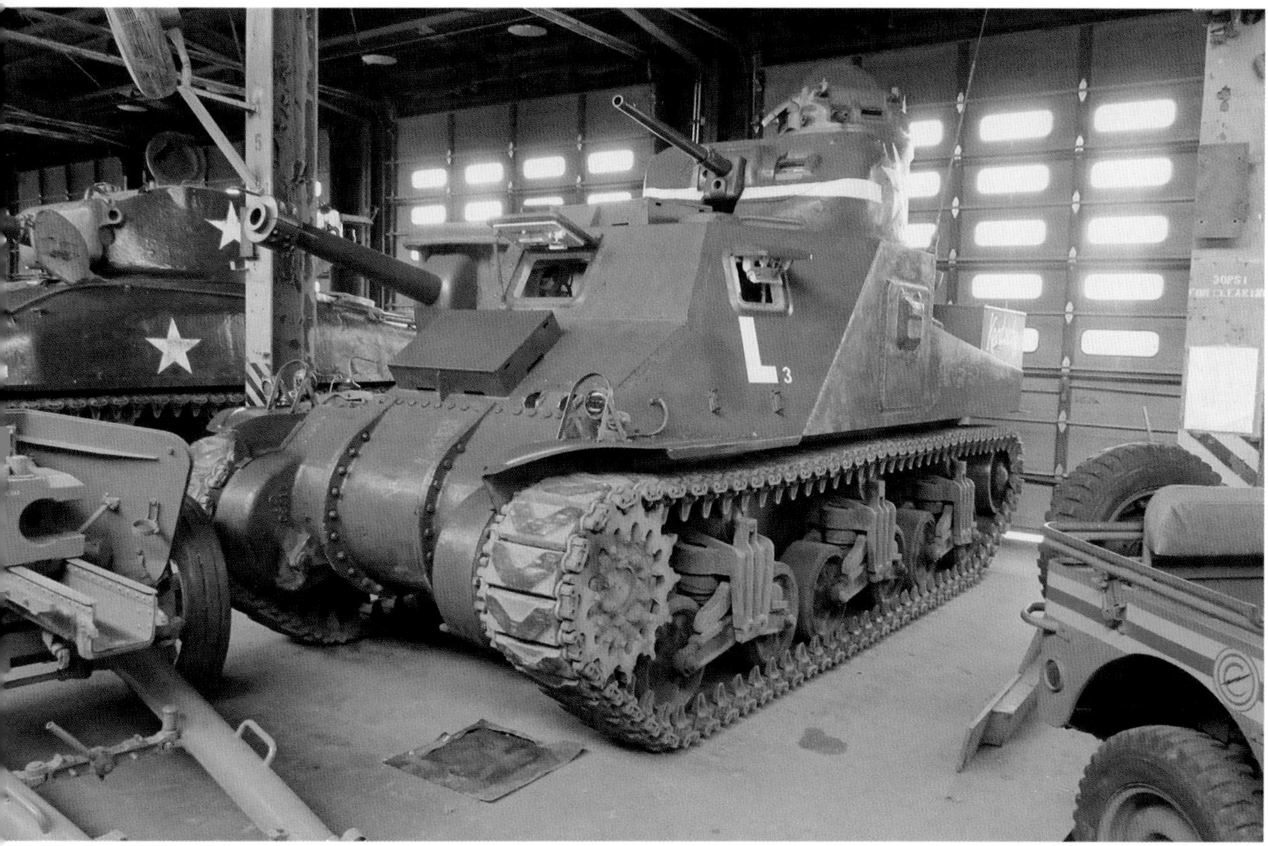
L
3

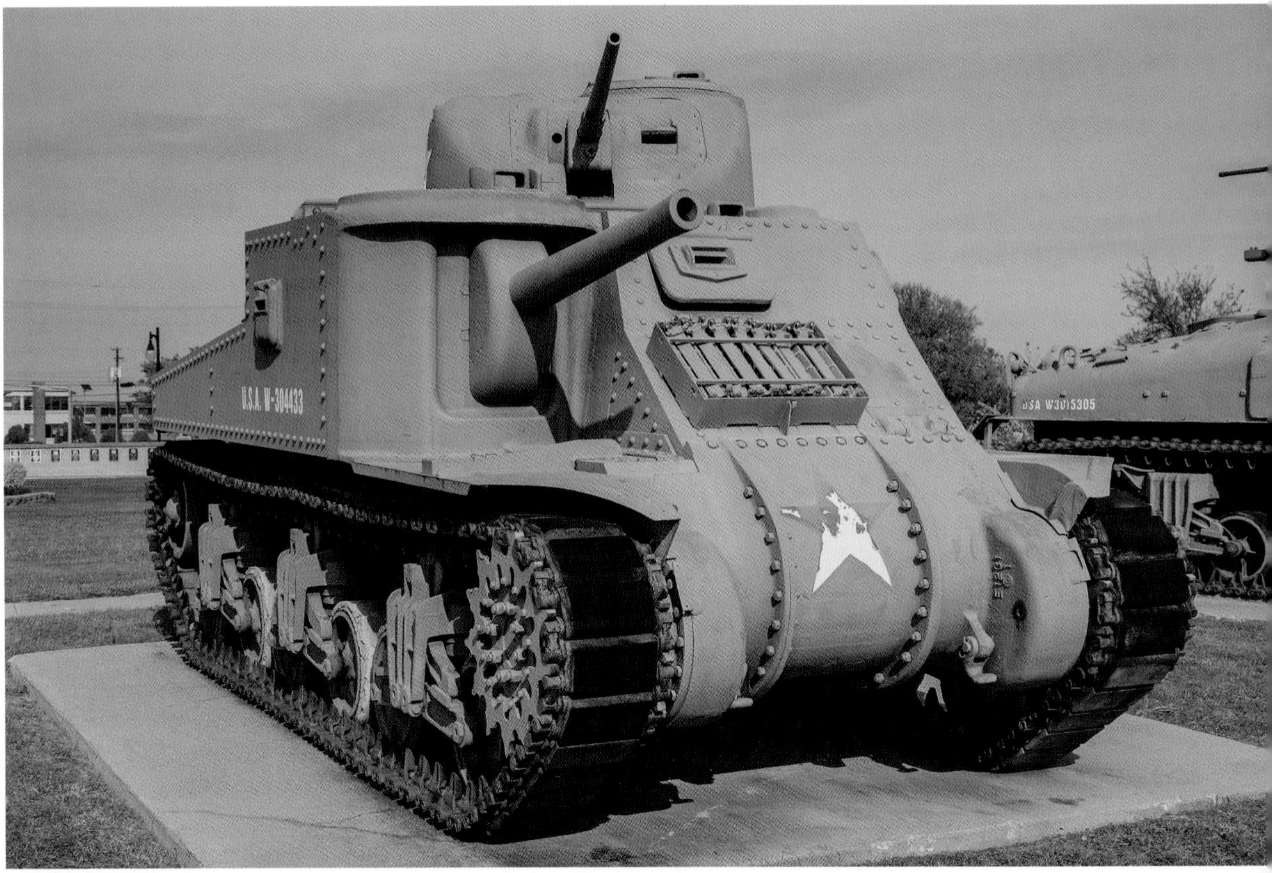
U.S.A. W-304433
USA W3015305

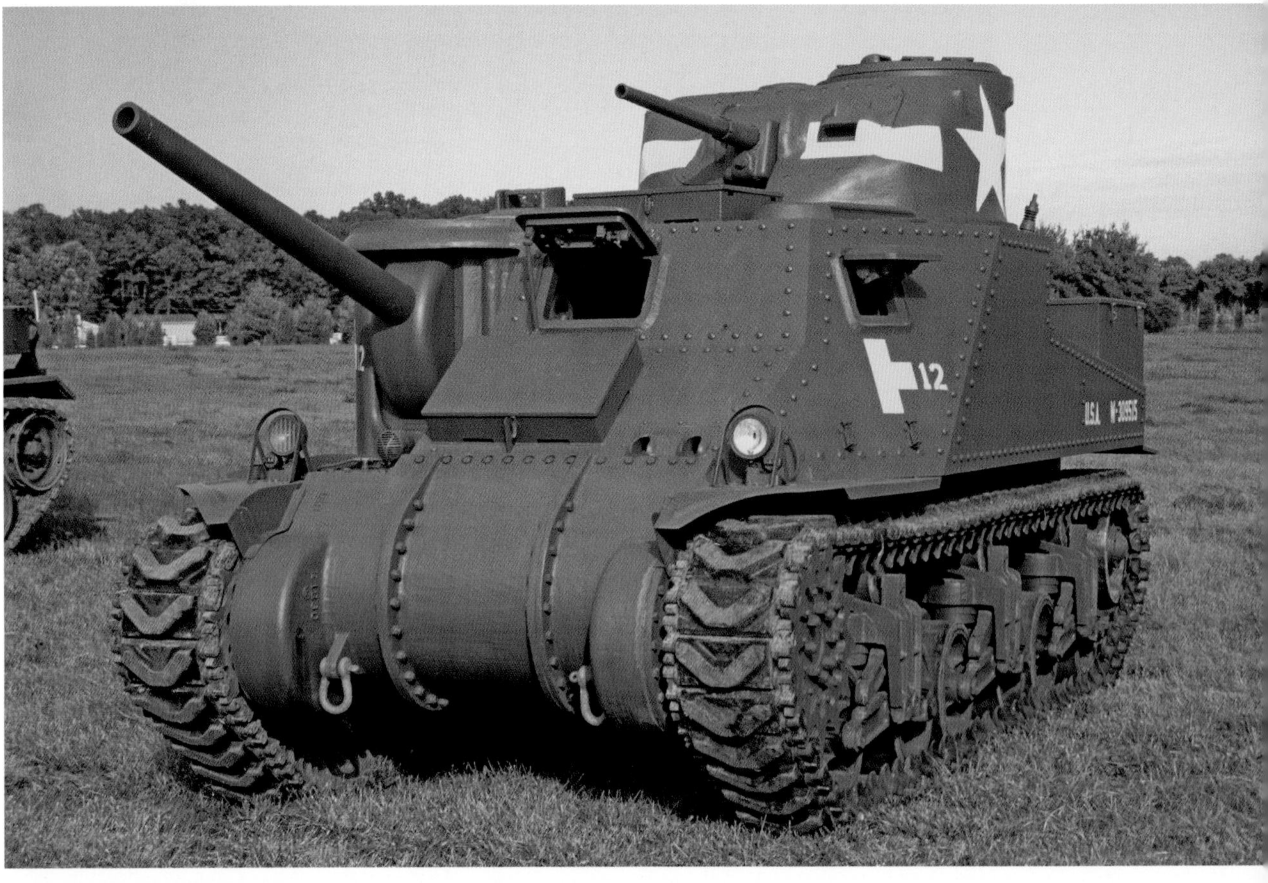
12

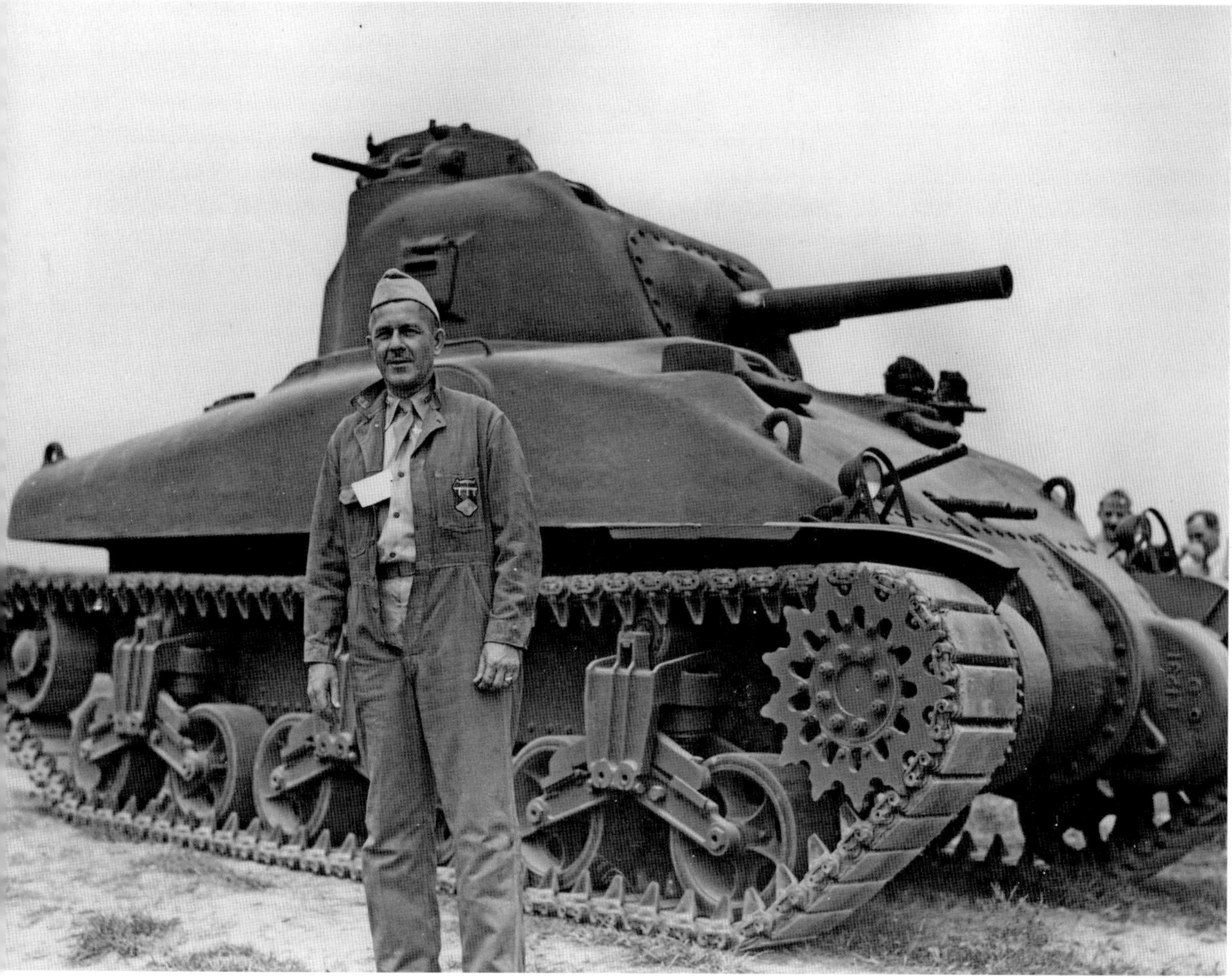

(*Opposite above*) On display at a US army museum located at Fort Hood, Texas is an M3 medium tank labelled the 'Lee' by the British army. This particular example is missing the cast armour cupola seen on all US army M3 series medium tanks during the Second World War. Rather, reflecting its employment by the British or Commonwealth armies during the conflict it has been fitted with the same split-cover circular turret hatch fitted to the turret of the Grant. *(Chris Hughes)*

(*Opposite below*) Belonging to the Virginia Museum of Military Vehicles is this restored M3 medium tank in US army markings. It is armed with the longer-barrelled 75mm gun that began showing up on late-production M3 series medium tanks and was 9ft 8in in length. The majority came off the assembly line fitted with the 75mm gun labelled as the M2 that was 7ft 8in long. *(Author's collection)*

(*Above*) US army Major General Jacob Devers, then head of the Armoured Force, poses in front of the medium tank M6, the prototype for the M4 series of medium tanks, on 3 September 1941. Devers played an important role in the development of American medium tanks before and during the Second World War. The M6 was armed with the short-barrelled M2 75mm main gun. *(National Archives)*

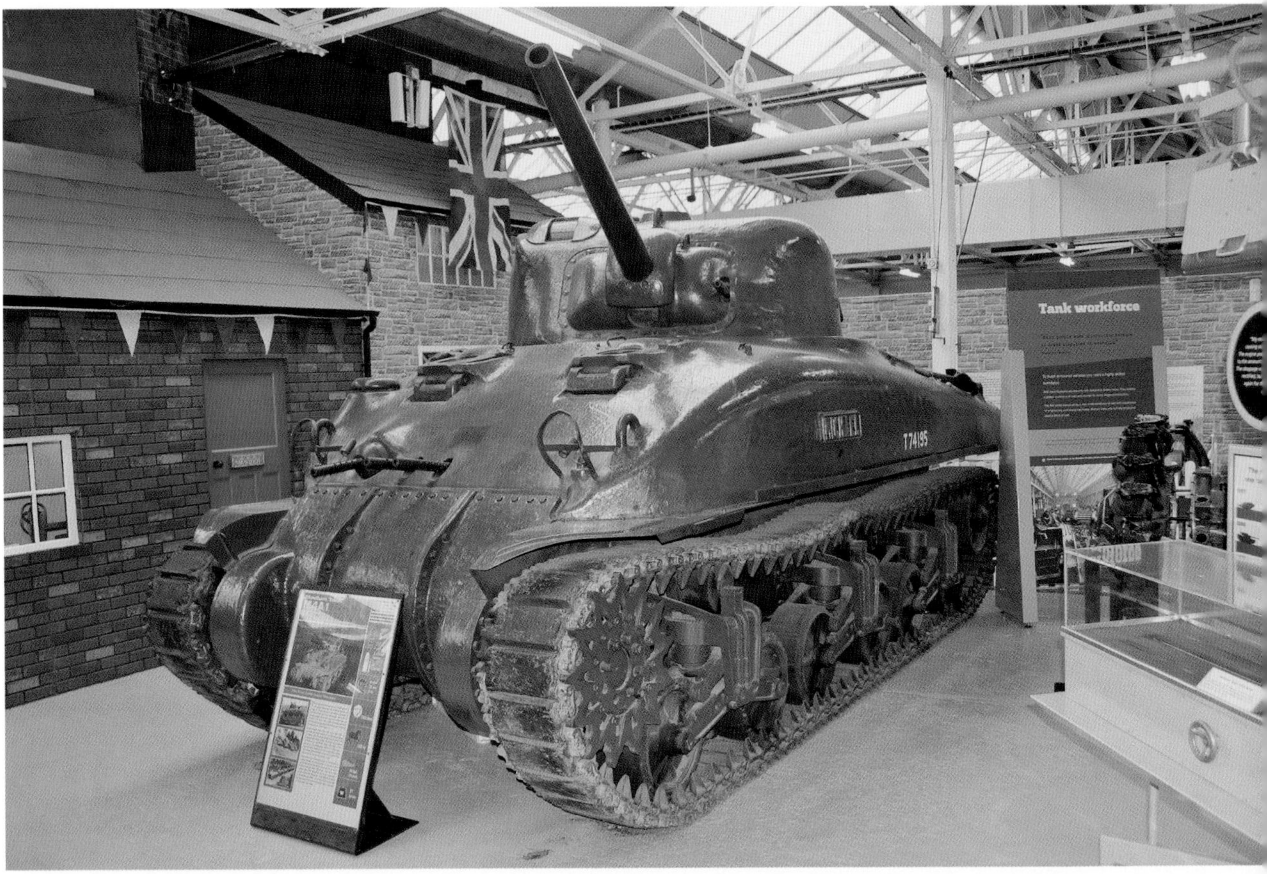
T74185
Tank workforce

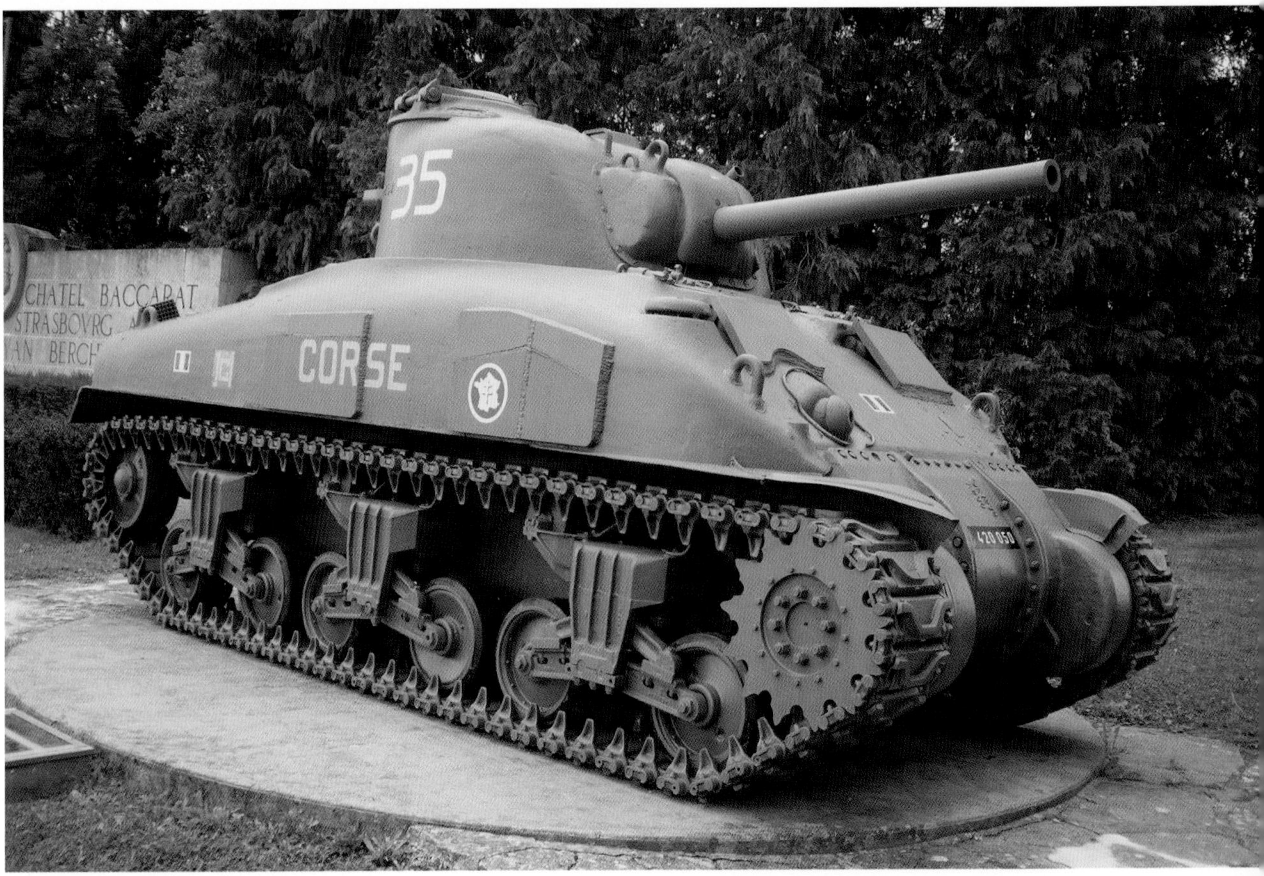
CHATEL BACCARAT
STRASBOVRG
35
CORSE

 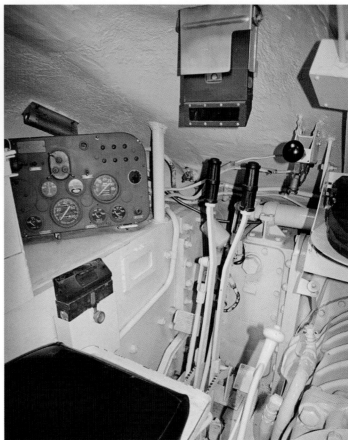

(*Opposite above*) The second M4A1 medium tank off the assembly line was built by the Lima Locomotive Works in March 1942 and was then shipped to England bearing the name 'MICHAEL' in honour of Michael Dewar, head of the British Tank Mission to the United States. It is seen here on display at the Tank Museum in Bovington, England. (*Tank Museum*)

(*Opposite below*) On display in France as a monument tank is this first-generation M4A1 medium tank. The vehicle has both very early-production and late-production features. An early-production feature is the M34 gun mount that featured a very narrow rotor shield. The vehicle commander's cupola is a very late-production feature added to some first-generation M4 series tanks upon being rebuilt. (*Pierre-Olivier Buan*)

(*Above left*) The gunner's controls of a first-generation M4A1 medium tank appear in this photograph. On the right is the gunner's manually-operated traverse grip and on the left the vertically-oriented elevation hand wheel. Above these controls are the gunner's direct-sight telescope and the overhead periscope sighting device. (*Author's collection*)

(*Above right*) Pictured is the driver's position on a first-generation M4A1 medium tank. On the far left is his instrument panel with the driver's two steering brake levers in front of his seat. On the bottom left of the steering brake levers is the floor-mounted clutch pedal. To the right of the steering brake levers are the driver's gearshift lever and accelerator pedal. (*Author's collection*)

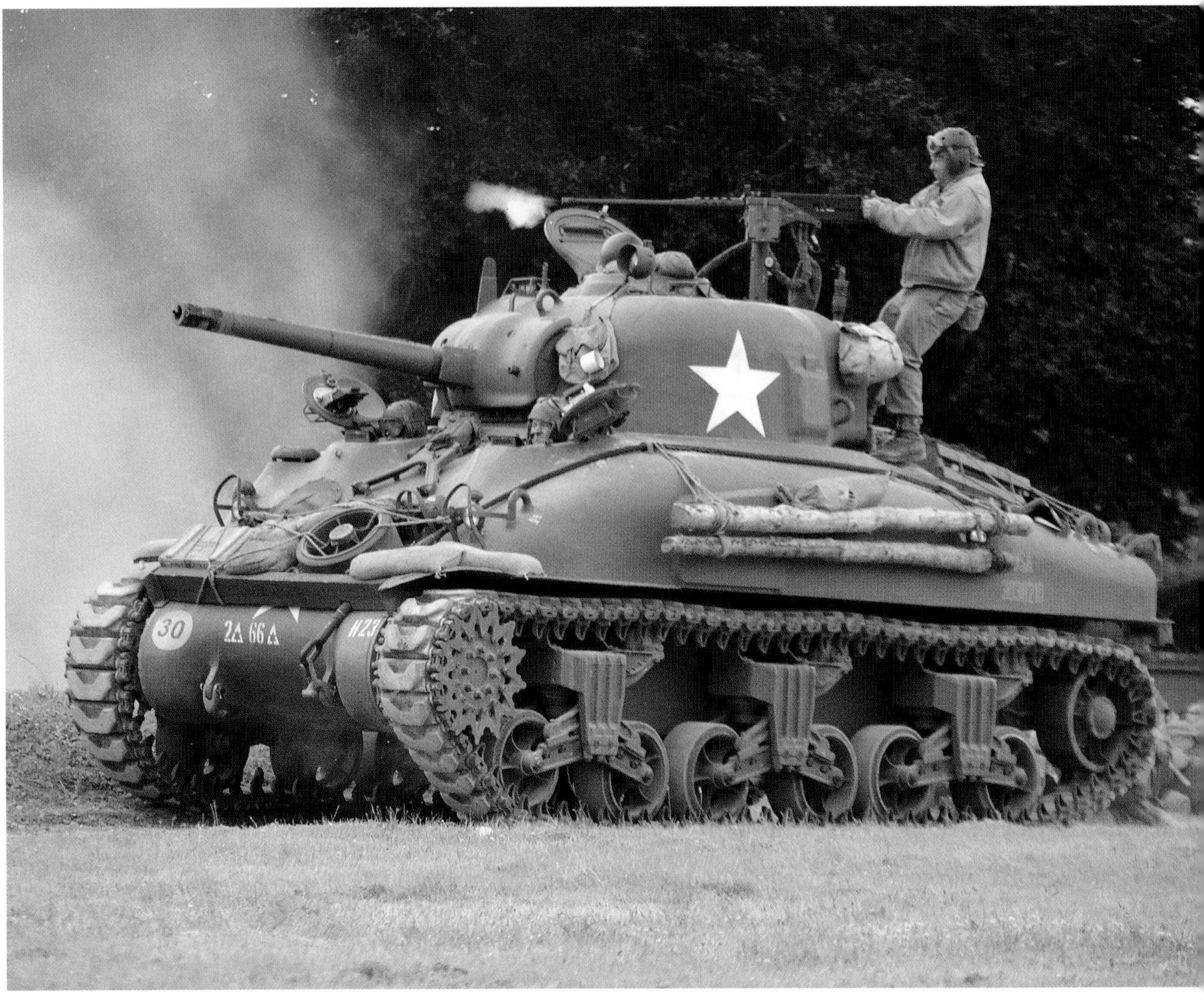

(*Above*) Taking part in a historical vehicle demonstration is this first-generation M4A1 medium tank. The black device fitted to the end of the tank's 75mm main gun is a blank-firing adapter. The re-enactor on the top of the tank's engine deck is firing blanks from an M2 air-cooled .50 calibre machine gun that had a maximum effective range of approximately 1,200 yards. *(Ian Wilcox)*

(*Opposite above*) Due to the more angular shape of the first-generation welded hull, the M4 had room for ninety-seven 75mm main gun rounds, whereas the rounded shape of the first-generation M4A1 cast armoured hull seen here allowed for the storage of only ninety. The upper and lower front hull on all first-generation M4 series tanks was 50mm thick. *(Author's collection)*

(*Opposite below*) Unlike the Red Army T-34 series of medium tanks that had its transmission located in the rear engine compartment, the transmission of the M4 series of medium tanks was located in the front hull in-between the driver and assistant driver/bow gunner. The tank's differential, steering brakes and final drive were integrated into an armoured housing that was bolted directly to the transmission and extended across the entire width of the lower front hull as seen on this M4A1 on display in France. *(Pierre-Olivier Buan)*

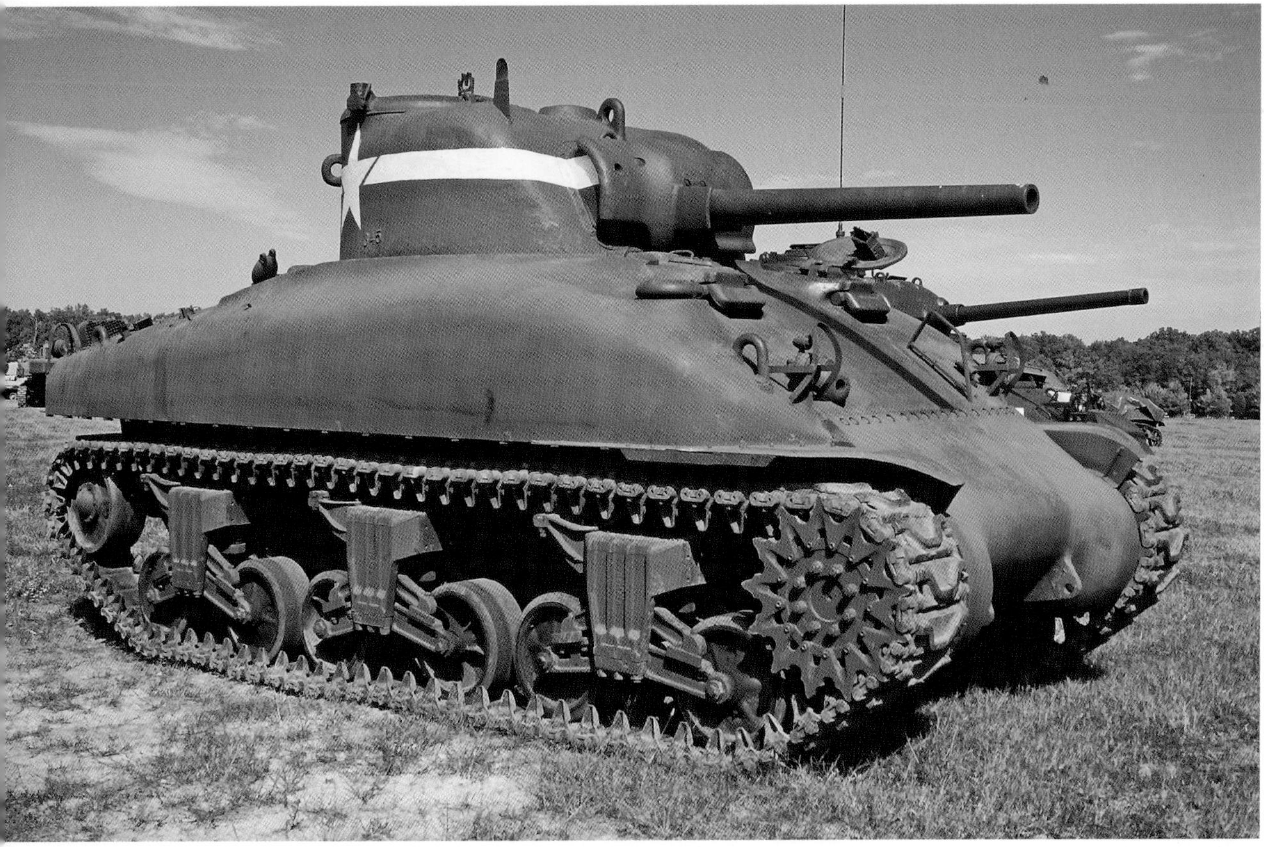

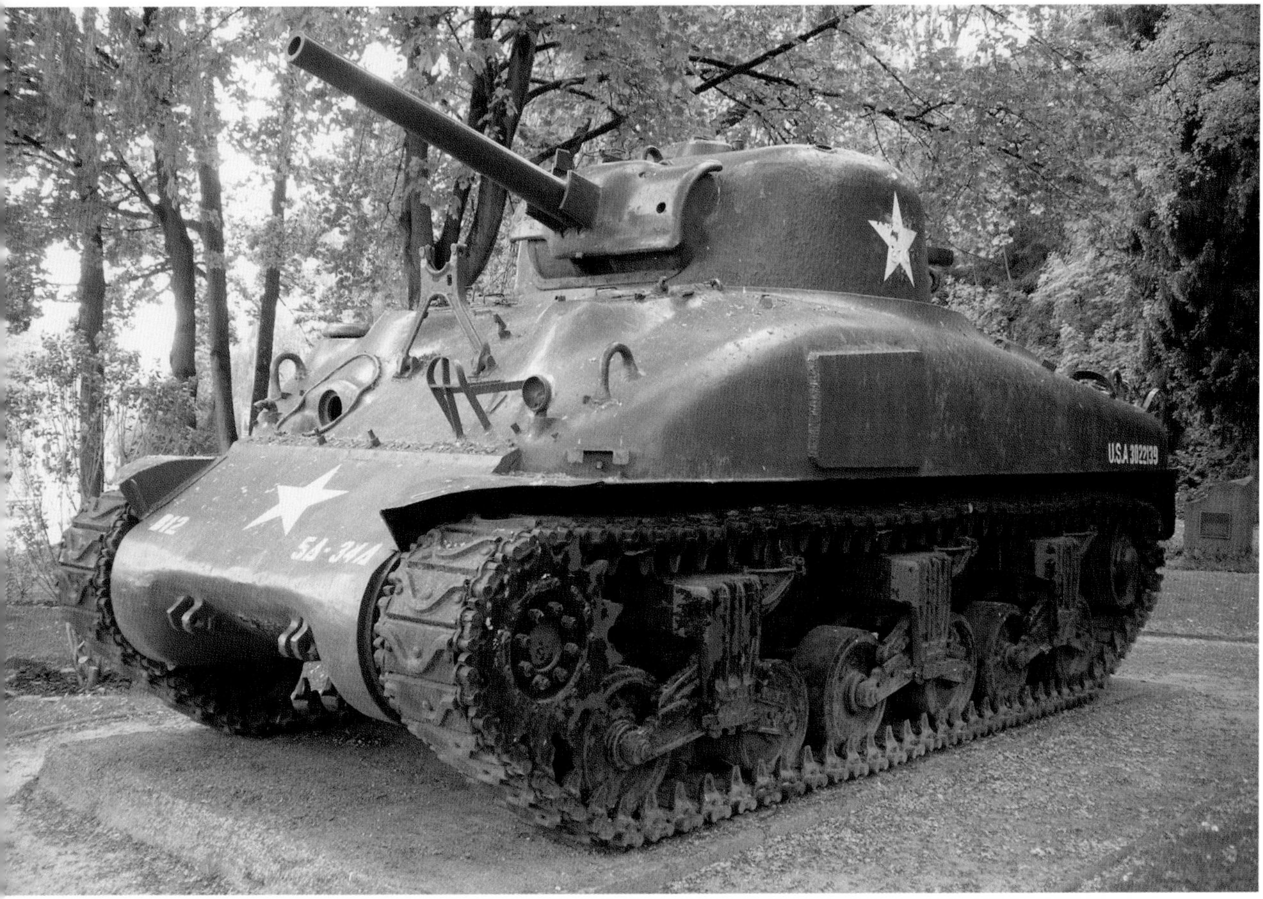
U.S.A 3022139

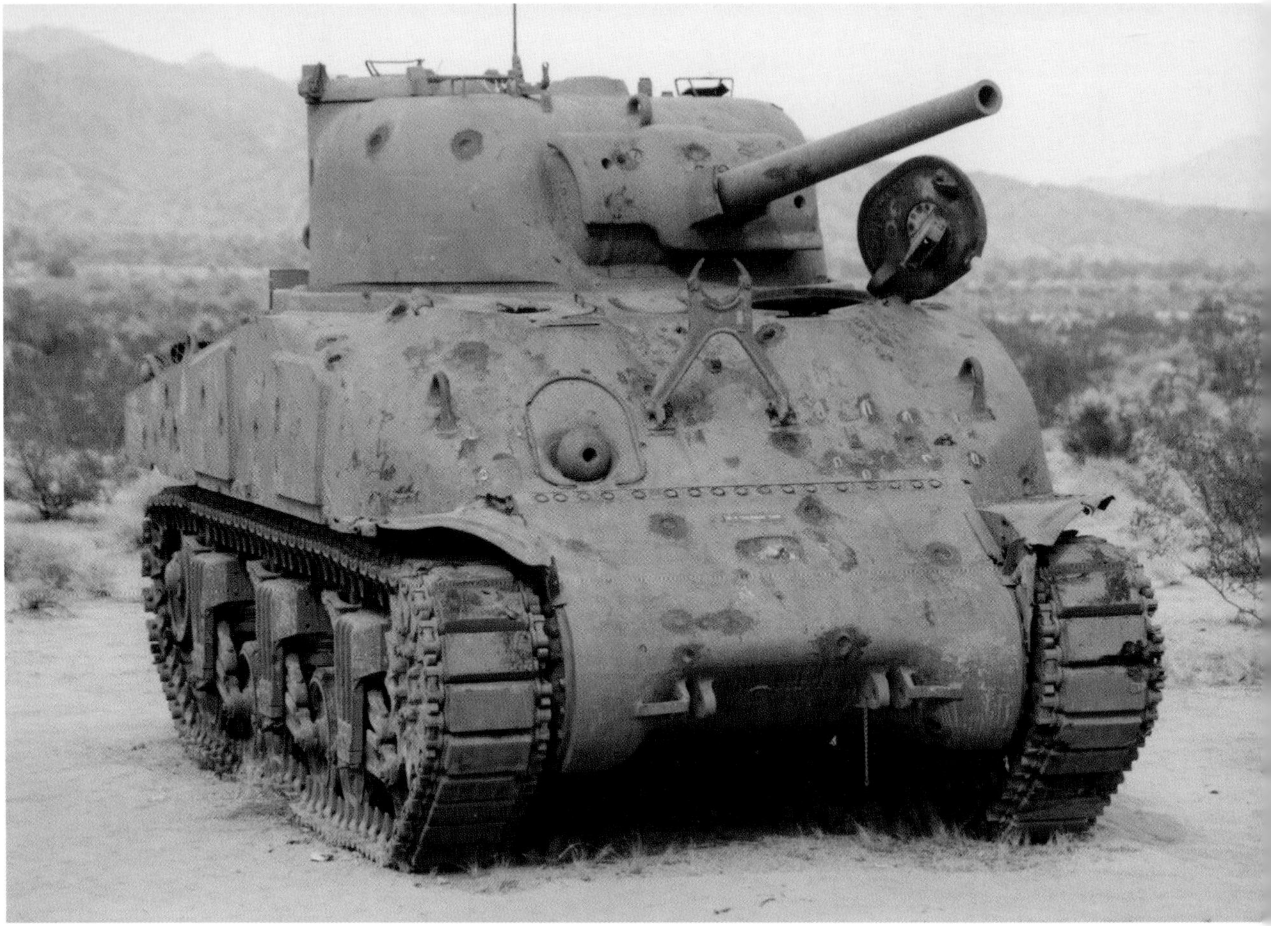

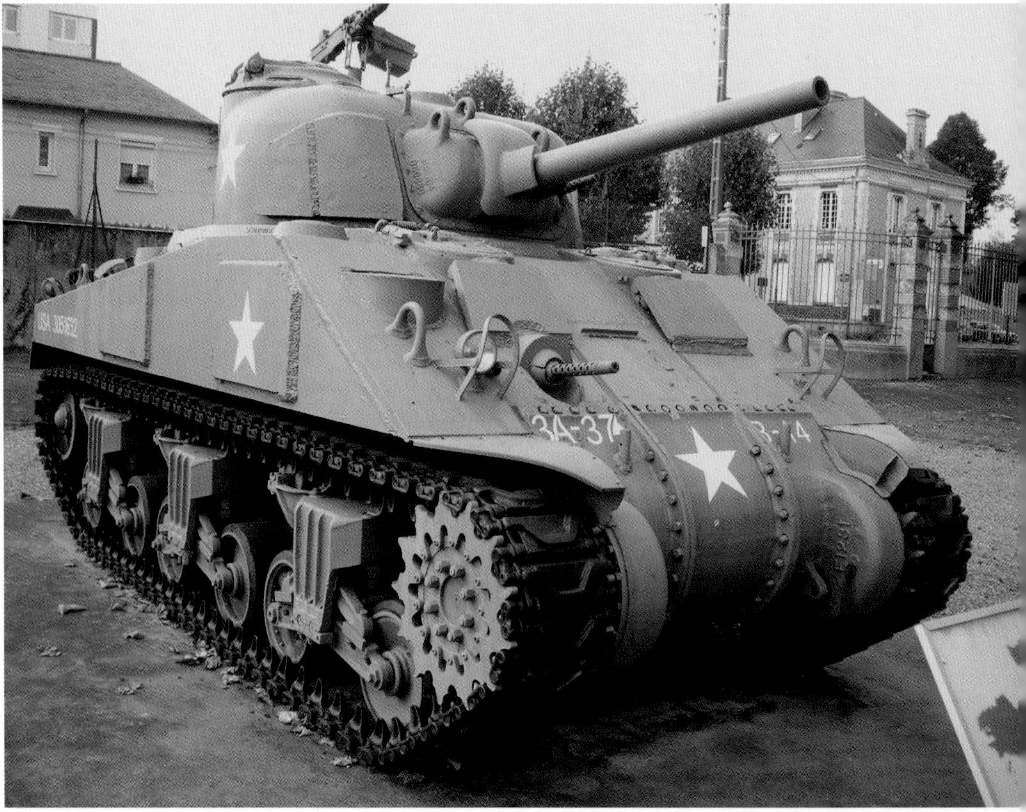

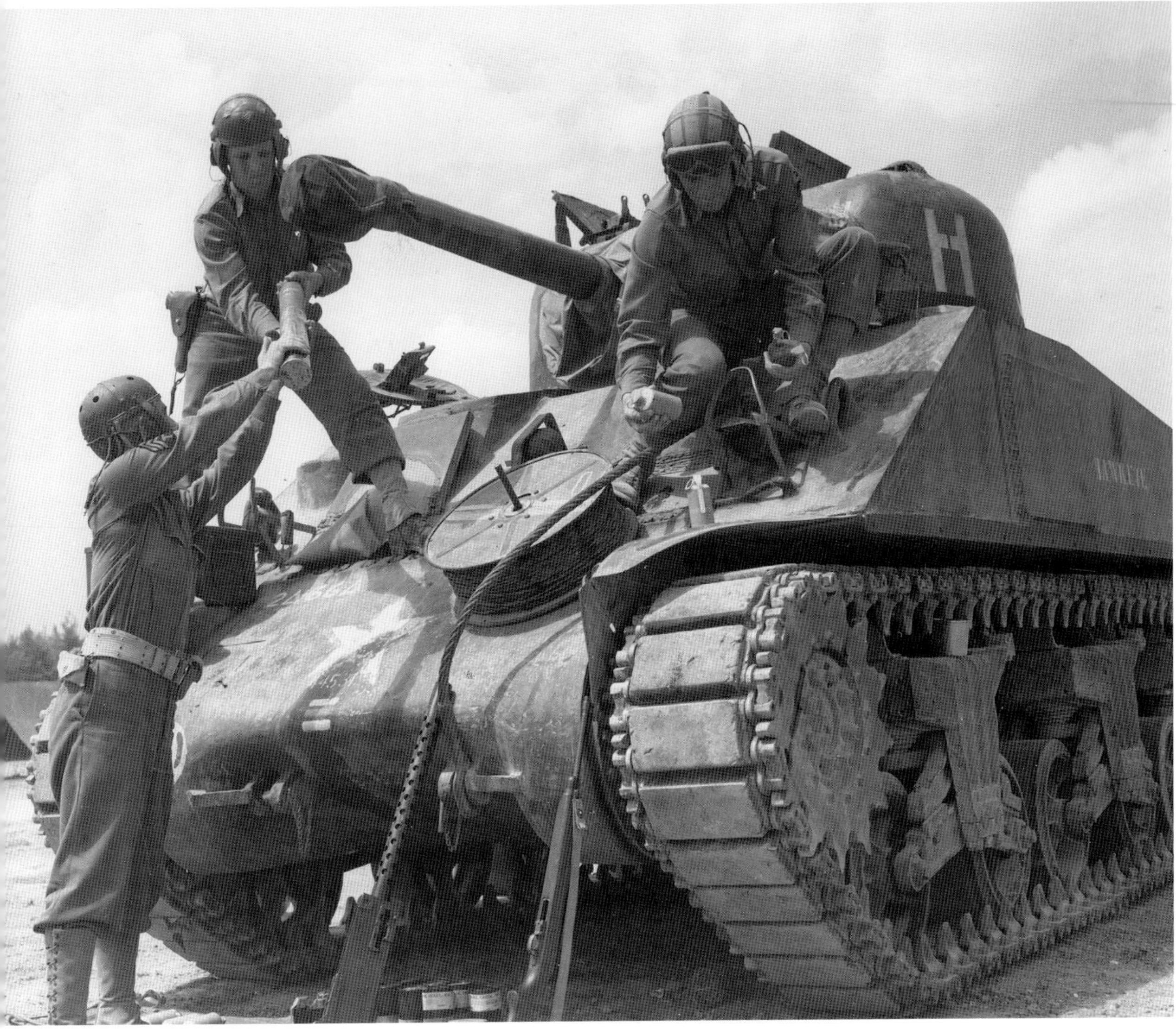

(*Opposite above*) On display at a privately-run military museum located in Southern California is this ex-range target, which is a welded armoured hull M4 medium tank that had been fitted with a single-piece cast armour front hull section from an M4A1 medium tank. Such vehicles are now commonly referred to as having a 'composite hull', although this was never an official US army designation. (*Chris Hughes*)

(*Above*) A posed wartime picture shows the crew of a US army welded armoured hull M4 in the process of loading up their tank with munitions, including 75mm main gun rounds and grenades. In the British army this process would be referred to as 'bombing up'. Typically, American tank crews had at least one submachine gun and not the M1 Carbine seen leaning on the lower front hull. (*Patton Museum*)

(*Opposite below*) Pictured on display in France is this first-generation welded armour hull M4 with a combination of early- and late-production features. As the protruding hatch hoods on the first-generation M4 series tanks proved to be a ballistic weak spot, they were up-armoured as seen on this vehicle with welded-on armour plates approximately 38mm thick. (*Pierre-Olivier Buan*)

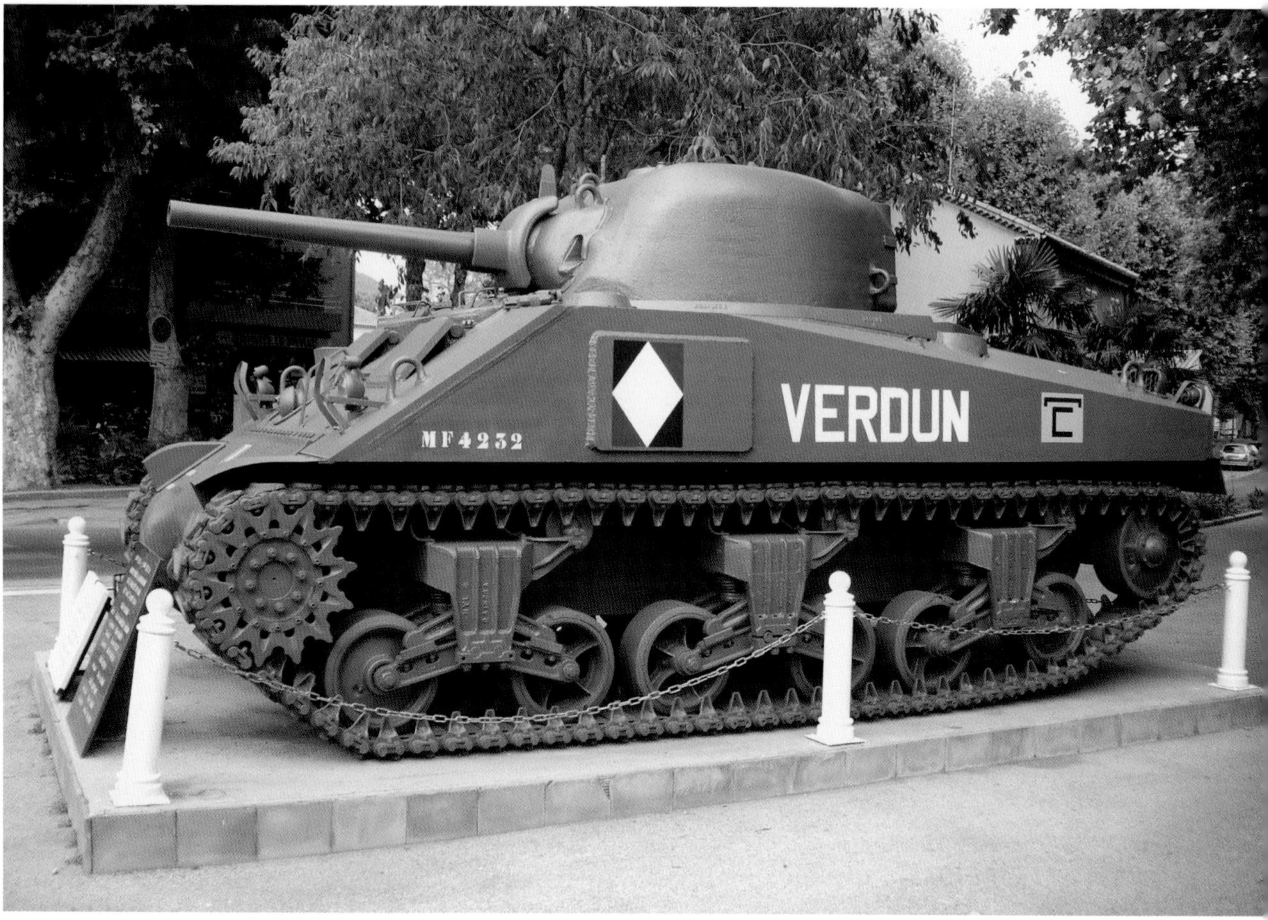
MF4232
VERDUN

All first-generation M4 series tanks rode on a vertical volute spring suspension (VVSS) system. An example is seen here on this welded armoured hull M4 on display in France. The big advantage of volute springs on tanks is the fact that they are compact and very damage-tolerant. Even if a portion of a volute spring is damaged, the broken pieces can carry at least part of the original load. *(Pierre-Olivier Buan)*

In this photograph we see the pilot model of the M4A2. The twin diesel-engine-powered tank came about due to a shortage of aircraft-type air-cooled radial gasoline engines. The two fixed forward-firing small-calibre machine guns in the front hull and the direct vision slits for the driver and the assistant driver/bow gunner did not last long on the production line. *(TACOM)*

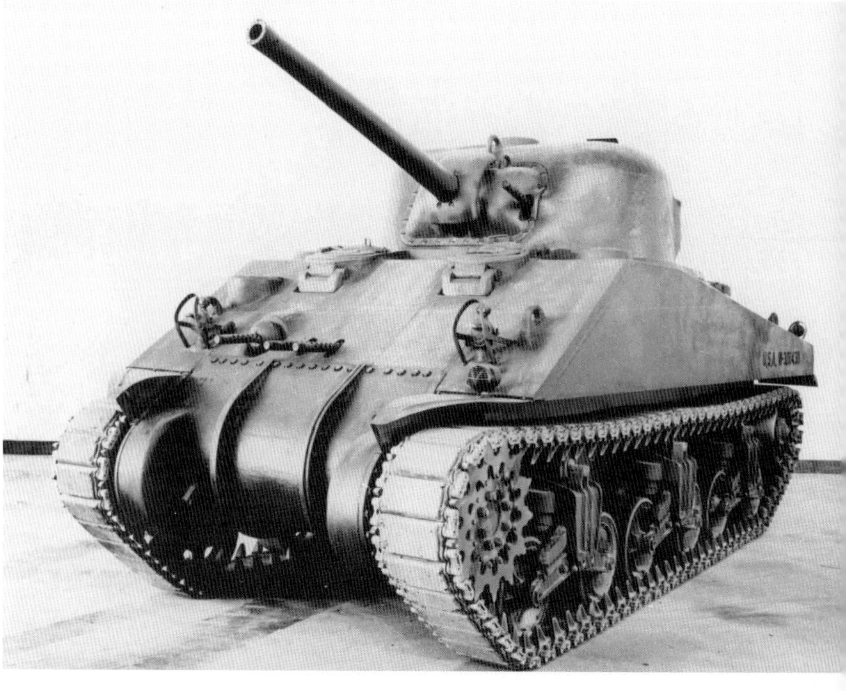

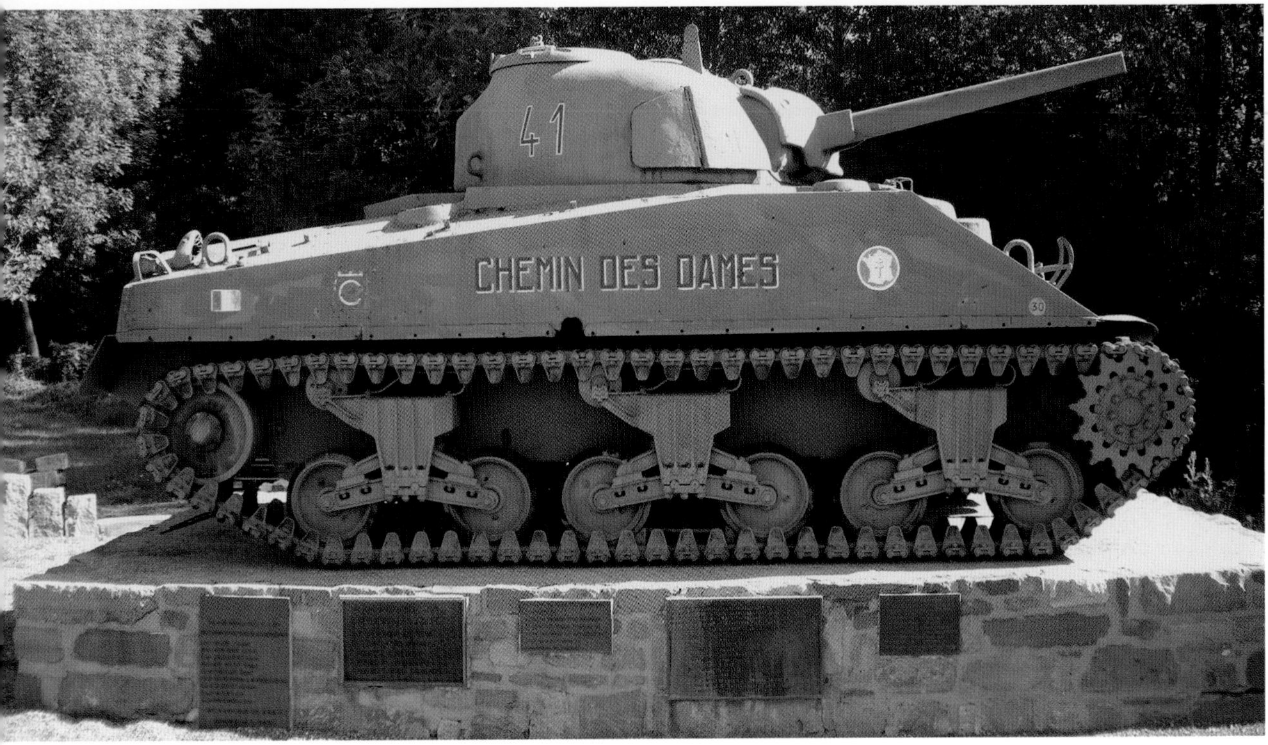
41
CHEMIN DES DAMES

On display in France is this battle-damaged first-generation M4A2. One of the biggest problems that beset the crews of all first-generation M4 series tanks was their propensity to burn. This was typically due to main gun ammunition fires caused when struck by various anti-tank weapons, ranging from armour-piercing projectiles to shaped-charge warheads. *(Pierre-Olivier Buan)*

Taking part in a historical vehicle demonstration is this welded armoured hull M4A2 in British army wartime markings. So serious was the problem of main gun ammunition fires in first-generation M4 series tanks that the Germans nicknamed those they encountered in British army service as the 'Tommy Cookers'. The term 'Tommy' was slang for British soldiers and tankers. *(Ian Wilcox)*

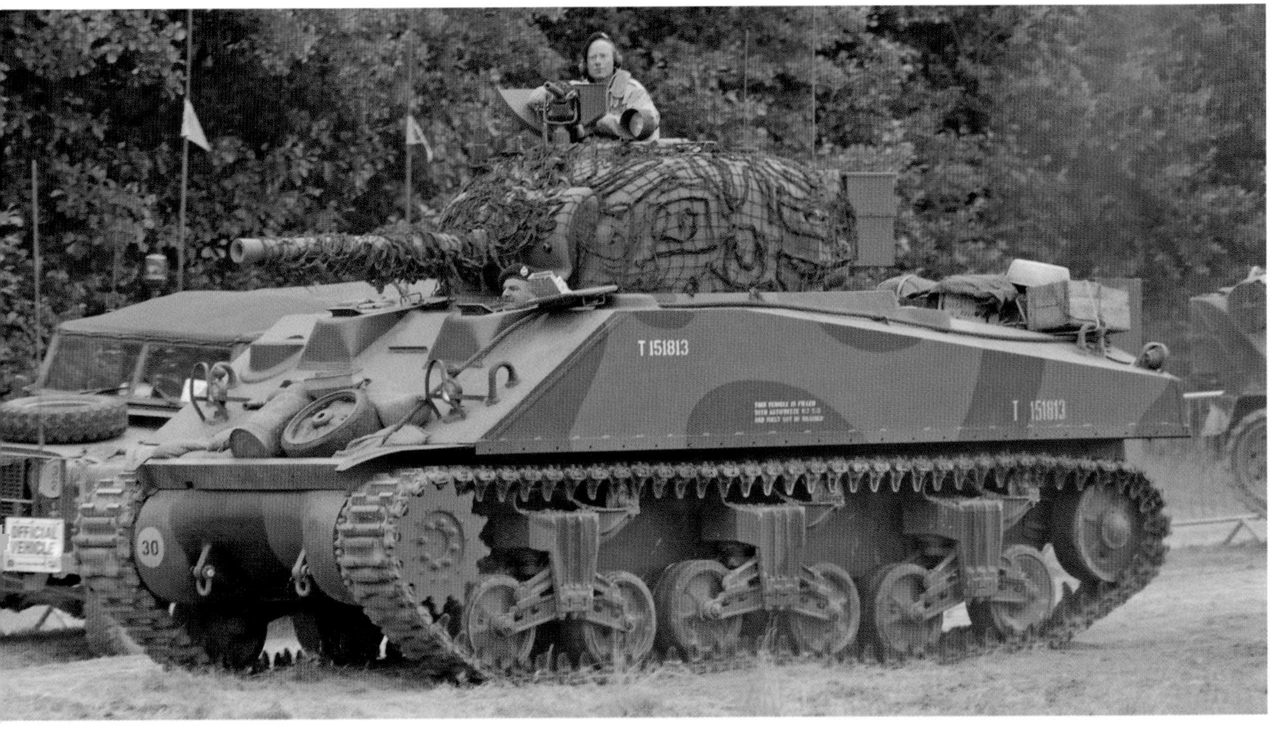
T 151813
T 151813
30

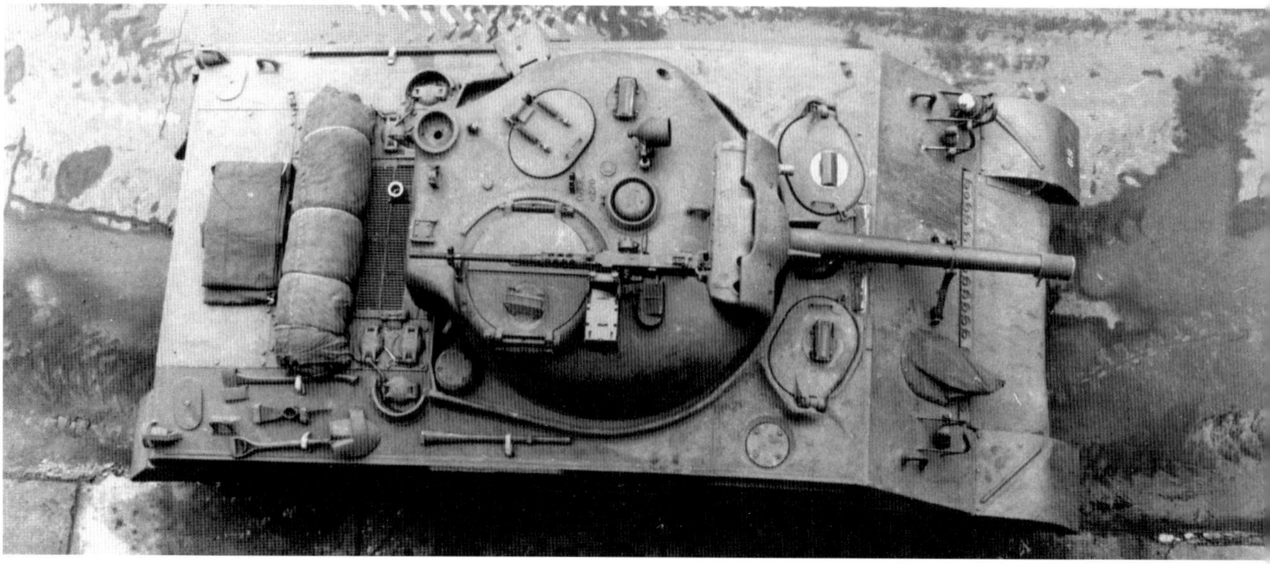

Visible on the turret of this late-production M4A2 is the original standard split-cover circular turret hatch for the vehicle commander. This particular example of the M4A2 features a reset glacis that was sloped at an angle of 47 degrees rather than the original 56 degrees of earlier production units. This glacis reset did away with the protruding hatch hoods of the driver and assistant driver/bow gunner. *(TACOM)*

Pictured is a wartime Ordnance Department display of all the stowage carried inside and outside the first-generation M4 series tanks. In early-production M4 series tanks the majority of 75mm main gun rounds were stored within light sheet-metal boxes, with another twelve stored vertically in clips along the inside wall of the turret basket. *(TACOM)*

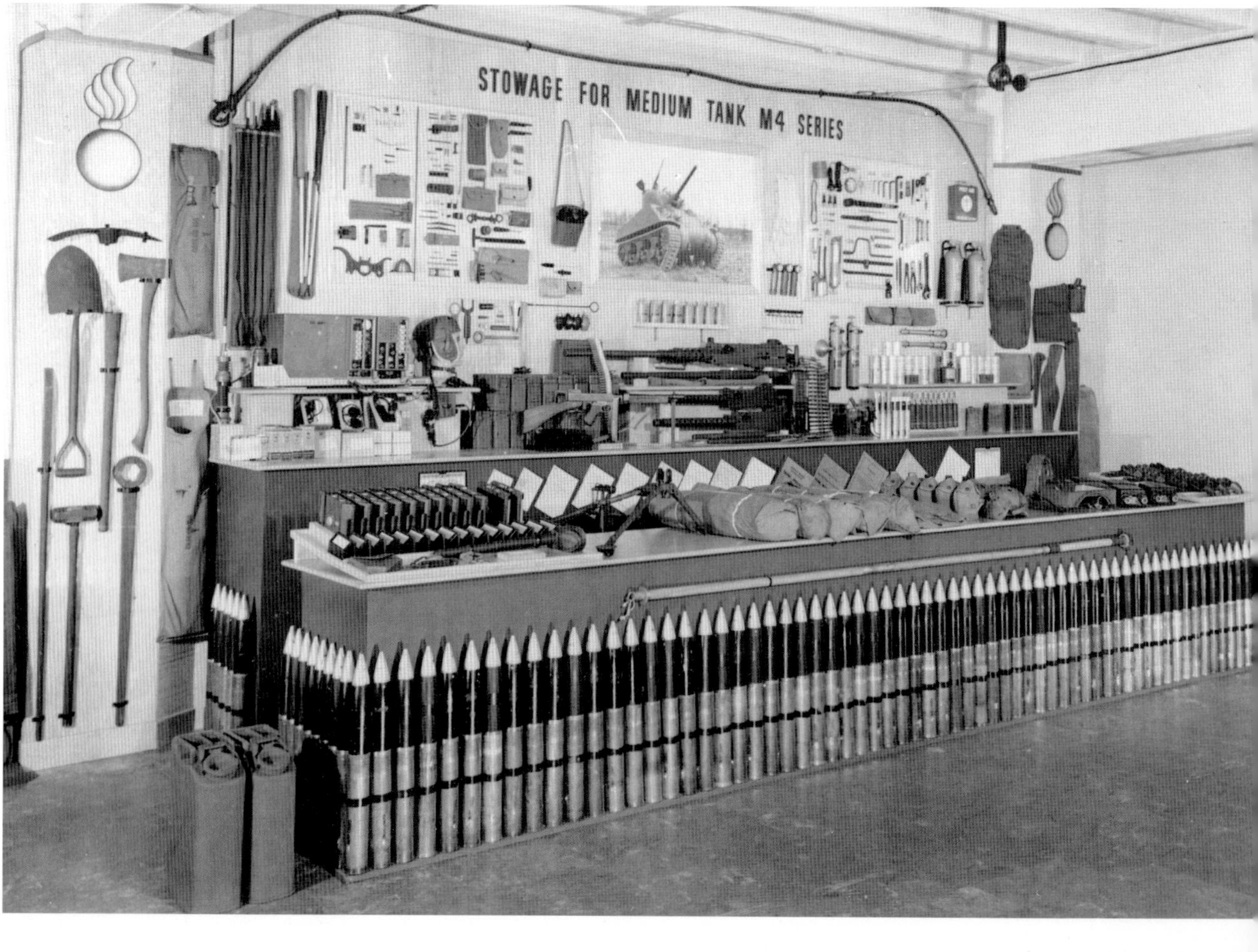
STOWAGE FOR MEDIUM TANK M4 SERIES

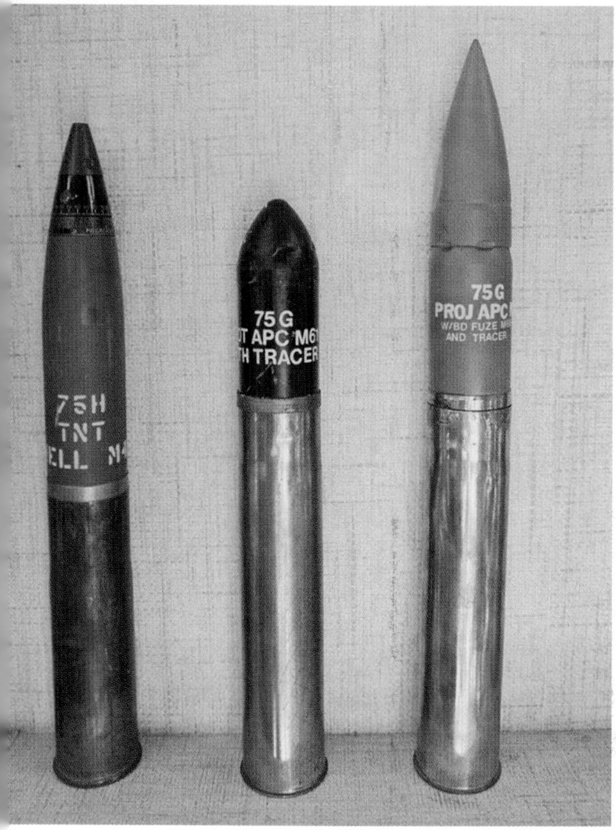
75H
TNT
75G
75G
PROJ APC

A close-up picture of three of the main gun rounds fired from the 75mm main guns of first-generation M4 series tanks. On the far left is the M48 high-explosive (HE) round as denoted by the fuse on the tip of the projectile. The other two are armour-piercing (AP) rounds; the one on the far right is fitted with a thin metal windshield referred to as a ballistic cap.
(Author's collection)

Belonging to the collection of the Virginia Museum of Military Vehicles (VMMV) is this first-generation M4A3. The liquid-cooled gasoline engine that powered the vehicle was labelled as the Ford GAA. It would turn out to be the preferred engine for the M4 series due to its high power output for its size and weight.
(Author's collection)

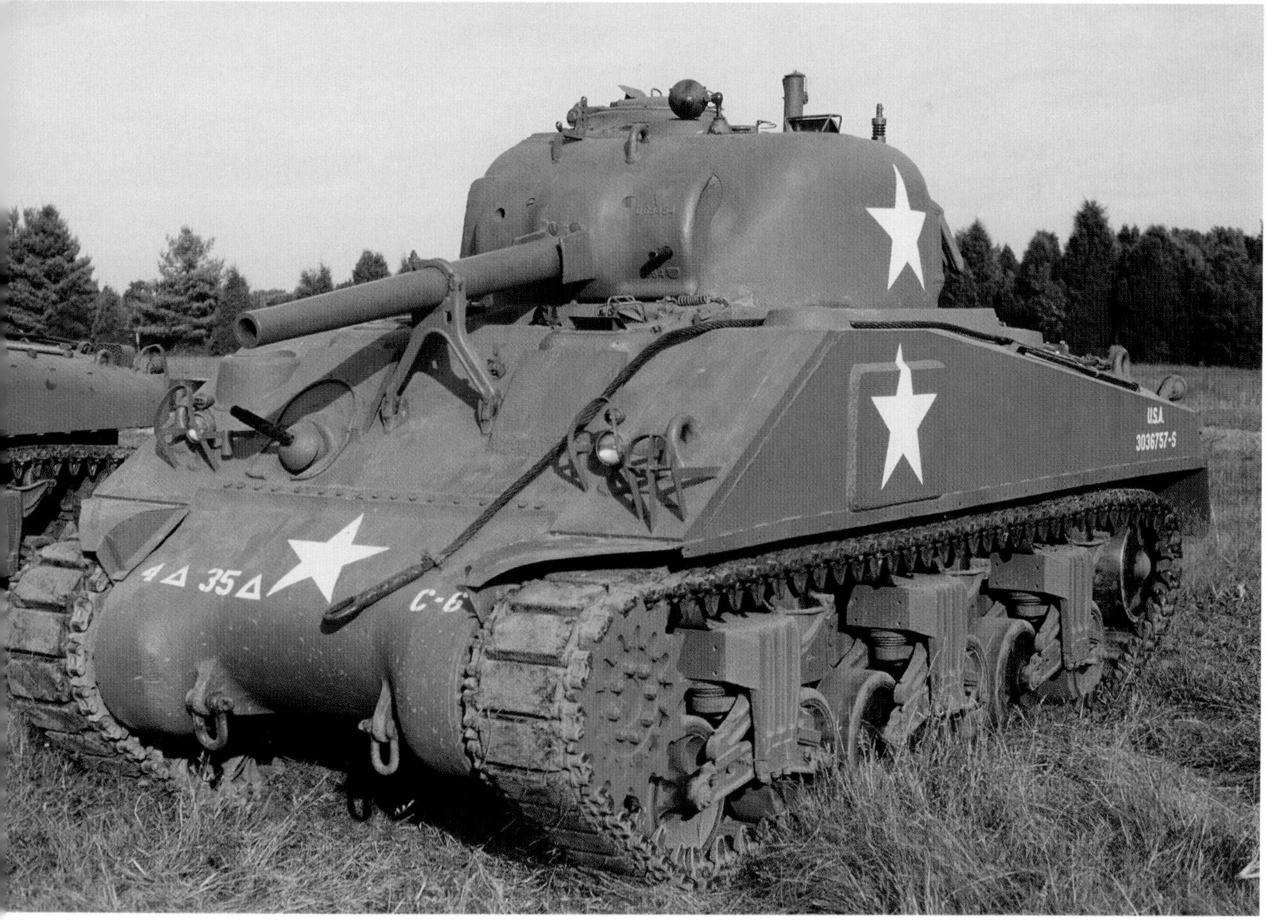
U.S.A.
3036757-S
C-6

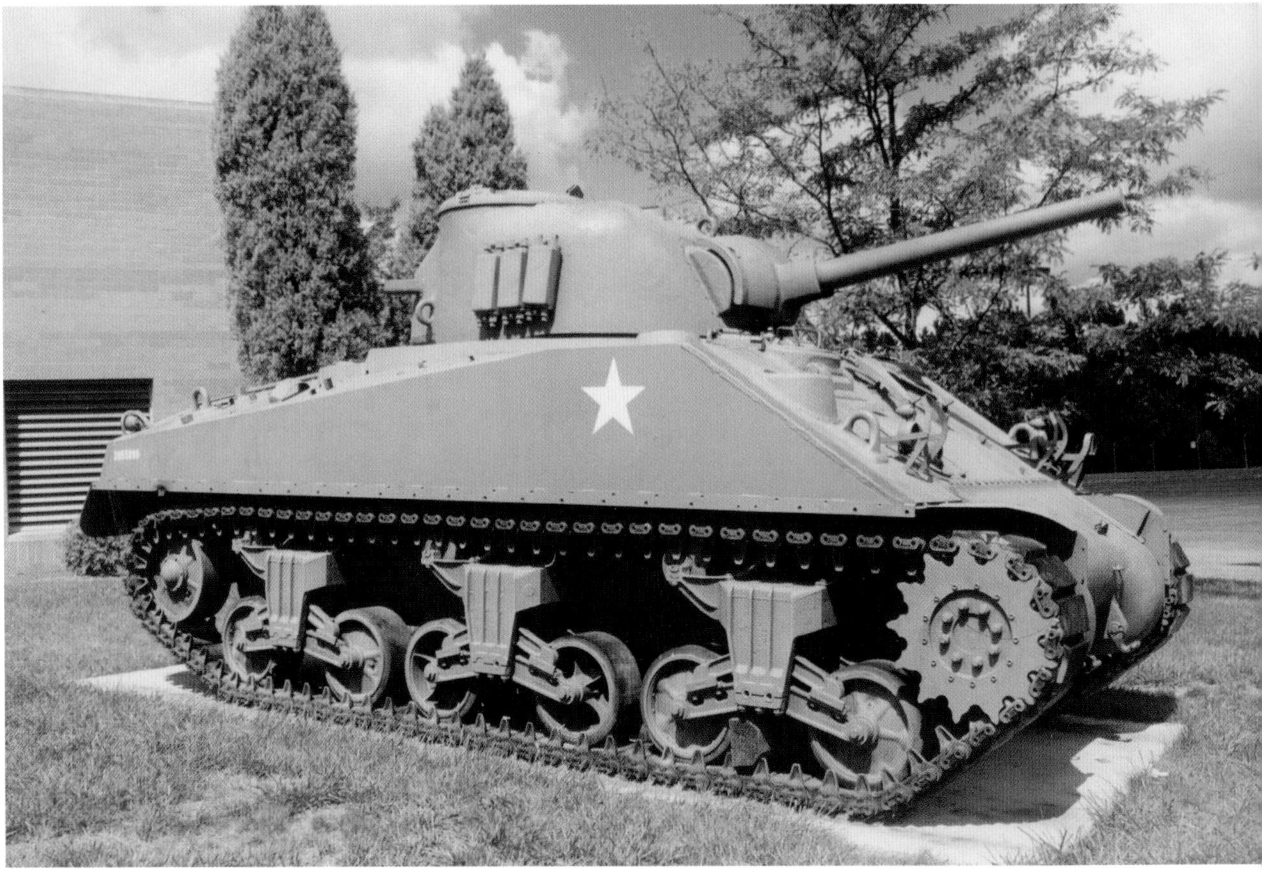

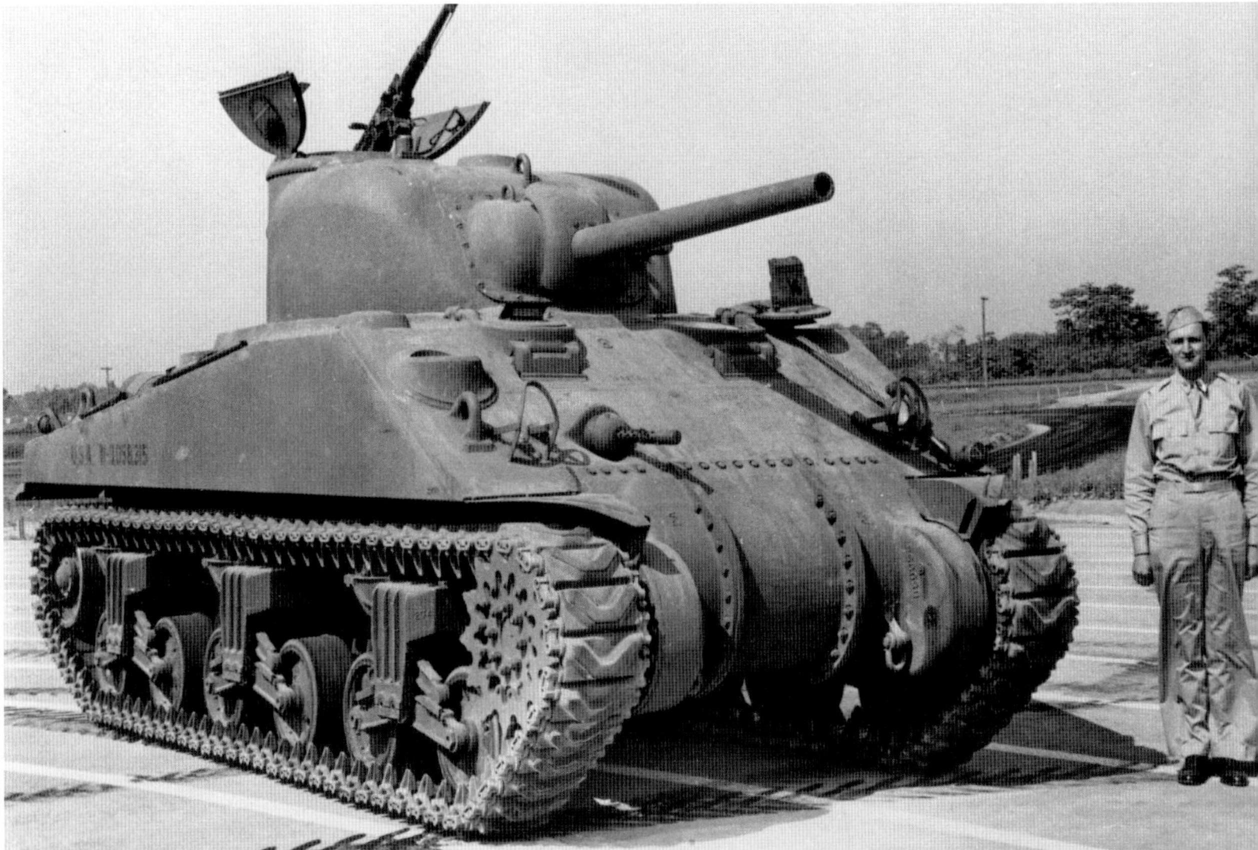

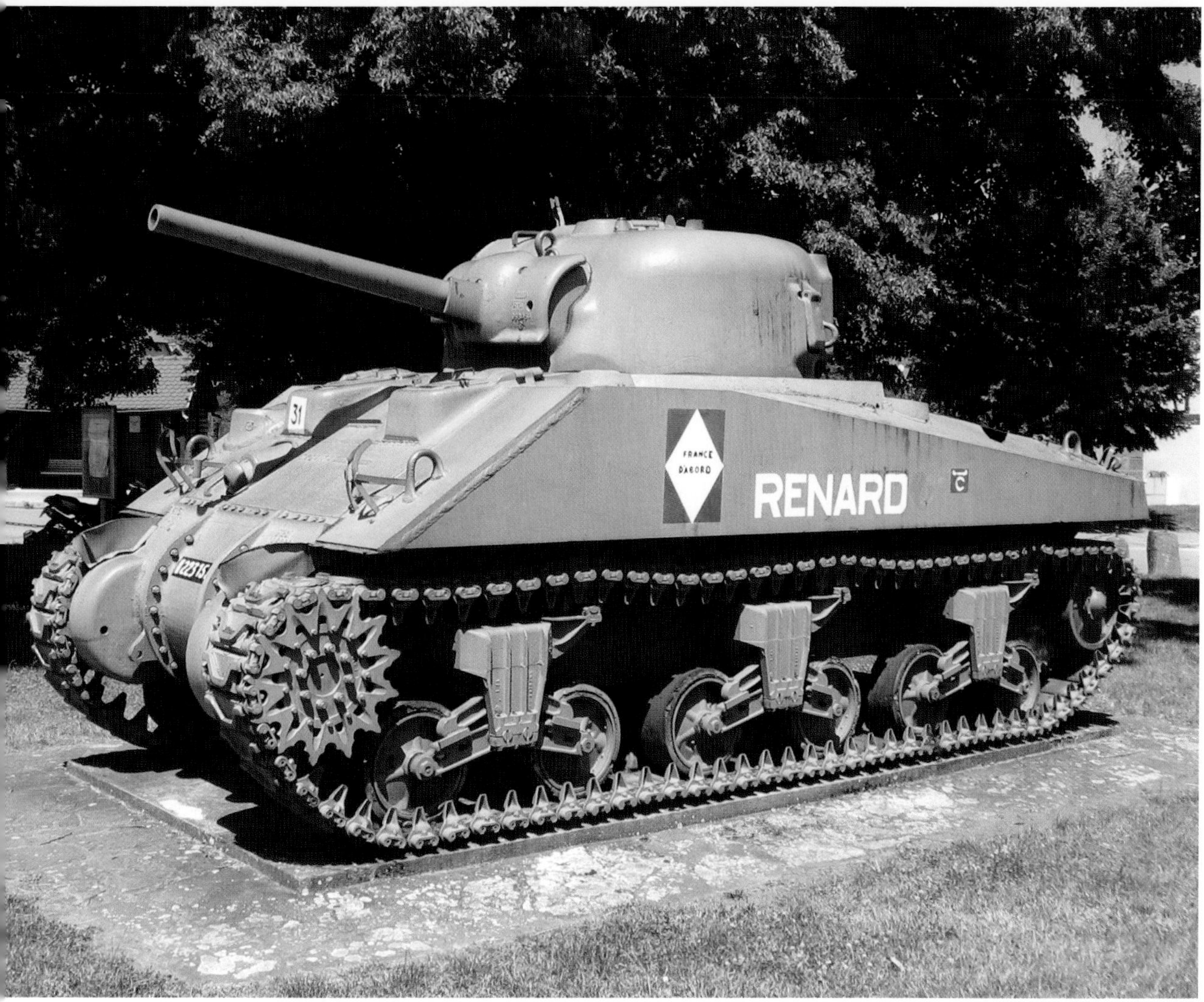
FRANCE
D'ABORD
RENARD
31

(*Opposite above*) On display somewhere in the American Mid-West is this first-generation M4A3. If sufficient production capacity had existed for the Ford GAA engine that powered the tank, the US army would have stopped production of all the other first-generation M4 series and had American industry concentrate solely on the building of the M4A3. The maximum gross horsepower of the Ford GAA engine was 500hp at 2,600rpm. *(Jim Mesko)*

(*Opposite below*) The third pilot of the M4A4 is pictured. To accommodate the large Chrysler A57 Multibank power plant, the welded hull of the M4A4 was lengthened by 11in. Ordnance Department testing of the engine arrangement on the M4A4 led them to conclude that it was the least satisfactory of all the engines that went into the M4 series of medium tanks. *(TACOM)*

(*Above*) On display in France as a monument is this M4A4. Due to a shortage of M4, M4A1 and M4A3 tanks during the Battle of the Bulge (December 1944 to January 1945), the British army returned a number of M4A2 and M4A4 tanks to the hard-pressed US army. Most of these returned Lend-Lease tanks went on to see service with General George S. Patton's Third Army. *(Pierre-Olivier Buan)*

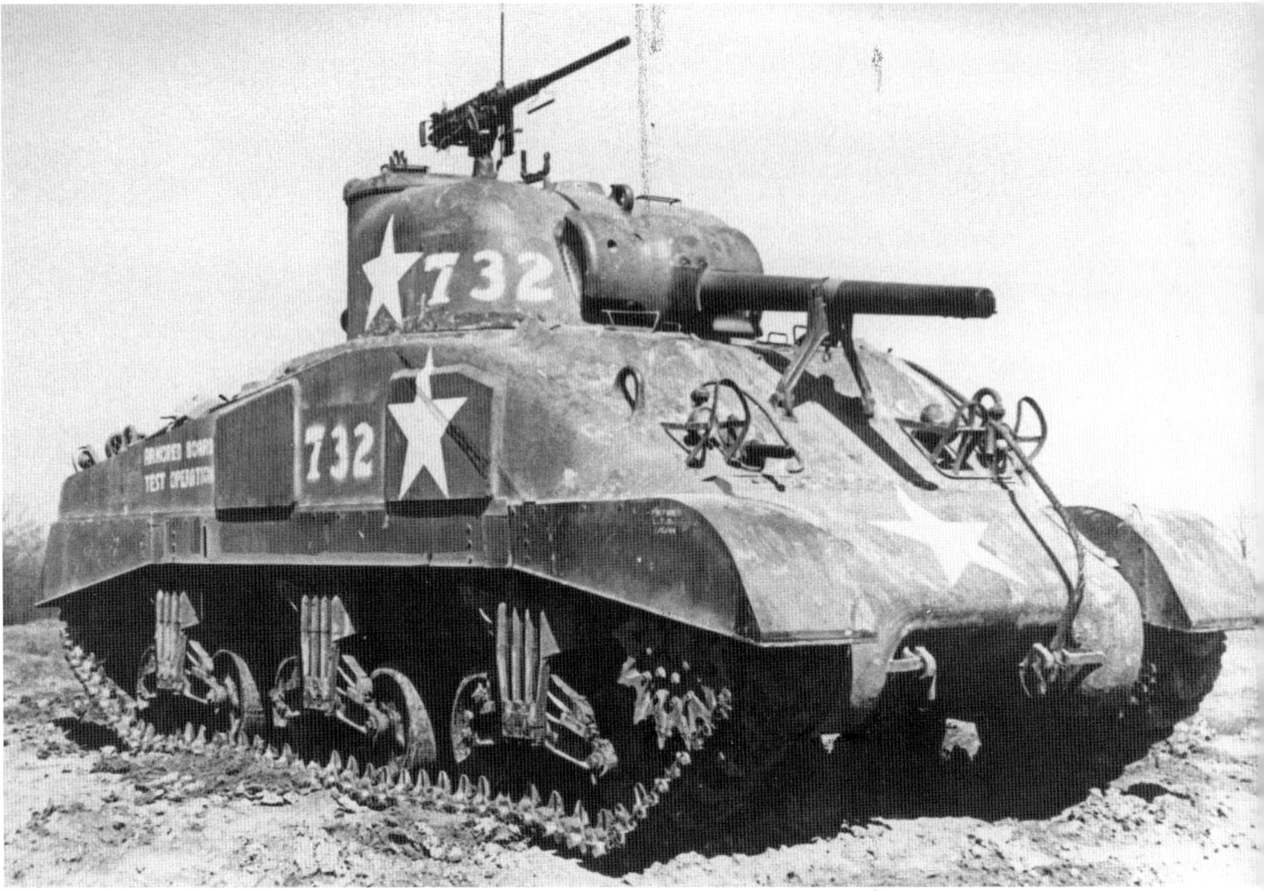
732
732

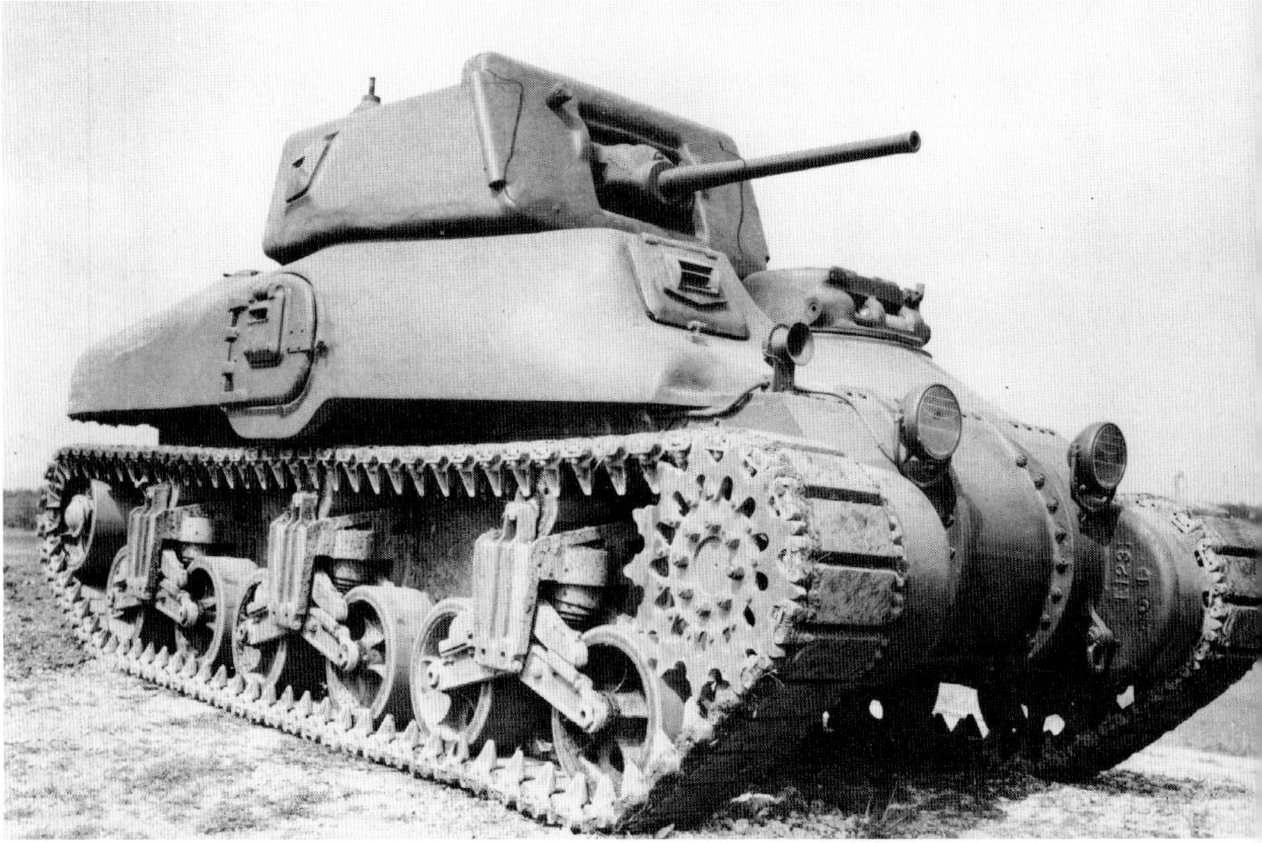

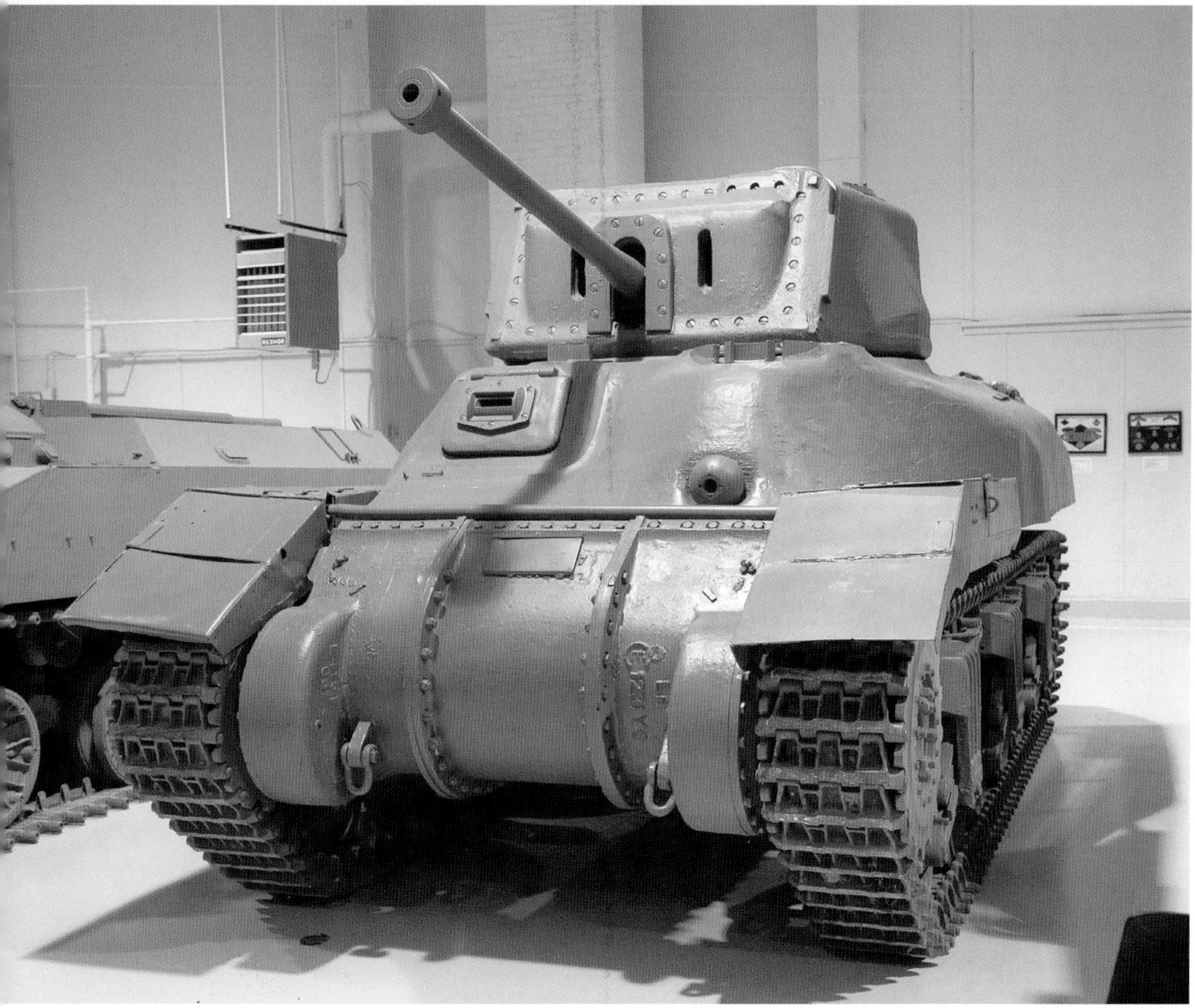

(*Opposite above*) The M4A6 pictured was powered by a Caterpillar Tractor Company radial diesel engine designated as the RD1820. Unlike any of the other types of engines that were employed to power the various models of the M4 series, the RD1820 could operate on a variety of petroleum products ranging from crude oil to gasoline, making it the first example of a multi-fuel tank power plant. *(TACOM)*

(*Opposite below*) Pictured is the Canadian-built Ram I medium pilot tank at the US army's Aberdeen Proving Ground in August 1941, armed with a 2-pounder main gun and a coaxial machine gun. Note the small one-man machine-gun-armed secondary turret borrowed from the US army version of the M3 medium tank series. The tank's chassis was based on the M3 series of medium tanks but the upper hull and turret were of Canadian design. *(TACOM)*

(*Above*) On display at a Canadian army museum is this Ram II medium tank armed with a 6-pounder main gun and coaxial machine gun. Gone is the small one-man machine-gun-armed secondary turret in the front hull. The US army eventually assigned the designation M4A5 medium tank to the Ram II. It could ride on either Canadian or American-built tracks. *(Paul Hannah)*

The tank pictured is the Canadian-built Grizzly I: a slightly modified copy of the American-designed and built M4A1. The Grizzly I can be distinguished from the American-built M4A1 by the different drive sprocket and tracks. Following British army practice the interior of the Grizzly I would be painted silver, whereas American military tanks had white interiors. *(Paul Hannah)*

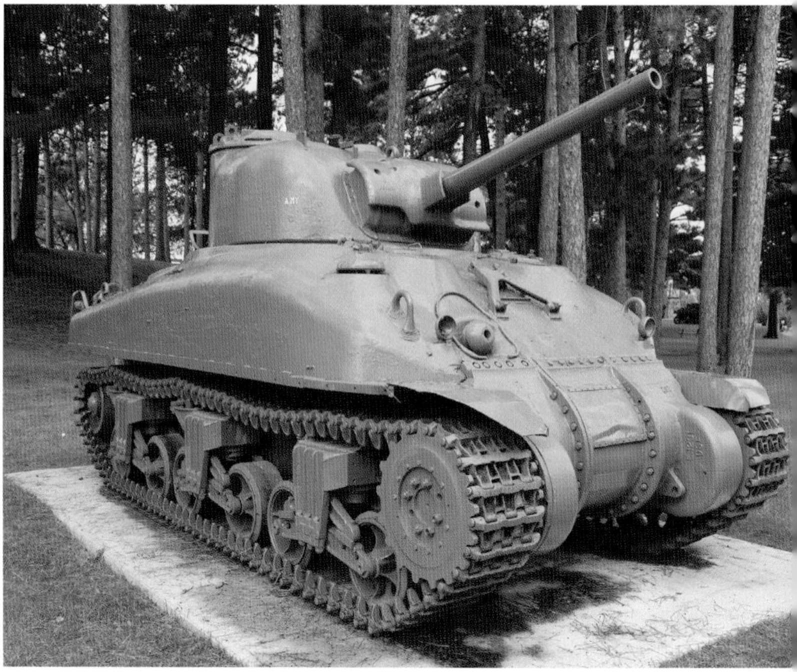

This is the first version of the Australian-designed and built Sentinel medium tank series labelled as the AC1 Cruiser. It is armed with a 2-pounder main gun and a coaxial machine gun. The phallic-looking device in the centre of the tank's front hull is the cast armour gun shield for a small-calibre machine gun. The vehicle had a length of 20ft 9in, a width of 9ft 1in and a height of 8ft 5in. *(Tank Museum)*

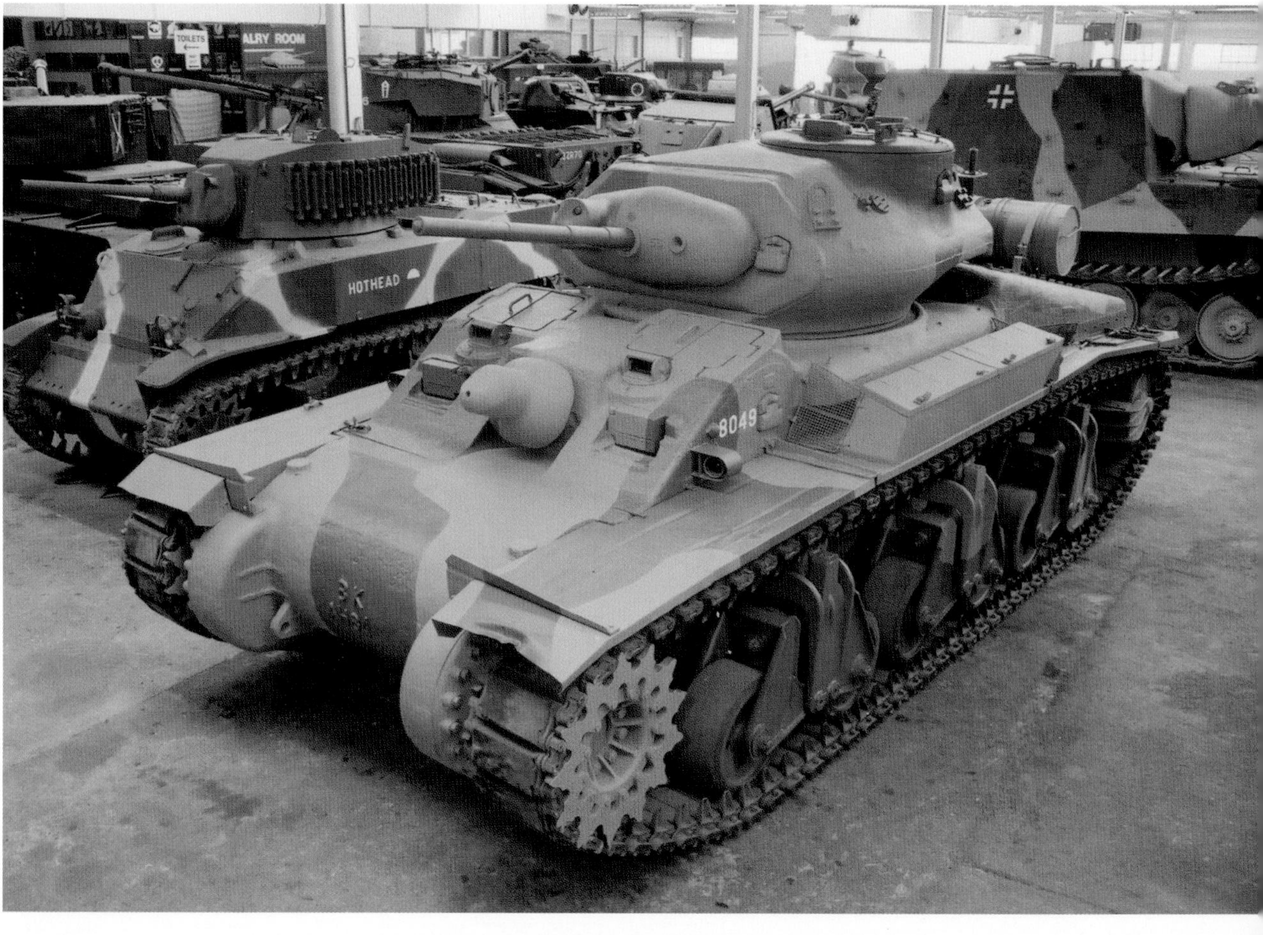
TOILETS
HOTHEAD
8049

Chapter Three

Late-War Medium Tanks

In an effort to stay ahead of German tank developments, the Red Army began in the spring of 1943 to look into up-arming the T-34 medium tank series. Between 15 May and 10 June 1943, the Design Bureau of the Artillery Plant #9 designed and built two prototypes of an 85mm gun labelled as the D5-T when intended for mounting in tanks and as the D5-S when fitting into self-propelled guns.

With the D5-T gun installed into a new and larger turret and fitted onto a modified T-34 hull, the Red Army created the T-34-85 medium tank in December 1943. Besides the 85mm main gun the tank was armed with two machine guns, one of which was the coaxial. A total of 255 units of the T-34-85 were armed with the D5-T gun before a new tank gun designated as the S-53 was introduced into the production line. It was chosen to replace the D5-T gun because it had a smaller breech and was simpler to manufacture.

A total of 23,213 units of the T-34-85 were built between January 1944 and May 1945. Due to the larger and heavier turret, the five-man T-34-85 weighed approximately 71,000lb. It would constitute the bulk of the late-war Red Army inventory of tanks. By comparison, the most numerous German medium tank of the war was the Panzer IV series of which 8,298 were built between 1939 and 1945.

Into Combat

The 85mm gun on the T-34-85 could easily penetrate the armour on the German army's Panzer IV. However, it remained at a serious disadvantage when confronting the German Panther. This was due to its substandard 85mm armour-piercing (AP) rounds that could only penetrate the sides and rear of the German tank. By contrast, the 75mm gun AP rounds of the Panther could penetrate any portion of the T-34-85's armour at a variety of ranges.

To redress the initial battlefield disadvantage the T-34-85 had when engaging the Panther, it was provided with a more potent 85mm round beginning in the summer of 1944. This allowed it to penetrate the frontal armour on the Panther at certain ranges. This improvement and the large numbers of T-34-85 tanks built outweighed any individual tactical advantages possessed by late-war German tanks.

American Second-Generation Medium Tanks

By early 1943 the US army concluded that there was no time to field a new medium tank. It would have to make do with the M4 series for the remainder of the Second World War. To this end the US army set out to upgrade the vehicle's design to improve its combat effectiveness. Those models of the original M4 series initially chosen for this upgrade programme included the M4, M4A1, M4A2 and M4A3. Eventually it was decided that the M4A4 and M4A6 were not to be part of the upgrade.

After making the decision to upgrade some of the M4 series tank models, it quickly became apparent that the large number of proposed changes would require a major redesign of the tank series. It was therefore decided in July 1943 to develop an improved 'ultimate' M4 series tank.

Rather than employ the word 'ultimate', the author will replace it with the term 'second-generation'. As not all the recommended design changes could be implemented at once, it was agreed to introduce them into the production lines of second-generation M4 series tanks in stages.

Design Improvements

A key upgrade to most of the second-generation M4 series was the mounting of a 76mm gun. As it was felt that the existing original (first-generation) M4 series turret did not provide enough room for a 76mm gun and turret crew, the larger cast armour turret from the failed T23 medium tank design was adopted to save time.

The turret from the T23 grafted onto the second-generation M4 series was complemented by a new full-width cast armour gun shield. In addition to the new turret and gun shield the second-generation M4 series were also fitted with a new raised vehicle commander's cupola. They were also designed with a thicker glacis.

An important external feature that marks all the second-generation M4 series is the absence of the driver and bow gunner hatch protrusions that are apparent on the glacis of the first-generation M4 series. This came about due to a reset of the glacis from an angle of 57 degrees on the first-generation M4 series to 47 degrees on the second-generation M4s.

An unseen second-generation M4 series improvement was a new main gun ammunition storage arrangement. Rather than being stored in the turret or upper hull, the majority of 76mm rounds were stored in the bottom of the tank's hull. Additional protection for these rounds came from being surrounded by liquid-filled canisters. In theory they would rupture upon being penetrated and quench ammunition fires. Tanks so fitted had the word 'Wet' stamped on their data plates.

Production Numbers

In total 10,883 units of the second-generation M4 series armed with a 76mm gun and having the wet ammunition storage arrangement were constructed. The breakdown between second-generation models is 3,426 units of the M4A1, 2,915 units of the M4A2 and 4,542 units of the M4A3.

The data plate on the second-generation M4A1 tanks identifies them as the M4A1 76 Gun, Wet. For the sake of brevity the author will convert this to M4A1(76)W and apply it to other second-generation M4 series tanks. Therefore the M4A2 becomes the M4A2(76)W and the M4A3 the M4A3(76)W. The latter was the preferred model employed by the US army during the last ten months of the war in North-West Europe.

Suspension Systems

To deal with the increased weight of the second-generation M4 series, the US army eventually had them fitted on the production line with the Horizontal Volute Spring Suspension (HVSS) system. Tests showed that it was far superior to the original vertical volute spring suspension (VVSS) system that the first-generation M4 series rode on, as well as early-production second-generation M4s.

The US army did not distinguish between second-generation M4 series tanks built with the VVSS system or the HVSS system. Research undertaken by Joe DeMarco at the American National Archives shows that there were 1,225 units of the M4A1(76)W built fitted with the HVSS system. Some 1,321 units of the M4A2(76)W and 2,167 units of the M4A3(76)W also received the HVSS system at the factory.

The new HVSS suspension system pushed up the weight of the tanks so fitted. As an example, the M4A3(76)W riding on the VVSS weighed approximately 67,000lb. When built with the HVSS system the tank's weight rose to approximately 74,000lb. Despite the added track width of the HVSS system, it still did not provide enough flotation for some of the off-road conditions encountered in Western Europe.

Combat Use

The initial deliveries of the second-generation M4 series to the US army forces based in England began in January 1944. They were the M4A1(76)W model that rode on the VVSS. However, none were issued to combat units in North-West France until late July 1944. This delay can be attributed to a number of different reasons. Some felt that it might cause logistical and training problems with the new 76mm gun. Others felt that the larger gun was not really necessary.

The belief that the first-generation M4 series armed with the 75mm gun would suffice till the end of the war in Western Europe lasted until July 1944. By that time US army tank units in North-West France began encountering many more Panther tanks than anticipated. As the armour on the German tank proved immune to the 75mm guns of the first-generation M4 series, the call went out to quickly field the second-generation M4 series armed with the 76mm gun.

Sadly, the much-hyped 76mm gun on the second-generation M4 series proved unequal to the task of penetrating the thick and often well-sloped armour of German late-war tanks. This problem would be partially remedied by the issue of more potent 76mm ammunition beginning in September 1944. Unfortunately, the improved 76mm ammunition would remain in short supply until the end of the war.

Some 140 units of the M4A3(76)W tank riding on the VVSS entered into service with US army tank units in Italy in August 1944. Another seventy units went to the American Seventh Army, which invaded Southern France that same month. The M4A3(76)W riding on the VVSS did not arrive in North-West Europe until September 1944. Those fitted with the HVSS system began showing up in North-West Europe in December 1944.

Second-Generation 75mm Gun Armed Tank

With the production of the second-generation M4A1, M4A2 and M4A3 tanks armed with the 76mm gun, the production of the first-generation M4 series armed with the 75mm gun came to an end: the M4 in January 1944, the M4A1 in December 1943, the M4A2 in May 1944, the M4A3 and M4A4 in September 1943, and the M4A6 in February 1944.

It was decided by the US army to continue to produce a single model of a second-generation M4 series armed with the 75mm gun, which the author will label as the M4A3(75)W. It had a wet stowage arrangement and the reset glacis of the 76mm gun armed versions.

The M4A3(75)W cast armour turret was almost the same as fitted on the original first-generation M4 series. It did feature a number of improvements; most notably, the addition of a loader's hatch. A total of 3,071 units were built between February 1944 and March 1945. Approximately 2,420 were produced with VVSS and 651 with the HVSS system.

Foreign Users

The bulk of the M4A1(76)W production run riding on the VVSS was provided to the British army under Lend-Lease. In British nomenclature, the M4A1(76)W was referred to as the 'Sherman IIA'. The British were also supplied with five units of the M4A2(76)W riding on the HVSS system. They designated it as the 'Sherman IIIAY'; however, none were ever used in combat.

Unhappiness with the poor penetrative abilities of the American 76mm gun on the M4A1(76)W led the British army to transfer the majority of them to British and Commonwealth army tank units fighting in Italy. This was done as it was felt that the threat from late-war German tanks in that theatre of operations was far less than would be encountered in North-West Europe.

The British army also transferred 180 units of their Lend-Lease-supplied M4A1(76)W tanks to the 1st Polish Armoured Division fighting in North-West

Europe. From US army stockpiles in Western Europe the Free French army would receive a small number of M4A1(76)W and M4A3(76)W tanks riding on the VVSS.

Of the 2,915 units built of the M4A2(76)W tanks riding on the VVSS, the Red Army was shipped 2,073 units under Lend-Lease. In addition, they received 183 units of the M4A2(76)W riding on the HVSS system between May and June 1945, too late to see combat on the Eastern Front.

The Sherman Firefly

The British army did not make the same mistake as the US army in underestimating the number of Panther tanks that might be encountered upon the invasion of the European continent. They therefore had in service prior to the invasion 350 units of a modified first-generation M4 series tank armed with a 17-pounder (76.2mm) gun. By the end of the war in Europe, approximately 2,000 units had been built.

The majority of the 17-pounder armed tanks were based upon the first-generation M4A4 tanks. In British army service they were referred to as the 'Sherman VC'. Less numerous were those constructed on the chassis of the M4 and labelled as the 'Sherman IC' by the British army. Both 17-pounder armed models were generally referred to by British tankers as the 'Firefly', although this name was never officially adopted by the British army.

The 17-pounder gun of the Firefly had the penetrative power to destroy both Panther and Tiger tanks. This was something that the 76mm main gun on the second-generation M4 series tanks could not do except at very close ranges. This fact prompted the US army to ask for a supply of Fireflies from the British army inventory in August 1944. The British responded that they could not afford to divert any of their Fireflies but that if the US army could supply first-generation M4 series tank 75mm of the appropriate types, 'a limited number of 17-pounder guns and conversion service may be available.'

The US army could not spare any first-generation M4 series of the appropriate types in the autumn of 1944 but could in February 1945. At that time an agreement was reached between the US army and the British army that 160 first-generation M4 and M4A3 tanks would be converted. Around 100 conversions were completed between March and April 1945 before the programme was cancelled due to the imminent collapse of Nazi Germany.

Of the 100 US army-supplied first-generation M4 series tanks that the British army had converted to be fitted with the 17-pounder, eighty units were shipped to the US army in North-West Europe, while the British army retained the remaining twenty units at Hayes Arsenal in the United Kingdom. It is not thought that any of the Fireflies converted for the US army were distributed to front-line units before the German surrender on 8 May 1945.

Crusader

With an urgent need to build as many tanks as possible in the shortest amount of time, the British army decided to base its first wartime-designed cruiser tank on the failed Covenanter. By tweaking the design of the tank, which included lengthening its hull and suspension system, British industry came up with the Cruiser Tank Mk VI (A15) that they named the 'Crusader'. A total of 5,300 units were built between 1940 and 1943.

There would be three models of the gun-armed Crusader built. The first was armed with a 2-pounder and two machine guns; one being the coaxial and the other mounted in a sub-turret at the front of the tank's hull. It had a five-man crew. The second model was still armed with a 2-pounder but had the machine-gun-armed sub-turret removed, bringing the crew down to four men. The final model of the Crusader was up-armed with a 6-pounder, causing the crew to drop to only three men.

Despite being up-gunned and having more armour protection than fitted to previous cruiser tanks, the approximately 44,000lb Crusader proved no match for the German medium tanks it encountered in North Africa between 1940 and 1943. As with all the other previous cruiser tanks, it also proved unreliable. The Crusader would be pulled from front-line service by the British army in May 1943 and there-after employed as a training tank or converted to other roles. The tank was powered by the Nuffield Liberty engine.

Cavalier

Using the Crusader as a base, British industry at the request of the British army sought to design and build a new more capable cruiser tank. Despite input from British army combat reports, British industry once again came up with another badly-botched tank design. It was designated as the Cruiser Tank Mk VII (A24) and named the 'Cavalier'.

Armed with a 6-pounder and up to two machine guns, the British army ordered 503 units of the five-man Cavalier in 1941. It was ordered without a trial test period, such was the urgent need for tanks. Much to the British army's dismay, the approximately 59,000lb Cavalier was even more mechanically unreliable than the Crusader. They quickly relegated it to the training role with about half the inventory later converted to other roles.

Centaur

There had been the expectation that the Cavalier could be equipped with a new transmission and a more powerful Rolls-Royce Meteor gasoline engine that would improve its reliability. However, a shortage of the Meteor engine caused the British army to order an interim tank fitted with the new transmission and the existing Nuffield Liberty engine. That interim tank was the Cruiser Tank Mk VIII (A27L) named the 'Centaur'. The letter 'L' in the vehicle's designation stood for the Liberty engine.

In anticipation of the Meteor engine becoming available for the Centaur in the near future, the tank's engine compartment was designed to accommodate both the existing Nuffield Liberty engine and the Meteor engine. The British army ordered 1,821 units of the Centaur with initial delivery of the tank beginning in 1942. As with the Cavalier, the Centaur had a five-man crew and most were armed with a 6-pounder and up to two machine guns.

The Centaur weighed approximately 64,000lb and was therefore even more under-powered than the Cavalier. Reflecting its obvious limitations, the British army restricted it to being used as a training vehicle or in other secondary roles until such time as the anticipated new and more powerful Meteor engine was available and could be retrofitted to the Centaur inventory.

Cromwell

The follow-up to the failed Centaur was the Cruiser Tank Mk VIII (A27M) named the 'Cromwell'. The letter 'M' in the vehicle's designation stood for its Meteor engine. Besides those late-production Centaurs brought up to the Cromwell standard with the fitting of a Meteor engine, 2,499 new-built units of the Cromwell were constructed between 1943 and 1945 in a number of different sub-variants.

The five-man Cromwell along with the American M4 series of tanks were the standard equipment for British army armoured divisions in 1944 and 1945. The first model of the Cromwell was armed with a 6-pounder with all subsequent models armed with a 75mm gun and up to two machine guns. The gun itself was a bored-out 6-pounder that was designed to use the same 75mm gun ammunition fired by the 75mm-gun-armed first-generation M4 series medium tanks.

The approximately 62,000lb Cromwell was a major improvement compared to other previous cruiser tanks, especially in terms of reliability. However, its 75mm gun lacked the penetrative power to deal with late-war German tanks. The majority of Cromwell tanks built were of riveted construction, with only 126 late-production units being of welded construction. By way of contrast, German industry had begun the construction of welded tanks in the early 1930s.

Challenger

To make up for the firepower disadvantage of the Cromwell, the British army rushed into production a stopgap variant named the Cruiser Tank (A30) and known as the 'Challenger'. It consisted of a lengthened Cromwell chassis fitted with a tall angular turret armed with a 17-pounder gun and a coaxial machine gun. The five-man tank weighed approximately 73,000lb; 200 units were ordered with the first production units appearing in early 1944.

The British army's unhappiness with the Challenger was due to it being plagued by numerous design flaws. This led to the decision in early 1944 to concentrate on the development and fielding of the Sherman Firefly in lieu of the Challenger. The Sherman Firefly had been the back-up tank if the Challenger failed to live up to expectations. In spite of the Challenger's design issues, the British army decided in August 1944 to issue the existing stock to those British army armoured divisions serving in Western Europe equipped with the Cromwell.

The constant design failures that came to be represented by the British army's pre-war and wartime-designed cruiser tanks and others is summed up nicely by respected British historian Alistair Horne in the following quote: 'The story of Britain's tank inferiority all through World War II is one of the great disgraces of her military history.'

Comet

Early on it became clear to some that the Challenger was a design dead-end. However, there remained a pressing requirement for a 17-pounder-armed version of the Cromwell in the British army. Vickers therefore came up with a modified 17-pounder gun labelled as the Gun, QF [Quick Firing], Tank 77mm that was just a bit less effective in its penetrative abilities than the original weapon.

A new larger and heavier turret was designed to accommodate the 77mm main gun and a coaxial machine gun on a Cromwell chassis. To compensate for the extra weight of the new turret the Cromwell's suspension system was upgraded. This included the addition of return rollers on what was still a Christie suspension system.

The combination of a new turret with an upgraded Cromwell chassis became the Cruiser Tank (A-34) and was named the 'Comet'. The five-man tank weighed approximately 79,000lb and was also armed with two machine guns. Construction of the Comet began in September 1944, with the first units being deployed in North-West Europe in December 1944. In total, 1,186 units of the tank were built.

The Comet was the first cruiser tank to be considered something of a success in service, being both reliable and mounting a gun that could defeat late-war German tanks. However, these features were offset by the fact that the tank remained poorly-protected compared to the Panther.

Centurion

The last of the wartime-designed British army cruiser tanks was named the 'Centurion' and assigned the General Staff designation A41. Its major design charac-teristics were laid down in October 1943. It was intended from the beginning that it should possess parity in both firepower and armour protection with the Panther. This meant it was to be armed with a 17-pounder and a coaxial weapon and also be heavily armoured.

At approximately 100,000lb the Centurion weighed about the same as the Panther, which the German army considered a medium tank. In the wartime Red Army and US army the Centurion would have been considered a heavy tank.

Due to the numerous tank design failures of British industry before and during the Second World War, the design of the four-man Centurion was entrusted to a government-sponsored tank design board. The engine for the tank was an up-rated version of the Meteor engine that powered the Cromwell. The final design of the Centurion was approved in February 1944. In reality, it was no longer a cruiser tank but a 'universal' that could perform both the role of cruiser and infantry tank.

Due to a shortage of industrial capacity, the building of the Centurion prototype did not start until January 1945 with delivery of the first prototype to the British army in April 1945. The testing process went so well that it was quickly decided to ship the first six prototypes to North-West Europe in the hope that they could engage German late-war tanks. However, this was not to be and they did not arrive until after the German surrender. The production version of the first Centurion model entered service in 1946.

Churchill

In the summer of 1941, the first production units of the Infantry Tank Mk IV (A22) which was assigned the name 'Churchill' were delivered to the British army. Reflecting the British army's desperate need for tanks at the time, it was rushed into service without a trial test period, as were so many of its tanks. As can be expected, this led to an endless series of early design changes to the early-production units of the tank.

The original production model of the Churchill was armed with a turret-mounted 2-pounder and a front hull-mounted 3-inch howitzer. In the second production model of the tank built in small numbers the gun positions were reversed, with the 2-pounder in the front hull and the 3-inch howitzer in the turret. As neither weapon possessed the penetrative powers to deal with German medium tanks, the third production model of the Churchill was armed only with a turret-mounted 6-pounder gun and two machine guns.

Eventually, the Churchill was armed with the same British-designed and built 75mm gun that had been fitted into later production units of the Cromwell. The Churchill was therefore under-gunned throughout its service life. On the positive side, it was a well-armoured tank; a feature that was much appreciated by those who served on it.

The Churchill had a five-man crew and weighed approximately 87,000lb. The final production tally of the tank is listed as 5,640 units, with many of those eventually converted to serve in a variety of secondary non-armed roles.

British industry was tasked in December 1943 to come up with a tank with enough firepower and armoured protection to deal with late-war German tanks on equal terms. The result of this development effort was the Infantry Tank (A43) named the 'Black Prince'. It was a five-man tank armed with a 17-pounder in a new turret design mounted on a widened chassis of a Churchill. Only six trial test units of the approximately 112,000lb vehicle were built before the project was cancelled in favour of the Centurion.

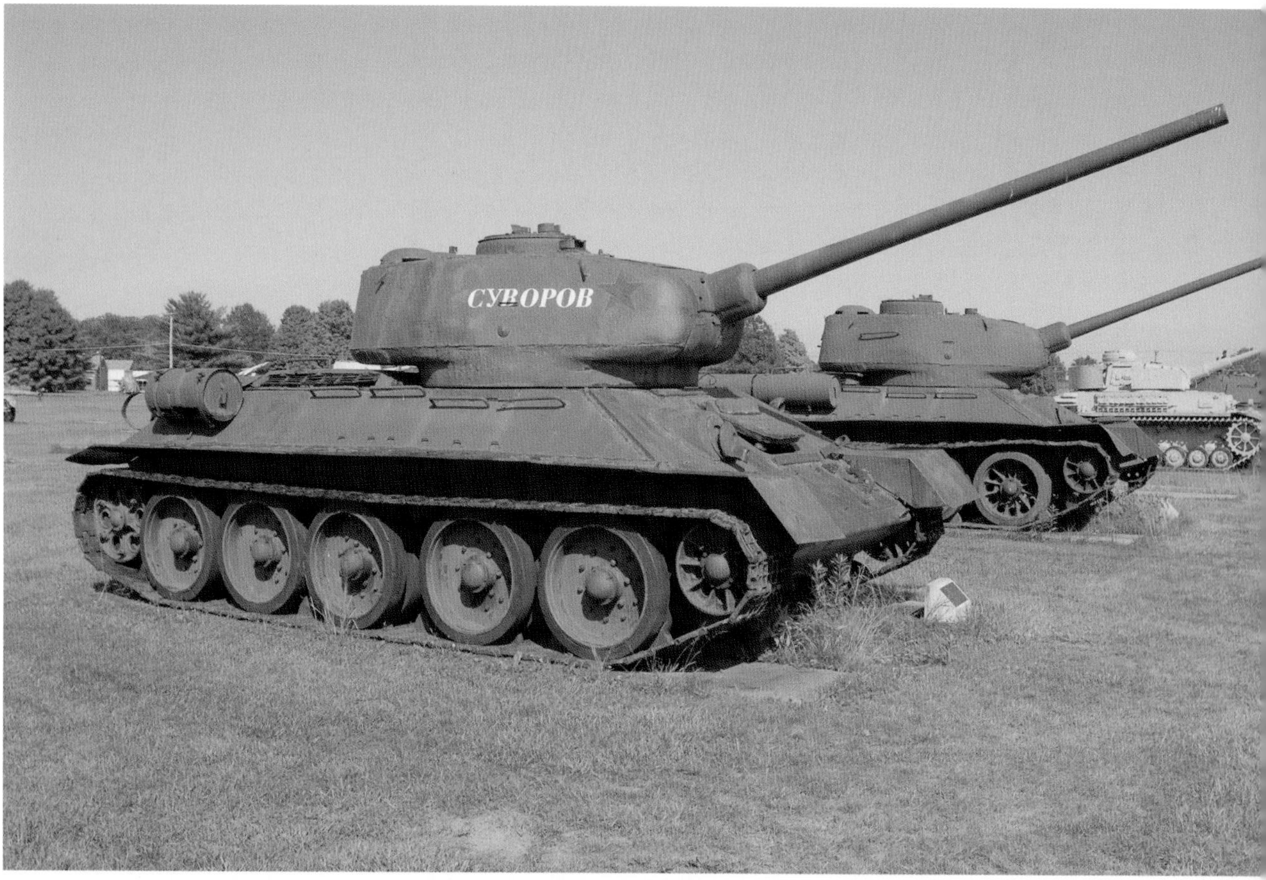
СУВОРОВ

(*Above*) Pictured are two late-production T-34-85 tanks. Both of these can be identified as the T-34-85 Model 1945 or later by their squared front fenders. Earlier models had rounded front fenders. The T-34-85 Model 1944 and all subsequent models were armed with the same S-53 85mm main gun, which had an armoured collar covering a portion of the gun where it protrudes from the tank's gun shield as seen in this image. *(Author's collection)*

(*Opposite above*) A number of very early-production T-34-85 Model 1943 tanks are visible in this picture. They were armed with the D5-T 85mm main gun that can be identified by the distinctive thick circular bolted collar covering a portion of the gun where it protrudes from the tank's gun shield. Note the large whip antenna on the right front hull of the tanks pictured. *(Bob Fleming)*

(*Opposite below*) Pictured in German hands is a captured T-34-85 Model 1944 armed with the S-53 85mm main gun which is indicated by its plain armoured collar. It is an early-production unit as indicated by the serrated and pierced rubber-rimmed road wheels and the two-piece overhead split hatch visible on the vehicle commander's cupola. *(Patton Museum)*

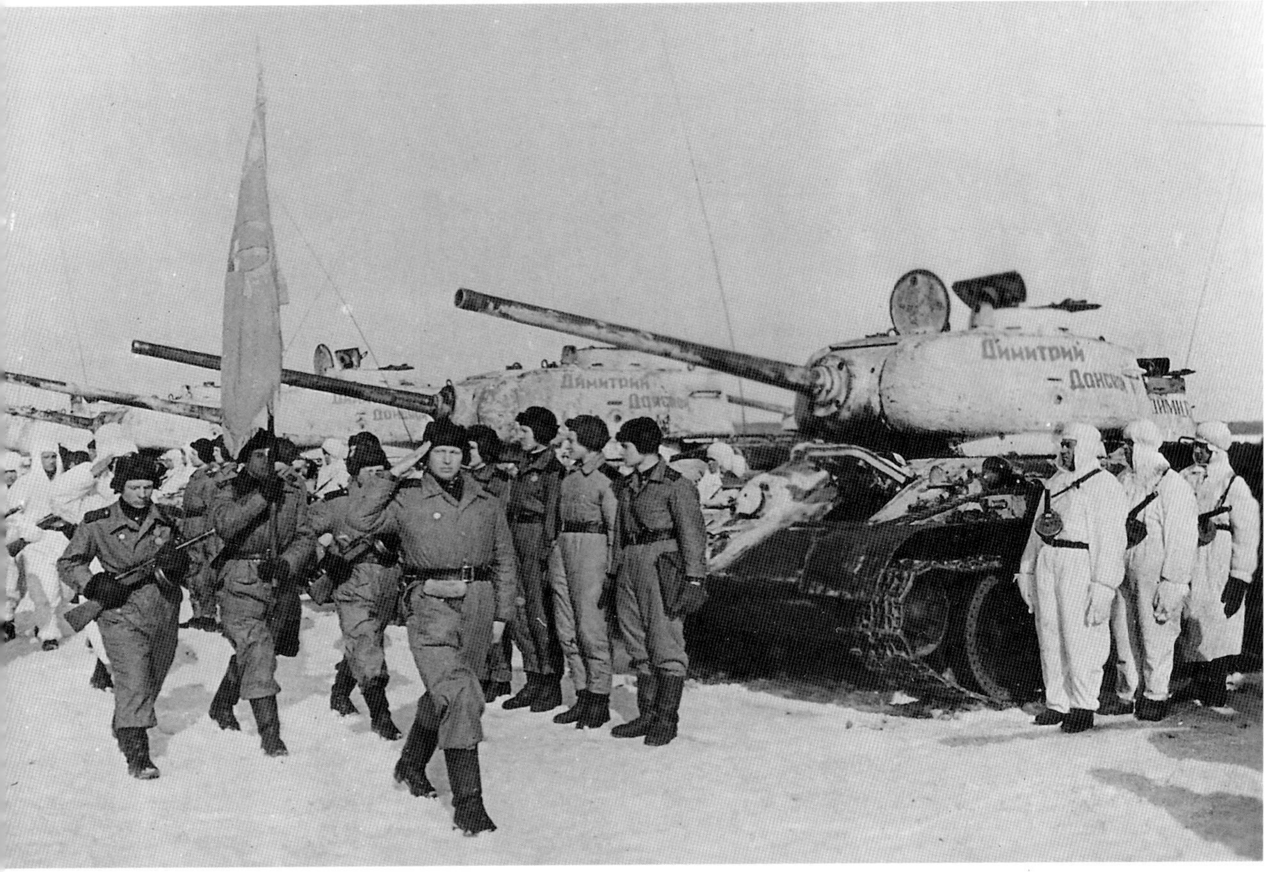
Димитрий

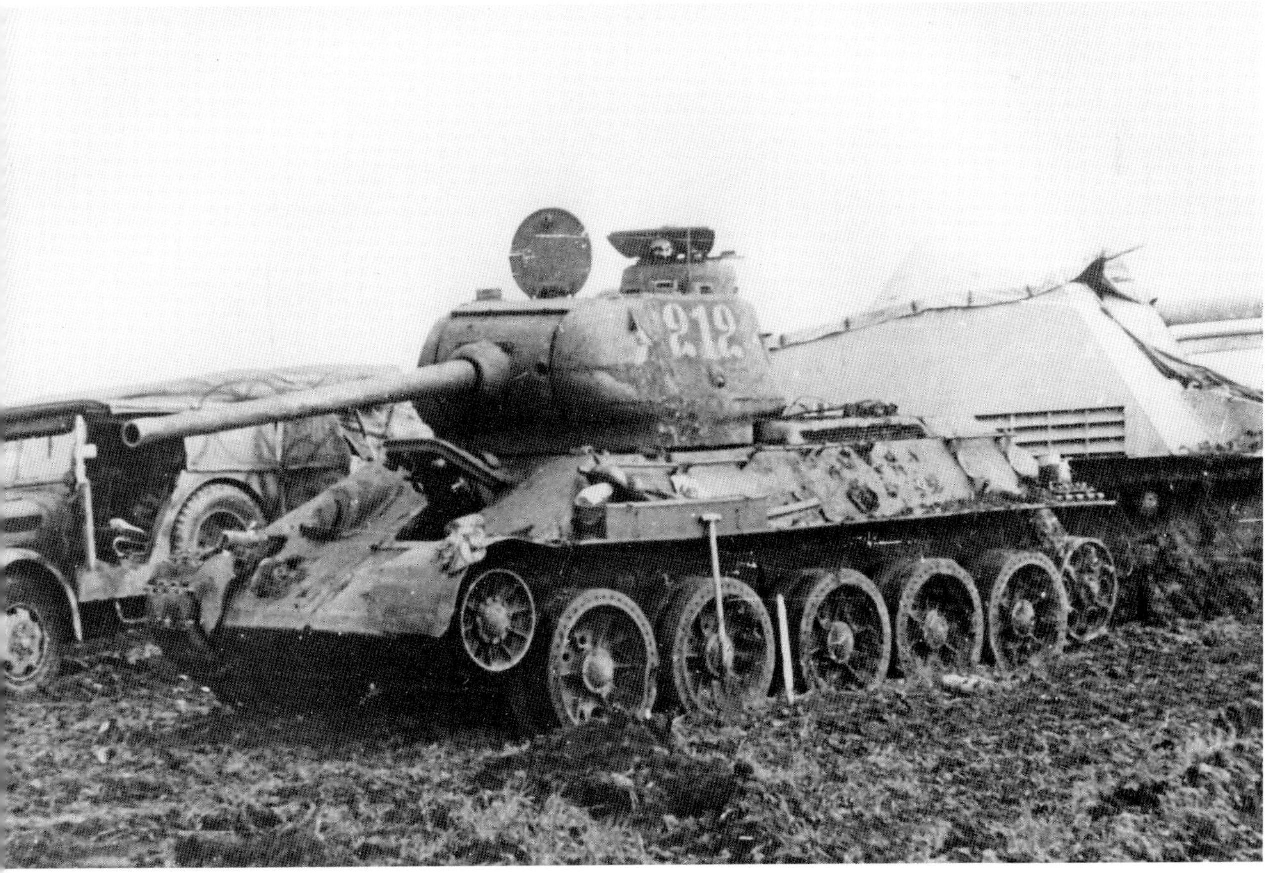
212

(*Above*) On display at a Canadian army museum is this T-34-85 Model 1945 or later. The sides and rear of the turret are 75mm thick. Side hull armour was 60mm thick, with the rear hull engine plate being 47mm thick. The solid rubber rims of the concave road wheels seen on this vehicle first appeared in 1945. They replaced the original serrated and pierced rubber-rimmed road wheels. (*Paul and Loren Hannah*)

(*Opposite above*) A column of Red Army T-34-85 tanks is pictured moving through a damaged Eastern European city on the way to Berlin, the capital of Nazi Germany. The vehicle in the foreground can be identified as a T-34-85 Model 1944 by the rounded front fenders. Beginning in early 1944 the radio for the T-34-85 series was moved from the right front hull to a position inside the turret. (*Patton Museum*)

(*Opposite below*) At the same time as the radio for the T-34-85 series was being relocated to the turret on the production line, the large whip antenna formerly positioned on the vehicle's right front hull was moved to a location just in front of the vehicle commander's cupola as visible in this picture. The rectangular bulge seen on the turret side indicates that this particular tank has an electric turret drive. The turrets on early production T-34-85 series tanks had only manual traverse. This tank also has the late-production one-piece overhead hatch cover for the vehicle commander's cupola. (*Chris Hughes*)

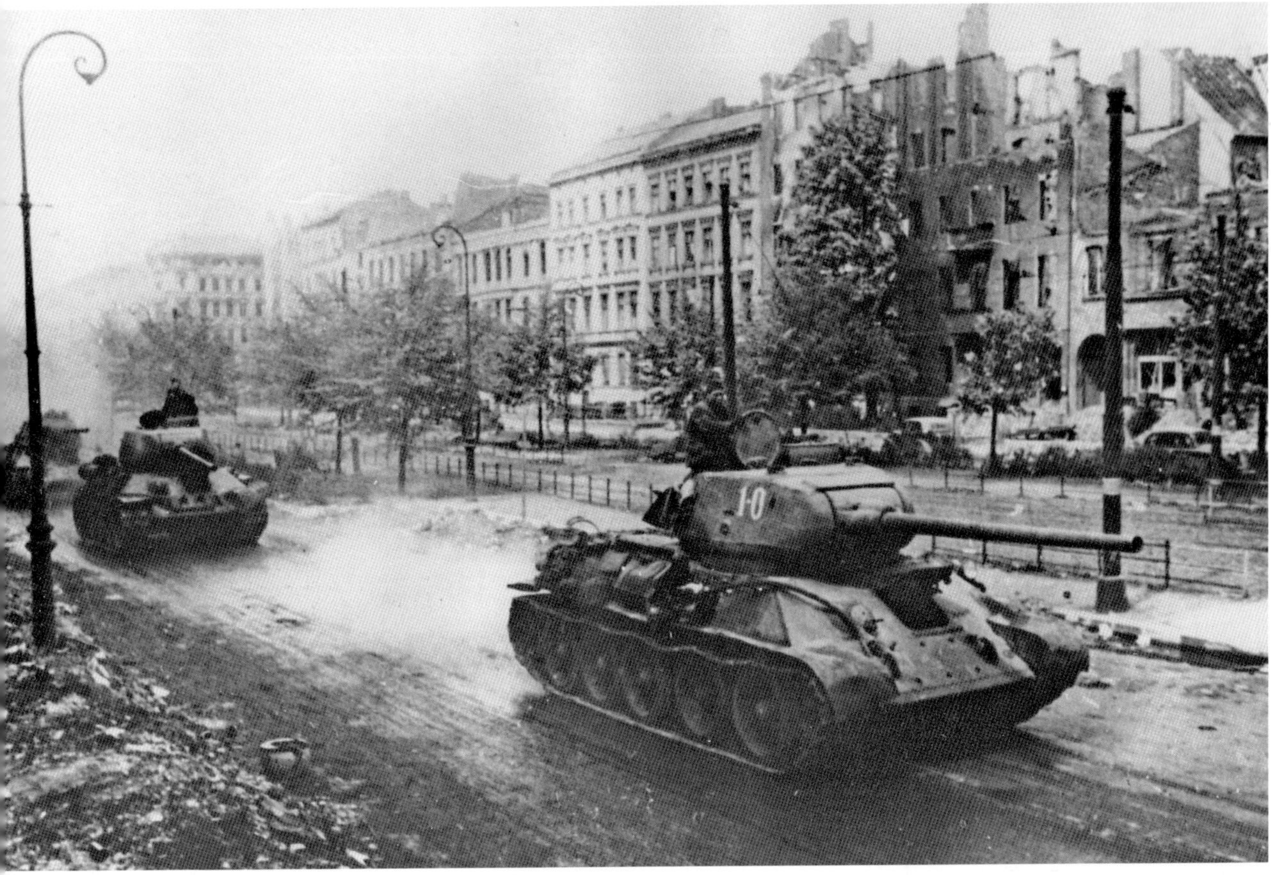

1-0

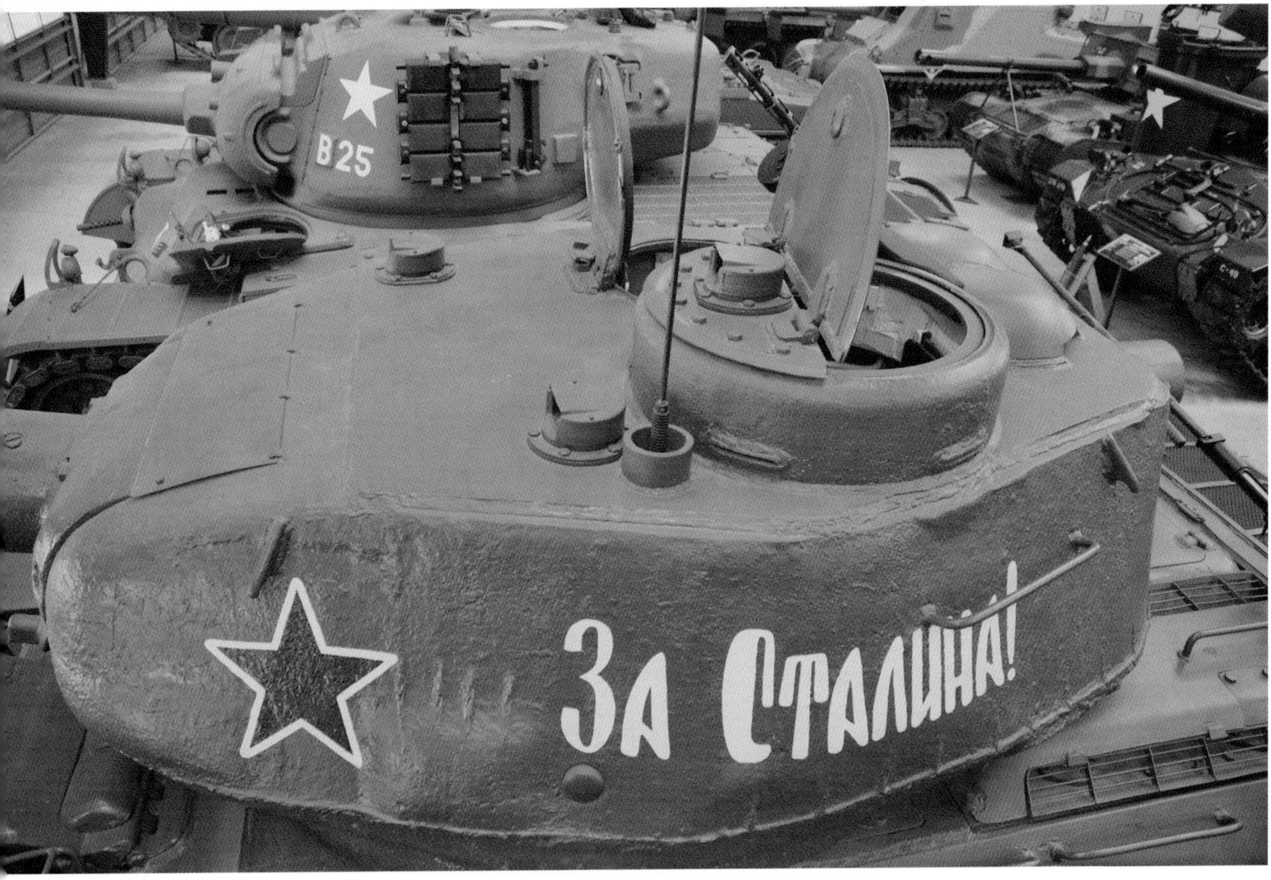

B25
За Сталина!

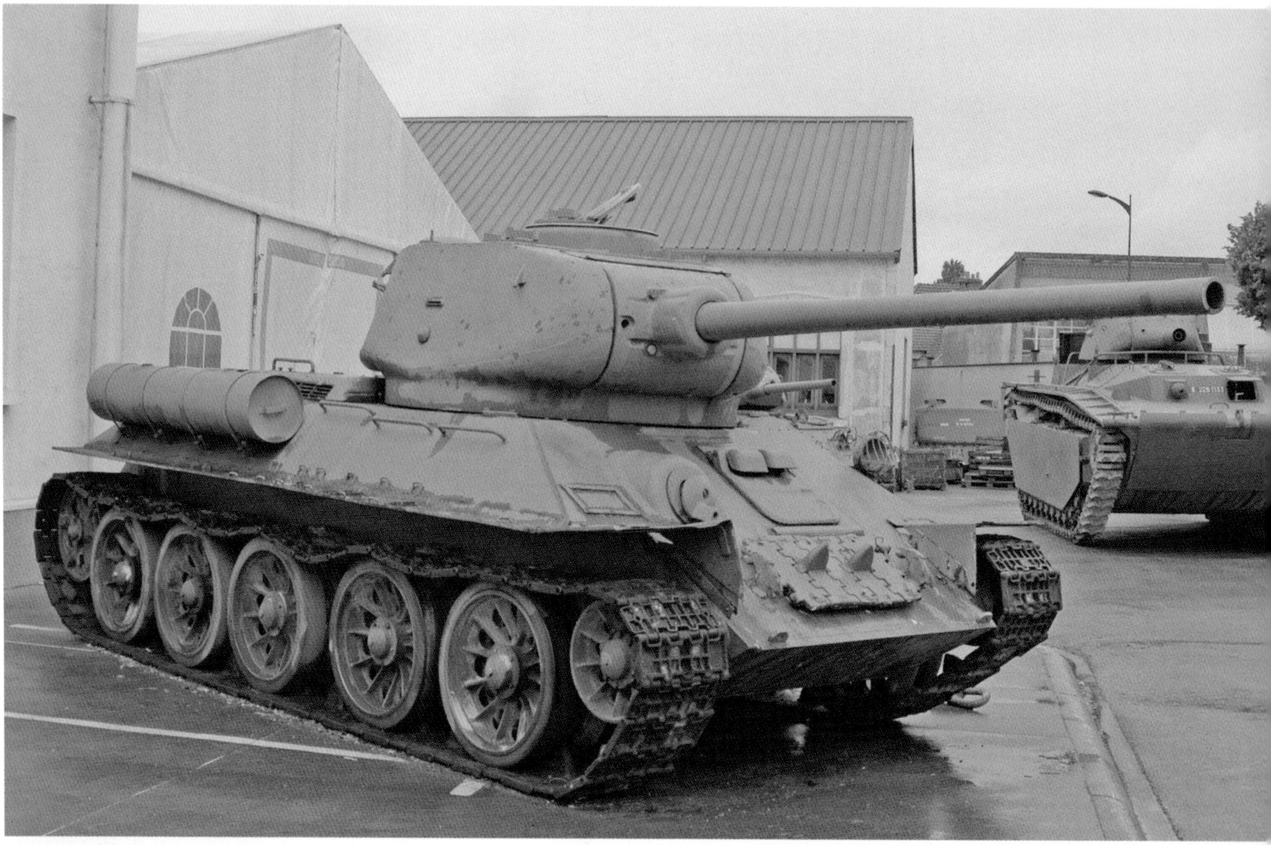

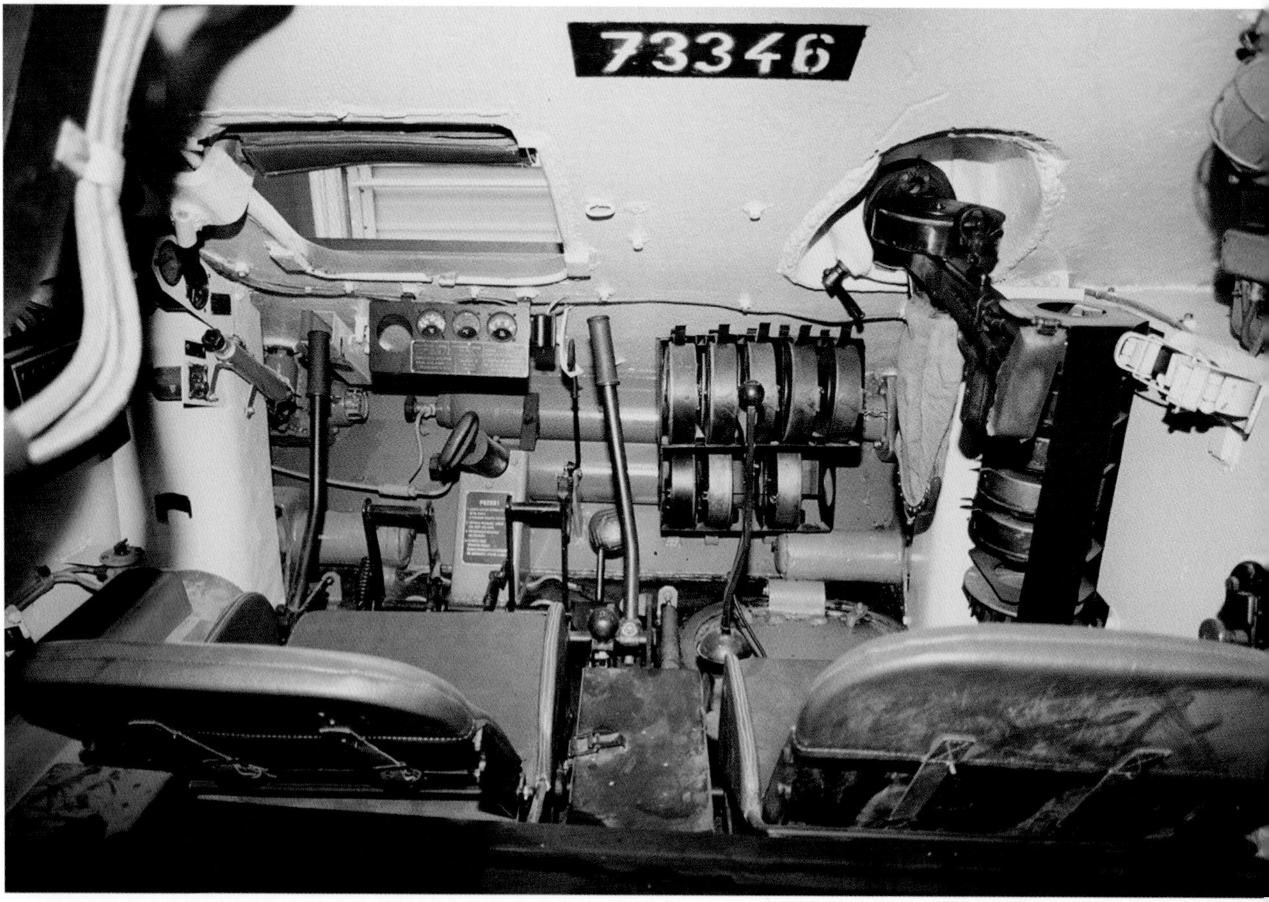
73346

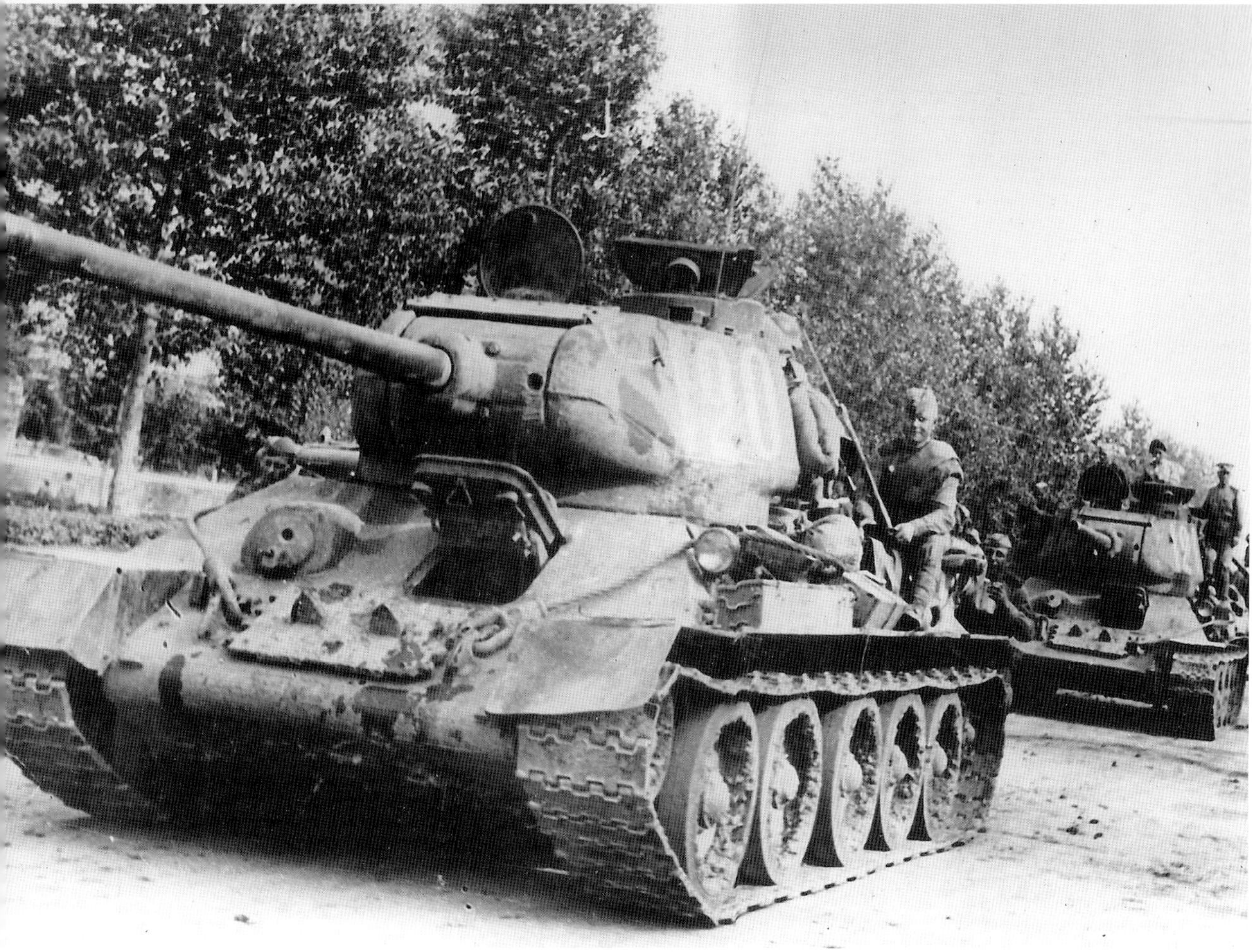

(*Opposite above*) Belonging to the French Army Tank Museum is this T-34-85 Model 1945 or later tank. It has the wartime production rubber-rimmed cast spoked road wheels built alongside the more common rubber-rimmed concave road wheels. The standard production T-34-85 series glacis plate formed a sharp angle where it was welded to the lower front hull plate as seen in this photograph. *(Christophe Vallier)*

(*Above*) This picture shows an early-production T-34-85 series tank turret with the original vehicle commander's cupola that had a two-piece overhead split hatch. Note that this T-34-85 turret is mounted on the original T-34 series hull as indicated by the rounded edge where the front hull glacis plate merges into the lower front hull of the tank. *(Bob Fleming)*

(*Opposite below*) This picture taken from under the breech ring of the 85mm main gun on a restored T-34-85 Model 1945 or later tank shows the driver/mechanic's position on the left and the machine-gunner's position on the right. Due to constant personnel shortages it was not uncommon to find the T-34-85 series tanks being operated by four-man crews with the machine-gunner's position being left vacant. *(Chris Hughes)*

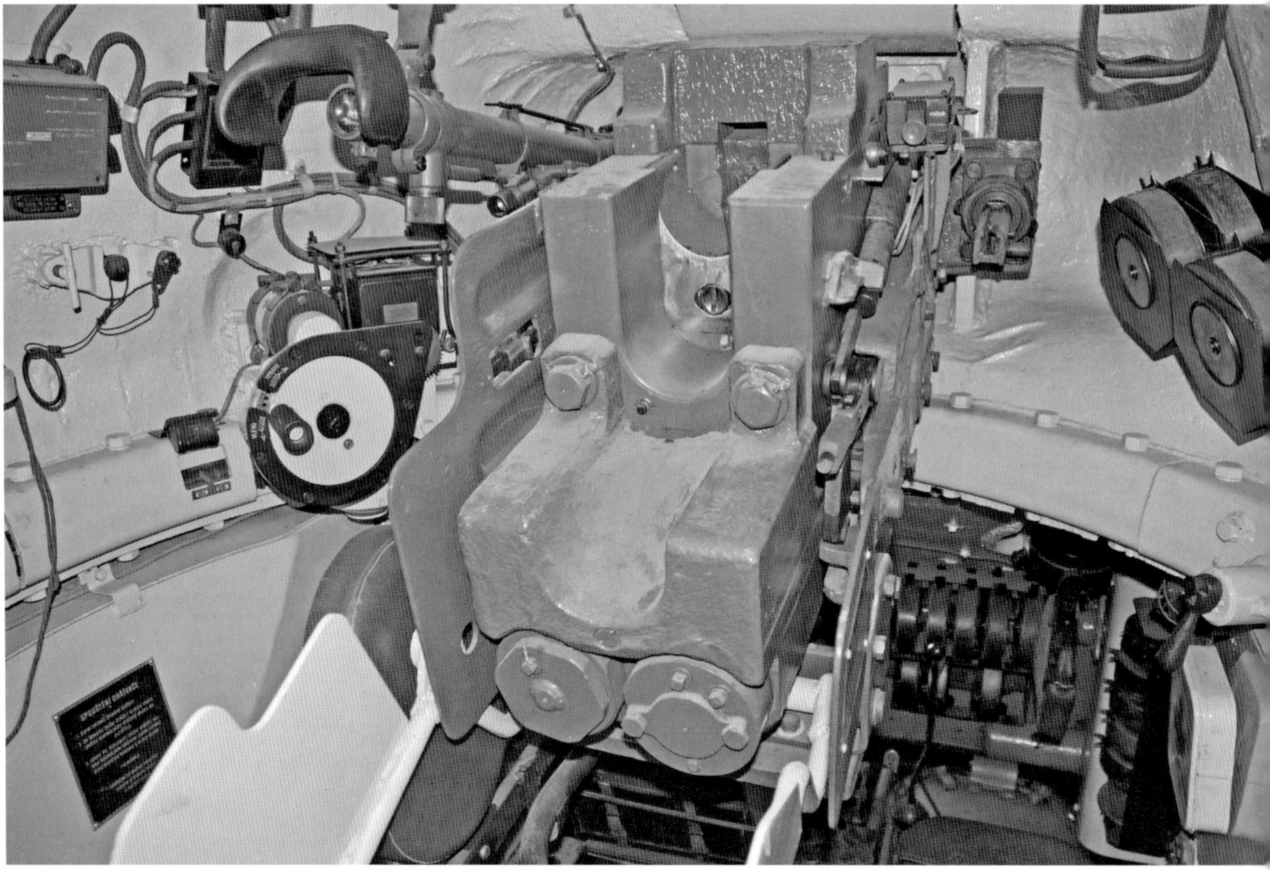

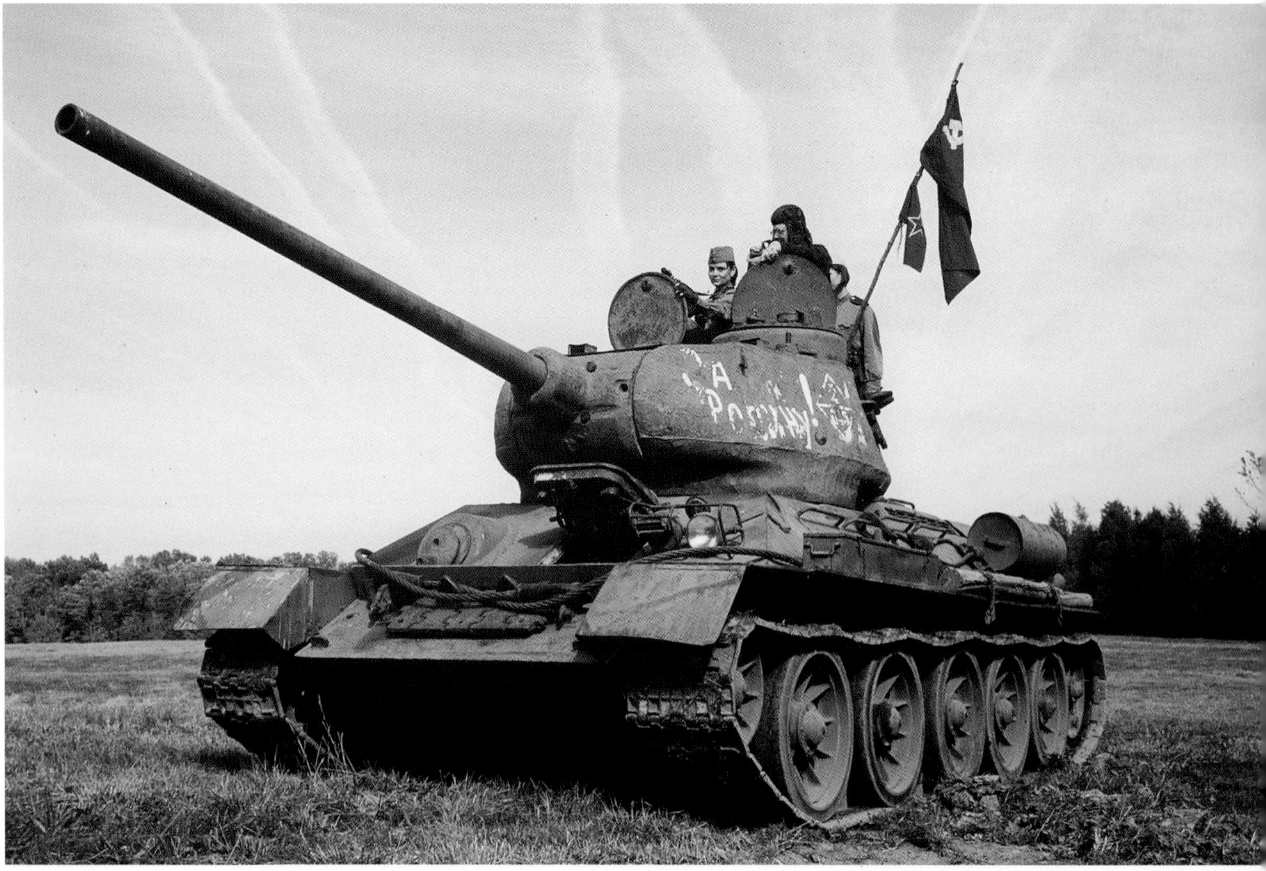

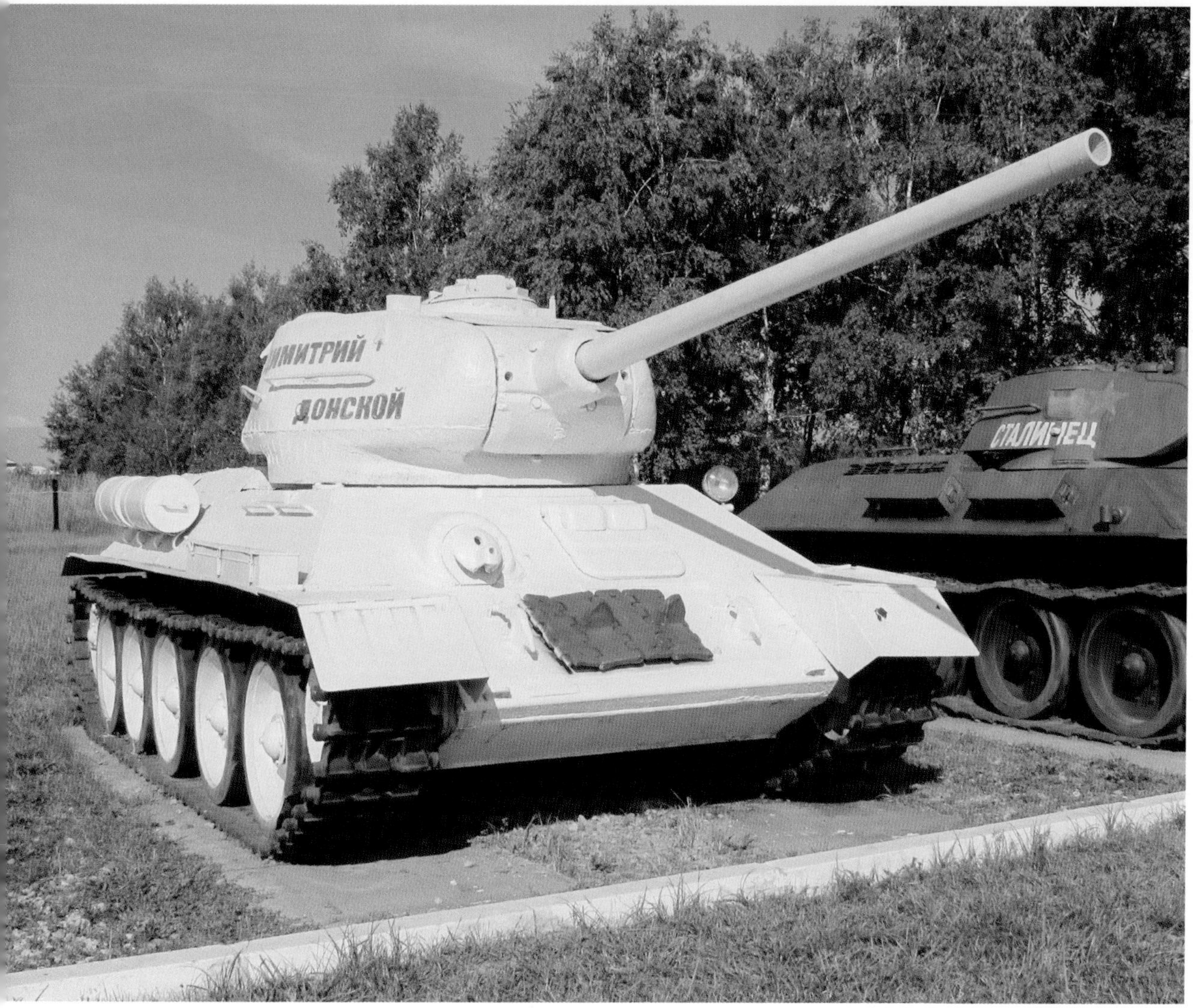
ДИМИТРИЙ
ДОНСКОЙ
СТАЛИНЕЦ

(*Opposite above*) Inside the turret of a T-34-85 Model 1945 or later can be seen the gunner's controls on the left-hand side of the breech end of the tank's S-53 85mm main gun. Visible behind and below the breech end of the gun is the white recoil guard. Note the various storage locations for the spare drum magazines for the tank's small-calibre machine guns in both the turret and hull. (*Chris Hughes*)

(*Opposite below*) Taking part in a museum demonstration is a T-34-85 Model 1945 or later with re-enactors in Second World War uniforms. Maximum armour thickness on the front of the T-34-85 series was 90mm. The tank's thicker armour and new larger and heavier turret pushed up the vehicle's weight, causing a minor loss in mobility compared to the original T-34 series armed with the 76.2mm main gun. (*Author's collection*)

(*Above*) On display at the Russian Army Tank Museum is this T-34-85 Model 1945 or later tank. In the immediate post-war years Soviet industry built both new units of the T-34-85 series tank and rebuilt wartime production vehicles. The vehicle had a length of 26ft 9in, a width of 9ft 5in and a height of 9ft. (*Vladimir Yakubov*)

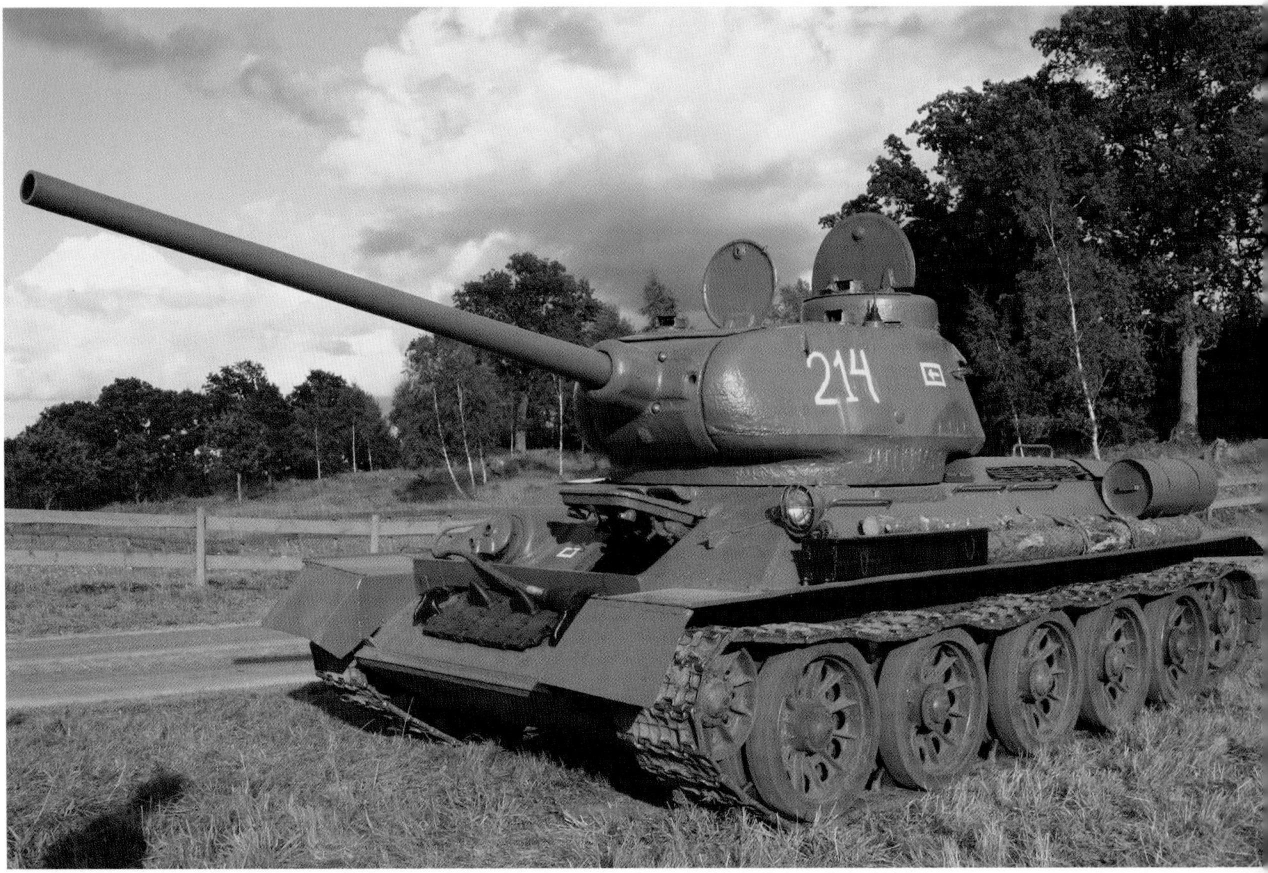
214

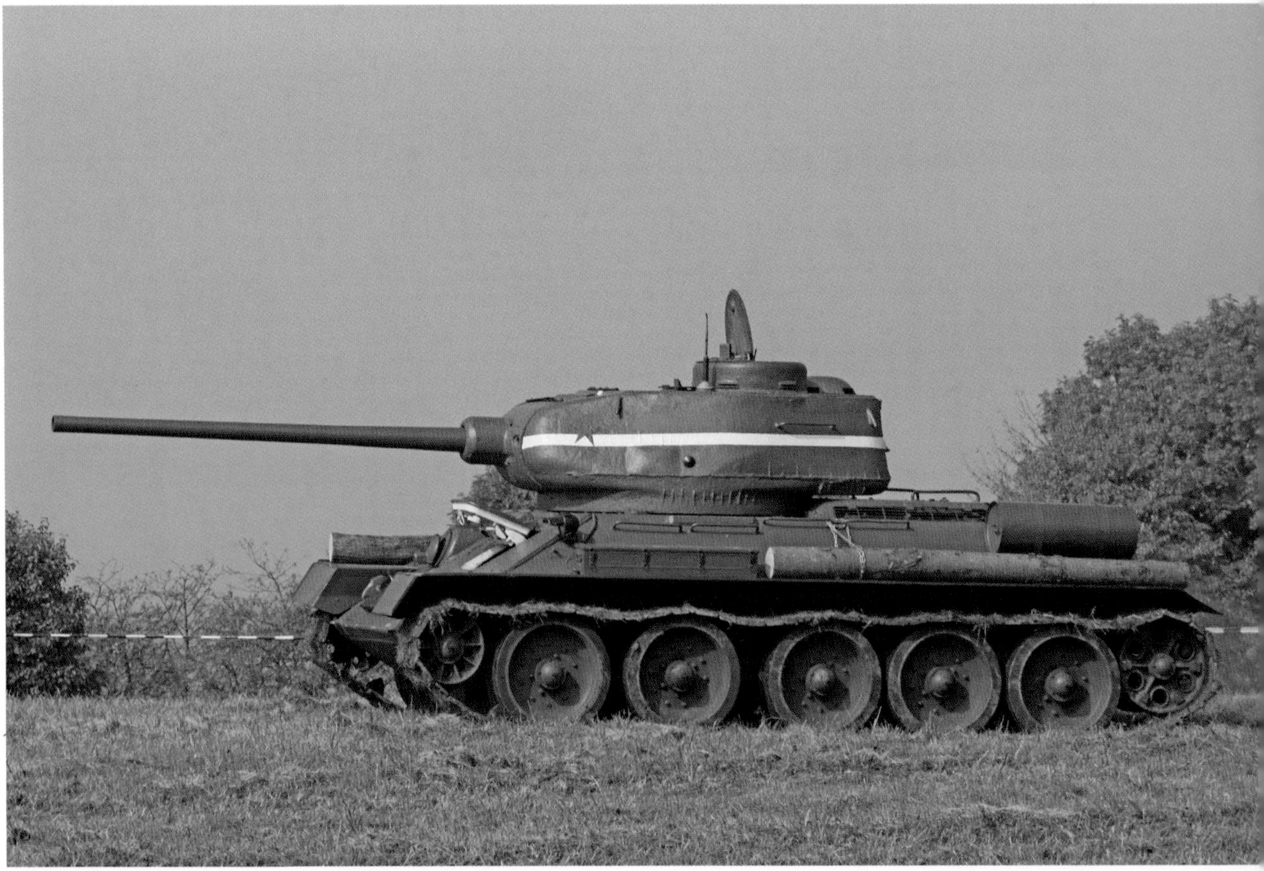

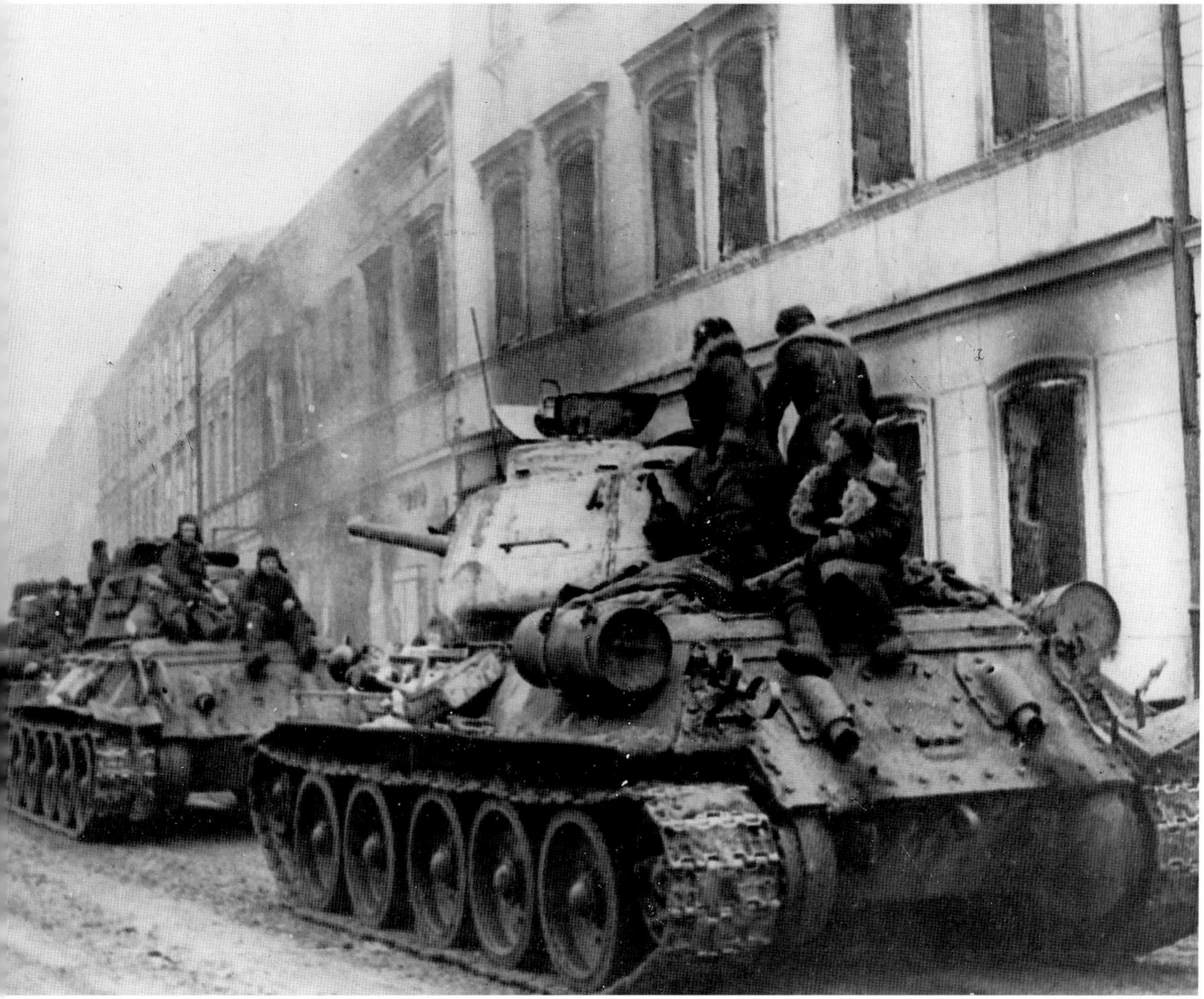

(*Opposite above*) The logs strapped to the upper side hull of this late-production and restored T-34-85 series tank are a somewhat common feature seen on wartime units of the tank. The logs were employed to assist the crews when bogged down in soft soil. Early-production T-34-85 series tanks had authorized onboard storage for fifty-five main gun rounds. Later-production units had authorized storage space for sixty main gun rounds. *(Andreas Kirchhoff)*

(*Above*) The rear tank in this late-wartime photograph is an early-production T-34-85 Model 1944 with the original two-piece overhead split vehicle commander's hatch. The metal brackets located just above the vehicle's rear fenders are for holding cylindrical smoke canisters that are missing from this tank. The tank directly in front of the T-34-85 Model 1944 is a T-34 Model 1943 armed with a 76.2mm main gun. *(Bob Fleming)*

(*Opposite below*) A late-production T-34-85 Model 1945 tank or later is shown being run during a historical military vehicle demonstration hosted by the German army museum system. Maximum speed of the tank was 34mph on level roads and 18mph off-road. Maximum range of the tank was approximately 186 miles (300km). *(Andreas Kirchhoff)*

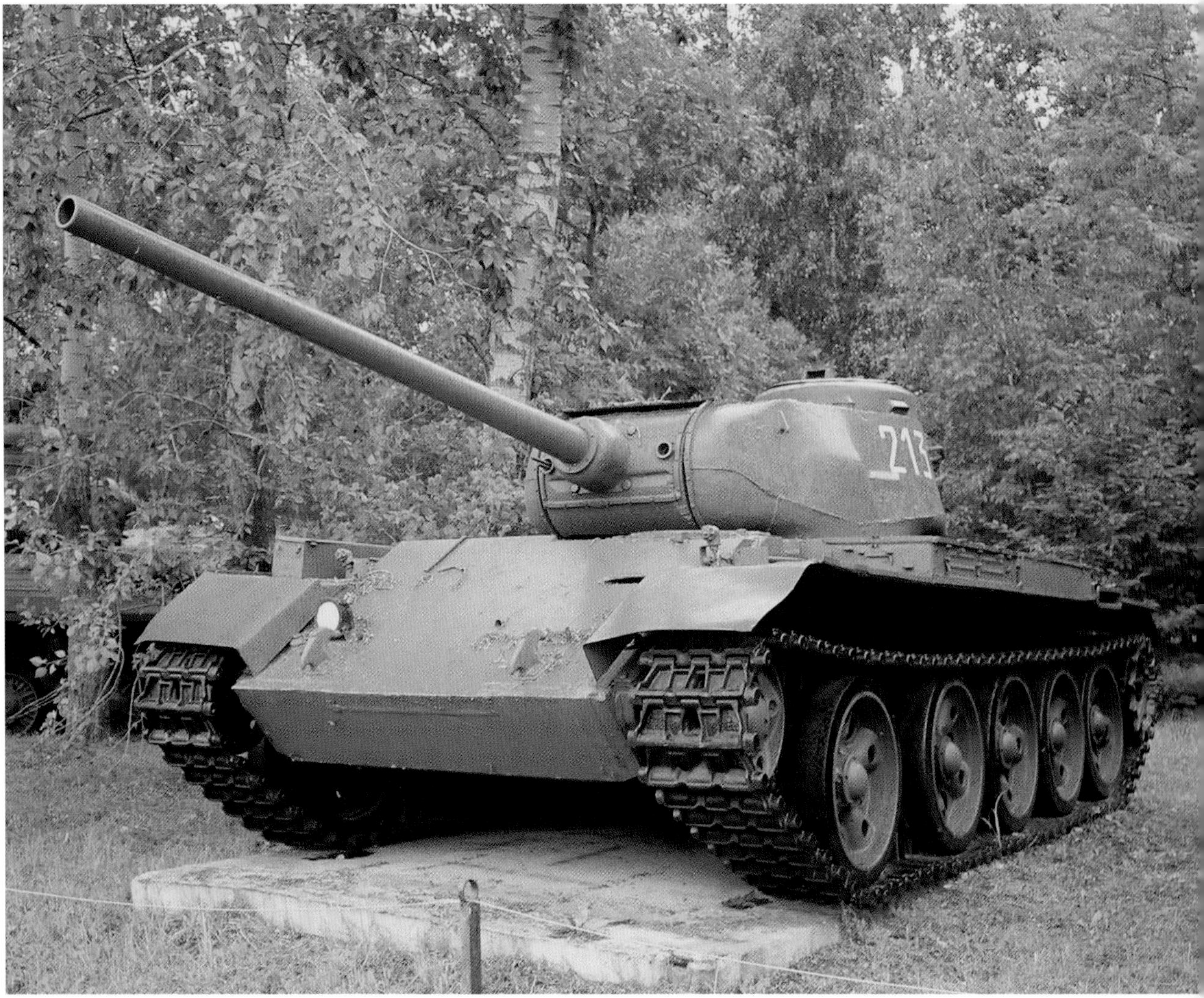
213

(*Above*) The planned wartime replacement for the T-34-85 series in Red Army service was supposed to have been the four-man T-44 medium tank seen here. It retained the 85mm main gun of the T-34-85 series but had a brand-new hull and a revised turret design. A total of 965 units were completed before the end of the Second World War but they did not see service in combat. *(Vladimir Yakubov)*

(*Opposite above*) Pictured during a historical military vehicle event in Europe is a privately-owned second-generation M4A1(76)W, which is a post-war rebuild. It is armed with a 76.2mm main gun referred to by the US army as a 76mm main gun. The vehicle is riding on the VVSS developed for the first-generation M4 series. The turret for the tank came from the experimental T23 medium tank that never went into production. *(Pierre-Olivier Buan)*

(*Opposite below*) On display in Belgium as a monument tank is this second-generation M4A1(76)W, which was rebuilt in the 1950s. Combat experience demonstrated that the standard armour-piercing round for the new 76mm main gun could only penetrate on average 1in more armour than the AP round fired by the 75mm main gun on the first-generation M4 series. *(Andreas Kirchhoff)*

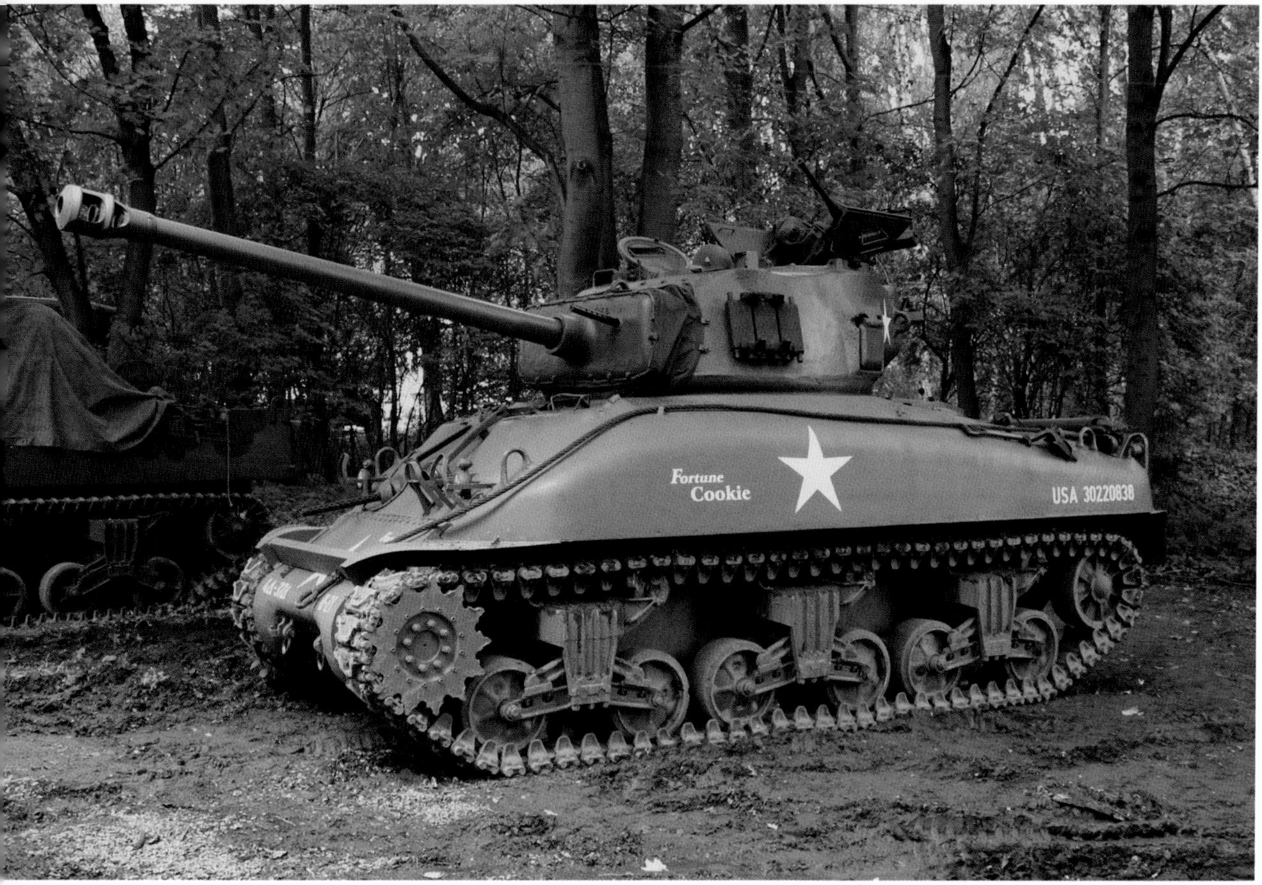
Fortune
Cookie
USA 30220838

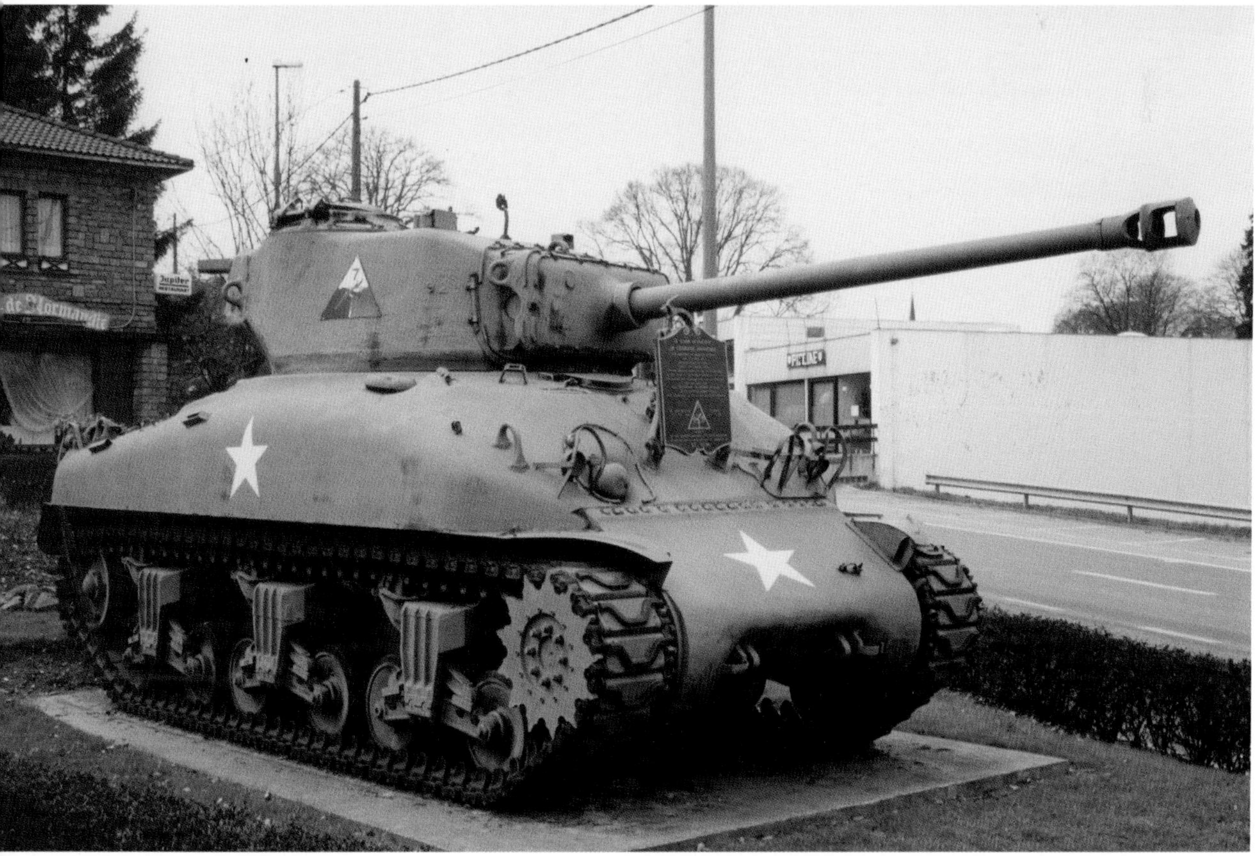

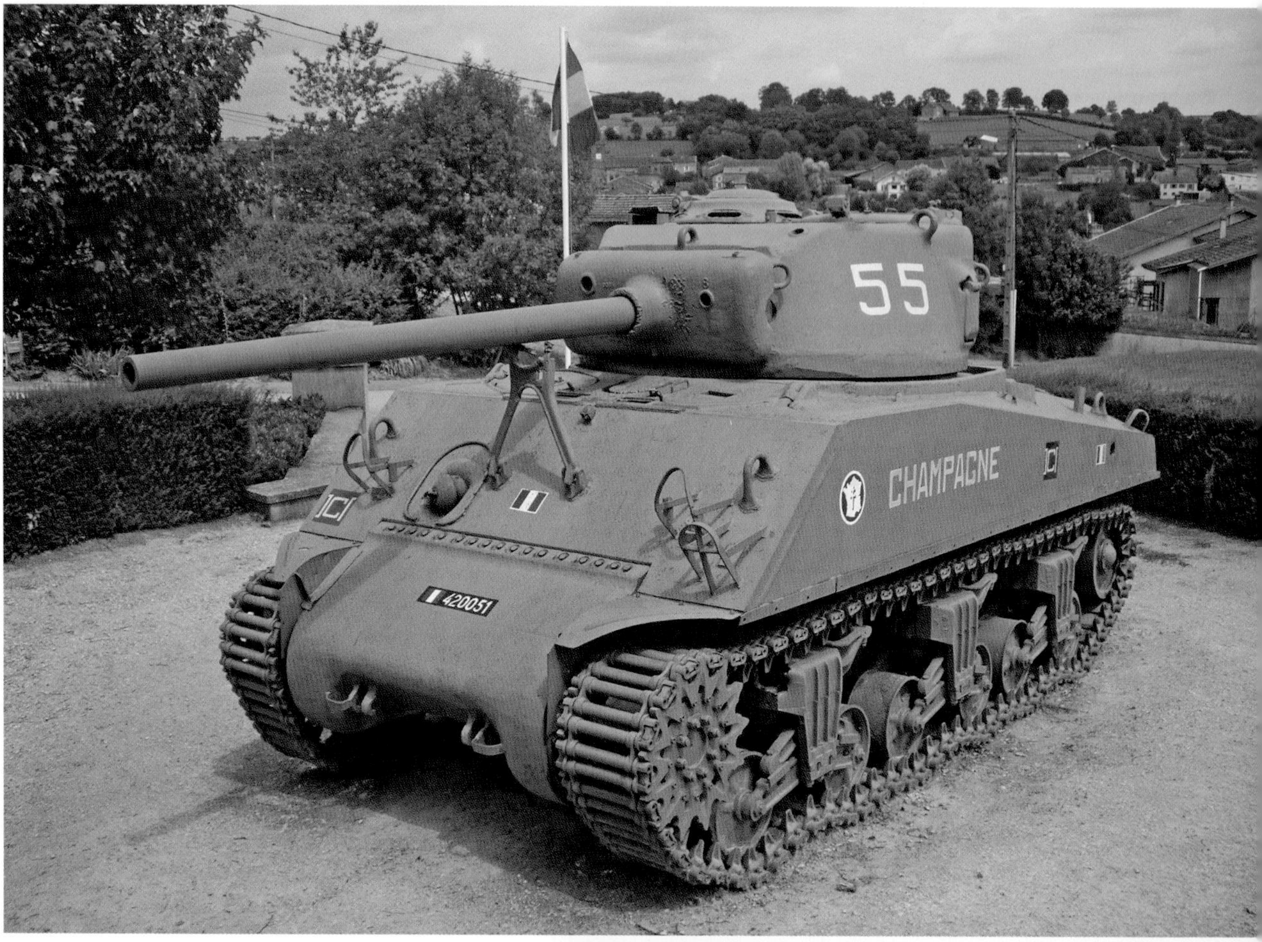
55
CHAMPAGNE
420051

One of the key external identifying features on all the second-generation M4 series was the disappearance of the protruding driver and assistant driver's hatch hoods seen on the glacis of the first-generation M4 series tanks. This was accomplished, as is visible on this M4A3(76)W tank on display in France, by resetting a new thicker-armoured glacis at a less steep angle. *(Pierre-Olivier Buan)*

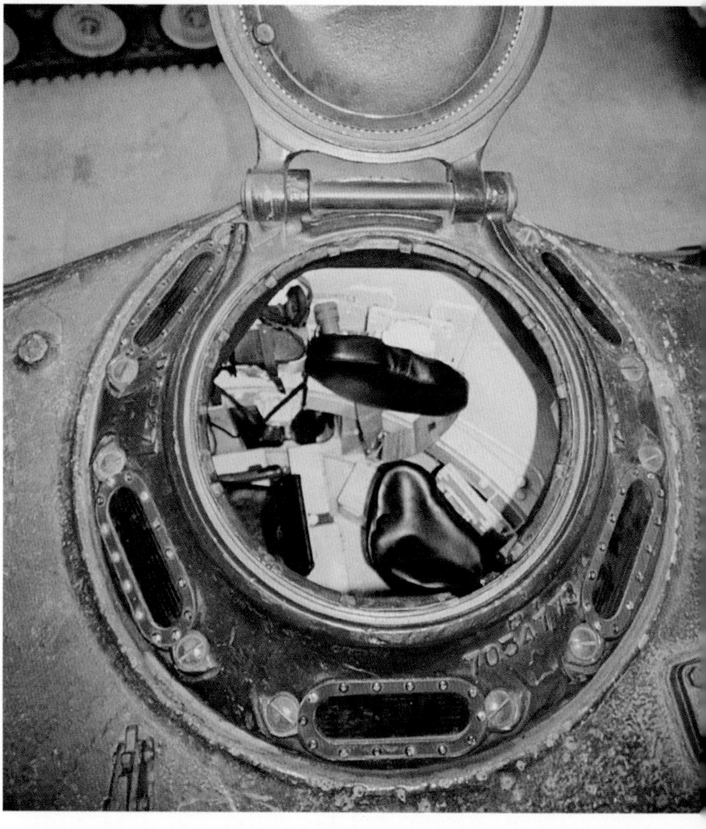

An important feature of most second-generation M4 series tanks was the addition of a new raised vehicle commander's cupola, as seen here. It had six laminated-glass vision blocks around its circumference. The overhead hatch contained a periscope with 360 degrees of rotation. This same vehicle commander's cupola was also retrofitted to many rebuilt first-generation M4 series tanks. *(Author's collection)*

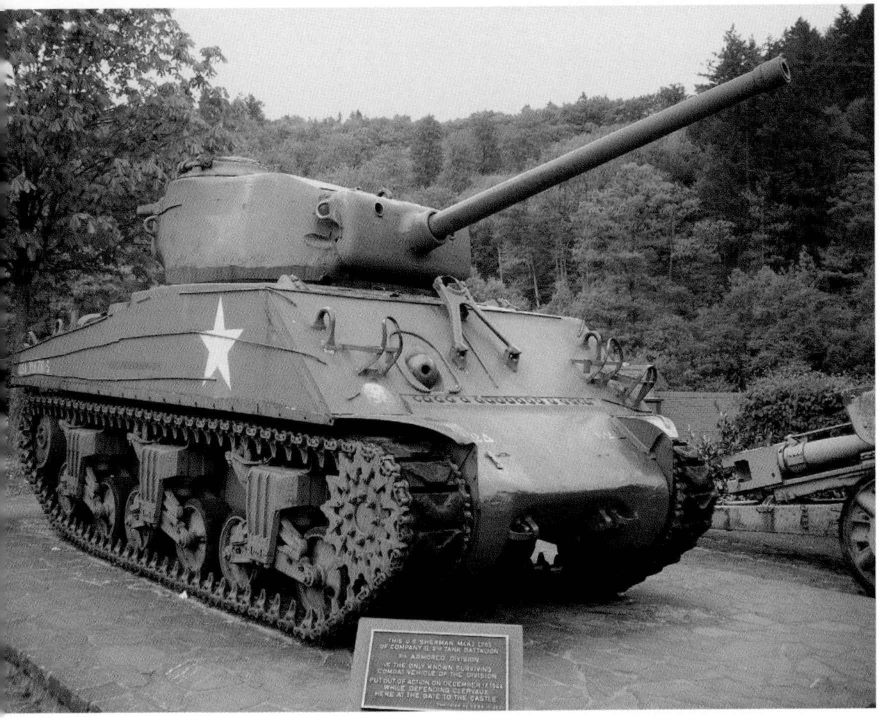
ARMORED DIVISION
IS THE ONLY KNOWN SURVIVING
COMBAT VEHICLE OF THE DIVISION
WHILE DEFENDING CLERVAUX
HERE AT THE GATE TO THE CASTLE

Unlike the first-generation M4 series that had cast armour rotor shields mounted in front of the cast armour gun shields, the second-generation M4 series tanks armed with the 76mm main gun did away with the rotor shield and relied solely on a full-width vertical cast armour gun shield for protection as can be seen on this M4A3(76)W monument tank in Europe. *(Pierre-Olivier Buan)*

Visible on the turret roof of an M4A3(76)W that almost toppled over into a large shell crater is the new raised vehicle commander's cupola. What makes the vehicle pictured here interesting is that instead of having the standard small flat oval loader's hatch, it has been replaced by the flat two-piece split vehicle commander's hatch from the first-generation M4 series. *(Patton Museum)*

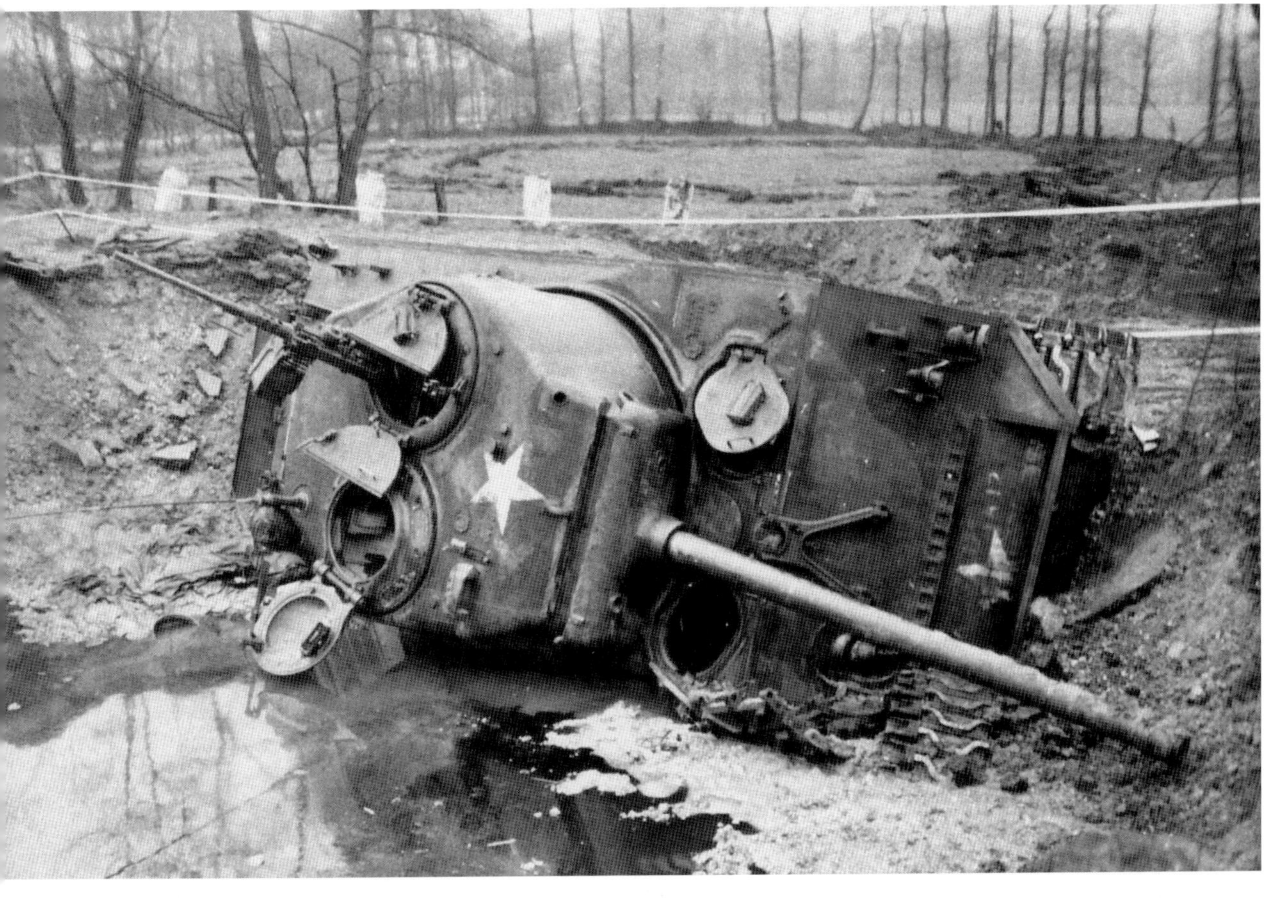

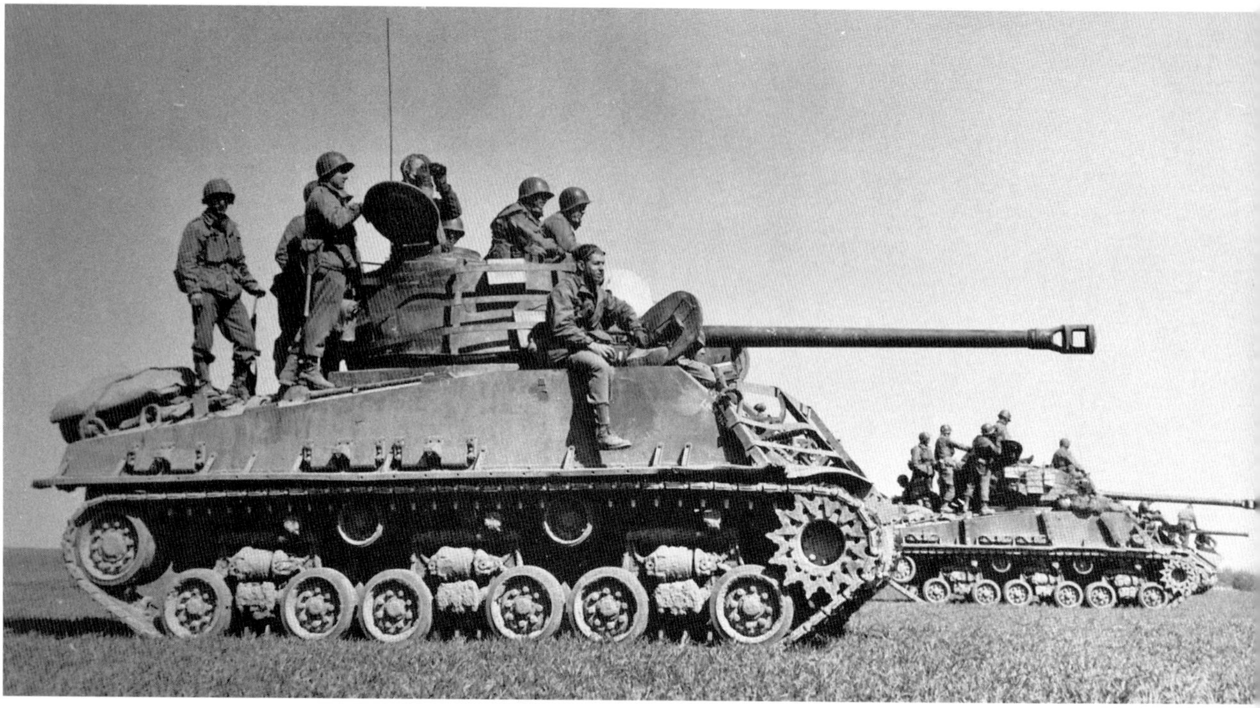

The early-production units of the second-generation M4 series tank armed with the 76mm main gun rode on the same VVSS as did the first-generation M4 series tanks armed with the 75mm main gun. Eventually, new-production second-generation M4 series tanks were fitted with the much-improved HVSS system as seen on this wartime image of M4A3(76)W tanks. *(Patton Museum)*

On the left side is a second-generation M4A1(76)W armed with a 76mm main gun and fitted with an HVSS system. On the right is a first-generation M4A3 armed with a 75mm main gun and fitted with the original VVSS. The tracks on the HVSS are 23in wide and those on the VVSS are 16.56in wide. Both tanks are privately owned and were restored by the late Fred Ropkey. *(Author's collection)*

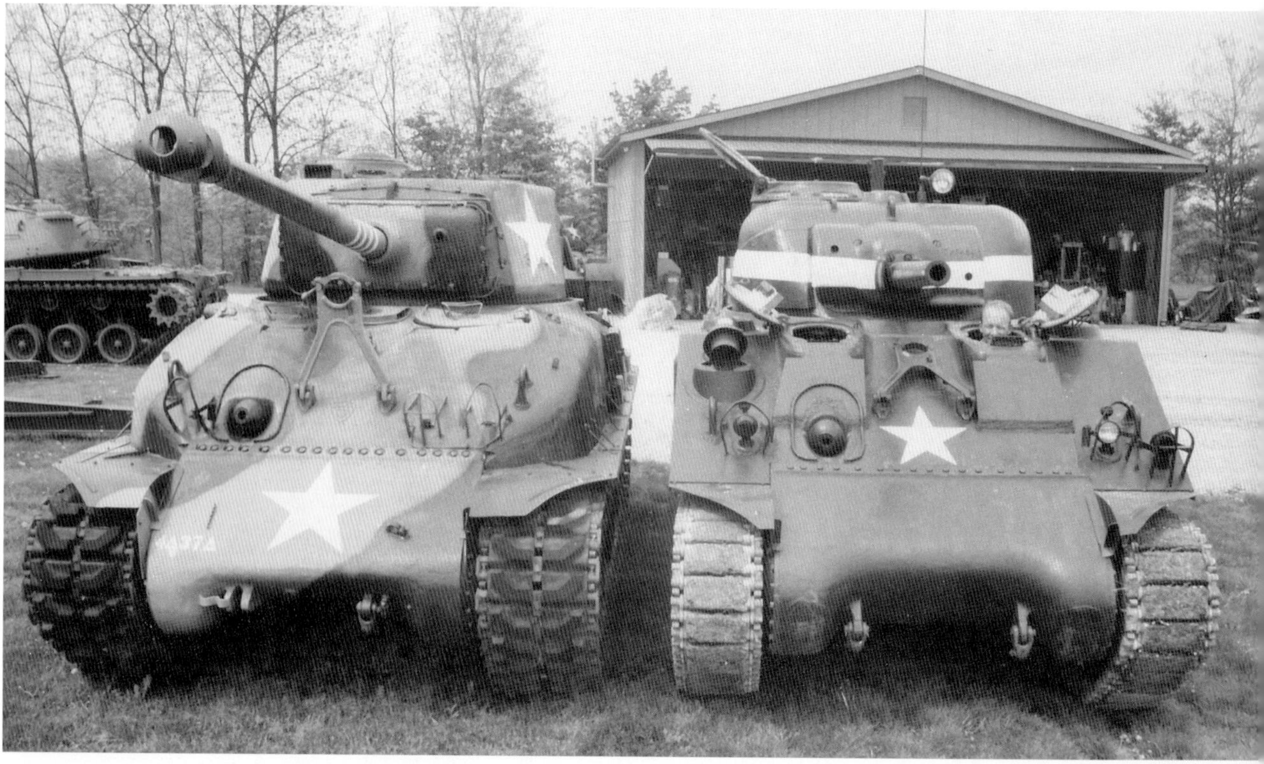

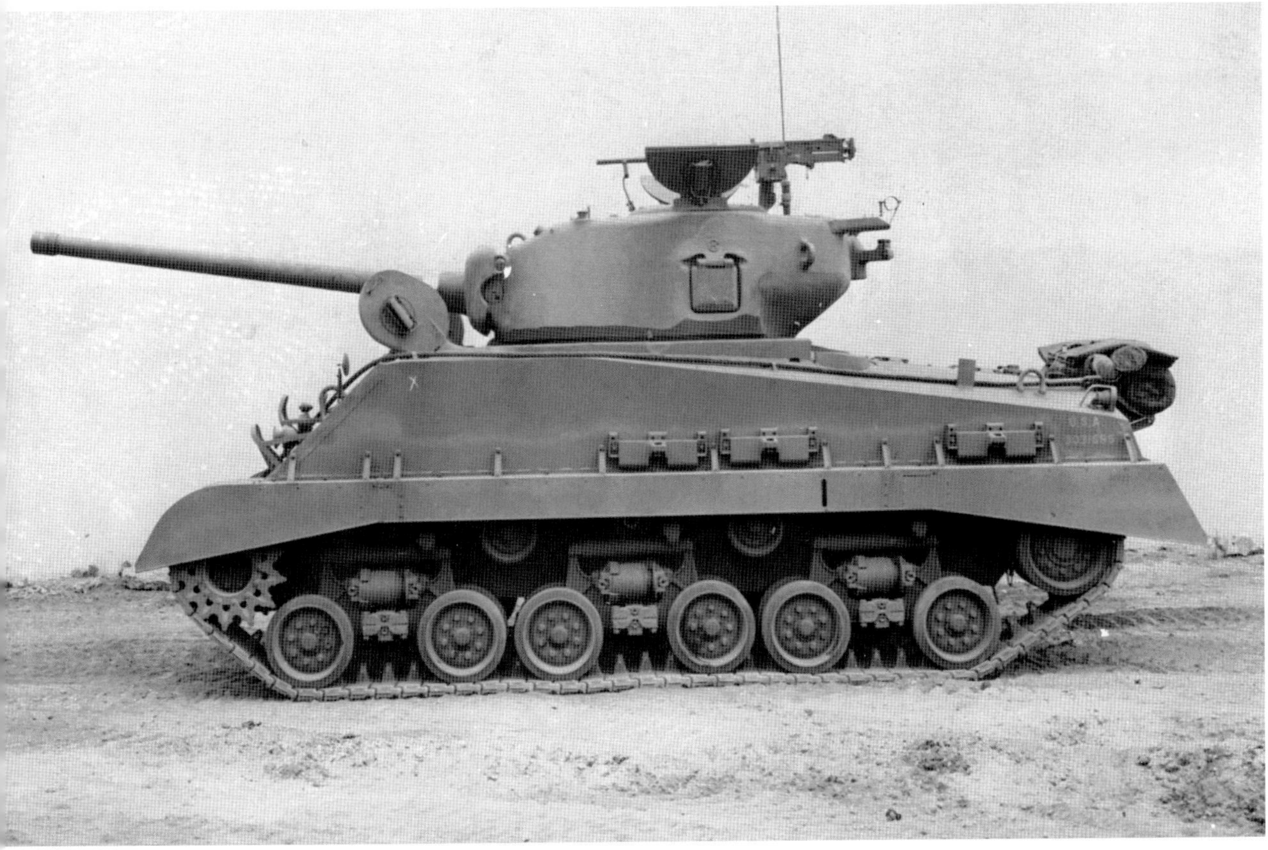

In this wartime US army Ordnance Department photograph we see the official designation for the M4A3(76)W tank. Most US army wartime documents do not distinguish between a second-generation M4 series tank riding on the VVSS or the HVSS system. A few wartime documents mention 'wide tracks' or '23-inch tracks' but never the HVSS system. The designation 'M4A3E8' was only intended for the pilot vehicles but is often employed incorrectly to describe the M4A3(76)W. *(TACOM)*

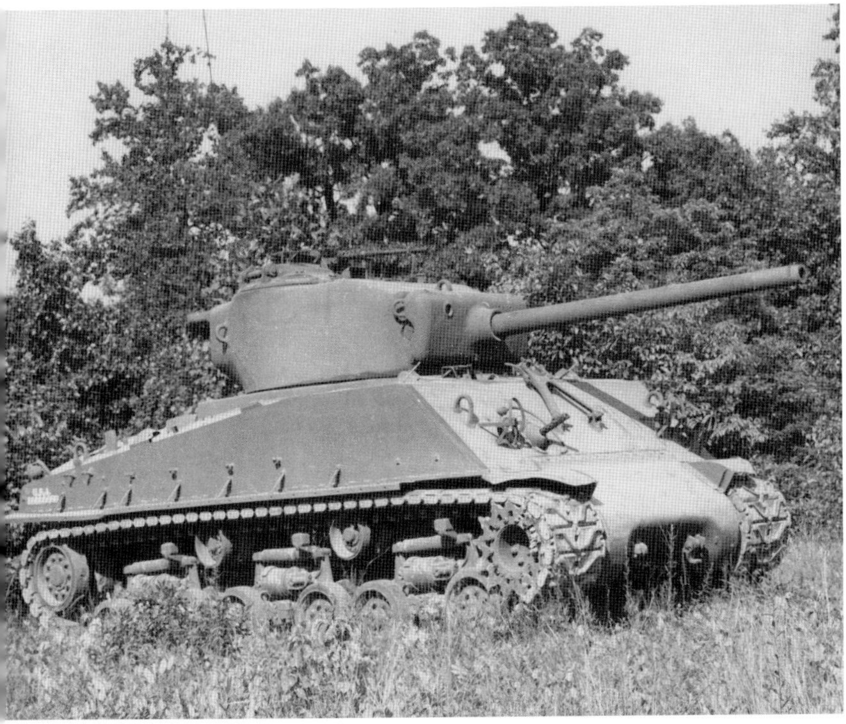

Pictured with an HVSS system is this M4A3(76)W. A serious problem with the 76mm main gun fitted to the early-production second-generation M4 series was the weapon's muzzle blast and the resulting target obscuration from smoke and dust. The solution was the addition of a muzzle brake that appeared on later-production vehicles. When muzzle brakes were not available the threaded barrel ends were fitted with a protective ring as seen in this photograph. *(TACOM)*

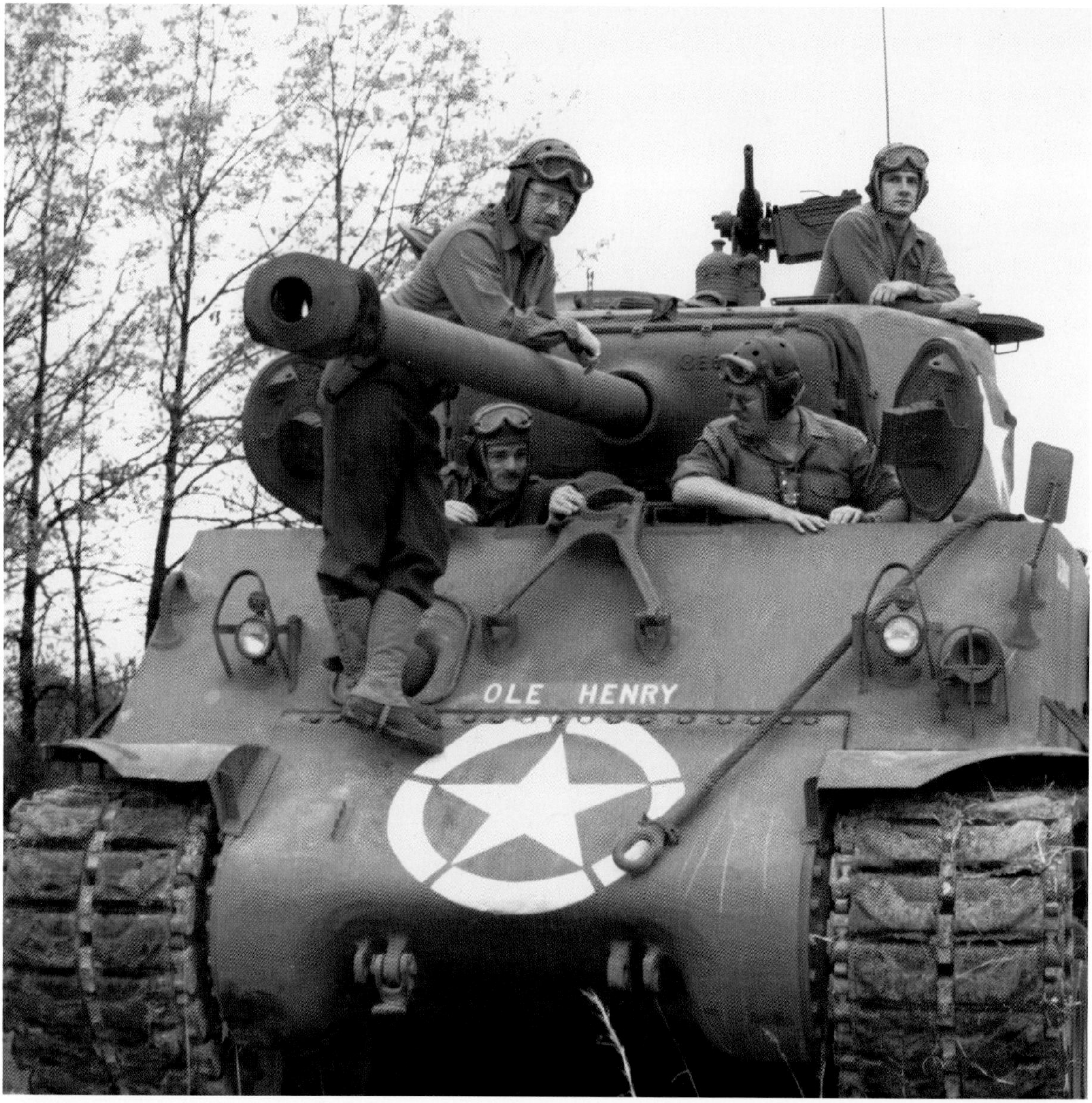
OLE HENRY

(*Above*) Volunteers in period uniform are shown manning an M4A3(76)W equipped with the HVSS system at the former Patton Museum of Armor and Cavalry during an open-house event. The muzzle brake at the end of the barrel was a late-production feature added to the second-generation M4 series armed with the 76mm main gun to cut down on target obscuration. (*Patton Museum*)

(*Opposite above*) The wider tracks of the HVSS system required the use of dual bogie wheels as are visible on the M4A3(76)W shown here. They distributed track wear more uniformly than with the earlier single bogie wheels of the VVSS. The addition of shock-absorbers with the HVSS system and other improvements such as the tracks now being centre-guided greatly decreased the odds of them being thrown on uneven ground. (*Patton Museum*)

(*Opposite below*) The driver's compartment of a restored M4A3(76)W. Both the driver and the assistant driver/bow gunner sat on foam-filled padded seats with padded back-rests. The seats themselves were attached on pedestals that were adjustable for height as well as backward and forward movement. Electrically-operated ventilating blowers located in the front hull provided some relief from the gases generated during weapon-firing. (*Author's collection*)

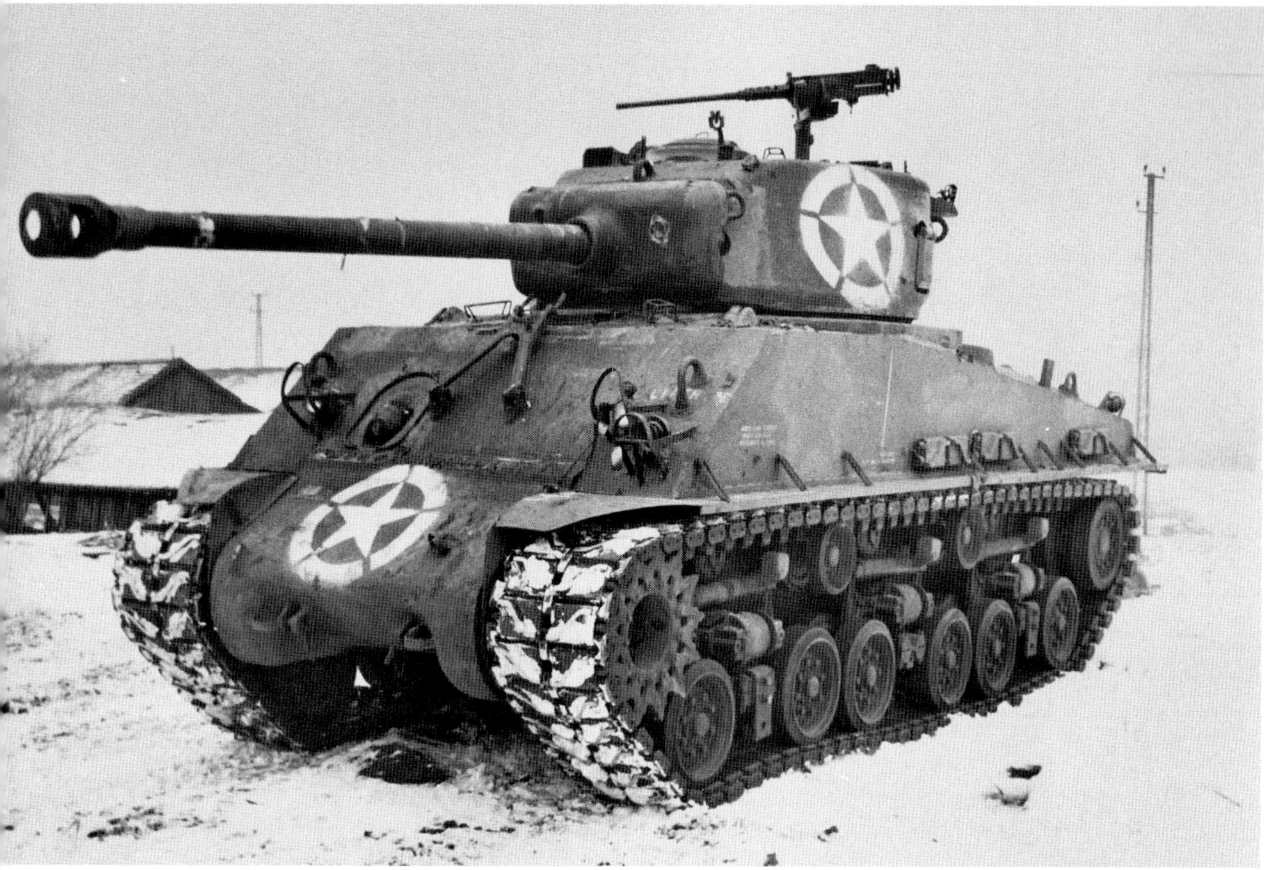

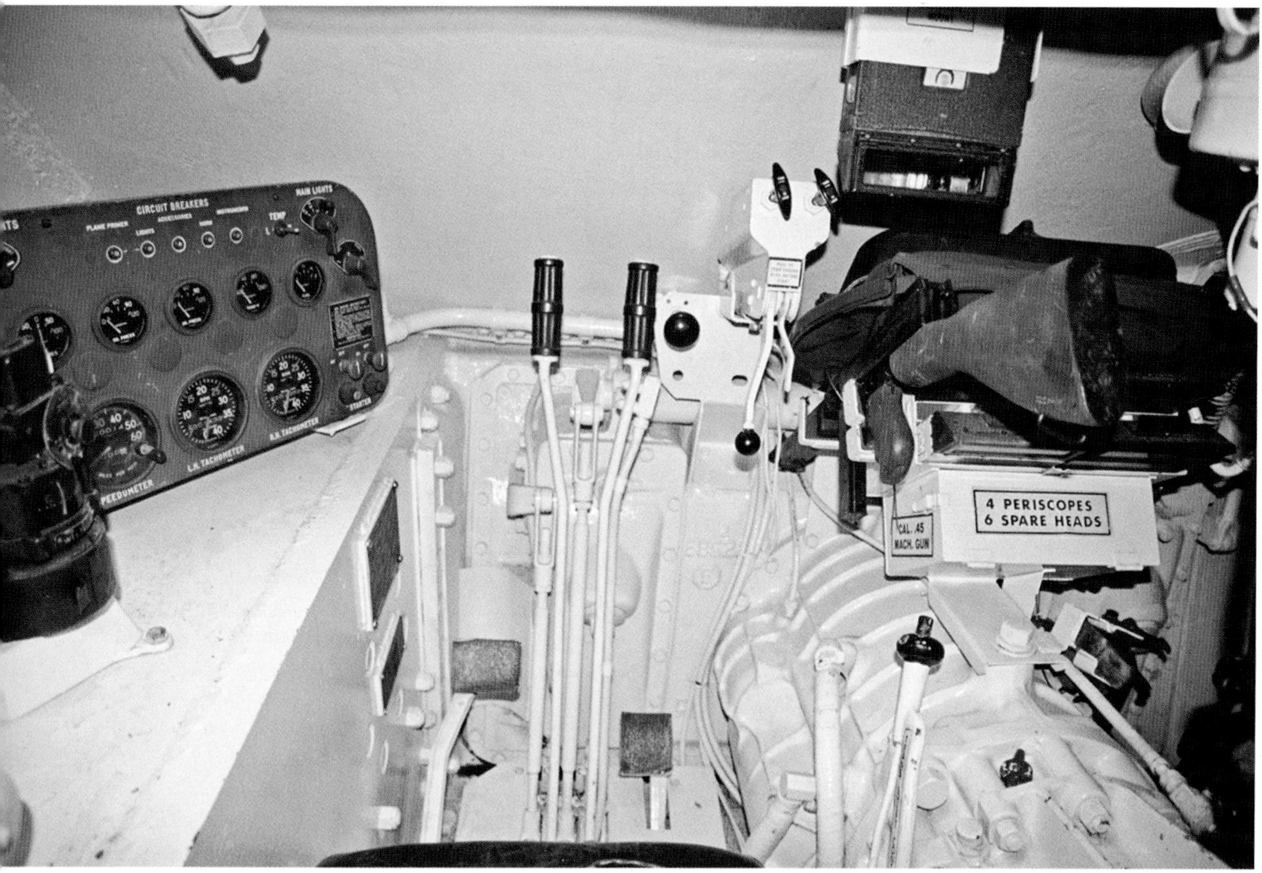
CIRCUIT BREAKERS
MAIN LIGHTS
TEMP
L.H. TACHOMETER
R.H. TACHOMETER
STARTER
4 PERISCOPES
6 SPARE HEADS
CAL. .45
MACH. GUN

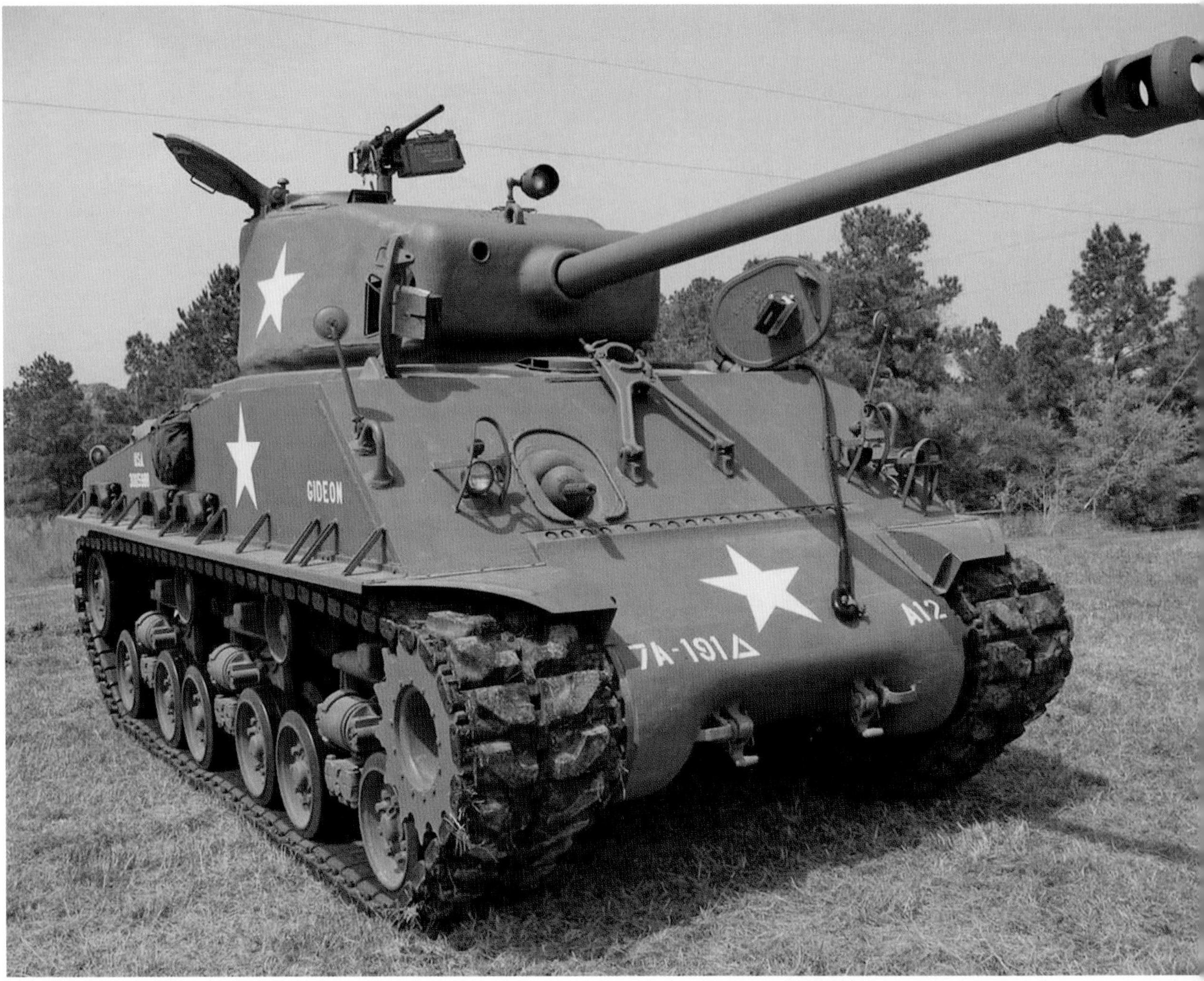
GIDEON
7A-191△
A12

Belonging to a private collector in Texas is this restored M4A3(76)W equipped with the HVSS system. The standard armour-piercing capped-tracer (APC-T) round for the 76mm main gun on the second-generation M4 series tanks so armed weighed approximately 25lb. It was designated as the M62. The approximately 15lb projectile portion of the round had a muzzle velocity of 2,030ft per second. *(Author's collection)*

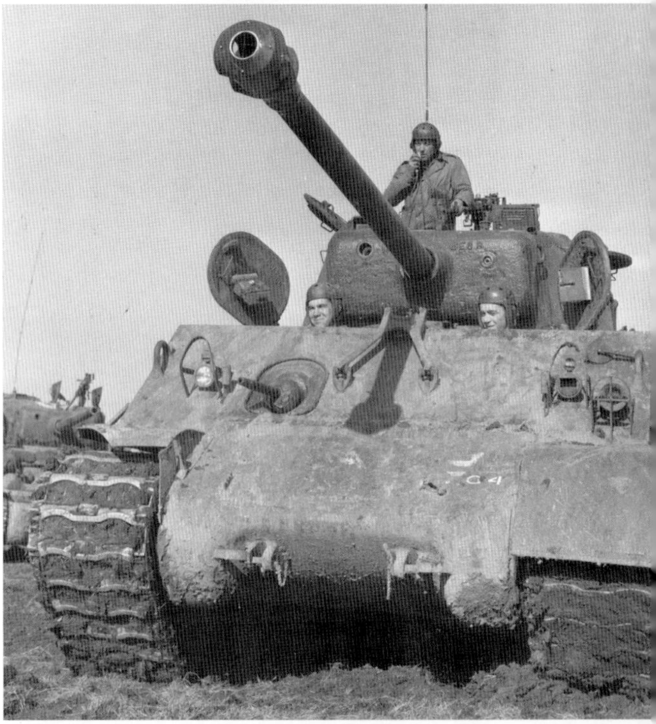

A wartime photograph of an M4A3(76)W equipped with the HVSS system. The addition of the HVSS system increased the weight of the tanks so fitted anywhere between 3,000lb and 5,000lb depending on the type of track used. The weight gain was offset by the fact that the HVSS system lowered the vehicle's ground pressure, which in turn improved the tank's off-road mobility. *(Author's collection)*

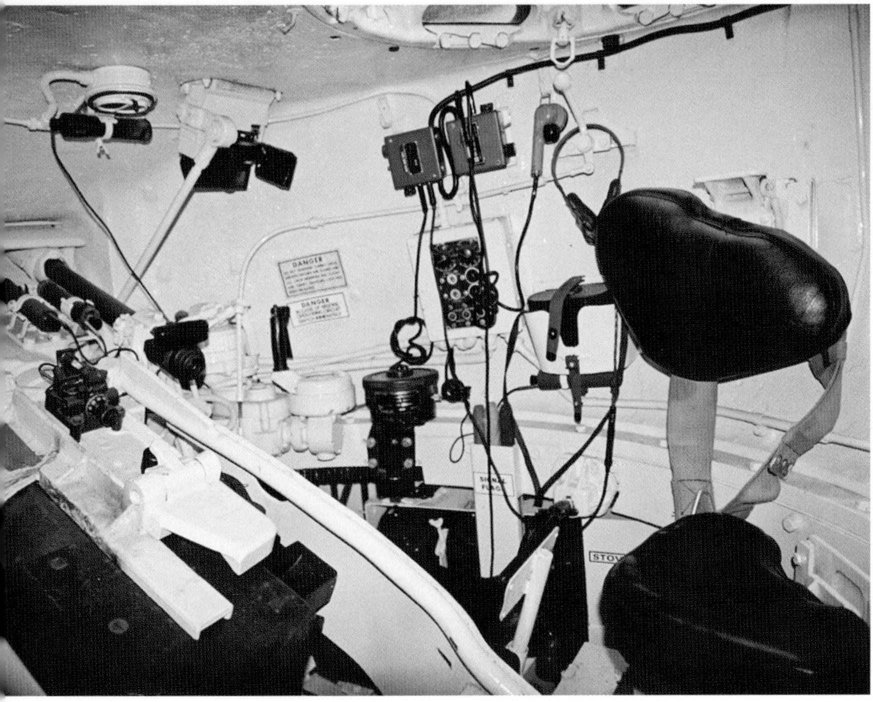
DANGER
DANGER

Inside the turret of a restored M4A3(76)W one can see the two different seats for the vehicle commander. The uppermost seat was employed by the vehicle commander when he had opened his overhead hatch. The bottom seat is for when he had his overhead hatch closed. Note the vehicle commander's hand-held microphone and cord stored against the turret wall. The small red handle visible in the picture is the turret locking device. *(Author's collection)*

On display in France is this post-war upgraded M4A1(76)W fitted with the HVSS system. This particular model of the second-generation series with the HVSS system did not enter service with the US army in Europe until after the German surrender in early May 1945. The glacis setback on the second-generation tanks with the cast hull is less noticeable than on those with the welded hulls. *(Author's collection)*

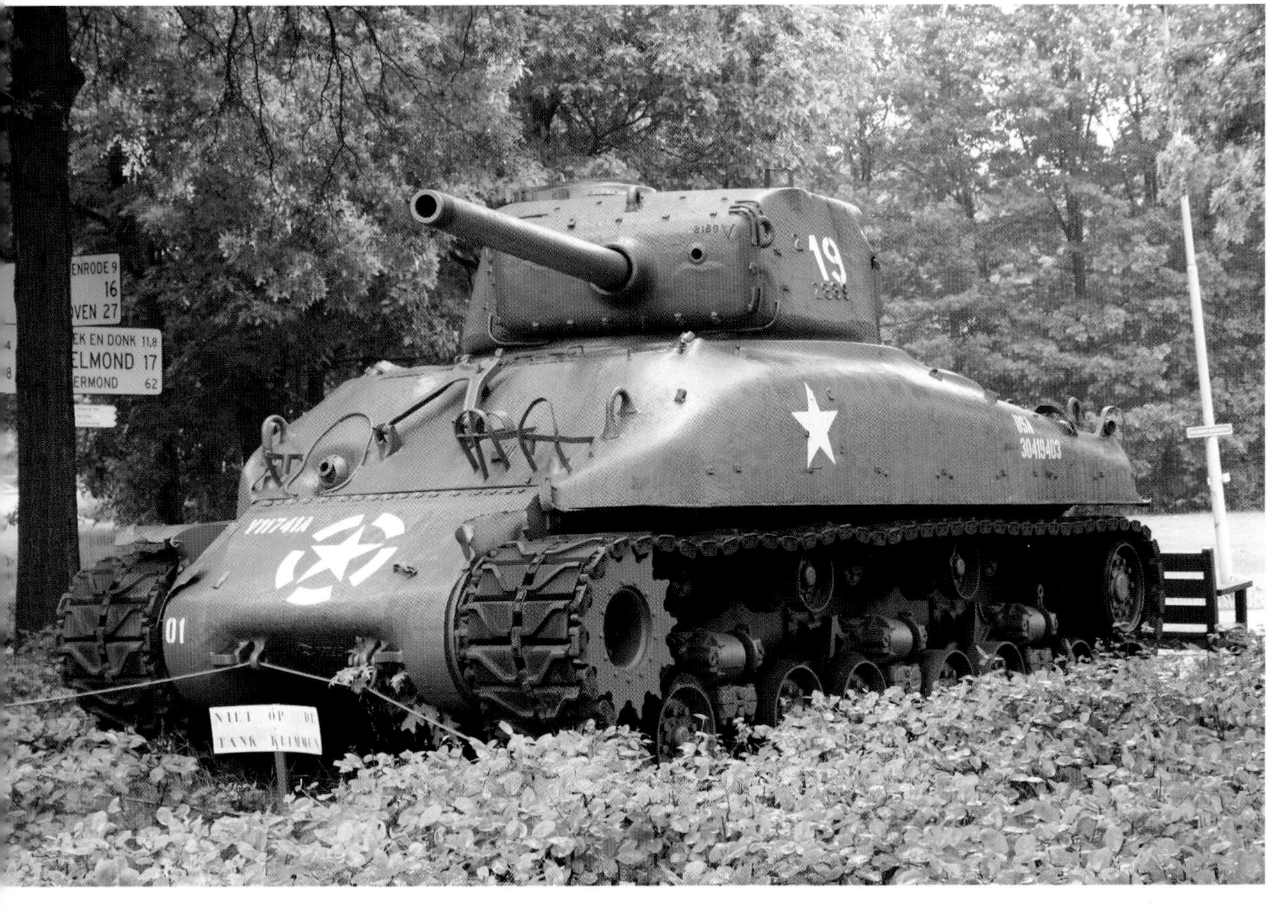
19
01

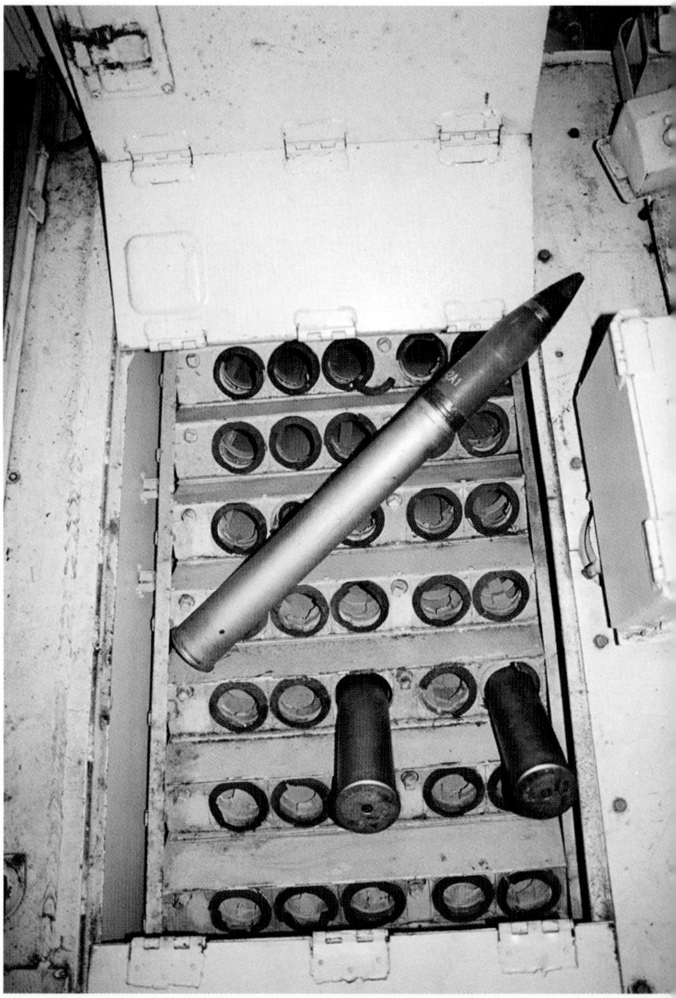

Located directly below the loader's position on all second-generation M4 series tanks armed with a 76mm main gun was a hull ammunition storage compartment seen here. Surrounding the openings for each main gun round was a liquid-filled container that would aid in quenching ammunition fires, hence the term 'wet' in the designation of second-generation gun-armed M4 series tanks. *(Author's collection)*

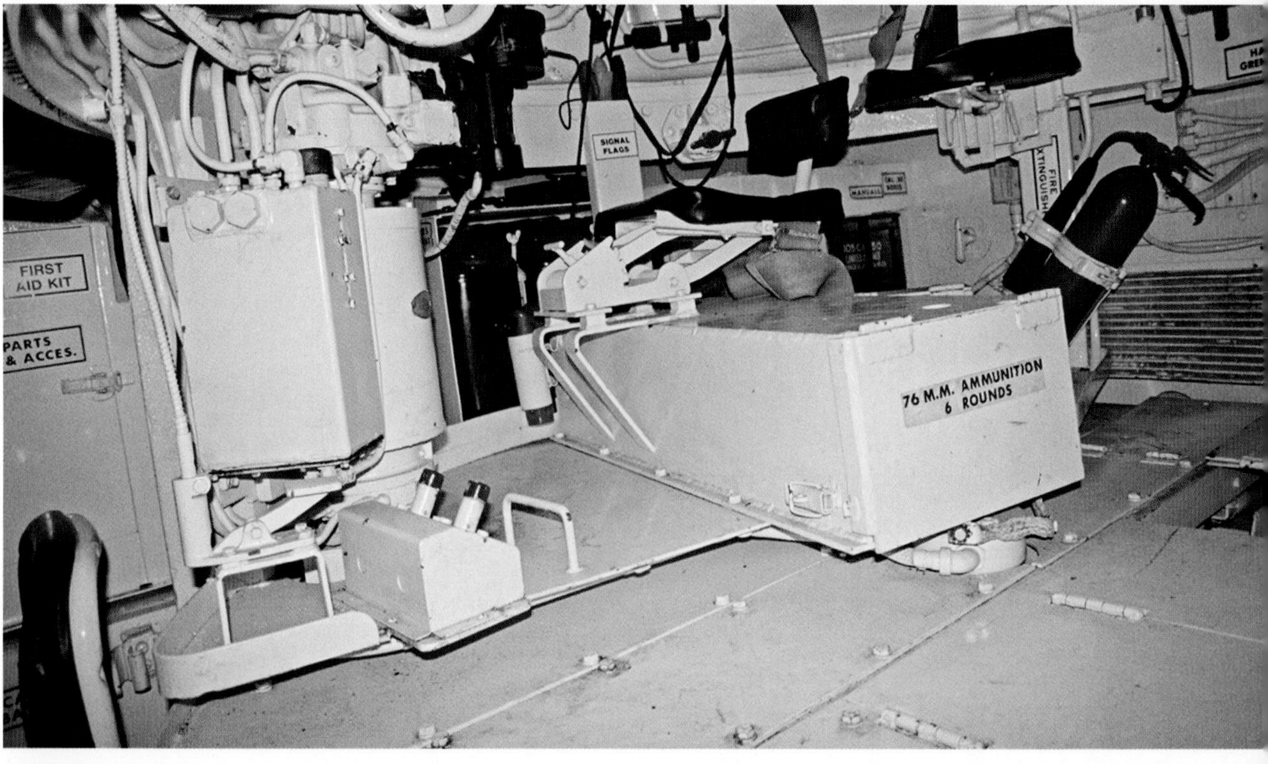
FIRST AID KIT
PARTS & ACCES.
SIGNAL FLAGS
76 M.M. AMMUNITION 6 ROUNDS

To allow the loader on gun-armed second-generation M4 series tanks to access the main gun rounds stored below him in the tank's hull, they had only a partial turret basket as seen in this picture. The vehicle commander and gunner were on the other half of the turret floor that turned with the turret. The loader had to walk atop the hull main gun storage compartment to keep up with turret rotation. *(Author's collection)*

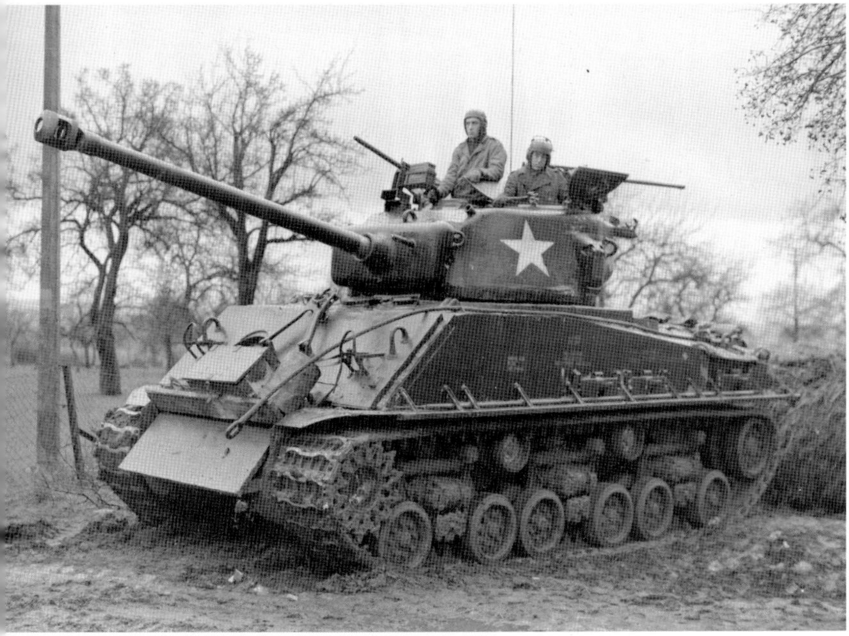

In this picture we see an M4A3(76)W crew that welded on what can be presumed to be a large armoured steel plate to the glacis of their tank. It extends all the way down to also cover the front hull-mounted cast armour differential. A non-standard pintle mount for a small-calibre machine gun has been fitted in front of the vehicle commander's cupola. *(Patton Museum)*

Pictured being refuelled is a M4A3(76)W. The crew had added to their vehicle an elaborate metal cage on the tank's turret that they filled with sandbags. While sandbags provided little protection from enemy armour-piercing projectiles, they did have some success in defeating enemy shaped-charge warheads fired from the German *Panzerschreck* ('Tank Terror') and *Panzerfaust* ('Tank Fist'). *(Patton Museum)*

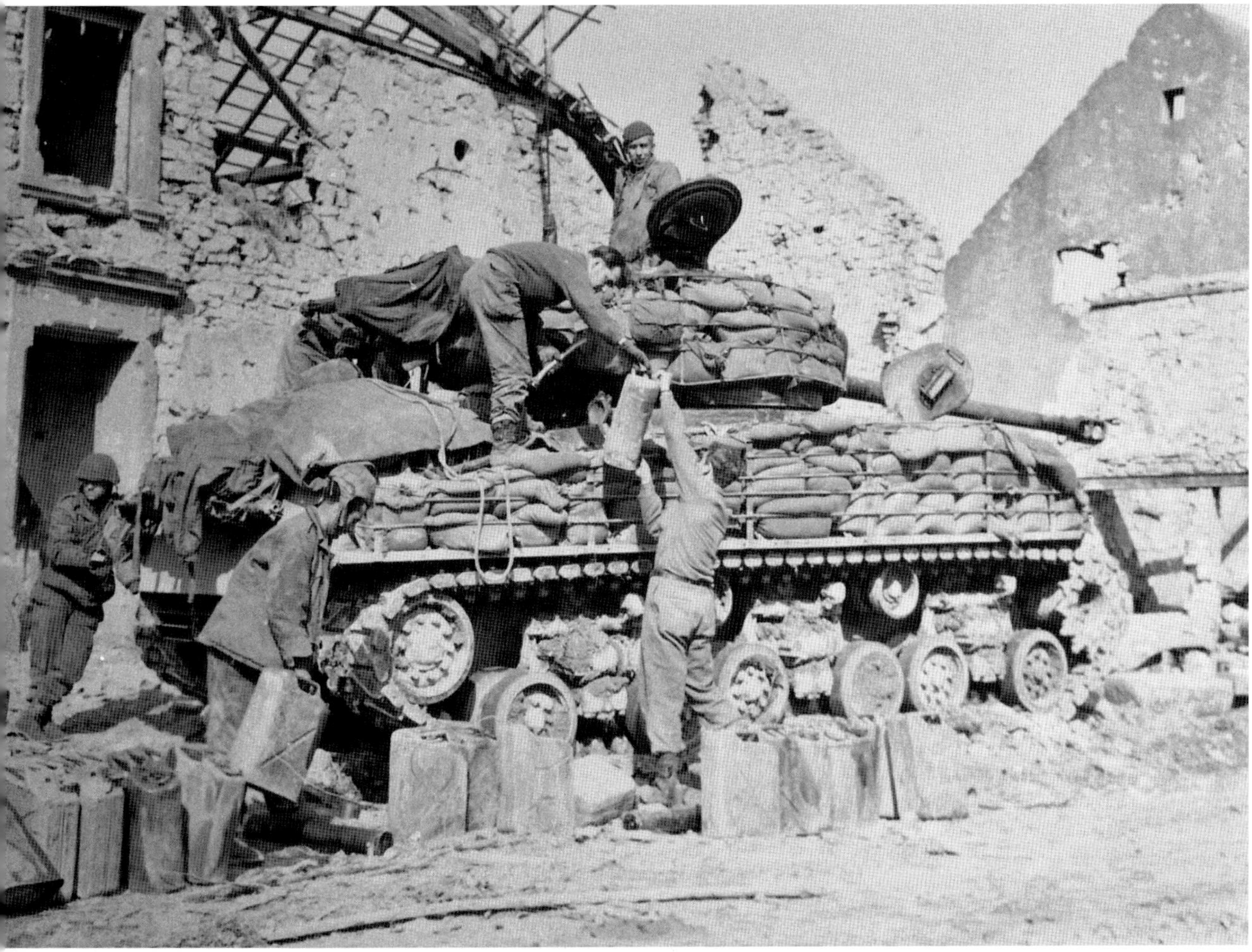

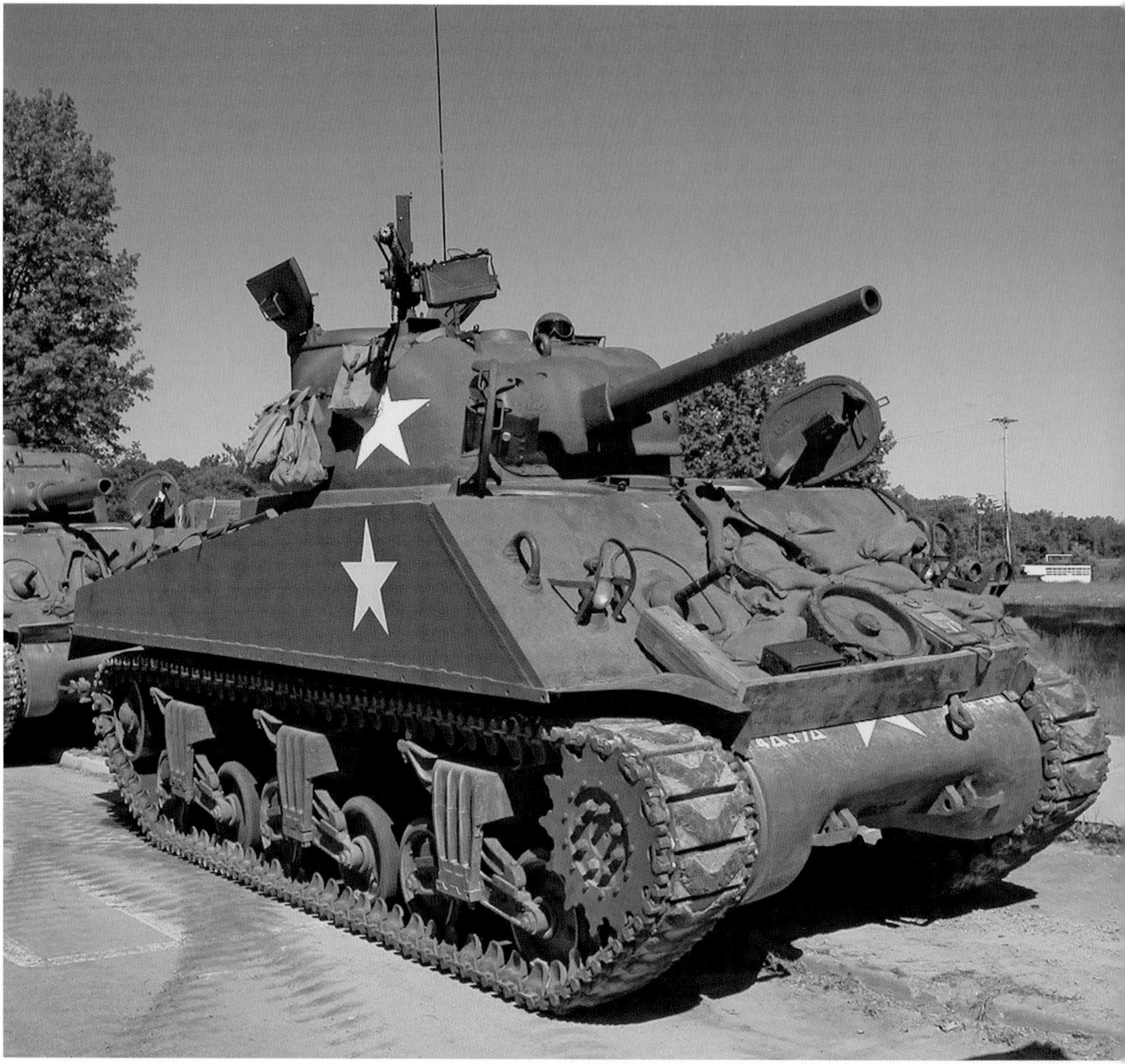

(*Above*) Belonging to the former Patton Museum of Armor and Cavalry is this restored second-generation M4A3 tank. While this second-generation model retained the first-generation M4 series cast armour turret and 75mm main gun, it was fitted with a second-generation wet main gun ammunition storage system. This is reflected in the tank designation as the M4A3(75)W. *(Chun-lun Hsu)*

(*Opposite page*) The crew of this unfortunate USMC M4A3(75)W had attached spare track links to both the tank's glacis and turret for additional protection. Note the large overhead hatches in the front hull. The hinge pins for these hatches were set at a compound angle which made them partially counterbalanced and therefore easier to open than the front hull hatches on first-generation M4 series tanks. *(National Archives)*

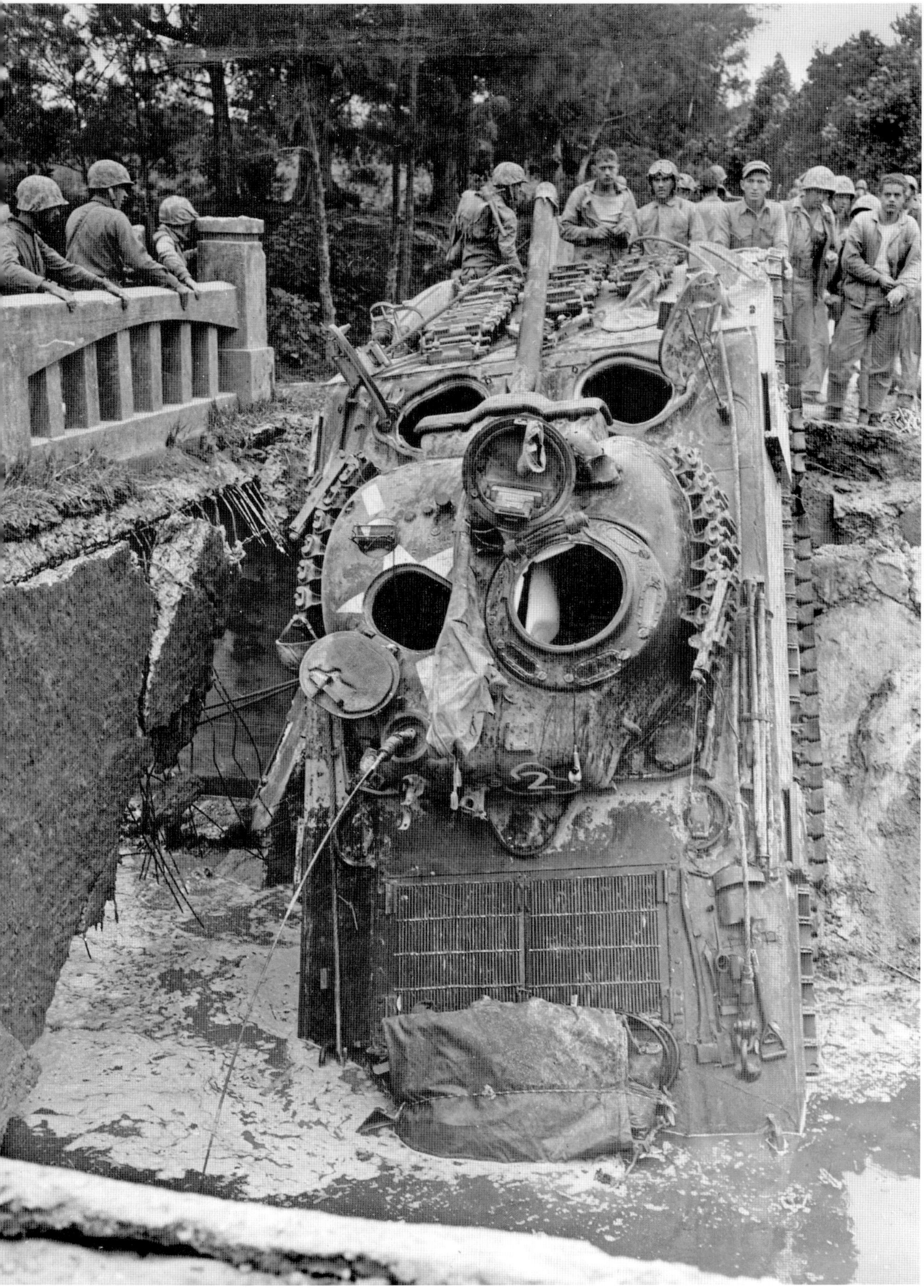

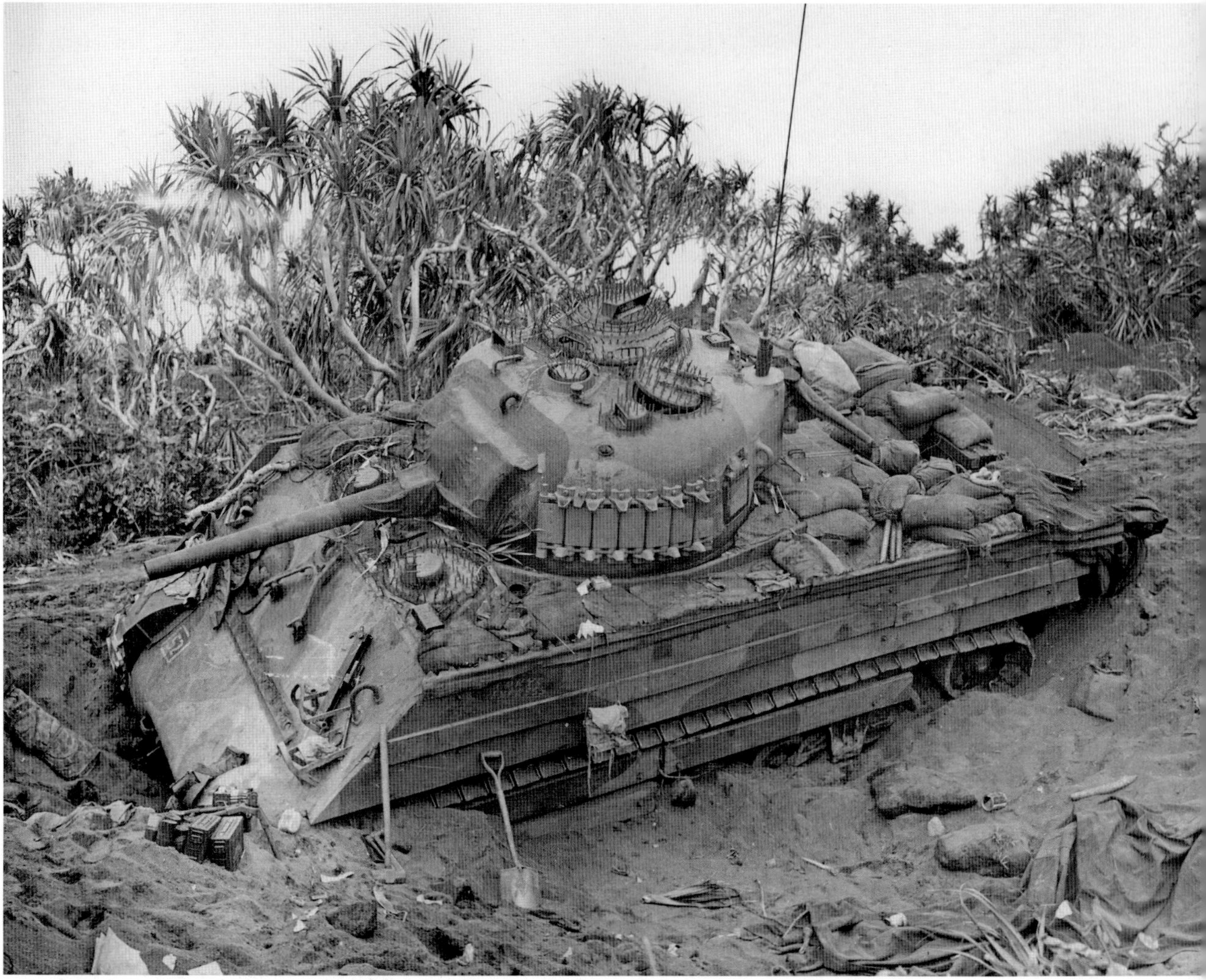

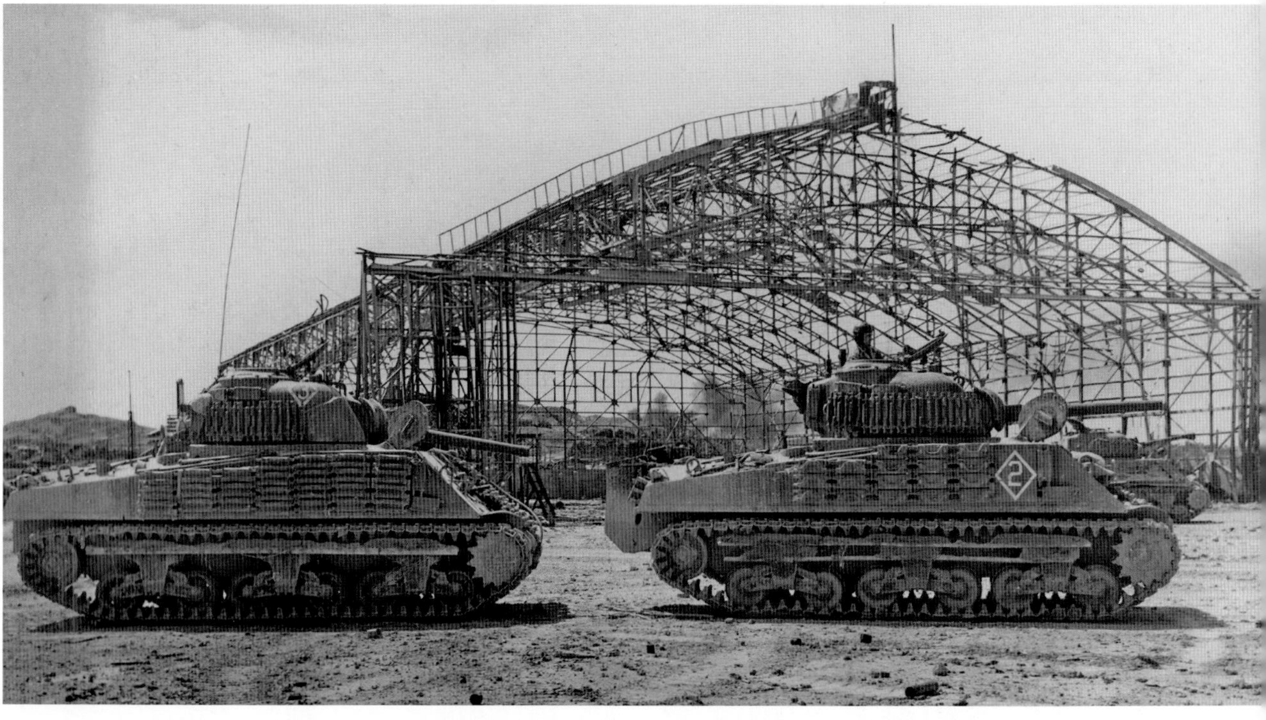
2

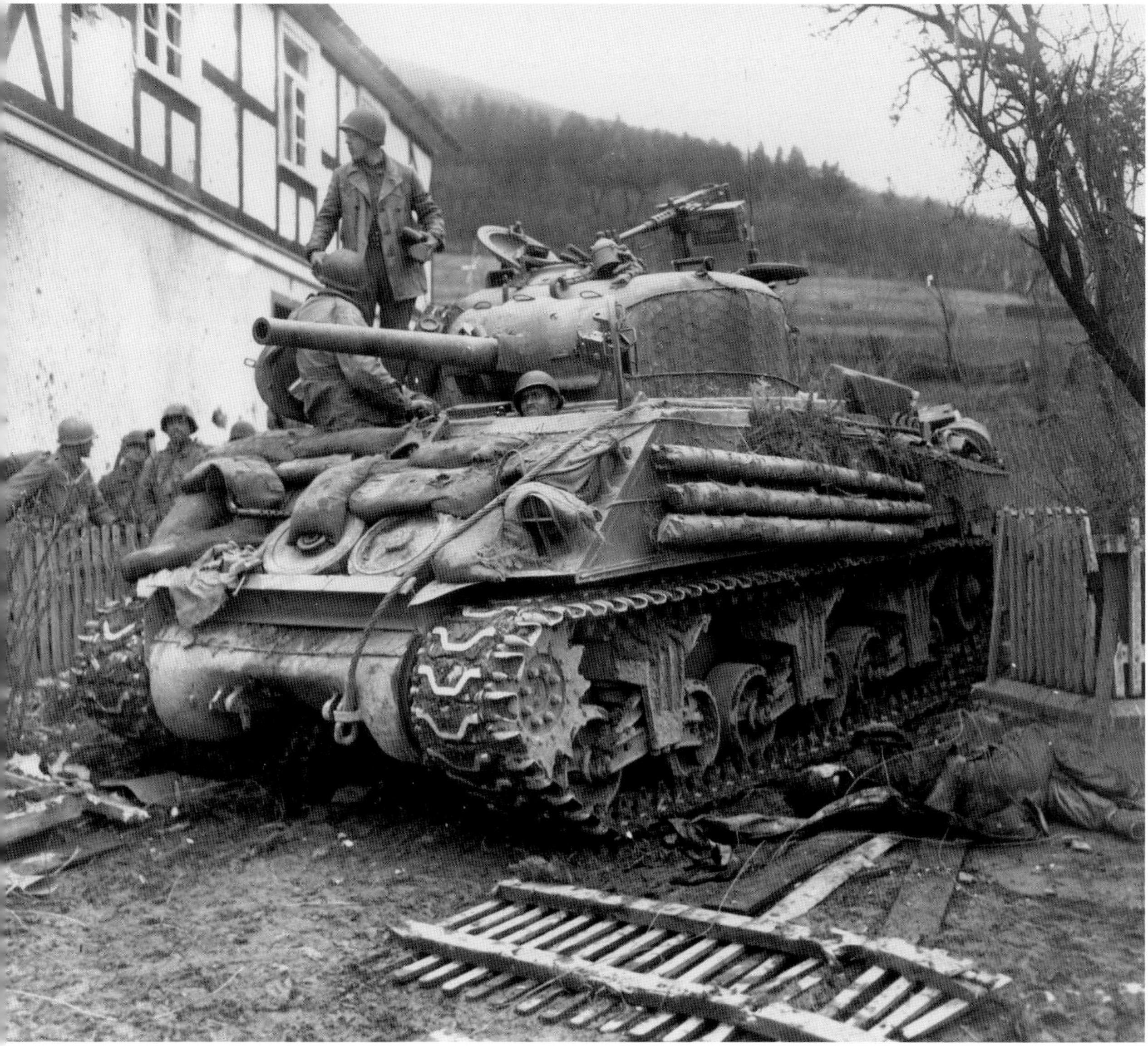

(*Opposite above*) To protect their tank from Japanese tank-hunter teams the crew of this USMC M4A3(75)W covered their turret roof with large nails to defeat satchel charges. Every other horizontal surface is covered with sandbags for the same reason. To prevent Japanese magnetic mines from adhering to the vertical hull sides of the tank they have covered it with wooden planks. *(National Archives)*

(*Opposite below*) Both of these USMC M4A3(75)W tanks have been covered by spare track links on their hulls and turrets. The horizontal metal bars seen welded to their suspension systems was for the attachment of wooden planks (missing here) aimed at preventing Japanese tank-hunter teams from throwing anti-tank mines and satchel charges under the vehicles. *(National Archives)*

(*Above*) Pictured is an M4A3(75)W tank in Europe during the last year of the war. To lower the ground pressure of the tracks on the M4 series, both first- and second-generation, the tank track could be fitted with extended steel end connectors as seen on the vehicle pictured. Note that the steel tracks also have a V-shaped chevron pattern on each track link to aid in off-road traction. *(Patton Museum)*

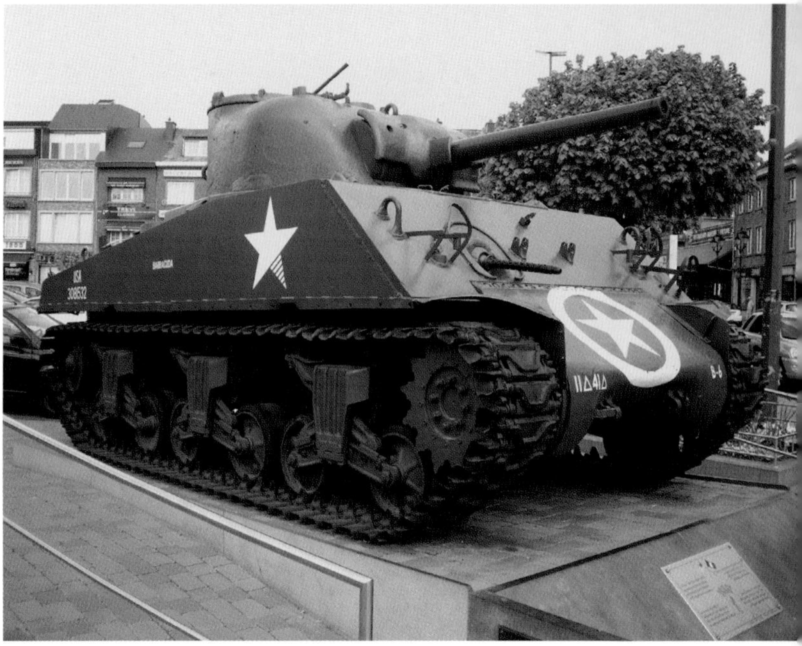

The small-calibre machine gun projecting out from the glacis of this monument tank on display in France was secured to the interior front hull by a bracket mount. As the mount did not have an aperture for sighting it could only be aimed by observing its tracer rounds. Of the typical complement of three machine guns on the M4 series, it was the small-calibre coaxial machine gun that was most often employed in combat. The gunner fired it with a foot-operated electrical switch but could also fire it manually if needed. *(Pierre-Olivier Buan)*

Belonging to the Belgian National Military Museum is this restored Sherman VC Firefly based on a first-generation M4A4 series tank. Due to the length of the 17-pounder main gun, the vehicle's radio, originally located in the turret bustle, was moved to a box seen in this picture attached to the rear of the turret. *(Michel Krauss)*

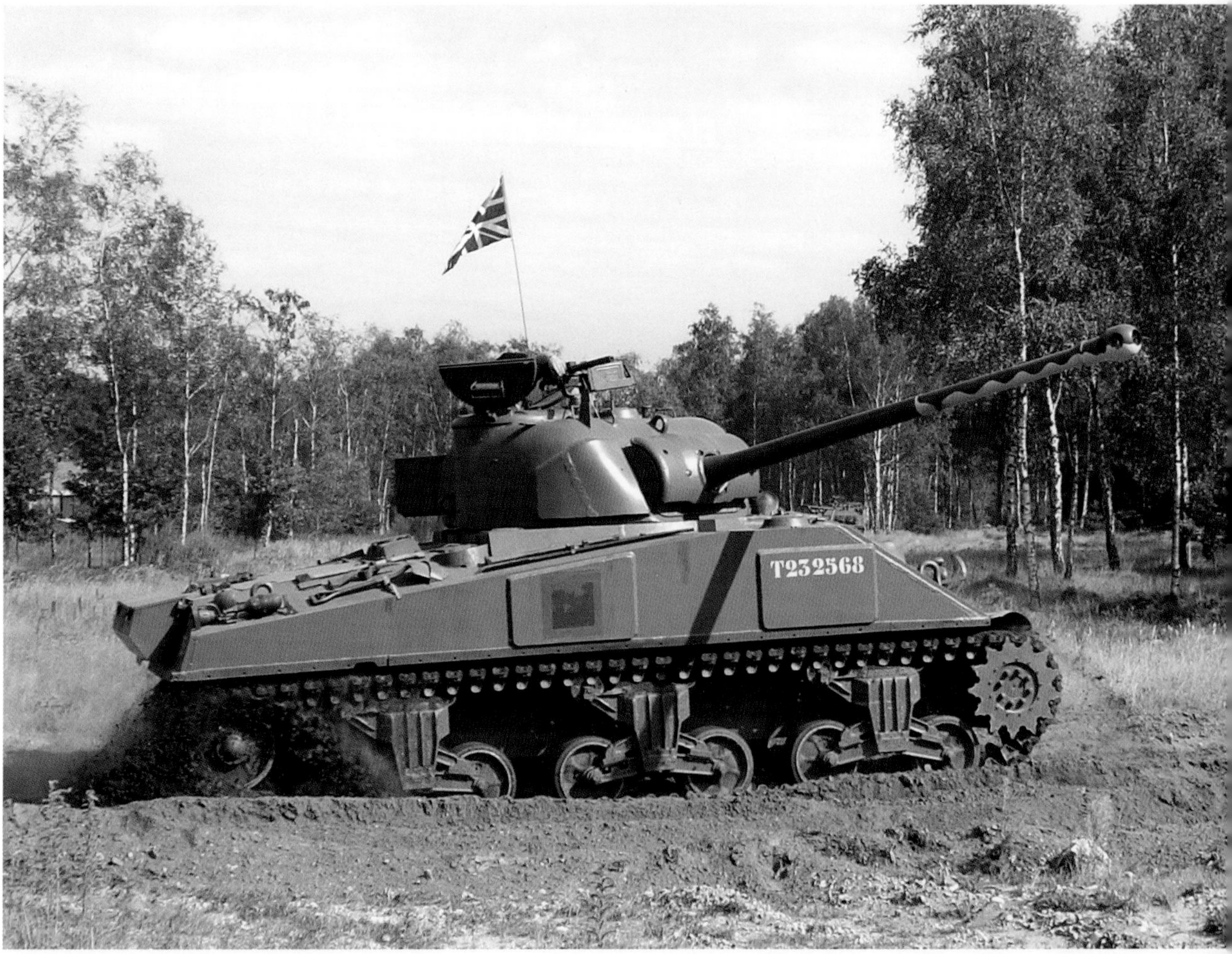
T232568

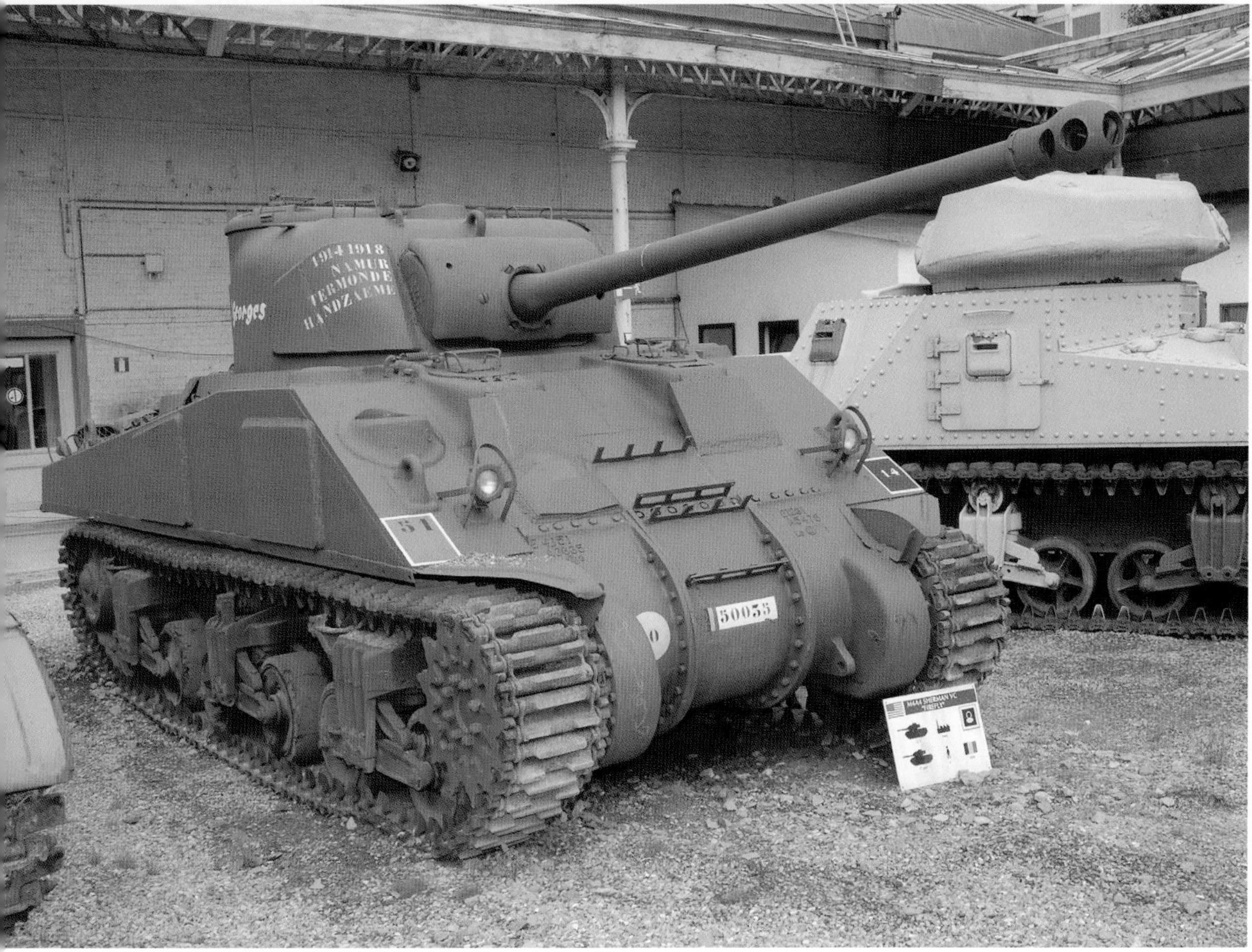
1914-1918
NAMUR
TERMONDE
HANDZAEME
51
50055

In order to place as many 17-pounder main gun rounds as possible in the Sherman Firefly, it was decided to eliminate the assistant driver/bow gunner's position. In his place was installed a main gun ammunition bin for fifteen rounds. This resulted in a plate of armour being welded over the machine-gun opening in the glacis as is visible in this image of a preserved Firefly VC. *(Michel Krauss)*

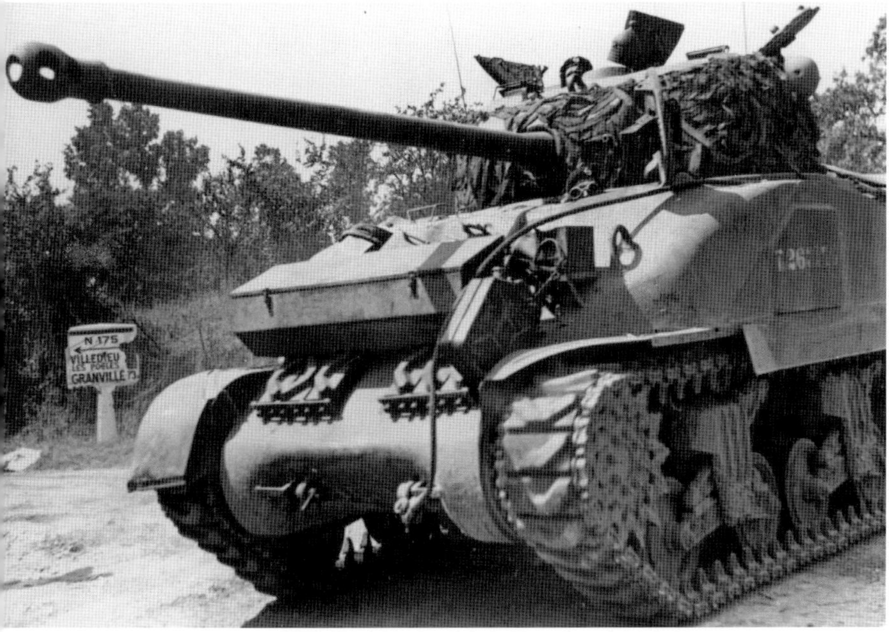
N 175
VILLEDIEU
GRANVILLE

Less common than the Sherman VC Firefly based on the first-generation M4A4 was the Sherman IC based on the first-generation M4. Those that were converted by the British army to the Firefly configuration that came with a composite hull as seen in this wartime photograph were referred to as the Sherman Hybrid IC. *(Tank Museum)*

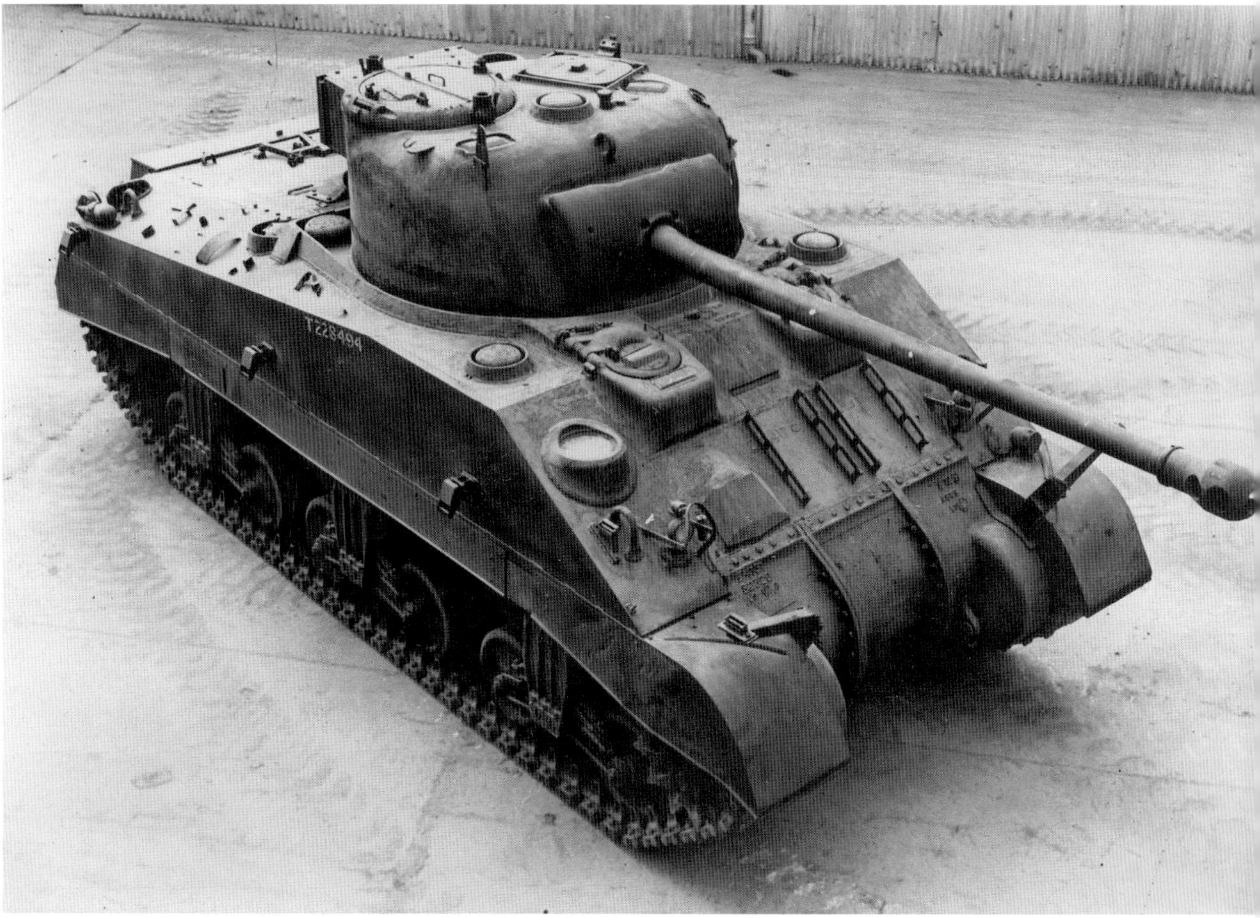

The standard first-generation M4 series tank turret lacked an overhead hatch for the loader. When the British army had their first-generation M4A4 and M4 tanks reconfigured as Fireflies they added a loader hatch as seen in this wartime image of a Sherman VC. The Firefly series had authorized main gun storage for seventy-eight rounds. *(Tank Museum)*

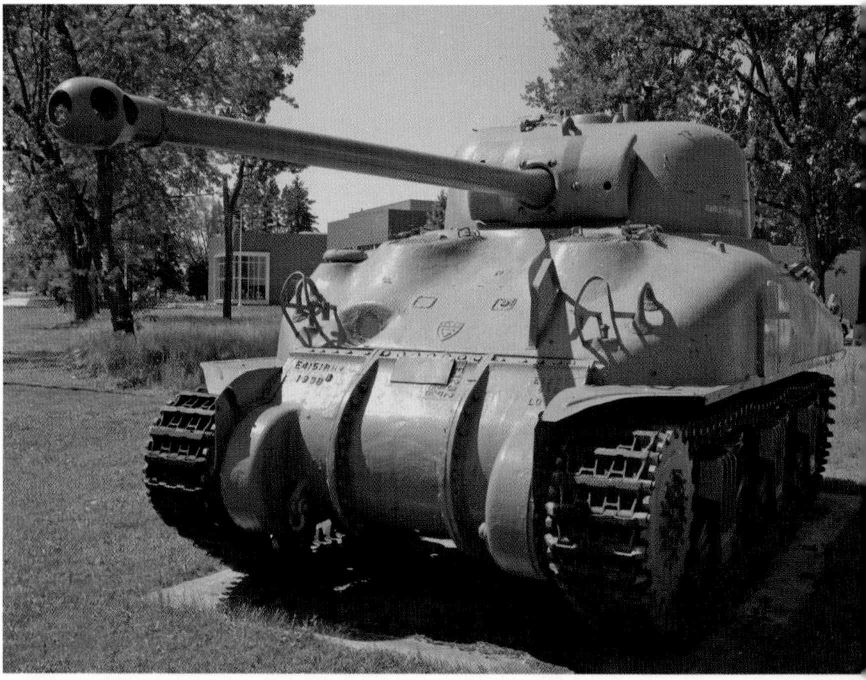

In anticipation of requiring more Sherman Fireflies than British industry could produce, the British army shipped a Firefly turret to Canada to see if it could be successfully fitted to the hull of a Canadian-built Grizzly I. That preserved test vehicle is seen here on display at a Canadian army museum. As events transpired the project was eventually cancelled. *(Paul and Loren Hannah)*

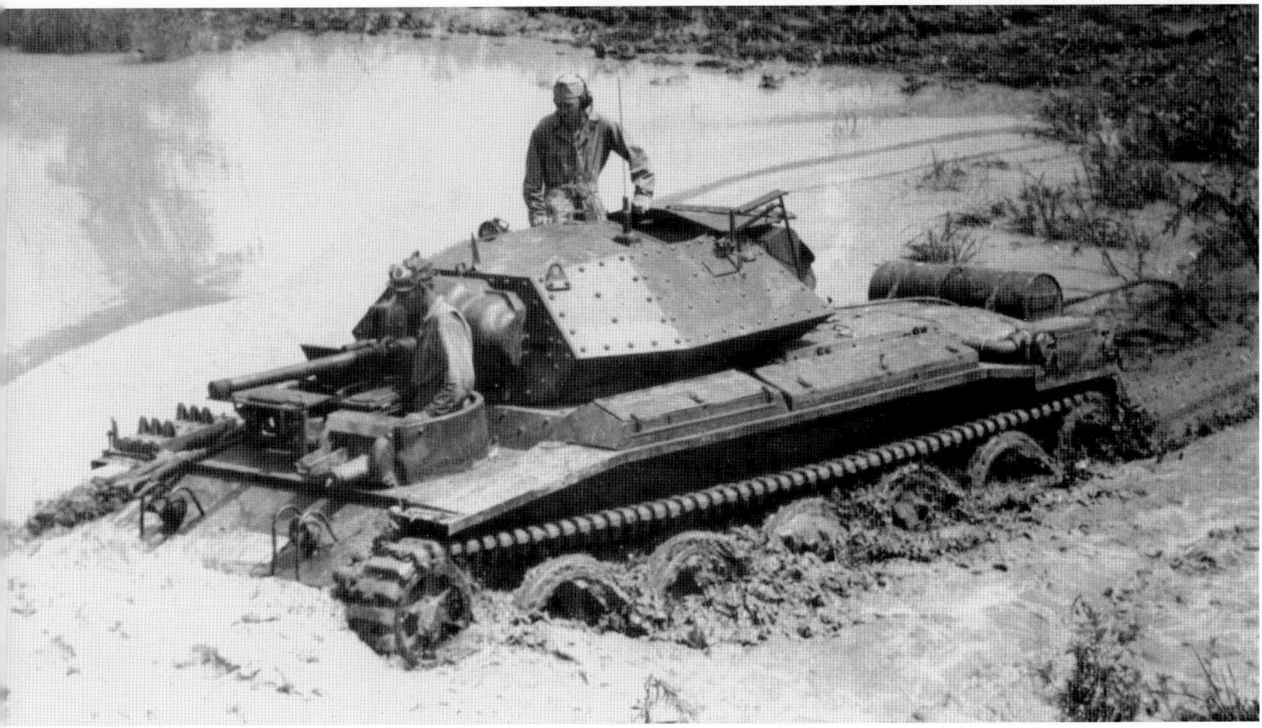

A British-built Cruiser Tank Mk VI (A15) named the 'Crusader' is shown being tested by US army personnel. This is the original model of the vehicle armed with a 2-pounder and a sub-turret armed with a small-calibre machine gun in the front hull. The sub-turret was subsequently removed from the original model in some cases and all follow-on versions. *(Patton Museum)*

The final production model of the Crusader, seen here, was up-armed with a 6-pounder. However, by the time it entered service the vehicle was already obsolete as a gun tank and was soon pulled from service. It was 19ft 8in in length, had a width of 8ft 8in and was 7ft 4in high. Top speed of the tank on level roads was 27mph. *(Tank Museum)*

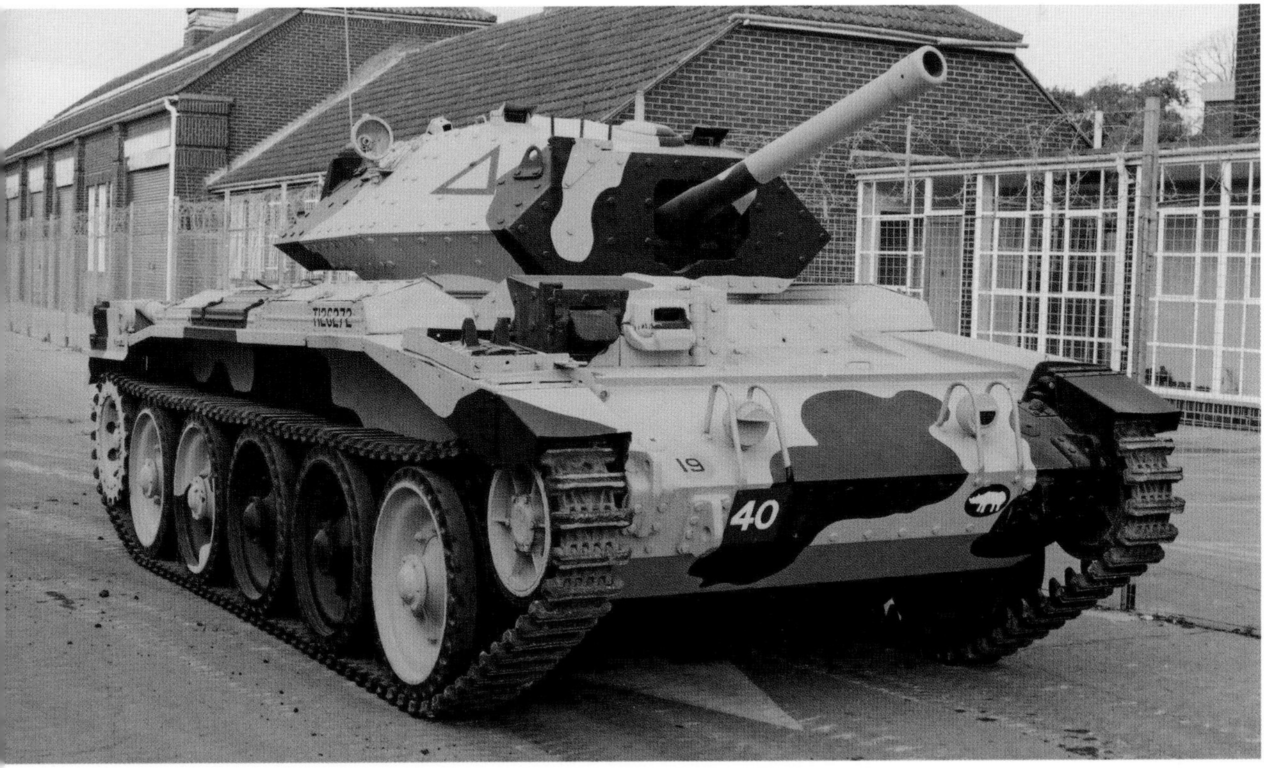
19
40

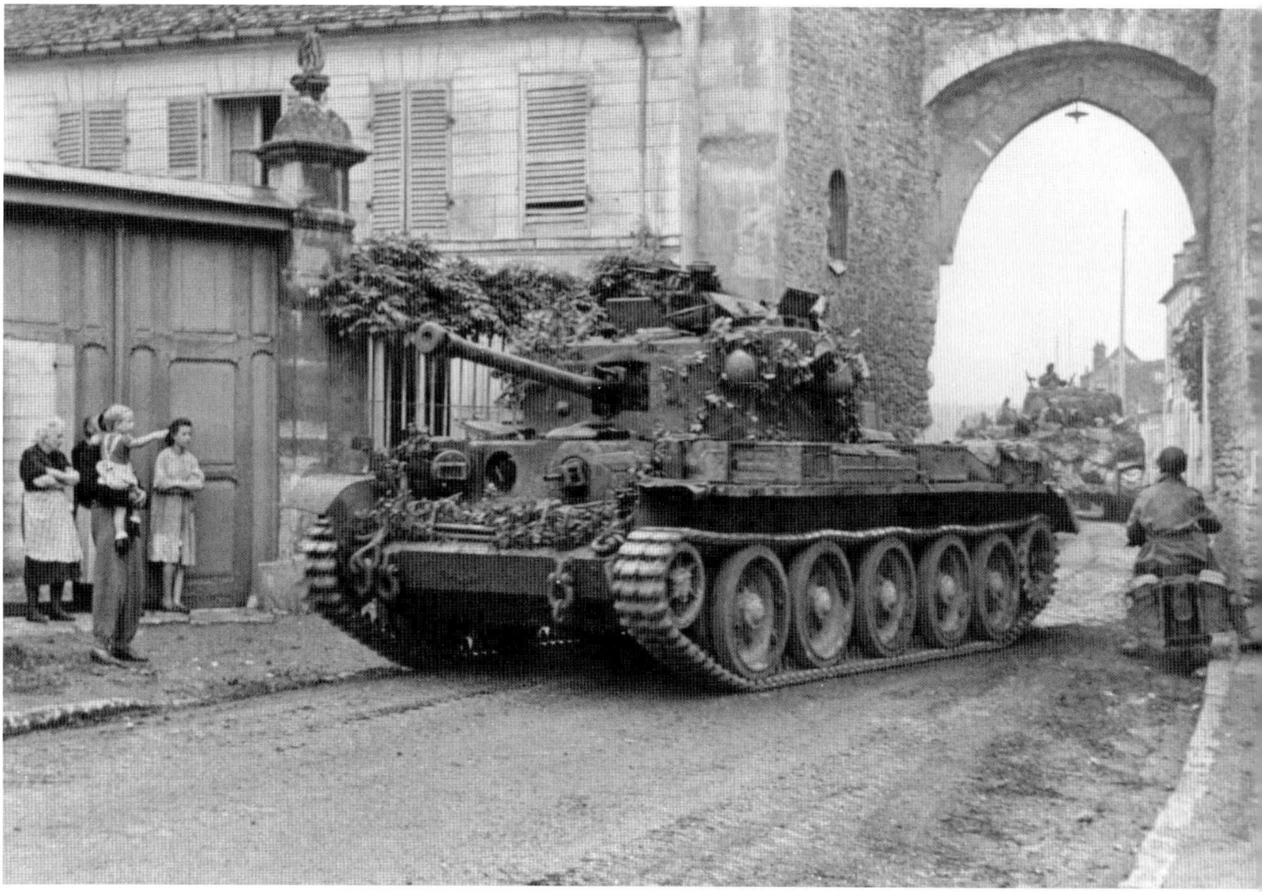

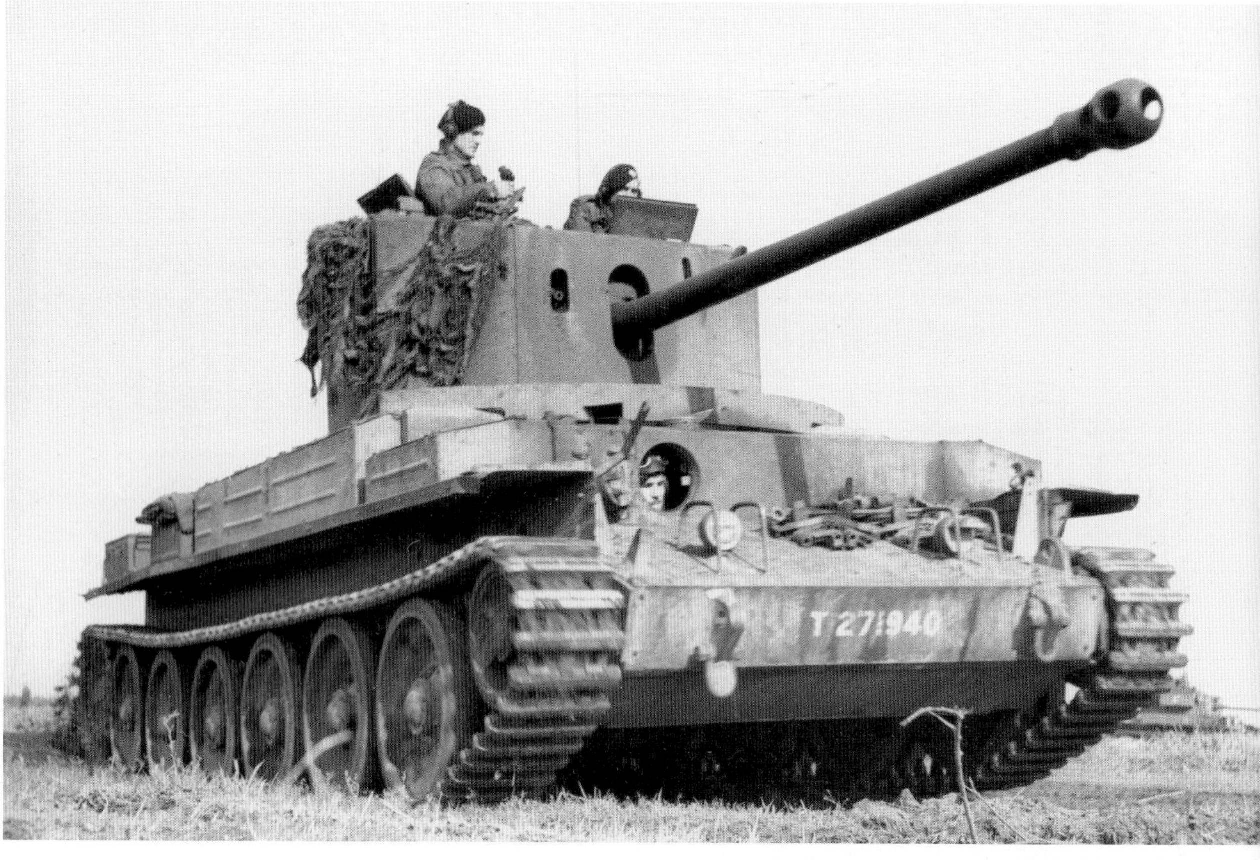
T 271940

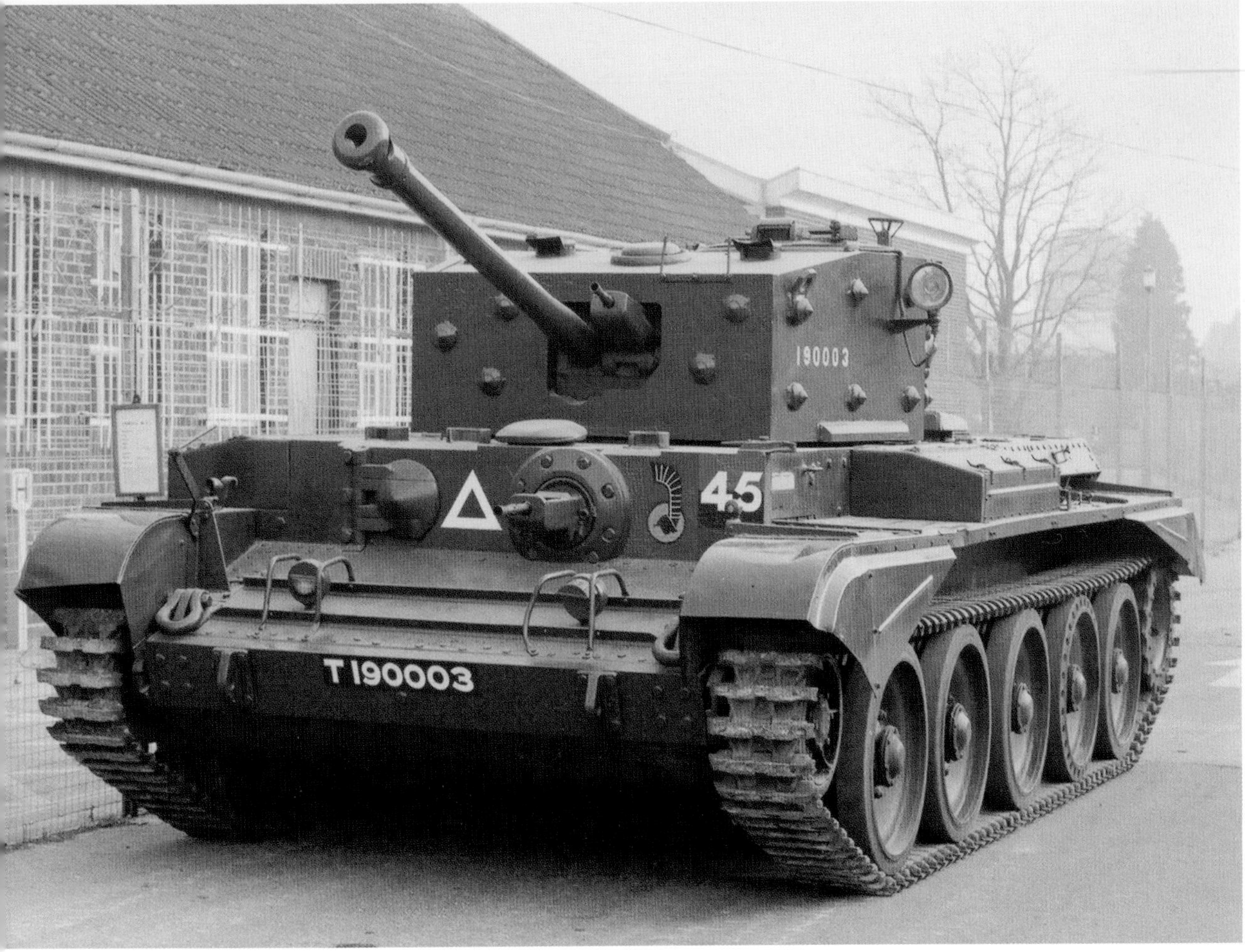

190003
45
T 190003

(*Opposite above*) The faster of the British army's long line of cruiser tanks was the Mk VIII (A27M) Cromwell seen here. It could reach a maximum speed on level roads of 40mph on early-production models. Unlike the American M4 series that had its transmission located in the front hull, the Cromwell transmission was, like that of the Soviet T-34 series, located in the rear hull along with the engine. (*Tank Museum*)

(*Above*) The Cromwell turret was a simple armoured steel box with add-on armour plates bolted to it as is evident from the large studs visible on this preserved example. With the add-on armour plate the turret had a maximum thickness of 101mm. The tank had a length of 20ft 10in, a width of 9ft 6in and a height of 8ft 2in. (*Tank Museum*)

(*Opposite below*) An extremely ungainly-looking tank was the Cruiser Tank (A30) shown here and named the 'Challenger'. It was the failed predecessor to the very successful Firefly series of 17-pounder armed tanks. Armed with a 17-pounder, it was based on the lengthened hull of the Cromwell. The turret was derived from a cancelled British heavy tank design. (*Tank Museum*)

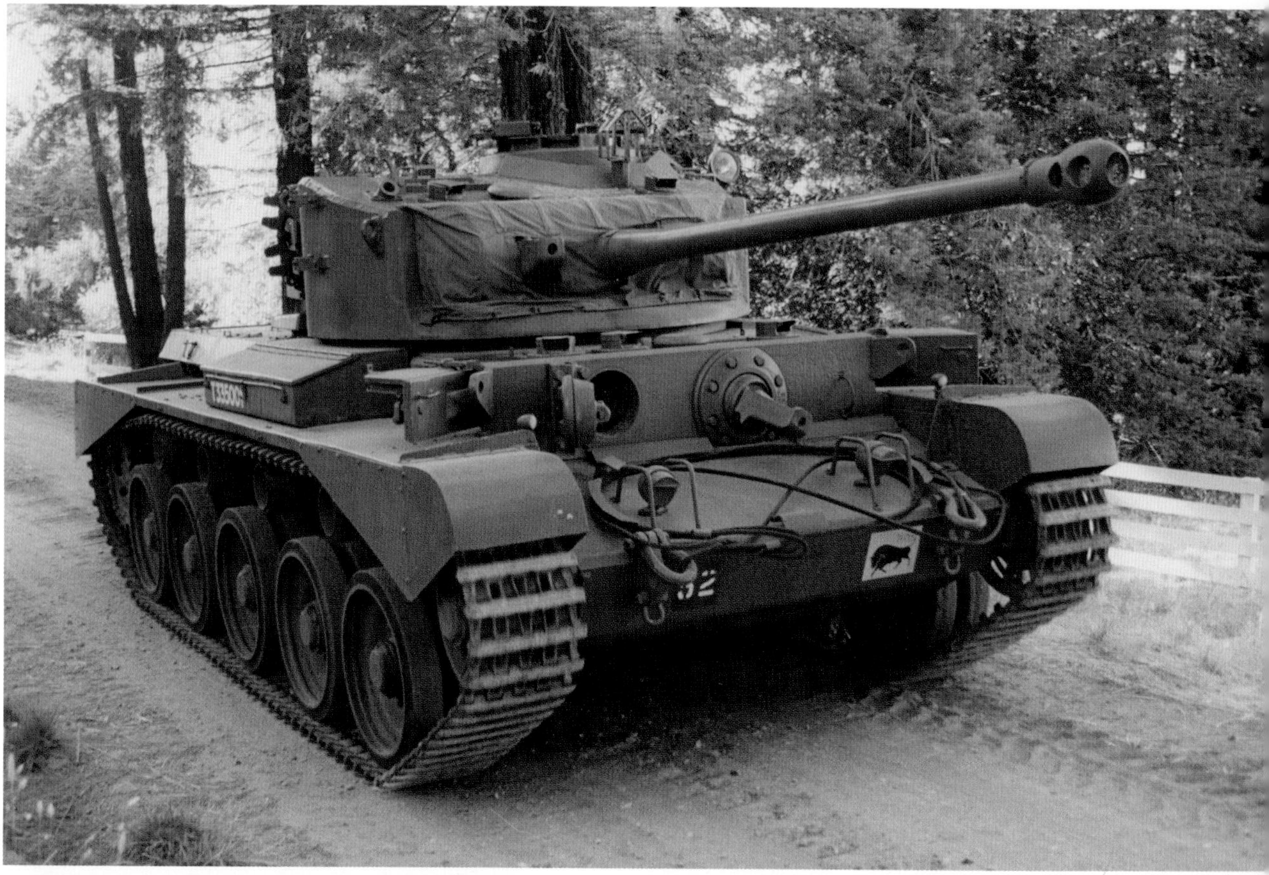

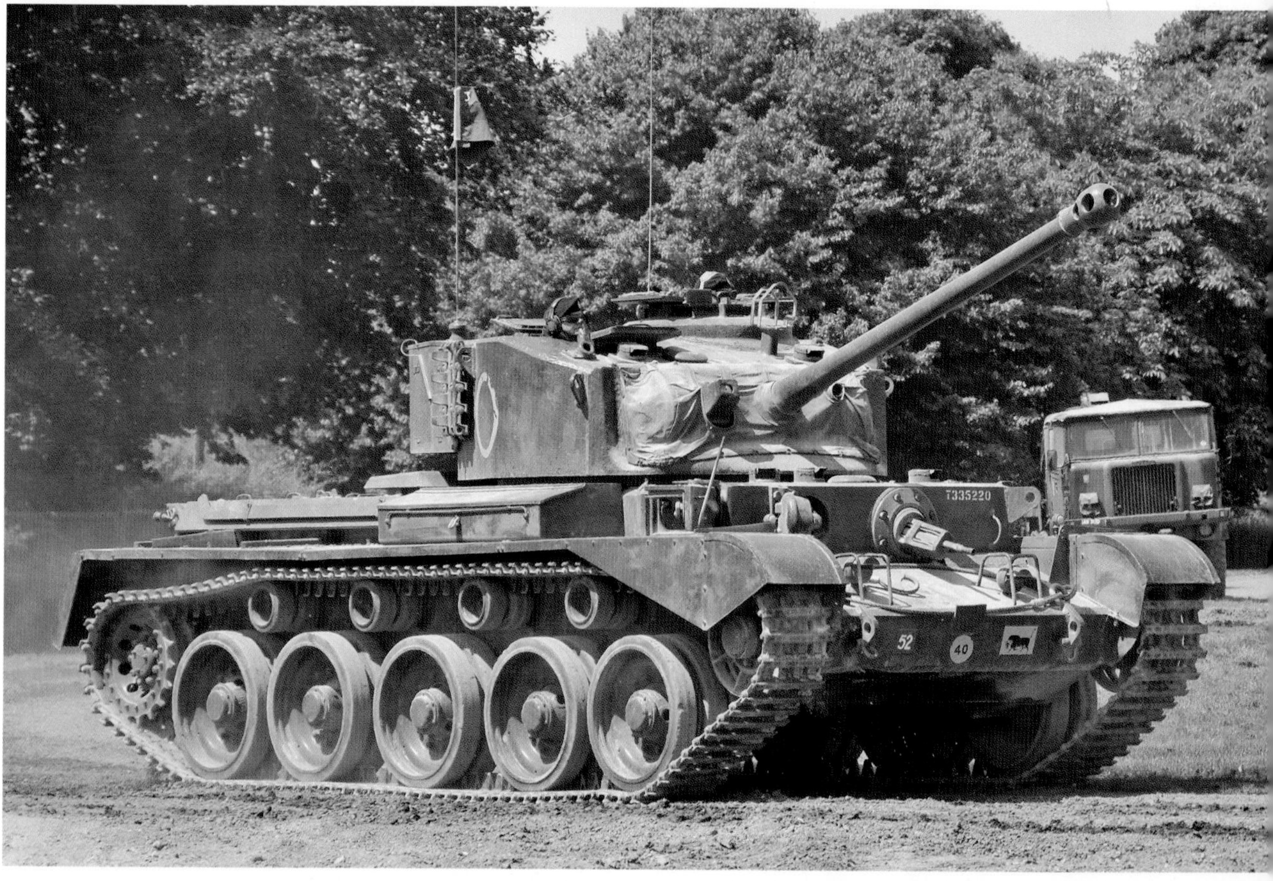
T335220
52
40

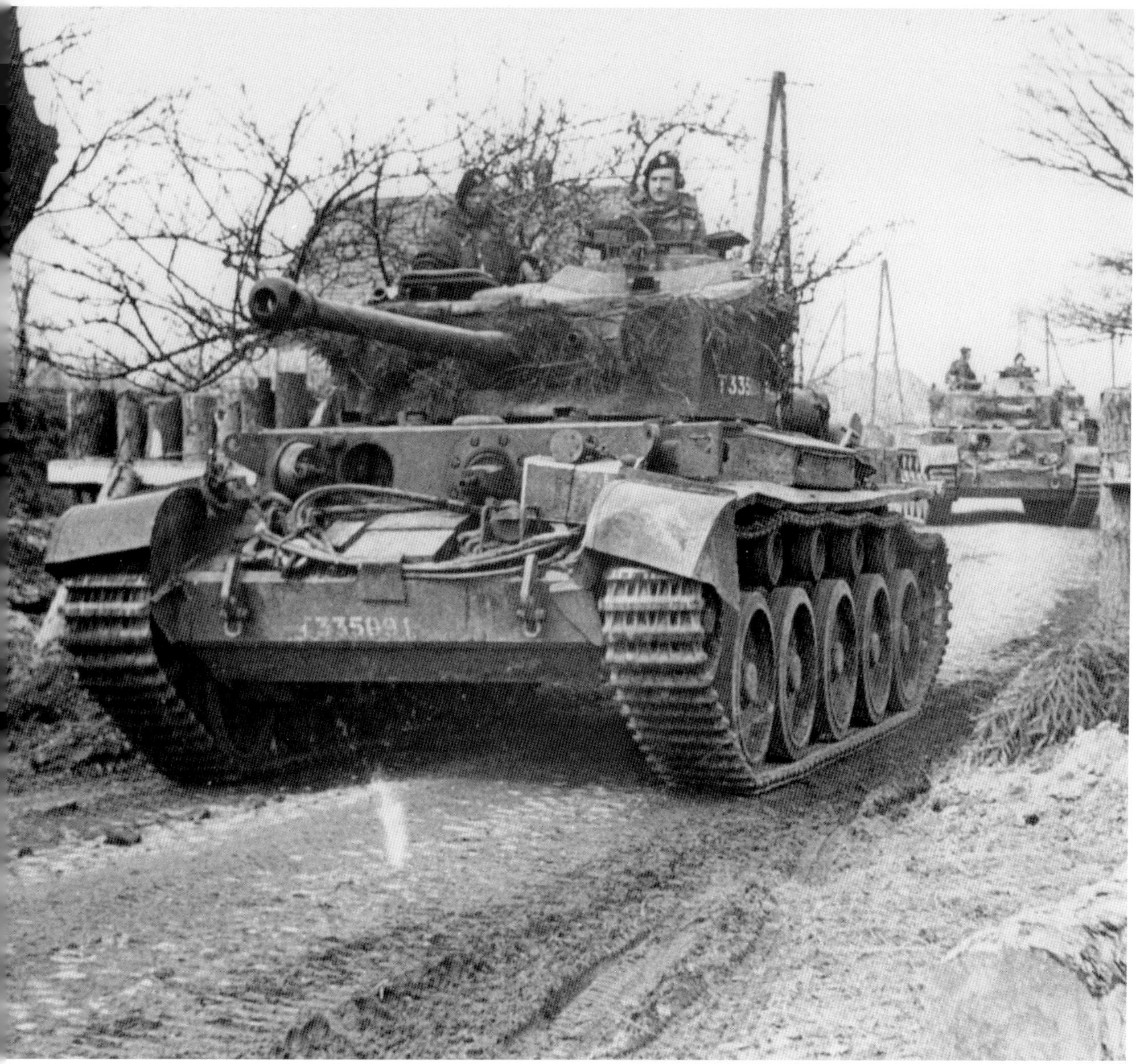

(*Opposite above*) Not wanting to give up on the concept of an up-armed Cromwell, the British army eventually fielded the Cruiser Tank (A-34) named the 'Comet'. A preserved example is pictured here. It was a much more successful design than the Challenger and was armed with a smaller and lighter version of the 17-pounder labelled as the 77mm gun. *(Author's collection)*

(*Above*) The Comet seen here in this wartime picture had a maximum speed on level roads of 29mph. However, like all tanks, its off-road maximum speed was much lower at approximately 16mph. It was the last British tank to ride on the American Christie suspension system. The thickest armour was 101mm at the turret front. *(Tank Museum)*

(*Opposite below*) Unlike the Christie suspension fitted to the Cromwell, that of the Comet was fitted with four return rollers as seen on this preserved example. Another external difference between the two related tanks included a vehicle commander's cupola on the Comet not present on the Cromwell. The vehicle length was 25ft 1.5in, width 10ft and its height was 9ft 5in. *(Ian Wilcox)*

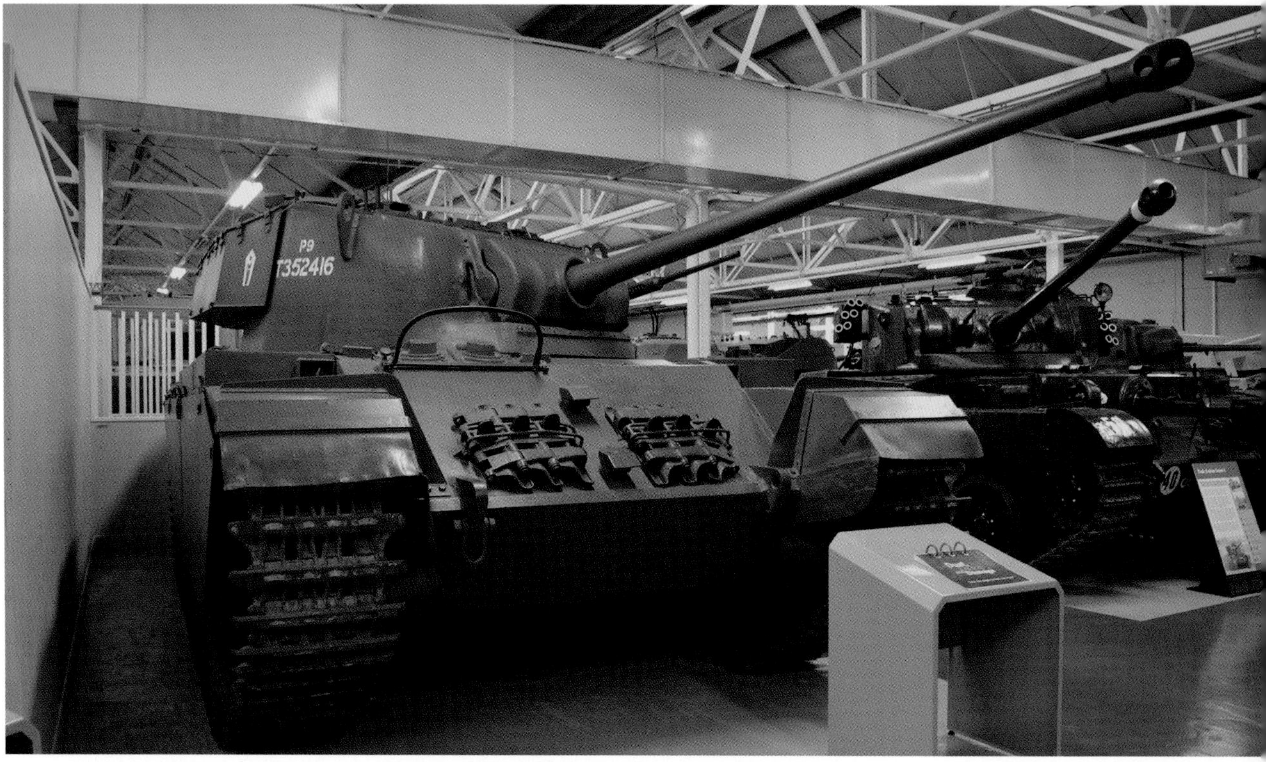
P9
T352416

The last of the cruiser tanks was the A41 Centurion. Like the Challenger and the Firefly, it was armed with a 17-pounder main gun. Pictured is a pilot tank also armed with a coaxial 20mm automatic cannon that did not make it into the production models. The tank had a length of 25ft 2in, a width of 11ft and a height of 9ft 8in. *(Tank Museum)*

Seen here on display at a Canadian army base museum is an early model of the British army tank named the 'Churchill' and designated as the Infantry Tank Mk IV (A22). The model of the Churchill pictured is the Mk I version armed with a 2-pounder in the turret and a 3-inch howitzer in the front hull. *(Tank Museum)*

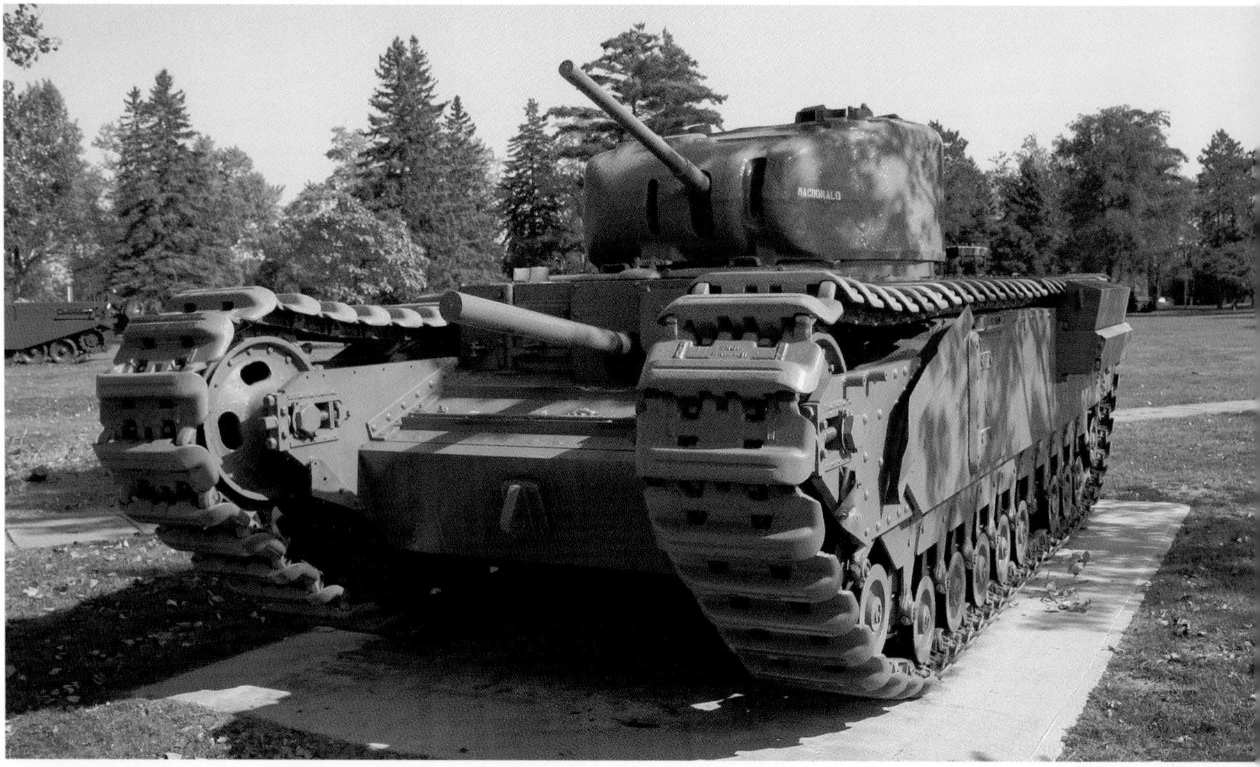
MACDONALD

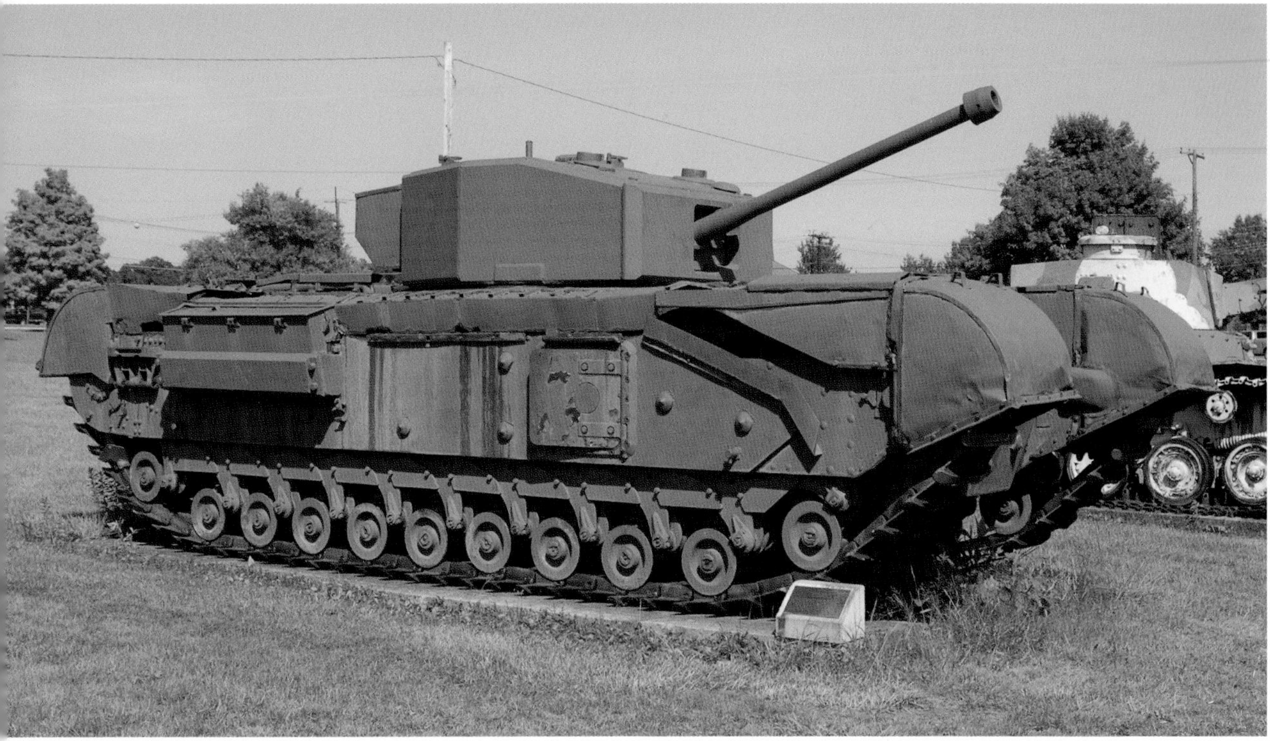

Pictured when it was on display at the now-closed US Army Ordnance Museum is this Churchill Mk III armed with a turret-mounted 6-pounder main gun. The tank was 24ft 5in long, had a width of 9ft and a height of 10ft 6in. The maximum turret armour thickness was 102mm. Top speed on level roads was 15.5mph. *(Author's collection)*

This preserved Churchill Mk IV tank is armed with a British-designed and built 75mm main gun as is evident from its unique muzzle brake design. With the 75mm main gun fitted it was labelled as the Mk IV(75), as early-production units had been armed with a 6-pounder main gun. The Churchill Mk IV, be it armed with the 6-pounder or 75mm main gun, was the most numerous version of the tank built. *(Tank Museum)*

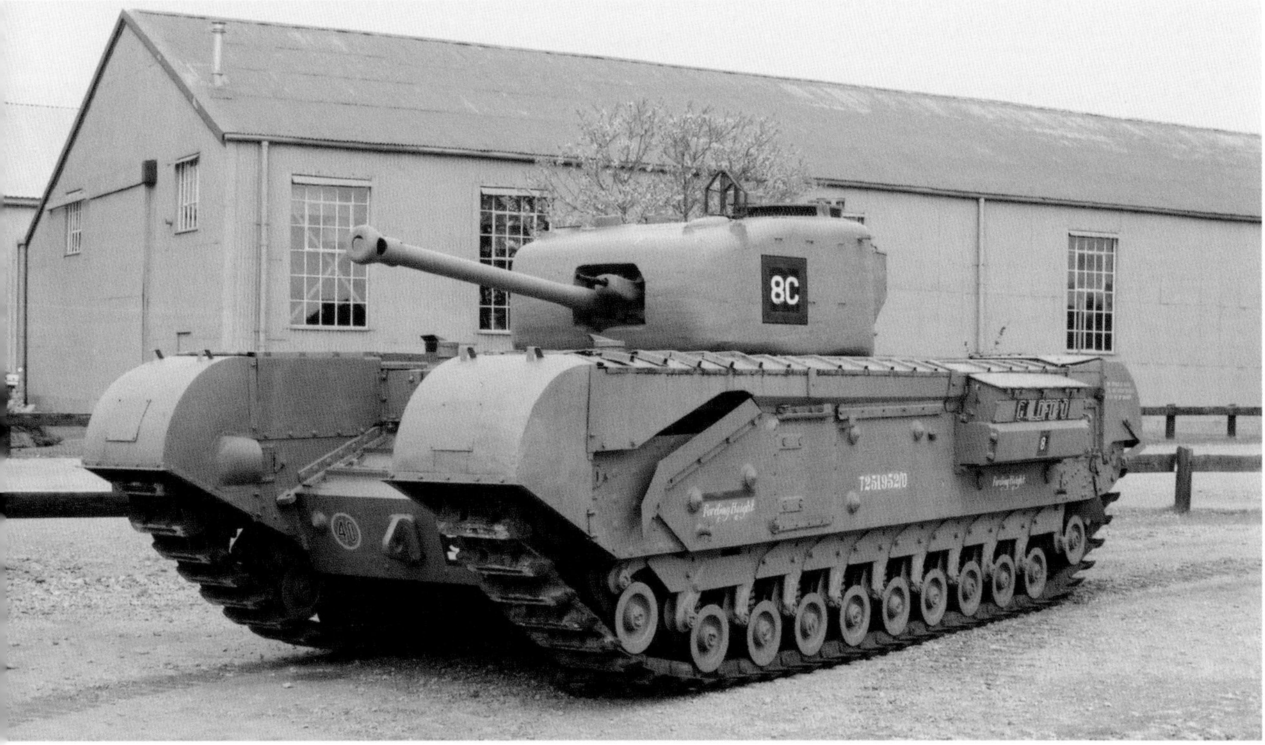
8C
T251952/0
40

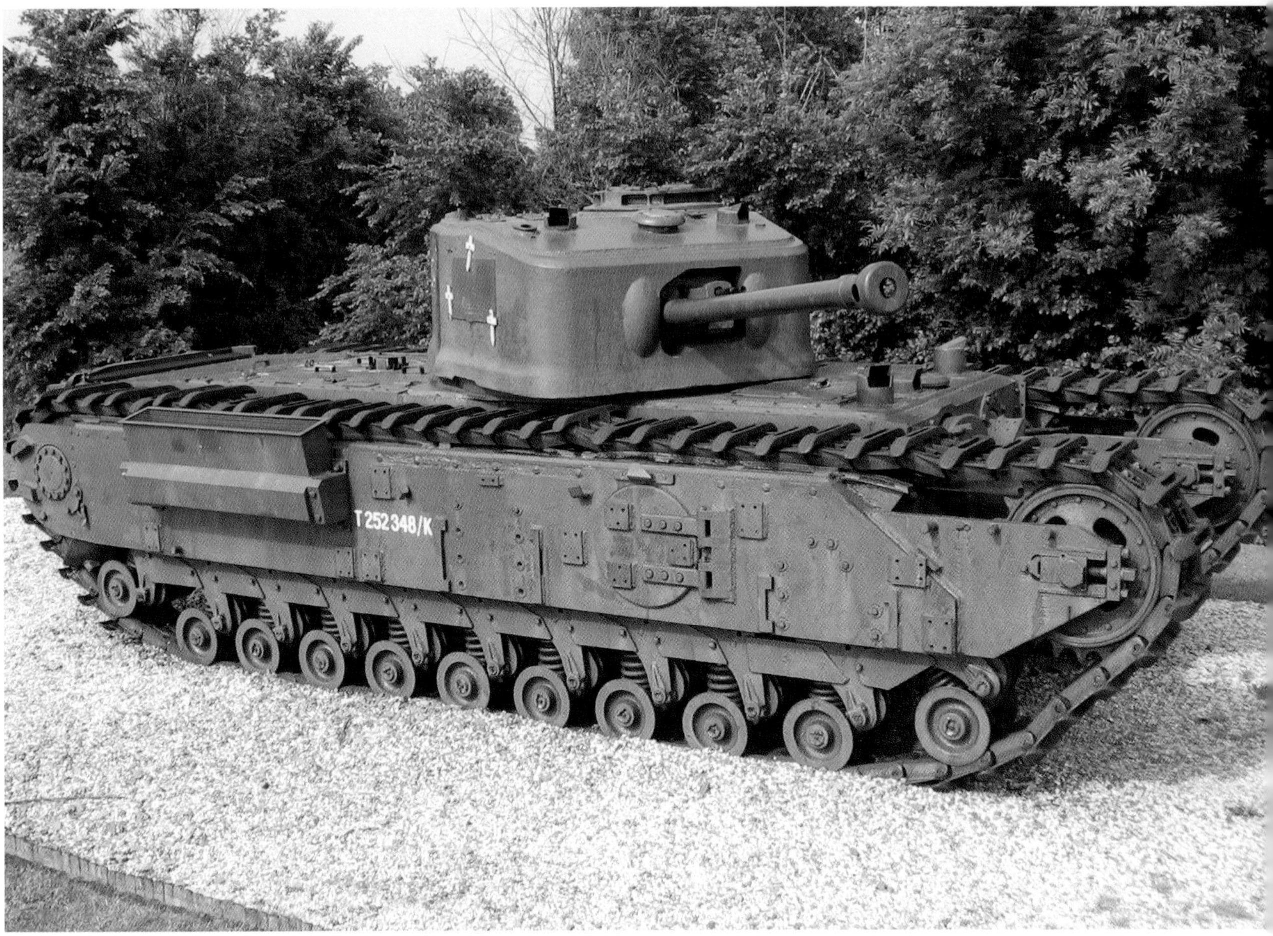
T 252 348/K

On display in France as a monument tank is this Churchill Mk VII armed with a British-built 75mm main gun. Reflecting lessons learned in combat, it featured much thicker turret armour up to a maximum of 152mm. Instead of the square hull escape hatches of earlier models of the tank, it had rounded hull escape hatches as seen on this particular vehicle. *(Pierre-Olivier Buan)*

One of the six prototypes of the Infantry Tank (A43) named the 'Black Prince' is seen here preserved at a museum. Production of this tank was supposed to have begun in early 1945. However, it soon became clear that the vehicle was badly underpowered and because the planned Centurion tank was judged a better design with more potential, the Black Prince never entered into production. *(Tank Museum)*

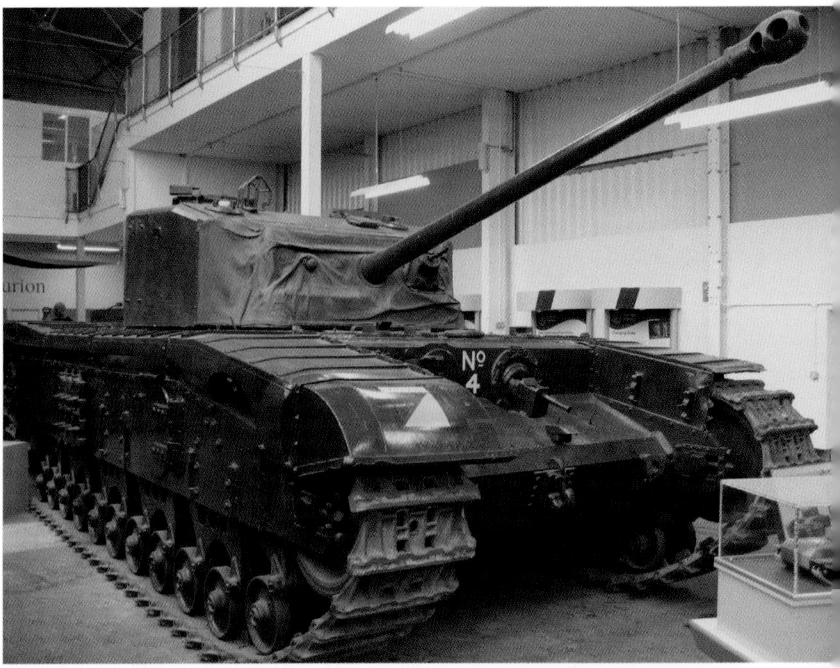
Nº
4

Chapter Four

Heavy Tanks

All the major allied armies before and during the Second World War had considered the design and construction of heavy tanks; however, not all successfully implemented their construction due to their cost and complexity. Some armies were not originally convinced of their need but changed their minds as the Second World War raged on.

T-35 Heavy Tank

The one allied force that totally embraced the concept of heavy tanks before and during the Second World War was the Red Army. It began design studies for its first heavy tank in 1930. This would lead to the fielding of the first production units of the multi-turreted T-35 in 1935. By the time production concluded in 1939 a total of sixty-one units of the tank had been constructed. In its final up-armed and up-armoured model the T-35 is reported to have reached a weight of approximately 121,000lb.

The T-35 had five turrets and was manned by a crew of eleven men. The largest turret on the tank was located on the top of its superstructure and was armed with a 76.2mm main gun. Of the other four turrets, the two mid-size ones were armed with 37mm guns later replaced by 45mm guns. The tank was also armed with at least five or more machine guns.

The Red Army did not deploy the T-35 during the Russo-Finnish War. It seemed to be generally reserved for use in pre-war parades in Moscow's Red Square. Upon the German invasion of the Soviet Union the T-35 tanks were thrown into action by the Red Army with most soon being lost to mechanical failure. A few would last long enough to see service as stationary pillboxes in October 1941.

Replacement Heavy Tank

In August 1938, the Red Army ordered Soviet industry to design and build prototypes of what was referred to as a 'breakthrough tank' and have wooden mock-ups ready for inspection by the end of 1938. The operational prototypes had to have three turrets: one armed with a 76.2mm main gun and the other two with 45mm main guns. In addition, they were to be fitted with at least three machine guns.

The job of designing and building the prototypes was assigned to two different factories. The Leningrad Kirov Plant prototype was assigned the designation SMK-1 and weighed 121,253lb. The other prototype was labelled as the T-100 and designed and built by Plant #185. It weighed 129,920lb. As time went on, the number of turrets mandated for a breakthrough tank dropped from three to two.

The building of a single-turreted prototype breakthrough tank by the Leningrad Kirov Plant was approved in February 1939 for consideration by the Red Army along with the SMK-1 and the T-100. This single-turreted breakthrough tank or heavy tank was referred to simply as the 'KV' in honour of Marshal of the Soviet Union Kliment Voroshilov. It was armed with a 76.2mm main gun and two machine guns, one being the coaxial. The KV series is now generally referred to as the KV-1 series.

When the three prototype breakthrough tanks were tested by the Red Army in September 1939, it was clear that the single-turreted KV-1 tank was greatly superior to the twin-turreted SMK-1 and T-100 tank. To verify the test results, all three prototype tanks were sent to participate in the early stages of the Russo-Finnish War, which began in November 1939.

Of the three prototypes sent to fight in Finland the KV-1 proved the most reliable. The thick frontal armour made it immune to destruction by all the existing direct-fire anti-tank guns. This brief demonstration of its combat effectiveness resulted in a December 1939 decision by the Red Army to place the KV-1 into service. The total number of KVs built between January 1940 and August 1942 was 3,167 units.

KV-1 Heavy Tank Series

The five-man KV-1 tank weighed approximately 95,000lb and was powered by the same diesel engine as the T-34 series. This meant that its mobility was inferior to the first-generation T-34 tanks it had been envisioned as working alongside. Adding to the Red Army's disappointment was the fact that the KV-1 series proved far less reliable than the T-34 series.

As with other Red Army tanks, the author has adopted the policy of assigning it model numbers based on the year it was introduced into service to distinguish between production versions. Therefore the first KV-1 production batch is labelled as the KV-1 Model 1939. It was armed with the same L-11 76.2mm main gun as fitted to the first-generation T-34 Model 1940 and early-production units of the T-34 Model 1941.

The next production KV-1 tank batch is labelled as the Model 1940. It was heavier at 101,000lb and beginning in January 1941 was armed with a 76.2mm main gun labelled as the F-32. In October 1941, the F-32 on the KV-1 Model 1940 production lines was replaced by a longer-barrelled and superior 76.2mm gun referred to as the ZiS-5. This was a near-identical version of the F-34 76.2mm main gun that went into late-production units of the T-34 Model 1941 and all the follow-on variants.

The up-armoured version of the KV-1 series armed with the ZiS-5 76.2mm main gun is now referred to as the Model 1941. It weighed approximately 105,000lb and was built with either a welded armour or a cast armour turret. Unfortunately, the armour upgrade for the KV-1 Model 1941 came at a price as the added weight only made the vehicle's existing powertrain problems much worse.

KV-1 Series Modifications

The replacement for the KV-1 Model 1941 was labelled as the KV-1S Model 1941. The 'S' suffix in the tank's designation was the abbreviation for the Russian word 'skorostnoi', which means 'speedy'. The KV-1S corrected some of the design problems found in the earlier versions of the KV-1 series with such things as a new transmission and clutch. Production of the tank began in August 1942 and continued until August 1943 with 1,086 units completed. It would remain in service with the Red Army until the end of the war in Europe.

To improve the automotive performance of the KV-1S, the designers did the only thing possible and thinned out the armour on the tank's turret and hull. This brought down the tank's weight to approximately 95,000lb. Another big improvement was the addition of an overhead armoured cupola for the vehicle's commander that greatly improved his situational awareness.

Cancelled Heavy Tanks

Approval had been given for the building of a heavily-armoured T-150 heavy tank armed with a 76.2mm main gun in June 1940. However, reports that the German military was testing a 105mm anti-tank gun led to its cancellation.

In place of the failed T-150, the Red Army issued a resolution in April 1941 ordering the development of three new heavy tanks labelled as the KV-3, KV-4 and KV-5, all to be armed with a 107mm main gun. According to available sources, the estimated weight of the KV-5 was to be approximately 370,000lb. The overrunning of the factories involved in the construction of these tanks in 1941 by the German army led to work being suspended and never restarted.

KV Series Replacement

By the autumn of 1942 it was clear to the Red Army that the KV-1 heavy tank series was a failure. A decree was issued on 24 February 1943 for Soviet industry to design and construct prototypes of a new heavy tank to be named the 'Joseph Stalin'.

To save time, two existing prototype tanks designated as the KV-13 were employed to assist in building the new Joseph Stalin heavy tank prototypes. One retained the existing KV-13 turret armed with a 76.2mm main gun and the other was fitted with the turret of an experimental tank labelled as the KV-9, which was armed with a 122mm howitzer. These two vehicles would become the base for the development of the future Red Army heavy tanks.

In the end it was decided to go with an 85mm gun installed in a new three-man turret for the first model of the Joseph Stalin heavy tank designated as the IS-85, later as the IS-1. The prefix 'IS' is the Russian abbreviation for 'Iosef Stalin'. The new turret had two machine guns, one coaxial and the other in the rear of the turret.

Due to production delays with the new hull design for the four-man IS-1, an interim heavy tank was approved that involved mounting an IS-1 turret on the widened hull of a KV-1S. The stopgap tank was designated as the KV-85 and 148 units were delivered to the Red Army between August and November 1943. Production of the IS-1 began in October 1943 and continued until January 1944 with approximately 100 units being completed.

IS-2

Doubts about the ability of the main gun on the IS-1 to penetrate the thick frontal armour on late-war German tanks led to the decision by the Red Army to look for a more powerful tank gun. The weapon chosen in November 1943 was a 122mm artillery piece modified as a tank gun. It was designated as the D-25T. With the new gun fitted into the existing IS-85 turret the tank became the IS-2, which weighed approximately 103,000lb.

Despite its large size, the armour penetration potency of the 122m main gun on the four-man IS-2 was not much more than that of the 75mm main gun on the Panther. Obviously, when firing at a non-armoured target, the high-explosive round of the IS-2 was much more effective due to its immense size.

The biggest fault with the 122mm main gun on the IS-2 was its large and heavy separate loading (two-piece) ammunition that made the loader's job extremely difficult. This meant that its rate of fire was much slower than the fixed (one-piece) smaller and lighter rounds employed by German late-war tanks.

The early-production units of the IS-2 can be identified by the stepped glacis that was eventually replaced by a sloped glacis. An important internal improvement to later-production IS-2 tanks was the replacement of the original artillery-type manually-operated screw-type breech with a semi-automatic breech block. Between December 1943 and May 1945, a total of between 3,380 and 3,385 units were built according to available reference sources.

IS-3

Even while production of the IS-2 continued, the Red Army sought out the next-generation heavy tank. The design benchmark set for the IS-2's replacement was that the vehicle had to resist fire on its front hull and turret from the armour-piercing projectiles fired by the 88mm KwK43 main gun mounted on the German Tiger B heavy tank. To achieve this goal Soviet tank designers came up with a new highly-sloped and thickly-armoured turret and hull design for its next-generation Joseph Stalin heavy tank assigned the designation IS-3.

Despite the new turret and hull design of the IS-3, the powertrain for the tank was only a slightly improved version of that on the IS-2. As with the IS-2, the IS-3 had a four-man crew and was armed with the same 122mm D-25T main gun plus two machine guns. As the first production units of the IS-3 did not come off the production line until May 1945, the same month in which the Germans surrendered, the tank did not see combat in the Second World War. As the IS-3 had been rushed into production it was troubled by a host of design flaws – mostly automotive – that were never resolved, even in the post-war era.

American Heavy Tanks

With the German invasion of Poland in September 1939, the US army began exploring the concept of a heavy tank. In May of the following year the head of the Infantry Branch of the US army recommended a heavy tank that might weigh somewhere between 100,000 and 160,000lb. Shortly thereafter the US army decided that there was a requirement for a heavy tank weighing 100,000lb. It was envisioned as having four turrets armed with a variety of guns ranging from 75mm to 20mm.

In July 1940, the proposed US army new heavy tank was approved for development as the T1. In quick order the idea of a multi-turreted heavy tank was dropped and it was to have only a single turret armed with a 3-inch main gun. Instead of a coaxial machine gun, it would be armed with a coaxial 37mm gun. As work progressed on the T1 it was eventually redesignated in April 1942 as the M6 or M6A1, depending on its hull construction.

The M6 Heavy Tank Series

Despite the funding being authorized in April 1942 for the construction of 1,804 units of the M6 series, the Armoured Force of the US army saw no need for a heavy tank and had the number of vehicles ordered dropped down to only 115 units. The US army Service of Supply for some reason then had that increased to 230 units.

The first production example of the M6 series came off the production line in December 1942. That same month the commander of the US army Armoured Force wrote a letter to the commander of the US Army Ground Forces (AGF) in which he stated his objections to a heavy tank: 'Due to its tremendous weight and limited tactical use, there is no requirement in the Armored Force for the heavy tank. The increase in the power of the armament of the heavy tank does not compensate for the heavier armor.'

It was at this point in time that the US army Service of Supply agreed with the commander of the US army Armoured Force that there was no pressing requirement for a heavy tank. The programme was terminated with only forty units having been built. None would leave the country and those built were retained only for testing purposes and then disposed of.

Assault Tanks

In March of 1942, an interest arose for a special assault tank (another name for a heavy tank) by the British army. The US army's Armoured Force had little interest in such a vehicle. In spite of this, in May 1942 the US army issued military characteristics for the proposed assault tank assigned the designation T14. It was based on the heavily up-armoured M4 series of first-generation tanks, with the suspension system from the M6 series heavy tank.

Two trial test units of the T14 appeared in July 1943. Due to the vehicle's weight of 84,000lb and the poor showing of its suspension system, the project was cancelled the following year. The T14 had a 75mm main gun and two machine guns.

Because a planned new heavy tank, which the US army had finally decided was needed, would not be ready for service until early 1945, they decided to up-armour the hull of an M4A3(75)W and provide it with a new heavily-armoured turret. This interim tank was assigned the designation Assault Tank M4A3E2 in March 1944.

The US army ordered 254 units of the M4A3E2. All were delivered between May and July 1944. However, they did not arrive in North-West Europe until the autumn of 1944. Due to all the additional armour fitted to the M4A3(75W), its weight is listed at approximately 84,000lb. This resulted in some problems with the VVSS system that was never intended to support such a weight. Warnings were issued to the crews about travelling off-road with the tank as the front volute springs could break if allowed to bottom out violently.

M26 Heavy Tank

The heavy tank that the US army had hoped to field in late 1944 started out as the T26E3. It would eventually be designated as the M26. Production of the five-man tank armed with a 90mm main gun and up to three machine guns did not begin until November 1944. The M26 weighed approximately 92,000lb and rode on a torsion bar suspension system. It was powered by the same 500hp gasoline engine fitted to both first- and second-generation M4A3 tanks, leaving it somewhat underpowered.

Twenty units of the M26 reached North-West Europe in January 1945, with their first combat engagement with an enemy tank occurring in the following month. Subsequent encounters between late-war German tanks and these first twenty units of the M26 to arrive were few and far between. By March 1945, an additional forty M26s arrived in North-West Europe. However, none of these would engage enemy tanks in battle before the German surrender in May 1945.

Some thought had been given to redirecting the existing inventory of M26s to the Pacific Theatre of Operations following the German capitulation. However, the Japanese surrender in September 1945 ended that plan, although a few M26s had been directed to the Pacific Theatre prior to the end of the Second World War.

In May 1946 the M26 was reclassified as a medium tank as the US army was envisioning placing into service much larger and heavier tanks. At this point in time the

US army had revised its weight classifications so that light tanks could weigh up to 50,000lb, medium tanks up to 110,00lb and heavy tanks up to 170,000lb.

Design Dead-Ends

In a complete turnaround from its refusal to even consider heavy tanks in 1942, the US army began considering heavy tanks once again in 1943. One of these was labelled as the T28 Heavy Tank. It was a turretless four-man vehicle weighing approximately 190,000lb and armed with a forward-firing 105mm main gun and up to two machine guns.

The T28 was intended to destroy the defensive works of the German Siegfried Line. Because it lacked a turret, the US army redesignated the vehicle as the T95 Gun Motor Carriage (GMC) in March 1945. It was originally anticipated that the US army would need to have twenty-five units constructed. That number was soon reduced to just three units with only two being completed between December 1945 and January 1946. Testing of the T95 continued until 1947 when the project was terminated. Post-war, the vehicle was redesignated as the Super Heavy Tank T28.

In response to the threat posed by late-war German tanks, the US army began work on the Heavy Tank T29 series with four trial test units ordered in the summer of 1944. Two units armed with a 105mm main gun were labelled the T29E1 and two units armed with a 155mm gun were referred to as the T29E2. In March 1945, the US army decided that it wanted 1,152 units of the six-man T29E1.

At the same time that the US army was anticipating ordering over 1,000 units of the T29E1, there developed an interest in a version of the T29 series to be armed with a 120mm main gun and labelled as the T53. Upon the end of the Second World War, the project was terminated with only one unit of the approximately 190,000lb tank completed.

The success of the M4A3E2 Assault Tank in late 1944 prompted the US army to consider a heavily-armoured assault tank version of the M26 which they labelled as the T26E5 in February 1945. It weighed approximately 102,000lb and retained the 90mm main gun and machine guns of the M26. However, testing of the tank quickly demonstrated that the existing suspension system could not cope with the weight of the increased armour and the programme was cancelled at the end of the Second World War with only twenty-seven units built.

French Heavy Tanks

From the tail-end of the First World War up until the German invasion of 1940, the French army had considered a wide variety of super-heavy tanks weighing up to an unbelievable 400,000lb. In the end only two heavy tanks saw service with the French army in the Second World War. The older of the two was the approximately 136,000lb Char 2 armed with a 75mm main gun.

Crewed by up to thirteen men, the Char 2 had been designed and built during the First World War but had not entered French army service until after the war had ended. Plans had originally called for 300 units to be built but the end of the conflict resulted in only ten units being completed. These tanks were upgraded during the 1930s and remained in service with the French army when the Germans invaded in May 1940. All would be lost to non-combat causes.

The post-First World War replacement for the Char 2 would be the Char B1 and the subsequent improved version designated as the Char B1-bis. Work on this series of heavy tanks began in the 1920s with the Char B1 entering service with the French army in 1931 and the upgraded version in 1935. Both four-man tanks had a 75mm gun in their front hulls, a turret-mounted 47mm gun and two machine guns.

Only thirty-four units of the 67,000lb Char B1 were delivered to the French army before production began of the up-armoured Char 1-bis, which weighed approximately 72,000lb. The French army had authorized the production of 1,114 units of the latter; only 258 units were in service by the time of the German invasion.

Although better-armed and armoured than the German medium tanks it encountered in combat during the Battle for France, a number of design flaws such as the one-man turret of the Char B1 and Char 1-bis and their general mechanical unreliability greatly reduced their battlefield effectiveness.

British Heavy Tanks

British industry produced two heavy tank prototypes for consideration by the British army during the Second World War. The first was designated as the 'TOG 1', with an improved version labelled as the 'TOG 2'. The acronym TOG stood for 'The Old Gang', referring to the fact that the designers of the TOG 1 and TOG 2 were the engineers responsible for the design of the British army tanks that had fought in the First World War.

The approximately 179,000lb TOG 1 and the follow-on TOG 2 built in 1940 had a crew that ranged from six to eight men. The TOG 1 was armed with a 75mm howitzer in its front hull and a turret-mounted 2-pounder. The TOG 2 was originally armed with a turret-mounted 6-pounder main gun, later replaced with a 17-pounder main gun. With the reasonably successful development of the Churchill, interest quickly waned in the old-fashioned and unpractical TOG 2 and it never progressed beyond the prototype stage.

The other heavy tank design dead-end was labelled as the Heavy Assault Tank (A39) and named the 'Tortoise'. Design work on the turretless vehicle armed with a 32-pounder (84mm) main gun began in 1942. Crewed by seven men, six trial units of the 175,000lb vehicle were delivered to the British army for testing only after the Second World War had ended. The test results were not impressive as the vehicle was too large and heavy to be practical and the programme was soon cancelled.

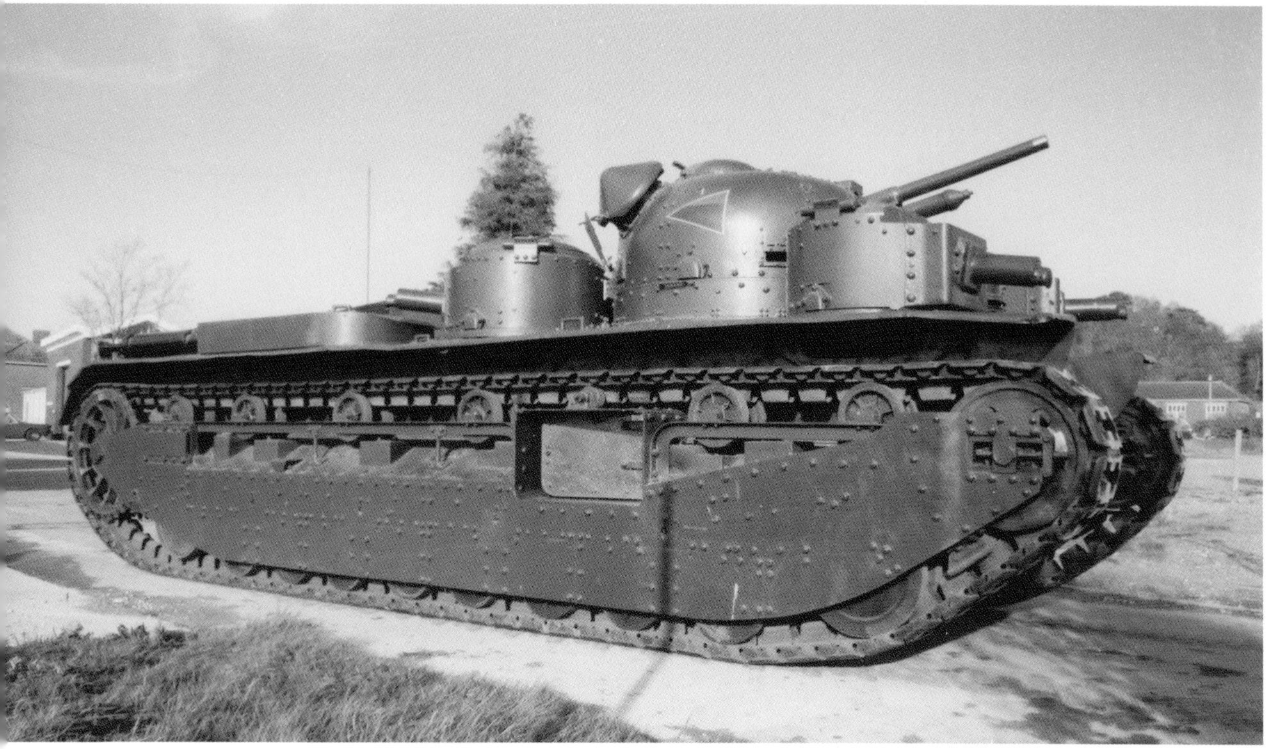

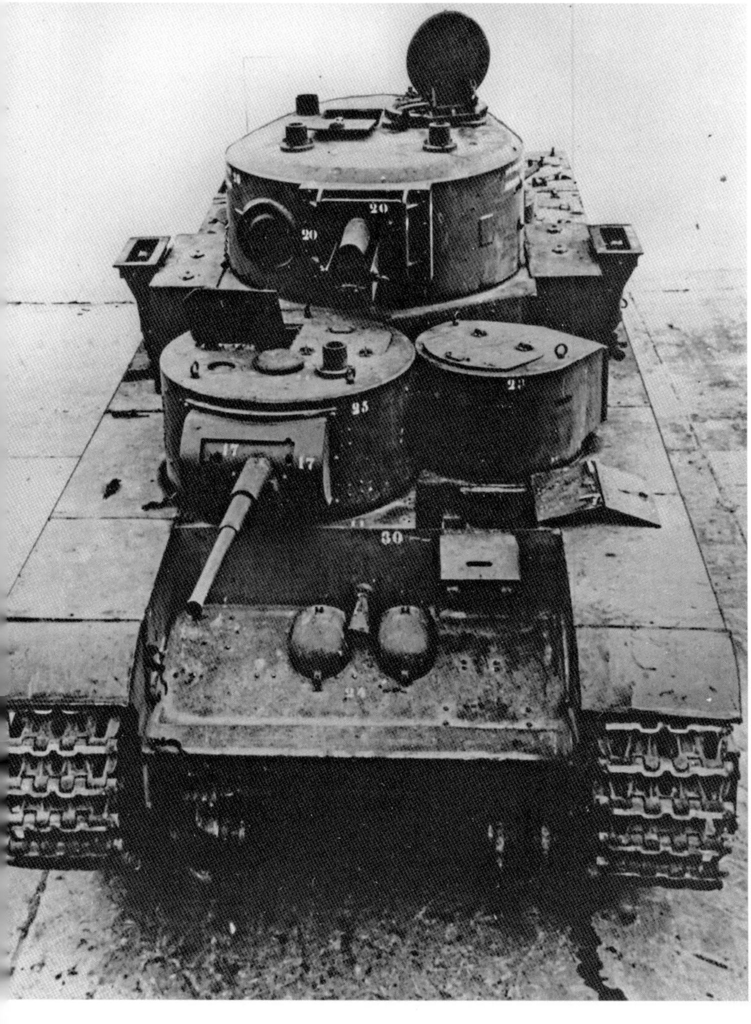

The inspiration for the Red Army's first heavy tank, the T-35, was a British-designed and built tank seen here that was designated as the A1E1 and named the 'Independent'. It was an experimental vehicle with five weapon-armed turrets that was not adopted by the British army. The tank had a length of 24ft 11in, a width of 8ft 9in and the vehicle height was 8ft 11in. *(Tank Museum)*

In this German army photograph of a captured T-35 heavy tank, the thickness of the armour on various portions of the vehicle is painted on. The uppermost and largest turret on the tank had 360 degrees of traverse and was armed with a 76.2mm main gun. On the front hull of the vehicle is a smaller turret armed with a 45mm main gun. *(Patton Museum)*

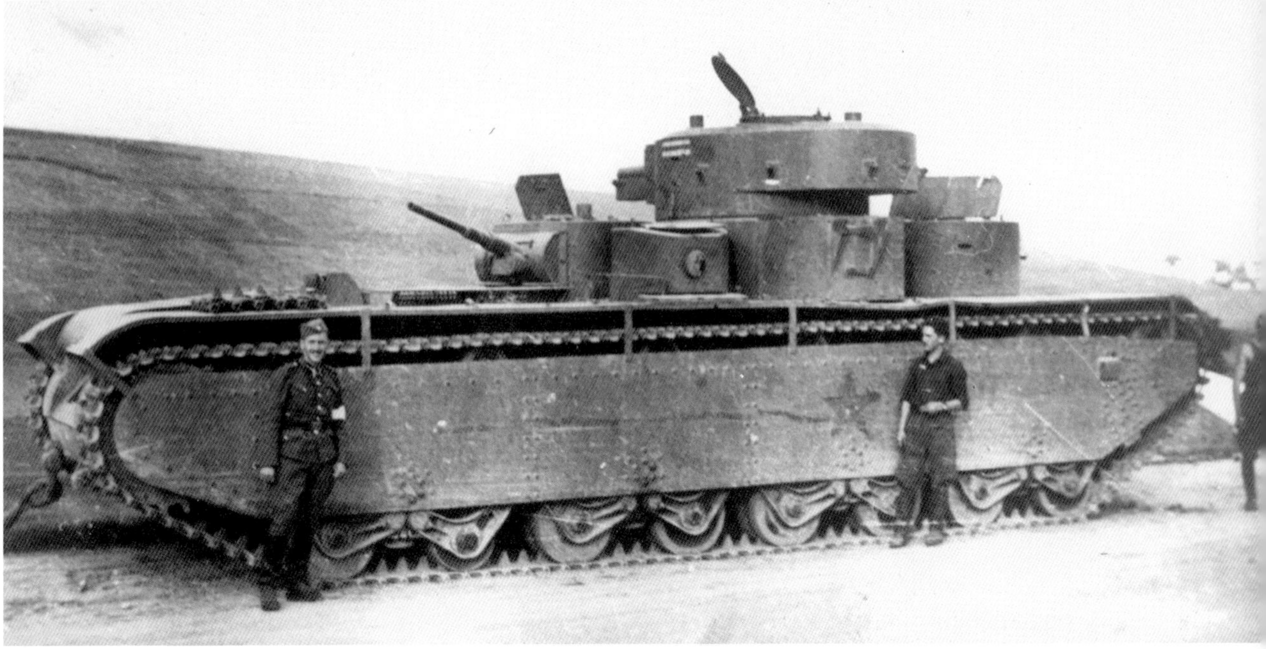

German soldiers pose next to an abandoned T-35 heavy tank. The vehicle pictured is now labelled as the T-35 Model 1935 and was the standard production version of the tank. There was an earlier version designated as the T-35 Model 1932 that can be identified by the fact that it had only three bogie wheel assemblies on either side of the hull rather than the four seen here. *(Patton Museum)*

Shown here on display at the Russian Army Tank Museum is a T-35 Model 1935 tank. The vehicle was 31ft 11in in length, had a width of 10ft 6in and a height of 11ft 3in. The maximum operational range of the tank was 93 miles, not an uncommon figure for all gasoline-engine-powered tanks of that time. *(Vladimir Yakubov)*

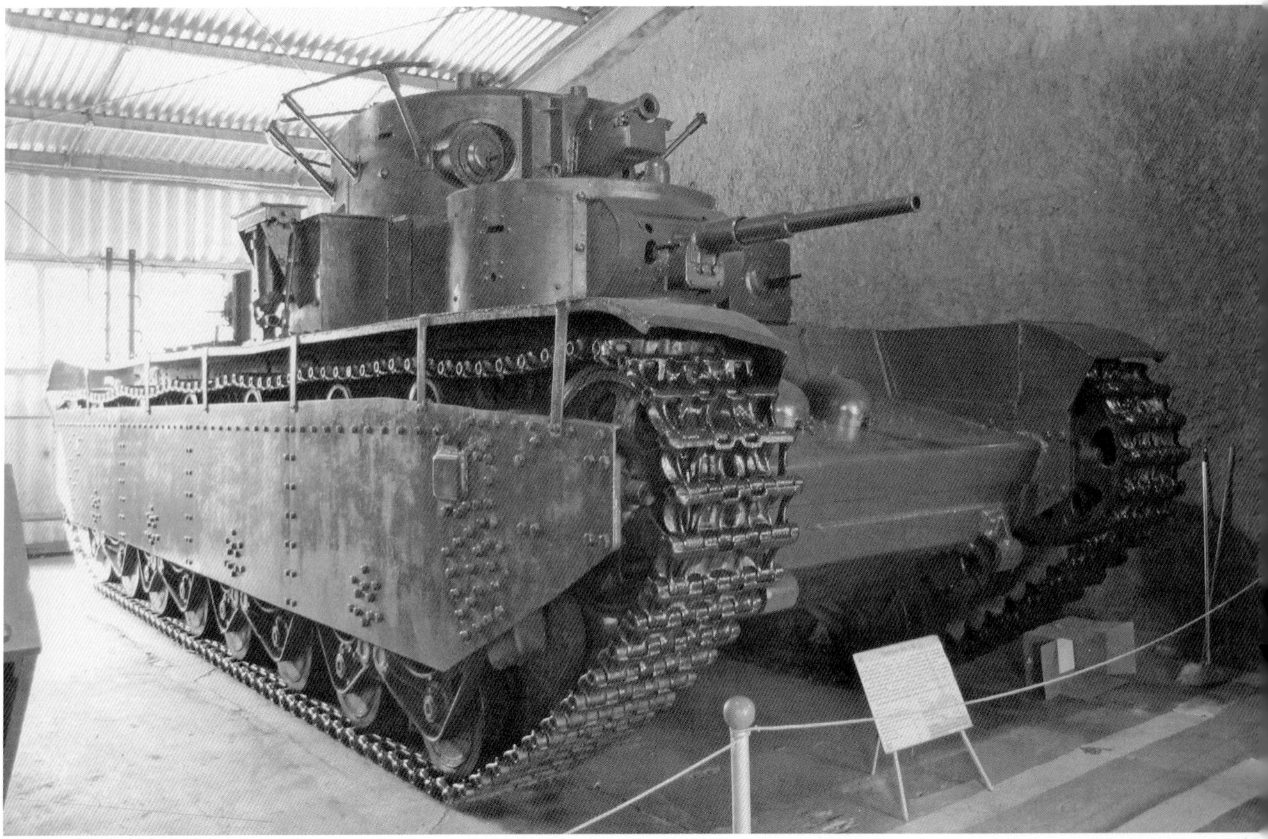

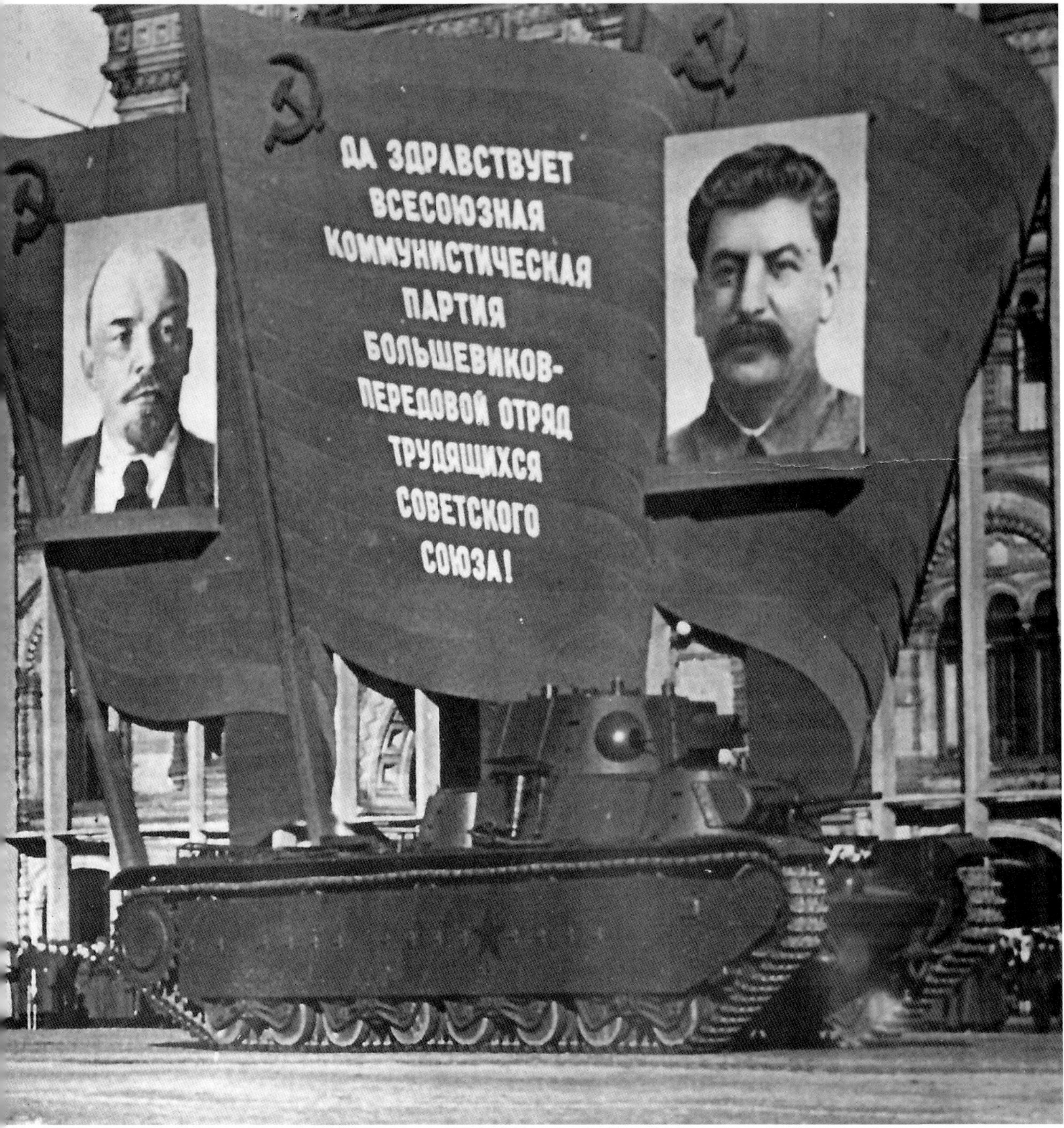
ДА ЗДРАВСТВУЕТ
ВСЕСОЮЗНАЯ
КОММУНИСТИЧЕСКАЯ
ПАРТИЯ
БОЛЬШЕВИКОВ-
ПЕРЕДОВОЙ ОТРЯД
ТРУДЯЩИХСЯ
СОВЕТСКОГО
СОЮЗА!

In its efforts to keep the T-35 series viable for the future, the Red Army had the last six production units fitted with new sloped-armour turrets as seen here in this pre-war parade photograph. These tanks were labelled as the T-35 Model 1938. The maximum armour thickness on this final version of the T-35 series was 70mm compared to the maximum armour thickness of only 30mm on the earlier variants of the tank. *(Patton Museum)*

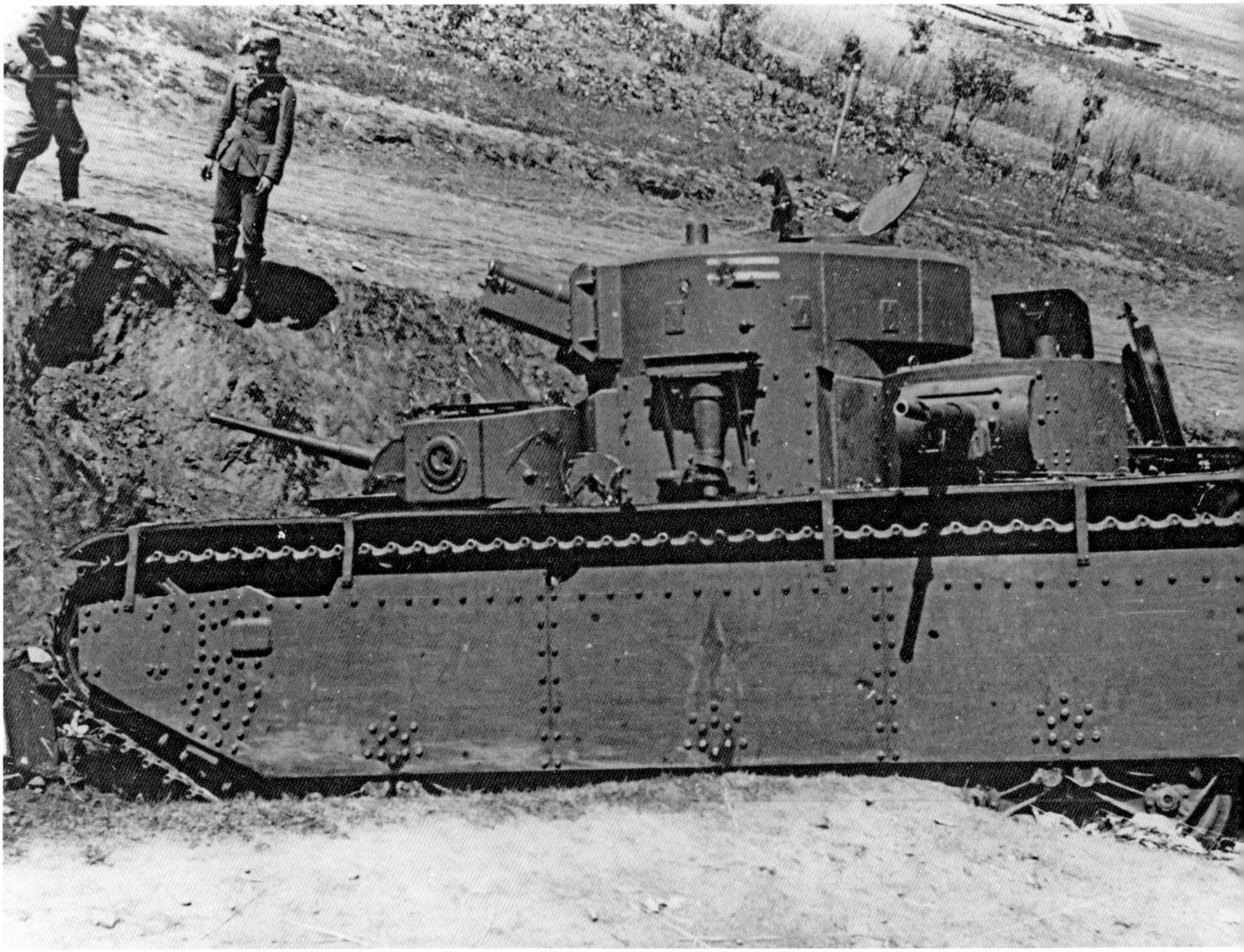

A German army photograph of a captured T-35 shows a second turret armed with a 45mm main gun located at the rear of the tank's hull. Never known for their reliability, the majority of T-35 series tanks lost during the early stages of the German invasion of the Soviet Union fell out due to mechanical problems or lack of fuel. *(Patton Museum)*

Unhappiness with the many shortcomings of the T-35 series of heavy tanks led the Red Army to seek out a new heavy tank. One of three prototype candidates submitted for consideration to the Red Army was the twin-turreted design shown here on field trials. It was labelled as the T-100. The upper turret was armed with a 76.2mm main gun and the lower turret with a 45mm main gun. *(Patton Museum)*

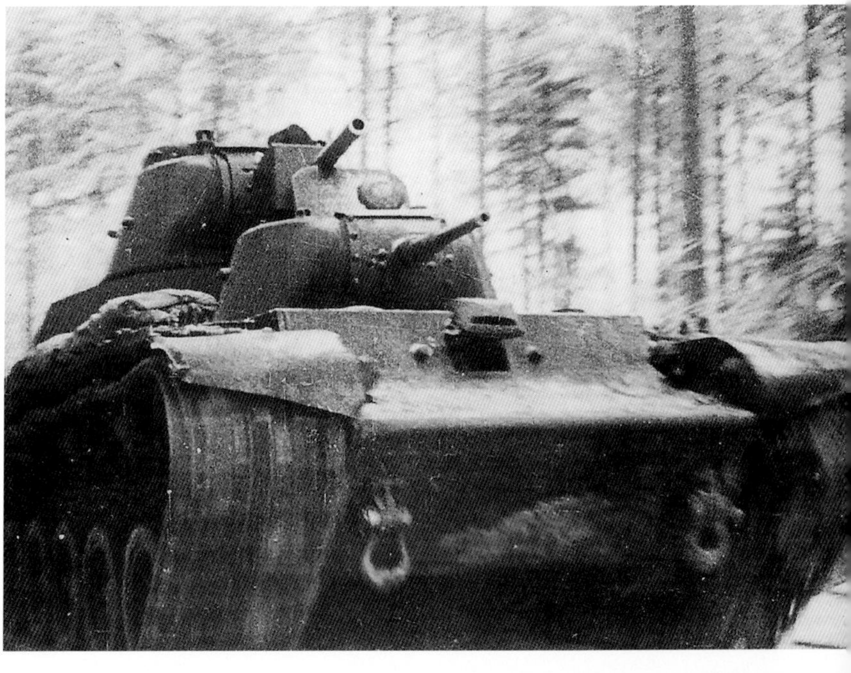

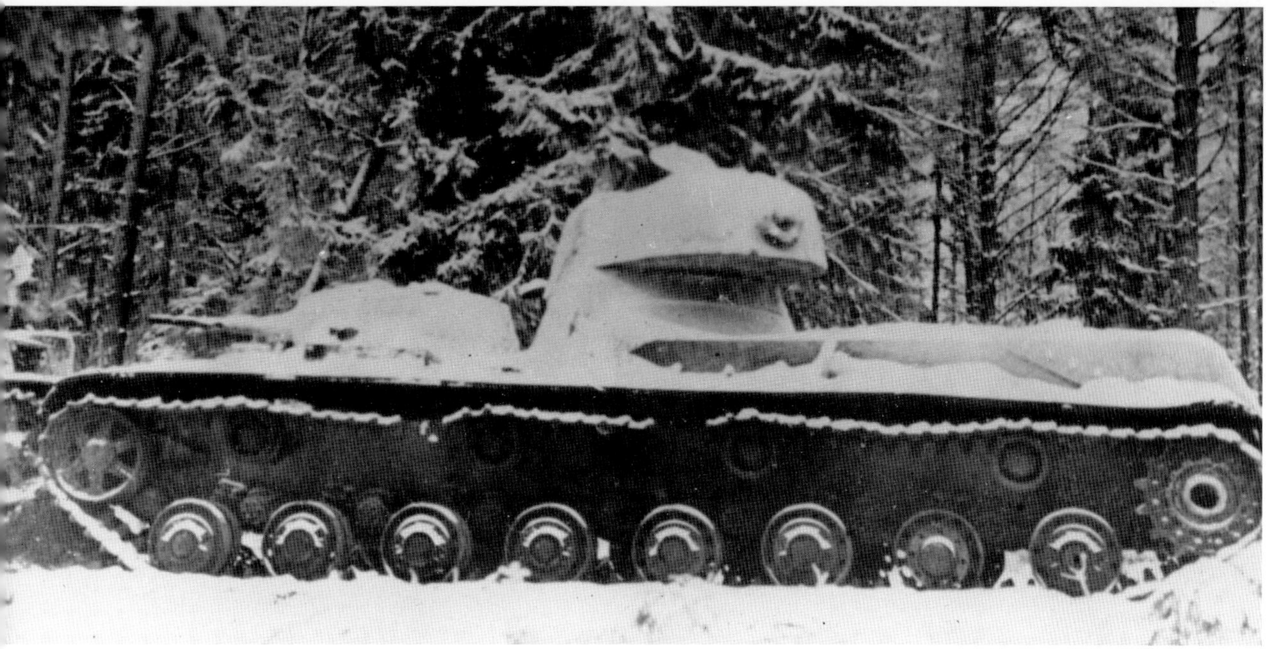

Pictured is the second of three prototype heavy tanks submitted to the Red Army as a replacement for the T-35 heavy tank series. It was labelled as the SMK and, like the T-100, had two turrets. Testing of both the T-100 and the SMK led the Red Army to conclude that both prototype heavy tanks would be too ungainly and complicated to be practical in service. *(Patton Museum)*

Of the three heavy tank prototypes provided to the Red Army for consideration as a replacement for the T-35 heavy tank series, the winning contender was the single-turreted version of the SMK seen here that was labelled as the 'KV' and is now popularly referred to as the 'KV-1'. The particular tank shown is from the initial production lot and now referred to as KV-1 Model 1939. *(Patton Museum)*

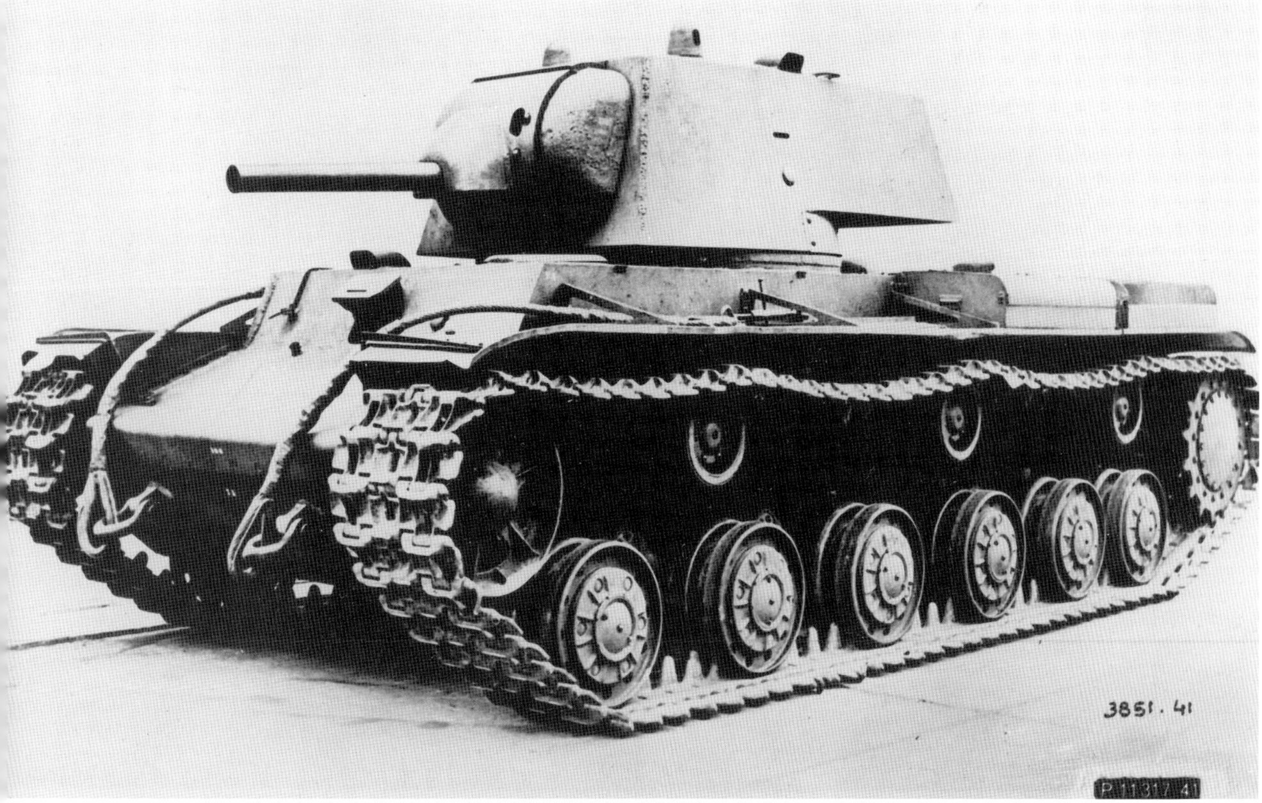
3851. 41
P 11317 41

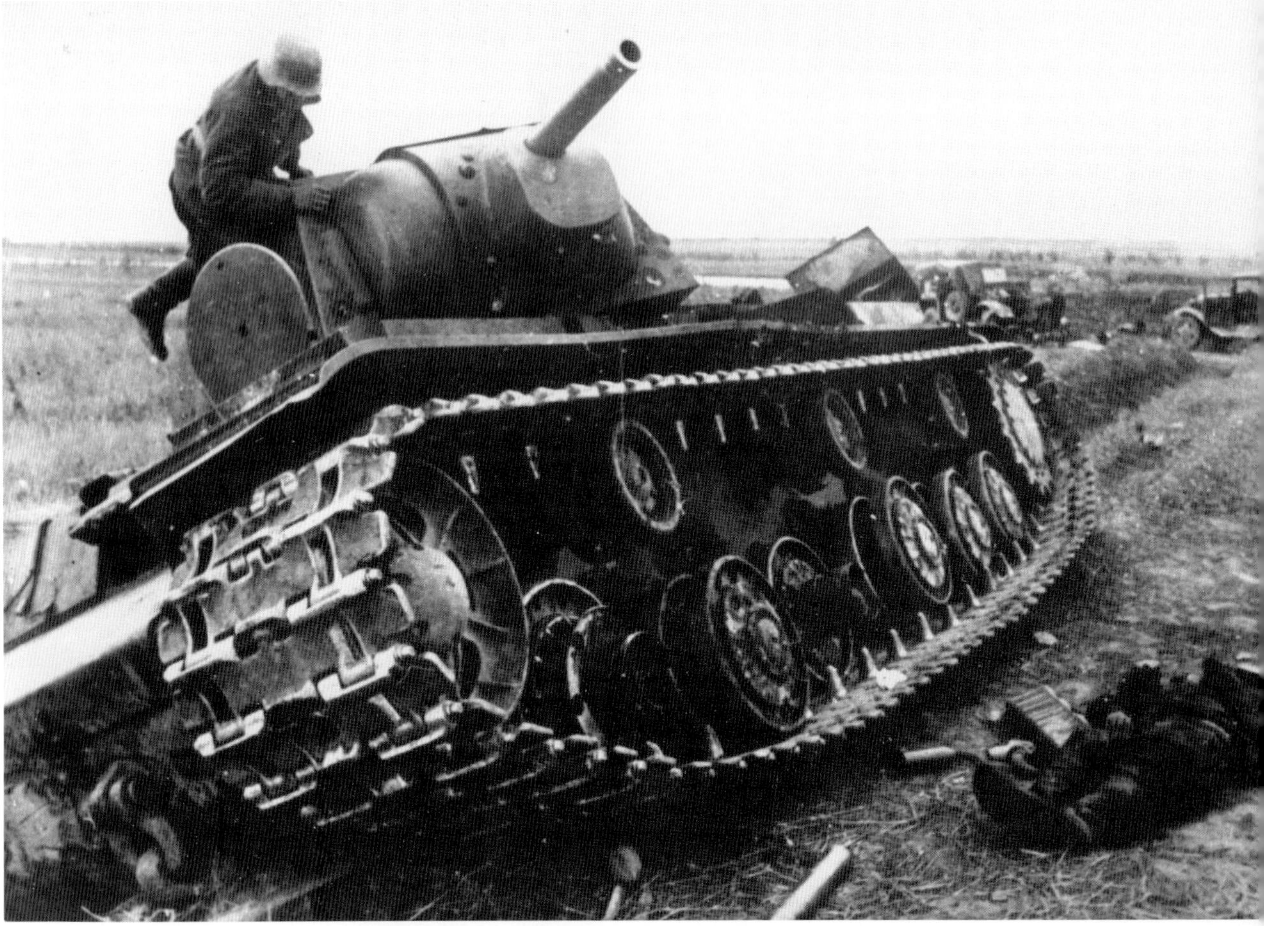

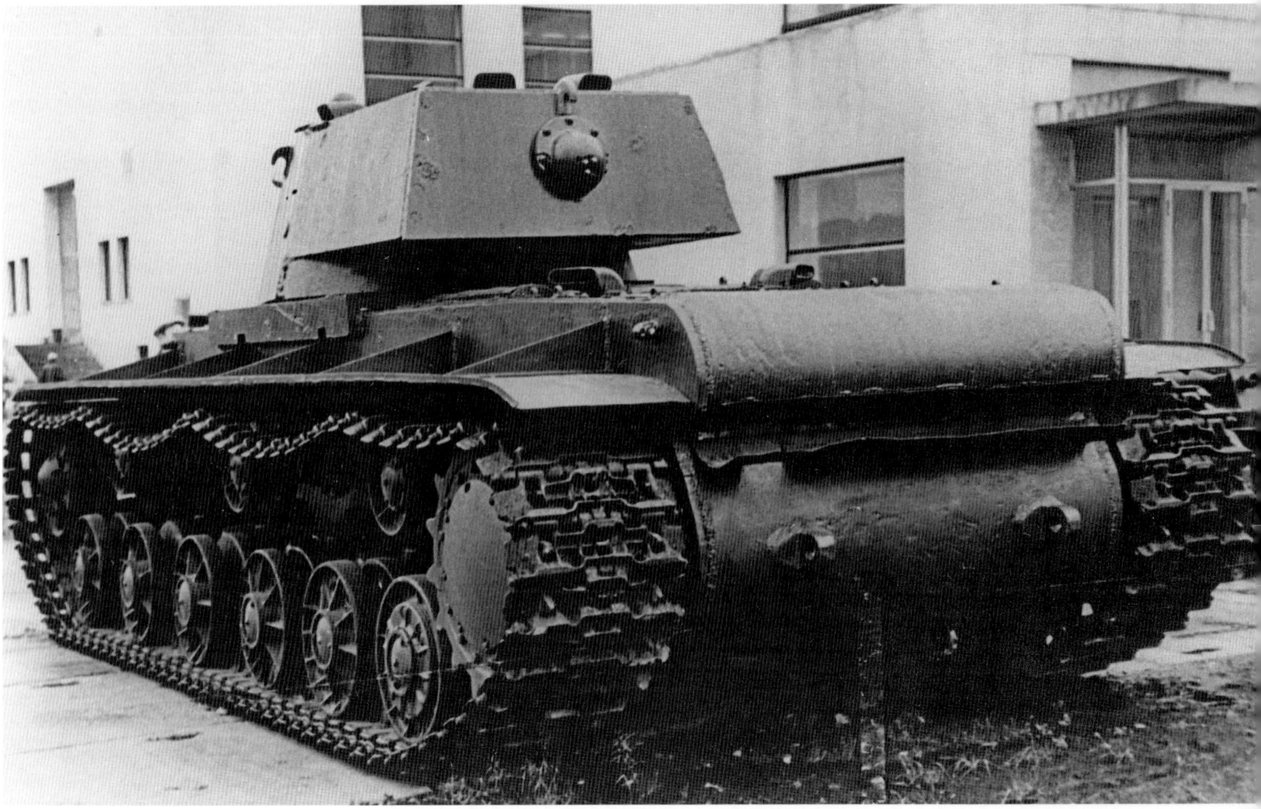

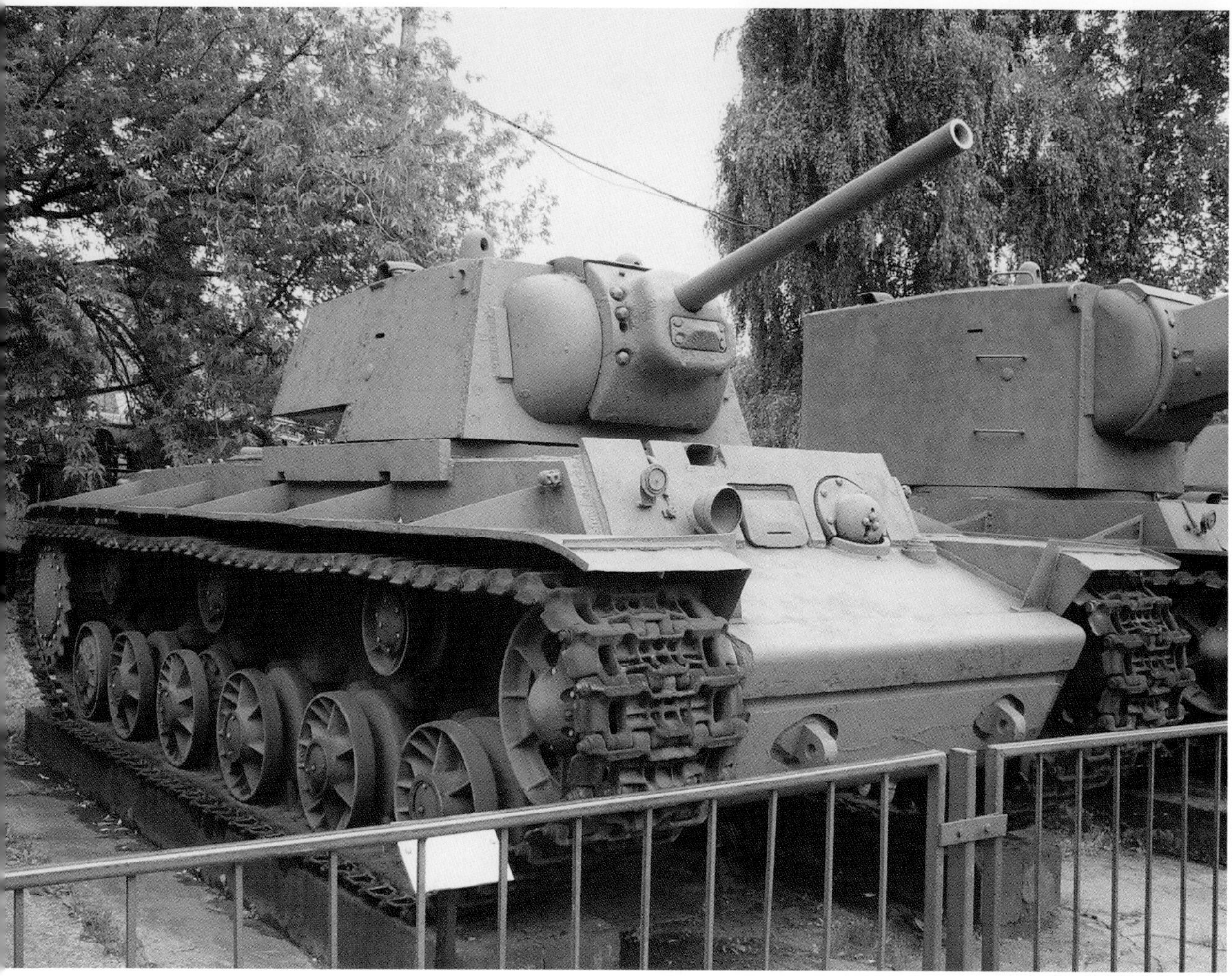

(*Opposite above*) A German soldier examines a knocked-out KV-1 Model 1940. This version of the KV-1 series can be identified by the welded armour box around the rearmost portion of the barrel that protected the weapon's hydro-pneumatic recuperator. A similar arrangement is also seen on all first-generation T-34 series tanks armed with a 76.2mm main gun. (*Patton Museum*)

(*Above*) On display at a Russian military museum in Moscow is this KV-1 Model 1940 upgraded to the Model 1941 standard by the addition of a new cast armour gun shield. It did away with the welded armour box that protected the 76.2mm main hydro-pneumatic recuperator on the KV-1 Model 1940. The entire KV-1 series was also armed with three small-calibre machine guns. (*Vladimir Yakubov*)

(*Opposite below*) Visibility out of the KV-1 series was extremely poor as it was for the T-34 series tanks armed with the 76.2mm main gun. The vehicle was 22ft 8in long, had a width of 10ft 11in and was 9ft 7in tall. One of the tank's three small-calibre machine guns was mounted in the rear turret wall as seen here on this KV-1 Model 1940. (*Patton Museum*)

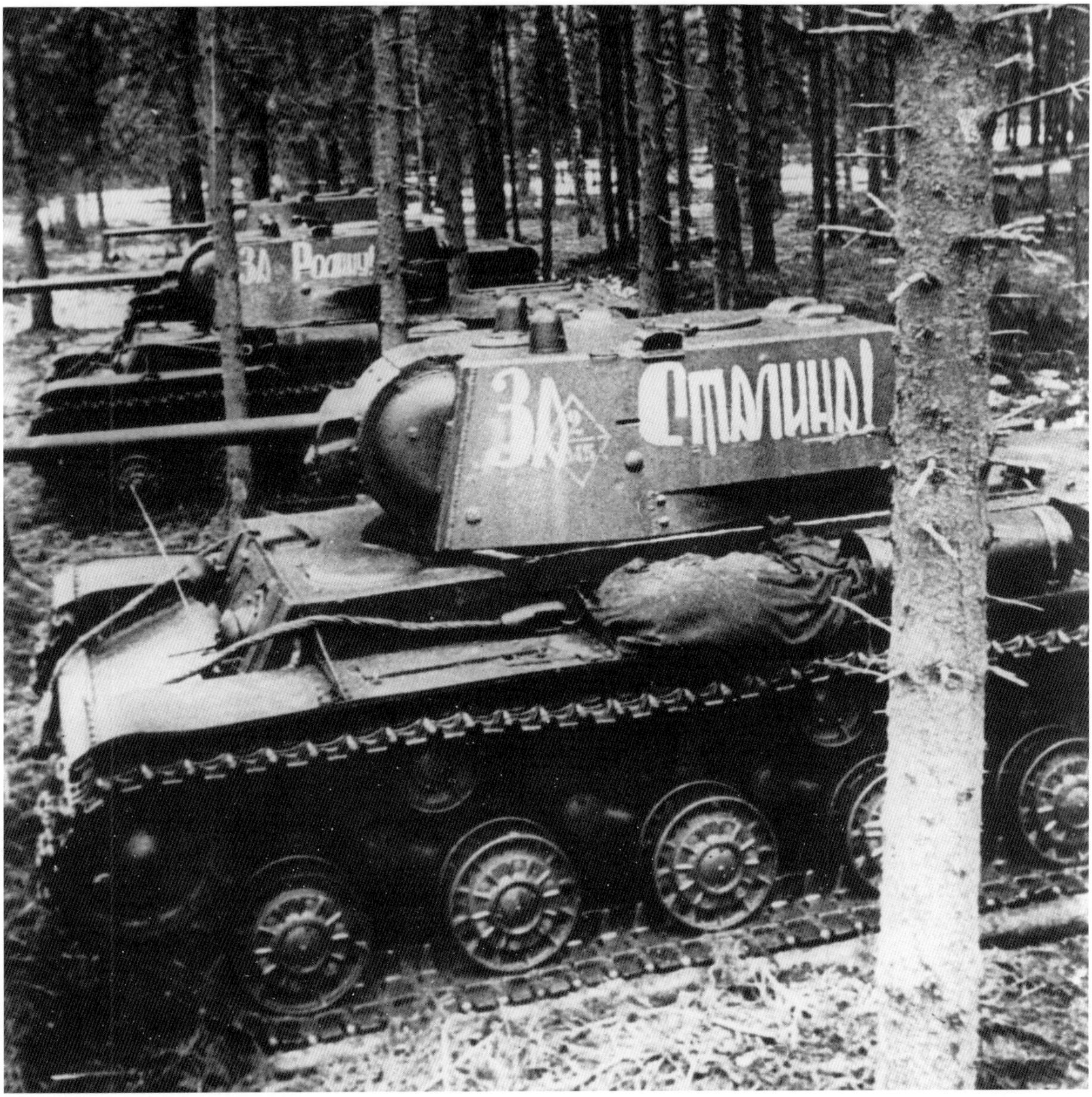
За Родину!
За Сталина!

(*Above*) Note the two overhead periscope sights on the turret roof of the KV-1 Model 1941 tank in the foreground. The one on the left-hand side of the turret roof was for the gunner who also had an articulated telescope to aim the 76.2mm main gun. The overhead periscope sight on the right-hand side of the turret was for the vehicle commander. *(Patton Museum)*

(*Opposite above*) This knocked-out KV-1 Model 1941 has an up-armoured turret that can be identified by the squared-off shape under the turret overhang. The original production unit turrets were bent around the bottom from a point mid-way on the lower portion of the turret. Throughout their time in service the entire KV-1 series was plagued by engine and transmission reliability problems that were never overcome. *(Bob Fleming)*

(*Opposite below*) To speed up production of the KV-1 series, Soviet industry introduced a new cast armour turret in 1942 as seen on this preserved KV-1 Model 1941. Armour thickness on the new cast armour turret was the same as on earlier welded armour turrets with 100mm on the gun shield and 75mm on the sides and rear of the turret. The turret roof was 30mm thick. *(Christophe Vallier)*

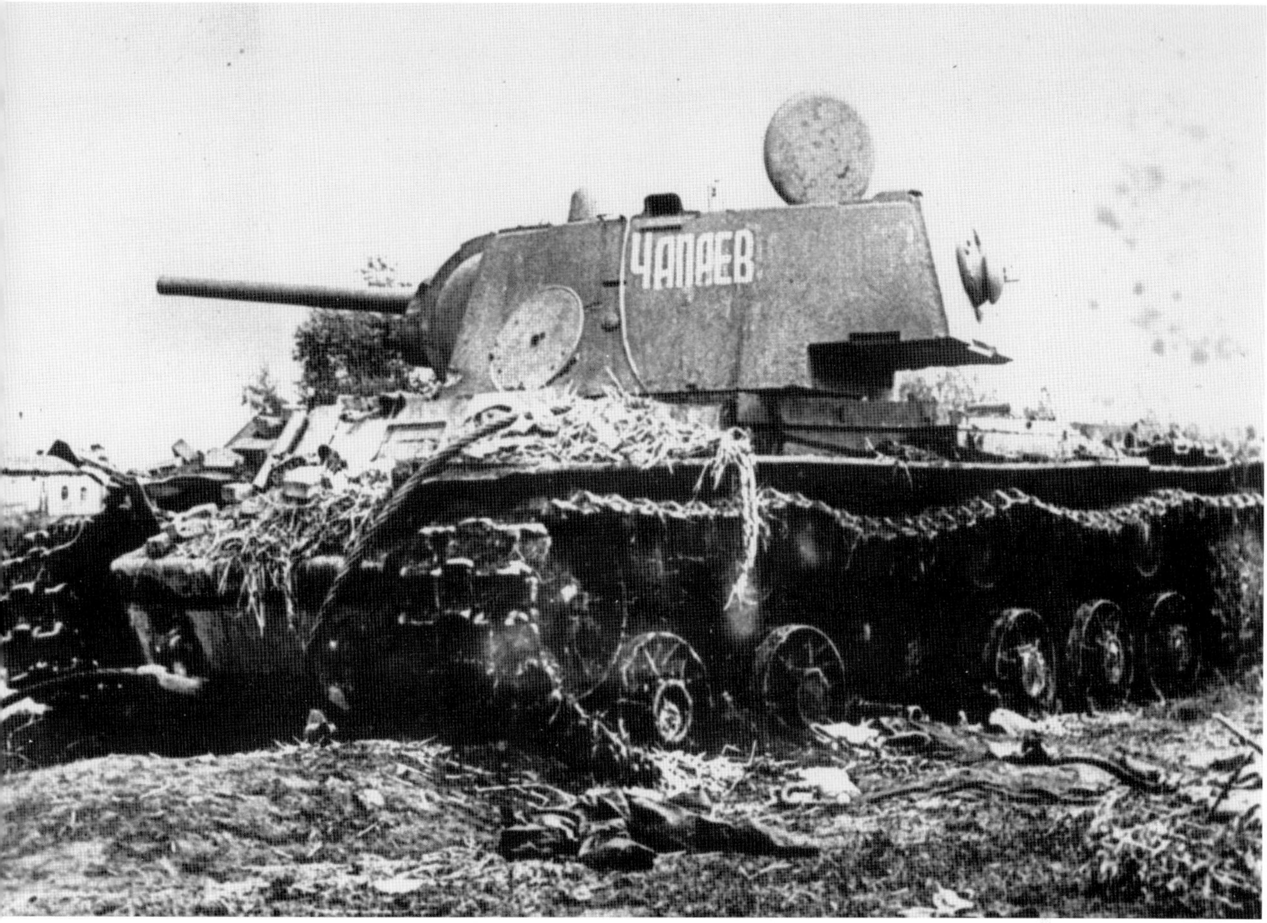
ЧАПАЕВ

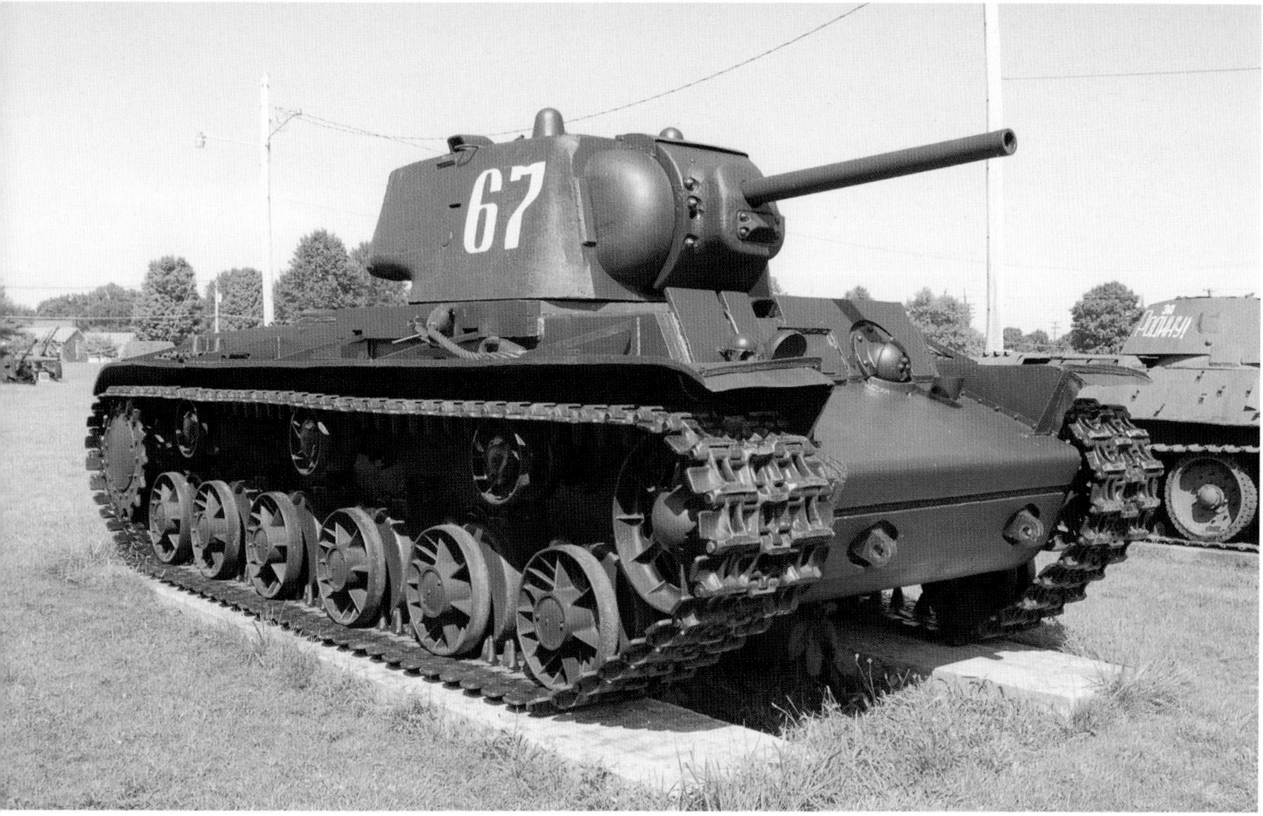
67

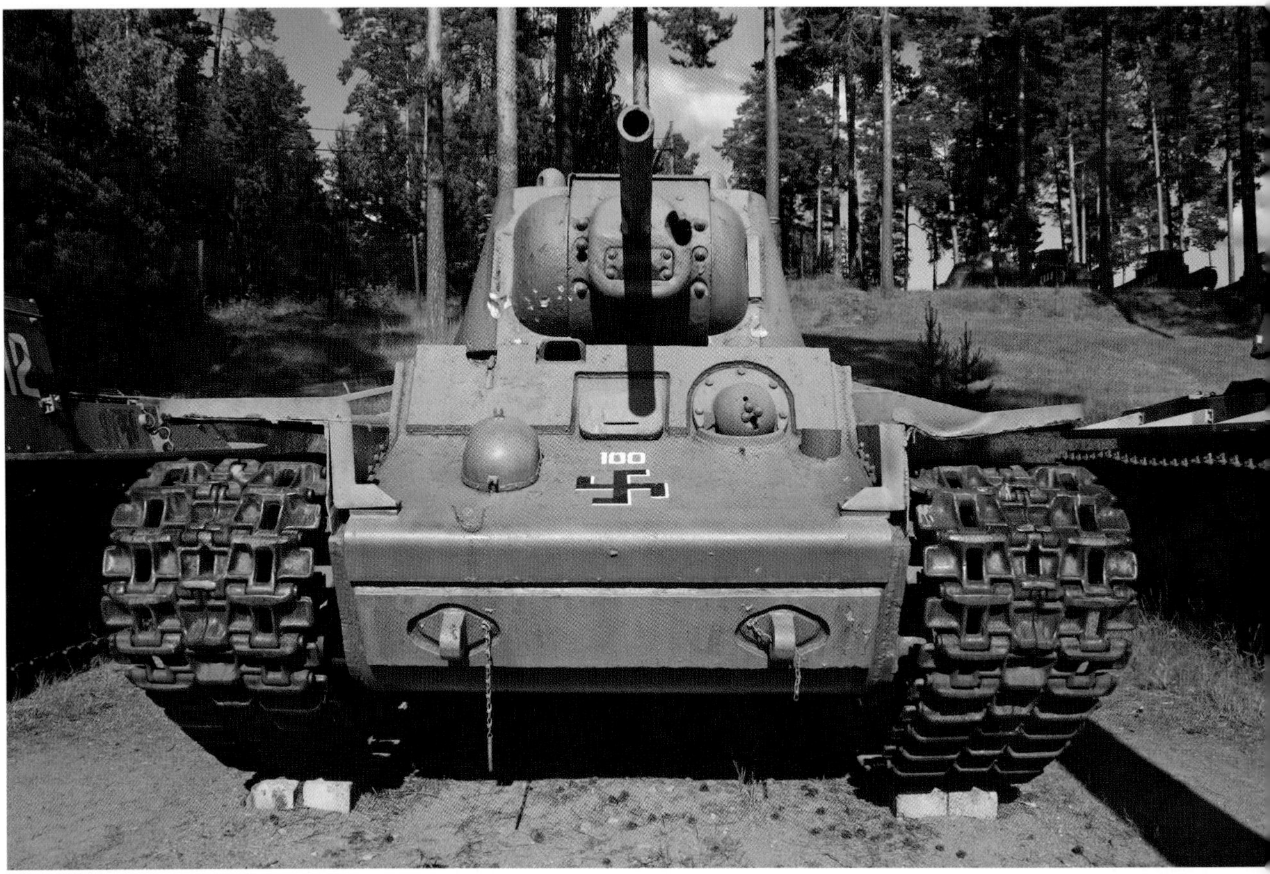
100

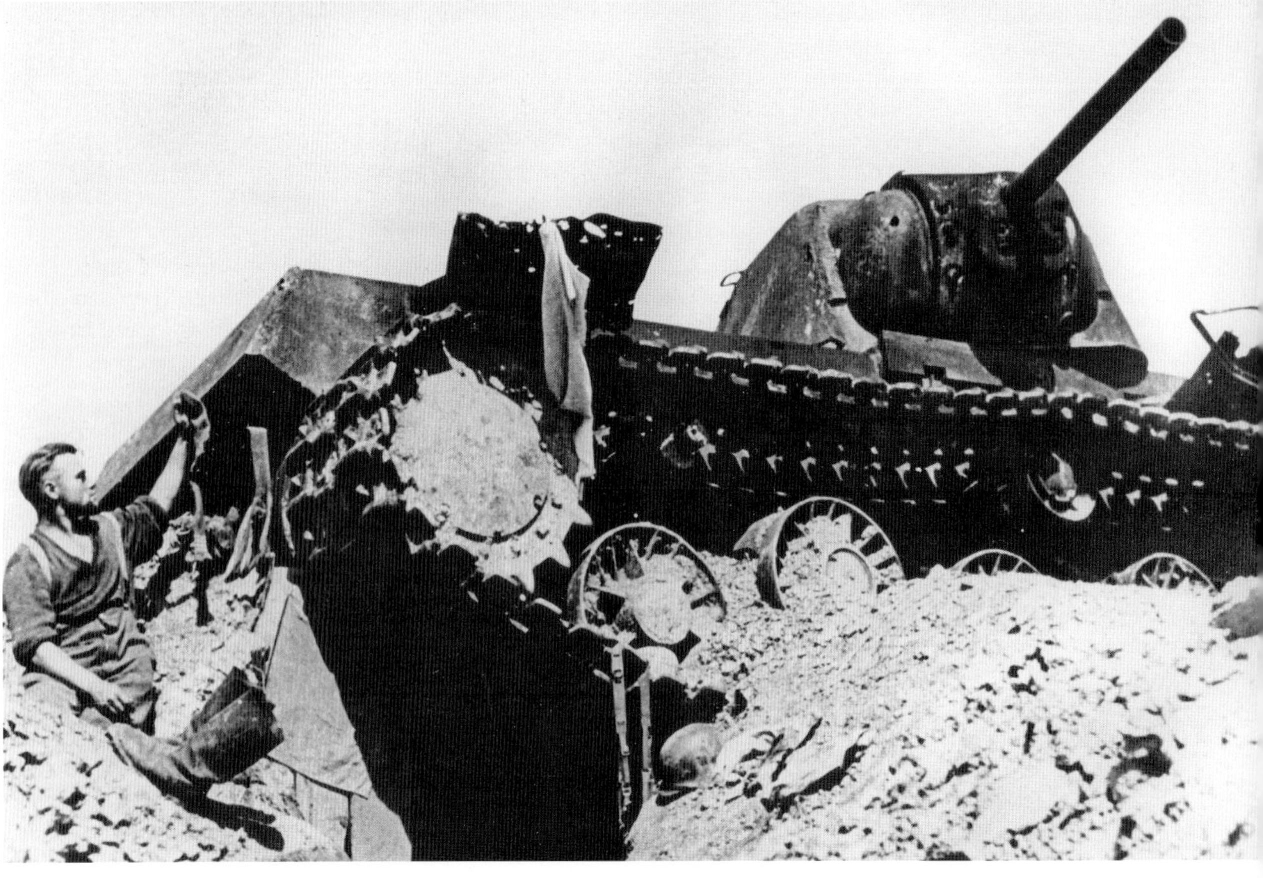

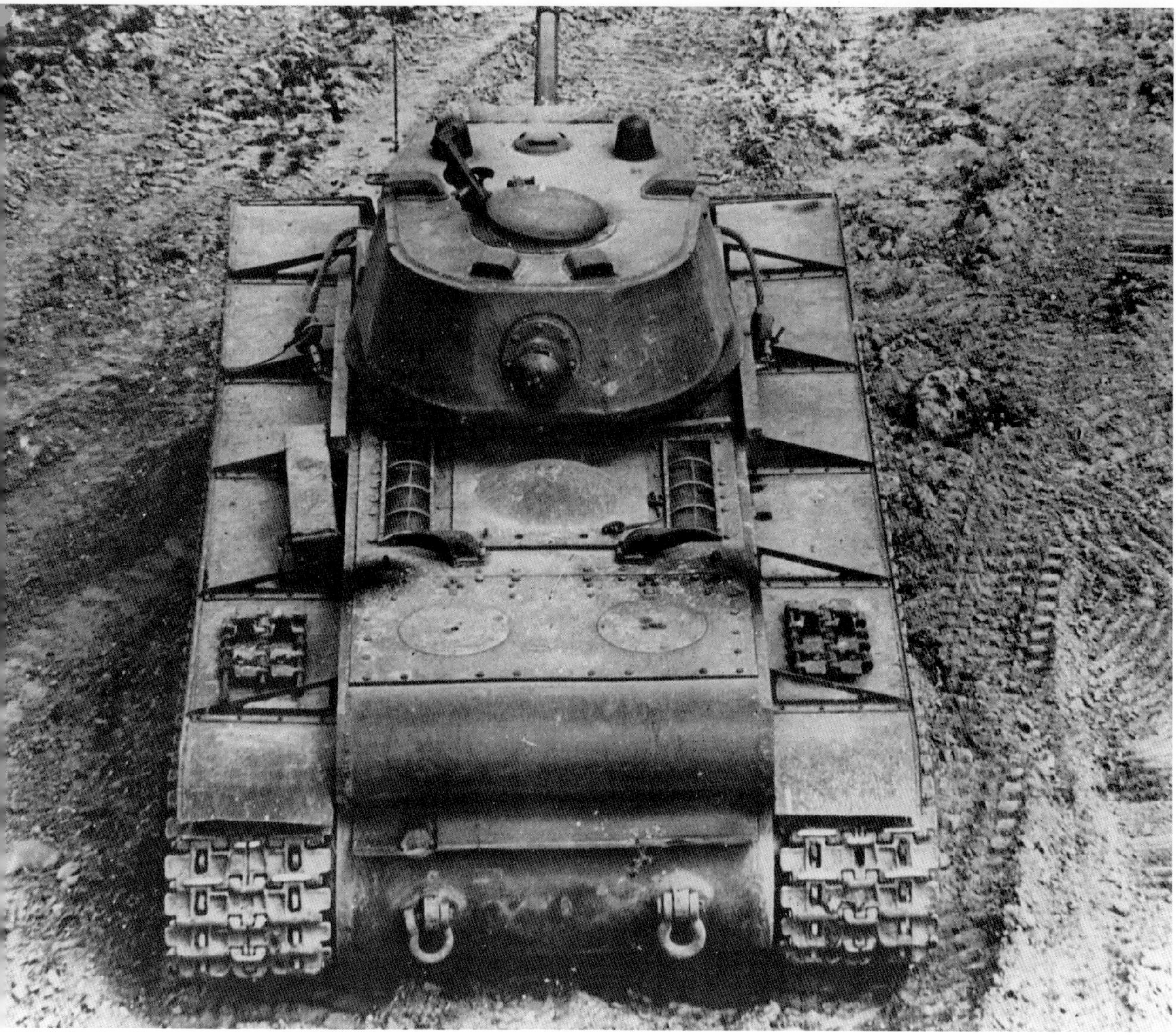

(*Opposite above*) The driver of the KV-1 series sat in the front centre of the vehicle's hull, as indicated by the direct-vision armoured flap seen in this picture of a preserved KV-1 Model 1941 with a cast armour turret. The radio-operator manned the front hull small-calibre machine gun. The KV-1 Model 1941 had authorized storage space for ninety-eight main gun rounds. *(Andreas Kirchhoff)*

(*Above*) The KV-1 Model 1941 pictured here, like the rest of the series, was powered by the same diesel engine that drove the lighter T-34 series, except with a different designation. The tank's maximum road speed on level ground was 21mph, dropping to approximately 10mph when off-road. The KV-1 series rode on a torsion bar suspension system instead of the Christie suspension system of the T-34 series. *(Patton Museum)*

(*Opposite below*) Later-production KV-1 Model 1941 tanks with welded turrets that had been up-armoured can be identified from the rear by the angled instead of rounded rear upper engine deck that covers the engine exhaust vents. That design feature is visible in this picture of a knocked-out KV-1 Model 1941 that has been turned into overhead cover for a German soldier's bunker. *(Patton Museum)*

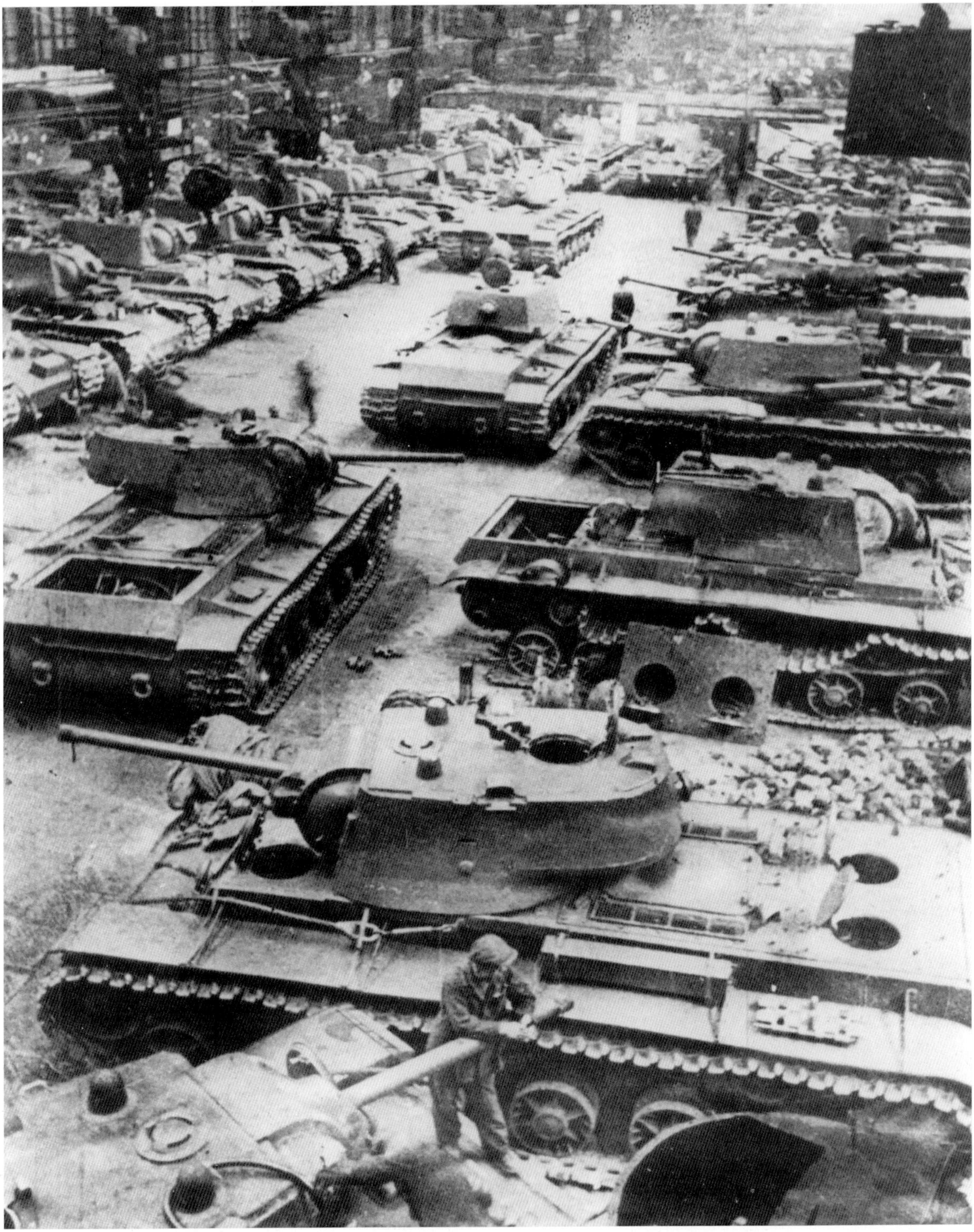

A factory overhauling KV-1 Model 1941 tanks with both cast and welded armoured turrets. Improved German tank and anti-tank guns forced the thickening of armour on later-production cast armour turreted KV-1 Model 1941 tanks. These up-armoured units can be identified in this photograph by the outward fairing at the bottom of the turret sides and the angled instead of rounded rear upper engine deck that covers the engine exhaust vents. *(Bob Fleming)*

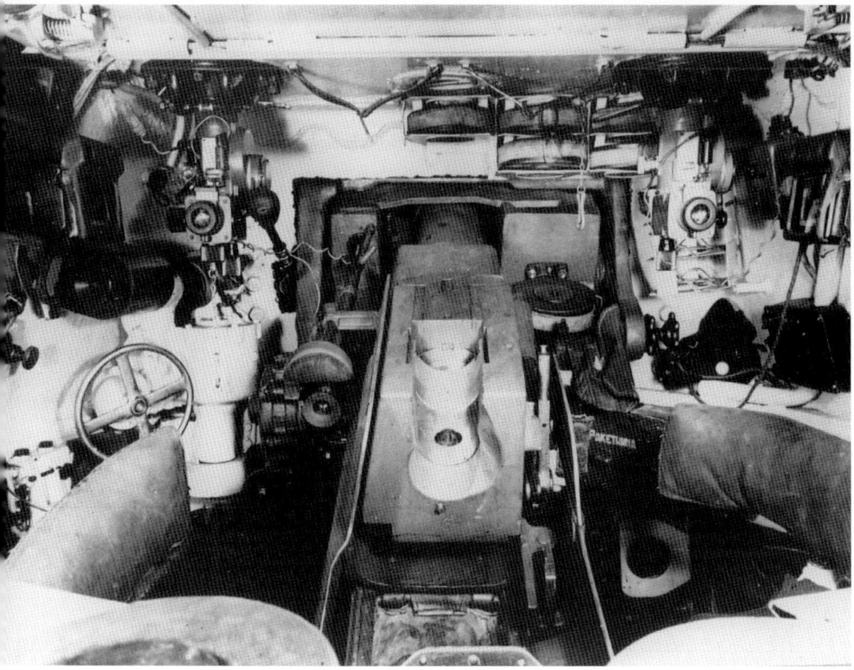

This picture shows the turret interior of a cast armour turreted KV-1 Model 1941 tank. The gunner's overhead periscope sight and his articulated telescope to aim the 76.2mm main gun are seen on the left-hand side of the picture. The vehicle commander, who also acted as the loader, was on the opposite side of the main gun breech. *(Patton Museum)*

In this photograph we see the rear turret bustle of a cast armour turreted KV-1 Model 1941 tank. Visible is the small-calibre machine gun fitted to the rear wall of the turret surrounded by the various drum magazines for the weapon. Also visible are some of the tank's 76.2mm main gun rounds stored in racks on either side of the turret's inner walls. *(Patton Museum)*

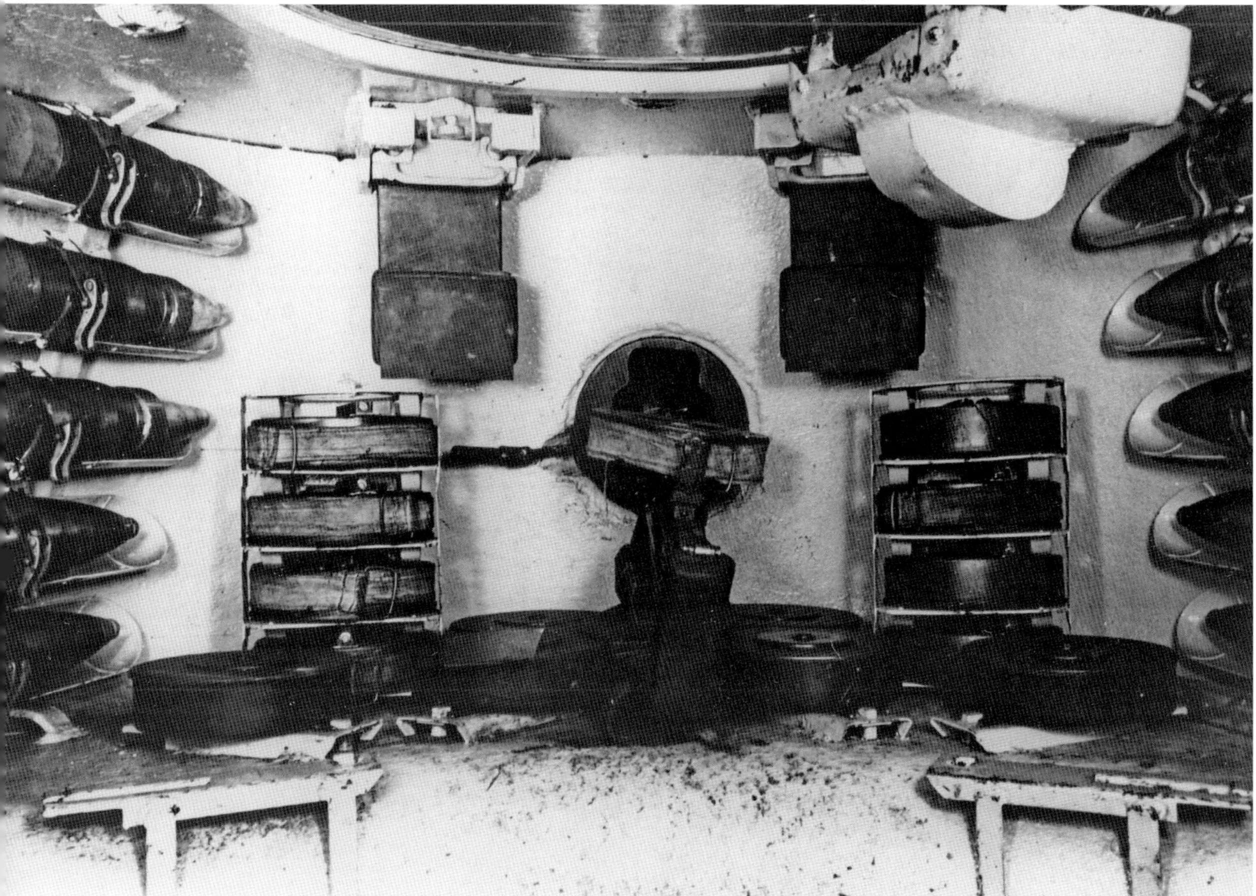

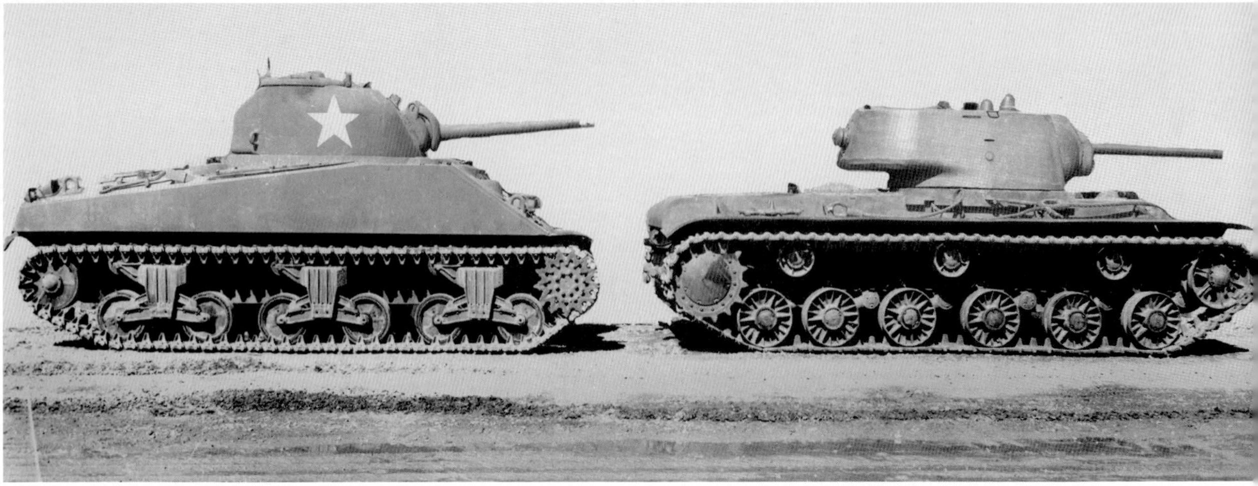

A comparison photograph of a US army first-generation M4A4 armed with a 75mm main gun and a cast armoured turreted KV-1 Model 1941 tank. Unlike the American tank, the Soviet tank had its transmission located in the rear hull along with its engine. On the American tank the drivetrain from the front-hull-mounted transmission to the rear-hull-mounted engine pushed up the turret basket, which in turn pushed up the vehicle height. *(Patton Museum)*

Seen here on display at a museum in Moscow is a KV-1S, the upgraded and lightened version of the KV-1 Model 1941. It had a new turret design but retained the 76.2mm main gun of the earlier models that was clearly obsolete by the time the tank was introduced into service. The hull of the KV-1S pictured is a reconstruction. *(Vladimir Yakubov)*

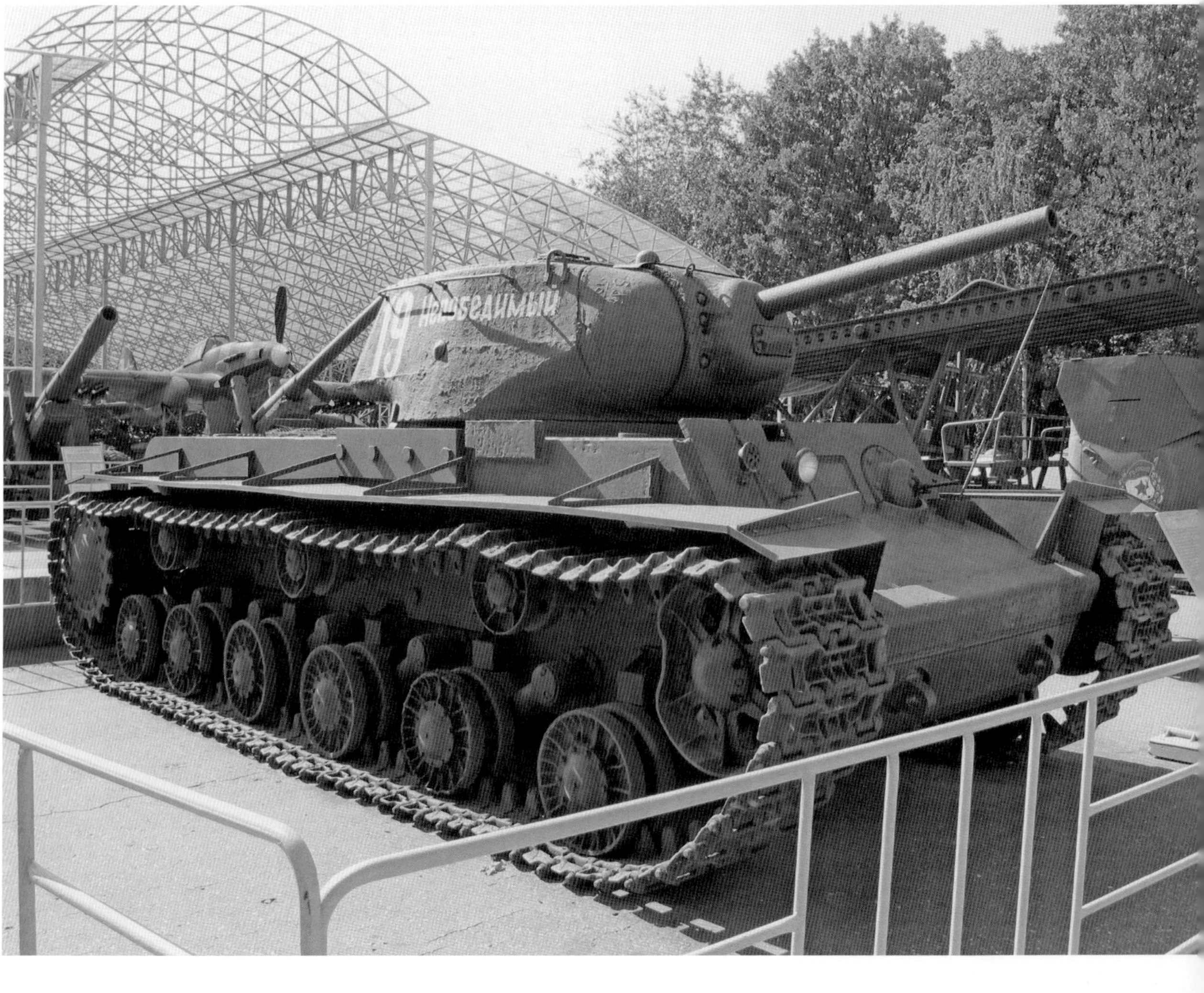
19
Непобедимый

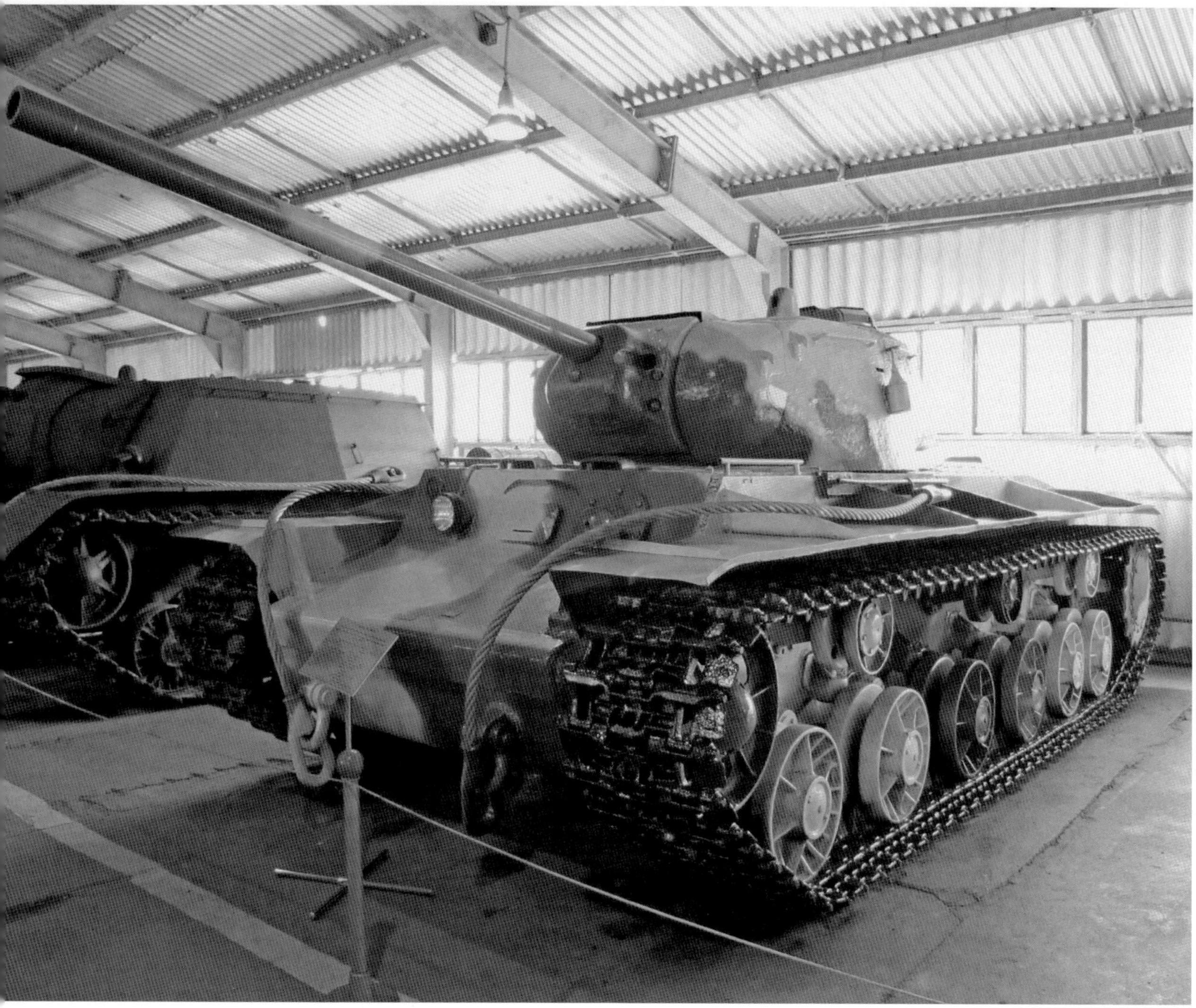

To rectify the problem of the KV-1S being under-gunned, there was an attempt to mount an 85mm main gun in its turret. This arrangement did not prove practical as the turret of the KV-1S proved too small. The single experimental prototype of that effort survived and is seen at the Russian Army Tank Museum. *(Vladimir Yakubov)*

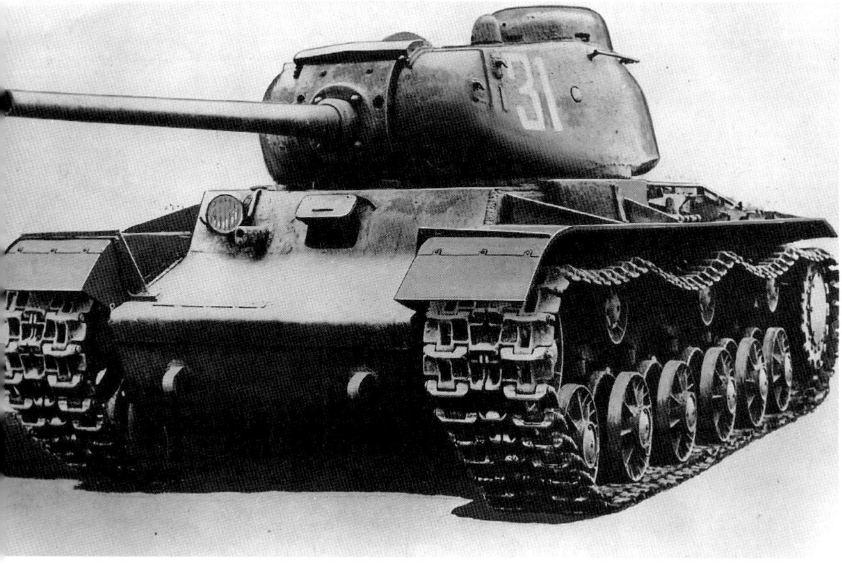
31

With the failure of up-gunning the KV-1S tank with an 85mm main gun, it was decided as a stopgap measure to take a KV-1S hull and mount on it a turret originally intended for the IS-1 Stalin heavy tank. This arrangement is pictured here and was designated as the KV-85. The vehicle commander was now absolved of the loader's role he had to perform on the KV-1 series and was provided with a cupola seen on the rear of the turret roof. *(Patton Museum)*

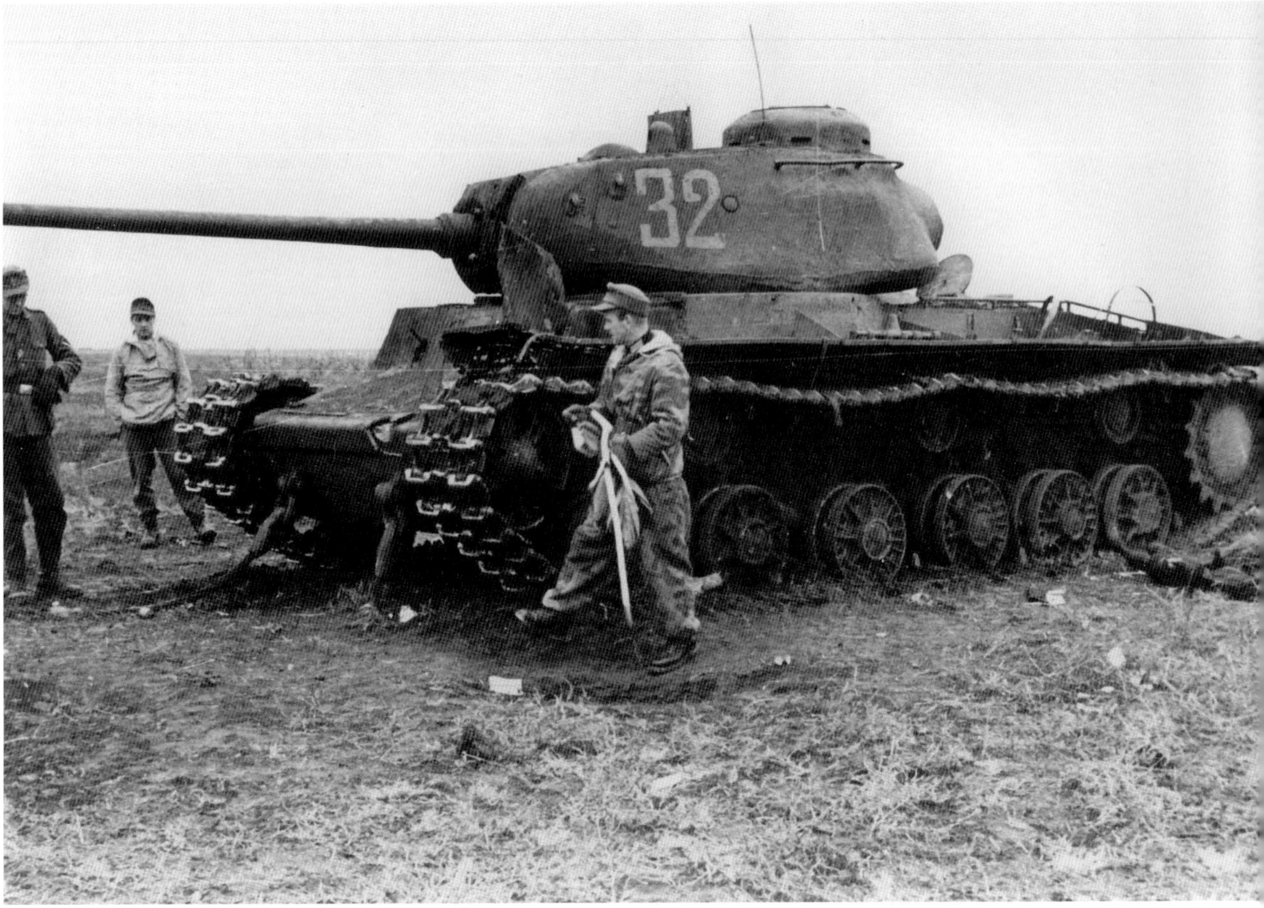
32

Curious German soldiers are shown looking over a knocked-out KV-85 tank. The vehicle was 28ft 2in in length, had a width of 10ft 8in and a height of 9ft 6in. Maximum armour thickness on the turret front was 110mm thick. Operational range was approximately 90 miles. *(Bob Fleming)*

The replacement for the KV-1S and the KV-85 was the IS-2 heavy tank armed with a 122mm main gun. The damaged example shown here was captured by the German army and has been marked with the thickness of its armour on various locations. The IS-2 featured both a redesigned hull and turret intended to better deflect German armour-piercing projectiles. *(Tank Museum)*

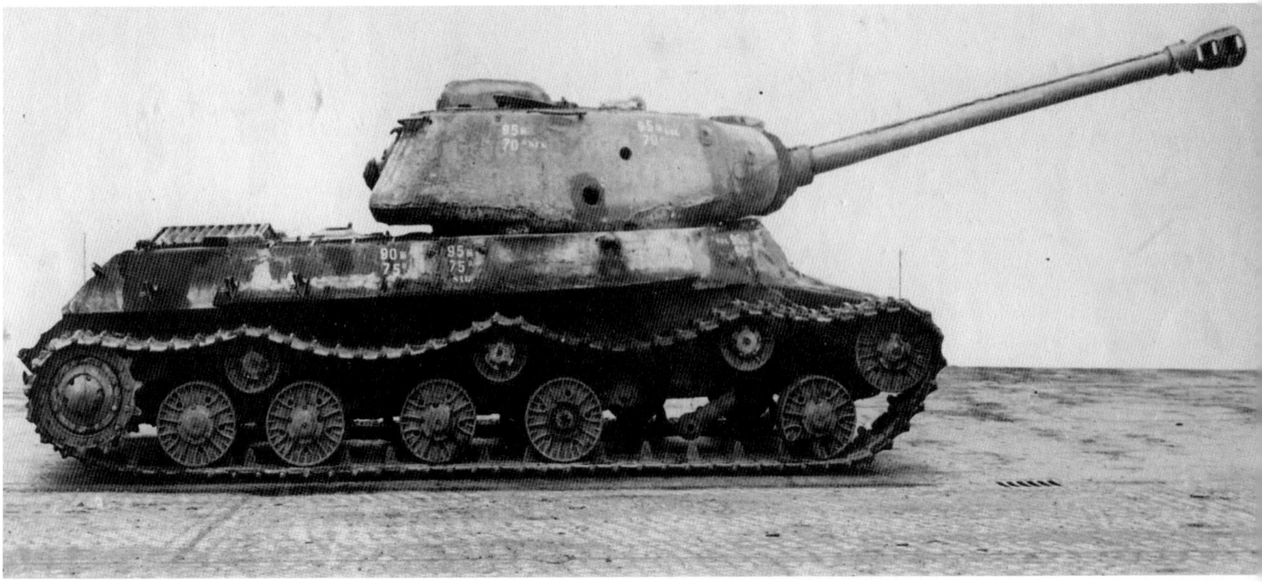

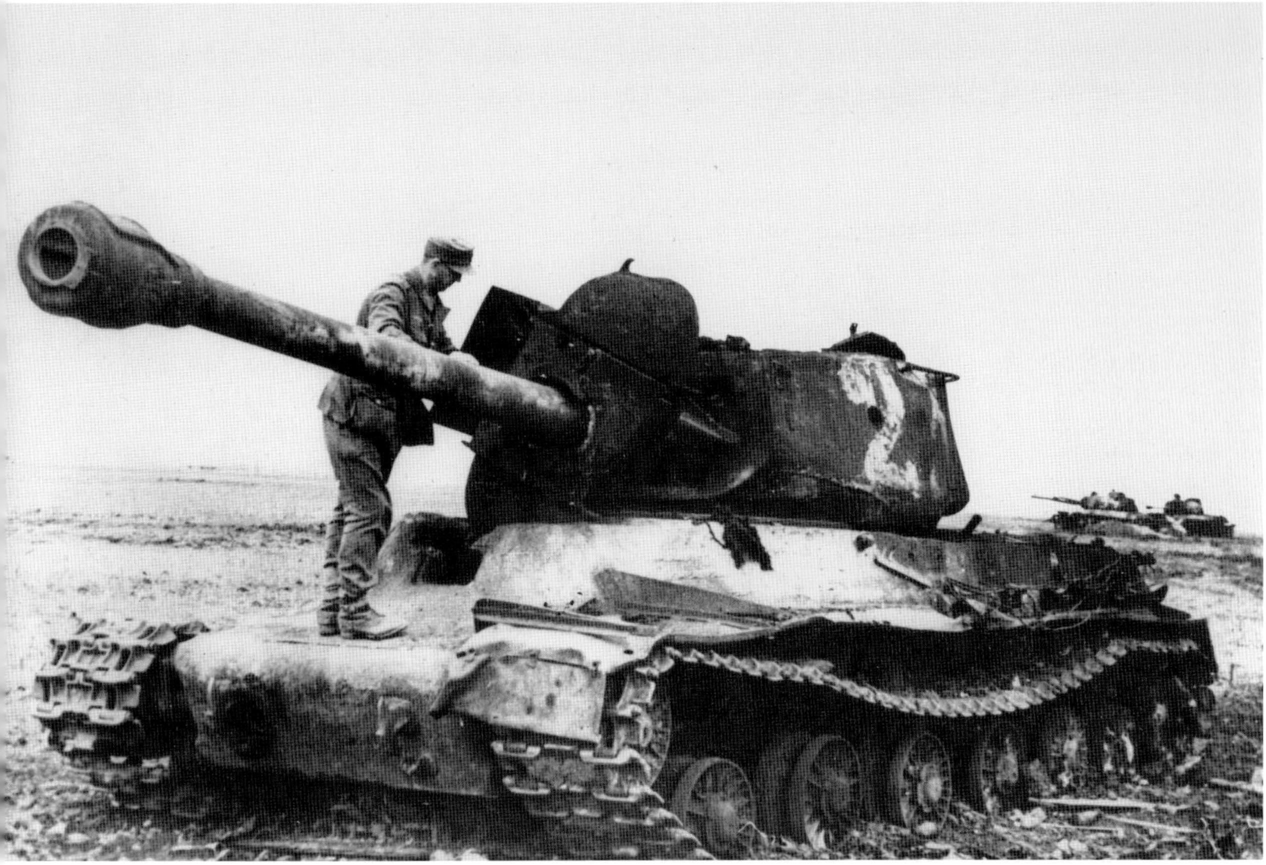

A German soldier is seen looking over a knocked-out early-production IS-2. It has no doubt suffered from its onboard main gun ammunition being detonated as the turret gun shield has been blown out of position and the blackened surface indicates a serious onboard fire. The maximum armour thickness on the front of the IS-2 turret was 160mm. *(Patton Museum)*

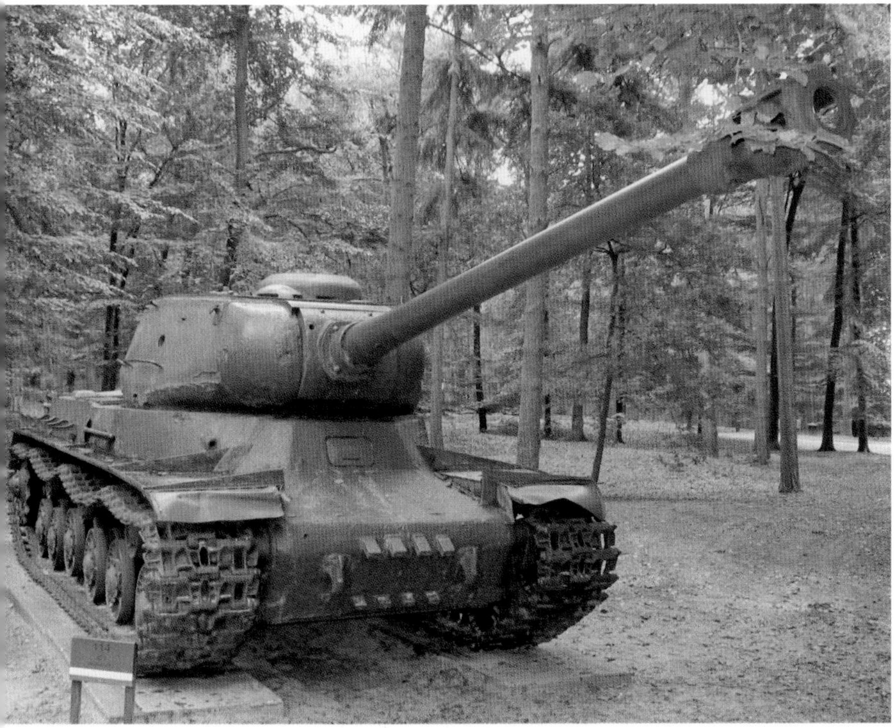

Pictured is a preserved early-production IS-2, which can be identified by its stepped glacis plate. The vehicle's crew consisted of four men: vehicle commander, gunner, loader and driver. The radio-operator/bow machine-gunner of the KV-1 series was dispensed with. Instead there was a fixed forward-firing small-calibre machine gun located in the right front hull. *(Frank Schultz)*

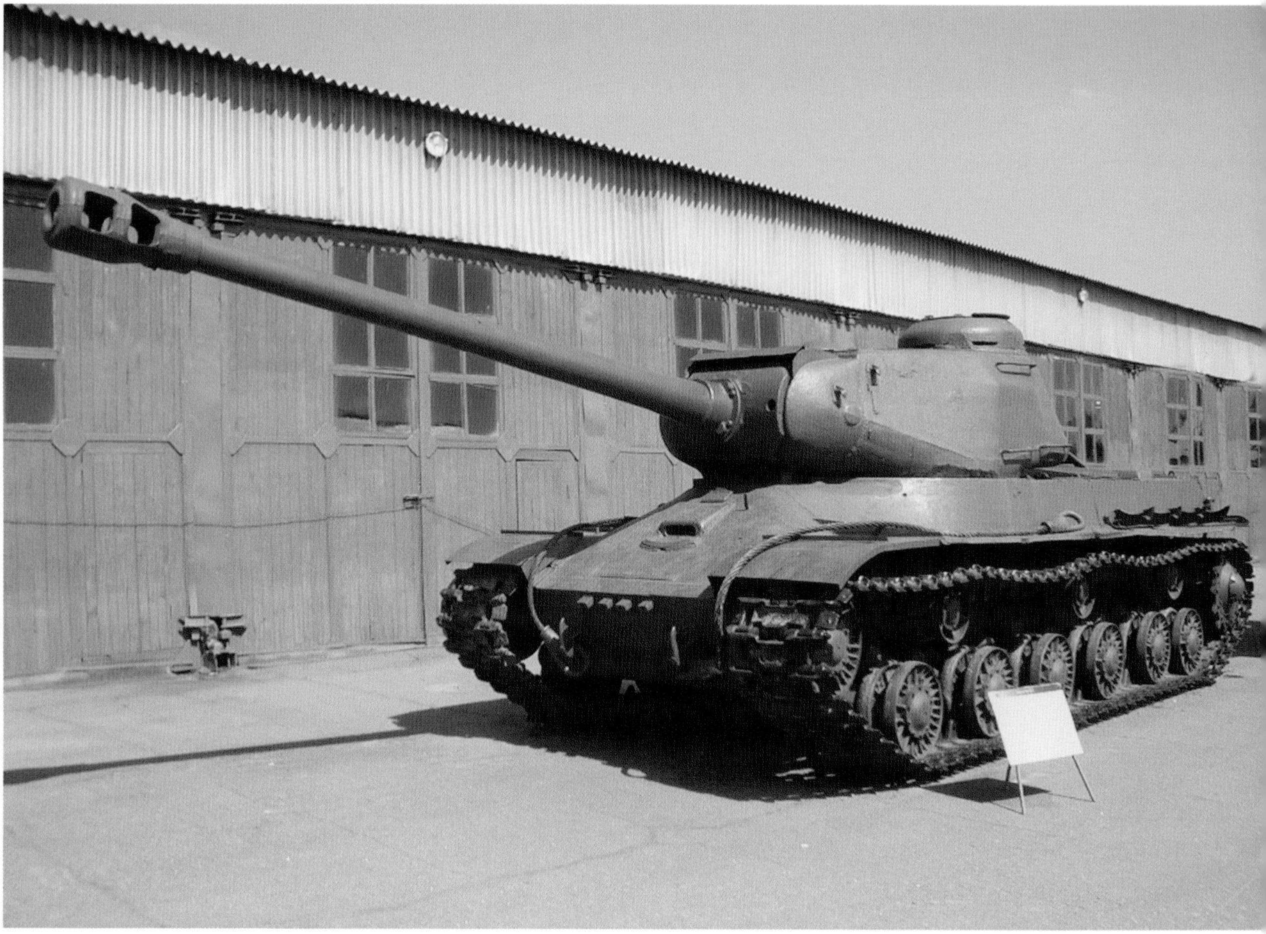

Belonging to the collection of the Russian Army Tank Museum is this Second World War vintage IS-2 with the later-production sloped glacis that replaced the original stepped glacis seen on early-production units. At its thickest point the turret armour was 160mm. The sides of the vehicle's hull were 95mm thick and the rear armour hull plate 60mm thick. *(Vladimir Yakubov)*

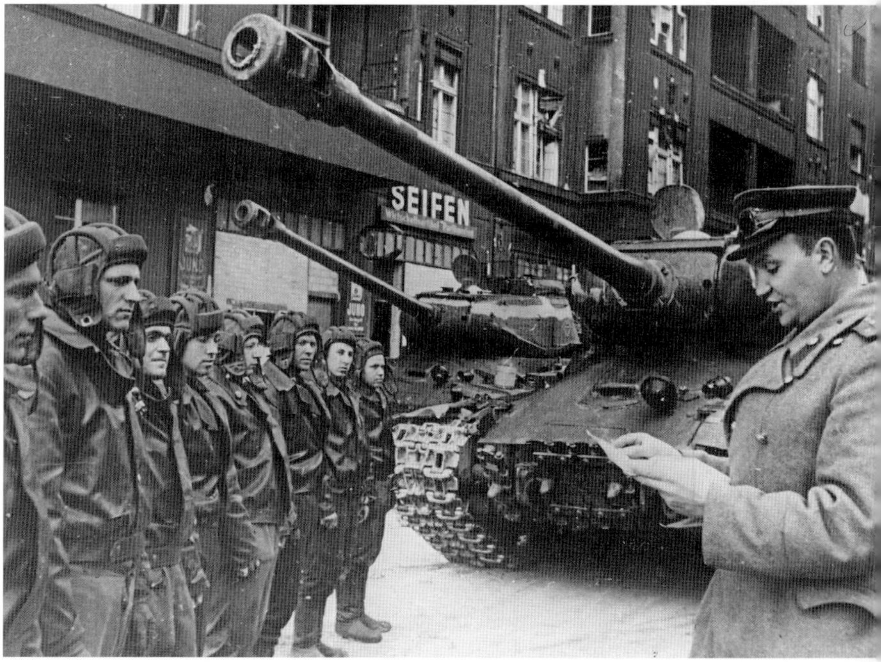
SEIFEN

A Red Army officer briefs the crews of his late-production IS-2 tanks at the end of the war in Europe. Due to the size of the separate-loading ammunition for the vehicle's 122mm main gun, it had authorized storage for only twenty-eight main gun rounds. In comparison, the German Tiger B heavy tank had authorized storage for eighty-six main gun rounds. *(Patton Museum)*

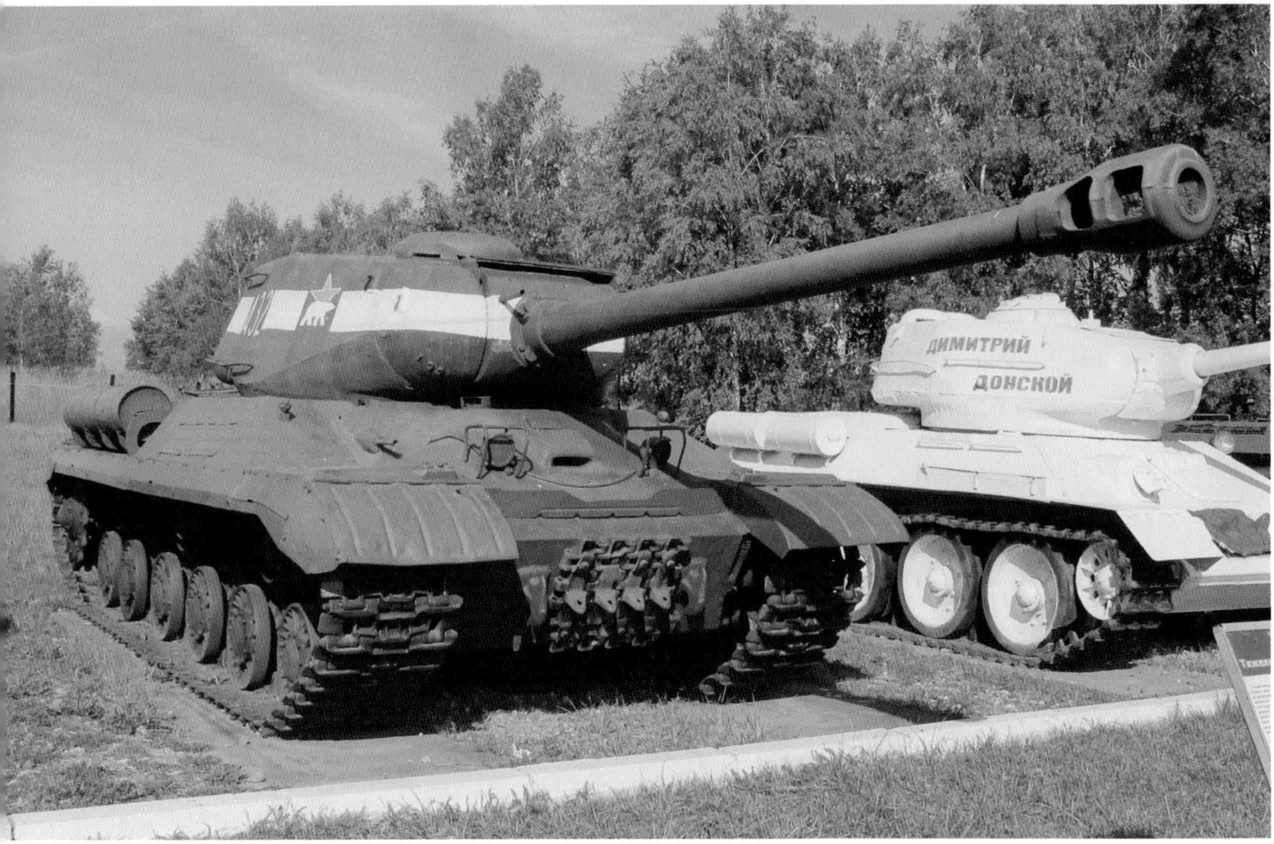
ДИМИТРИЙ
ДОНСКОЙ

On display at the Russian Army Tank Museum is this post-war upgraded IS-2 labelled as the IS-2M. This version of the tank can be identified by the storage bins built into the upper hull sides of the tanks. An unseen improvement to the IS-2M was the reconfiguration of the main gun ammunition storage arrangement that allowed the tank to carry thirty-five main gun rounds. *(Vladimir Yakubov)*

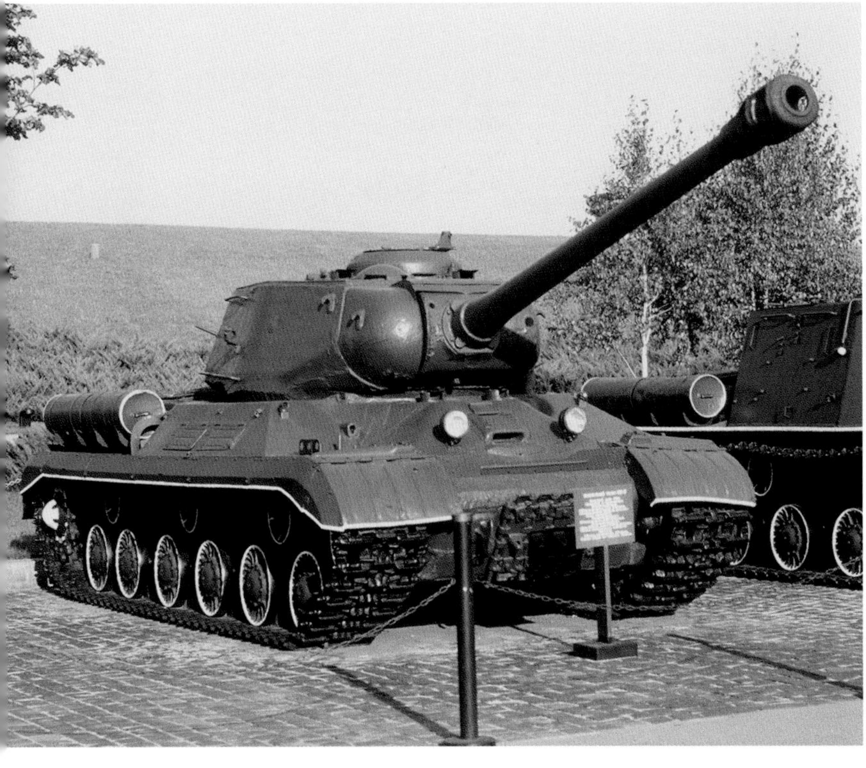

A post-war upgraded IS-2M is shown on display. The white paint outlining such things as the road wheels and the fuel tanks was often applied to tanks assigned to take part in important parades. The red highlight at the vehicle's muzzle brake is also a parade feature. The turret of the IS-2 series was made of cast steel armour to help minimize vehicle weight. *(Department of Defense)*

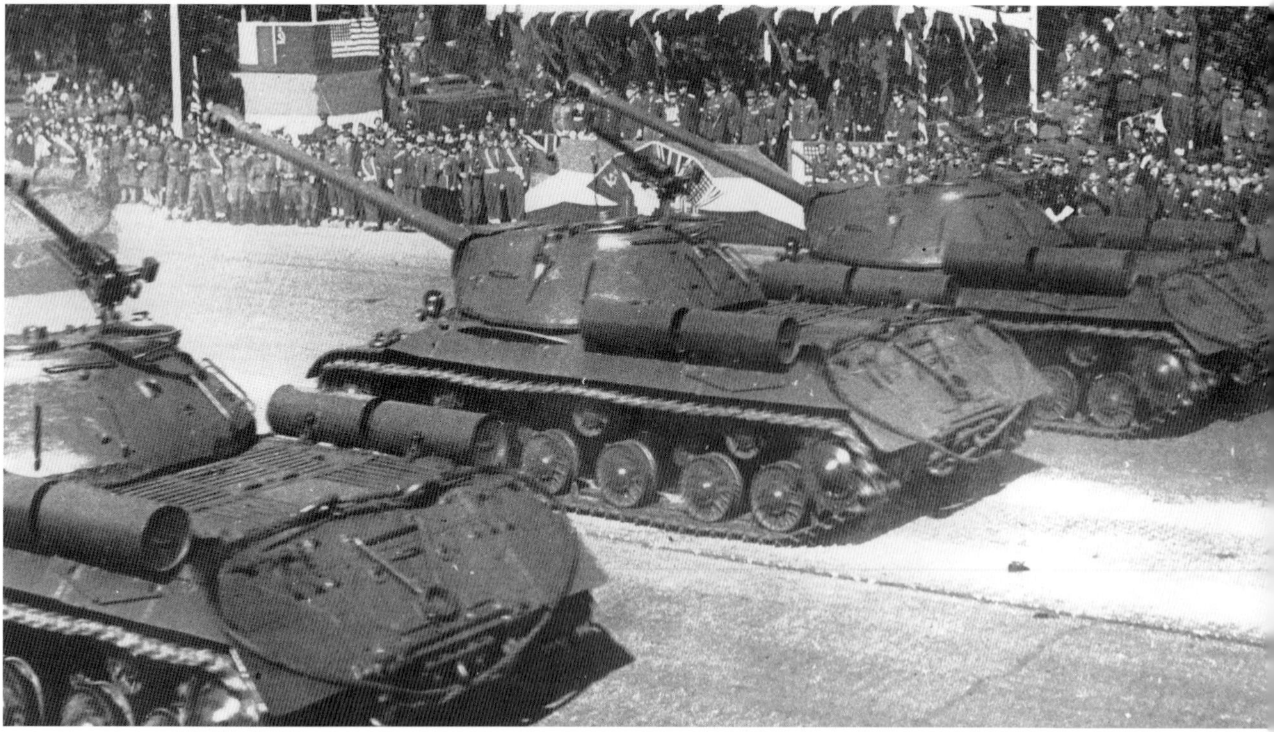

The Red Army replacement for the IS-2 tank was the IS-3 heavy tank, several of which are seen here on parade during a 7 September 1945 victory parade in Berlin. The low-slung and sleek appearance of this heavily-armoured tank was a rude shock to the Western Allied military leadership as up to that point in time they were not aware of its existence. *(Patton Museum)*

The IS-3 is 32ft 3in long and has a width of 10ft 5in. The vehicle height is 8ft without a turret roof-mounted machine gun fitted. Maximum armour thickness on the front of the turret is 220mm. Pictured is a post-war upgraded IS-3 heavy tank labelled as the IS-3M which is taking part in a military vehicle demonstration in Russia. *(R. Bazalevsky)*

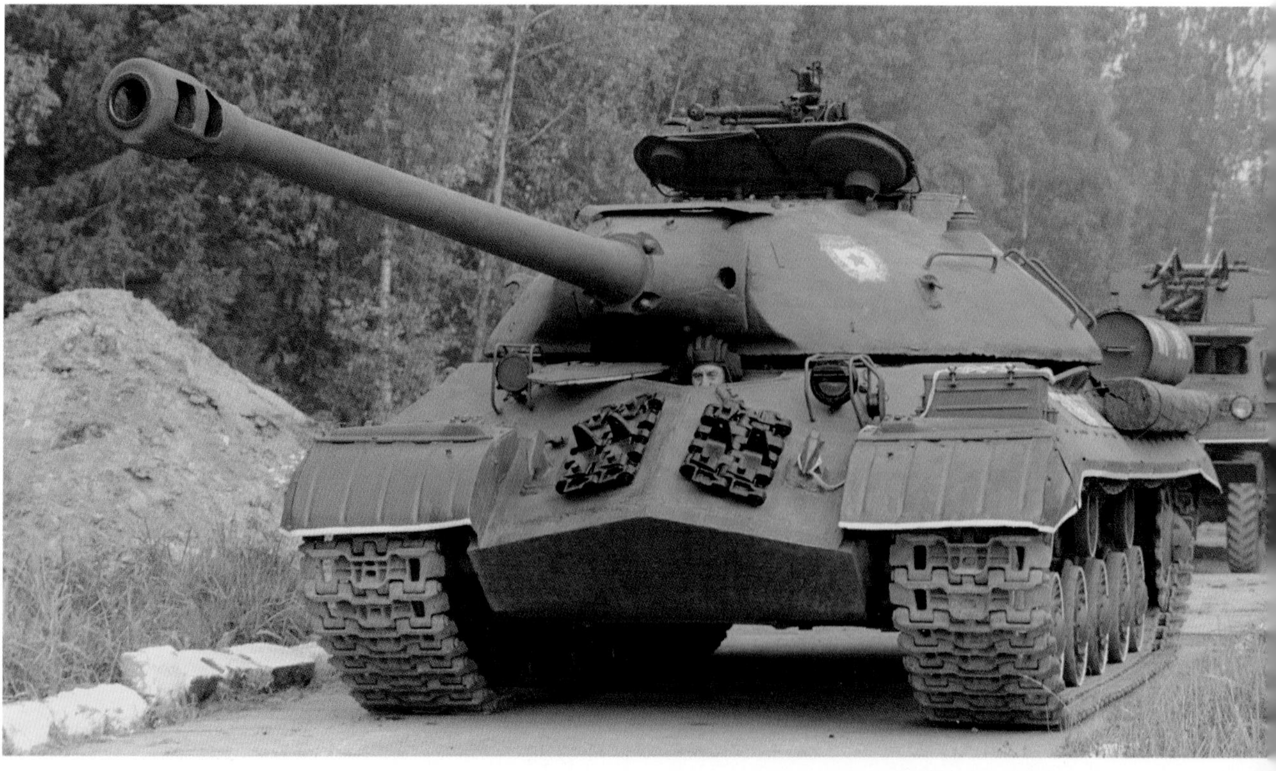

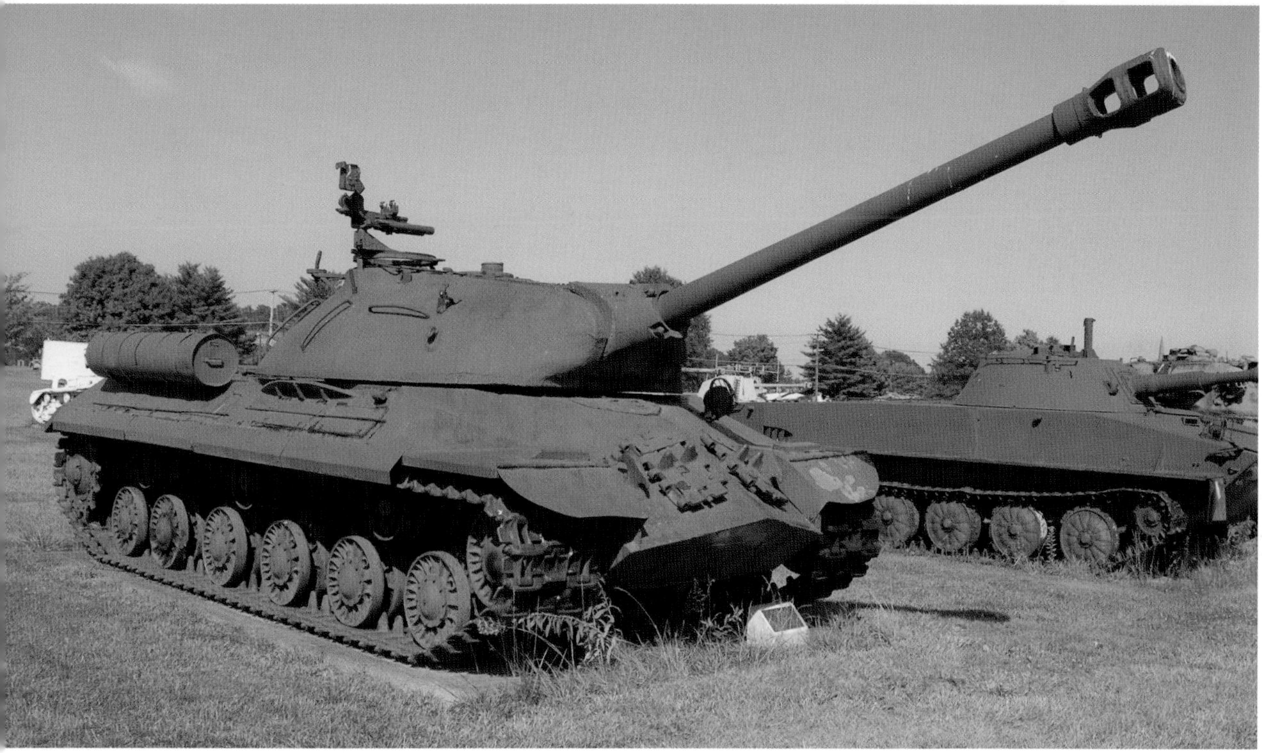

Shown here on display at the now-closed US Army Ordnance Museum is an IS-3M that can be identified by the upper hull side storage bins. Due to the very sharply-pointed bow of the tank Red Army tankmen nicknamed it the *Shchuka* ('Pike'). The bracket on the top of the tank's turret was for a large machine gun, which when fitted raised the tank's height to 9ft 8in. *(Author's collection)*

Pictured is the pilot model T1E2 that eventually became the US army's M6 heavy tank. It was 27ft 8in in length, had a width of 10ft 3in and the vehicle height was 9ft 10in. Maximum armour thickness was 127mm on the front of the turret. It was armed with a 3-inch main gun and a coaxial 37mm gun in lieu of a machine gun. *(TACOM)*

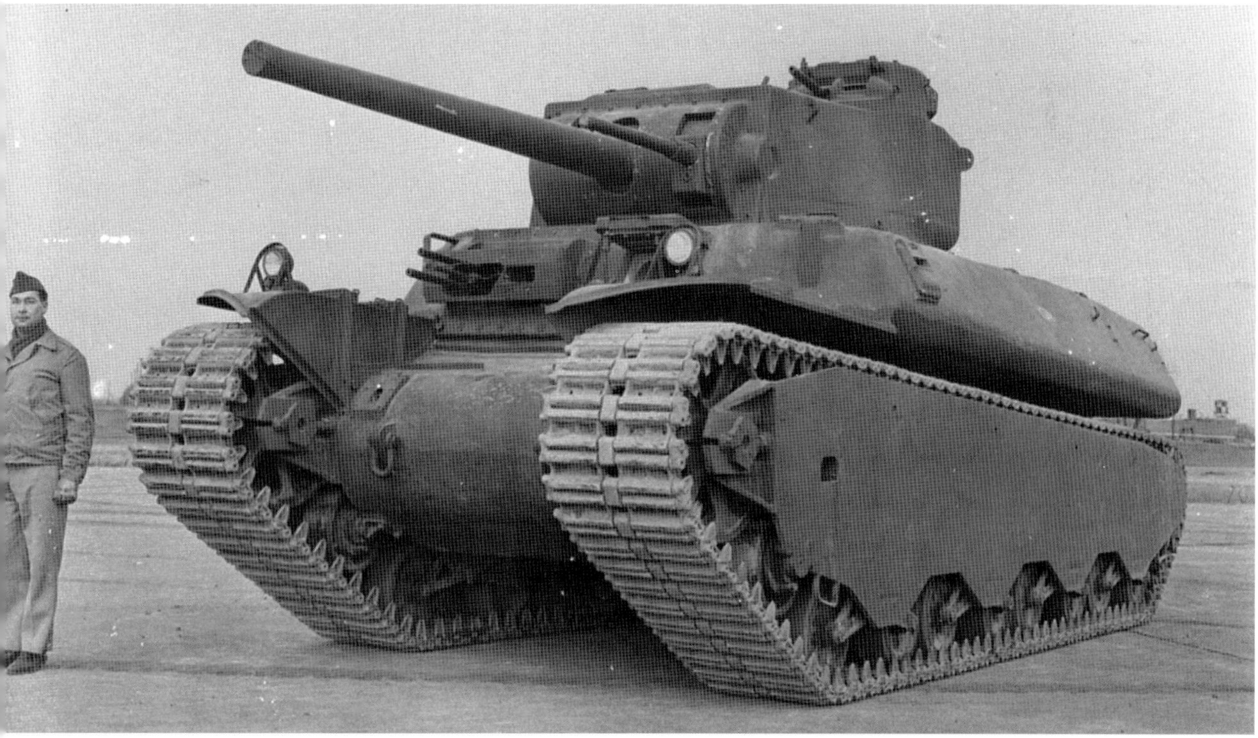

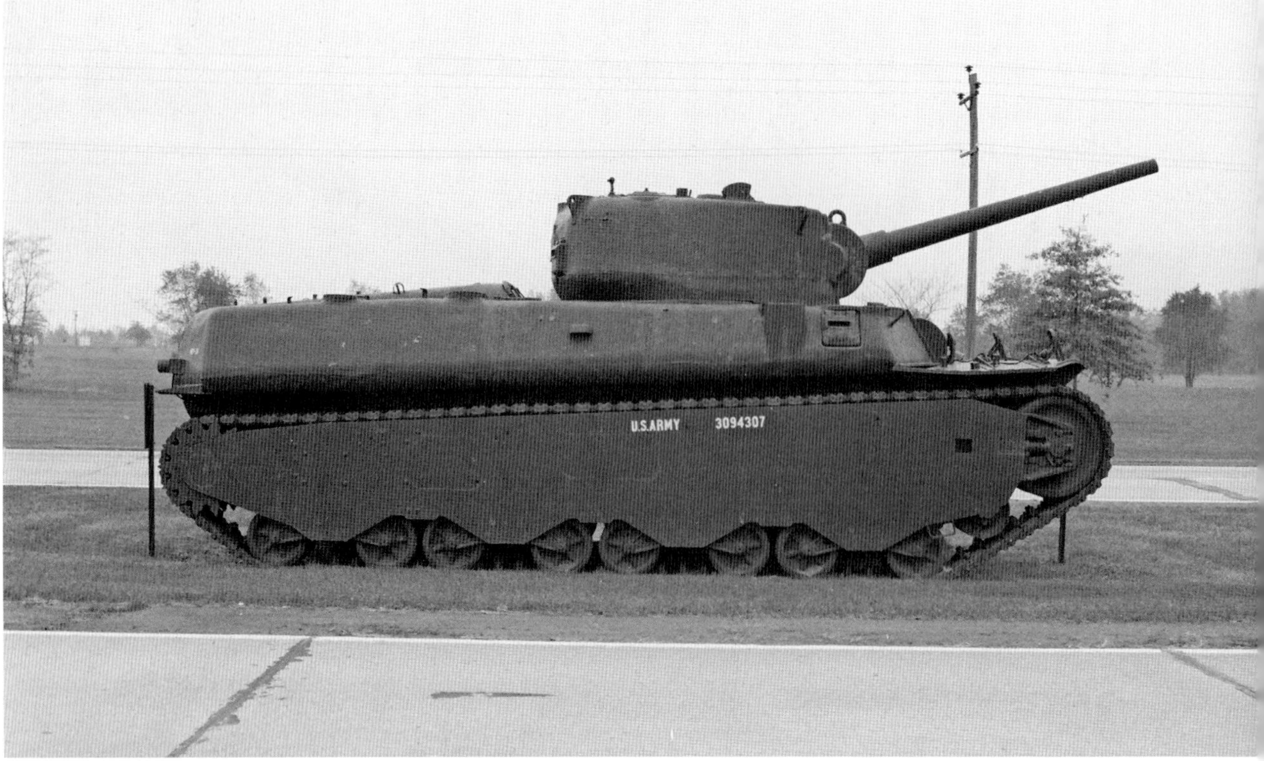
U.S.ARMY
3094307

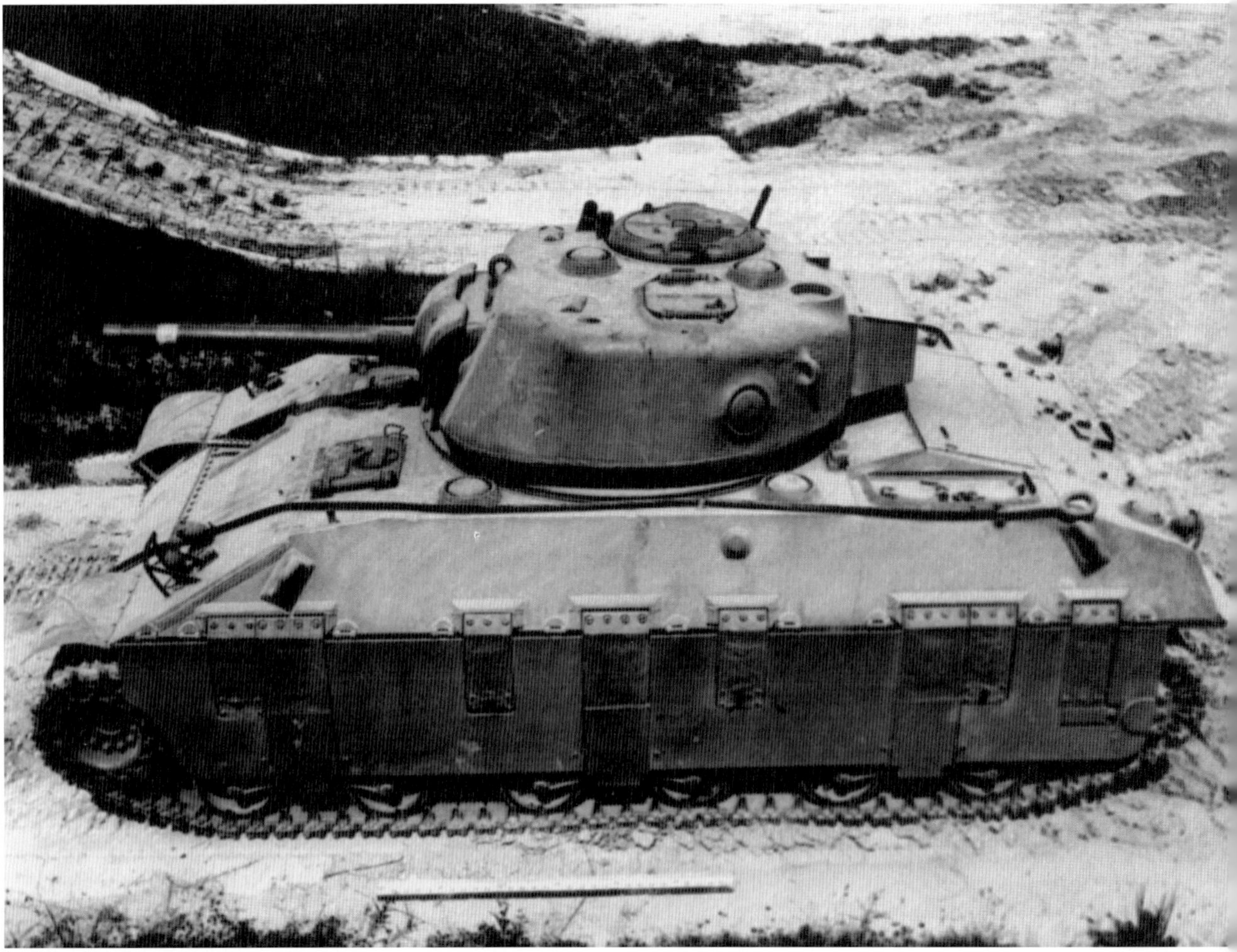

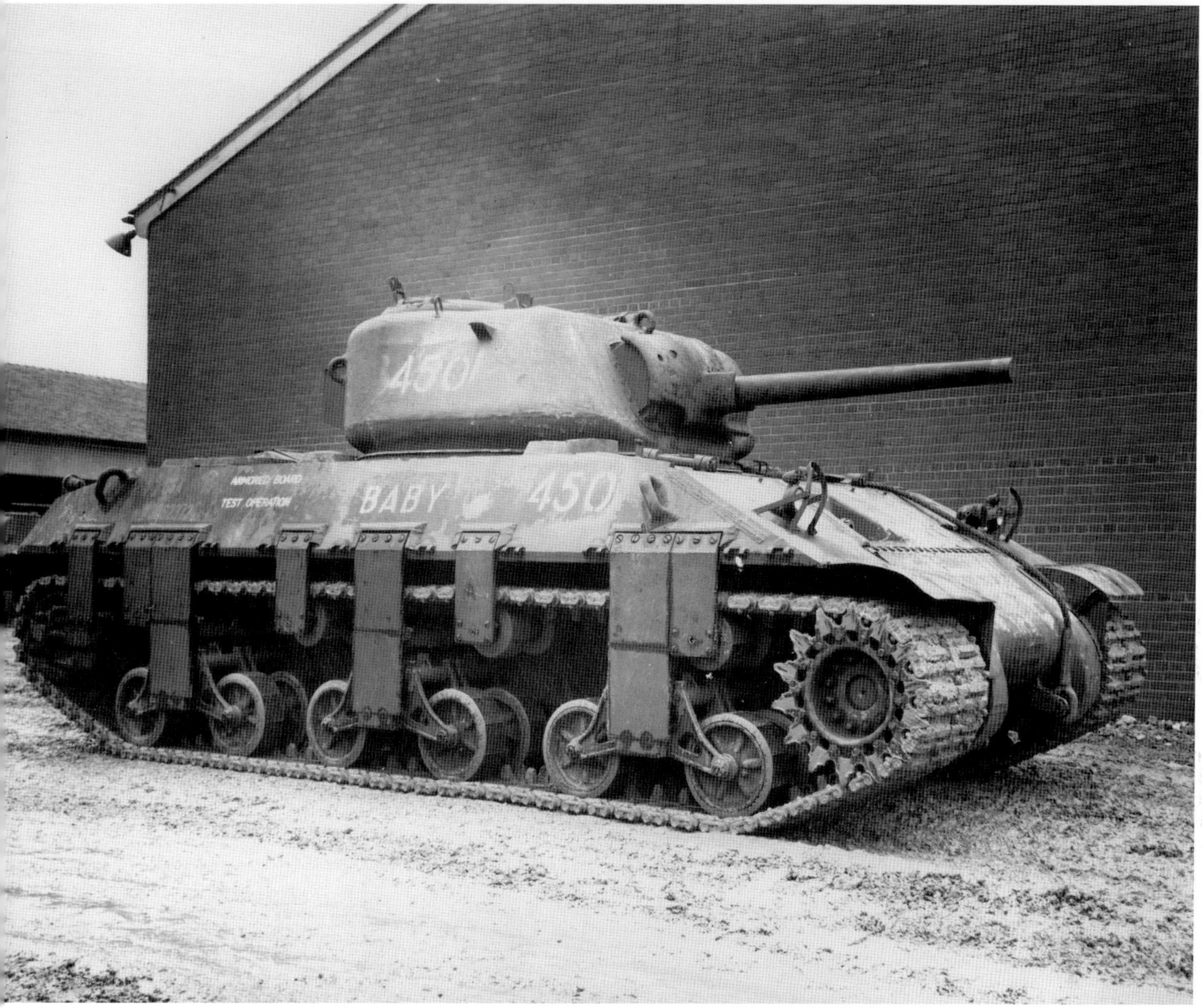
450
ARMORED BOARD
TEST OPERATION
BABY 450

(*Opposite above*) On display at the famous 'Tank Mile' that was in place at Aberdeen Proving Ground, Maryland for many decades is the sole example of the production model of the M6 heavy tank. The cast armour vehicle commander's cupola seen on the T1E2 pilot model was dispensed with on the production units as is evident from this photograph. *(Richard Hunnicutt)*

(*Opposite below*) In this official US army Ordnance Department picture we see one of the two T-14 assault tank pilots constructed in the summer of 1942 by the American Locomotive Company. They were built because of the perceived requirement for such a vehicle by both the American and British armies. Testing of the tank failed to impress anybody of importance, and other than the pilots none were ordered into production. *(TACOM)*

(*Above*) To allow for the servicing of the suspension system on the T-14 assault tank pilots, the armoured panels on either side of the hull could be removed as seen in this photograph. Like the M4 series, the T-14 was intended to have a crew of five. Both pilots of the T-14 were armed with a 75mm main gun. However, plans had been made to arm the pilots with 90mm main guns when further work on the vehicles was halted. *(TACOM)*

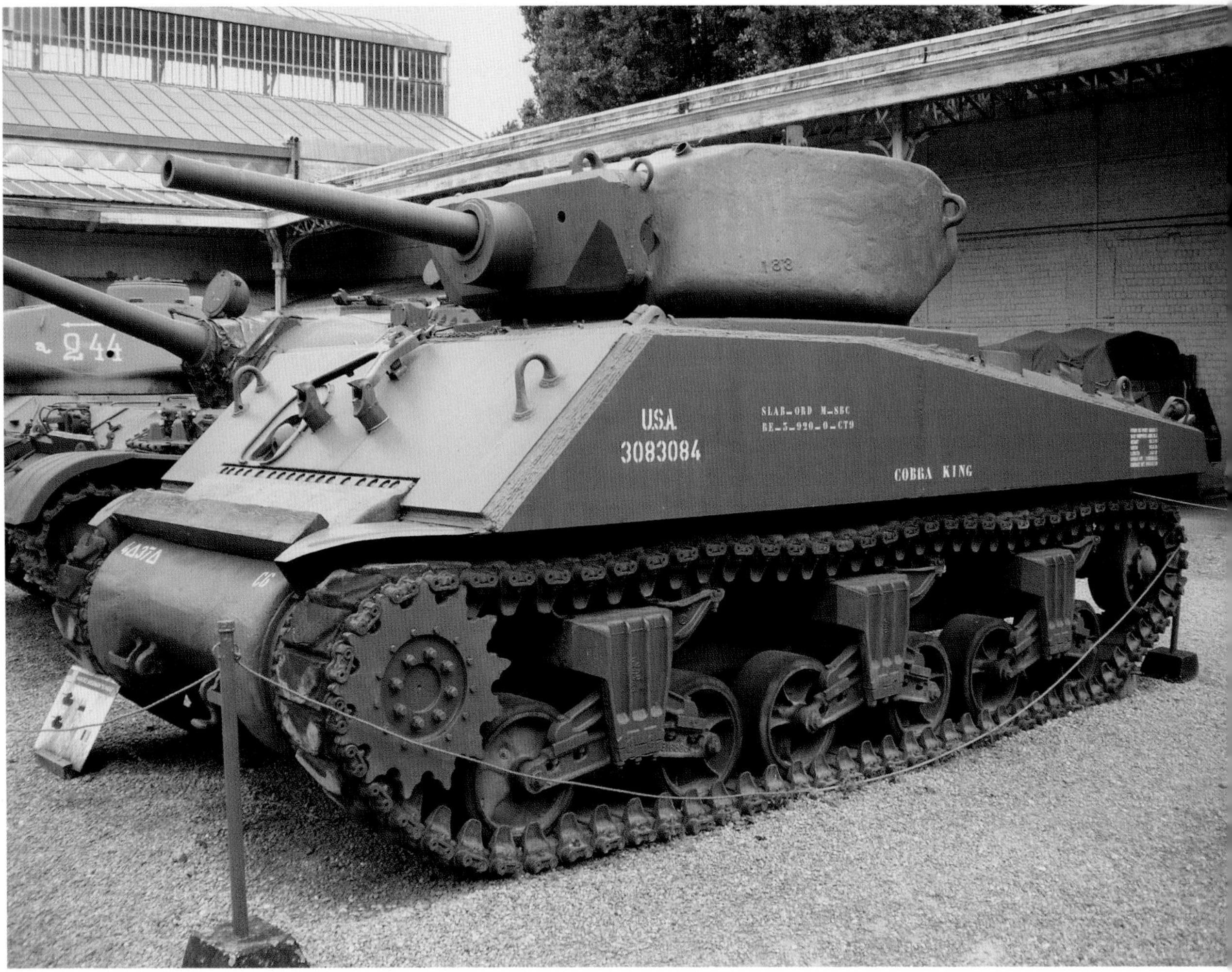
U.S.A.
3083084
COBRA KING

(*Above*) An assault tank that did make it into production for the US army was designated as the M4A3E2. A preserved example is seen here in a European military museum. It featured 101mm of armour on its glacis, with the final drive armour casting being 140mm at its thickest horizontal point. The cast armour gun shield on the tank's turret was 178mm thick. *(Pierre-Olivier Buan)*

(*Opposite above*) Pictured is an M4A3E2 that has been up-armed with a 76mm main gun as indicated by the length of the barrel fitted. To offset the additional weight of the vehicle due to the additional armour applied, all were fitted with extended steel end connectors as seen on the tank pictured to increase their flotation across soft soil. The maximum speed of the M4A3E2 on level roads was 25mph. *(Patton Museum)*

(*Opposite below*) The heavy tank that had been so long in gestation for the US army was the five-man M26 seen here in Germany on 1 March 1945. It was armed with a 90mm main gun. The vehicle was 28ft 4.5in in length and had a width of 11ft 6in, which was a problem for the US army's existing portable bridges. The height of the tank was 9ft 1.5in. *(Patton Museum)*

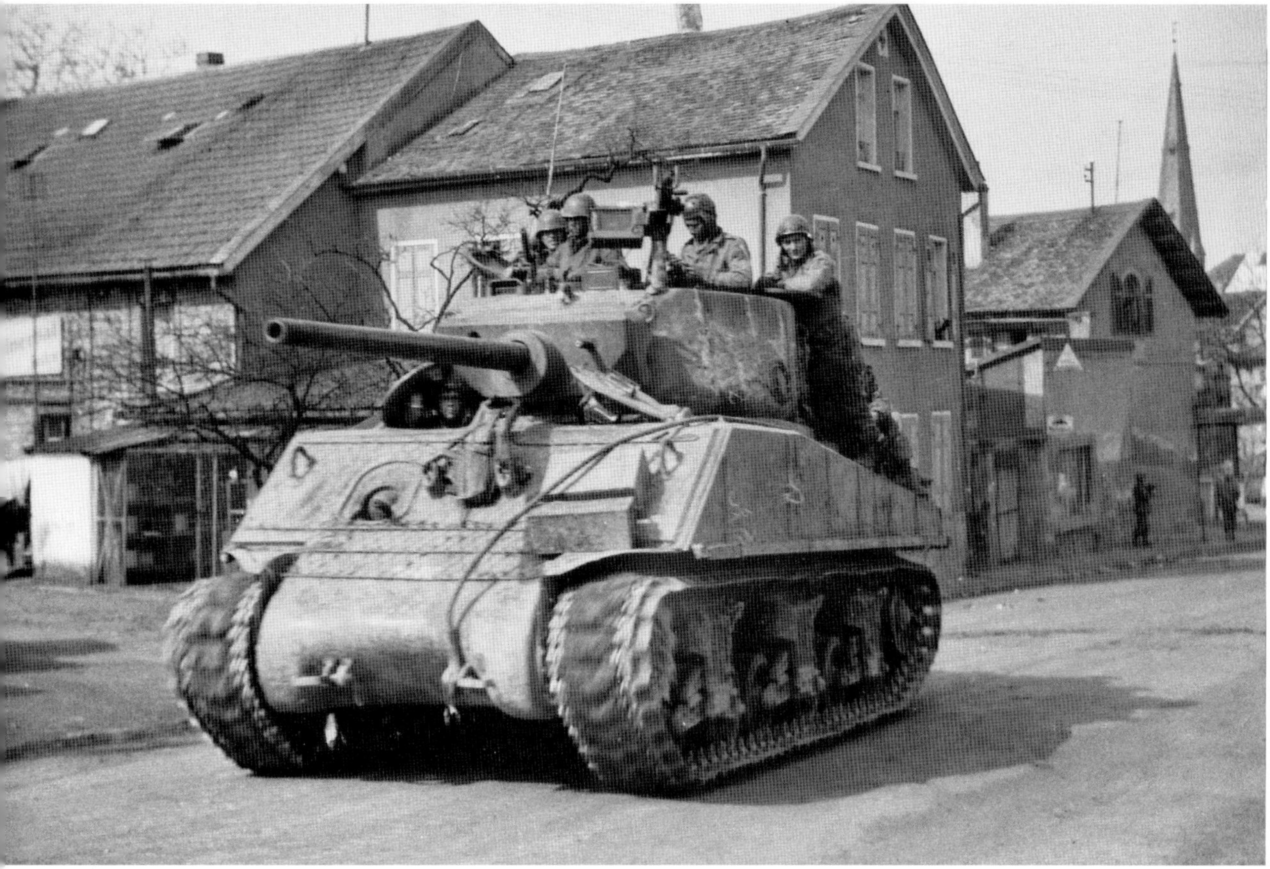

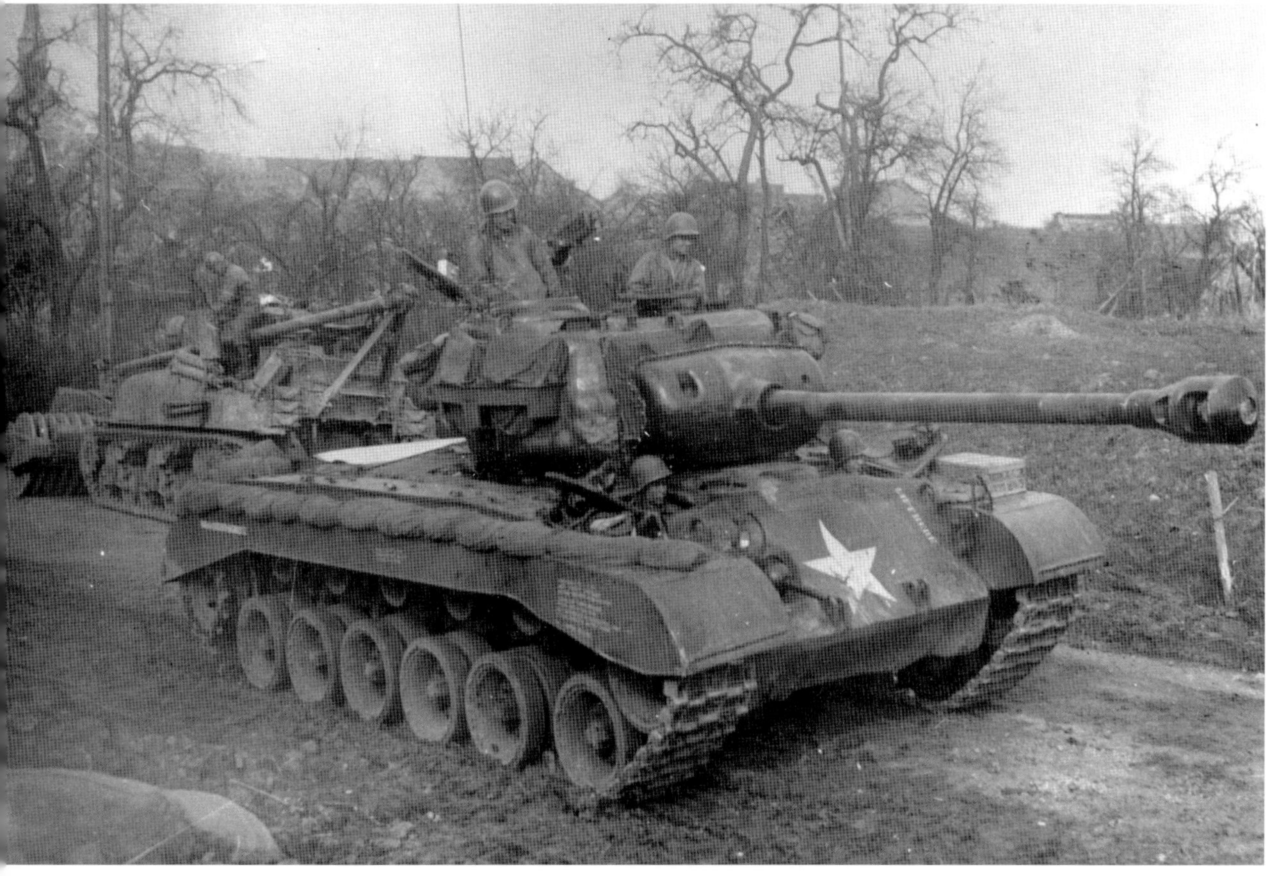

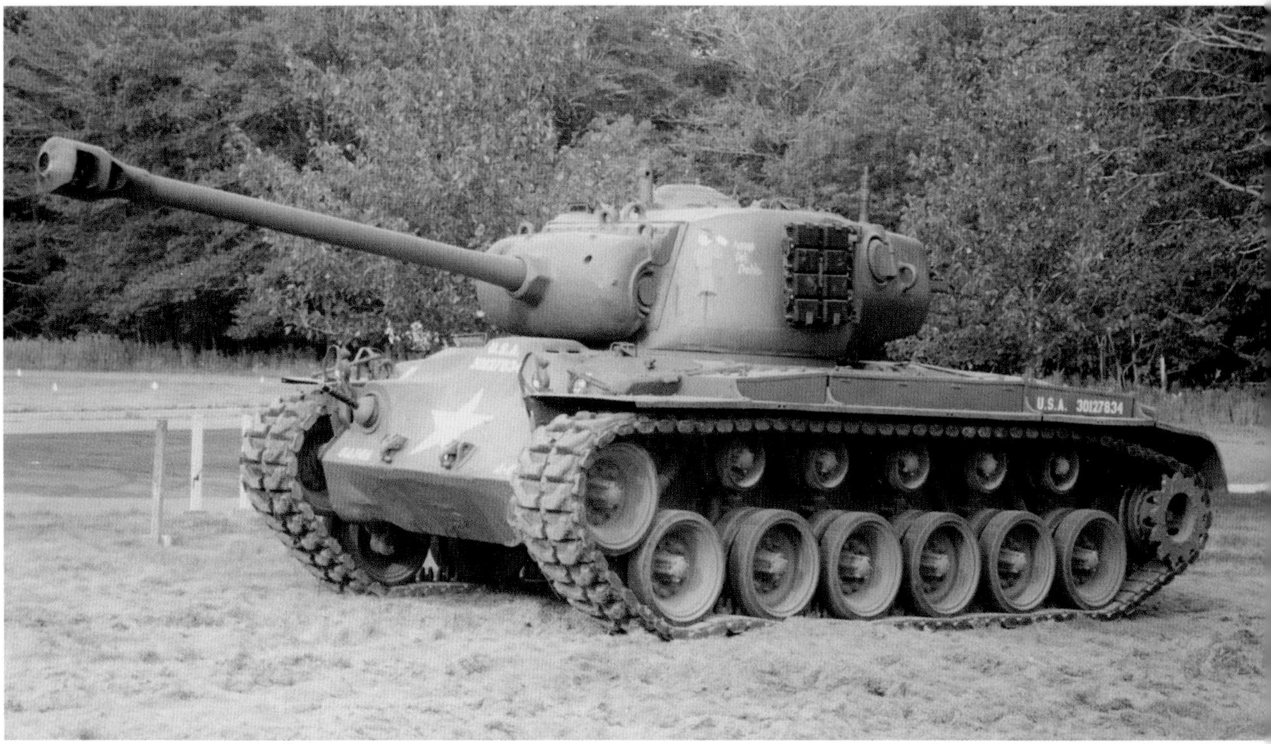
U.S.A. 30127834

Belonging to a private collector is this restored M26 heavy tank in US army markings. The 90mm main gun on the M26 series was designated as the M3. With the muzzle brake fitted the 90mm gun was approximately 17ft long. Early-production armour-piercing rounds from the weapon had a muzzle velocity of 2,650 feet per second with later-production AP rounds reaching 2,800 feet per second. *(Bob Fleming)*

The first combat engagement between a US army M26 heavy tank and a German Tiger E heavy tank took place on 26 February 1945. The American tank was the loser, taking three hits, one of which gouged out a chuck of armour from the front of the turret as seen here. Of the other two 88mm armour-piercing projectiles fired, one penetrated through the coaxial machine-gun port and the other the American tank's muzzle brake. *(Patton Museum)*

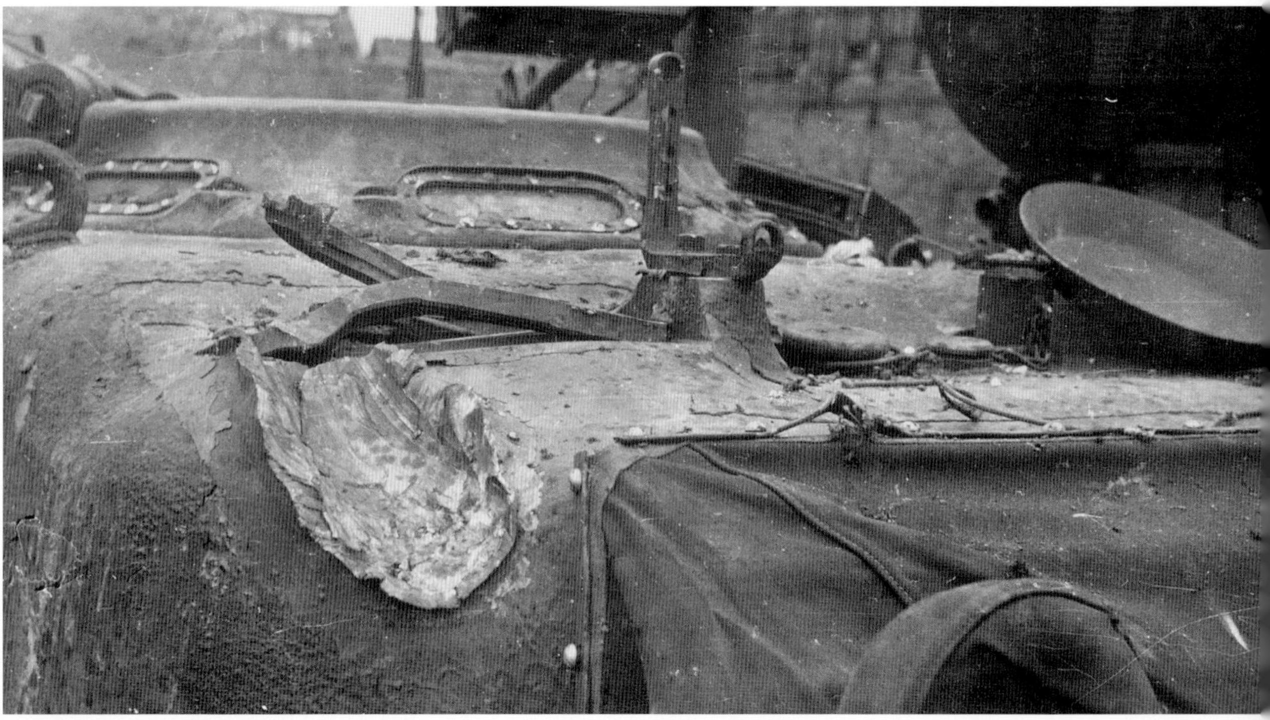

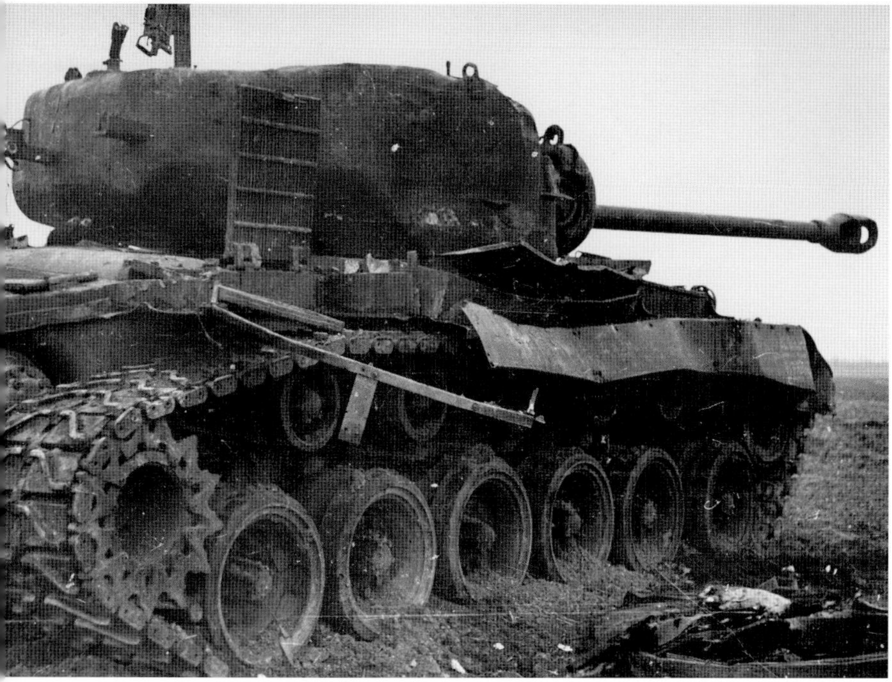

On 1 March 1945 one of the initial batch of M26 heavy tanks deployed to North-West Europe was damaged by two German high-explosive (HE) artillery rounds as seen in this picture. The first damaged the tank's right-hand-side suspension system. When the crew left their tank to inspect the damage, a second HE round struck the tank's turret and blew off the vehicle commander's cupola and killed the vehicle commander. *(Patton Museum)*

A second batch of M26 heavy tanks arrived in North-West Europe in late March 1945. Pictured are some that were allocated to the US army's 11th Armored Division that formed part of General George S. Patton's Third Army. By the time the crews of these M26 heavy tanks had mastered the skills required to operate the vehicle, it was 21 April 1945 and the war would end just a few weeks later. *(Patton Museum)*

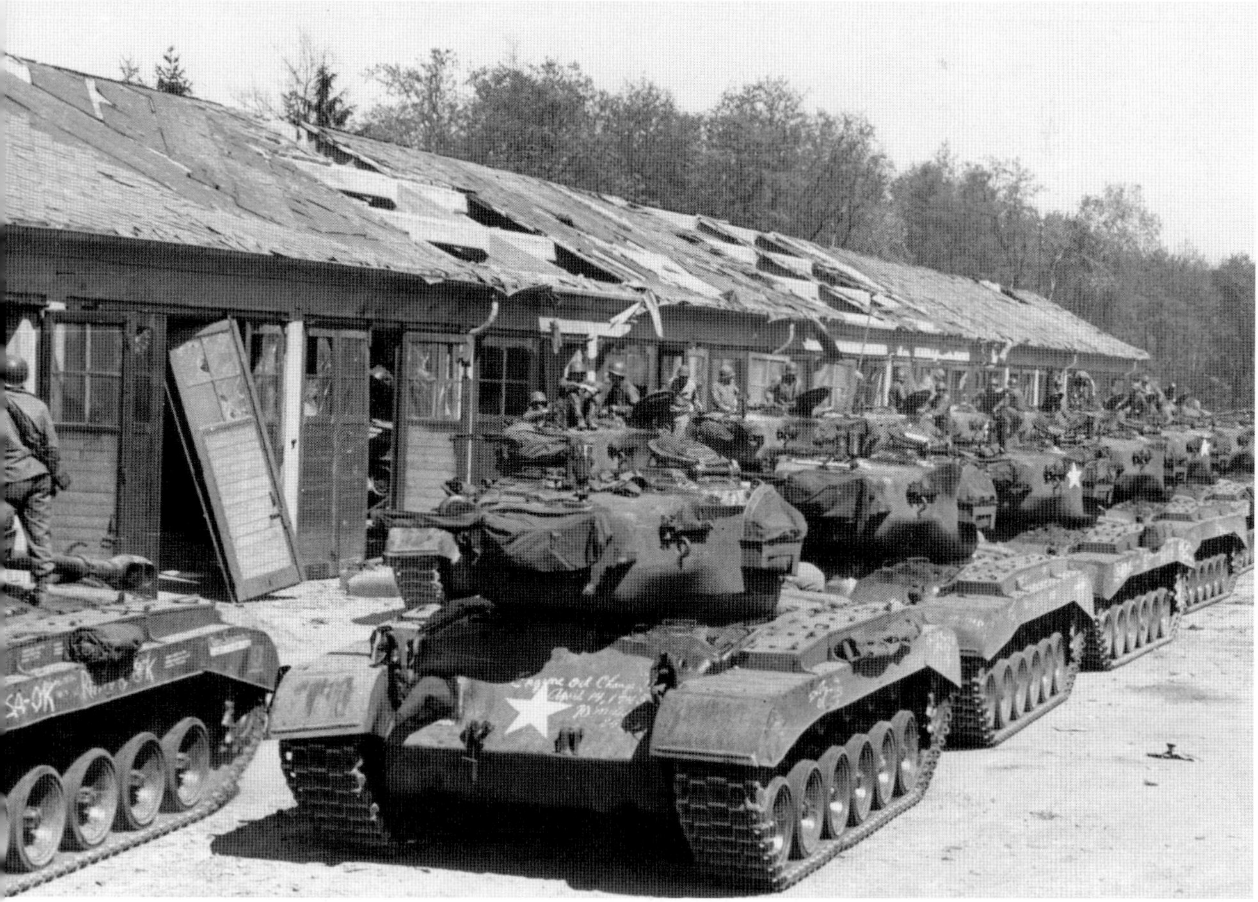

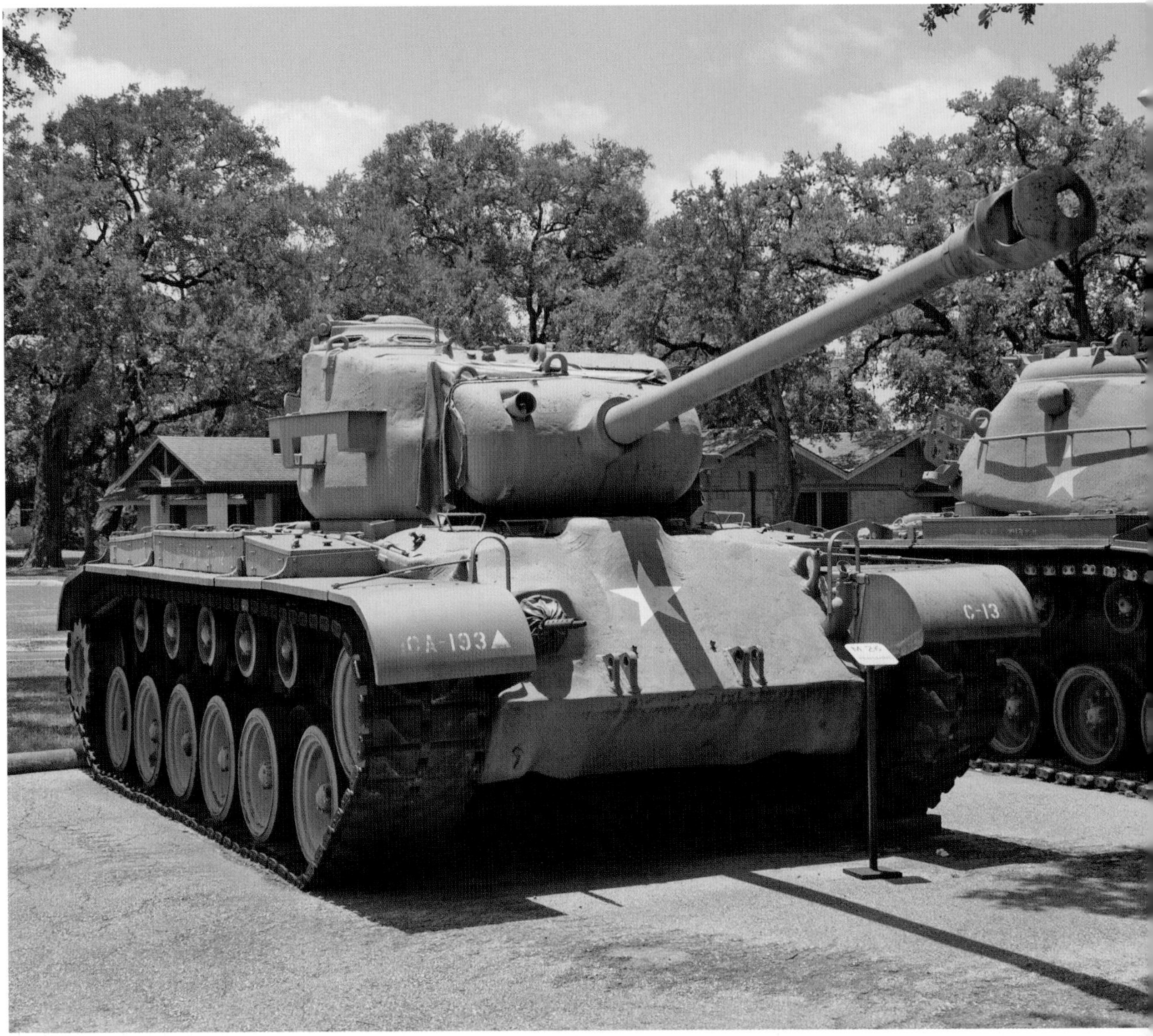

(*Above*) On display at a US army museum located at Fort Hood, Texas is this M26 heavy tank. It had authorized storage for seventy main gun rounds and 550 for the turret-mounted heavy-calibre machine gun. In addition, the tank had authorized storage for 5,000 small-calibre rounds for the coaxial and front-hull-mounted machine guns. (*Paul and Loren Hannah*)

(*Opposite page*) An impressive image of an M26 heavy tank production line on the left-hand side of the factory floor, with second-generation M4 series medium tanks fitted with the HVSS system being put together on the right-hand side. Unlike the M4 series, the M26 was fitted with dual driver's controls because it was fitted with an automatic transmission. (*TACOM*)

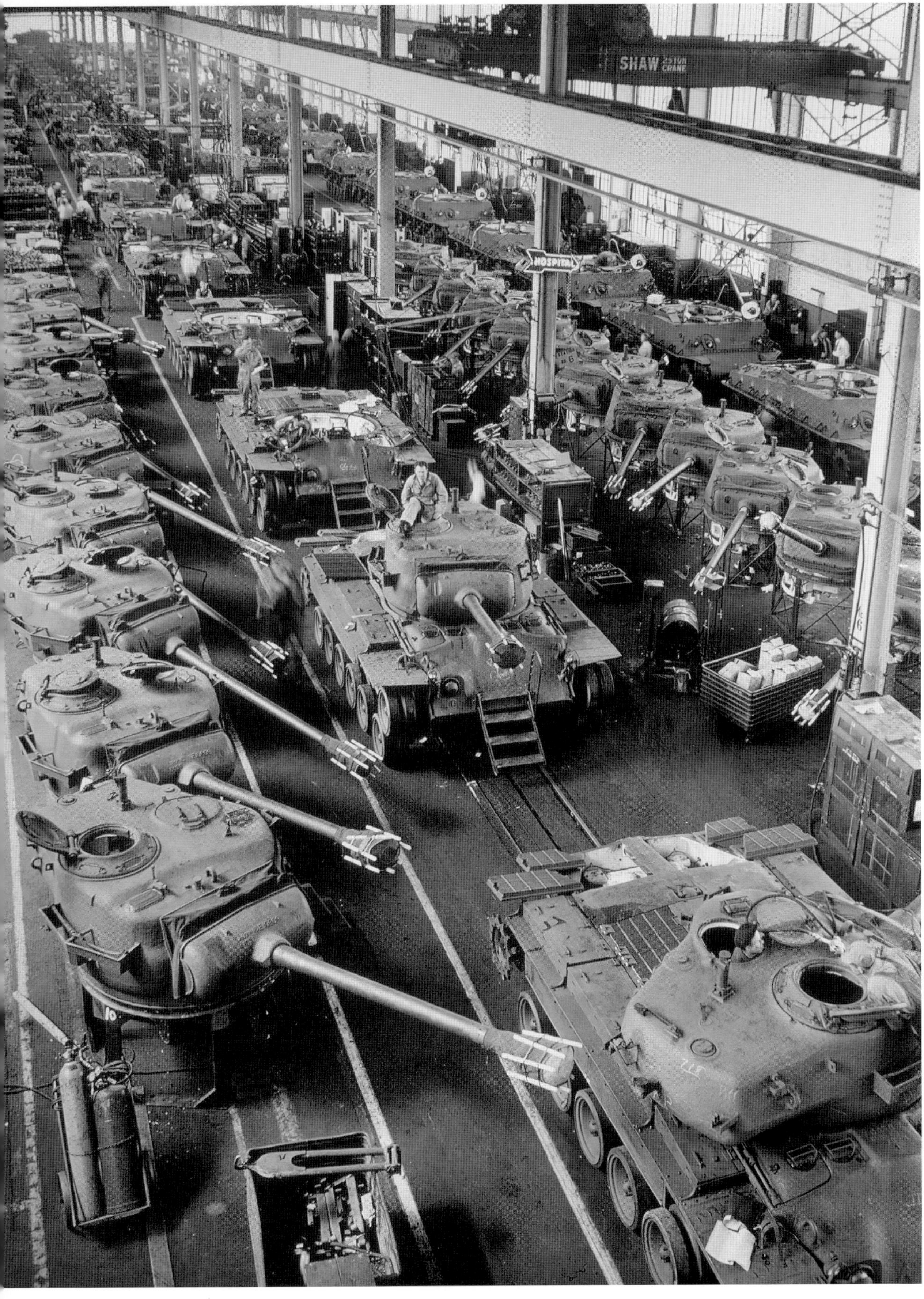
SHAW 25 TON CRANE
HOSPITAL

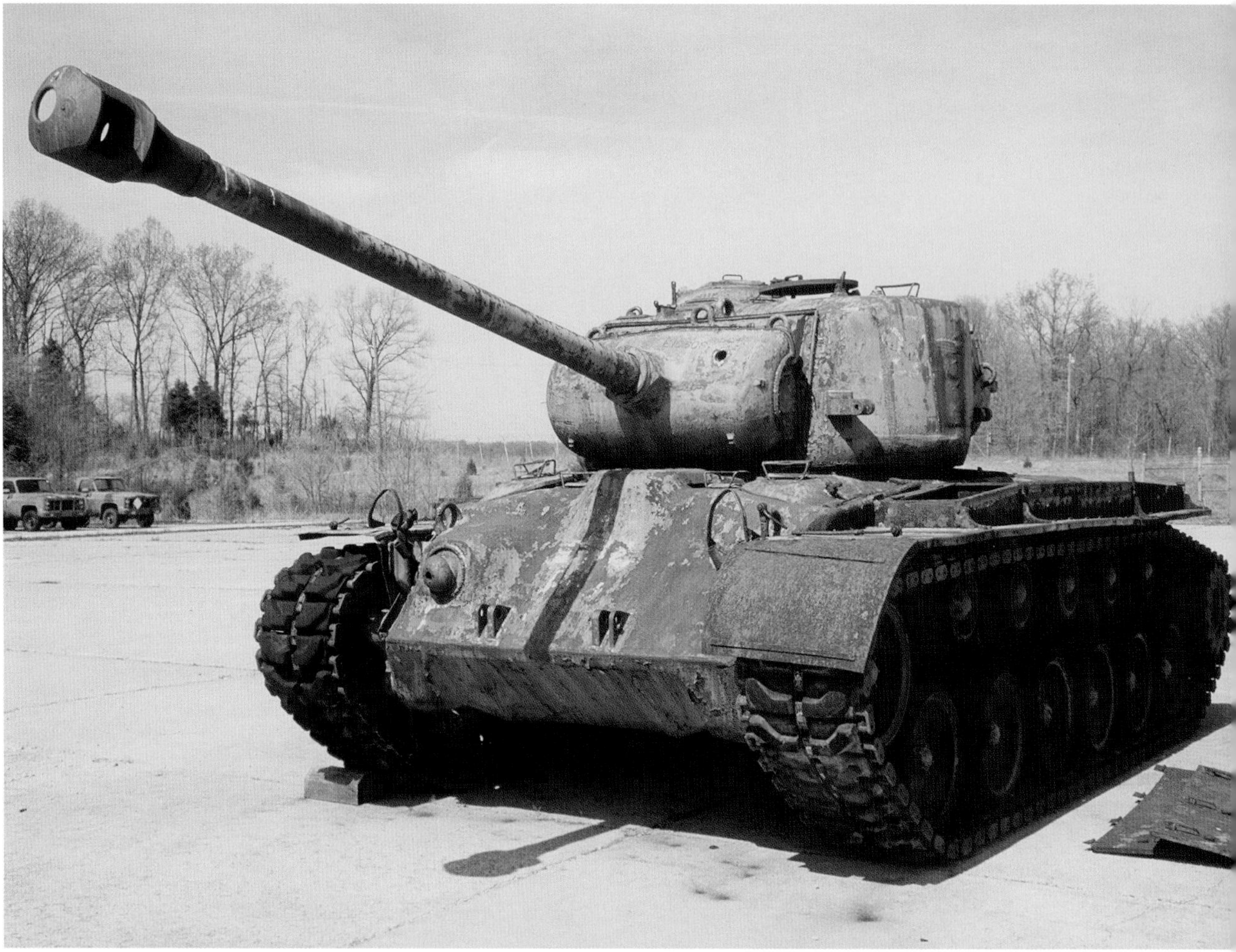

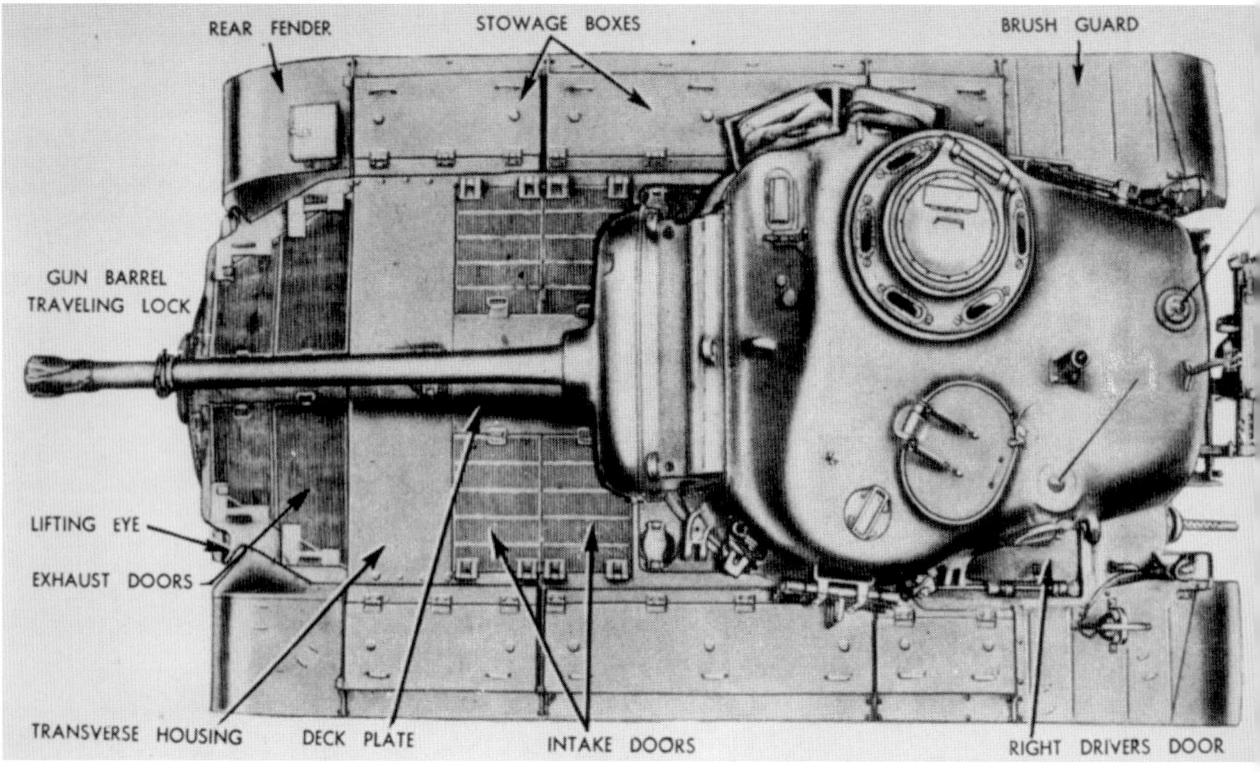
REAR FENDER
STOWAGE BOXES
BRUSH GUARD
GUN BARREL
TRAVELING LOCK
LIFTING EYE
EXHAUST DOORS
TRANSVERSE HOUSING
DECK PLATE
INTAKE DOORS
RIGHT DRIVERS DOOR

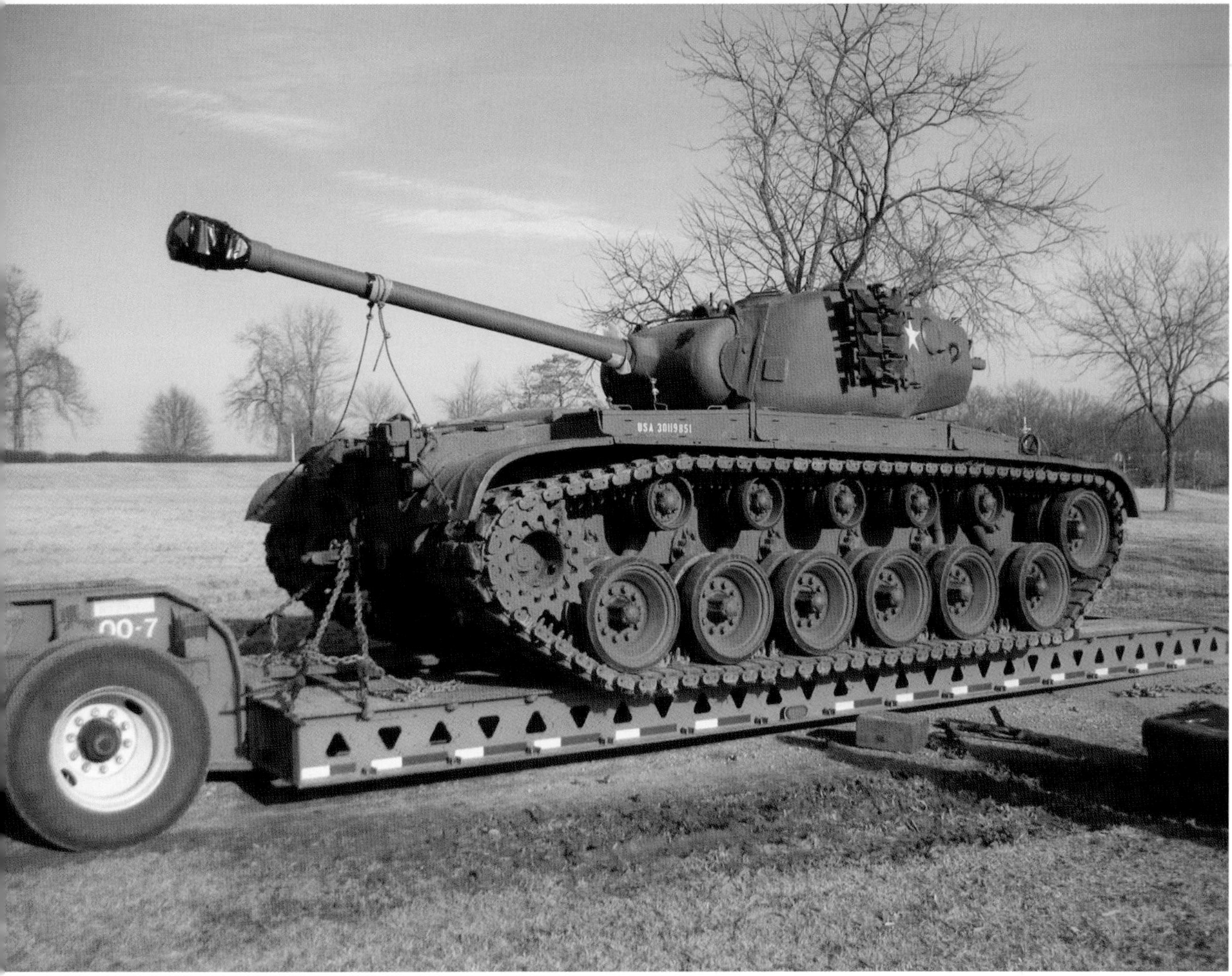
USA 30119851
00-7

(*Opposite above*) Shown here in storage at the now-closed Patton Museum of Armor and Cavalry is this unrestored M26 heavy tank. It and a number of others had been recovered from a US Air Force target range. The cast armour gun shield on the tank at its thickest point is 114mm. The near-vertical sides of the M26 tank turret are 76mm thick and the glacis at its thickest point is 101mm and sloped at 46 degrees. *(Author's collection)*

(*Opposite below*) From a US army manual comes this picture of an M26 heavy tank with its various external features labelled. At a range of 500 yards the 90mm main gun on the tank was in theory supposed to be able to penetrate 120mm of steel armour sloped at 30 degrees at 500 yards and 3.8 inches at 2,000 yards with the M82 armour-piercing projectile that weighed approximately 24lb. *(Patton Museum)*

(*Above*) Shown loaded on a trailer is an M26 heavy tank that had for many years been on interior display at the now-closed Patton Museum of Armor and Cavalry. All the assets of the museum were shipped to Fort Benning, Georgia to be placed into long-term storage until such time that a new museum could be funded to house the collection. *(Chun-lun Hsu)*

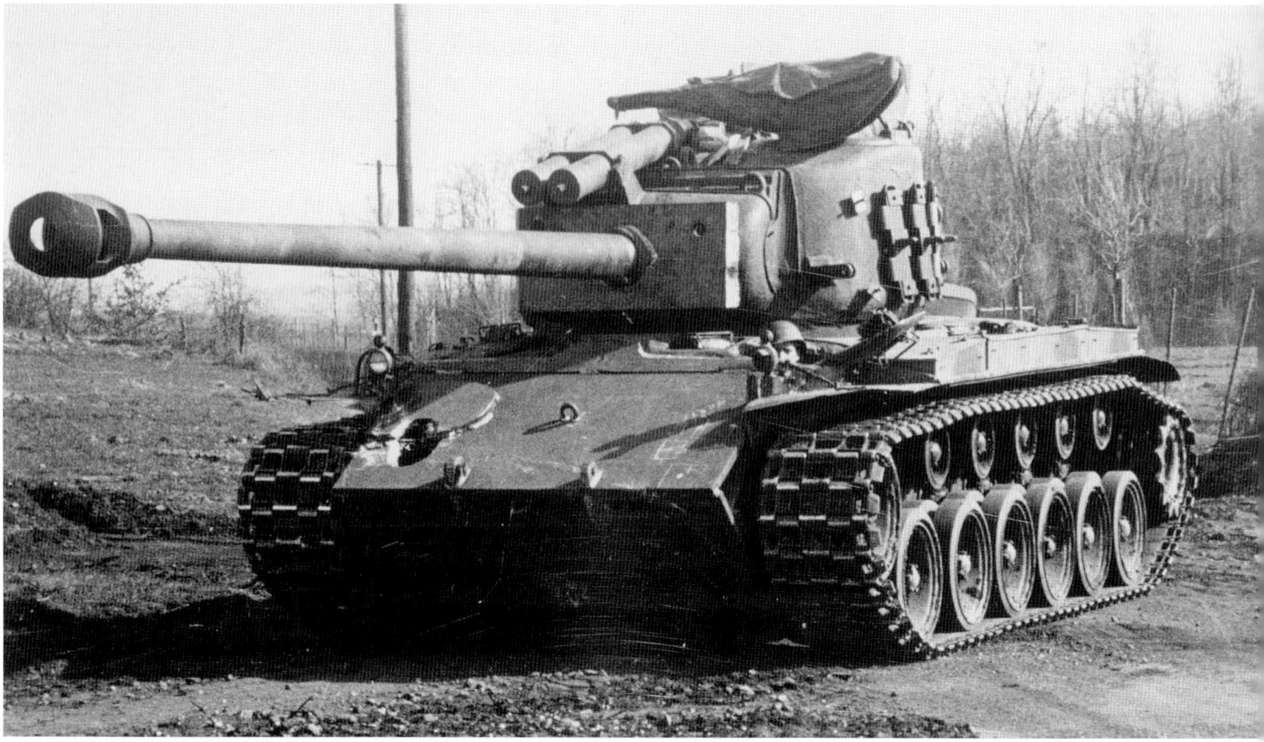

A single pilot example of the heavy tank T26E4 was sent to Germany just before the war concluded in that part of the world. It was armed with a longer-barrelled and more powerful 90mm main gun than that mounted on the M26 heavy tank. Extra armour was welded onto both the turret and hull of the T26E4 as is evident in this picture prior to being placed into combat. *(Patton Museum)*

Formerly on display for many decades outside the now-closed Patton Museum of Armor and Cavalry was this impressive-looking vehicle, initially classified as heavy tank T28. It was designated by the US army as the 105mm gun motor carriage T95 in 1945. Finally, in 1946 the vehicle was relabelled as the super-heavy tank T28. *(Author's collection)*

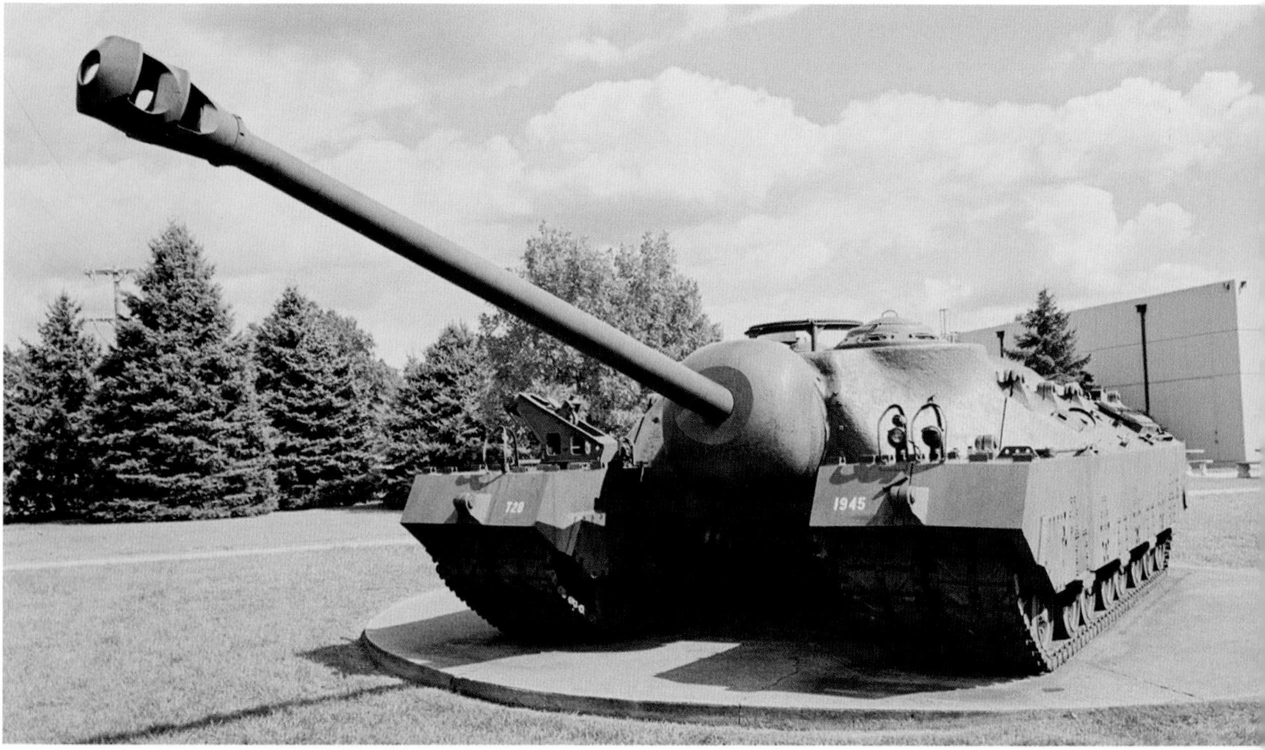
T28
1945

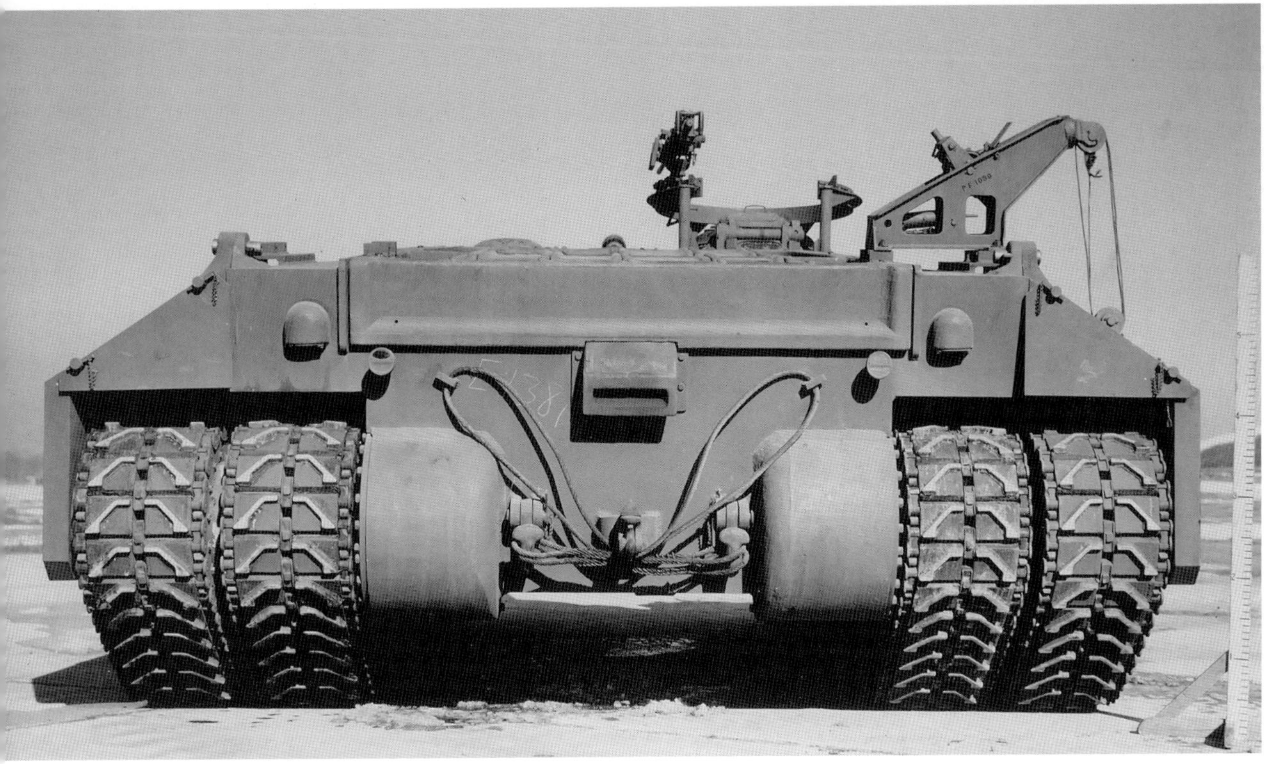

A rear view of the massive heavy tank T28 with its four sets of track. The crane seen on the roof of the vehicle is for helping to load the sixty main gun rounds it was authorized. Tank length was 36ft 5in with a width of 14ft 9in and a height of 9ft 3in. The maximum armour thickness on the tank's gun shield was 292mm. *(Patton Museum)*

A US army heavy tank that was first envisioned in 1944 is seen here in this artist's impression and labelled the T29. It was to be armed with a 105mm main gun. The pilot examples of the T29 were approximately 38ft long with their main guns pointed forward. They had a width of 12ft 5in and a height of 10ft 6in. *(Patton Museum)*

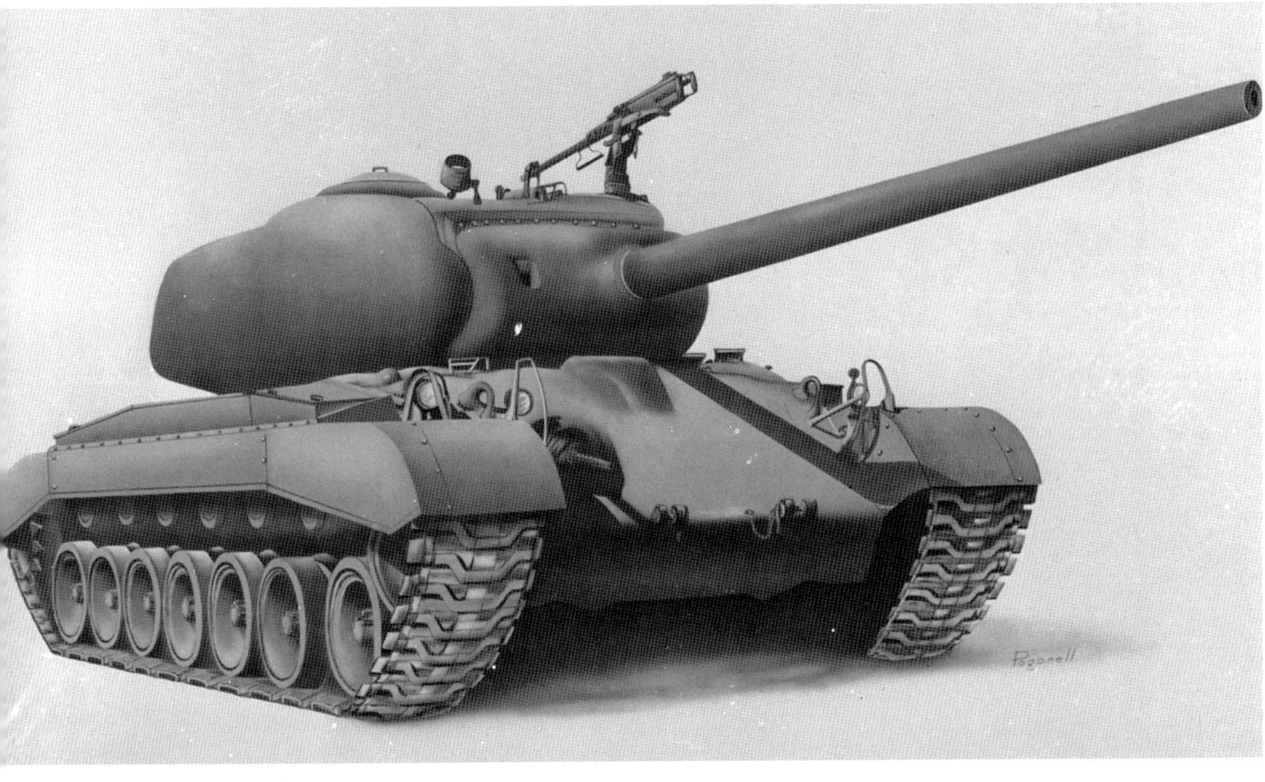

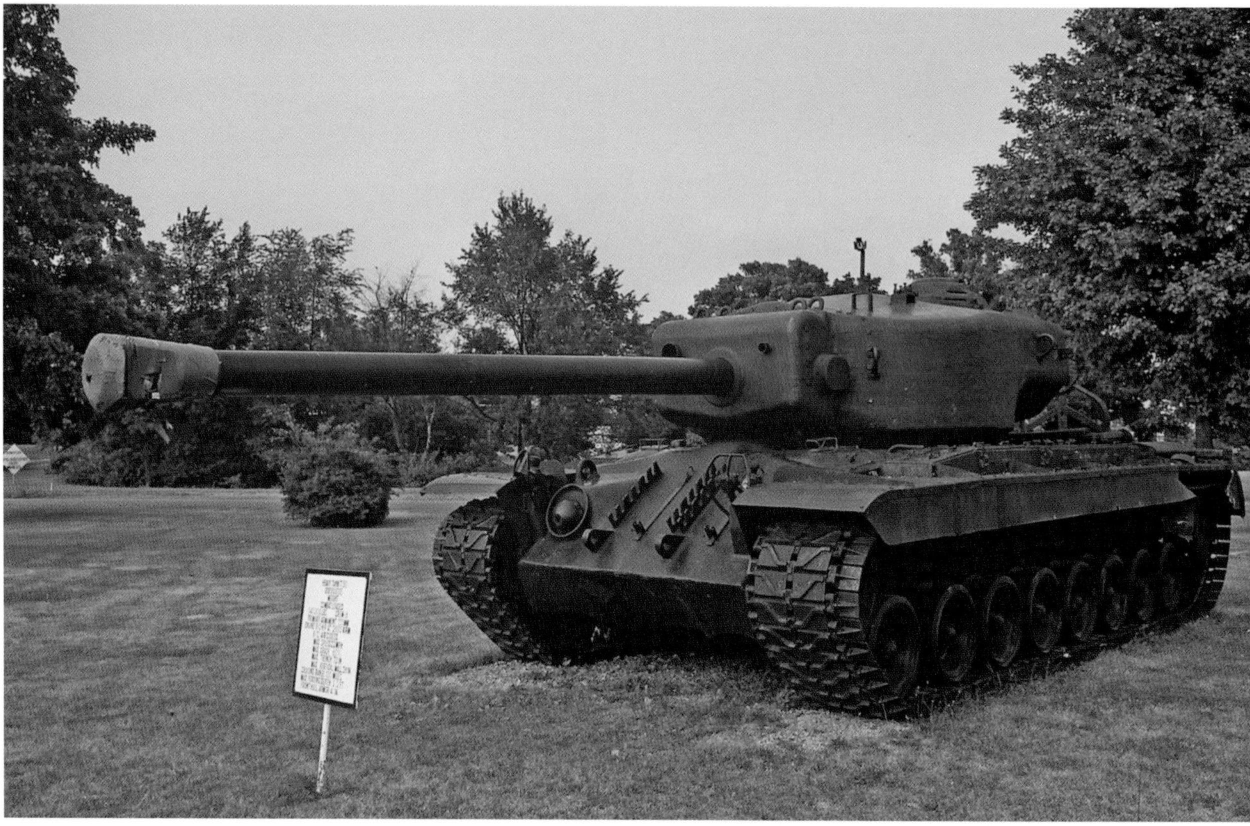

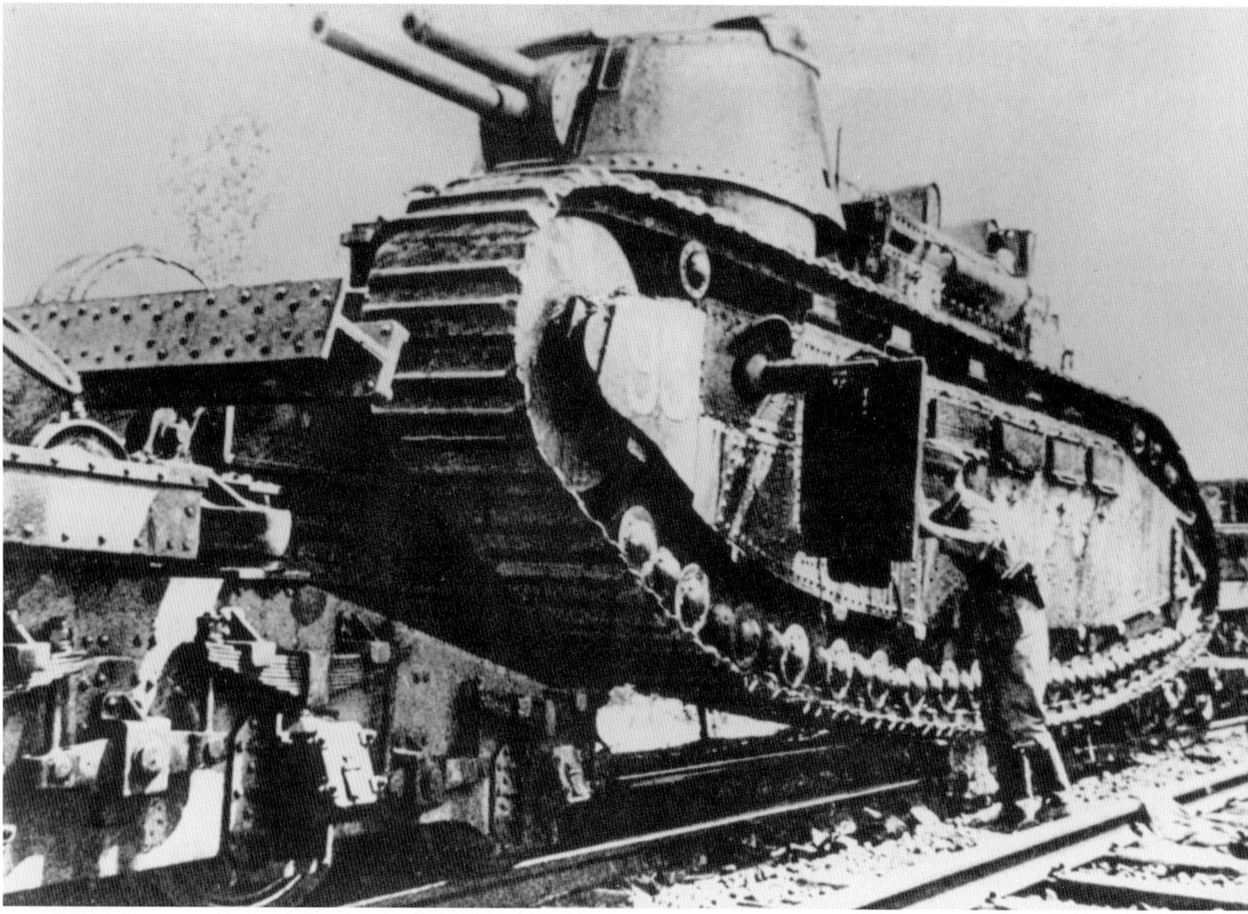

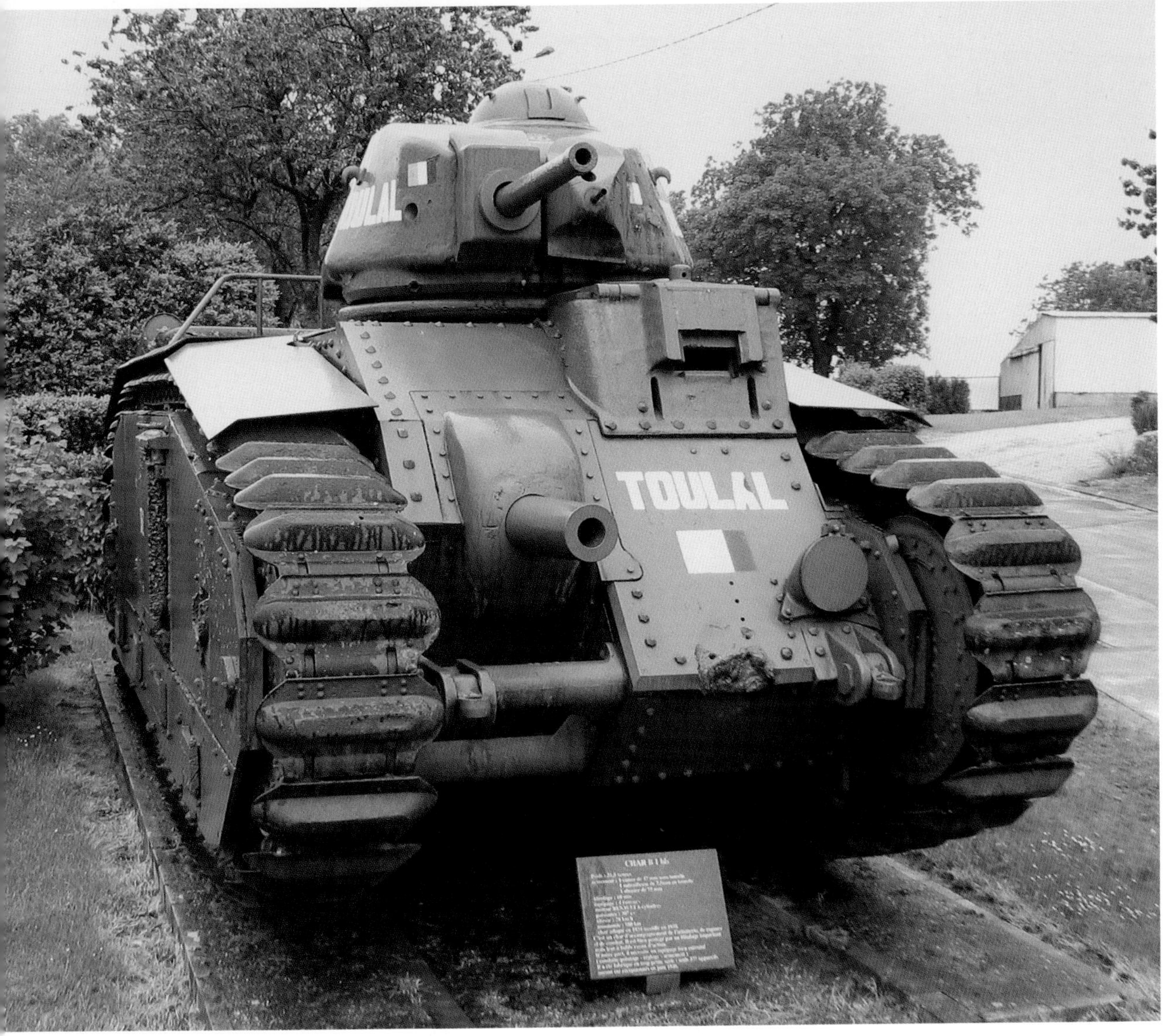
TOULAL

(*Opposite above*) The heavy tank T30 is seen here when it was on display at the former US army Armor School located at Fort Knox, Kentucky. The T30 was basically a heavy tank T29 armed with a 155mm main gun and a new air-cooled engine that developed 810 gross horsepower. It was also armed with a large-calibre coaxial machine gun. *(Dean and Nancy Kleffman)*

(*Opposite below*) Pictured is a destroyed French army Char 2C heavy tank that was lost during the German military invasion of France in the summer of 1940. The tank was a late-First World War design with ten being built but not entering into operational service until after the conflict. They were 33ft 8in in length, had a width of 9ft 8in and the height of the tank was 13ft 1in. *(Tank Museum)*

(*Above*) The follow-on to the Char 2C heavy tank in the French army was the Char B1-bis. Pictured is a preserved example in France. Armed with a 75mm main gun in its front hull, it was supplemented by a turreted 47mm gun operated by the vehicle commander. The maximum armour on the tank was 60mm thick. Top speed on level roads was 17.4mph. *(Pierre-Olivier Buan)*

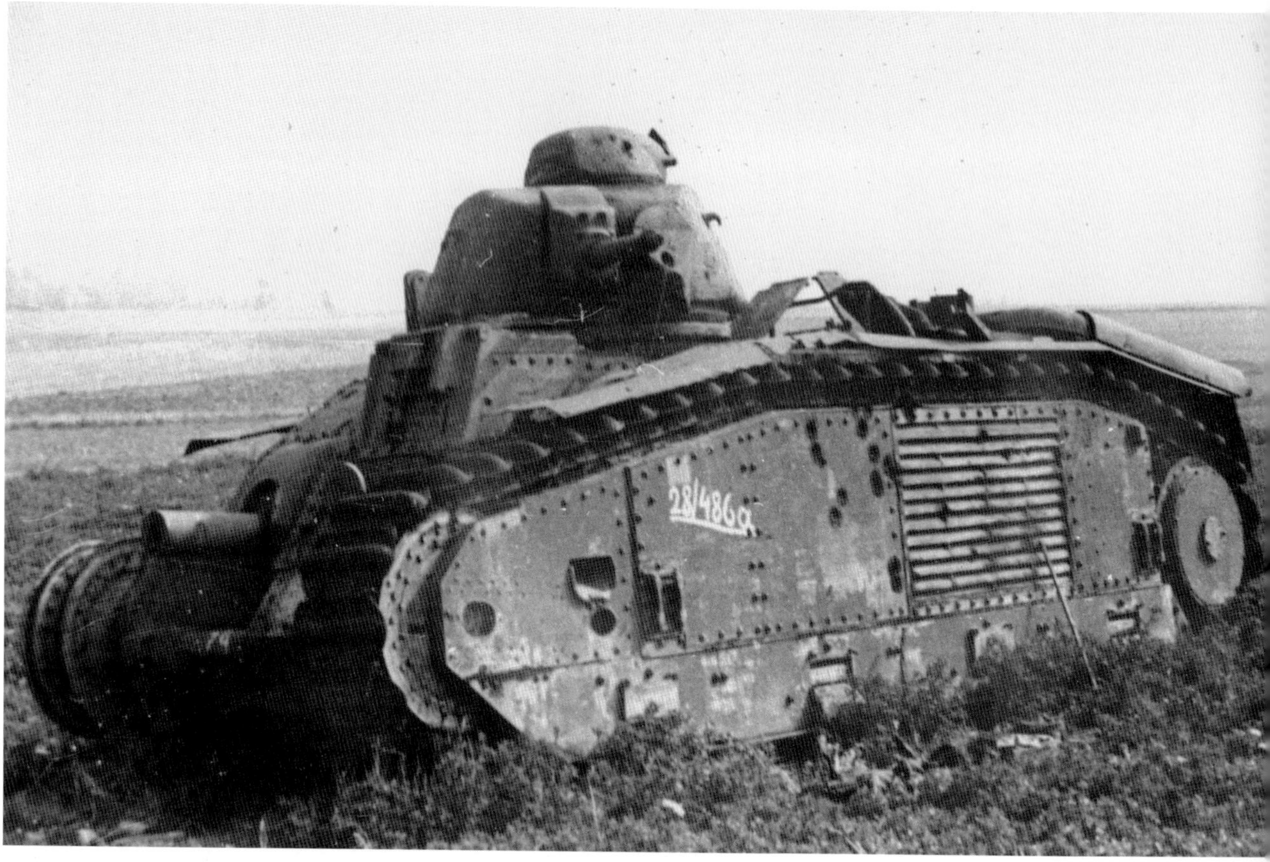
28/486a

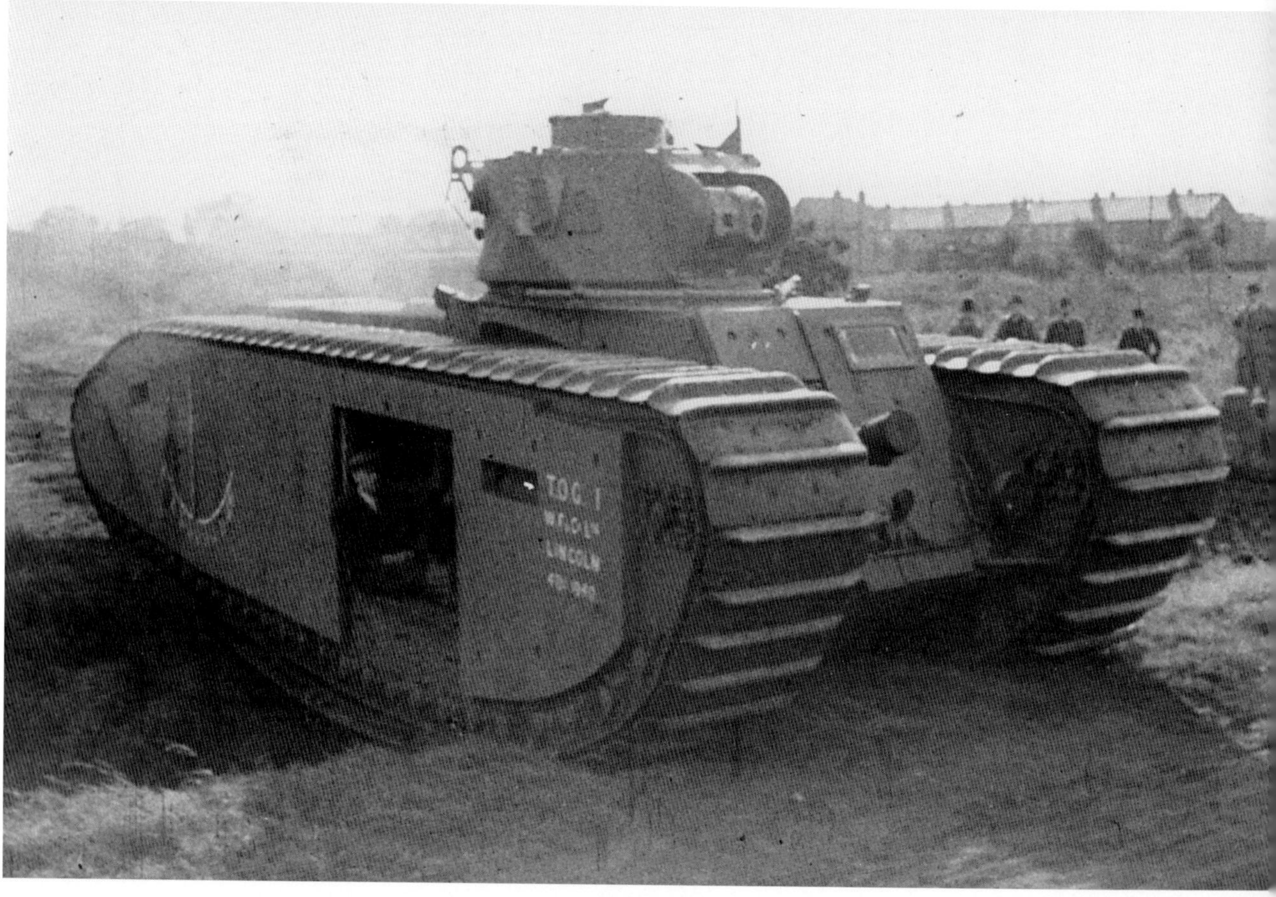
T.O.G. 1

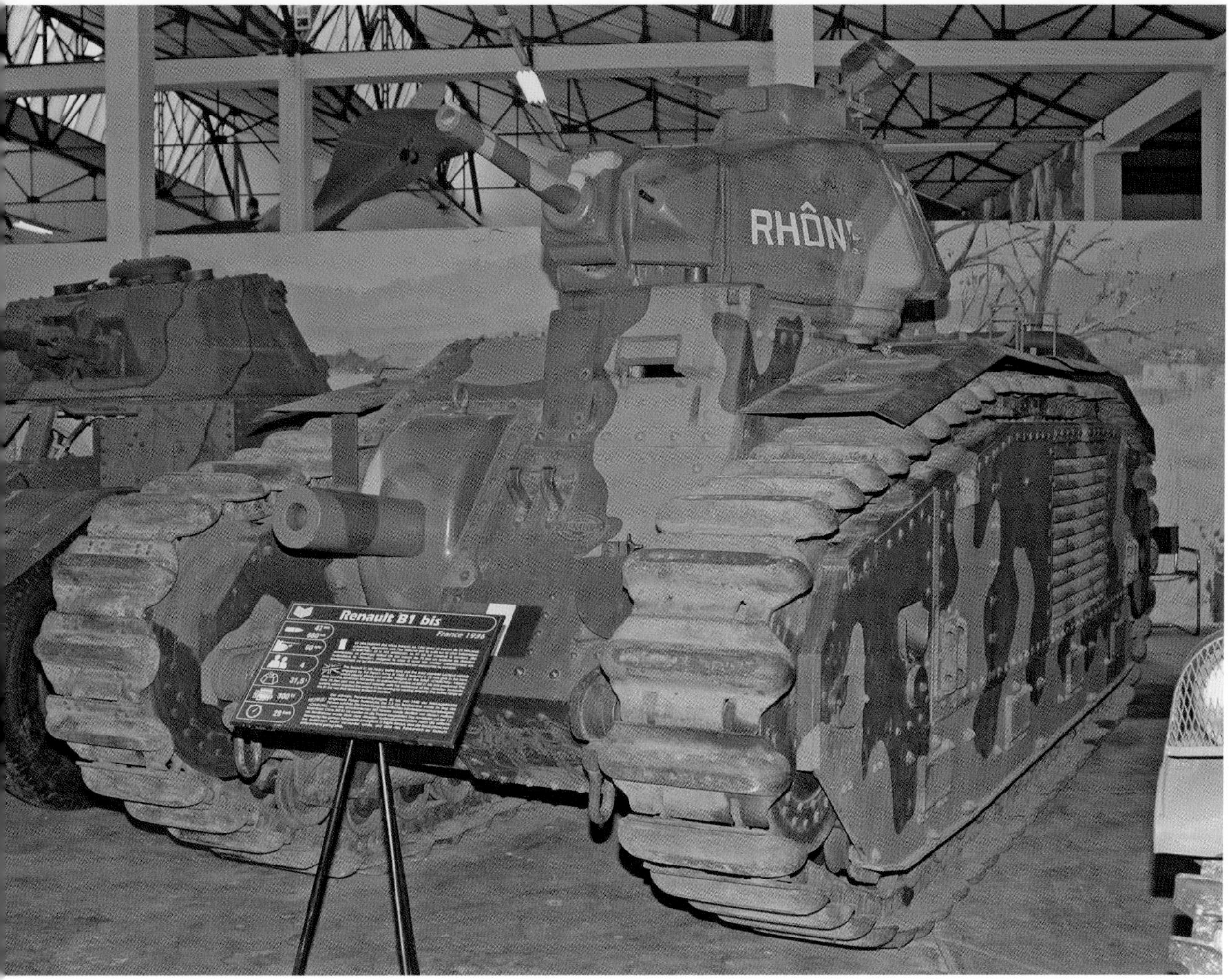
RHÔN
Renault B1 bis
France 1936

(*Opposite above*) In a French farmer's field is a knocked-out Char 2C heavy tank that took a large number of penetrating hits. The tank is 21ft 5in long, has a width of 8ft 2in and a height of 9ft 2in. There was authorized storage in the vehicle for seventy-four of the 75mm gun rounds and fifty for the turret-mounted 47mm gun. (*Patton Museum*)

(*Above*) On display at the French Army Tank Museum is a colourfully-painted Char B1-bis heavy tank. Unlike the front-hull-mounted 75mm main gun in the American M3 medium tank series that had some limited traverse, the 75mm gun on the Char B1-bis was fixed in position, which meant that the entire tank had to be turned to aim the 75mm main gun of the vehicle. (*Christophe Vallier*)

(*Opposite below*) A view of the British-designed and built TOG1 heavy tank demonstrating its trench-crossing abilities. The large square opening seen here that was duplicated on the other side of the vehicle was originally intended to be fitted with armoured sponsons armed with 2-pounder anti-tank guns and machine guns. This design feature was later deemed unnecessary and deleted from the design. (*Tank Museum*)

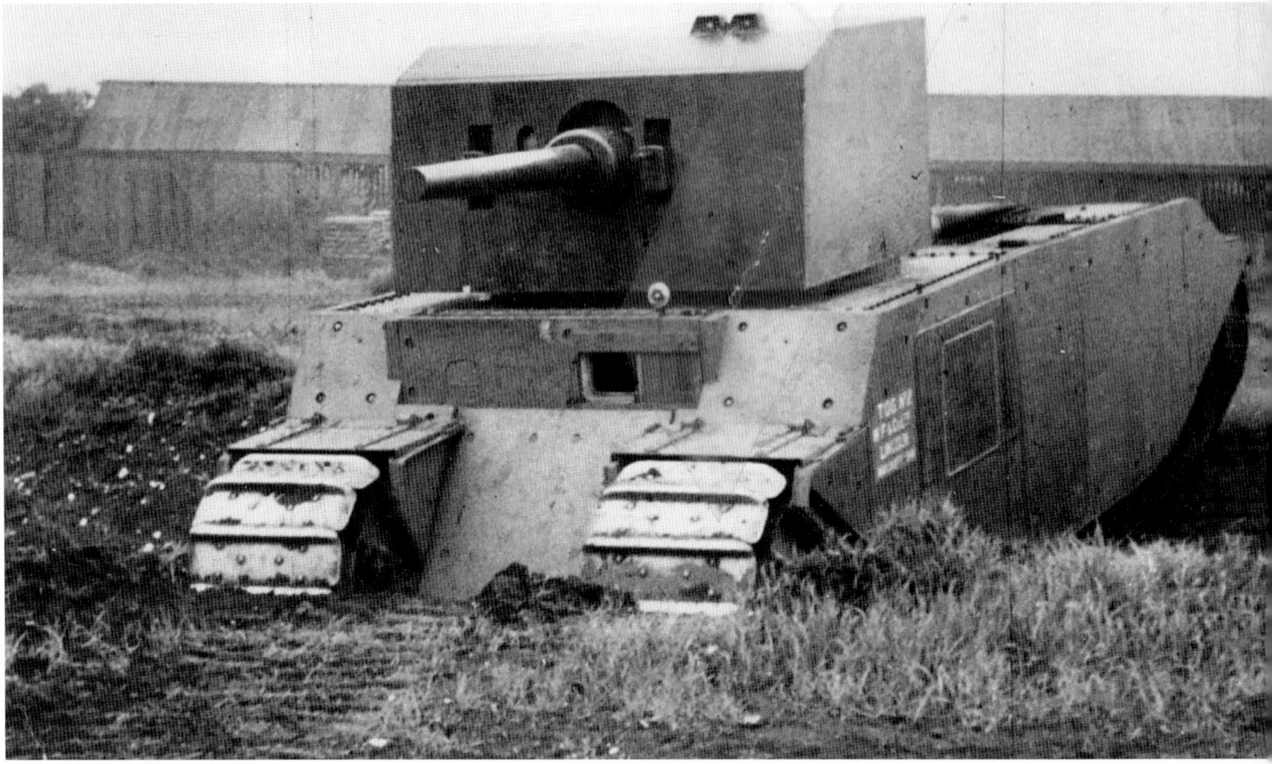

Undergoing mobility testing is this TOG2 armed with a 3-inch gun in a new turret design. The prototype tank had a length of 33ft 3in, a width of 10ft and the vehicle height was 10ft. The maximum armour on the tank was 75mm thick. Power came from a diesel engine that gave the TOG2 a top speed on level roads of 8.5mph. *(Tank Museum)*

Joining the list of failed British-designed heavy tanks is the vehicle pictured here that was labelled as the A39 Heavy Assault Tank named the 'Tortoise'. The Tortoise was armed with a forward-firing 32-pounder (94mm) main gun and protected by as much as 225mm thick armour. Driven by a single gasoline-powered engine, the vehicle had a top speed of 12mph. *(Tank Museum)*

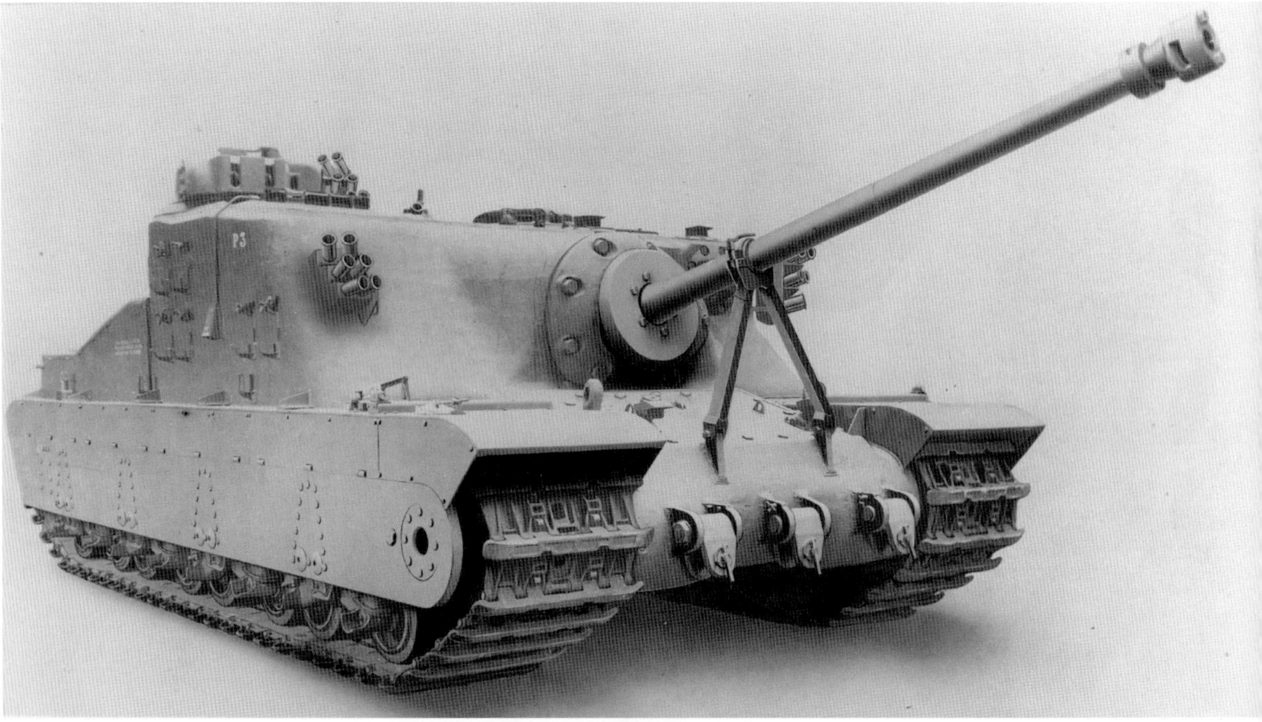

Notes

Notes

Notes

Notes

Notes

Notes